MODERN METHODS
FOR BUSINESS RESEARCH

Edited by

George A. Marcoulides
California State University, Fullerton

LEA LAWRENCE ERLBAUM ASSOCIATES, PUBLISHER
1998   Mahwah, New Jersey   London

QUANTITATIVE METHODOLOGY SERIES
Methodology for Business and Management

George A. Marcoulides, Series Editor

Marcoulides • Modern Methods for Business Research

Introduction to Methodology for Business and Management

The volumes in this new series will present methodological techniques that can be applied to address research questions in business and management. The series is aimed at investigators and students from all functional areas of business and management as well as individuals from other disciplines. Each volume in the series will focus on a particular methodological technique or set of techniques. The goal is to provide detailed explanation and demonstration of the techniques using real data. Whenever possible, computer software packages will be utilized.

Series Editor
George A. Marcoulides, *California State University, Fullerton*

Lawrence Erlbaum Associates, Inc., Publishers
10 Industrial Avenue
Mahwah, New Jersey 07430

Library of Congress Cataloging-in-Publication Data

Modern methods for business research / edited by George A.
Marcoulides.
    p.   cm. — (Methodology for business and management)
Includes bibliographical references and index.
ISBN 0-8058-2677-7 (cloth : alk. paper). 0-8058-3093-6 (pbk : alk. paper).
1. Business—Research—Methodology. I. Marcoulides, George A.
II. Series.
HD30.4.M627 1998
650'.07'2—dc21   97-31706
                                                        CIP

Books published by Lawrence Erlbaum Associates are printed on acid-free paper,
and their bindings are chosen for strength and durability.

Printed in the United States of America
10 9 8 7 6 5 4 3 2 1

Contents

Preface

The purpose of this volume is to introduce a selection of the latest popular methods for conducting business research. The goal is to provide an understanding and working knowledge of each method with a minimum of mathematical derivations. It is hoped that the volume will be of value to a wide range of readers and will provide the stimulation for seeking a greater depth of information on each method presented.

The chapters in this volume provide an excellent addition to the methodological literature. Each chapter was written by a leading authority in the particular topic. Interestingly, despite the current popularity of each method in business, a good number of the methods were first developed and popularized in other substantive fields. For example, the factor analytic approach was originally developed by psychologists as a paradigm that was meant to represent hypothetically existing entities or constructs. And yet, these days one rarely sees an article in a business journal that does not refer to some type of exploratory or confirmatory factor analytic model.

Although each chapter in the volume can be read independently, the chapters selected fall into three general interrelated topics: measurement, decision analysis, and modeling. The decision regarding the selection and the organization of the chapters was quite challenging. Obviously, within the limitations of a single volume, only a limited number of topics could be addressed. In the end, the choice of the material was governed by my own belief concerning what are currently the most important modern methods for conducting business research. The first topic, measurement, contains three chapters; generalizability theory, latent trait and latent class models, and multifaceted Rasch modeling. The second topic includes chapters on location theory models, data envelopment analysis, and heuristic search procedures. Finally, the modeling topic contains the following chapters: exploratory and confirmatory factor analysis, dynamic factor analysis, partial least squares and structural equation modeling, multilevel data analysis, growth modeling, and modeling of longitudinal data.

ACKNOWLEDGMENTS

This book could not have been completed without the assistance and support provided by many people. First, I thank all of the contributors for their time and effort in preparing chapters for this volume. They all provided excellent chapters and worked diligently through the various stages of the publication process. I also thank the numerous reviewers who provided comments on initial drafts of the various chapters. Thanks are also due to Larry Erlbaum, Ray O'Connell, Kathryn Scornavacca, and the rest of the editorial staff at Lawrence Erlbaum Associates for their assistance and support in putting together this volume. Finally, I would like to thank Laura and Katerina for their love and support with yet another project.

—George A. Marcoulides

CHAPTER ONE

Applied Generalizability
Theory Models

George A. Marcoulides
California State University, Fullerton

Generalizability (G) theory is a statistical theory about the dependability of behavioral measurements (Shavelson & Webb, 1991). Although many psychometricians can be credited with paving the way for G theory (e.g., Burt, 1936, 1947; Hoyt, 1941; Lindquist, 1953), it was formally introduced by Cronbach and his associates (Cronbach, Gleser, Nanda, & Rajaratnam, 1972; Cronbach, Rajaratnam, & Gleser, 1963; Gleser, Cronbach, & Rajaratnam, 1965) as an extension of classical reliability theory. Since the major publication by Cronbach et al. (1972), G theory has gained increasing attention, as evidenced by the growing number of studies in the literature that apply it (Shavelson, Webb, & Burstein, 1986). The diversity of measurement problems that G theory can solve has developed concurrently with the frequency of its application (Marcoulides, 1989a). Some researchers have gone so far as to consider G theory "the most broadly defined psychometric model currently in existence" (Brennan, 1983, p. xiii). Clearly, the greatest contribution of G theory lies in its ability to model a remarkably wide array of measurement conditions through which a wealth of psychometric information can be obtained (Marcoulides, 1989c).

The purpose of this chapter is to review the major concepts in G theory and illustrate its use as a comprehensive method for designing, assessing, and improving the dependability of behavioral measurements. To gain a perspective from which to view the application of this measurement procedure and to provide a frame of reference, G theory is compared with the more traditionally used classical reliability theory. It is hoped, by providing

1

a clear and understandable picture of G theory, that the practical applications of this technique will be adopted in business and management research. Generalizability theory most certainly deserves the serious attention of all researchers involved in measurement studies.

OVERVIEW OF CLASSICAL RELIABILITY THEORY

Classical theory is the earliest theory of measurement and the foundation for many modern methods of reliability estimation (Cardinet, Tourneur, & Allal, 1976). Despite the development of the more comprehensive G theory, classical theory continues to have a strong influence among measurement practitioners today (Suen, 1990). In fact, many tests currently in existence provide psychometric information based on the classical approach. Classical theory assumes that when a test is administered to an individual the observed score is comprised of two components. The first component is the true underlying ability of the examinee, which is the intended target of the measurement procedure. The second component is some combination of unsystematic error in the measurement, which somehow clouds the estimate of the examinee's true ability. This relationship can be symbolized as:

$$\text{Observed score } (X) = \text{True score } (T) + \text{Error } (E)$$

The better a test is at providing an accurate indication of an examinee's ability, the more accurate the T component will be and the smaller the E component. Classical theory also provides a reliability coefficient that permits the estimation of the degree to which the T component is present in a measurement. The reliability coefficient is expressed as the ratio of the variance of true scores to the variance of observed scores and as the error variance decreases the reliability coefficient increases. Mathematically this relationship is expressed as:

$$r^2_{xt} = \frac{\sigma^2_T}{\sigma^2_X}$$

or

$$r^2_{xt} = \frac{\sigma^2_T}{\sigma^2_T + \sigma^2_E}$$

The evaluation of the reliability of a measurement procedure is basically a question of determining how much of the variation in a set of observed scores is a result of the systematic differences among individuals and how much is the result of other sources of variation. Test–retest reliability estimates provide an indication of how consistently a test ranks examinees over time. This type of reliability requires administering a test on two different occasions and examining the correlation between the two test occasions to determine stability over time. Internal consistency is another method for estimating reliability and measures the degree to which individual items within a given test provide similar and consistent results about an examinee. Another method of estimating reliability involves administering two "parallel" forms of the same test at different times and examining the correlation between the forms.

The preceding methods for estimating reliabilities of measurements suggest that it is unclear which interpretation of error is the most appropriate. Obviously, the error variance estimates will vary according to the measurement designs used (i.e., test–retest, internal consistency, parallel forms), as will the estimates of reliability. Unfortunately, because classical theory provides only one definition of error, it is unclear how one should choose between these reliability estimates. Thus, in classical theory one often faces the uncomfortable fact that data obtained from the administration of the same test to the same individuals may yield three different reliability coefficients.

To make this discussion concrete, an example is in order. A personnel manager wishes to measure the job performance of five salespersons by using a simple rating form. The rating form covers such things as effective communication, effectiveness under stress, meeting deadlines, work judgments, planning and organization, and initiative. Two supervisors independently rate the salespersons in terms of their overall perfomance using the rating form on two occasions, with ratings from "not satisfactory" to "superior." The ratings comprised a 5-point scale. Table 1.1 presents data from the hypothetical example.

Using the preceding data, how might classical theory calculate the reliability of these jobs performance measures? Obviously, with performance measurements taken on two different occasions, a test–retest reliability can be calculated. A test–retest reliability coefficient is calculated by correlating

TABLE 1.1
Data From Hypothetical Job Performance Example

Salesperson	Occasion 1		Occasion 2	
	Rater 1	Rater 2	Rater 1	Rater 2
1	2	2	3	3
2	4	4	5	3
3	4	5	5	5
4	2	1	3	1
5	5	4	3	2

the salespersons' scores from Occasion 1 with the scores from Occasion 2, after summing over all other information in the table. This value is approximately 0.73. Of course, an internal consistency reliability can also be calculated. This value is approximately 0.87. Thus, it appears that not only are the estimates of reliability in classical theory different, but they are not even estimates of the same quantity (Webb, Rowley, & Shavelson, 1988). Although classical test theory defines reliability as the ratio of the variance of true scores to the variance of observed scores, as evidenced by the earlier example, one is confronted with changing definitions of what constitutes true and error variance. For example, if one computes a test–retest reliability coefficient, then the day-to-day variation in the salespersons' performance is counted as error, but the variation due to the sampling of items is not. On the other hand, if one computes an internal consistency reliability coefficient, the variation due to the sampling of different items is counted as error, but the day-to-day variation in performance is not. So which is the right one?

As it turns out, G theory is a theory of multifaceted errors in measurements. As such, it explicitly recognizes that multiple sources of error may exist simultaneously (e.g., errors due to the use of different occasions, raters, items) and can estimate each source of error and the interaction among sources of error (Brennan, 1983; Marcoulides, 1987; Shavelson & Webb, 1981). Generalizability, therefore, extends classical theory and permits the estimation of the multiple sources of error that measurements may contain.

OVERVIEW OF GENERALIZABILITY THEORY

Generalizability theory is considered a theory of the multifaceted errors of measurement. In G theory, any measurement is a sample from a universe of admissible observations described by one or more facets. These facets, for example, could be one of many possible judges rating an examinee on one of several possible rating scales on one of many possible occasions. According to Cronbach et al. (1972), the conceptual framework underlying G theory is that "an investigator asks about the precision or reliability of a measure because he wishes to generalize from the observation in hand to some class of observations to which it belongs" (p. 15).

Thus, the classical theory concept of reliability is replaced by the broader notion of generalizability (Shavelson, Webb, & Rowley, 1989). Instead of asking "how accurately observed scores reflect corresponding true scores," G theory asks "how accurately observed scores permit us to generalize about persons' behavior in a defined universe" (Shavelson et al., 1989, p. 922). For example, in performance assessment the universe to which an investigator wishes to generalize relates to how well an individual is performing on the job. Generalizability, then, is the extent to which one can generalize from performance measures to the actual job. It is essential, therefore, that the universe an investigator wishes to generalize about be defined by specifying which facets can change without making the observation unacceptable or unreliable. For example, if supervisor ratings might be expected to fluctuate from one occasion to another, then multiple rating occasions need to be included in the measurement procedure. Additionally, if the choice of items included in the rating scale might affect the score an employee receives, then an adequate sample of items must be included in the measurement procedure. Ideally, one would like to know an employee's score (the universe score) over all combinations of facets and conditions (i.e., all possible raters, all possible items, all possible occasions). Unfortunately, because the universe score can only be estimated, the choice of a particular occasion, rater, or item will inevitably introduce error in the measurement of performance. Thus, the basic approach underlying G theory is to separate the variability in measurement that is due to error. This is accomplished by decomposing an observed score into a variance component for the universe score and variance components for any other errors associated with the measurement study.

To illustrate this decomposition, consider a one-facet crossed design. This is the simplest and most common of all measurement designs. A common example of this one-facet design is a paper-and-pencil, multiple-choice test with n_i items administered to some sample of subjects. If X_{pi} is used to denote the score for any person in the population on any item in the universe, the expected value of a person's observed score is $\mu_p \equiv \underset{i}{E} X_{pi}$. In a similar manner, the population mean for item i is defined as $\mu_i \equiv \underset{p}{E} X_{pi}$, and the mean over both the population and the universe is $\mu \equiv \underset{p}{E}\underset{i}{E} X_{pi}$ (Brennan, 1983). An observed score for one person on one item can be expressed in terms of the following linear model:

$$
\begin{aligned}
X_{pi} &= \mu & & (\textit{grand mean}) \\
&+ \mu_p - \mu & & (\textit{person effect}) \\
&+ \mu_i - \mu & & (\textit{item effect}) \\
&+ X_{pi} - \mu_p - \mu_i + \mu & & (\textit{residual}).
\end{aligned}
$$

In this model, for each score effect there is an associated variance component of the score effect. For example, the variance component for persons is:

$$
\sigma_p^2 = \underset{p}{E}(\mu_p - \mu)^2.
$$

The total variance of the observed scores is equal to the sum of each variance component:

$$\sigma^2 X_{pi} = \underset{p}{E}\,\underset{i}{E}\,(X_{pi} - \mu)^2 = \sigma_p^2 + \sigma_i^2 + \sigma_{pi,e}^2 .$$

The focus of G theory is on these variance components because their magnitude provides information about the sources of error variance influencing a measurement. Variance components are determined by means of a G study and can be estimated from an analysis of variance (ANOVA) of sample data (although other methods of estimation can also just as easily be used to provide the same information; see Marcoulides, 1987, 1989b, 1990, 1996). Estimation of the variance components is achieved by equating the observed mean squares from an ANOVA to their expected values and solving the set of linear equations; the resulting solution for the components comprises the estimates. The estimation of variance components for the aforementioned one-facet design is illustrated in Table 1.2 (for complete details see Cornfield & Tukey, 1956).

Because estimated variance components are the basis for indexing the relative contribution of each source of error and determining the dependability of a measurement, the estimation of variance components is considered to be the "Achilles heel of G theory" (Shavelson & Webb, 1981, p. 138). Although ANOVA is the most commonly used method, several other approaches have been proposed in the literature. These include Bayesian methods, minimum variance methods, and restricted maximum likelihood (Marcoulides, 1987; Shavelson & Webb, 1981). Because the computational requirements involved in estimating variance components increase geometrically for more complex designs, preference should be given to the use of computer packages. For example, the programs GENOVA (Brennan, 1983), SAS-PROC VARCOMP and SAS-PROC MIXED (SAS Institute, 1994), and even a general-purpose structural equation modeling program like LISREL (Marcoulides, 1996) can be used to obtain the estimated variance components.

TABLE 1.2
ANOVA Estimates of Variance Components for One-Facet Design

Source of Variation	Mean Square	Expected Mean Square
Person (p)	MS_p	$\sigma_{pi,e}^2 + n_i\sigma_p^2$
Items (i)	MS_i	$\sigma_{pi,e}^2 + n_i\sigma_i^2$
Residual (pi,e)	$MS_{pi,e}$	$\sigma_{pi,e}^2$

Note. The estimates for each variance component are obtained from the ANOVA as follows:

$$\hat{\sigma}_p^2 = \frac{MS_p - MS_{pi,e}}{n_i}$$

$$\hat{\sigma}_i^2 = \frac{MS_i - MS_{pi,e}}{n_p}$$

$$\hat{\sigma}_{pi,e}^2 = MS_{pi,e}$$

Generalizability theory also considers two types of error variance corresponding to two different types of decisions: relative and absolute. Relative error is of primary concern when one is interested in a decision that involves rank ordering individuals (not uncommon, as rank ordering may be used for selecting the top two employees). With this type of error definition, all the sources of variation that include persons are considered measurement error. Accordingly, relative error is defined as σ_δ^2 and includes the variance components due to the interaction of persons with items averaged over the number of items used in the measurement; that is:

$$\sigma_\delta^2 = \frac{\sigma_{pi,e}^2}{n_i}$$

Absolute error allows one to concentrate on a decision to determine whether an employee can perform at a prespecified level (rather than knowing only whether the individual has performed better than others). The absolute error variance, therefore, reflects not only the disagreements about the rank ordering of persons, but also any differences in average ratings. Absolute error is defined as σ_Δ^2 and includes all variances in the design; that is:

$$\sigma_\Delta^2 = \frac{\sigma_i^2}{n_i} + \frac{\sigma_{pi,e}^2}{n_i}$$

Although G theory stresses the importance of variance components, it also provides a G coefficient analogous to the classical theory reliability coefficient. The G coefficient also ranges from 0 to 1.0 and is influenced by the amount of error variation observed in an individual's score and by the number of observations made. As the number of observations increase, error variance decreases and the generalizability coefficient increases. The generalizability coefficient can be intepreted as the ratio of universe score variance to expected observed score variance ($E\rho^2 = \sigma_p^2/E\sigma^2 X_{pi}$), and is somewhat analogous to the traditional reliability coefficient (Marcoulides, 1989d). However, unlike classical theory, G theory recognizes that error variance is not a monolithic entity but that multiple sources can contribute error to a measurement design (Shavelson & Webb, 1991). Thus, a G coefficient can be determined for each type of decision, relative or absolute:[1]

$$E\rho_\delta^2 = \frac{\sigma_p^2}{\sigma_p^2 + \dfrac{\sigma_{pi,e}^2}{n_i}}$$

[1]The notation presented for the absolute coefficients is often used interchangeably.

and

$$\rho_\Delta^2 = \Phi = \cfrac{\sigma_p^2}{\sigma_p^2 + \cfrac{\sigma_i^2}{n_i} + \cfrac{\sigma_{pi,e}^2}{n_i}}.$$

Of course, sample estimates of the parameters in the G coefficients are used to estimate the appropriate level of generalizability. Thus, once the sources of measurement error have been pinpointed through estimating the variance components, one can determine how many conditions of each facet are needed to obtain an optimal level of generalizability (Goldstein & Marcoulides, 1991; Marcoulides, 1993, 1995, 1997; Marcoulides & Goldstein, 1990, 1991, 1992b).

In G theory, there is also an important distinction between a G study and a decision (D) study. Whereas G studies are associated with the development of a measurement procedure, D studies apply the procedure in practical terms (Shavelson & Webb, 1981). If the results of a G study show that some sources of error in the design are very small, then one may elect to reduce the number of levels of that facet (e.g., occasion of observation), or may even ignore that facet in a D study. Thus, resources might be better spent by increasing the sample of conditions (especially in multifaceted designs) that contribute large amounts of error in order to increase generalibility. A major contribution of G theory, therefore, is that it permits one to pinpoint the sources of measurement error and increase the appropriate number of observations accordingly in order to obtain a certain level of generalizability (Shavelson et al., 1986).

Although Cronbach et al. (1972) indicated that generalizability will generally improve as the number of conditions in a facet are increased, this increment can ultimately enter the realm of fantasy. More important is the question of the "exchange rate" or "trade-off" between conditions of a facet within some cost considerations (Cronbach et al., 1972). Typically, in multifaceted studies there can be several D study designs that yield the same level of generalizability. For example, if one desires to develop a measurement procedure with a G coefficient of 0.90, there might be two distinct D study designs from which to choose. Clearly, in such cases one must consider resource constraints in order to choose the appropriate D study design. The question then becomes how to maximize generalizability within a prespecified set of limited resources. Of course, in the one-facet person by item ($p \times i$) design, the question of satisfying resource constraints while maximizing generalizability is simple. One chooses the greatest number of items needed to give maximum generalizability without violating the budget (Cleary & Linn, 1969). When other facets are added to the design, obtaining a solution can be quite complicated. Extending on this idea, Goldstein and Marcoulides

(1991), Marcoulides and Goldstein (1990, 1991), and Marcoulides (1993, 1995) recently developed procedures that can be used in any measurement design to determine the optimal number of conditions that maximize generalizability under limited budget and other constraints (see next section for an example application).

A TWO-FACETED GENERALIZABILITY STUDY

Generalizability theory provides a framework for examining the dependability of measurements in almost any type of design. This is because G theory explicitly recognizes that multiple sources of error may be operating in a measurement design. As such, G theory can be used in multifaceted designs to estimate each source of error and the interactions among the sources of error. For example, in a study of the dependability of measures of brand loyalty (Peter, 1979), the investigator considered items and occasions to be important factors that could lead to the undependability of the measurement procedure (Marcoulides & Goldstein, 1992a). Such a study would be considered a person by items by occasions ($p \times i \times o$) two-faceted crossed design.[2]

The following two-faceted study of the dependability of measures of job performance is used to illustrate G theory's treatment of multifaceted error (Marcoulides & Mills, 1986). In this study ratings of job performance are obtained for 15 secretaries employed in the business school of a large state university. The rating forms contain 10 items that are used to assess overall job performance. Three supervisors independently rate the secretaries in terms of their performance on each of the items with ratings from "not satisfactory" to "superior"—the ratings comprising a 5-point scale. This design is a person (secretaries) by items by supervisors ($p \times i \times s$) two-faceted crossed design.

For this study there are several sources of variability that can contribute to error in determining the dependability of the measures of job performance. Because secretaries are the object of measurement, their variability does not constitute error variation. In fact, we expect that secretaries will perform differently. However, items and supervisors are considered potential sources of error because they can contribute to the undependability of the measurement design.

Using the ANOVA approach, seven variance components must be estimated. These correspond to the three main effects in the design (persons,

---

[2]It is important to note that in a crossed design every condition of the Item facet occurs in combination with every condition of the Occasion facet. This is in contrast to a nested design where certain conditions of the Item facet occur with only one condition of the Occasion facet.

items, supervisors), the three two-way interactions between effects, and the three-way interaction confounded with random error (due to the one observation per cell design). Thus, the total variance of the observed score would be equal to the sum of each of these variance components:

$$\sigma^2 X_{pis} = \sigma_p^2 + \sigma_i^2 + \sigma_s^2 + \sigma_{pi}^2 + \sigma_{ps}^2 + \sigma_{is}^2 + \sigma_{pis,e}^2 .$$

As discussed in the previous section, estimation of these variance components is achieved by equating the observed mean squares from an ANOVA to their expected values and solving the sets of linear equations; the resulting solution for the components comprises the estimates. Table 1.3 provides the expected mean square equations for the preceding two-faceted design. The estimated variance components for the aforementioned sources of variation are provided in Table 1.4. Appendix A contains a LISREL (Jöreskog & Sörbom, 1992) script for obtaining estimates using the covariance structure approach and Appendix B contains a Statistical Analysis System (SAS) procedure setup (for a complete discussion see Marcoulides, 1996).

As can be seen in Table 1.4, supervisor ratings are a substantial source of error variation (19.7%). It appears that some supervisors are rating secretaries using different criteria. In addition, supervisors are rank ordering secretaries differently as evidenced by the large variance component of the person (secretary) by supervisor interaction (12.4%). On the other hand, the item variance is quite small (1%), indicating that the items used to measure performance are providing consistent results. This is also reflected in the small variance components due to the person by item interaction (2.3%), and the item by supervisor interaction (0.8%). There is no doubt that the number of supervisors has the greatest effect on generalizability, whereas items have little effect.

TABLE 1.3
ANOVA Estimates of Variance Components for Two-Facet Design

Source of Variation	Mean Square	Expected Mean Square
Person (p)	MS_p	$\sigma_{pis,e}^2 + n_i\sigma_{ps}^2 + n_s\sigma_{pi}^2 + n_in_s\sigma_p^2$
Items (i)	MS_i	$\sigma_{pis,e}^2 + n_i\sigma_{is}^2 + n_s\sigma_{pi}^2 + n_pn_s\sigma_i^2$
Supervisors (s)	MS_s	$\sigma_{pis,e}^2 + n_i\sigma_{ps}^2 + n_s\sigma_{is}^2 + n_pn_i\sigma_s^2$
Two-Way Interactions		
pi	MS_{pi}	$\sigma_{pis,e}^2 + n_o\sigma_{pi}^2$
ps	MS_{ps}	$\sigma_{pis,e}^2 + n_i\sigma_{ps}^2$
is	MS_{is}	$\sigma_{pis,e}^2 + n_p\sigma_{is}^2$
Residual (pis,e)	$MS_{pis,e}$	$\sigma_{pis,e}^2$

Note. The estimates for each variance component are obtained from the ANOVA by solving the sets of linear equations.

TABLE 1.4
ANOVA Variance Component Estimates and Percentage Contribution

Component	Estimate	Percentage
σ_p^2	6.30	48.7
σ_i^2	0.13	1.0
σ_s^2	2.55	19.7
σ_{pi}^2	0.30	2.3
σ_{ps}^2	1.60	12.4
σ_{is}^2	0.10	0.8
$\sigma_{pis,e}^2$	1.95	15.0

Generalizability theory also permits the development of decisions about measurement designs based on information provided from the G study. These decisions (called D studies) allow one to optimize the measurement procedure on the basis of information about variance components derived through a G study. Table 1.5 provides the estimated variance components and G coefficients for a variety of D studies using different combinations of number of items and number of supervisors. For example, if one decided that absolute decisions were essential in determining the performance of secretaries, the absolute error variance would be determined as:

$$\sigma_\Delta^2 = \frac{\sigma_i^2}{n_i} + \frac{\sigma_s^2}{n_s} + \frac{\sigma_{pi}^2}{n_i} + \frac{\sigma_{ps}^2}{n_s} + \frac{\sigma_{is}^2}{n_i n_s} + \frac{\sigma_{pis,e}^2}{n_i n_s}$$

or simply:

TABLE 1.5
Variance Components and Generalizability
Coefficients for a Variety of Decision Studies

n_i	1	1	10	10
n_s	1	3	3	6
σ_p^2	6.30	6.30	6.30	6.30
σ_i^2	0.13	0.13	0.13	0.13
σ_s^2	2.55	0.85	0.85	0.42
σ_{pi}^2	0.30	0.30	0.30	0.30
σ_{ps}^2	1.60	0.53	0.53	0.27
σ_{is}^2	0.10	0.03	0.00	0.00
$\sigma_{pis,e}^2$	1.95	0.65	0.06	0.03
σ_δ^2	3.85	1.48	0.62	0.33
σ_Δ^2	6.63	2.49	1.48	0.76
$E\rho_\delta^2$	0.62	0.81	0.91	0.95
ρ_Δ^2	0.49	0.72	0.81	0.90

$$\sigma_\Delta^2 = \frac{0.13}{10} + \frac{2.55}{3} + \frac{0.30}{10} + \frac{1.60}{3} + \frac{0.10}{30} + \frac{1.95}{30} = 1.48.$$

The G coefficient for such an absolute decision would be determined to be:

$$\rho_\Delta^2 = \Phi = \frac{\sigma_p^2}{\sigma_p^2 + \sigma_\Delta^2} = \frac{6.30}{6.30 + 1.48} = 0.81$$

Similarly, using only one item and one supervisor will produce an estimated absolute G coefficient of 0.49, compared to 0.72 when using one item and three supervisors.

There is no doubt that the items in the study are contributing very little error variability and can be reduced in subsequent measurements of job performance with little loss of generalizability. However, in order to increase generalizability, it appears that an increase in the sample of supervisors is needed because they do contribute large amounts of error variance. Of course, as indicated by Marcoulides and Goldstein (1990), one cannot ignore potential resource constraints imposed on the measurement procedure. For example, if the total available budget (B) for the preceding measurement procedure is $100 and if the cost per item per supervisor (c) is $20, then the optimal number of items and supervisors can be determined using the following equations (for a complete discussion see Marcoulides, 1993, 1995):[3]

$$n_i = \sqrt{\frac{\sigma_{pi}^2}{\sigma_{ps}^2}\left(\frac{B}{c}\right)} = \sqrt{\frac{0.30}{1.60}\left(\frac{100}{20}\right)} = 1$$

and

$$n_s = \sqrt{\frac{\sigma_{ps}^2}{\sigma_{pi}^2}\left(\frac{B}{c}\right)} = \sqrt{\frac{1.60}{0.30}\left(\frac{100}{20}\right)} = 5$$

Of course, additional constraints, for example on the upper bounds of the number of supervisors, could easily be imposed on the problem before optimizing the solution. Such additional constraints might become important when, besides the budgetary constraints, one is aware of other design restrictions (such as the actual number of available supervisors). Thus, D studies are very important when attempting to improve the dependability

---

[3]When the values of n_i and n_s are nonintegers, they must be rounded to the nearest feasible integer values—see Marcoulides and Goldstein (1990) for discussion of optimality when rounding integers. Marcoulides (1993) also illustrated optimization procedures for more complex designs.

of measurement procedures because they provide values for both realistic and optimum number of conditions.

MULTIVARIATE GENERALIZABILITY STUDIES

Behavioral measurements often involve multiple scores in order to describe individuals' aptitude or skills (Webb, Shavelson, & Maddahian, 1983). For example, the Revised Stanford–Binet Intelligence Scale (Terman & Merrill, 1973) uses 15 subtests to measure four dimensions: short-term memory, verbal reasoning, quantitative reasoning, and abstract/visual reasoning. Although multiple scores in behavioral measurements may be conceived as vectors to be treated simultaneously, the most common procedure used in the literature is to assess the dependability of the scores separately (Shavelson et al., 1989). Shavelson et al. have indicated that perhaps this is because both the multivariate approach is not easily comprehended and there are limited computer programs available to perform multivariate generalizability analysis. There is no doubt that the analysis of a multivariate G study is not as straightforward as that of a univariate G study. Nevertheless, a multivariate analysis can provide information that cannot be obtained in a univariate analysis, namely information about facets that contribute to covariance among the multiple scores. Such information is essential for designing optimal D studies that maximize generalizability.

The two-faceted study of the dependability of measures of job performance examined in the previous section attempted to measure performance using a rating form with 10 items. As illustrated in the previous section, the dependability of this measurement procedure was assessed using a univariate approach (i.e., one in which the items were treated as a separate source of error variance—as a facet). By treating the items as a separate source of error variance, however, no information was obtained on the sources of covariation (correlation) that might exist among the items. Such information may be important for correctly determining the magnitude of sources of error influencing the measurement procedure. In other words, when obtaining behavioral measurements, the covariance for the sampled conditions and the unsystematic error might be a nonzero value. To illustrate this point further, suppose that the aforementioned two-faceted design were modified so that each supervisor rated the 15 secretaries on two occasions: O1 and O2. If some supervisors give higher ratings on the average than other supervisors do, then the constant errors in rating O1 will covary with the constant errors in rating O2. As it turns out, this correlated error can influence the estimated variance components in a generalizability analysis (Marcoulides, 1987). One way to overcome this problem is to conduct a multivariate G study and compare the results with the univariate results.

Perhaps the easiest way to explain the multivariate case is by analogy to the univariate case (Marcoulides & Hershberger, 1997). As illustrated in the previous section, the observed score for a person in the two-faceted person by items by supervisor ($p \times i \times s$) design was decomposed into the error sources corresponding to items, supervisors, and their interactions with each other and persons. In extending the notion of multifaceted error variance from the univariate case to the multivariate, one must not treat items as a facet contributing variation to the design but as a vector of outcome scores (i.e., 10 dependent variables). Thus, using v to symbolize the items in the measurement design provides:

$$
\begin{aligned}
vX_{ps} = \; & v\mu & & (\textit{mean for } v) \\
& + (v\mu_p - v\mu) & & (\textit{person effect}) \\
& + (v\mu_s - v\mu) & & (\textit{supervisor effect}) \\
& + (vX_{ps} - v\mu_p - v\mu_s + v\mu) & & (\textit{residual}).
\end{aligned}
$$

The total variance of the observed score $\sigma_v^2 X_{ps}$ is analogous to $\sigma^2 X_{pis}$ in the univariate case and is:

$$
\sigma_v^2 X_{ps} = \sigma_{vp}^2 + \sigma_{vs}^2 + \sigma_{vps,e}^2 \, .
$$

For example, expanding the preceding formula for any pair of observed scores provides:

$$
\begin{aligned}
{}_1X_{ps} = {}_1\mu + ({}_1\mu_p - {}_1\mu) + ({}_1\mu_s - {}_1\mu) + ({}_1\textit{residual}) \\
{}_2X_{ps} = {}_2\mu + ({}_2\mu_p - {}_2\mu) + ({}_2\mu_s - {}_2\mu) + ({}_2\textit{residual}).
\end{aligned}
$$

The variance-covariance components for this pair of observed scores are $\sigma_1^2 X_{ps}$, $\sigma_2^2 X_{ps}$, $\sigma_1 X_{ps2} X_{ps}$ and are equal to:

$$
\begin{aligned}
\sigma_1^2 X_{ps} &= \sigma_{1p}^2 + \sigma_{1s}^2 + \sigma_{1ps,e}^2 \\
\sigma_2^2 X_{ps} &= \sigma_{2p}^2 + \sigma_{2s}^2 + \sigma_{2ps,e}^2 \\
\sigma_1 X_{ps2} X_{ps} &= \sigma_{1p2p} + \sigma_{1s2s} + \sigma_{1ps,e\,2ps,e} \, .
\end{aligned}
$$

It is important to note that if $\sigma_1 X_{ps2} X_{ps} = 0$, the previous estimates for $\sigma_1^2 X_{ps}$, $\sigma_2^2 X_{ps}$ would be equivalent to the observed score variance in which each item is examined separately.

As discussed in the previous section, univariate G theory focuses on the estimation of variance components because their magnitude provides information about the sources of error influencing a measurement design. In contrast, multivariate G theory focuses on variance *and* covariance components. As such, a matrix of both variances and covariances among observed scores is decomposed into matrices of components of variance and covariance. And, just as the ANOVA can be used to obtain estimates of variance components, multivariate analysis of variance (MANOVA) provides estimates of variance and covariance components. For example, the decomposition of the variance-covariance matrix of observed scores with two dependent variables (i.e., two items) is equal to:

$$
\begin{pmatrix} \sigma_1^2 X_{ps} & \sigma_1 X_{ps2} X_{ps} \\ \sigma_1 X_{ps2} X_{ps} & \sigma_2^2 X_{ps} \end{pmatrix} = \begin{pmatrix} \sigma_{1p}^2 & \sigma_{1p2p} \\ \sigma_{1p2p} & \sigma_{2p}^2 \end{pmatrix} + \begin{pmatrix} \sigma_{1s}^2 & \sigma_{1,2s} \\ \sigma_{1,2s} & \sigma_{2s}^2 \end{pmatrix} + \begin{pmatrix} \sigma_{1ps,e}^2 & \sigma_{1ps,e2ps,e} \\ \sigma_{1ps,e2ps,e} & \sigma_{2ps,e}^2 \end{pmatrix}.
$$

Once again, the components of variance and covariance are of primary importance and interest in a multivariate generalizability analysis because they provide information about the sources of error influencing a measurement. For example, they provide the essential information needed to decide whether the items in the earlier measurement design involving job performance should be treated as a composite or as separate scores.

It is also easy to extend the notion of a G coefficient to the multivariate case (Joe & Woodward, 1976; Marcoulides, 1995; Woodward & Joe, 1973). For example, the G coefficient for the aforementioned study could be computed as:

$$
\rho^2 = \frac{a' \Sigma_p a}{a' \Sigma_p a + \dfrac{a' \Sigma_{ps,e} a}{n_s}}
$$

where a = a weighting scheme for the content categories or items used in the measurement design (i.e., a weighting vector), n_s = the number of supervisors,

$$
\Sigma_p = \begin{pmatrix} \sigma_{1p}^2 & \sigma_{1p2p} \\ \sigma_{1p2p} & \sigma_{2p}^2 \end{pmatrix},
$$

and

$$
\Sigma_{ps,e} = \begin{pmatrix} \sigma_{1ps,e}^2 & \sigma_{1ps,e2ps,e} \\ \sigma_{1ps,e2ps,e} & \sigma_{2ps,e}^2 \end{pmatrix}.
$$

According to Joe and Woodward (1976), one way to find the multivariate G coefficient for any design is to solve the following set of equations:

$$[\Sigma_p - \rho^2 (\Sigma_p + \Sigma_{ps,e})]a = 0$$

where the ρ^2 (i.e., the multivariate G coefficient) refers to the characteristic root (eigenvalue) and a its associated eigenvectors (i.e., the weighting vector). Thus, for each multivariate generalizability coefficient corresponding to a characteristic root in the previous equation, a set of canonical coefficients defines a composite of scores in the design. The number of composites defined by the coefficient is equal to the number of different measures (i.e., items used) entered in the analysis. By definition, the first composite will be the most reliable (Short, Webb, & Shavelson, 1986; Webb et al., 1983).

Unfortunately, one problem with weightings (i.e., canonical coefficients a) based on the eigenvalue solution of the G coefficient is that the weights (composites) are "blind" to the theory that originally gave rise to the profile of measurements (Shavelson et al., 1989). That is to say, statistical criteria for composites do not necessarily make conceptual sense. In real applications, the weights or structure of composites are generallly determined by some combination of at least two basic factors: issues of content coverage and importance (some item or items deserve extra weight) and theoretical issues (some items may be considered especially relevant to the meaning of a construct).

To date, a considerable amount of research has been conducted in an attempt to settle the weighting issue, and different approaches have been proposed in the literature. A detailed discussion of different approaches to the estimation of weights is provided by Blum and Naylor (1968), Srinivasan and Shocker (1973), Shavelson et al. (1989), Weichang (1990), and Marcoulides (1994). The different approaches presented are based on either empirical or theoretical criteria. These approaches include: (a) weightings based on expert judgment, (b) weightings based on models confirmed through factor analysis, (c) equal or unit weights, (d) weightings proportional to observed reliability estimates, (e) weightings proportional to an average correlation with another subcriteria, and (f) weightings based on eigenvalue criteria. In general, criticisms of the various approaches can be based on three criteria (relevance, multidimensionality, and measurability) and discussion concerning which approach to use continues in the literature (Weichang, 1990). Marcoulides (1994) recently examined the effects of different weighting schemes on selecting the optimal number of observations in multivariate-multifaceted generalizability designs when cost constraints are imposed and found that all weighting schemes produce similar optimal values (see also Marcoulides & Goldstein, 1991, 1992b, for further discussion concerning procedures to determine the optimal number of conditions that maximize multivariate generalizability). Based on these results Marcoulides suggested that in practice selecting a weighting scheme should be guided more by underlying theory than by empirical criteria.

GENERALIZABILITY THEORY
AS EVIDENCE OF VALIDITY

There is no doubt that in any type of behavioral measurement validity should also be considered alongside dependability (reliability). This is particularly true because a precise estimate of the wrong behavior is much less useful than a relatively imprecise estimate of an intended behavior (Marcoulides, 1989d). Therefore, although reliability (dependability) is an extremely important issue (especially because it places a ceiling on validity), the validity of a measurement procedure is an interrelated issue that must also be addressed. Although most researchers make a distinction between reliability and validity, it is my contention (for further discussion see Marcoulides, 1989d) that this distinction should not occur because reliability and validity are regions on the same continuum. Cronbach et al. (1972) also supported this notion when they indicated that "the theory of 'reliability' and the theory of 'validity' coalesce; the analysis of generalizability indicates how validly one can interpret a measure as representative of a set of possible measures" (p. 234).

Of the many approaches to validity that have been presented in the literature (e.g., content, criterion-related), construct validity is considered to be the most general and includes all others (Cronbach, 1971). Cronbach and Meehl (1955) summarized construct validity as taking place "when an investigator believes that his (or her) instrument reflects a particular construct, to which are attached certain meanings. The proposed interpretation generates specific testable hypotheses, which are a means of confirming or disconfirming the claim" (p. 255). As such, this definition implies an inferential approach to construct validity, one in which a statement of confidence in a measure is made (Marcoulides, 1989a, 1989c, 1989d).

A considerable number of researchers have proposed statistical methods that can be used to assess the degree of validity. Campbell and Fiske (1959), in a what is considered a classic reference, introduced the multitrait-multimethod (MTMM) approach for establishing construct validity (see also Marcoulides & Shumacker, 1996). According to Campbell and Fiske, in order to establish construct validity both convergent and divergent validation are required. Validation is convergent when confirmed by independent measurement procedures. Of course, independence of a measurement procedure is a matter of degree, and evaluation of validity can still take place even if measurements are not entirely independent (Campbell & Fiske, 1959). This is because "a split-half reliability is little more like a validity coefficient than is an immediate test–retest reliability, for the items are not quite identical. A correlation between dissimilar subtests is probably a reliability measure, but it still closer to the region called validity" (p. 83).

Boruch, Larkin, Wolins, and MacKinney (1970) and Dickinson (1987), however, suggested that the MTMM approach is rather complicated and the results are often ambiguous. Instead they proposed that the ANOVA approach should be used. Basically, they indicated that construct validity is the extent to which variability in a measure is a function of the variability in the construct—a definition that obviously opens up the way for G theory. Cronbach et al. (1972) also realized the potential application of G theory for examining validity issues when they indicated that "generalizability theory—even though it is a development of the concept of reliability—clarifies both content and construct validation" (p. 380). Recently, Haertel (1985), Kane (1982), Marcoulides (1989a, 1989d), and Marcoulides and Mills (1986, 1988) also noted the potential usefulness of G theory to studies of construct validity. As such, G theory should basically be viewed as part of a general effort to determine both the reliability and validity of measurement procedures.

APPENDIX A

```
LISREL SCRIPT FOR ESTIMATING VARIANCE COMPONENTS
DA NI=8 NO=25 MA=CM
;
; THE COVARIANCE MATRIX S APPEARS BELOW OR USE FI=FILENAME
;
CM
*
10
3 10
3 3 10
3 3 3 10
3 2 2 2 10
2 3 2 2 3 10
2 2 3 2 3 3 10
2 2 2 3 3 3 3 10
;
MO NX=8 NK=7 LX=FU,FI PH=DI,FR TD=DI,FR
;
; THE MODEL STATEMENT INCLUDES THE DEFAULT VALUES
;
; THE LAMBDA MATRIX HAS THE FOLLOWING FORM
;
VA 1.0 LX(1,1) LX(1,2) LX(1,6)
VA 1.0 LX(2,1) LX(2,3) LX(2,6)
VA 1.0 LX(3,1) LX(3,4) LX(3,6)
VA 1.0 LX(4,1) LX(4,5) LX(4,6)
VA 1.0 LX(5,1) LX(5,2) LX(5,7)
VA 1.0 LX(6,1) LX(6,3) LX(6,7)
VA 1.0 LX(7,1) LX(7,4) LX(7,7)
VA 1.0 LX(8,1) LX(8,5) LX(8,7)
OU ML
```

APPENDIX B

```
SAS SETUP FOR ESTIMATING VARIANCE COMPONENTS
DATA EXAMPLE;
INPUT RATER OCCASION PERSON RATING;
LINES;
1 1 1 4.8
1 1 2 5.6
1 1 3 5.2
. .   . . .
. .   . . .
;
PROC ANOVA;
CLASS RATER OCCASION PERSON;
MODEL RATING=RATER|OCCASION|PERSON;
PROC VARCOMP METHOD=REML;
CLASS RATER OCCASION PERSON;
MODEL RATING=RATER|OCCASION|PERSON;
```

REFERENCES

Blum, M. L., & Naylor, J. C. (1968). *Industrial psychology—its theoretical and social foundations.* New York: Harper & Row.

Boruch, R. F., Larkin, J. D., Wolins, L., & MacKinney, A. C. (1970). Alternative methods of analysis: Multitrait-multimethod data. *Educational and Psychological Measurement, 30,* 833–853.

Brennan, R. L. (1983). *Elements of generalizability theory.* Iowa City, IA: American College Testing.

Burt, C. (1936). The analysis of examination marks. In P. Hartog & E. C. Rhodes (Eds.), *The marks of examiners* (pp. 245–314). London: Macmillan.

Burt, C. (1947). Factor analysis and analysis of variance. *British Journal of Psychology, 1,* 3–26.

Campbell, D. T., & Fiske, D. W. (1959). Convergent and discriminant validation by the multitrait-multimethod matrix. *Psychological Bulletin, 56,* 81–105.

Cardinet, J., Tourneur, Y., & Allal, L. (1976). The symmetry of generalizability theory: Application to educational measurement. *Journal of Educational Measurement, 13,* 119–135.

Cleary, T. A., & Linn, R. L. (1969). Error of measurement and the power of a statistical test. *British Journal of Mathematical and Statistical Psychology, 22,* 49–55.

Cornfield, J., & Tukey, J. W. (1956). Average values of mean squares in factorials. *Annals of Mathematical Statistics, 27,* 907–949.

Cronbach, L. J. (1971). Test validation. In R. L. Thorndike (Ed.), *Educational measurement* (2nd ed., pp. 443–507). Washington, DC: American Council on Education.

Cronbach, L. J., Gleser, G. C., Nanda, H., & Rajaratnam, N. (1972). *The dependability of behavioral measurements: Theory of generalizability scores and profiles.* New York: Wiley.

Cronbach, L. J., & Meehl, P. E. (1955). Construct validity in psychological tests. *Psychological Bulletin, 52,* 281–302.

Cronbach, L. J., Rajaratnam, N., & Gleser, G. C. (1963). Theory of generalizability: A liberalization of reliability theory. *British Journal of Statistical Psychology, 16,* 137–163.

Dickinson, T. L. (1987). Designs for evaluating the validity and accuracy of perfomance ratings. *Organizational Behavior and Human Decision Processes, 40,* 1–21.

Gleser, G. C., Cronbach, L. J., & Rajaratnam, N. (1965). Generalizability of scores influenced by multiple sources of variance. *Psychometrika, 30*(4), 395–418.

Goldstein, Z., & Marcoulides, G. A. (1991). Maximizing the coefficient of generalizability in decision studies. *Educational and Psychological Measurement, 51*(1), 55–65.

Haertel, E. (1985). Construct validity and criterion referenced testing. *Review of Educational Research, 55,* 23–46.

Hoyt, C. J. (1941). Test reliability estimated by analysis of variance. *Psychometrika, 6,* 153–160.

Joe, G. W., & Woodward, J. A. (1976). Some developments in multivariate generalizability. *Psychometrika, 41,* 205–17.

Jöreskog, K. G., & Sörbom, D. (1992). *LISREL8 user's reference guide.* Chicago: Scientific Software International, Inc.

Kane, M. T. (1982). A sampling model for validity. *Applied Psychological Measurement, 6*(2), 125–160.

Lindquist, E. F. (1953). *Design and analysis of experiments in psychology and education.* Boston: Houghton Mifflin.

Marcoulides, G. A. (1987). *An alternative method for variance component estimation: Applications to generalizability theory.* Unpublished doctoral dissertation, University of California, Los Angeles.

Marcoulides, G. A. (1989a). The application of generalizability theory to observational studies. *Quality & Quantity, 23*(2), 115–127.

Marcoulides, G. A. (1989b). The estimation of variance components in generalizability studies: A resampling approach. *Psychological Reports, 65,* 883–889.

Marcoulides, G. A. (1989c). From hands-on measurement to job performance: Issues of dependability. *Journal of Business and Society, 1*(2), 1–20.

Marcoulides, G. A. (1989d). Performance appraisal: Issues of validity. *Performance Improvement Quarterly, 2*(2), 3–12.

Marcoulides, G. A. (1990). An alternative method for estimating variance components in generalizability theory. *Psychological Reports, 66*(2), 102–109.

Marcoulides, G. A. (1993). Maximizing power in generalizability studies under budget constraints. *Journal of Educational Statistics, 18*(2), 197–206.

Marcoulides, G. A. (1994). Selecting weighting schemes in multivariate generalizability studies. *Educational and Psychological Measurement, 54*(1), 3–7.

Marcoulides, G. A. (1995). Designing measurement studies under budget constraints: Controlling error of measurement and power. *Educational and Psychological Measurement, 55*(3), 423–428.

Marcoulides, G. A. (1996). Estimating variance components in generalizability theory: The covariance structure analysis approach. *Structural Equation Modeling, 3*(3), 290–299.

Marcoulides, G. A. (1997). Optimizing measurement designs with budget constraints: The variable cost case. *Educational and Psychological Measurement, 57*(5), 808–812.

Marcoulides, G. A., & Goldstein, Z. (1990). The optimization of generalizability studies with resource constraints. *Educational and Psychological Measurement, 50*(4), 782–789.

Marcoulides, G. A., & Goldstein, Z. (1991). Selecting the number of observations in multivariate measurement designs under budget constraints. *Educational and Psychological Measurement, 51*(4), 573–584.

Marcoulides, G. A., & Goldstein, Z. (1992a). Maximizing the reliability of marketing measures under budget constraints. *SPOUDAI: The Journal of Economic, Business, Statistics and Operations Research, 42*(3–4), 208–229.

Marcoulides, G. A., & Goldstein, Z. (1992b). The optimization of multivariate generalizability studies under budget constraints. *Educational and Psychological Measurement, 52*(3), 301–308.

Marcoulides, G. A., & Hershberger, S. L. (1997). *Multivariate statistical methods: A first course*. Mahwah, NJ: Lawrence Erlbaum Associates.

Marcoulides, G. A., & Mills, R. B. (1986, November). Employee performance appraisals: Improving the dependability of supervisors ratings. *Proceedings of the Decision Sciences Institute, 1*, 670–672.

Marcoulides, G. A., & Mills, R. B. (1988). Employee performance appraisals: A new technique. *Review of Public Personnel Administration, 9*(4), 105–113.

Marcoulides, G. A., & Schumacker, R. E. (1996). *Advanced structural equation modeling: Issues and techniques*. Mahwah, NJ: Lawrence Erlbaum Associates.

Peter, J. P. (1979). Reliability: A review of psychometric basics and recent marketing practices. *Journal of Marketing Research, 16*, 7–17.

SAS Institute, Inc. (1994). *SAS user's guide, version 6*. Cary, NC: Author.

Shavelson, R. J., & Webb, N. M. (1981). Generalizability theory: 1973–1980. *British Journal of Mathematical and Statistical Psychology, 34*, 133–166.

Shavelson, R. J., & Webb, N. M. (1991). *Generalizability theory: A primer*. Newbury Park, CA: Sage.

Shavelson, R. J., Webb, N. M., & Burstein, L. (1986). Measurement of teaching. In M. C. Wittrock (Ed.), *Handbook of research on teaching* (pp. 50–91). New York: Macmillan.

Shavelson, R. J., Webb, N. M., & Rowley, G. L. (1989). Generalizability theory. *American Psychologist, 44*(6), 922–932.

Short, L., Webb, N. M., & Shavelson, R. J. (1986, April). *Issues in multivariate generalizability: Weighting schemes and dimensionality*. Paper presented at the annual meeting of the American Educational Research Association, San Francisco.

Srinivasan, V., & Shocker, A. D. (1973). Estimating weights for multiple attributes in a composite criterion using pairwise judgements. *Psychometrika, 38*(4), 473–493.

Suen, H. K. (1990). *Principles of test theories*. Hillsdale, NJ: Lawrence Erlbaum Associates.

Terman, L. M., & Merrill, M. A. (1973). *Stanford–Binet Intelligence Scale*. Chicago: Riverside.

Webb, N. M., Rowley, G. L., & Shavelson, R. J. (1988). Using generalizability theory in counseling and development. *Measurement and Evaluation in Counseling and Development, 21*, 81–90.

Webb, N. M., Shavelson, R. J., & Maddahian, E. (1983). Multivariate generalizability theory. In L. J. Fyans, Jr. (Ed.), *Generalizability theory: Inferences and practical applications* (pp. 67–81). San Francisco: Jossey-Bass.

Weichang, L. (1990). *Multivariate generalizability of hierarchical measurements*. Unpublished doctoral dissertation, University of California, Los Angeles.

Woodward, J. A., & Joe, G. W. (1973). Maximizing the coefficient of generalizability in multi-facet decision studies. *Psychometrika, 38*(2), 173–181.

CHAPTER TWO

Latent Trait and Latent Class Models

Karen M. Schmidt McCollam
University of Virginia

Latent trait and latent class models are widely accepted within social and behavioral sciences because of the theoretical nature of research concepts. Latent variables, or variables not directly observed (e.g., verbal ability), are typically concepts researchers want to understand, but are regarded as being indicated by observed, or manifest variables, such as vocabulary or paragraph comprehension. Latent trait and latent class models elegantly link the observed variables to the variable of interest, the latent variable.

Although latent trait and class models similarly link latent variables to manifest variables, the two types of models have distinguishing features. As discussed by Andersen (1990), there are two main differences. The first stems from differences in latent variable measurement level. For latent trait models, the latent variable is assumed to be continuous, whereas the latent class latent variable is assumed to have discrete categories. The second difference is related to the method in which individual response probabilities relate to the latent variable. For latent trait models, functional relations model the relationship of the response probabilities to the latent value, but for latent class analysis, these functional relations are not relevant.

The overview of this chapter on latent trait and latent class models is as follows. First, latent trait, or item response theory (IRT) models are described, beginning with the one-parameter (Rasch), two-parameter, and three-parameter models, all for dichotomous responses. Second, models for polytomous responses, including the nominal response model (Bock, 1972), the graded response model (Samejima, 1969), and the partial credit model (Masters, 1982) are described. Due to the introductory nature of this chapter and relative model complexity, more attention is given to dichotomous IRT models. And, because a thorough discussion of estimation requires extensive exposition, estimation procedures are summarized only briefly. An application of the one-parameter logistic model is presented. Third, latent class models are described, beginning with standard, formal latent class models, then restricted latent class models. Finally, for completion, a hybrid of a latent trait and latent class model, the Mixed Rasch Model (Rost, 1990), is examined and applied to data.

An in-depth examination of all latent trait models and latent class models is not possible in a single book chapter. For some detailed examinations of various latent trait and latent class models, see Hambleton, Swaminathan, and Rogers (1991), Andrich (1988), Heinen (1996), Langeheine and Rost (1988), Lord (1980), Lord and Novick (1968), Haberman (1979), and Rasch (1960).

ITEM RESPONSE MODELS: CONTINUOUS LATENT TRAITS

Item response theorists are concerned with examining the behavior of a person, defined as a trait, an ability, or a proficiency score. These traits are latent, or unobserved, and the underlying variable is assumed continuous. Using a test or scale designed to measure, for example, attitude toward workplace flexibility, attitude toward abortion, verbal ability, vocational aptitude, math achievement, credit risk, and so on, the item response theorist desires placing each person on a trait continuum using *theta* (θ) obtained from the IRT model.

Advantages of IRT Over Classical Test Theory

Why should anyone use IRT methods over classical test theory procedures? Several advantages of IRT models over classical test theory exist (Hambleton et al., 1991). First, classical test theory results are group-dependent. If item i on test X indicates difficulty in endorsement or success, this difficulty index depends on the particular group being tested. The meaning of the index will differ depending on the dissimilarity of a new population from the original population tested. IRT results, however, are not group-dependent. Item indices are comparable across groups if the IRT model fits the population data.

Second, classical test theory results are test-dependent. If person j_1 takes a paragraph comprehension test, and person j_2 takes a vocabulary test, how can we compare the verbal ability of these two persons completing different tests when the scaling and content of the two tests differ, particularly if the tests are unequally difficult? In addition, as Hambleton et al. (1991) noted, comparing a person failing every aptitude test item to a person with partial success is problematic because classical test theory indicates nothing about how low the zero-score person scores, whereas performance of the partial-success person provides some information about ability. Because these two scores have different amounts of precision, it is problematic to compare them. Regarding precision, IRT models provide estimates of departure from population trait values with standard errors for each person's trait score. With IRT, scores are not test-dependent. An ability score for a vocabulary test can be compared to another ability score for a paragraph comprehension test. Hence, both item properties and trait score properties do not vary with respect to population or test items. This property is known as the *property of invariance.*

A third problem for classical test theory lies in the raw test score's scale. Raw test scores allow for ordinal scale interpretations, whereas IRT scaling, using logistic functions relating response probabilities to the latent variables, allows theta interpretation on an interval scale. Therefore, all three of these classical test theory measurement problems are alleviated through latent trait analysis: group dependency, test dependency, and test score scaling.

IRT Model Assumptions

Local Independence. IRT models assume that a latent (unobserved) variable is responsible for all relationships between manifest (observed) variables. Hence, after accounting for the latent variable responsible for the manifest test performance, a person's responses are statistically independent. Similarly, this assumption holds between persons with the same level of the latent trait. This assumption is known as *local independence.* Local independence assumes the latent variables postulated in the IRT model are fully specified, and that after the latent variables are held constant, persons' responses are independent. The meaning of local independence is indicated by the conditional probability of a response pattern for a set of items equaling the product of the conditional response probabilities for the individual items.

To express local independence mathematically with a response pattern for a set of i items for a person, for example, for four items, if $X_1 = 0$, $X_2 = 1$, $X_3 = 1$, and $X_4 = 0$, the following property of the joint probability of a response pattern can be stated:

$$P(X_1 = 0, X_2 = 1, X_3 = 1, X_4 = 0 | \theta_j) =$$
$$P(X_1 = 0 | \theta_j)P(X_2 = 1 | \theta_j)P(X_3 = 1 | \theta_j)P(X_4 = 0 | \theta_j) =$$
$$Q_1 P_2 P_3 Q_4,$$

where $P_i = P(X_i = 1 | \theta_j)$ and $Q_i = 1 - P_i$.

Hence, when the assumption of local independence holds, information about the conditional individual response probabilities is sufficient for computing the conditional probability of a particular response pattern for a set of i items.

When these joint probabilities are observed for a person, the joint probability is denoted a *likelihood function,* and the maximum value of the logarithmic transformation of this likelihood function is known as the maximum likelihood estimate of θ.

Unidimensionality. The assumption of unidimensionality states that one ability or trait underlies a person's test performance. This assumption is difficult to meet, as is often the case when more than one ability accounts for performance, such as a physics test requiring high verbal skills, a math test requiring cultural knowledge, or personality traits influencing test performance. Lord and Novick (1968) stated that when the unidimensionality assumption is met, local independence holds. Local independence also holds when all latent dimensions accounting for performance are factored in the model (Hambleton et al., 1991).

Acknowledging that unidimensionality assumptions are hard to meet, some IRT researchers have developed multidimensional IRT models to account for performance. Among these models is Embretson's (1984, 1995) *multicomponent latent trait model for covert processes* (MLTM–CP). Embretson's MLTM–CP postulates that two or more abilities can be decomposed from item responses, given theoretical assumptions of performance. For a description of the model's details and application, see Embretson (1984, 1995).

LATENT TRAIT MODELS
FOR DICHOTOMOUS RESPONSES

This section introduces the three most widely used unidimensional IRT models for dichotomous responses. These three IRT models differ with respect to the number of parameters estimated. Dichotomous IRT models provide the foundation for understanding more complex models, such as polytomous response models and multidimensional IRT models. Therefore, more detail is given to the dichotomous models. For some sources with more thorough examination of these models, see Lord (1980), Lord and Novick (1968), Rasch (1960), and Heinen (1996).

One-Parameter Logistic Model

The one-parameter (1P) logistic model, identical to the IRT model developed by Rasch (1960), specifies an item characteristic curve (ICC) modeled by the following:

$$P(X_{ij} = 1 \mid \theta_j) = \frac{\exp(\theta_j - b_i)}{1 + \exp(\theta_j - b_i)} \tag{1}$$

where $P(X_{ij} = 1 \mid \theta_j)$ is the probability that person j with a given ability or trait level θ answers item i correctly, b_i is the difficulty parameter for item i, θ_j is the ability for person j, and *exp* is the exponent of the constant e, with a value of 2.7181.

This ICC is a response function giving the probability of a correct response for a person for a particular item, conditional on ability or trait level. The 1P logistic model's only parameter determining performance is the b_1 parameter, also known as a threshold or difficulty parameter, the location on the response function where the probability of success (or endorsement) is .50 for dichotomous responses. Figure 2.1 shows the ICC for one item. Note the point on the response function for a 50% probability of success corresponds to the trait level 1.29. Hence, to have a 50% chance of item success, one needs a theta, or ability, of 1.29. For any ICC, as one departs from the .50 threshold, the probability of success on an item increases as ability increases, and the probability of success on an item decreases as ability decreases. Estimation procedures for this model and others are summarized in a later section.

As an illustration, consider the following. Suppose a 17-item aptitude test designed to measure abstract reasoning ability is given to 100 persons. Each of the questions is scored 1,0 for correct/incorrect. Sample data for 10 persons are shown in Table 2.1. Note that Person 8 solved 14 of the 17 abstract reasoning items correctly, whereas Person 2 solved only 4 items correctly. Theta estimates from the MIRA computer program (Rost & von Davier, 1993) for these 10 persons are given. Theta estimates for dichotomous models will

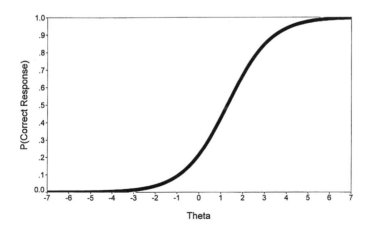

FIG. 2.1. A one-parameter logistic item characteristic curve.

TABLE 2.1
Dichotomous Item Responses and Theta Estimates for a 17-Item Test

Person	Responses	Theta
1	01011000111110001	+0.131
2	01010000000001001	−1.303
3	10001000011101011	−0.132
4	00101100111101111	+0.676
5	00000100001011001	−0.972
6	00100010100000101	−0.972
7	00100000011110000	−0.972
8	01111100111111111	+1.694
9	10000000010100011	−0.972
10	10100000010101001	−0.675

be the same for persons with the same total score, but with greater precision than the raw total score. Note that the four persons successful on five items receive the same ability score, −0.972, and the person scoring 14 receives a theta of 1.694 on abstract reasoning.

Table 2.2 shows a brief annotated output for these data from the MIRA computer program (Rost & von Davier, 1993). Comments and descriptions of the output are given to the right of the "!" symbols. The reader should be informed that some IRT computer packages, such as MIRA, scale item b-values as *easiness,* rather than difficulty, hence, high-positive item b-values indicate easier success than low-negative b-values. Therefore, the positive and negative signs are reversed from the b-scale to the ability scale.

To illustrate, Fig. 2.2 shows ICCs for five selected items across a range of easiness. The corresponding θ threshold values for the ICCs from left to right are $\theta_1 = -1.29$, $\theta_2 = -0.65$, $\theta_3 = -0.23$, $\theta_4 = +0.17$, and $\theta_5 = +1.06$. Hence, Item 1 is easier than Item 5. The corresponding b-values are +1.29, +0.65, +0.23, −0.17, and −1.06, respectively. For example, if a person has an ability score of −0.50, this person has a greater than 50% chance of solving Item 2 correctly, but a less than 20% chance of solving Item 5 correctly. Note in Fig. 2.2 that a feature of the 1P model is that the ICCs are parallel, and all items are assumed to discriminate equally. Overall, ICCs should be inspected for their placement on the ability continuum to determine relative ICC clustering for the ability level of interest (Hambleton et al., 1991).

Two-Parameter Logistic Model

Often researchers believe test items discriminate among persons differently, cases for which the 1P model may be inadequate. The two-parameter (2P) logistic model has an item discrimination parameter that can vary across items. Researchers examining the 2P model include Lord (1952), Birnbaum (1968), and Bock and Lieberman (1970). Lord formulated the 2P model using the

TABLE 2.2
Brief Annotated Output From MIRA for a One-Parameter Logistic Model

Number of Persons	:	100	!100 respondents
Number of Items	:	17	!17 abstract reasoning items
Number of Categories	:	2	!items are scored 1,0
Reduced N. of Persons	:		!2 persons had perfect scores
			!and so their thetas are not
		98	!estimable
Random Startvalue	:	1234	!start value for estimation
Max. N. of Iterations	:	100	!program defaults
Max. Dev. of Likelihood	:	0.001000	!program defaults
Number of Different Patterns	:		!all persons had !different
			!response patterns,
			!except for
			!the two with perfect
		99	!scores
Number of Possible Patterns	:	131072	!2^{17} possible response !patterns

SCORE FREQUENCIES

0:	0.*	1:	0.*	2:	1.*	3:	3.*	4:	11.*	5:	7.*
6:	8.*	7:	7.*	8:	8.*	9:	9.*	10:	8.*	11:	5.*
12:	8.*	13:	6.*	14:	9.*	15:	6.*	16:	2.*	17:	2.*

! There were 0 persons with a score of 0, 11 persons with a score of 4, 5 persons with a
score of 11, 2 persons with a score of 17 (perfect score).

Expected Score Frequencies and Personparameters

*	Raw-*	Expected *	Para- *	Standard*	Comments
*	score*	freq. *	meter *	error *	
*	1*	0.010*	−2.978*	1.044*	!a person with a
*	2*	1.000*	−2.193*	0.771*	!score of 1 receives
*	3*	3.000*	−1.692*	0.657*	!−2.978 for an
*	4*	11.000*	−1.303*	0.595*	!ability estimate
*	5*	7.000*	−0.972*	0.557*	!and 1.044 for a
*	6*	8.000*	−0.675*	0.534*	!standard error
*	7*	7.000*	−0.399*	0.520*	
*	8*	8.000*	−0.132*	0.514*	
*	9*	9.000*	0.131*	0.514*	
*	10*	8.000*	0.398*	0.520*	
*	11*	5.000*	0.676*	0.535*	
*	12*	8.000*	0.973*	0.558*	
*	13*	6.000*	1.304*	0.596*	
*	14*	9.000*	1.694*	0.658*	
*	15*	6.000*	2.197*	0.771*	
*	16*	2.000*	2.983*	1.044*	!A person with a !total
					score of 16 !has an
					!estimated ability !of
					2.983

Mean: 0.205 Stdev: 1.168 Rel: 0.79485
Expected Score = 9.07

!expected score for
!the
!sample is 9.07

(Continued)

TABLE 2.2
(Continued)

	* Thr.1 *	!threshold 1, or 1
	●●●	!item parameter =
ITEM 1	0.13 +	!item difficulty
ITEM 2	−0.17 +	
ITEM 3	1.29 +	!Item 3 is the easiest item to answer
ITEM 4	0.23 +	!correctly
ITEM 5	0.65 +	
ITEM 6	−1.06 +	!Item 6 is the least easiest item to answer
ITEM 7	−0.17 +	!correctly
ITEM 8	−1.00 +	
ITEM 9	−0.73 +	
ITEM 10	0.87 +	
ITEM 11	−0.07 +	
ITEM 12	0.81 +	
ITEM 13	−0.02 +	
ITEM 14	0.54 +	
ITEM 15	−1.06 +	
ITEM 16	−0.68 +	
ITEM 17	0.43 +	

Goodness of fit table

●●

LogLik.	*	−1012.306 *	!log likelihood
N.of Para	*		!Number of parameters =
			!k−1 items for item !parameters, and
			!2 + k−2 items for class- !specific
		33 *	!score probabilities
G-square	*	1106.352 *	
d.f.	*		!2^17 possible patterns minus
		131038 *	!33
			!estimated parameters minus 1
AIC	*	2090.612 *	!Aikake's information !criterion

normal ogive, and later, Birnbaum extended the 2P model to use the logistic function.

The model, similar in form to the 1P model, is as follows:

$$P(X_{ij} = 1 \mid \theta_j) = \frac{\exp (Da_i(\theta_j - b_i))}{1 + \exp (Da_i(\theta_j - b_i))} \qquad (2)$$

where a_i = a discrimination parameter, D = 1.7, a scaling factor used to approximate the normal ogive distribution, and all other parameters are defined in Equation 1.

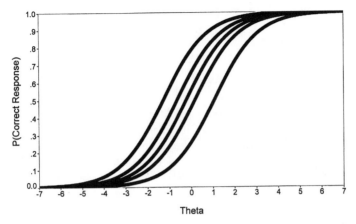

FIG. 2.2. One-parameter logistic item characteristic curves for five items with varying difficulty.

Hambleton et al. (1991) described some of the properties of the 2P model, namely, (a) discrimination parameters are usually between the values of 0 and 2, (b) higher discrimination parameter values indicate steep ICCs, and (c) negative discrimination parameter values indicate item problems, such as miskeying, as mentioned by Hambleton et al., or item content problems, such as distractor item endorsement associated with ability.

Two 2P logistic ICCs are shown in Fig. 2.3. The left-hand item has a difficulty b-value of 1.25, and an a-value of .7, and the right-hand item has a b-value of 2.5, and an a-value of 1.2. Note that the right-hand ICC requires a higher ability for a 50% chance of success, and a steeper slope. Therefore, the right-hand item discriminates better among examinee levels than does

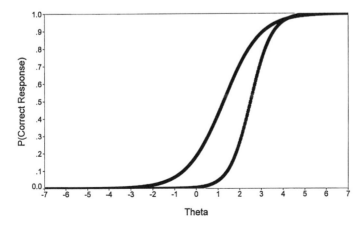

FIG. 2.3. Two-parameter logistic item characteristic curves for two items.

the left-hand item. The discrimination parameter of the 2P logistic model is an excellent tool for researchers interested in developing and modifying efficient test item banks.

Three-Parameter Logistic Model

The three-parameter (3P) logistic model includes an additional item parameter, which estimates, if present, an ICC lower asymptote that is greater than zero. This parameter is of interest to researchers and practitioners in multiple-choice aptitude test settings, in which persons can respond correctly by guessing, therefore increasing the lowest probability of response. Hambleton et al. (1991) described the third parameter as *pseudo-chance-level,* which could be influenced by item distractor set, social desirability of item choices (Heinen, 1996), ability level, and other nonability factors.

The 3P logistic model is as follows:

$$P(X_{ij} = 1 \mid \theta_j) = c_i + (1 - c_i) \frac{\exp(Da_i(\theta_j - b_i))}{1 + \exp(Da_i(\theta_j - b_i))} \tag{3}$$

where c_i is the pseudo-chance-level parameter, and all other definitions are as in Equations 1 and 2. Figure 2.4 shows trace lines for three items with different pseudo-chance-level parameters. The parameters, from left to right, are as follows: For item 1, $a_1 = 1.75$, $b_1 = -1.30$, and $c_1 = .00$; for item 2, $a_2 = 1.10$, $b_2 = -.25$, and $c_2 = .20$; and, for item 3, $a_3 = .75$, $b_3 = 1.20$, and $c_3 = .25$. Note that the probability of getting a correct response never goes below 20% for item 2, and 25% for item 3, whereas the lower asymptote for item 1 is zero.

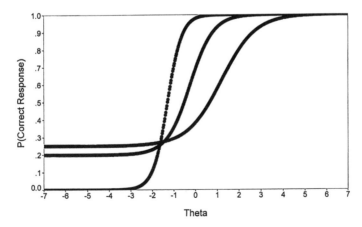

FIG. 2.4. Three-parameter logistic item characteristic curves for three items.

LATENT TRAIT MODELS
FOR POLYTOMOUS RESPONSES

In this section, three commonly used IRT models for scale analyses using polytomous responses are described. The graded response model, the partial credit model, and the nominal response model are defined, with example category trace lines given for the graded response model. Each model has different assumptions, based on the nature of the categorical responses. The interpretation of theta for many polytomous models applied to attitude and personality scales changes from theta as an *ability* to theta as an indicator of the *degree to which one possesses a latent trait*. For example, if a polytomous scale measures altruism, a relatively high positive theta value indicates a high degree of altruism.

The Graded Response Model

Samejima (1969) proposed the graded response model to account for ordered categorical responses. It is an extension of the 2P model, but is designed for m > 2 categorical responses, and uses the normal ogive, and not a logistic distribution. The graded response model is designed to assess, for each response category k, the probability of a response in category k or above. Hence, if $P^*_{jk}(\theta)$ and $P^*_{jk+1}(\theta)$ are defined as the regression of the dichotomous item scoring in which all response categories less than category k and $k + 1$, respectively, are scored 1 for each item j, a probability curve of the graded item scoring over the latent trait, θ, is $P_{jk}(\theta) = P^*_{jk}(\theta) - P^*_{j,k+1}(\theta)$, for $1 \leq k \leq m - 1$, where m is the highest category for item j. Hence, $P_{jk}(\theta)$ is a difference between two cumulative probabilities.

The extreme categories are found by $P_{j0}(\theta) = 1 - P^*_{j1}(\theta)$ and $P_{jm}(\theta) = P^*_{jm}(\theta)$. The corresponding form of the graded response model is:

$$P_{jk}(\theta) = \frac{1}{1 + \exp\left[(-Da_j(\theta - b_j + c_k)\right]} - \frac{1}{1 + \exp\left[(-Da_j(\theta - b_j + c_{k+1})\right]} \quad (4)$$

where a_j = slope, or discrimination parameter for item j, b_j = location, or difficulty parameter for item j, c_k = intercept, or k category parameter for item j, c_{k+1} = intercept, or $k + 1$ category parameter for item j, and all other values are as in Equation 3.

The models in the preceding equations are latent response functions for items scored in k and $k + 1$ categories. It is important to note that graded response model slopes must be equal within each item so that the differences between cumulative probabilities do not become negative. Negative probabilities result from normal ogives with different slopes crossing each other.

Heinen (1996) described some of the appealing properties of the graded response model, namely, the probability of a response in the greatest category increases as a function of the latent variable, the probability of the lowest category decreases as a function of the latent variable, and the middle categories having well-ordered maxima related to the ordering of the response categories. These features allow greater understanding and interpretation by researchers and practitioners.

Suppose a scale item reflects attitude measurement, with response options 0 = completely agree, 1 = somewhat agree, 2 = somewhat disagree, 3 = completely disagree. With the graded response model, the item has four categories, and three category c_k parameters. For example, suppose an item's parameters are as follows: $a = 1.00$, $b = 0.00$, $c_1 = 2.20$, $c_2 = 0.25$, and $c_3 = -2.00$. The plots of the item category trace lines, or category characteristic curves, are shown in Fig. 2.5. The item category trace lines are drawn from left to right, as P_{j0}, P_{j1}, P_{j2}, and P_{j3}, for the four response categories, respectively. Once a person's theta has been estimated, the item category parameters designate regions of most probable response to the item. Because category boundaries are defined in terms of differences between cumulative probabilities, it can be noted from Fig. 2.5 that, for example, if a person's theta is -3.00, the most probable response to the item is in the lowest category, 0.00. Similarly, if a person's theta is 1.00, the most probable response to the item is in the third category, 2.00. Note that the distances between the category thresholds are unequal, and the P_{j2} trace line is flatter than the P_{j1} trace line. This indicates a lower probability of endorsement over theta for the category 2 and higher than for category 1.

Two other widely used polytomous models, the partial credit model and the nominal response model, are described briefly next.

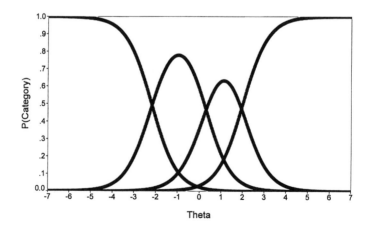

FIG. 2.5. Graded response model trace lines for a four-category item.

The Partial Credit Model

The partial credit model (Masters, 1982) was designed for ordered polytomous item responses, with the scheme that the ordered item response categories 0 through m correspond to processing stages the test examinee makes in responding to the item. For example, if an item measures the degree to which a person's attitude reflects a developmental level in a sequence of thinking processes, the partial credit model is well suited to this application.

Thissen and Steinberg (1986) clarified the difference between the partial credit model and the graded response model's item category trace lines. For the partial credit model, the trace lines indicate "category k given that the response is in category $k - 1$ or category k," rather than "category k or higher" for the graded response model (Thissen & Steinberg, 1986, p. 570). Hence, the focus in the partial credit model is on step transitions between response categories.

The assumption of the partial credit model as the probability of a person passing the threshold between category $m - 1$ and m depends on the person's latent trait and the threshold location. As in the previously described dichotomous models, the relationship between the probability of passing the threshold and latent ability and threshold location is postulated as a logistic function.

The partial credit model is as follows:

$$P(\delta_{im} = 1 \mid \theta_j) = \frac{P_{im}(\theta_j)}{P_{i,m-1}(\theta_j) + P_{im}(\theta_j)} = \frac{\exp(\theta_j - \delta_{im})}{1 + \exp(\theta_j - \delta_{im})} \tag{5}$$

where $P(\delta_{im} = 1 \mid \theta_j)$ is the probability of passing the threshold between $m - 1$ and m for item i, P_{im} is the probability of a response in category m for item i, $P_{i,m-1}$ is the probability of a response in category $m - 1$ for item i, δ_{im} is the value of the threshold for item i, and all other values are as in Equation 1. A constraint for the probabilities of response categories for $P_{im}(\theta_j)$ is $P_{i0}(\theta_j) + P_{i1}(\theta_j) + \ldots + P_{im}(\theta_j) = 1$.

The Nominal Response Model

The nominal response model, designed by Bock (1972), is a polytomous model in which response categories for an item are not ordered. Thissen and Steinberg (1986) conceptualized the partial credit model as a special case of the nominal response model, in which the item slope parameters are constrained to increase in steps of one. The purpose of developing the nominal response model is to use information from endorsed correct responses as well as endorsed incorrect responses.

The nominal response model is as follows:

$$P(X_{ik} = 1 \mid \theta_j) = \frac{\exp\left(a_{ik}(\theta_j - b_{ik})\right)}{\displaystyle\sum_{b=1}^{m} \exp\left(a_{ib}(\theta_j - b_{ib})\right)} \qquad (6)$$

where a_{ik} is a discrimination parameter related to the kth option, b_{ik} is a threshold parameter related to the kth option, m is the number of categorical response options, and all other parameters are as previously defined in Equation 1. In addition, for each level of theta, the sum of the probabilities of the response options equals one.

Estimation of Parameters and Model Fit Assessment

The item and person parameters estimated in these IRT models are commonly estimated in several ways, with maximum likelihood estimation procedures being the most widely used. When both person and item parameters must be estimated simultaneously, *joint maximum likelihood estimation* (Lord, 1974, 1980) is used. Sufficient statistics from examinee right to wrong score ratios are used as start values for theta estimation. Then, treating person parameters as known, item parameters are estimated. Next, treating item parameters as known, theta estimates are made. These steps are repeated until estimates between successive stages are stable.

Some other item and person parameter estimation methods include *marginal maximum likelihood* (Bock & Aitkin, 1981), which assumes a known, normal distribution of θ, and therefore θ is removed from the likelihood function, resulting in estimation of item parameters, and *conditional maximum likelihood* (Andersen, 1972), in which raw total score sufficient statistics are used for θ, and the likelihood function for item parameters is conditioned on these sufficient statistics. The MIRA program (Rost & von Davier, 1993) used in this chapter's illustration uses conditional maximum likelihood estimation. For a thorough discussion of other estimation procedures, see Heinen (1996).

IRT model fit assessment approaches vary widely, and techniques of model fit are constantly being developed. Approaches commonly used are the loglikelihood, the likelihood ratio or G^2, and Aikake's information criterion (AIC; Bozdogan, 1987). Relative comparison of these fit indices between models (e.g., 1P vs. 2P), given the parameters estimated in the model, provides information about increases and decreases in model fit, given the differences between constraints. For a thorough discussion of various model fit assessment techniques, see Langeheine and Rost (1988) and Hambleton et al. (1991).

LATENT CLASS ANALYSIS

As mentioned in the introduction, latent class and latent trait variables both link observed variables to latent variables of interest, but a main difference between the two models stems from the measurement level of the latent variable. For latent trait models, the variable is assumed to be continuous, and for latent class models, the variable is assumed to have discrete categories. As was demonstrated earlier, the latent score for trait models is denoted as θ_j. For latent class models, the latent variable for a person is a category, denoted as t. Latent class analyses are appropriate for anyone interested in understanding persons placed in discrete classes based on patterns of responses. As Heinen (1996) explained, with discrete latent variables, the latent structure models are parameterized with a fixed number of T classes, and θ_t is used to represent a latent class. These θ_t classes can be metrical or nominal.

LATENT CLASS MODEL ASSUMPTIONS

Local Independence

As with IRT models, the assumption of local independence is expressed as the conditional probability of an arbitrary response pattern for a set of items equaling the product of the conditional response probabilities for the individual items. For example, for four dichotomously scored items, if $X_1 = 1$, $X_2 = 0$, $X_3 = 1$, and $X_4 = 0$, the following property can be stated:

$$P(X_1 = 1, X_2 = 0, X_3 = 1, X_4 = 0 \mid \theta_t) =$$
$$P(X_1 = 1 \mid \theta_t) \, P(X_2 = 0 \mid \theta_t)$$
$$P(X_3 = 1 \mid \theta_t) \, P(X_4 = 0 \mid \theta_t) =$$
$$P_1 Q_2 P_3 Q_4,$$

where $P_i = P(X_i = 1 \mid \theta_t)$ and $Q_i = 1 - P_i$. Hence, the goal for latent class analysis is to determine a set of θ_t's such that the manifest variables in each class are locally independent.

Latent Class Models

In this section, two types of basic latent class models are presented: a formal latent class model, followed by a restricted latent class model. Next, a hybrid of latent class and latent trait models are illustrated by a concrete example, and the link between the two approaches is discussed.

First, an illustration of the logic underlying latent class analysis can be given by presenting a simple two-item cross-tabulation of data for discrete data. This approach was nicely illustrated in McCutcheon (1987). For example, suppose questionnaire data designed to measure business ethical attitude are collected from 200 persons. Responses to two dichotomously scored questions are presented in Table 2.3. A chi-square test of independence

TABLE 2.3
Two-Item Cross-Tabulation

	Item 2		
Item 1	60	70	130
	80	50	130
	140	120	260

indicates a significant association between cell frequencies ($\chi^2 = 6.19$, $df = 1$, $p < .05$). An interpretation of this association can be thought of as a symmetrical relationship, as the variables are indicators of the same factor, are part of a system, have functional interdependence of elements, are effects of a common cause, or simply have a spurious relationship (Rosenberg, 1968). As described by McCutcheon, latent class analysis can be described as a means of examining symmetrical relationships among discrete variables, to the extent these relationships form classes of persons.

The Standard Unrestricted Latent Class Model

The standard latent class model (Clogg, 1981; Goodman, 1974; Haberman, 1979; Lazarsfeld & Henry, 1968) postulates that within a latent class θ_t, responses to manifest variables are independent. The relationship is designated as a product of the probability of being at a particular level on each of the measured variables and the probability of falling in a particular category of the latent variable, θ_t. The standard latent class model is unrestricted because the conditional probabilities and the latent class probabilities are not specified in any hypotheses. For this reason, the unrestricted model analysis is exploratory.

For a four-variable case, this unrestricted model is expressed as follows:

$$\pi_{ijklt}^{ABCD\theta} = \pi_{it}^{\bar{A}\theta} \times \pi_{jt}^{\bar{B}\theta} \times \pi_{kt}^{\bar{C}\theta} \times \pi_{lt}^{\bar{D}\theta} \times \pi_t^{\theta} \tag{8}$$

where $\pi_{ijklt}^{ABCD\theta}$ is the probability that a randomly selected person will reside in the i,j,k,l,t cell, $\pi_{it}^{\bar{A}\theta}$ is the conditional probability of a case being in level t of θ having level i of variable A, and so on for variables B, C, and D, and π_t^{θ} is the probability of a randomly selected person at level t of θ.

These latent class probabilities are informative of the relative size and number of classes. For example, it is informative to note how the class membership probability is related to the relative class size, and how the latent strucures differ across classes. Some interesting properties of latent class analysis include: (a) The probabilities of the latent class membership sum to 1.00, and (b) within each of the latent classes, the conditional probabilities for the items sum to 1.00.

Estimation and Model Fit

Estimation of the latent class probabilities is performed using maximum likelihood procedures with such numerical procedures as the EM algorithm (Dempster, Laird, & Rubin, 1977) and Newton–Raphson (Hambleton & Swaminathan, 1985). A thorough examination of these procedures is not feasible with the goals of this chapter. To summarize, the researcher gives start values for the class probabilities given in Equation 8, and iteratively, the conditional probabilities for patterns and the latent class probabilities are estimated and reestimated until some stopping criterion is reached. For a detailed description of estimation see McCutcheon (1987), Heinen (1996), and Langeheine and Rost (1988).

Model fit of standard latent class analysis is performed by comparing the test statistics across class analyses, for example, comparison of a two-class versus a three-class analysis. Using chi-square-based statistics such as the Pearson chi-square or the loglikelihood ratio, G^2, fit across class model analyses can be examined. To understand the nature of the differences across classes, the response patterns of the separate classes should be explored.

Restricted Class Models

Suppose after one has performed an unrestricted class analysis, he or she is interested in latent class comparisons across conditional probabilities of observed variables. For example, suppose a questionnaire assesses attitude toward men and women in work settings. One question addresses the extent to which women should be paid equally to men for the same position and with equal experience. A second question addresses men's and women's salaries in holding the same job in an upper management position, both with the same experience. Perhaps a question a researcher would test is the extent to which two different classes respond similarly to salary equity but differently to upper management salary equity. This hypothesis test allows the researcher to set constraints, or restrictions, on the conditional probabilities, to determine whether the nature of the latent classes differ.

Two methods of restriction across conditional probabilities exist: equality constraints and specific value constraints. The first method tests whether latent class probabilities or conditional probabilities are the same, and the second method tests whether latent class probabilities or conditional probabilities have a specific value (Goodman, 1974). So, in our example, one could test the extent to which two latent classes respond equally to general gender salary equity and management gender salary equity, or, test whether the conditional probabilities across classes are .40, for example.

To assess the effectiveness of the constraints, a comparison is made between latent class model fit, using chi-square, or likelihood ratio statistics, with the constraints, and without the constraints, to determine improvement in model fit with reduced number of parameters. This assessment allows the researcher the ability to understand the nature of differences and similarities in conditional probabilities and latent class probabilities between groups. For methods explaining the procedures for setting equality and specific value constraints within latent class computer programs, see McCutcheon (1987).

An interesting hybrid model combining the strengths of latent class and latent trait theory has been developed by Rost (1990). This latent structure model is examined next.

A HYBRID MODEL: THE MIXED RASCH MODEL

Rost (1990) proposed a Rasch-type model in which latent class and latent trait models are combined. The purpose of this model, called the Mixed Rasch Model, allows the estimation of different item difficulties and thetas for persons on the latent trait side and allows class memberships designating different patterns of responses on the latent class side. Within each class, item difficulties are constant for all persons, but these item difficulties differ between classes of persons.

The Mixed Rasch Model is well suited toward applications in which researchers believe item responses differ between groups due to solution strategies, for example. Suppose a sample of persons is given a musical aptitude test. Some aptitude items measure classical musical aptitude, and other items measure technical musical aptitude. Assuming some of the sample represents a class of persons oriented toward one item type and others in the sample are oriented toward another, subgroups should solve more oriented items than nonoriented items.

The Mixed Rasch Model is as follows:

$$P(X_{ij} = 1) = \sum_g \pi_g \frac{\exp{(\theta_{jg} + b_{ig})}}{1 + \exp{(\theta_{jg} + b_{ig})}} \tag{9}$$

where θ_{jg} = theta for person j in group g, b_{ig} = easiness for item i in group g, π_g = the class size parameter or mixing proportion, and all other values are as in Equation 1. Note that b_{ig} in this model is designated as item easiness.

The b-value has a reverse sign from item difficulty. The constraint $\sum_{g}\pi_{g} = 1$ designates the sum of the mixing proportions over all groups is equal to one.

Mixed Rasch Model analyses enable estimation of class membership based on different patterns of responses. An example application well suited toward this goal is a study done by McCollam and Embretson (1995). Item responses for a 27-item spatial visualization test of varying spatial transformation, given to 211 persons, were analyzed using the Mixed Rasch Model (Rost, 1990). Because it is well known that spatial solution strategies differ among persons, the authors hypothesized that latent classes exist in the population based on these strategy differences. MIRA (Rost & von Davier, 1993) class estimates were obtained for one, two, and three classes. Fit indices indicated the two-class solution best fit the data. Post-MIRA examination of class item responses indicated a low- and high-spatial transformation proficiency between groups, with differing ability relationships to outside aptitude tests, indicating solution

TABLE 2.4
Brief Annotated Output for Mixed Rasch Model

Number of Persons	:	211	
Number of Items	:	27	
Number of Categories	:	2	!2 categories, right & wrong
From Number of Classes	:	1	!fit 1, 2, & 3 classes
To Number of Classes	:	3	
Reduced N. of Persons	:	210	!1 person had a perfect score
Number of Different Patterns	:	211	!No patterns were identical
Number of Possible Patterns	:	134217728	!2^{27} possible patterns

SCORE FREQUENCIES

* 0:	0.*	1:	0.*	2:	0.*	3:	0.*	4:	0.*	5:	0.
* 6:	0.*	7:	9.*	8:	5.*	9:	11.*	10:	13.*	11:	13.
*12:	7.*	13:	13.*	14:	10.*	15:	10.*	16:	13.*	17:	9.
*18:	14.*	19:	11.*	20:	21.*	21:	9.*	22:	11.*	23:	7.
*24:	13.*	25:	5.*	26:	6.*	27:	1.*				

!9 persons got a raw total score of 7. 13 persons got a raw total
!score of 16. 1 person received a raw total score of 27.

!2-class model estimation is shown

Number of Classes: 2
****

Statistics of Class Membership:
* Class * Percent * N. of Cl. * average P *
****

1 *	0.379	80	0.8743	!about 38% are in class
2 *	0.616	130	0.9537	!1, and about 62% are
				!in class 2

(Continued)

TABLE 2.4
(Continued)

Expected Score Frequencies and Personparameters:

		!Class 1			!Class 2	
*Raw-	* Exp.	* Para-	* Stand.	* Exp.	* Para-	* Stand.
*score	* freq.	* meter	* error	* freq.	* meter	* error
1	0.010	−4.360	1.074	0.010	−3.644	1.039
2	0.010	−3.508	0.815	0.010	−2.873	0.760
3	0.010	−2.934	0.711	0.010	−2.390	0.641
4	0.010	−2.472	0.653	0.010	−2.025	0.572
5	0.010	−2.072	0.613	0.010	−1.724	0.527
6	0.010	−1.717	0.580	0.010	−1.463	0.495
7	6.670	−1.397	0.552	2.330	−1.230	0.472
8	1.807	−1.105	0.528	3.193	−1.016	0.455
9	7.356	−0.838	0.506	3.644	−0.815	0.442
10	9.490	−0.591	0.489	3.510	−0.625	0.432
11	6.597	−0.360	0.474	6.403	−0.441	0.425
12	4.746	−0.140	0.463	2.254	−0.262	0.421
13	7.664	0.069	0.454	5.336	−0.086	0.419
14	4.875	0.273	0.448	5.125	0.089	0.419
15	2.137	0.472	0.445	7.863	0.265	0.421
16	0.010	0.669	0.444	12.992	0.444	0.425
17	5.968	0.866	0.446	3.032	0.627	0.432
18	6.738	1.067	0.451	7.262	0.818	0.441
19	3.095	1.275	0.460	7.905	1.018	0.454
20	0.010	1.493	0.474	20.993	1.232	0.472
21	0.010	1.727	0.494	8.992	1.465	0.495
22	0.010	1.985	0.523	10.992	1.725	0.526
23	4.491	2.280	0.566	2.509	2.025	0.571
24	0.010	2.636	0.633	12.996	2.388	0.639
25	0.010	3.107	0.751	4.996	2.869	0.758
26	4.299	3.862	1.030	1.701	3.636	1.037

Mean: 0.261 Stdev: 1.286   Mean: 0.921 Stdev: 1.050
Expected Score = 13.81   Expected Score = 17.87

!Each class has a different distribution of ability scores
!for raw score total. For class 1, a person with a raw score of 1
!gets an ability score of −4.360. For class 2, a person with a raw
!score of 19 gets an ability score of 1.018

		!Class 1						!Class 2		
		-Expected-				*	*	-Expected-		
Item	Item's	*	Category		*	Item*	Item's	*	Category	*
*No. *	Score	* Stdev *	Freq.		*	No. *	Score *	Stdev	Freq.	*
			*	0	1			*	0	1
1 *	0.56	* 0.50 *	33.8	42.2		1 *	0.68 *	0.47 *	43.2	90.8
2 *	0.27	* 0.44 *	55.4	20.5		2 *	0.31 *	0.46 *	92.6	41.5
3 *	0.93	* 0.26 *	5.4	70.6		3 *	0.67 *	0.47 *	44.6	89.4
4 *	0.24	* 0.42 *	58.1	17.9		4 *	0.46 *	0.50 *	71.9	62.1
5 *	0.94	* 0.23 *	4.3	71.7		5 *	0.88 *	0.33 *	16.7	117.3

(Continued)

TABLE 2.4
(Continued)

	!Class 1						!Class 2		
*		-Expected-		*	*		-Expected-		
Item	Item's	*	Category	*	Item*	Item's	*	Category	*
*No. *	Score *	Stdev *	Freq.	*	No. *	Score *	Stdev	Freq.	*
6 *	0.91 *	0.28 *	6.6	69.4	6 *	0.75 *	0.43 *	33.4	100.6
7 *	0.30 *	0.46 *	53.5	22.4	7 *	0.68 *	0.47 *	42.5	91.6
8 *	0.93 *	0.25 *	5.2	70.7	8 *	0.88 *	0.32 *	15.8	118.3
9 *	0.44 *	0.50 *	42.7	33.2	9 *	0.74 *	0.44 *	34.3	99.8
10 *	0.30 *	0.46 *	53.5	22.4	10 *	0.70 *	0.46 *	40.5	93.6
11 *	0.70 *	0.46 *	22.7	53.3	11 *	0.78 *	0.41 *	29.3	104.7
12 *	0.36 *	0.48 *	48.8	27.2	12 *	0.64 *	0.48 *	48.2	85.8
13 *	0.46 *	0.50 *	41.2	34.7	13 *	0.84 *	0.37 *	21.8	112.3
14 *	0.93 *	0.25 *	5.2	70.8	14 *	0.93 *	0.25 *	8.8	125.2
15 *	0.45 *	0.50 *	41.6	34.4	15 *	0.36 *	0.48 *	85.4	48.6
16 *	0.36 *	0.48 *	48.8	27.2	16 *	0.57 *	0.50 *	58.2	75.8
17 *	0.31 *	0.46 *	52.2	23.7	17 *	0.55 *	0.50 *	60.8	73.3
18 *	0.72 *	0.45 *	21.3	54.7	18 *	0.72 *	0.45 *	37.7	96.3
19 *	0.44 *	0.50 *	42.6	33.4	19 *	0.66 *	0.47 *	45.4	88.6
20 *	0.39 *	0.49 *	46.0	29.9	20 *	0.70 *	0.46 *	40.0	94.1
21 *	0.30 *	0.46 *	52.9	23.1	21 *	0.35 *	0.48 *	87.1	46.9
22 *	0.59 *	0.49 *	31.1	44.9	22 *	0.68 *	0.47 *	42.9	91.1
23 *	0.33 *	0.47 *	51.2	24.7	23 *	0.49 *	0.50 *	67.8	66.3
24 *	0.31 *	0.46 *	52.7	23.3	24 *	0.59 *	0.49 *	54.3	79.7
25 *	0.66 *	0.47 *	26.1	49.9	25 *	0.86 *	0.35 *	18.9	115.1
26 *	0.35 *	0.48 *	49.6	26.4	26 *	0.77 *	0.42 *	30.4	103.6
27 *	0.35 *	0.48 *	49.6	26.3	27 *	0.62 *	0.48 *	50.4	83.7

!note the differences between classes for item success
!42.2% of class 1 members got item 1 correct
!90.8% of class 2 members got item 2 correct

	!Class 1			!Class 2		
Item	* Thr.1	*	Item	* Thr.1	*	!Thr.1 = b-value
1	0.11		1	−0.02		!for class 2,
2	−1.41		2	−1.83		!item 2 is hardest
3	2.67	!for class 1,	3	−0.07		
4	−1.66	!item 4 is hardest	4	−1.06		
5	2.92	!item 5 is easiest	5	1.34		
6	2.44		6	0.40		
7	−1.25		7	0.01		
8	2.70		8	1.42		
9	−0.47		9	0.36		
10	−1.25		10	0.09		
11	0.84		11	0.60		
12	−0.89		12	−0.21		
13	−0.37		13	1.01		
14	2.72		14	2.09		!item 14 is esiest
15	−0.39		15	−1.55		
16	−0.89		16	−0.58		

(Continued)

TABLE 2.4
(Continued)

!Class 1			!Class 2			
Item	* Thr.1	*	Item	* Thr.1	*	!Thr.1 = b-value
17	−1.15		17	−0.67		
18	0.94		18	0.21		
19	−0.46		19	−0.11		
20	−0.69		20	0.12		
21	−1.20		21	−1.62		
22	0.28		22	−0.01		
23	−1.07		23	−0.92		
24	−1.18		24	−0.44		
25	0.61		25	1.19		
26	−0.95		26	0.54		
27	−0.95		27	−0.29		

!Recall that Rost scales b-values as easiness, not difficulty, so
!the signs are reversed from difficulty

	!overall fit statistics									
Class	* LOG-LIKE	*	NPAR	*	LIKE.RATIO	*	DF	*	AIC	*
1	−3121.232	*	53	*	3983.980	*	134217674	*	6348.465	*
2	−3068.596	*	105	*	3878.708	*	134217622	*	6347.193	*
3	−3025.659	*	157	*	3792.834	*	134217570	*	6365.319	*

!For Number of parameters, or npar.:
!Each model has h − 1 class parameters, where h = number of classes
!Each model has (k − 1)h class-specific item parameters, where k =
!number of items.
!Each model has 2 + h(k − 2) class-specific score probabilities
!DF = 2^{27} − npar, or 134217728 − npar
!Aikake's information criterion is lowest for the two-class model.
!Therefore the 2-class model would be considered the best !model

strategy differences. A brief annotated output for the two-class solution is in Table 2.4, with comments made to the right of "!" symbols.

SUMMARY

The goal of this chapter was to introduce widely used latent trait and latent class models to unfamiliar readers, informing readers about the strength and power of such models for understanding item response phenomena. It is believed that as more exposure is given to these models and methods, researchers and practitioners will find their value and apply them to substantive issues and problems. Further repeated exposure to latent trait and latent class models is recommended.

REFERENCES

Andersen, E. B. (1972). The numerical solution of a set of conditional estimation equations. *Journal of the Royal Statistical Society, Series B, 34,* 42–54.

Andersen, E. B. (1990). *The statistical analysis of categorical data.* Berlin: Springer-Verlag.

Andrich, D. (1988). *Rasch models for measurement.* Newbury Park, CA: Sage.

Birnbaum, A. (1968). Some latent trait models and their use in inferring an examinee's ability. In F. M. Lord & M. R. Novick (Eds.), *Statistical theories of mental test scores.* Reading, MA: Addison-Wesley.

Bock, R. D. (1972). Estimating item parameters and latent ability when responses are scored in two or more nominal categories. *Psychometrika, 37,* 29–51.

Bock, R. D., & Aitkin, M. (1981). Marginal maximum likelihood estimation of item parameters: Application of an EM algorithm. *Psychometrika, 46,* 443–459.

Bock, R. D., & Lieberman, M. (1970). Fitting a response model for n dichotomously scored items. *Psychometrika, 35,* 179–197.

Bozdogan, H. (1987). Model selection and Akaike's information criterion (AIC): The general theory and its analytical extensions. *Psychometrika, 52,* 345–370.

Clogg, C. C. (1981). New developments in latent structure analysis. In D. J. Jackson & E. G. Borgatta (Eds.), *Factor analysis and measurement in sociological research* (pp. 215–246). Newbury Park, CA: Sage.

Dempster, A. P., Laird, N. M., & Rubin, D. B. (1977). Maximum likelihood estimating with incomplete data via the EM algorithm. *Journal of the Royal Statistical Society, Series B, 39,* 1–38.

Embretson, S. E. (1984). A general multicomponent latent trait model for response processes. *Psychometrika, 49,* 175–186.

Embretson, S. E. (1995). Working memory capacity versus general control processes in abstract reasoning. *Intelligence, 20,* 169–189.

Fischer, G. (1973). Linear Logistic test model as an instrument in educational research. *Acta Psychologica, 37,* 359–374.

Goodman, L. A. (1974). The analysis of systems of qualitative variables when some of the variables are unobservable: Part I. A modified latent structure approach. *American Journal of Sociology, 79,* 1179–1259.

Haberman, S. J. (1979). *Analysis of qualitative data: Vol. 2. New developments.* New York: Academic Press.

Hambleton, R. K., & Swaminathan, H. (1985). *Item response theory: Principles and applications.* Boston: Kluwer.

Hambleton, R. K., Swaminathan, H., & Rogers, H. J. (1991). *Fundamentals of item response theory.* Newbury Park, CA: Sage.

Heinen, T. (1996). *Latent class and discrete latent trait models: Similarities and differences.* Thousand Oaks, CA: Sage.

Langeheine, R., & Rost, J. (Eds.). (1988). *Latent trait and latent class models.* New York: Plenum.

Lazarsfeld, P. F., & Henry, N. W. (1968). *Latent structure analysis.* Boston: Houghton Mifflin.

Lord, F. M. (1952). A theory of test scores. *Psychometrika Monograph No. 7, 17*(4, Pt. 2).

Lord, F. M. (1974). Estimation of latent ability and item parameters when there are omitted responses. *Psychometrika, 39,* 247–264.

Lord, F. M. (1980). *Applications of item response theory to practical testing problems.* Hillsdale, NJ: Lawrence Erlbaum Associates.

Lord, F. M., & Novick, M. R. (1968). *Statistical theories of mental test scores.* Reading, MA: Addison-Wesley.

Masters, G. N. (1982). A Rasch model for partial credit scoring. *Psychometrika, 47,* 149–174.

McCollam, K. M., & Embretson, S. E. (1995, August). *Analysis of spatial strategies using the Mixed Rasch Model.* Poster presented at a meeting of the American Psychological Association, New York.

McCutcheon, A. L. (1987). *Latent class analysis.* Newbury Park, CA: Sage.

Rasch, G. (1960). *Probabilistic models for some intelligence and attainment tests.* Copenhagen: Danish Institute of Educational Research.

Rosenberg, M. (1968). *The logic of survey analysis.* New York: Basic Books.

Rost, J. (1990). Rasch models in latent classes: An integration of two approaches to item analysis. *Applied Psychological Measurement, 14,* 271–282.

Rost, J., & von Davier, M. (1993). *MIRA: A PC-program for the Mixed Rasch Model: User manual.* Kiel, Federal Republic of Germany: Institute for Science Education.

Samejima, F. (1969). Estimation of latent ability using a response pattern of graded scores. *Psychometrika Monograph No. 17, 34*(4, Pt. 2).

Thissen, D., & Steinberg, L. (1986). A taxonomy of item response models. *Psychometrika, 51,* 567–577.

CHAPTER THREE

Measurement Designs Using Multifacet Rasch Modeling

Mary E. Lunz
American Society of Clinical Pathologists

John M. Linacre
MESA, University of Chicago

The purpose of an assessment is to make generalizable inferences about people, products, or information. Whether the goal is to assess knowledge and skill, determine product quality, or make promotion, marketing, productivity, or usage decisions, the assessment must be designed to measure as accurately as possible. How the assessment is structured and analyzed has a substantial impact on the interpretation and accuracy of the results.

The structure of the assessment determines the validity and reproducibility of the results. Therefore, it is useful to understand the impact of each facet of the assessment on the outcome. There are several factors that influence outcomes, namely, (a) who is observed (employees), (b) what they do (tasks), (c) who performs the evaluation (evaluator), (d) how the rating scale is defined (number of rating scale points), and (e) number of observations (ratings). The unique contribution of the multifacet Rasch model is that all facets are placed in the same measurement framework so that comparisons among the elements comprising the facets can be made. How the facet elements combine to produce the ratings can be observed, and the impact of each facet on the results of the study can be understood.

The purpose of the multifacet Rasch model is to account for variations, so that context bias is accounted for and removed from the interpretation of the results. When the characteristics of the facets are accounted for, the results generalize beyond the specific elements of the assessment, such as the particular evaluators, questions, or situations encountered. The actual unbiased amount of ability, value, or quality possessed is measured. Multifacet assessments occur as a regular activity in business applications even though they are called by many different names. Among the most obvious examples are performance appraisals, marketing interviews, assessments of employee skills and/or management styles, and survey data for many variables such as organizational climate, informal communication, and job satisfaction.

The primary specifications of the multifacet Rasch model are as follows: First, more able individuals will perform better than less able individuals. Generally, scores increase as ability increases regardless of the subset of knowledge and skill sampled. For example, a more able automobile driver should be able to turn right or left with greater efficiency than a less able driver. On a test, the able candidate will answer more questions correctly than the less able candidate. The second specification is that one particular question does not affect how an individual performs on any other particular question. This is called *local independence*. In tests in which each problem deals with a discrete topic, local independence does not present a problem. However, in tests in which performance is based on previous responses, local independence may become an issue. A third specification is *unidimensionality,* which refers to the assertion that a single underlying latent trait or ability is being assessed. The underlying trait is the ability to perform competently in whatever area is being assessed. Problems are designed to test all aspects of this ability, and unidimensionality is controlled by adherence to carefully determined specifications. The sample of problems may be small, but should be representative.

Assessments that require an evaluator cause indirect interaction between the individual and the problems presented by the evaluation. The individual performs the skill, but the evaluator rates the quality of the performance. Because evaluators have different perceptions and/or expectations, their differences must be accounted for to achieve a contextually unbiased, objective estimate of the person's ability to perform. When the bias of the evaluator is not removed, the outcome of the assessment does not generalize, and is not objective. Rather, the outcome is dependent on the perception of the particular evaluator's assessment of how well a particular task was performed.

FACETS OF AN ASSESSMENT

The focus of the assessment depends on its purpose and the expected outcomes. There are typically at least four separate facets in an assessment that must be accounted for to ensure generalizability of the results. The first facet is *person ability* or characteristic being measured. The knowledge and skill possessed by the person with regard to the problem, skill, or product is measured. It is expected that persons will vary in their ability to perform selected skills. The goal of assessment is often to describe these differences so that decisions about the person's ability can be accurate and reproducible.

The second facet is the *item*, which may take many forms. Some items have detailed specifications, whereas others are general. Examples of items may be case studies, job satisfaction items, product characteristics, science, or business projects. Another example may be survey items to evaluate "viewer" satisfaction or other situational characteristics.

The third facet is the *evaluator*. Evaluators are an intricate part of assessment, because they are directly responsible for providing the rating. Ratings may be given to the quality of an employee's ability to perform defined tasks, a survey item, a product characteristic, or any other pertinent item. Evaluators have unique physical and mental characteristics, as well as unique reactions, all of which affect their ratings. In some situations, evaluators' training focuses and directs an evaluator's attention, but is usually unable to alter permanently the knowledge and skill that has developed over a lifetime (Stahl & Lunz, 1994). In other situations, differences among evaluators provide the information necessary to understand different reactions to the same product.

A fourth facet may be the *skills* or *qualities* rated for each project, product, or person. Considerations for this facet include the number of skills or qualities rated, the extent of detail in the definition of the skills or qualities, the relevance of the skills or qualities, and whether or not the skills are observable. Personal skills such as using punctuation correctly or operating a drill press may be relatively easy to observe and assess, whereas ethical standards are more difficult to assess. In a product evaluation, the qualities of the product may be evaluated to determine marketability.

A fifth component is the *definition of the rating scale*. Rating scales provide a "disciplined dialogue" that encourages evaluators to assign meaning to each point on the scale. Rating scales may have as few as 2 points (0/1) or an infinite number (0/∞). Each point on the scale usually has a specific definition. The definitions of the rating scale points are important, because they govern how evaluators assign points for quality of performance. The distance between rating scale points impacts the ratings given. For example, there is a great distance between "unacceptable" and "excellent," or 1 and 100 points. Definitions of points between the extremes provide focus for the evaluator. The more points on the rating scale, the more detailed the observation, as long as the evaluator can discern the differences. The fewer points on the rating scale, the more general the observation. The number of points on the scale has a significant impact on the scoring and outcomes of the assessment.

The structuring of the facets of the measurement design is the basis for the analysis. Data come from the ratings given by those who observe or respond. There are many ways of structuring facets into an assessment so that the purpose of the study is accomplished.

In the multifacet analysis, each of the facets is considered for its contribution to the observed rating. The unique contribution of the multifacet analysis is that the impact of the combination of facet elements each person encounters is accounted for. After context bias is accounted for, the ability of the individual or the desirability of the product, and so forth, is measured more accurately. Another issue is the potential for unique combinations of facet elements that occur within an assessment. When each person is assessed by different groups of evaluators, each person challenges a different form of the assessment. When a product is assessed, the characteristics of the evaluators are likely to impact on their response. Accounting for these differences provides more valid and reliable results.

Statistical Reliability of the Assessment

Reliability depends on the number of observations combined with the rating scale definition. Increasing the number of observations increases the precision of the assessment and the statistical confidence associated with any decision. Although this is basic mathematical truth, the reality of what this means in practice must be carefully considered in terms of cost in time and money. The number of points on the rating scale impacts the specificity of the observations and therefore impacts the reliability of the results. For example, a 2-point scale (0/1) requires broad judgments such as right or wrong, good or bad. As the number of points on the rating scale increases, so does the specificity of the judgment. A 4-point scale may be defined as 4 = excellent, 3 = satisfactory, 2 = marginal, 1 = unsatisfactory, thus requiring more definitive distinctions among performances and increasing the reliability of the assessment.

Another way to increase statistical reliability is to increase the number of ratings. The number of items could be increased, the number of skills rated could be increased, and/or the number of evaluators could be increased. The larger the number of observations, the more precise the results are likely to be.

Facets are related to each other in the assessment, so other considerations such as linking patterns must be considered in the assessment design. For example, if evaluator A rated projects 1 and 2 on skills 1, 2, and 3, whereas evaluator B rated projects 3 and 4 on skills 4, 5, and 6, there is no overlap and no opportunity to statistically remove the effects of the interaction among evaluators, projects, and skills. An alternative and more useful design may be to have evaluators A and B rate the projects using the same skills, for example, skills 1–6. This design provides a common basis for measurement and a common dialogue for assessing performance, even if the projects are different.

The issue of what to standardize in an assessment is a pertinent concern for improving reliability. Increasing the number of observations is useless without some standardization. In order for consistency to be achieved, the rating scale must be standardized. All evaluators must use the same rating scale, understand the definitions assigned to the point levels, and be willing to use the scale for assessment purposes. The skills rated are the next level to be standardized. Pertinent skills must be defined explicitly and agreed on. If three skills are defined, then all evaluators must be willing to assess those skills. If six skills are defined, then all evaluators must use the six skills. The question is how much standardization is sufficient to produce reliable measurement.

Attempts to standardize evaluators through extensive training and retraining have not been consistently successful. In fact, even if evaluators correlate perfectly, there is still no guarantee that they rate the same way (Lunz, 1992). It is interesting to note that forcing evaluator agreement, the least reliable of all methods of achieving measurement objectivity, has been suggested as the method of choice. Interjudge reliability correlations have been used to demonstrate reliability, when the goal is to measure differences among persons or products with as little measurement error as possible.

METHODS

The Facets Model: Background and Explanation

The basic Rasch model (Rasch, 1960/1992) is a mathematical representation of the person and item interaction. The log-odds of a person answering a particular dichotomous item correctly is modeled as:

$$\log(P_{ni}/(1 - P_{ni})) = (B_n - D_i) \tag{1}$$

where (P_{ni}) is the probability of answering the item correctly, $(1 - P_{ni})$ is the probability of answering the item incorrectly, B_n is the ability of the person, and D_i is the difficulty of the item.

The probability of a correct response is a function of the difference between the ability of a person and the difficulty of the item. If a person's ability is greater than the difficulty of the item, then the probability of answering correctly is greater than 50%. If the difficulty of the item is greater than the ability of the person, the probability of answering the item correctly is less than 50%. The use of the logarithmic function in the equation transforms ordinal observations to a linear scale. The unit of measurement is the log-odds unit or "logit" (Wright & Stone, 1979).

For analysis of assessments the basic Rasch model is extended to the multifacet Rasch model (Linacre, 1989), so that facets for skill and item difficulty, evaluator severity, and rating scale usage can be added to the model equation. Severity is the term used to encompass the factors that influence the way evaluators rate. The difficulty of the item is the impediment to responding correctly. Easy items represent low-level tasks or general knowledge. More difficult items require more knowledge and skill or are more complex to perform. When a person or product is rated, the log odds of succeeding is modeled:

$$\log(P_{nmjik}/P_{nmjik-1)}) = (B_n - T_m - C_j - D_i - R_k) \qquad (2)$$

where P_{nmjik} is the probability of being rated in category k, $P_{nmjik-1)}$ is the probability of being rated in category $k - 1$, B_n is the ability of the person, T_m is the difficulty of the item, C_j is the severity of the evaluator, D_i is the difficulty of the skill, and R_k is the difficulty of rating category k compared to category $k - 1$.

The probability of a satisfactory person performance is a function of the difference between the ability of the person and the difficulty of the skills after adjustment for the severity of the evaluator and the difficulty of the items. If the person's ability is higher than the difficulty of the item after adjustment for the difficulty of the skill and the severity of the evaluator, then the probability of being rated in a high category is greater than 50%. Conversely, if the difficulty of the item after adjustment for the difficulty of the skill and the severity of the evaluator, is greater than the ability of the person, the probability of being rated in a high category is less than 50%.

The location of the persons, projects, evaluators, and skills on a linear scale provides a frame of reference for understanding the relationship of the facets of the performance examination, using the observed ratings. It makes it possible to observe estimated person ability (B_n) from highest to lowest, estimated item difficulty (T_m) from most to least difficult, estimated evaluator severities (C_j) from most to least severe, and estimated skill difficulties (D_i) from most to least difficult.

When all persons perform the same skills and are evaluated by all evaluators, everyone takes the same examination so adjustments are not necessary. However, scores must still be linearized to measures to insure objective measurement. Typically, fully crossed designs are too expensive or logistically or organizationally impossible. Therefore, assessment designs in which persons interact with particular evaluators and/or selected skills are often constructed. To make the person ability estimates objective, the influence of the various facets must be systematically accounted for so that differences in person ability can be measured accurately and without contextual bias.

In the multifacets analysis, person ability measures are estimated concurrently with the evaluator severities and skill difficulties. By placing all person performances on the same linear measurement scale, comparable standards can be implemented, even when the particular facet elements (e.g., evaluators) vary.

The multifacet Rasch model also provides estimates of the consistency of the evaluator rating patterns. This is reported as the fit of the data to the model. It is expected that observed ratings will be consistent; that is, able persons should earn higher ratings than less able persons, and more difficult items or skills should cause lower ratings to be awarded than easier items or skills. When ratings on any of the facets are inconsistent, fit statistics flag these ratings.

Two fit statistics are reported. The Outfit mean-square is a conventional chi-square statistic divided by its degrees of freedom. Thus, under Rasch model conditions, the modeled variance of an observation around its expectation is:

$$Var(x_{nij}) = \sum_{k=0}^{m_i} (k - E(x_{nij}))^2 \, P_{nijk} \tag{3}$$

where $Var(x_{nij})$ is the variance of the observation, x_{nij}, awarded to person n on item i by judge j; m_i is the highest numbered category for observations on item, $k = 0$, m_i; $E(x_{nij})$ is the expected value of the observation; P_{nijk} is the probability that person n will be observed on item i by judge j in category k. The Outfit mean-square, U_i, for item i (and similarly for person v and judge j) is:

$$U_i = \sum_{n=1}^{N} \sum_{j=1}^{J} \frac{(x_{nij} - E(x_{nij}))^2 / Var(x_{nij})}{NJ} \tag{4}$$

where N is the number of persons and J is the number of observations of performance on item i per person. Similarly, the Infit mean-square is an information-weighted chi-square statistic divided by its modeled degrees of freedom. The Infit mean-square, V_i, for item i (and similarly for person n and evaluator j) is

$$V_i = \frac{\displaystyle\sum_{n=1}^{N} \sum_{j=1}^{J} (x_{nij} - E(x_{nij}))^2}{\displaystyle\sum_{n=1}^{N} \sum_{j=1}^{J} Var(x_{nij})} \tag{5}$$

The Infit compares the sum of squared rating residuals with their expectation. It is sensitive to an accumulation of small deviations that are less or more consistent than expected. The Outfit compares the sum of standardized residuals with their count and is sensitive to off-target responses due to extremism or misunderstanding. The range of these fit statistics is 0 to infinity with a modeled expectation of 1.00 and a variance inversely proportional to the degrees of freedom.

Because the interpretation of fit is situationally dependent, there are no fixed levels for fit acceptance or rejection. Situational considerations include the type of test or rating scale, type of observation, examination design, and/or expectations for evaluator agreement (see Wright, 1995; Wright & Linacre, 1994). The criteria for acceptable fit used in this study are mean-squared residuals between .5 and 1.5. Evaluators and skills with fit statistics beyond these criteria are reviewed for inconsistency or overconsistency in their rating pattern.

The fit statistics for evaluators are calculated from all ratings given by an evaluator, and indicate the degree to which each evaluator is internally self-consistent when making judgments (intrajudge consistency). Evaluators who award what are for them unexpectedly high or low ratings to a particular person on a particular skill or project are identified and the effect of the unexpected ratings on the person ability estimates reviewed. The fit statistics for each skill are calculated from all ratings given for that skill and indicate interjudge consistency when grading that skill. Misfit indicates that some evaluators deviated significantly from others when grading some items or persons. The fit statistics for each skill indicate interjudge consistency when rating skills within items across persons. Person misfit indicates interjudge disagreement on the quality of that person's performance.

The fit statistics evaluate the suitability of the data for the construction of a variable. The fit statistics for evaluators indicate the degree to which each evaluator is internally self-consistent across persons, skills, and items (intrajudge consistency). Evaluators who award unexpectedly high or low ratings to a particular person on a particular skill or item can be flagged and the effect of the unexpected ratings on the person ability estimates reviewed. The fit statistic for each skill indicates interjudge consistency when grading that project. Misfit indicates that some evaluators deviated significantly from others when grading the skill for some persons. The fit statistics for each project also indicate interjudge consistency when rating skills within items across persons. Misfit indicates that some evaluators were inconsistent in their use of the rating scale when assessing that skill for some persons.

Three examples of multifacet Rasch analysis are provided. The data are unique for each example. The examples were selected to show how the information from some business analyses can be increased using the multifacet Rasch model. These are not the only applications for this powerful analysis tool, but are a useful sample.

Each application was analyzed using FACETS, a computer program for the analysis of data with more than two facets (Linacre, 1990). This program has been used in general education, medical education, certification and licensure, rehabilitation therapy, occupational therapy, as well as business applications for analysis of survey, person, and product data. Its unique contribution is to produce objective, unbiased estimates of the characteristics of the entity being measured.

The first example is educational and discusses how the evaluation of individuals can be made objective. The second example demonstrates how product evaluation for marketing studies can be more objective and therefore provide more information about the data collection process as well as the results. The third example presents an application to survey analysis, in this case job satisfaction, and how patterns become more informative by using the multifacet model.

EXAMPLE 1: PERSON ASSESSMENT

The purpose of this assessment was to ascertain and differentiate among the ability of a group of employees to perform skills necessary for acceptable job performance. The multifacet model used in this analysis was $\log(P_{nijk}/P_{nij(k-1)}) = (B_n - D_i - C_j - R_k)$. A group of 74 employees are assessed by 31 evaluators on their ability to perform three skills. Six evaluators assess the work of each person on the three skills. The multifacet analysis is properly linked because all persons are rated on the same skills using the same rating scale, and there is random overlap among the six evaluators who rate the performance of the persons. Employees were evaluated on their ability to perform three tasks: cut, press, and assemble. Employees were rated by random subsets of six of the 31 evaluators on each of the tasks. The rating scale used by the evaluators included 5 points: 0 = unsatisfactory, 1 = marginal, 2 = satisfactory, 3 = very good, and 4 = excellent. All evaluators rated employees on all of the tasks, but different employees were rated by different subsets of evaluators, so the multifacet correction was used to account for differences in evaluators, giving all employees a comparable opportunity to demonstrate satisfactory achievement on each of the tasks. Also, information about the difficulty of the skills and the severity of the evaluators was obtained. These measured differences were based on all of the ratings given by evaluators to all skills across all employees. Thus, the severity of the evaluator was based on all ratings given across all skills to employees. The difficulty of the skills was based on all ratings given by all evaluators across all employees.

Figure 3.1 shows the graphic representation of the assessment results. The variable is defined in logits listed in the left column. Employees are distributed according to their measured ability after adjustment for differences in the subsets of evaluators who observed their performance on the

Map of all Evaluation Facets

```
----------------------------------------------------------------------
|Measr |+PERSONS                |-EVALUATOR    |-SKILL    |S.1 |
----------------------------------------------------------------------
+  5 + 405  Most Able           + Most Severe  + Most     +(4) +
     | 412                      |              | Difficult|
     |                          |              |          |
     |                          |              |          |
     |   304                    |              |          |
+  4 +                          +              +          +     +
     |   305                    |              |          |
     |   505  506               |              |        --- 
     |   104                    |              |          |
     |   112  211  214  513  515 |             |          |
     |   308                    |              |          |
     |   504                    |              |          |
+  3 + 310  311                 +              +          +     +
     |   208  408  512          |              |          |
     |   313  501               |              |          |
     |   212  314  502  514     |              |          |
     |   303  509               |              |          |
     |   102  205  507          |              |          |
     |   103  108  210  302  510 |             |        + 3  +
+  2 + 114                       +              +          +     +
     |   508                    |              |          |
     |   306  309  403          |              |          |
     |   201  315  410          |              |          |
     |   203  206               |              |          |
     |   109  111  209          | 3   34       |          |
+  1 + 106  407                 +              +          +     +
     |   207  307  402          | 18  27  29  9|          |
     |   503                    |              |          |
     |   115                    | 11  16  8    |        --- 
     |   113  404  411  414     | 25           |          |
     |   105  110               | 1  10  12  15| PRESS    |
     |   204  406  511          |              |          |
*  0 * 107  202  215  409  413  * 20          * ASSEMBLE *     *
     |   415                    | 28  33       |          |
     |   401                    | 13  21  23   | CUT      |
     |                          | 26  32       |          |
     |                          | 30  31  6  7 |        + 2  +
     |   312                    |              |          |
     |   213                    | 22  24       |          |
+ -1 +                          + 19           +          +     +
     |                          | 4            |          |
     |   301                    | 14           |        --- 
     |                          |              |          |
     |                          |              | Least    |
+ -2 + Least Able               + Least Severe +Difficult +(0) +
----------------------------------------------------------------------
|Measr |+PERSONS                |-EVALUATOR    |-SKILL    |S.1 |
----------------------------------------------------------------------
```

FIG. 3.1. Employee performance assessment: map of all evaluation facets.

three skills. The ability estimates are statistically independent of the perceptions of the particular evaluators who gave the ratings. The most able employee (405) had more than a 50% probability of achieving a satisfactory rating from the most severe evaluators (3 and 34). The three tasks (press, assemble, and cut) were close to 0.00 and relatively comparable in difficulty. Figure 3.2 shows the comparison of unadjusted scores to adjusted ability estimates. The overall correlation is .95; however the scores for an ability estimate of 2.25 logits range from approximately 50 to 60 points. This is due to the adjustment for evaluator severity.

Tables 3.1, 3.3, and 3.4 show the details for each facet. The statistics shown for each facet of the assessment are generally comparable. Table 3.1 is used for explanation; however, the same data are shown for all comparable tables for all three examples. The *Obsvd Score* is the raw score or sum of

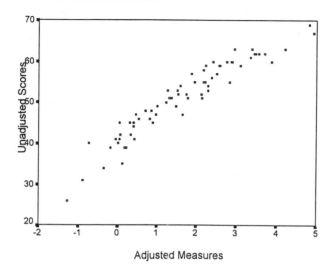

FIG. 3.2. Comparison of adjusted ability estimates to unadjusted scores.

ratings earned by the employee. The *Obsvd Count* is the number of observations or ratings of the employee. The *Obsvd Average* is the average rating,
the Obsvd Score divided by the Obsvd Count. The *Fair Average* is the logit
ability estimate converted back to a raw score average, after the effects of
the other facets have been accounted for. This enables a "fair" comparison
in raw score points. The *Measure Logit* is the logit estimate of employee
ability when the impact of the evaluators or other facets are accounted for.
The *Model Error* is the standard error or precision of the Measure Logit. The
Infit MnSq is the information-weighted mean-square fit statistic. The *Outfit
MnSq* is a conventional mean-squared statistic that is more sensitive to outliers. Both of these statistics relate observed to expected. When expected
and observed match statistically, the result is a fit of 1.00. Fit statistics below
1.00 usually indicate greater than expected consistency, in the form or over-
use of 1 or 2 points on the rating scale. Fit statistics greater than 1.5 usually
indicate less than expected consistency, usually in the form of giving extremely high or extremely low ratings unexpectedly. *Std* is a standardized
form of the mean-square statistic, distributed N(0,1).

   At the bottom of the table are several statistics also useful for interpreting
the data. The *RMSE* $((\Sigma se/N)^{1/2})$ is the root mean-square standard error (se) for
all nonextreme measures. The *Adj S.D.* $(SD^2 - MSE)^{1/2}$ is the standard deviation
of measures for nonextreme scores after removing the measurement error,
thus a statistically unbiased standard deviation. *Separation* is an estimate of
the spread of the estimates relative to their precision (Adj. S.D/RMSE).
Separation Reliability is the equivalent to the KR-20 or Cronbach Alpha
statistic, that is, the ratio of True Variance to Observed Variance (R = (SD² −

TABLE 3.1
Ability Estimates of Employees to Perform the Skills

PERSONS	Obsvd Score	Obsvd Count	Obsvd Average	Fair Avrge	Measure Logit	Model Error	Infit MnSq	Std	Outfit MnSq	Std
405	67	18	3.7	3.8	4.94	0.53	1.2	0	1.3	0
412	69	18	3.8	3.8	4.82	0.63	1.1	0	1.2	0
304	63	18	3.5	3.7	4.21	0.46	1.8	2	3.2	4[a]
305	60	18	3.3	3.6	3.87	0.43	1.9	2	2.0	2[a]
505	62	18	3.4	3.5	3.70	0.45	0.9	0	0.9	0
506	62	18	3.4	3.5	3.70	0.45	0.5	−2	0.5	−2[b]
104	62	18	3.4	3.5	3.56	0.45	0.6	−1	0.5	−1
214	62	18	3.4	3.5	3.48	0.45	1.3	0	1.3	0
211	62	18	3.4	3.5	3.45	0.45	1.1	0	1.0	0
513	62	18	3.4	3.5	3.45	0.44	1.5	1	1.5	1
515	62	18	3.4	3.5	3.45	0.44	1.0	0	0.9	0
112	63	18	3.5	3.4	3.38	0.45	0.8	0	0.8	0
308	61	18	3.4	3.4	3.35	0.44	0.9	0	1.0	0
504	59	18	3.3	3.4	3.11	0.44	1.1	0	1.2	0
310	63	18	3.5	3.3	2.96	0.44	0.9	0	0.9	0
311	63	18	3.5	3.3	2.96	0.44	0.9	0	0.9	0
408	60	18	3.3	3.3	2.90	0.43	1.6	1	1.6	1
208	60	18	3.3	3.3	2.87	0.43	1.0	0	1.0	0
512	55	18	3.1	3.3	2.84	0.42	1.5	1	1.5	1
313	60	18	3.3	3.3	2.77	0.43	0.7	−1	0.7	−1
501	60	18	3.3	3.3	2.76	0.43	1.2	0	1.2	0
314	59	18	3.3	3.2	2.59	0.43	0.4	−2	0.4	−2[b]
502	59	18	3.3	3.2	2.57	0.43	0.5	−1	0.5	−1
212	57	18	3.2	3.2	2.52	0.42	1.3	0	1.2	0
514	57	18	3.2	3.2	2.52	0.43	1.9	2	1.9	2[a]
509	60	18	3.3	3.2	2.42	0.43	1.1	0	1.1	0
303	56	18	3.1	3.1	2.39	0.42	1.8	1	1.8	1
102	53	18	2.9	3.1	2.30	0.41	0.3	−2	0.3	−2[b]
205	54	18	3.0	3.1	2.30	0.42	0.9	0	1.0	0
507	59	18	3.3	3.1	2.24	0.43	0.7	−1	0.7	−1
302	55	18	3.1	3.1	2.21	0.42	0.7	0	0.7	0
108	58	18	3.2	3.1	2.17	0.43	1.4	1	1.4	1
210	55	18	3.1	3.1	2.17	0.42	1.0	0	1.0	0
510	51	18	2.8	3.1	2.15	0.40	0.3	−2	0.3	−2[b]
103	52	18	2.9	3.1	2.13	0.41	0.6	−1	0.5	−1
114	55	18	3.1	3.0	1.96	0.42	0.9	0	1.0	0
508	57	18	3.2	3.0	1.88	0.43	0.5	−1	0.5	−1
403	51	18	2.8	3.0	1.78	0.40	1.1	0	1.1	0
309	52	18	2.9	2.9	1.75	0.41	0.6	−1	0.6	−1
306	47	18	2.6	2.9	1.66	0.38	0.9	0	0.9	0
401	54	18	3.0	2.9	1.59	0.42	0.5	−1	0.5	−1
201	52	18	2.9	2.9	1.53	0.41	0.3	−2	0.3	−2[b]
315	53	18	2.9	2.9	1.52	0.41	1.4	0	1.4	0
206	49	18	2.7	2.9	1.48	0.39	1.1	0	1.2	0
203	51	18	2.8	2.8	1.36	0.41	0.4	−1	0.4	−1
209	51	18	2.8	2.8	1.32	0.40	1.0	0	1.1	0

(Continued)

TABLE 3.1
Ability Estimates of Employees to Perform the Skills

PERSONS	Obsvd Score	Obsvd Count	Obsvd Average	Fair Avrge	Measure Logit	Model Error	Infit MnSq	Std	Outfit MnSq	Std
109	53	18	2.9	2.8	1.28	0.41	0.6	−1	0.6	−1
111	50	18	2.8	2.8	1.24	0.40	1.8	1	1.7	1[a]
407	49	18	2.7	2.7	1.01	0.39	0.8	0	0.8	0
106	47	18	2.6	2.7	0.98	0.38	0.6	−1	0.5	−1
402	45	18	2.5	2.6	0.89	0.37	1.0	0	1.1	0
207	48	18	2.7	2.6	0.86	0.38	1.2	0	1.3	0
307	46	18	2.6	2.6	0.83	0.37	1.7	1	1.6	1[a]
503	48	18	2.7	2.6	0.70	0.39	0.9	0	0.8	0
115	46	18	2.6	2.5	0.54	0.37	2.4	2	2.4	2[a]
411	47	18	2.6	2.5	0.46	0.38	1.4	0	1.4	1
404	41	18	2.3	2.5	0.43	0.34	1.1	0	1.1	0
414	44	18	2.4	2.5	0.41	0.36	0.5	−1	0.5	−1
113	45	18	2.5	2.5	0.40	0.37	0.5	−1	0.6	−1
105	42	18	2.3	2.4	0.33	0.35	0.7	0	0.8	0
110	45	18	2.5	2.4	0.32	0.37	0.4	−2	0.4	−2[b]
406	39	18	2.2	2.4	0.21	0.33	0.9	0	0.9	0
204	39	18	2.2	2.4	0.18	0.33	0.4	−2	0.4	−2[b]
511	35	18	1.9	2.3	0.13	0.31	1.6	1	1.6	1[a]
409	42	18	2.3	2.3	0.06	0.35	2.3	2	2.3	2[a]
107	45	18	2.5	2.3	0.05	0.37	0.6	−1	0.6	−1
413	41	18	2.3	2.3	0.04	0.34	0.6	−1	0.6	−1
215	40	18	2.2	2.3	0.01	0.33	1.2	0	1.1	0
202	41	18	2.3	2.3	−0.04	0.34	0.5	−1	0.5	−1
415	39	18	2.2	2.2	−0.18	0.33	1.2	0	1.1	0
401	34	18	1.9	2.1	−0.34	0.31	1.1	0	1.2	0
312	40	18	2.2	1.9	−0.72	0.34	0.4	−2	0.4	−2[b]
213	31	18	1.7	1.8	−0.88	0.30	0.7	−1	0.7	0
301	26	18	1.4	1.5	−1.27	0.28	1.1	0	1.1	0

	Obsvd Score	Obsvd Count	Obsvd Average	Fair Avrge	Calib Logit	Model Error	Infit MnSq	Std	Outfit MnSq	Std
Mean	51.9	18.0	2.9	2.9	1.77	0.40	1.0	−0.2	1.0	−0.2
S.D.	9.1	0.0	0.5	0.5	1.40	0.05	0.5	1.4	0.5	1.5

Note. RMSE 0.41, Adj S.D. 1.34, Separation 3.29, Reliability 0.92, Fixed (all same) chi-square: 942.77, d.f.: 73, significance: .00, Random (normal) chi-square: 72.78, d.f.: 72, significance: .45.
[a]Evaluators disagreed on the quality of the performance of these employees.
[b]Evaluators gave very similar ratings on the quality of performance of these employees.

MSE)/SD^2). This statistic indicates how well the estimated measures are differentiated from each other by the scoring system. It is desirable to show reliable separation or difference for person and item estimates, but it is usually not desirable to show reliable separation for evaluator estimates, because it is usually assumed the evaluators, when they have had proper training, will give comparable ratings to employees who demonstrate the same level of skill.

Unfortunately, this assumption is not always supported by data. The *Fixed Chi-Square* is a test of the hypothesis that there is no difference among measures after measurement error is accounted for. The significance is the probability that this dispersion of the measures would occur by chance when the hypothesis holds. *Random Chi-Square* is a test of the hypothesis that the set of measures can be regarded as a random sample from a normal distribution. The significance is the probability that the observed distribution of the measures would occur by chance when the hypothesis holds.

Table 3.1 shows employees in "Measure Logit" order or ability estimate order. The most able employee (#405) earned an Observed Score of 67 for 18 ratings and an ability estimate of 4.94 logits after correction for the severity of the subset of six evaluators who rated this employee's performance. The least able employee (#301) earned an observed score of 26 on 18 ratings and an ability estimate of −1.27 logits after correction for the severity of the subset of six evaluators. The fit statistics for both employees were within range, indicating that the evaluators generally agreed on the quality of the performances. Six employees had fit statistics that exceeded the criteria for consistency among evaluators, indicating that there was disagreement among evaluators on the performance of these employees. Employee #304 is an excellent example. The evaluators were 25, 9, 4, 29, 34, 18 (see Table 3.3 for evaluator statistics) with an average severity of .54 logits. Evaluator 4 was the most lenient (severity −1.21 logits), but gave this able employee an unexpectedly low rating for task 3 (Cut). Thus an able employee (estimated ability = 4.21 logits) received a low rating from the most lenient evaluator causing the misfit.

The reliability of person separation is .92 indicating that the assessment design yielded reliable distinctions among employees. Table 3.2 provides details on two of the employees, #408 and #509, who earned the same total raw scores, but different estimated ability measures after the severity of their evaluators was accounted for. This adjustment "levels the playing field" or gives all employees an equal opportunity for success. It also removes the dependence between the rating given and the particular evaluator.

Table 3.3 shows the evaluators in Severity order (*Measure Logit*). The most severe evaluator was approximately 33% more severe than the most lenient evaluator. Therefore, the evaluators assigned to assess employee performance could have a noticeable impact on employee ability ratings. Two evaluators did not meet the criteria for consistency, 26 and 4. Evaluator 26 was a moderate evaluator who gave several lower than expected ratings to an able employee. Evaluator 4 was a lenient evaluator who gave several lower than expected ratings to several employees. Several evaluators (Numbers 29, 18, 10, 33, 23, 13) show overconsistency. This usually means that they used the two middle points on the scale very heavily, so that able as well as less able employees all earned similar ratings regardless of their

TABLE 3.2
Accounting for Examination Differences

Person	Total Raw Score	Estimated Measure	Evaluator Severity		Task Ratings			Fit Mean Sq
			#	Sev	1	2	3	1.6[d]
408	60	2.90[a]	27	.89	4	3	4	
			6	−.59	4	4	4	
			7	−.51	3	3	4	
			30	−.58	4	4	4	
			26	−.45	3	3	3	
			16	.51	2	2	2[d]	
			Mean −.12[b]					
509	60	2.42[a]	26	−.45	4	3	4	1.1[d]
			14	−1.22	4	4	4[c]	
			13	−.35	3	4	3	
			30	−.58	2	3	3	
			32	−.48	3	3	3	
			7	−.51	3	3	4	
			Mean −.59[b]					

[a]Estimated ability measures adjusted for the severity of the evaluators. [b]Candidate 408 had more severe evaluators, on average, than candidate 509. [c]It is expected that more severe evaluators will give lower ratings whereas more lenient evaluators will give higher ratings. [d]Candidate 408 had relatively high fit because he was an able person who got lower than expected scores from a severe evaluator.

actual ability. This indicates that these evaluators were not able to distinguish among employee performances on the skills tested.

Table 3.4 shows the skills in difficulty order. "Cut" was the easiest skill on which to earn a high rating. It had the highest Observed Score for the number of ratings given. All skills were rated fairly consistently across employees by evaluators.

Evaluators are unique humans, who try to be accountable for the ratings they give. They attempt to follow instructions and use the rating scale as it is intended. However, evaluators see the world uniquely and so have somewhat different definitions for the meaning of the points on the rating scale and the requirement for satisfactory performance. This has been demonstrated consistently by low evaluator interrater reliability coefficients for performance assessment studies (Burger & Burger, 1994; Koretz, 1992), and multifacet Rasch analysis (Lunz & Stahl, 1990, 1993). Evaluators are the facet of performance assessment that is the most difficult to standardize, making accounting for differences more expeditious than attempting to train similarities.

The use of a multifacet model analysis does not diminish the importance of training evaluators and planning the assessment process carefully. It does,

TABLE 3.3
Severity and Consistency of Evaluators

EVALUATOR	Obsvd Score	Obsvd Count	Obsvd Average	Fair Avrge	Measure Logit	Model Error	Infit MnSq	Infit Std	Outfit MnSq	Outfit Std
					Most Severe					
34	116	42	2.8	1.5	1.35	0.25	1.1	0	1.1	0
3	77	33	2.3	1.5	1.32	0.25	0.9	0	1.0	0
27	113	45	2.5	1.8	0.89	0.23	1.5	1	1.3	1
29	109	42	2.6	1.8	0.89	0.24	0.4	-3	0.4	-3[b]
18	109	45	2.4	1.8	0.87	0.22	0.6	-2	0.7	-1
9	125	45	2.8	1.8	0.83	0.24	0.7	-1	0.8	-1
8	118	45	2.6	2.0	0.59	0.23	1.2	0	1.1	0
11	114	45	2.5	2.0	0.58	0.23	1.4	1	1.5	1
16	117	42	2.8	2.0	0.51	0.25	0.8	0	0.8	0
25	123	48	2.6	2.0	0.50	0.22	1.0	0	1.0	0
1	119	42	2.8	2.1	0.31	0.25	1.4	1	1.3	1
12	130	45	2.9	2.1	0.27	0.25	0.6	-2	0.6	-2[b]
15	127	45	2.8	2.1	0.26	0.24	1.3	1	1.3	1
10	127	45	2.8	2.2	0.25	0.25	1.3	1	1.3	1
20	130	45	2.9	2.3	-0.01	0.25	1.0	0	1.0	0
33	127	42	3.0	2.3	-0.15	0.27	0.6	-1	0.6	-2
26	122	42	2.9	2.4	-0.18	0.26	1.6	2	1.6	2[a]
21	129	45	2.9	2.4	-0.23	0.25	0.7	-1	0.7	-1
23	137	45	3.0	2.4	-0.26	0.26	0.5	-2	0.5	-2[b]
13	139	45	3.1	2.4	-0.35	0.26	1.4	1	1.3	1
26	142	45	3.2	2.5	-0.45	0.27	0.5	-2	0.5	-2[b]
32	135	45	3.0	2.5	-0.48	0.26	0.9	0	1.1	0
7	138	45	3.1	2.5	-0.51	0.26	1.1	0	1.2	0
30	128	42	3.0	2.5	-0.58	0.27	0.8	-1	0.8	0
31	139	45	3.1	2.5	-0.58	0.26	1.1	0	1.1	0
6	145	48	3.0	2.5	-0.59	0.25	1.4	1	1.3	1
24	137	45	3.0	2.6	-0.80	0.26	0.9	0	0.9	0
22	138	42	3.3	2.6	-0.87	0.29	0.9	0	0.9	0
19	85	27	3.1	2.7	-0.94	0.34	0.9	0	0.9	0
4	105	30	3.5	2.8	-1.21	0.39	2.0	2	2.5	2[a]
14	142	45	3.2	2.8	-1.22	0.27	1.0	0	1.0	0
					Least Severe					

Num EVALUATOR	Obsvd Score	Obsvd Count	Obsvd Average	Fair Avrge	Measure Logit	Model Error	Infit MnSq	Infit Std	Outfit MnSq	Outfit Std
Mean	123.9	43.0	2.9	2.2	0.00	0.26	1.0	-0.2	1.0	-0.1
S.D.	15.5	4.6	0.3	0.3	0.70	0.03	0.4	1.5	0.4	1.5

[a]Inconsistent evaluators: gave some unexpected higher or lower than expected ratings.

[b]Overconsistent evaluators: Gave a higher percent of 0, 1, 2, 3, 4 ratings than expected. Indicates the evaluator had difficulty differentiating among performances.

TABLE 3.4
Difficulty and Consistency of Tasks

SKILL	Obsvd Score	Obsvd Count	Obsvd Average	Fair Avrge	Measure Logit	Model Error	Infit MnSq Std		Outfit MnSq Std	
PRESS	1240	444	2.8	2.2	0.25	0.08	1.0	0	1.0	0
ASSEMBLE	1271	444	2.9	2.2	0.07	0.08	1.0	0	1.0	0
CUT	1331	444	3.0	2.4	−0.32	0.08	1.0	0	1.0	0
Mean	1280.7	444.0	2.9	2.3	0.00	0.08	1.0	−0.2	1.0	0.2
S.D.	37.8	0.0	0.1	0.1	0.24	0.00	0.0	0.4	0.0	0.1

Note. RMSE 0.08, Adj *S.D.* 0.22, Separation 2.83, Reliability 0.89, Fixed (all same) chi-square: 26.60, *d.f.*: 2, significance: .00, Random (normal) chi-square: 2.00, *d.f.*: 1, significance: .16.

however, redefine their role. Instead of being the final, individual arbiter on quality, they are an element in the research design. This does not eliminate the need for evaluators to be accountable; indeed, the fit statistics flag incoherent ratings. Decisions can be reproduced (decision reproducibility) because the effect of the interaction among particular evaluators, items, and skills is measured and equated so all decisions can be made using a defined performance standard.

The assessment design must balance a number of concerns simultaneously. An adequate number of observations must be made. Skills and rating scale must be defined. Evaluators must be trained. The overlap among facets must be such that analysis is possible. For example, performance appraisals done within departments by individual managers cannot provide the overlap necessary for this objective analysis, even though the same skills are rated using defined rating scales. There must be some connection among departments through a common manager or common employees.

EXAMPLE 2: PRODUCT ANALYSIS

The purpose of this study was to evaluate six product samples for their qualities of attractiveness and consistency. The goal was to determine which product would be most acceptable to the consumer. The study used 43 consumer evaluators who worked during four time periods. The multifacet analysis was used to account for differences in evaluator criticality when rating product samples, so that a more accurate assessment of the quality of the product samples would result. The product samples with higher quality estimates, after the impact of evaluator criticality and the time period during which the ratings were made are accounted for, should be most acceptable to consumers in general.

The multifacet model used in this analysis was $\log(P_{niqmk}/P_{niqm(k-1)}) = (B_n - D_i - Q_q - T_m - R_k)$ was used. The facets included in the analysis were: evaluator criticality (B_n), product sample overall quality (D_i), quality assessment (Q_q), time period (T_m), and rating scale usage (R_k). The necessary linking was accomplished by having all evaluators rate all product samples using the same criteria for quality. Samples were rotated among evaluators across time periods, so that all samples were evaluated during each time period.

The 43 evaluators were familiar with the definitions for the qualities being rated (attractive and consistent). A 4-point rating scale was used by all evaluators on which 1 indicated "grossly deficient," 2 indicated "poor," 3 indicated "adequate," and 4 indicated "excellent," with regard to each aspect of quality. Definitions for each point on the rating were provided. The analysis model was defined so that products with the highest scores earned the highest overall quality estimates after the criticality of evaluators was accounted for. The product with the highest overall estimate has the highest probability of earning a higher rating from even the most critical evaluator, regardless of the time period during which it is rated. When the context bias due to the evaluator criticality, aspects of quality, and time period are accounted for, an unbiased assessment of the product sample results. Also useful information on variance among evaluators, aspects of quality, and impact of time period are available.

Figure 3.3 shows the map of the results of the analysis. The time periods had no effect as there was no statistical difference in their calibration (0.00), and quality characteristics were rated comparably and calibrated at 0.00. The aspects of attractiveness and consistency were apparently equally rated, or evaluators could not distinguish between them in the context of these products. However, the pattern of overall ratings was different among products. Product A was significantly better liked than Product D after the impact of the other facets was accounted for.

Table 3.5 shows the evaluators in order of criticality. Evaluator 20 was significantly less critical than Evaluator 15 who tended to give lower ratings to all products. This difference in rating style was accounted for when products were ordered for overall quality. Table 3.6 shows the ordering of the products. The reliability of Separation (.96) indicates that overall, the samples were statistically significantly different in overall rated quality. Tables 3.7 and 3.8 show that there was no difference in the patterns of rating attractiveness and consistency, across time periods. It was as likely that a product would be highly rated on Friday morning as on Saturday morning. This confirmed that the time period during which a product was rated had no effect on the rating. The qualities of attractiveness and consistency were not more or less likely to earn a high rating. This means that rating patterns were different across products, but tended to be at similar levels on both qualities within product samples. If the product earned a high or low rating

```
|Logit|-Evaluators      |+Product   |-Quality   |-PERIOD: 1 |AVERAGE
+   2 + Most Critical    +Most Liked +           +          +(4)  +
    |    Evaluator       |Product    |           |          |     |



    |                    |PRODUCT A  |                      ---
    |  15                |
+   1 +                  + PRODUCT F +           +          +     +
    |                    |PRODUCT B  |
    |  21                |
    |                    |PRODUCT C  |
    |  38                |PRODUCT E  |
    |  13  30  32        |PRODUCT D             3
    |  36  41            |
    |  23  33  43  6     |
    |  17  19   2  28    |
    :  :  29  31         :           :          :          :     :
    |  |  12  40   9     |           |          |          |     |
*   0 * 10  14  27  34   *           * ATTRACTIVE * FRIDAY AM    *
    :  :  45             :           : CONSISTENT : FRIDAY PM    :
    :  :                 :           :          : SATURDAY AM :  :
    :  :                 :           :          : SATURDAY PM :  :
    |   3  42            |                      ---
    |  39   4            |
    |   1  16  44   5    |
    |  22   8            |

    |  11  24  26  35    |                      2

    |  20  25   7        |
    |    Least Critical  |Least liked|
+  -1 + Evaluator        |+Product   +          +          +(1)  +

|Meas|-Evaluators       |+Product   |-Quality   |-PERIOD: 1 |S.1  |
```

FIG. 3.3. Map of product assessment analysis.

on attractiveness, the probability is that it earned a comparable rating on consistency and vice versa. However, the ratings overall, across product samples, were different. Since many ratings ($n = 614$) were given to each product, the measurement errors were small (.05 logits).

Table 3.9 shows the usage of the rating scale. Eighty-two percent of the ratings were 3 or 4. This suggests that the use of the rating scale was limited in this example, and that the products were rated as adequate or excellent 82% of the time, or that the evaluators could not use this rating scale to distinguish the aspects of quality. Rating scale definitions that encouraged better use of the rating scale might have promoted more definitive assessment of the products.

The fit statistics provide additional information about the products and evaluators. Some evaluators were consistent in their ratings, whereas others were less consistent. Consistency indicates the ability to rate products according to the qualities defined. Evaluators 24, 25, 27, 36, and 39 have high outfit statistics indicating that they gave some unexpectedly high or low ratings. Further analysis identified that Evaluator 24 gave lower than expected ratings to Products A, E, and F. Evaluator 25 gave a lower than expected ratings to Product E, and Evaluator 27 gave a lower than expected rating to

TABLE 3.5
Product Assessment Analysis

Customer Evaluators	Obsvd Score	Obsvd Count	Obsvd Average	Fair Avrge	Measure Logit	Model Error	Infit MnSq Std		Outfit MnSq Std	
					Most Critical					
15	222	96	2.3	1.6	1.08	0.10	0.9	−1	0.9	−1
2	252	96	2.6	1.8	0.77	0.11	0.8	−2	0.8	−1
38	236	84	2.8	2.0	0.57	0.12	1.2	1	1.2	1
32	270	96	2.8	2.0	0.54	0.11	0.7	−2	0.7	−2[b]
30	278	96	2.9	2.1	0.47	0.11	0.9	0	0.9	0
13	244	84	2.9	2.1	0.46	0.12	0.9	0	0.9	0
36	282	96	2.9	2.2	0.40	0.11	1.6	4	1.6	3[a]
41	250	84	3.0	2.2	0.37	0.12	1.3	1	1.3	2
33	254	84	3.0	2.3	0.31	0.12	0.5	−4	0.5	−4[b]
23	272	90	3.0	2.3	0.30	0.12	0.8	−1	0.8	−1
43	202	66	3.1	2.3	0.30	0.14	0.3	−6	0.3	−6[b]
6	256	84	3.0	2.3	0.28	0.13	0.8	−1	0.8	−1
2	294	96	3.1	2.3	0.24	0.12	0.9	0	1.0	0
28	260	84	3.1	2.4	0.21	0.13	0.3	−6	0.3	−6[b]
31	316	102	3.1	2.4	0.20	0.12	1.2	1	1.2	1
19	280	90	3.1	2.4	0.18	0.12	1.0	0	1.0	0
29	262	84	3.1	2.4	0.18	0.13	0.9	0	1.0	0
17	206	66	3.1	2.4	0.16	0.15	0.7	−1	0.7	−1
9	266	84	3.2	2.5	0.11	0.13	1.3	1	1.2	1
12	266	84	3.2	2.5	0.11	0.13	0.9	0	0.9	0
40	268	84	3.2	2.5	0.08	0.13	0.9	0	0.9	0
27	250	78	3.2	2.5	0.04	0.14	1.4	2	1.4	2
45	254	78	3.3	2.6	0.01	0.14	1.0	0	1.0	0
10	330	102	3.2	2.6	0.00	0.12	1.4	2	1.3	1
14	332	102	3.3	2.6	−0.03	0.13	1.0	0	0.9	0
34	274	84	3.3	2.6	−0.03	0.14	0.9	0	0.8	0
42	218	66	3.3	2.6	−0.06	0.16	1.5	2	1.4	1
3	258	78	3.3	2.7	−0.10	0.15	0.5	−3	0.5	−3[b]
4	284	84	3.4	2.8	−0.24	0.15	0.7	−1	0.8	−1
39	304	90	3.4	2.8	−0.25	0.14	1.9	3	1.7	3[a]
44	266	78	3.4	2.8	−0.26	0.16	0.9	0	1.0	0
16	306	90	3.4	2.8	−0.27	0.15	1.0	0	1.0	0
1	306	90	3.4	2.8	−0.29	0.15	0.9	0	0.9	0
5	328	96	3.4	2.9	−0.31	0.14	1.2	0	1.1	0
8	290	84	3.5	2.9	−0.38	0.16	0.9	0	0.9	0
22	230	66	3.5	2.9	−0.38	0.18	0.6	−1	0.7	−1
11	318	90	3.5	3.1	−0.58	0.16	1.5	2	1.4	1
35	276	78	3.5	3.1	−0.59	0.18	0.7	−1	0.8	−1
26	298	84	3.5	3.1	−0.60	0.17	0.7	−1	0.7	−1
24	320	90	3.6	3.1	−0.63	0.17	2.0	4	2.1	4[a]
25	282	78	3.6	3.2	−0.77	0.19	1.7	2	1.8	2[a]
7	304	84	3.6	3.2	−0.80	0.19	1.0	0	0.9	0
20	304	84	3.6	3.2	−0.80	0.19	1.4	1	1.3	1
					Least Critical					

(Continued)

TABLE 3.5
(*Continued*)

	Obsvd Score	Obsvd Count	Obsvd Average	Fair Avrge	Measure Logit	Model Error	Infit MnSq Std		Outfit MnSq Std	
Mean	273.7	85.7	3.2	2.6	−0.00	0.14	1.0	−0.3	1.0	−0.3
S.D.	32.4	9.2	0.3	0.4	0.43	0.02	0.4	2.4	0.4	2.3

Note. Evaluators are presented in order of criticality. RMSE 0.14, Adj *S.D.* 0.40, Separation 2.82, Reliability 0.89, Fixed (all same) chi-square: 398.90, *d.f.*: 42, significance: .00, Random (normal) chi-square: 41.59, *d.f.*: 41, significance: .45.

[a]Evaluators gave unexpectedly high or low ratings. The information provided by these evaluators may not be as useful as information from more consistent evaluators.

[b]Evaluators gave very similar rating, indicating some inability to differentiate among product quality.

Product F. Evaluators 3, 28, 32, 33, and 43 show high-negative standardized fit statistics. This means that they tended to give similar ratings to all products. Thus, the information they provided is probably less useful when deciding which product to market. Evaluators who use the rating scale consistently and can make distinctions among products provide the most useful information for decision makers.

Fit statistics for products indicate the consistency of the evaluators in assessing the quality of products across time periods. Product D shows high-positive misfit, indicating that some evaluators gave lower than expected ratings to the product. Further investigation indicated that Evaluators 7, 11, 20, and 24 all gave lower than expected ratings to this product. Because

TABLE 3.6
Product Assessment Analysis

N Product	Obsvd Score	Obsvd Count	Obsvd Average	Fair Avrge	Quality Logit	Model Error	Infit MnSq Std		Outfit MnSq Std	
				Highest Ratings						
1 PRODUCT A	2128	614	3.5	3.5	1.28	0.06	0.9	−1	0.9	0
6 PRODUCT F	2046	614	3.3	3.4	1.01	0.05	1.1	1	1.1	1
2 PRODUCT B	1974	614	3.2	3.3	0.86	0.05	1.0	0	1.0	0
3 PRODUCT C	1922	614	3.1	3.2	0.74	0.05	0.9	−1	0.9	−1
5 PRODUCT E	1898	614	3.1	3.1	0.63	0.05	0.9	−2	0.9	−1
4 PRODUCT D	1800	614	2.9	3.0	0.47	0.05	1.2	3	1.2	3[a]
				Lowest Ratings						
Mean	1961.3	614.0	3.2	3.2	0.83**	0.05	1.0	−0.1	1.0	0.4
S.D.	105.4	0.0	0.2	0.2	0.26	0.00	0.1	1.8	0.1	1.7

Note. Products are presented in order of rated quality. RMSE 0.05, Adj S.D. 0.26, Separation 5.02, Reliability 0.96, Fixed (all same) chi-square: 147.93, *d.f.*: 5, significance: .00, Random (normal) chi-square: 4.99, *d.f.*: 4, significance: .29.

[a]Product D was rated inconsistently. This means that evaluators did not agree on the quality of this product.

TABLE 3.7
Product Assessment Analysis

N Quality	Obsvd Score	Obsvd Count	Obsvd Average	Fair Avrge	Measure Logit	Model Error	Infit MnSq Std		Outfit MnSq Std	
1 CONSISTENT	5884	1842	3.2	2.6	0.00	0.03	1.0	0	1.0	0
2 ATTRACTIVE	5884	1842	3.2	2.6	0.00	0.03	1.0	0	1.0	0
Mean	5884.0	1842.0	3.2	2.6	0.00	0.03	1.0	−0.1	1.0	0.6
S.D.	0.0	0.0	0.0	0.0	0.00	0.00	0.0	0.0	0.0	0.0

Note. Aspects of quality are calibrated. RMSE 0.03, Adj S.D. 0.00, Separation 0.00, Reliability 0.00*, Fixed (all same) chi-square: .00 *d.f.*: 1, significance: 1.00.
*There was no difference in the aspects of quality based on ratings across all products and all evaluators. However, some products earned higher overall ratings than others.

product D earned the lowest ratings overall and showed evidence of disagreement among evaluators, this may be the least desirable product to market. The fit statistics for aspects of quality and time periods show no unexpected rating patterns.

In this analysis, the research design and multifacet analysis confirmed that the time the rating was given had little impact on the outcome. Also, the ratings for attractiveness and consistency were generally comparable within products. This may indicate that other elements of quality could be more informative for assessing the quality of these products. Evaluators varied in their criticality when rating products. That means that some evaluators tended to give lower ratings to all the products, whereas others gave higher ratings. After these differences in evaluators are accounted for, there is still a difference in the overall quality of the products. This is an absolute difference because the perceptual biases of the evaluators have been accounted for in the assessment. This should be useful information for a

TABLE 3.8
Product Assessment Analysis: Ordering of Time Periods

N PERIOD: 1	Obsvd Score	Obsvd Count	Obsvd Average	Fair Avrge	Measure Logit	Model Error	Infit MnSq Std		Outfit MnSq Std	
1 FRIDAY AM	3110	1008	3.1	2.6	0.02	0.04	1.0	0	1.1	1
2 FRIDAY PM	2566	828	3.1	2.6	0.01	0.04	1.1	1	1.0	0
3 SATURDAY AM	3336	1014	3.3	2.6	0.01	0.04	0.9	−1	0.9	−1
4 SATURDAY PM	2756	834	3.3	2.6	−0.03	0.05	1.0	0	1.1	1
Mean	2942.0	921.0	3.2	2.6	0.00	0.04	1.0	−0.0	1.0	0.4
S.D.	299.8	90.0	0.1	0.0	0.00	0.00	0.1	1.1	0.1	1.0

Note. There was no systematic difference in the way products were assessed across time periods. RMSE 0.04, Adj *S.D.* 0.00, Separation 0.00, Reliability 0.00, Fixed (all same) chi-square: .84, *d.f.*: 3, significance: .84.

TABLE 3.9
Rating Scale Analysis Usage

Response Category Name	OBSERVED CATEGORIES				MOST PROBABLE	THURSTONE THRESHOLD	EXPECTATION		SCALE CALIBRATIONS		
	Categ Label	Found	Used	%	from	at	Measure Category	at +0.5	Step	Measure	S.E.
GROSSLY DEFICIENT	1	216	216	6%	low	low	(−1.85)	−1.26	1	−0.28	0.07
POOR	2	448	448	12%	no	−0.87	−0.59	−0.08	2	−0.49	0.05
ADEQUATE	3	1424	1424	39%	−.39	−0.18	0.47	1.29	3	0.77	0.03
EXCELLENT	4	1596	1596	3%	.77	1.01	(2.04)				

Note. The majority of ratings were 3 or 4 indicating relatively high perceived quality for the products.

69

marketing manager who is faced with a decision concerning which product to market.

EXAMPLE 3: JOB SATISFACTION SURVEY ANALYSIS

The purpose of this study was to measure job satisfaction in a way that accounts for differences in the groups to which the employee belongs. A four-facet model in which log $(P_{nwcik}/P_{nwci(k-1)}) = (B_n - T_w - G_c - D_i - R_k)$ was used. The facets were: employee overall job satisfaction (B_n), effect of wage grouping on job satisfaction (T_w), effect of title or role on job satisfaction (G_c), difficulty of agreeing with the job satisfaction items (D_i), and the use of the rating scale (R_k). All facets, except the job satisfaction items, were analyzed such that higher scores imply higher measures, so that comparisons across people and groups could be made. Measures for the job satisfaction items were scored such that higher scores imply lower estimated measures, so that the employee with the highest job satisfaction estimate has the highest probability of being satisfied with the items that are most difficult to agree with.

The job satisfaction survey contained 17 items, all of which were worded positively. Therefore, a higher score indicated more job satisfaction than a lower score. A sample of 371 employees from health care institutions across the country completed the survey using a 4-point rating scale on which 4 = very satisfied, 3 = satisfied, 2 = dissatisfied, and 1 = very dissatisfied. Employees were placed in four salary groups based on their reported hourly wage for 1995: Group 1 = $10–12, Group 2 = $13–15, Group 3 = $16–18, and Group 4 = $19–21 per hour. Employees were also placed in groups based on their title in the organization: staff, supervisor, manager. All employees responded to all job satisfaction items. Employees were in discrete groups with regard to title and salary, but there was overlap among the groups. For example, employees with a title of staff could fall into any of the salary groups.

A common belief is that individuals who earn higher salaries and have more job responsibility are more satisfied with their jobs. The goal was to determine whether or not the data support this expectation.

The multifacet analysis provides two types of information not available in standard analysis of variance or regression. First, the impact of group membership is accounted for in the calibration of job satisfaction items. Thus, context bias is removed from the analysis and items are easy or hard to agree with regardless of group membership. Second, the ordering of employees with regard to their job satisfaction is independent of the groups to which they belong, or how difficult the item is to agree with. This provides a more accurate estimate of the employee's job satisfaction.

Figure 3.4 shows the map of the multifacet analysis. The general pattern confirms the belief that employees who earn higher salaries and who have

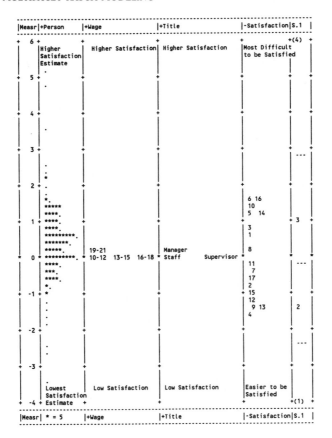

FIG. 3.4. Map of job satisfaction survey analysis.

more responsibility tend to be more satisfied than individuals with lower salaries and less responsibility. The most satisfied employee had a satisfaction estimate of 5.17 logits with a score of 66 out of 68 points (average rating 3.9). The least satisfied employee had a satisfaction estimate of −3.37 logits from a raw score of 22 out of 68 points (average rating 1.3). The average satisfaction estimate was .43 logits (score about 46) with a standard deviation of .92 logits and a standard error of .40 logits. The reliability of employee job satisfaction separation was .81 indicating that the job satisfaction scale was reasonably reliable in terms of detecting differences in job satisfaction among employees when differences for wage and title are accounted for.

Tables 3.10, 3.11, and 3.12 show the detail of the other facets. The average differences in job satisfaction among salary groups and title groups were small and not really meaningful (Tables 3.10 and 3.11), although there were some differences in the overall satisfaction among groups. Table 3.12, however, shows that the job satisfaction items varied significantly in measured level of

TABLE 3.10
Wage Groups in Satisfaction Order

N Wage $	Obsvd Score	Obsvd Count	Obsvd Average	Fair Avrge	Measure Logit	Model S.E.	Infit MnSq	Std	Outfit MnSq	Std
					Most Satisfied					
4 19–21	1,188	425	2.8	2.7	.15	.08	1.0	0	1.0	0
1 10–12	2,291	850	2.7	2.6	−.01	.06	1.1	1	1.1	1
2 13–15	10,549	3,978	2.7	2.6	−.07	.03	1.0	0	1.0	0
3 16–18	2,801	1,054	2.7	2.6	−.07	.05	1.0	0	1.0	0
					Least Satisfied					
Mean	4,207.3	1,576.8	2.7	2.6	.00	.05	1.0	0.1	1.0	−0.0
S.D.	3,707.5	1,404.8	0.1	0.0	.09	.02	0.0	0.8	0.0	0.8

Note. RMSE .06, Adj *S.D.* .07, Separation 1.28, Reliability .62, Fixed (all same) chi-square: 7.6, *d.f.*: 3, significance: .05, Random (normal) chi-square: 2.6, *d.f.*: 2, significance: .27.

satisfaction. "I like the people I work with" (Q4) and "I like doing the job" (Q9) were the items with which employees were most likely to be satisfied, indicating a high probability of satisfaction from most employees. "Satisfaction with chance for promotion" (Q16) and "Stand a chance for promotion" (Q6) were the items with which employees were least likely to be satisfied, even when the differences among the title and wage groups are accounted for in the analysis, indicating a low probability of satisfaction for all but the most satisfied employees. The items of the job satisfaction survey were highly differentiated, and the reliability of item separation was .99.

Table 3.13 shows the usage of the rating scale. Ratings of 1 and 4 were used much less frequently than ratings of 2 and 3. This indicates that extreme feelings of satisfaction or dissatisfaction were not the norm in this sample. Most employees were somewhere in the middle with regard to their job satisfaction, although they were clearly more satisfied with some items than others.

TABLE 3.11
Title Groups in Satisfaction Order

N Title	Obsvd Score	Obsvd Count	Obsvd Average	Fair Avrge	Measure Logit	Model S.E.	Infit MnSq	Std	Outfit MnSq	Std
					Most Satisfied					
3 Manager	478	170	2.8	2.7	.15	.13	1.2	1	1.2	1
2 Supervisor	1,220	459	2.7	2.6	−.07	.08	1.2	3	1.2	3
1 Staff	15,131	5,678	2.7	2.6	−.08	.02	1.0	−1	1.0	−1
					Least Satisfied					
Mean	5,609.7	2,102.3	2.7	2.6	.00	.07	1.1	1.3	1.1	1.1
S.D.	6,739.4	2,531.1	0.1	0.0	.10	.04	0.1	2.0	0.1	2.0

Note. RMSE .09, Adj *S.D.* .06, Separation .67, Reliability .31, Fixed (all same) chi-square: 3.0, *d.f.*: 2, significance: .22, Random (normal) chi-square: 1.6, *d.f.*: 1, significance: .21.

TABLE 3.12
Job Satisfaction Items in Satisfaction Order

Satisfaction	Obsvd Score	Obsvd Count	Obsvd Average	Fair Avrge	Measure Logit	Model S.E.	Infit MnSq	Infit Std	Outfit MnSq	Outfit Std
					Least Satisfied					
Q6 Stand a chance for promotion	744	371	2.0	1.8	1.64	.08	0.8	-2	0.8	-2
Q16 Sat chance for promotion	744	371	2.0	1.8	1.64	.08	0.8	-3	0.8	-2
Q10 People get ahead as fast	791	371	2.1	2.0	1.35	.08	0.9	0	1.0	0
Q5 Communication seem good	804	371	2.2	2.0	1.28	.08	1.1	1	1.1	2
Q14 Sat chance salary increase	815	371	2.2	2.1	1.21	.08	0.9	0	0.9	0
Q3 I receive recognition	892	371	2.4	2.3	.74	.08	0.9	-1	0.9	-1
Q1 I am being paid fairly	910	371	2.5	2.3	.62	.08	1.3	3	1.3	3
Q8 Efforts seldom blocked	977	371	2.6	2.5	.18	.08	1.1	1	1.1	1
Q11 Benefit package is equitable	1036	371	2.8	2.7	-.23	.09	1.0	0	1.0	0
Q7 Benefits good as other orgs	1052	371	2.8	2.7	-.35	.09	1.2	2	1.2	2
Q17 Job is enjoyable	1091	371	2.9	2.9	-.65	.09	0.8	-3	0.8	-3
Q2 My supervisor is competent	1113	371	3.0	2.9	-.83	.09	1.6	6	1.6	6
Q15 I like my supervisor	1136	371	3.1	3.0	-1.01	.09	0.9	-1	0.9	-1
Q12 I enjoy my coworkers	1167	371	3.1	3.1	-1.27	.09	0.8	-2	0.8	-2
Q13 I feel sense of pride	1171	371	3.2	3.1	-1.31	.09	0.8	-2	0.8	-2
Q9 I like doing job	1190	371	3.2	3.1	-1.47	.09	1.0	0	0.9	0
Q4 I like people I work with	1196	371	3.2	3.1	-1.52	.09	0.9	-2	0.8	-2
					Most Satisfied					

Satisfaction	Obsvd Score	Obsvd Count	Obsvd Average	Fair Avrge	Measure	Model S.E.	Infit MnSq	Infit Std	Outfit MnSq	Outfit Std
Mean	989.9	371.0	2.7	2.6	.00	.08	1.0	-0.2	1.0	-0.3
S.D.	161.1	0.0	0.4	0.5	1.12	.01	0.2	2.5	0.2	2.6

Note. RMSE .09, Adj S.D. 1.12, Separation 13.13, Reliability .99, Fixed (all same) chi-square: 2,979.5, d.f.: 16, significance: .00, Random (normal) chi-square: 16.0, d.f.: 15, significance: .38.

TABLE 3.13
Rating Scale Analysis for Job Satisfaction

Response Category Name	Category Score	DATA Counts Used	%	Cum. %	Avge Meas Diff	OUTFIT MnSq	STEP CALIBRATIONS Measure	S.E.	EXPECTATION Measure at Category	-0.5	MOST PROBABLE from	THURSTONE THRESHOLD at
Strongly Disagree	1	605	10%	10%	-1.43	1.1			(-3.28)		low	low
Disagree	2	1735	28%	37%	-.61	.9	-2.09	.05	-1.31	-2.43	-2.09	-2.25
Agree	3	3114	49%	86%	.75	.9	-.50	.03	1.08	-.26	-.50	-.38
Strongly Agree	4	853	14%	100%	1.84	1.1	2.59	.04	(3.69)	2.69	2.59	2.62

Fit to the expectation of the multifacet model provides an estimate of consistency within groups or consistency of rating across groups depending on the facet under consideration. In this study, the wage groups (T_w) (Table 3.10) are consistent in their ratings of job satisfaction. The title groups (G_c) (Table 3.11) were not always consistent. The supervisor group $(n = 27)$ apparently rated several items differently than expected for members of that group (Outfit = 1.2, Std = 3.00). For example, two supervisors rated item Q8, "My efforts are seldom blocked" as very dissatisfied (rating = 1) indicating that their efforts were frequently blocked. Misfit occurred because other supervisors did not share this perception.

The job satisfaction items showed misfit for "my supervisor is competent" (Q2) (Outfit = 1.6, Std = 6), and "I am being paid fairly" (Q1) (Outfit = 1.3, Std = 3). Seven of the 334 staff and 1 of the 17 managers gave lower than expected ratings to item Q2 compared to their normal pattern of responses. These unexpected responses represented individuals in all wage groups. For item Q1, one staff member gave a higher than expected rating and another gave a lower than expected rating. The misfit occurred because respondents held significantly diverse perceptions regarding the fairness of their wages, even after controlling for their reported wage group.

The extremely consistent responses to items Q6 and Q16 occurred because ratings of 1 and 2 (dissatisfied) were given by 77% of the respondents. Items Q12, Q13, and Q14 were given ratings of 3 or 4 (satisfied) by 87%, 84%, and 87% of the respondents, respectively. Item Q17 was rated as 3 (satisfied) by 67% of the respondents. Items that showed inconsistent patterns or high-positive fit statistics were Q1, Q7, and Q2. The misfit occurred because the ratings were distributed between 2 and 3 (satisfied and dissatisfied) by 78%, 79%, and 64% of respondents, respectively. The patterns of fit are directly parallel to the response patterns for satisfaction or dissatisfaction on these items.

The limitation of this use of the multifacet model is that the wage and title groups may be mutually exclusive for some employees. Although crossover among groups occurred, it is possible that only managers earn wages as high as $19–$21 per hour, although that is unlikely because the sample was drawn from institutions across the country. All employees answered all of the job satisfaction items. It is clear that satisfaction with the opportunity for promotion is low regardless of the wage or salary group to which an employee belongs. Lack of satisfaction with opportunity for promotion has been noted in other national studies, thus, these data support those from other studies. If organizations are concerned with improving employee job satisfaction, promotion opportunity may be an area in which to work for all levels of personnel and all wage groups. It seems clear that employees enjoy doing their jobs, but wish to have opportunities to advance.

The advantage of using the multifacet model is that differences in groups are accounted for in the employee satisfaction estimates. The mean satisfaction estimate without accounting for salary and wage facets was .31 logits ($SD = .93$ range $= -3.52$ to 5.08 logits), whereas the mean satisfaction estimate with these facets accounted for was .43 logits ($SD = .92$, range $= -3.37$ to 5.17 logits). Thus accounting for pertinent facets may provide a more accurate estimate for individual employee satisfaction as well as providing a picture of the results.

SUMMARY

Measurement is the process that uses observations, such as raw scores or survey data, to make distinctions within a linear frame of reference among persons and other entities. Objectivity is the foundation of valid measurement. If the measured difference is independent of the particular (e.g., the rater) condition, it is objective. The chapter demonstrated construction of measurement processes that are objective, because context bias is removed from the person or product estimates using the multifacets model. The same principles apply to all three examples even though the data are different. The examples do not generalize to each other because the research designs are completely separate. An individual value must be interpreted within the context of the study for which it was scaled. Even with this limitation, substantially more information is available when patterns are observable within the data. The maps and tables provide pictures of how the elements within each study work together or apart to produce the outcomes. Other statistical methods often identify the same statistical differences, but only multifacet Rasch modeling shows the patterns that produce the statistically significant differences.

By using the multifacet Rasch model, differences in the difficulty of the examination forms can be identified. It is easy to see that a candidate encountered two severe evaluators. The qualities that make products appear to be more or less acceptable can be identified. This could lead to a better research design and/or more specific information about the product. Finally for survey analysis, the multifacet approach can show, graphically, who finds the survey items easier or more difficult to agree with, in addition to accounting for differences among groups.

The opportunities for objective measurement using the multifacet model are limited only by our imaginations. Almost everything in life, other than a multiple-choice test, probably has more than two facets. The process of identifying the facets and developing a research design that produces data amenable to the analysis requires careful planning. The three examples were selected to demonstrate diverse applications of the multifacet methods. The multifacet methods are useful whenever the research design has more than two facets by necessity or design. Necessity means the need for an evaluator to give ratings to performances, products, or the like. Design means that designated group membership may have an implication for how individuals respond to a survey item or rate a product or person. The multifacet model separates the impact of each facet on the outcomes so that better and more specific information is available to the researcher or the decision makers.

REFERENCES

Burger, S. E., & Burger D. L. (1994). Determining the validity of performance-based assessment. *Educational Measurement Issues and Practice, 13*(1), 9–15.

Koretz, D. (1992). New report on Vermont portfolio project documents challenges. *National Council on Measurement in Education Quarterly Newsletter, 1*(4), 1–2.

Linacre, J. M. (1989). *Many-facet Rasch measurement.* Chicago: MESA Press.

Linacre, J. M. (1990). *FACETS, a computer program for analysis of examinations with multiple facets.* Chicago: MESA Press.

Lunz, M. E. (1992). New ways of thinking about reliability. *Professions Education Researcher Quarterly, 13*(4), 16–18.

Lunz, M. E., & Stahl, J. A. (1990). Judge consistency and severity across grading periods. *Evaluation and the Health Professions, 13*(4), 425–444.

Lunz, M. E., & Stahl, J. A. (1993). Impact of examiners on candidate scores: An introduction to the use of multifacet Rasch model analysis for oral examinations. *Teaching and Learning in Medicine, 5*(3), 174–181.

Lunz, M. E., Wright, B. D., & Linacre, J. M. (1990). Measuring the impact of judge severity on examination scores. *Applied Measurement in Education, 3*, 331–345.

Rasch, G. (1992). *Probabilistic models for some intelligence and attainment tests.* Chicago: MESA Press. (Original work published 1960)

Stahl, J. A., & Lunz, M. E. (1994). Judge performance reports: Media and message. In G. Engelhard & M. Wilson (Eds.), *Objective measurement: Theory into practice* (Vol. 3). Norwood, NJ: Ablex.

Wright, B. D. (1995). Diagnosing person misfit. *Rasch Measurement Transactions, 9*(2), 430–431.

Wright, B. D., & Linacre, J. M. (1994). Reasonable mean-square fit values. *Rasch Measurement Transactions, 8*(30), 370.

Wright, B., & Stone, M. (1979). *Best test design.* Chicago: MESA Press.

CHAPTER FOUR

Applied Location Theory Models

Zvi Drezner
Tammy Drezner
California State University, Fullerton

Optimization of a company's operations is essential to its long-term survival and profitability. Operations researchers develop more efficient ways for such operations that involve modeling these operations and finding the optimal way to perform them. An important aspect of optimizing company operations is locating its facilities in their optimal location. This is part of analyzing the logistics aspects of the company's operations. The area of operations research has benefited significantly from the introduction of digital computers. Optimization techniques became more accessible, more powerful, and therefore more useful. The last 20 to 30 years witnessed a vast increase in interest in operations research problems in general and location problems in particular among researchers from a variety of disciplines including economics, marketing, engineering, urban planning, geography, and management. This diverse interest yielded a multitude of research approaches and solutions to such problems.

A location problem is a spatial resource allocation problem. In the general location paradigm, one or more service facilities serve a spatially distributed set of demands ("customers"). The objective is to locate facilities to optimize a spatially dependent objective. Location decisions include the addition of new facilities to an existing infrastructure, rearranging an existing layout, or planning a completely new system.

The application of location theory to industrial problems was first introduced by Alfred Weber (1909), who considered locating a single warehouse so as to minimize the total travel distance between the warehouse and a set of spatially distributed customers. This work was reconsidered by Isard

(1956) in his study of industrial location, land use, and related problems. Another early location problem was formulated by Hotelling (1929), an economist, who considered locating two competing stores on Main Street.

The classic application of locational analysis is Weber's (1909) location of a warehouse (or a distribution center) servicing a set of retail facilities. Other service type location examples include the location of schools, day-care facilities, bank branches, and telephone switchboards; the location of emergency facilities such as hospitals, ambulance depots, or fire stations; the location of military and naval installations, international couriers, and international airline hubs. These location decisions represent different company objectives. The location objectives range from minimizing total travel time as is the case in school location, to the minimization of travel time for the farthest customer as is the case in emergency facility location, to location on a globe for airline routing or military installations. Other location models are used in competitive environments where companies compete for customers such as grocery stores, department stores, shopping malls, restaurants, or gas stations. There are situations where facilities are considered "obnoxious." Such obnoxious facility location models are used for locating airports, recycling centers, nuclear power plants, prisons, waste disposal sites, pollution generating factories, or refineries. In this case, the location represents a balance between two conflicting objectives: protecting residents but still being within commute range.

In his article, Eiselt (1992) listed scores of applications of various location models. Some of these applications include: steam generators in large heavy oil fields, postal relay boxes, newspaper transfer points, trucking terminals, solid waste transfer points, check-processing sites, computer service centers, oil spill removal equipment, and rain gauges.

For many types of facilities, when distances are straight line (or Euclidean), there is a "sphere of influence," a circle within which they are effective in servicing customers. Such facilities are cellular telephone signal detectors, forest fire detectors, emergency sirens, television and radio stations, lawn sprinklers, and others. Because the "radius of influence" is fixed, the problem of locating such facilities leads to an objective of covering the demand by the minimum number of circles of a given radius. For example, a metropolitan area needs to be covered by cellular telephone detectors or a grass area needs to be covered by lawn sprinklers. In order to minimize cost, the configuration utilizing the minimal number of detectors is sought. The problem is solved by checking sequentially whether one, two, three, and so on detectors will suffice to cover the area. The first configuration that covers the whole area is the solution. To apply this procedure, we need a method to determine the largest area that is covered by a given number of detectors.

To facilitate the demonstration, we consider the simple case of a square-shaped metropolitan area. The largest square covered by one detector is the square circumscribed inside the circle. The best location for two detectors is at the centers of two identical rectangles obtained by drawing a vertical (or horizontal) line through the center of the square (a simple analysis shows that this configuration is superior to dividing the square into two triangles by drawing a diagonal and covering each triangle by a detector). Four detectors should be located at the centers of four identical small squares. These squares are obtained by dividing the larger square by horizontal and vertical lines through its center. Following the same pattern, the intuitive solution for nine detectors is to divide the square into nine identical squares and place a detector at the center of each. However, by employing location analysis tools a better solution is obtained. See the best solution in Fig. 4.1. Assume that the detector's radius of coverage is "one." The intuitive arrangement covers a square area of 18 whereas the configuration shown in Fig. 4.1 covers a square area of 18.81. If the area to be covered is between 18 and 18.81 it can be covered by 9 detectors, whereas using the intuitive solution will require at least 10 detectors.

What is the best configuration for a large number of detectors in a generally shaped area? Most location solutions of this type tend to result in an hexagonal (or beehive) pattern (Z. Drezner & Zemel, 1992; Losch, 1944, 1954). The best strategy for area coverage by facilities is to arrange them in an hexagonal pattern rather than in a square grid. In a square grid each

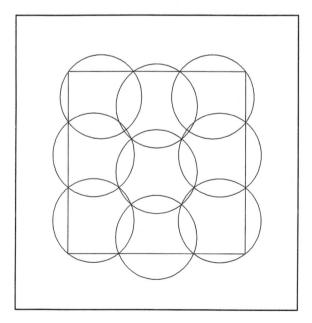

FIG. 4.1. Covering a square with nine facilities. Adapted from Suzuki and Z. Drezner (1996).

circle intersects four other circles whereas in a hexagonal pattern each circle intersects six other circles. The solution for nine facilities can be interpreted as a transition to a beehive configuration. In the intuitive solution the center circle intersects only the four other circles, whereas in the solution depicted in Fig. 4.1 the center circle intersects six other circles rather than four. The hexagonal pattern is more easily observed for a larger number of facilities (see such diagrams in Suzuki & Drezner, 1996, and in Fig. 4.2).

It is common practice to use square grids in planning and design. Buildings have a square shape. Roads usually follow a square grid pattern of North–South (N–S) and East–West (E–W) arteries. However, this is not the best configuration for area coverage. For a large number of facilities, a hexagonal pattern covers approximately a 30% larger area than a square grid pattern with the same number of facilities. This generic result is useful for a decision maker even if unfamiliar with the intricacies of locational analysis. A planner of ATM (Automatic Teller Machine) sites should prefer a beehive pattern for his or her machines. A planner of the location of gas stations, restaurant chains, and convenience store chains should prefer hexagonal patterns. Using hexagonal patterns, when distances are close to straight line (or Euclidean) distances, reduces by 30% the number of facilities required to cover an area.

The examples just discussed provide an insight into optimization problems in general and into location problems in particular. A systematic discussion of optimization problems using location analysis for illustration follows. The

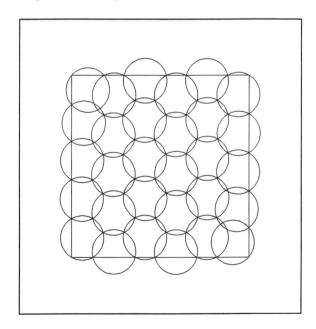

FIG. 4.2.   Covering a square with 30 facilities.

remainder of the chapter is organized as follows: In the first section we provide an overview and classification of facility location models. Next, we illustrate how various location models can be solved using Excel. A sample problem is solved using various models. Then specially selected models for specific location models are presented. These models can also be used as part of more complicated scenarios that require special algorithms for solving basic location models, or they can be part of a spreadsheet coded in visual basic. An Appendix contains a discussion of convexity and nonlinear programming models as a tool for solving location problems.

CLASSIFICATION OF LOCATION MODELS

Figure 4.3 is an organized classification of the field of locational analysis into its major subareas. The various branches in the figure represent the dimensions along which the models and solution approaches vary. These dimensions consist of the following:

1. Facility location models and facility layout: The distinction between facility location and facility layout consists of the presence or absence of demand. Whereas facility location models deal with locating facilities among customers who require service, facility layout models are concerned with the optimal layout of facilities in a given area in relation to each other. In facility layout problems, the facilities are interrelated and there are no demand points. Examples of facility layout include the layout of a firm's offices, the layout of an instrument control panel in an airplane, and the layout of a building complex. The facility layout problem is sometimes referred to in the literature as the "quadratic assignment problem." For a review, see the chapter by Burkard (1990) in Mirchandani and Francis (1990), and Z. Drezner (1987a).

Facilities can be either desirable or obnoxious. Desirable facility location models assume that the closer the facility is to demand the better the objective is met. There are two main objectives for desirable facilities models: minisum and minimax. The first and most common one is the "classical" model of minimizing the sum of weighted distances (sometimes called "the Weber problem" named after Alfred Weber, 1909). The second, the minimax model, is concerned with minimizing the maximal distance between facilities and demand points. This is the appropriate model for locating emergency facilities where the level of service to the farthest customer is the relevant criterion. For a review of these two models, see Love, Morris, and Wesolowsky (1988), and Francis, McGinnis, and White (1992).

Another type of desirable facility is the competitive facility such as the retail outlet. One or more facilities are to be located in an area in which

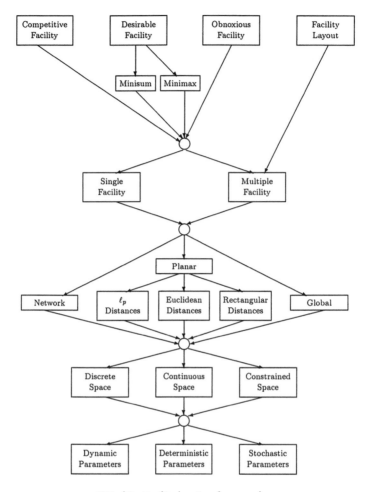

FIG. 4.3. Facility location framework.

competition already exists. Competitive facility location models are applied mainly by marketers. Facilities compete for customers and their objective is to maximize the market share they capture. Assuming that profit increases when market share increases, maximizing profit is equivalent to maximizing market share. It follows that the location objective is to locate the retail outlet at the location that maximizes its market share. One unique feature of competitive facility models is facility attractiveness (its appeal to customers). Facility attractiveness level, therefore, needs to be incorporated in the model. Other location models do not consider differences in attractiveness among facilities and therefore allocate customers to facilities by proximity. Also unique to competitive facility location is the modeling of demand in terms of buying power. Income levels and discretionary spending become a measure of demand. For a review of competitive models see Z. Drezner (1995b), especially the chapters by T. Drezner (1995), Ghosh, McLafferty, and Craig (1995), and Serra and ReVelle (1995).

Obnoxious facility location models seek to locate facilities as far as possible from customers. Commonly, a secondary consideration is that the facilities are still within reach. The airport location is a good example of this type. An airport is a source of noise pollution and traffic congestion, yet it needs to be easily accessible. Both objectives need to be accommodated. For a review of obnoxious facility location models, see Erkut and Neuman (1989) and Z. Drezner (1995b).

It becomes clear that facility location analysis is useful for both public and private sector facilities. A common objective in the public sector is equity, such as in service provision; therefore, the minimax objective is used. There exist other equity objectives appropriate for public sector applications. For a review of such applications, see Marsh and Schilling (1994) and Eiselt and Laporte (1995). A common objective in the private sector is minimization of cost (e.g., transportation cost) thus the minisum objective is appropriate.

2. The number of facilities: A distinction exists in the analysis between locating one facility and locating multiple (two or more) facilities. Multiple-facility location is conceptually and mathematically more complex. Applications for single-facility location problems usually become multiple-facility problems when the area covered is large and one facility cannot service the whole area. The area is then divided between several facilities and the problem becomes a combination of simultaneously finding both the proper allocation of customers to facilities and the best location for the facilities. In the location literature this is referred to as the location-allocation model (Ghosh & Rushton, 1987). The covering problem described in the introduction (the cellular telephone detectors) is a multifacility location problem. It is quite common that several new facilities need to be located in an area in which some existing facilities are already located. Such problems are called conditional location problems (Berman & Simchi-Levi, 1990; Chen & Handler, 1993).

3. Location environment: Three main environments are considered in location analysis. Customers and facilities can be located on a network, in the plane, or on the surface of the globe. Each environment entails its own formulation. The nature of the environment determines the measure of distance between customers and facilities.

Network problems deal with facility location on a network such as a road or a rail system, a communication network, or a computer chip. A graph (or a network) is defined by nodes and arcs of given lengths. Movement from one point on the graph to another is restricted to arcs of the network. The location of facilities is usually restricted to arcs and nodes. The shortest distance between two points on the graph needs to be calculated as part of each network modeling. For a review of network problems, see Daskin (1995).

Planar problems, where demand points and facilities are located in the plane, have received the most attention by researchers. There are three main distance measures on the plane: Euclidean distance or the distance along a straight line between two points, rectangular distance (sometimes called rectilinear or Manhattan distance) where movement between two points is allowed only along N–S or E–W axes roads, and the general ℓ_p distance, which approximates actual road distances most accurately (Brimberg & Love, 1995). Some other distance measures such as block norms (Ward & Wendell, 1985), or ring-radial distances, which are modeled after the street grid in Moscow, (Mittal & Palsule, 1984) are rarely used in such analyses. For a review of planar models, see Love et al. (1988) and Francis et al. (1992).

Global facility location deals with location on a sphere for air travel or naval operations. The facilities and the demand are located on the surface of the earth. Facility location on a sphere is an extension of facility location on the plane. Whereas planar problems deal with demand points and facilities on a small scale (where they are relatively close and can be assumed to be on a plane), spherical models deal with long-range distances where location on the plane can no longer be assumed. In this case distance is measured along great circles. For a review of spherical algorithms, see Wesolowsky (1983).

4. Solution domain: The locations of the new facilities can be found in either a discrete space, continuous space, or constrained space. Discrete models seek the optimal location from among a prespecified set of possible sites. Continuous models seek the best location anywhere in the problem space (planar, spherical, or network). Some models restrict the location of the new facilities by imposing constraints on their location. Some recent models consider barriers to travel (Aneja & Parlar, 1994; Katz & Cooper, 1981), which entails circumventing the barriers rather than traveling on a straight line. Such barriers can be rivers, lakes, parks, and so forth.

5. The nature of the parameters: In most location models it is assumed that problem parameters (such as demand level or its distribution) are deterministic (known). Other models deal with uncertainty about the parameters assuming that some parameters are drawn from some statistical distribution and are not deterministic. These are referred to as stochastic models (Z. Drezner & Wesolowsky, 1981). In dynamic models (Z. Drezner, 1995a; Z. Drezner & Wesolowsky, 1991), it is assumed that the parameters change over time in a predictable way. The problem becomes finding the best location that will minimize cost over a time horizon.

These models constitute the bulk of the location literature. There are other problems that lend themselves to formulation as a location model:

Finding the smallest square box that will contain a given number of soft-drink bottles/cans is a multifacility location problem where the smallest distance needs to be maximized (Z. Drezner & Erkut, 1995); building a road that will best serve a given number of demand points is the location of a linear facility rather than the location of a point facility. One might require a road to pass as far as possible from a set of demand points. This is the obnoxious version of the linear facility location problem (Z. Drezner & Wesolowsky, 1989). An additional example is the Steiner tree problem. The problem was introduced by Gauss in the early 1800s. Gauss inquired about the most efficient way to build a railroad system to connect four cities in Germany. In general terms, the Steiner tree problem is based on n points in the plane that need to be connected by rail or road system of minimal length. Electrical and pipeline connections are another common example. Steiner tree problems are complex and their solutions are usually not intuitive. See Fig. 4.4 for an example of a Steiner tree solution connecting four vertices of a square.

An important issue in all location models is the modeling of demand. For the distribution center problem, demand is generated as a finite set of users called demand points. For many other applications, demand is generated over an area because it is prohibitive to use each household as a separate demand point. For that purpose the area is partitioned into small subareas and each is assigned one demand point at its center. This demand point represents the total demand generated by all households in that subarea. In competitive location models, demand is modeled in terms of aggregated buying power. For many practical applications census data are available for

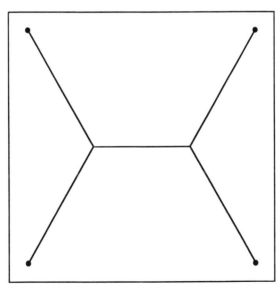

FIG. 4.4. The Steiner tree.

census tracts, zip codes, or cities. In such cases the demand points are defined by the type of available data.

For further and more in-depth discussion of the various location issues, we recommend Daskin (1995) for network problems, Love et al. (1988) and Francis et al. (1992) for planar problems, and Wesolowsky (1983) for spherical problems. The book by Z. Drezner (1995b) provides a state-of-the-art discussion on location analysis models and provides an excellent bibliography of over 1,200 references. For a review of location models, we recommend the chapters by Plastria (1995) and Eiselt and Laporte (1995).

SOLVING LOCATION PROBLEMS USING EXCEL

The introduction of the "Solver" option in Excel provides users with a simple and powerful tool for the solution of optimization problems in general and location problems in particular. In this section, we demonstrate the use of Excel for the solution of various facility location problems.

An important issue in optimization solvers is whether the functions in the model are convex or not. A function is convex if a line connecting any two points on the function graph is "above" the function graph. If the functions are convex, the solution obtained by Excel is guaranteed to be optimal. Otherwise, Excel might provide a solution that is not optimal. (For a discussion of convexity see the Appendix.) To help determine whether the formulation functions are convex, several basic rules regarding the property of convexity are offered:

Property 1: Euclidean, rectilinear, and ℓ_p distances are convex.

Property 2: Multiplying a convex function by a positive constant retains convexity.

Property 3: The sum of several convex functions is a convex function.

Property 4: The maximum of several convex functions is a convex function.

Note that the minimum of several convex functions is usually *not* convex.

Basic Notation

- n is the number of demand points.
- (a_i, b_i) is the location coordinates of demand point i, for $i = 1, \ldots, n$.
- w_i is the weight associated with demand point i, for $i = 1, \ldots, n$.
- (x, y) is the unknown location of the facility.
- $d_i(x,y)$ is the distance between demand point i and the facility location (x, y).

An Example Problem

Consider 16 communities in central and northern Orange County, California. Orange County is located in Southern California between Los Angeles and San Diego. Each community's population is represented as its associated weight. Data for these communities are given in Table 4.1.

Solution of the Minisum Problem

Minisum objectives are appropriate when total customer transportation cost is to be minimized. Consider the location of a service center, such as a federal building, serving the 16 communities. The objective is to minimize the total travel distance for all residents of these communities.

For Euclidean distances:

$$d_i(x,y) = \sqrt{(x - a_i)^2 + (y - b_i)^2} \qquad (1)$$

The objective is to minimize:

$$\sum_{i=1}^{n} w_i d_i(x,y) \qquad (2)$$

TABLE 4.1
Data for an Example Problem

Number	Name	Location a	b	w
1	Anaheim	3	5	234
2	Brea	3	7	32
3	Buena Park	2	6	65
4	Costa Mesa	3	2	86
5	Cypress	1	5	42
6	Fullerton	3	6	107
7	Garden Grove	3	4	129
8	Huntington Beach	2	2	179
9	Irvine	5	2	138
10	Mission Viejo	7	1	48
11	Newport Beach	4	1	66
12	Orange	4	4	102
13	Placentia	4	6	37
14	Santa Ana	4	3	225
15	Tustin	5	3	39
16	Yorba Linda	6	6	57

This objective function (Equation 2) is convex by applying properties 1, 2, and 3. Therefore, the solution found by Excel is the optimal solution.

In order to solve this problem by Excel, a spreadsheet that calculates the objective function is designed, and the Solver option in Excel is used to find the best location. The constructed spreadsheet is shown in Fig. 4.5. The spreadsheet is constructed applying the following steps:

1. In columns A, B, and C, the coordinates of the demand points and the weight associated with each are entered.

2. The unknown coordinates x and y for the facility will be calculated by the solver in cells D1 and E1, respectively. These cells are kept empty.

3. In cells E2:E17 (the ":" in Excel signifies a range of cells) the individual terms of Equation 2, to be summed up for all demand points, are entered. The terms are the weight multiplied by the distance $[w_i d_i(x,y)]$. Specifically, we enter: =C2*sqrt((D$1-A2)^2+(E$1-B2)^2) in cell E2. (The "*" is the multiplication sign, the "$" signifies that when the cell is copied, the address following the "$" is not changed, and the "^" signifies raising to a power.) This cell is copied (or dragged down) to cover all cells from E2 to E17.

4. The objective function (Equation 2) is calculated in cell F1 by entering =SUM(E2:E17) in that cell.

5. The spreadsheet is now ready to find the optimal solution. The optimal location is the point that minimizes the function calculated in F1. The optimal location coordinates will be calculated in D1 and E1. We now call Solver and the window shown in Fig. 4.6 appears on the screen. In Excel 5.0 or

	A	B	C	D	E	F	G	H
1	a	b	w			8447.113		
2	3	5	234		1364.443			
3	3	7	32		243.7047			
4	2	6	65		411.0961			
5	3	2	86		310.0774			
6	1	5	42		214.1588			
7	3	6	107		717.7778			
8	3	4	129		645			
9	2	2	179		506.2885			
10	5	2	138		743.1527			
11	7	1	48		339.4113			
12	4	1	66		272.125			
13	4	4	102		576.9991			
14	4	6	37		266.8108			
15	4	3	225		1125			
16	5	3	39		227.4071			

FIG. 4.5. The Excel spreadsheet.

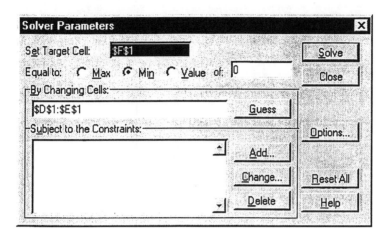

FIG. 4.6. The Solver window.

7.0 the Solver option appears under "tools." If you cannot find it, try "add ins" under "tools," and if this fails to bring Solver, you need to reinstall Excel and make sure that the Solver option is installed.

6. Because the objective function is calculated in cell F1, F1 is entered in the box following "Set Target Cell."

7. Because it is a minimization objective, the option "Min" is selected for "Equal to."

8. The variables are stored in cells D1 and E1. Variables D1:E1 are entered in the space below the line reading "By Changing Cells." Cells D1 and E1 contain no values so the program starts with the values of zero for both. If any values are entered in these cells as an "initial guess," then Solver will use the provided initial values.

9. The spreadsheet is now ready to find the solution. The button "Solve" in the upper right corner of the window is clicked, and the solution shown in Fig. 4.7 is obtained. The optimal location is shown in cells D1 and E1. The minimal sum of weighted distances at that location is shown in cell F1. The best location for the federal building is approximately at x = 3.5 and y = 3.7, southwest of Orange. The minimal sum of weighted distances is 2,919.349. The best location is depicted in Fig. 4.8.

Let us now assume that the road system in Orange County resembles a grid of N–S and E–W arteries. In this case, the distance between any two points is best modeled by the rectilinear or "Manhattan" distance. The expression for the distance needs to be changed from Euclidean, or straight line, distance to the rectilinear distance, which is:

$$d_i(x,y) = |x - a_i| + |y - b_i| \qquad (3)$$

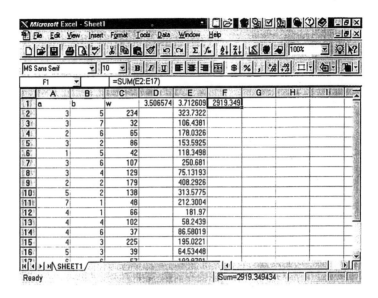

FIG. 4.7. The Excel solution spreadsheet.

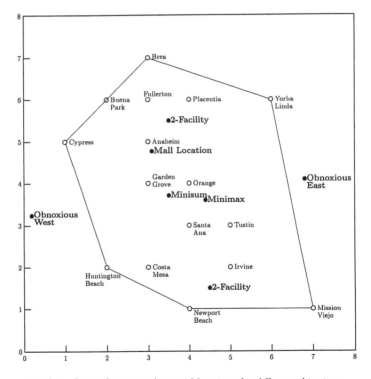

FIG. 4.8. The study area and optimal locations for different objectives.

92

The objective function is given by Equation 2. This problem is convex as well. The only change required in the spreadsheet is replacing the expression of the distance in cell E2 with the sum of absolute values (Equation 3) and recopy to cells E2:E17. The solution to the rectilinear problem is at (3,4), which is in the city of Garden Grove.

The two solutions are quite close to one another. This is common because the solution for any minisum problem tends to be close to the center of the geographical area.

Solution of the Minimax Problem

Minimax models are appropriate for locating facilities whose objective is to serve the farthest customer in the best way, such as emergency facilities. Suppose that the service center to be constructed is an emergency center, such as a major hospital. The distance from the farthest patient to the hospital is to be minimized. Minimax formulations are usually unweighted because the farthest customer is independent of the number of customers at that demand point. The minimax formulation is to minimize: $\max\{d_i(x,y)\}$. The minimax problem with either Euclidean (Equation 1) or rectilinear (Equation 3) distances is a convex problem by properties 1, 2, and 4. Therefore, the location solution found by Excel is optimal.

To solve this model using Excel, the weight C2 in the formula in E2 is removed and the SUM in the objective function F1 is replaced by MAX. The solution is at (4.4, 3.6), southeast of Orange, with a maximum distance of 3.677. Three cities—Brea, Cypress, and Mission Viejo—are all at the maximum distance from the solution point. See Fig. 4.8.

The rectilinear version of the minimax problem is solved by replacing the Euclidean distances with rectilinear distances. The solution obtained by Excel is (4, 3) (in Santa Ana) with a maximum distance of 5.

Solution of the Multiple-Facility Problem

Multiple-facilities models are required when one facility cannot service the whole service area. These models are applicable for both minisum and minimax objectives. Assume, for example, that it is determined ahead of time that one federal building cannot handle all the services requested by the residents of northern and central Orange County. It is decided that p buildings need to be built. It is assumed that each customer patronizes the facility closest to him or her. The aggregated customer travel time is to be minimized. Let the best location for facility j be at (x_j, y_j). The objective function of the minisum problem is therefore the minimization of:

$$\sum_{i=1}^{n} w_i \min_{1 \le j \le p} \{d_i(x_j, y_j)\} \qquad (4)$$

Suppose that $p = 2$; that is, two federal buildings need to be simultaneously located in the area. The corresponding changes in the minisum spreadsheet are:

1. The coordinates of the first center will be stored in D1 and E1 as before, and the coordinates of the second center will be stored in F1 and G1.
2. The objective function is moved from F1 to H1.
3. The weighted distances to the second service station are calculated in column G.
4. The minimum value between columns E and G is calculated in column H.
5. The objective function in cell H1 is the sum of the values in column H.

This problem (Equation 4) is not convex because the minimum of a set of convex functions is not convex. Therefore, Excel may find a nonoptimal solution (see the Appendix for a discussion of the implications of nonconvexity). As a result, a repeated solution procedure, starting each time with different randomly generated locations, is proposed. We first solve the minisum Euclidean distance version (Equation 1) of the problem. By applying Excel several times to randomly generated starting locations we find two local minima: One configuration is to locate one facility at (3,5) (Anaheim) and the other at (3.91, 2.52) south of Santa Ana. The sum of weighted distances is 1,886. The other configuration is to locate one facility in Anaheim and the other at a location closer to Santa Ana at (3.99, 2.96) with an objective function value of 1,871. Because the objective is to minimize total distance, the latter is likely to be the global optimum—the solution to the minisum Euclidean problem.

The solution to the minisum problem using rectilinear distances (Equation 3) is to locate one facility in Anaheim (3,5), and the other at (4,2) which is halfway between Costa Mesa and Irvine.

The minimax version of the problem is to minimize

$$\max_{1 \leq i \leq n} \left\{ \min_{1 \leq j \leq p} \{d_i(x_j, y_j)\} \right\}, \tag{5}$$

which is also nonconvex. Excel does not handle this particular formulation well unless a good starting point is given. The solution to the Euclidean version (Equation 1) of the problem found by Excel is to locate the two centers at (3.5, 5.5) and (4.5, 1.5) with a maximum distance of 2.55. It is interesting that the rectilinear distance solution was at the same coordinates with a maximum distance of 3. This solution to the minimax objective is also depicted in Fig. 4.8.

The Conditional Location Problem

In many applications, several facilities already exist in the area and one or more facilities are to be added. These problems are referred to as *conditional location problems.* These problems are not convex. Solving such problems using Excel is similar to solving the multiple-facility problem. The only change is in the Solver window: The coordinates of the new facilities are defined as variables whereas the existing facilities are assigned to their present location and are not changed by the Solver.

Assume that one federal building exists in Orange [at (4,4)], and another is planned to be located in the area. The spreadsheet used for the multiple-facility location is also used for the conditional location problem. The coordinates (4,4) are entered in D1 and E1, whereas only cells F1 and G1 are used as variables. Using Euclidean distances we obtain three local minima with almost identical values of the objective function. These are Anaheim (3,5) with an objective function value of 2,378.439, Costa Mesa (3,2) with an objective function value of 2,378.663, and Huntington Beach (2,2) with an objective function value of 2,378.221. The best location is Huntington Beach (2,2).

Competitive Facility Location

To demonstrate the nature of retail location problems, we consider the location of a new mall in the area. As was discussed in the section Classification of Location Models, unique features of competitive facility location models include modeling of demand in terms of buying power, incorporating a measure of facility attractiveness, and defining market share as the objective function. We employ the following additional notation:

- B_i is the buying power of customers located at demand point i, for $i = 1, \ldots, n$.
- k is the number of existing facilities (malls).
- (x_j, y_j) is the location of existing facility j, for $j = 1, \ldots, k$.
- A_j is the attractiveness of existing facility j, for $j = 1, \ldots, k$.
- (x,y) is the unknown location of the new facility.
- A is the known attractiveness of the new facility.
- ε is the correction to the distance (explained later).
- M is the market share captured by the new facility (mall).

A common approach used by marketers to estimate market share is by using the gravity-based model first proposed by Huff (1964, 1966). The gravity-based model is based on the observation: "The probability that a customer patronizes a certain facility is proportional to the facility's floor area and inversely proportional to a power of the distance to it." Floor area is a surrogate for facility attractiveness. See T. Drezner (1995) for a review of various gravity models. The original gravity model assumes that the power is "2"; that is, the probability is inversely proportional to the square of the distance. Euclidean distances (Equation 1) are used for this model. A more accurate allocation of demand is obtained when a constant ε is added to the square of the distance (T. Drezner & Z. Drezner, 1997). This constant should be approximately $R^2/2$ where R is the radius of the demand point.

The market share, M, attracted by the new facility is:

$$M = \sum_{i=1}^{n} B_i \frac{\dfrac{A}{d^2(x,y) + \varepsilon}}{\dfrac{A}{d^2(x,y) + \varepsilon} + \sum_{j=1}^{k} \dfrac{A_j}{d_i^2(x_j,y_j) + \varepsilon}} \tag{6}$$

The objective function (Equation 6) is the maximization of market share. The market share is not a concave function and therefore there may be several local maxima (see the Appendix for a discussion of concavity and local maxima).

There are six existing major shopping malls in the study area with the parameters given in Table 4.2. A new shopping mall with an attractiveness of 5 is planned for the area. The location that will maximize the market share captured by the new facility (by Equation 6) is sought. Equation 6 is easily constructed as an Excel spreadsheet. The solution found by Excel, using $\varepsilon = 1$, is south of Anaheim at (3.09, 4.77) with a market share captured of 241.62 (see Fig. 4.8). Though the objective function is not concave, only one local maximum was identified by Excel regardless of the starting solution.

TABLE 4.2
Existing Shopping Malls

| Mall Number | Location | | Attractiveness |
	x	y	
1	2.7	6.8	7
2	3.9	4.5	3
3	3.6	4.2	7
4	3.2	2.2	10
5	4.0	1.5	7
6	6.1	1.2	3

Obnoxious Facility Location

Suppose a prison is planned to be built in the study area. On one hand, public safety requires that the prison is "as far as possible" from the communities. This will lead to a solution at infinity (say, at the east coast of the United States). On the other hand, guards employed at the facility and visitors should be able to conveniently access it. Therefore, the model should specify restrictions on the location of the obnoxious facility. A common approach is to require the solution to be within the convex hull of demand points. The convex hull is the smallest convex polygon that encloses all points (communities). For this specific problem, the convex hull is the polygon whose vertices are (see Fig. 4.8): Yorba Linda, Brea, Cypress (Buena Park, which lies on the side connecting Brea and Cypress, is not required for the polygon definition), Huntington Beach, Newport Beach, and Mission Viejo. The polygon has six vertices and therefore six sides. Restricting the solution to the inside of this polygon requires the addition of six linear constraints to the model, one for each side of the polygon. These constraints are added to the formulation in the Solver window (see Fig. 4.6). The bottom half of the window allows for constraints in the model. One needs to specify "Add" and a window opens. One can either enter the formula in the provided space, or code the formula into a cell in the spreadsheet and just specify the cell (or cells) in which the formula is entered. The constraint is usually an expression that is either $\leq$, or $\geq$, or = some value. For example, the line connecting Yorba Linda [located at $(6,6)$] and Brea [located at $(3,7)$] is $x + 3y = 24$. Therefore, the constraint is $x + 3y \leq 24$. This can be entered as =D1+3*E1 in the left-hand side of the window and the number 24 on the right-hand side. Adding six such constraints guarantees that the solution is in the convex hull and not at infinity.

Alternatively, similar results can be achieved by constraining the total sum of weighted distances (which is the single-facility minisum objective) to be less than a certain value. Such a constraint is logical if services are provided to the prison and employees and visitors need to travel to it. Although the main objective is not to minimize the travel costs for visitors, some consideration of that issue is warranted. The minimum possible sum of weighted distances was found to be 2,919.349 (see Fig. 4.7). We can, for example, specify that all visitors combined (for simplicity we assume the same proportion of visitors from all communities) are not required to travel more than about double this value or a weighted sum of 6,000. This can be added as one constraint to the problem.

Two objectives are commonly used for such problems. One possible objective is to maximize the minimal distance from all communities (the maximin objective). This will guarantee minimum safety for all communities. A second objective is based on the assumption that the nuisance is decreasing with the square of the distance from the obnoxious facility. This is especially true for pollution-generating facilities. The objective here is to minimize the total "harm" to the communities (the minisum obnoxious objective). This leads to the objective function of the minimization of:

$$\sum_{i=1}^{n} \frac{w_i}{d_i^2(x,y)} \tag{7}$$

All obnoxious facility models are nonconvex. The feasible region is convex in both our constraint types, but the objective function is not. Therefore, there may be several local minima to the problem. Obnoxious facility location problems need to be solved repeatedly from randomly generated starting solutions and the best solution selected this way. We elected to illustrate the solution procedure for the second constraint ($\sum_{i=1}^{n} w_i d_i(x,y) \leq 6,000$) rather than the convex hull. The problem is solved twice, once for each objective. Euclidean distances (Equation 1) were used. The solution for the maximin problem is at (6.81, 4.06) at the eastern part of the county with an equal distance of 2.10 from Yorba Linda and Tustin (see Fig. 4.8). A very close second is a location on the western side of the county at (0.20, 3.07) with equal distance of 2.09 from Cypress and Huntington Beach. Note that these two solutions are outside the convex hull. The value of the weighted sum of distances is 6,000 in both cases. There are many more local minima to the problem, each closer to the nearest community. Every "space" between communities contains such a local minimum. For example, inside the area between Santa Ana, Tustin, Irvine, Newport Beach, and Costa Mesa (see Fig. 4.8) there is a local minimum at (4,2). However, the distance to the nearest community is only 1.

The minisum obnoxious problem (Equation 7) also has many local minima. In this case two main local minima are obtained, one in the east county and one in the west county in locations very close to those obtained for the maximin objective. Again, the eastern site is a little better than the western one. The optimal location is at (6.80, 4.11), which is very close to the solution by the maximin objective, with an objective function value of 136.4. The western site is at (0.16, 3.41) with an objective function value of 143.4. The constraint in this case also has a value of 6,000 in both cases.

Facility Location on the Globe

So far we have discussed location models in the plane. One group of location models deals with distances measured on the globe. Locating an international airport or naval base is best modeled by using spherical distances. Spherical distances are flight distances, or shortest arc distances. International distances are not well approximated by planar distances. For example, the shortest route from New York to Tokyo passes close to the North Pole rather than in a straight line across the United States and the Pacific Ocean drawn on a flat map.

The coordinates of each location on the sphere are expressed as longitude (x) and latitude (y). Using the same notation as earlier, the distance between a demand point and a facility (Drezner & Wesolowsky, 1978) is:

$$\cos[d_i(x,y)] = \sin b_i \sin y + \cos b_i \cos y \cos(x - a_i).$$

The distance can be easily calculated by Excel using the functions COS, SIN, and the inverse of the cosine function ACOS.

Location problems on a sphere are generally not convex and may have several local minima. The distance function is convex inside a circle on the surface of the sphere with a radius smaller than one fourth of the circumference of the sphere. Therefore, problems that do not cover a large region are convex in that region. However, one should try several starting points when using a Solver to solve problems that span over more than one fourth of the circumference of the earth. For a complete discussion of this issue see Drezner and Wesolowsky (1978).

Consider the problem of establishing a worldwide courier network such as Federal Express. Suppose that the courier uses its own aircraft and provides service to many cities worldwide. We selected the 21 largest metropolitan areas in the world with a population of over 8 million people each for the problem. The cities are listed in Table 4.3. A negative longitude means a longitude east of Greenwich, England, and west of the international date line east of New Zealand, whereas a positive longitude means west of Greenwich to the international date line. A negative latitude means south of the equator.

It is prohibitive to have a daily flight between every pair of cities. This will amount to over 400 flights a day and require a fleet of over 200 airplanes. It is therefore proposed to establish a hub (Federal Express originally used Memphis as the hub for U.S. operations) and have daily round-trip flights from each city to the hub. The planes arrive at the hub at the same time, packages are exchanged, and the planes leave the hub on their way back to their origin at the same time. Using a hub requires a fleet of 21 planes. Where is the optimal location for the hub? The appropriate objective, when the shortest service time is required, is the minimax objective, that is, finding a location that minimizes the maximum distance to all cities.

The location solution to the minimax problem obtained by Excel is at 35.67 North, and 13.00 East. This location is close to Tunis in Northern Africa on the southern part of the Mediterranean Sea. Using an Earth radius of 3,959 miles, this point is at a maximum distance of 6,684 miles from all cities (see Table 4.4). Three cities—Los Angeles, Buenos Aires, and Jakarta—are at the maximum distance. All other cities are closer to the hub but a few not by much. For example, Manila is 6,598 miles away from this hub, and

TABLE 4.3
Largest Metropolitan Areas

City	Longitude (x)	Latitude (y)	Population
Tokyo	−139.75	35.67	28.4
Mexico City	99.12	19.43	23.9
Sao Paolo	46.52	−23.52	21.5
Seoul	−127.00	37.57	19.1
New York	73.97	40.78	14.6
Osaka	−135.50	34.53	14.1
Bombay	−72.80	19.00	13.5
Calcutta	−88.40	22.57	12.9
Rio De Janiero	43.20	−22.95	12.8
Buenos Aires	58.37	−34.58	12.2
Tehran	−51.75	35.75	11.7
Manila	−120.95	14.58	11.3
Jakarta	−106.80	−6.27	11.2
Cairo	−31.35	30.03	11.2
Moscow	−37.60	55.75	10.8
Los Angeles	118.25	34.05	10.4
Delhi	−77.18	28.62	10.1
Lagos	−3.40	6.45	9.8
Karachi	−67.05	24.87	9.3
London	0.08	51.53	8.9
Paris	−2.33	48.80	8.8

Mexico City is 6,593 miles away. This is the fastest way to provide service between any two cities with a fleet of 21 airplanes only.

If the objective is minimizing the total mileage traveled by these 21 airplanes, one should minimize the total sum of distances (unweighted). This objective yields a solution at 44.76 North and 48.48 East (in Russia at the northwest corner of the Caspian Sea) with a total of 86,075 one-way miles flown. The weighted minisum objective (under the assumption that the cost is proportional to the populations and more than one aircraft will service each city daily) leads to a solution at 52.55 degrees North and 50.67 degrees East, which is farther north of the Caspian Sea in Russia. This remote location does not seem appropriate, and one may choose a city in Turkey, or in Eastern Europe instead.

Steiner Trees

Consider the Steiner tree problem for connecting four cities located at the vertices of a square with a side of 1. What is the best way to connect these cities by roads or rails? Building all four sides of the square has a total length of 4. However, three sides suffice to connect all points with a total length of 3. If the two diagonals are constructed, the total length is $2\sqrt{2} = 2.828$. Is this the best solution? There is yet a better solution (see Fig. 4.4) with a

TABLE 4.4
Distances from Optimal Hub Locations

City	Distance From Hub (Miles)		
	Minimax	Minisum	Weighted Minisum
Tokyo	6,436	4,599	4,278
Mexico City	6,593	7,555	7,144
Sao Paolo	5,642	7,583	7,790
Seoul	5,848	3,954	3,681
New York	4,531	5,537	5,191
Osaka	6,334	4,461	4,168
Bombay	3,788	2,263	2,606
Calcutta	4,534	2,720	2,868
Rio De Janiero	5,467	7,399	7,623
Buenos Aires	6,684	8,615	8,836
Tehran	2,160	646	1,162
Manila	6,598	4,658	4,596
Jakarta	6,684	5,038	5,218
Cairo	1,132	1,380	1,838
Moscow	1,806	897	572
Los Angeles	6,684	6,929	6,417
Delhi	3,721	1,926	2,136
Lagos	2,109	3,782	4,150
Karachi	3,270	1,723	2,095
London	1,272	2,244	2,113
Paris	1,056	2,168	2,092

total length of $\sqrt{3} + 1 = 2.732$. For general arrangement of cities, it may be difficult to "guess" the right configuration of connecting lines, but once a certain configuration is hypothesized, Excel can be used to determine the exact location of the two center points in Fig. 4.4.

Let the two center points be (x, y) and (u, v). The objective function is the minimization of:

$$\sqrt{x^2 + y^2} + \sqrt{x^2 + (y-1)^2} + \sqrt{(u-1)^2 + v^2} + \sqrt{(u-1)^2 + (v-1)^2} + \sqrt{(x-u)^2 + (y-v)^2}.$$

This problem is nonconvex with two equal valued local minima: one parallel to the x-axis and the other parallel to the y-axis. A solution is $(x,y) = (0.2887, 0.5)$ and $(u,v) = (0.7113, 0.5)$ as depicted in Fig. 4.4. The combined road length is 2.732.

The Capacitated Plant Location Problem

The capacitated plant location problem is different from the problems discussed in the previous sections in many ways. First, there is a list of locations where the plants can be located rather than be located anywhere in the plane. Consequently, the distances in the model are not functions of the plants' locations but rather given values for each pair of demand location and potential site. Also, each potential site for the location of a plant may have a different construction and maintenance cost, and may have a different available capacity. Second, the number of plants is not predetermined but is a variable of the model sites.

Demand is generated at demand points and all demand must be satisfied by the plants. There are two costs considered in the model: One is the transportation cost between the plants and demand points and the other is the fixed construction and maintenance cost. Both costs are calculated on an annual basis (i.e., construction costs are converted to an annual expense). The objective is to minimize the total cost. The capacitated plant location problem is formulated as a mixed 0–1 programming (for a discussion of this type of problem, see the Appendix to this chapter).

Notation.

- n is the number of demand points.
- w_i is the demand at demand point i, for $i = 1, \ldots, n$.
- m is the number of potential plant sites.
- C_j is the capacity at potential site j, for $j = 1, \ldots, m$.
- d_{ij} is the distance between demand point i and potential site j for $i = 1, \ldots, n; j = 1, \ldots, m$.
- B_j is the construction cost at potential site j, for $j = 1, \ldots, m$.
- x_{ij} is the proportion of demand generated at demand point i assigned to the plant at potential site j for $i = 1, \ldots, n; j = 1, \ldots, m$.
- y_j is a 0–1 variable indicating whether a plant will be constructed at potential site j. $y_j = 1$ if a plant is built at potential site j, and $y_j = 0$ if not.

The optimization formulation is:

$$\min \left\{ \sum_{j=1}^{m} B_j y_j + \sum_{i=1}^{n} \sum_{j=1}^{m} w_i d_{ij} x_{ij} \right\}$$

subject to:

$$\sum_{j=1}^{m} x_{ij} = 1 \quad \text{for } i = 1, \ldots, n$$

$$\sum_{i=1}^{n} w_i x_{ij} \le C_j y_j \quad \text{for } j = 1, \ldots, m \tag{8}$$

$$x_{ij} \ge 0; \ y_j \in \{0,1\}$$

The first term in the objective function represents the construction cost and the second term represents the transportation cost. The first constraint set specifies that all the demand at demand point i is satisfied. The second constraint set limits the demand assigned to plant j to its capacity. Note that the capacity of plant j is $C_j y_j$, which is equal to C_j if $y_j = 1$ and zero otherwise. The last constraints specify that (a) there cannot be negative demand (note that $x_{ij} \leq 1$ because of the first constraint) and (b) the y_j is either zero or one. No "partial" plant is allowed. This formulation allows for demand at one demand point to be divided among several plants. This is termed the *divisible problem*. If all demand at a demand point has to be assigned to one facility only, the constraint $x_{ij} \geq 0$ is replaced by $x_{ij} \in \{0,1\}$. This problem becomes the *integer problem*.

Consider building one or more plants in Orange County to satisfy customer demand. Demand is equal to the population in each community (in thousands) as given in Table 4.1. There are four proposed sites for these plants: Cypress, Mission Viejo, Yorba Linda, and Huntington Beach. Each such proposed plant can serve $C_j = 800$ people (in thousands) and costs $B_j = 1,000$ annually to build. Distances between demand points and the plants at each potential site are calculated by rectilinear distance (Equation 3).

The spreadsheets for both the divisible and integer problems are given in Figs. 4.9 and 4.10, respectively. For both spreadsheets:

1. Columns B and C contain the locations of the demand points.

2. Rows 1 and 2 (columns E–H) contain the locations of the potential plant locations.

3. In the array E4:H19, the distances d_{ij} between the demand points and the potential sites are calculated by Equation 3.

4. Column J contains the population w_i of each city.

5. In the array L4:O19 the product $w_i d_{ij}$ of the distance and the population is calculated.

6. Capacity of each plant is entered in row E21:H21.

7. Construction cost at each potential site is entered in row E40:H40.

8. The y variables will be calculated at E23:H23, which is empty. (The spreadsheet shows the solution.)

9. The x variables will be calculated in the array E24:H39, which is empty.

10. In preparation for the constraints: Row 22 is the product of row 23 and row 21 ($C_j y_j$). Row E20:H20 contains the total demand assigned to each potential site (the left-hand side of the second constraint). Cell E20, for example, is the scalar product of column E24:E39 by column J4:J19 using the command =SUMPRODUCT(E24:E39,J4:J19).

11. The objective function of Equation 8 is programmed in cell B1.

	A	B	C	D	E	F	G	H	I	J	K	L	M	N	O
1		6149			1	7	6	2							
2					5	1	6	2							
3															
4	Anaheim	3	5		2	8	4	4		234		468	1872	936	936
5	Brea	3	7		4	10	4	6		32		128	320	128	192
6	Buena Park	2	6		2	10	4	4		65		130	650	260	260
7	Costa Mesa	3	2		5	5	7	1		86		430	430	602	86
8	Cypress	1	5		0	10	6	4		42		0	420	252	168
9	Fullerton	3	6		3	9	3	5		107		321	963	321	535
10	Garden Grove	3	4		3	7	5	3		129		387	903	645	387
11	Huntington Beach	2	2		4	6	8	0		179		716	1074	1432	0
12	Irvine	5	2		7	3	5	3		138		966	414	690	414
13	Mission Viejo	7	1		10	0	6	6		48		480	0	288	288
14	Newport Beach	4	1		7	3	7	3		66		462	198	462	198
15	Orange	4	4		4	6	4	4		102		408	612	408	408
16	Placentia	4	6		4	8	2	6		37		148	296	74	222
17	Santa Ana	4	3		5	5	5	3		225		1125	1125	1125	675
18	Tustin	5	3		6	4	4	4		39		234	156	156	156
19	Yorba Linda	6	6		6	6	0	8		57		342	342	0	456
20					786	0	0	800							
21					800	800	800	800		1586					
22					800	0	0	800							
23					1	0	0	1							
24	Anaheim				1	0	0	0	1						
25	Brea				1	0	0	0	1						
26	Buena Park				1	0	0	0	1						
27	Costa Mesa				0	0	0	1	1						
28	Cypress				1	0	0	0	1						
29	Fullerton				1	0	0	0	1						
30	Garden Grove				0.85	0	0	0.15	1						
31	Huntington Beach				0	0	0	1	1						
32	Irvine				0	0	0	1	1						
33	Mission Viejo				0	0	0	1	1						
34	Newport Beach				0	0	0	1	1						
35	Orange				1	0	0	0	1						
36	Placentia				1	0	0	0	1						
37	Santa Ana				0	0	0	1	1						
38	Tustin				0	0	0	1	1						
39	Yorba Linda				1	0	0	0	1						
40					1000	1000	1000	1000							

FIG. 4.9. The spreadsheet for the plant location problem (divisible).

The Solver window is depicted in Fig. 4.11 and contains:

1. The objective function ("Set Target Cell") is programmed in B1.

2. The variables (both x and y) are in the array E23:H39 ("By Changing Cells").

3. In the window "Subject to Constraints" the constraints of Equation 8 are entered.

4. The constraint E20:H20<=22:H22 corresponds to the second constraint of Equation 8.

5. The constraint E23:H23<=1 specifies that $y_j \le 1$.

	A	B	C	D	E	F	G	H	I	J	K	L	M	N	O
1	6341				1	7	6	2							
2					5	1	6	2							
3															
4	Anaheim	3	5		2	8	4	4		234		468	1872	936	936
5	Brea	3	7		4	10	4	6		32		128	320	128	192
6	Buena Park	2	6		2	10	4	4		65		130	650	260	260
7	Costa Mesa	3	2		5	5	7	1		86		430	430	602	86
8	Cypress	1	5		0	10	6	4		42		0	420	252	168
9	Fullerton	3	6		3	9	3	5		107		321	963	321	535
10	Garden Grove	3	4		3	7	5	3		129		387	903	645	387
11	Huntington Beach	2	2		4	6	8	0		179		716	1074	1432	0
12	Irvine	5	2		7	3	5	3		138		966	414	690	414
13	Mission Viejo	7	1		10	0	6	6		48		480	0	288	288
14	Newport Beach	4	1		7	3	7	3		66		462	198	462	198
15	Orange	4	4		4	6	4	4		102		408	612	408	408
16	Placentia	4	6		4	8	2	6		37		148	296	74	222
17	Santa Ana	4	3		5	5	5	3		225		1125	1125	1125	675
18	Tustin	5	3		6	4	4	4		39		234	156	156	156
19	Yorba Linda	6	6		6	6	0	8		57		342	342	0	456
20					787	0	0	799							
21					800	800	800	800		1586					
22					800	0	0	800							
23					1	0	0	1							
24	Anaheim				1	0	0	0	1						
25	Brea				1	0	0	0	1						
26	Buena Park				1	0	0	0	1						
27	Costa Mesa				0	0	0	1	1						
28	Cypress				1	0	0	0	1						
29	Fullerton				1	0	0	0	1						
30	Garden Grove				1	0	0	0	1						
31	Huntington Beach				0	0	0	1	1						
32	Irvine				0	0	0	1	1						
33	Mission Viejo				0	0	0	1	1						
34	Newport Beach				0	0	0	1	1						
35	Orange				1	0	0	0	1						
36	Placentia				1	0	0	0	1						
37	Santa Ana				0	0	0	1	1						
38	Tustin				1	0	0	0	1						
39	Yorba Linda				0	0	0	1	1						
40					1000	1000	1000	1000							

FIG. 4.10. The spreadsheet for the plant location problem (integer).

6. The next (highlighted) constraints specifies that all variables (both x and y) are integer. This is the integer formulation. For the continuous formulation only the ys are required to be integers. The only change in the whole formulation is to change the range of this constraint from E23:H39 to E23:H23.

7. The next constraint requires that all variables are non-negative.

8. The last constraint corresponds to the first constraint in Equation 8.

9. To facilitate Excel's solution, one needs to select "Options" in the Solver window and select "Assume Linear Model." Failure to select this

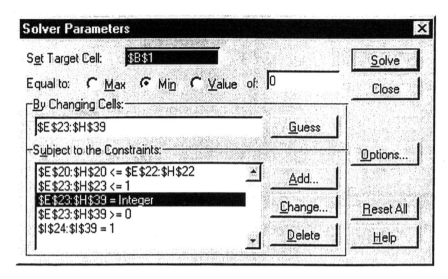

FIG. 4.11. The Solver window for the plant location problem.

option causes an excessive solution time by Solver and may result in a wrong solution.

The divisible (when demand is allowed to be divided between facilities) solution is shown in Fig. 4.9. The objective function value is 6,149. Two plants should be opened, one in Cypress and one in Huntington Beach (the two ys, which are equal to 1 in row 23). No demand point is assigned to another potential location (columns F and G between rows 24 and 39 are 0). Only demand in Garden Grove (row 30) is divided between the two plants.

The integer formulation (each demand point must be assigned to only one plant) yields the spreadsheet in Fig. 4.10. The objective function value is 6,341. Two plants are established at the same sites, but the allocation of demand to plants is slightly altered. All variables in rows 24 to 39 are either 0 or 1.

SELECTED SPECIAL ALGORITHMS

As discussed in the previous section, many location problems can be solved by Excel. However, when the number of demand points or facilities is large the problem contains too many variables or constraints, which exceed Excel's capacity. In such cases a special program is needed for the solution of these problems. In this section we review selected special, but simple, algorithms for solving various location problems. These methods are independent of Excel and require coding a special program. They can be coded in any programming language such as Basic, Fortran, Pascal, or others. If coded in

Basic (or Visual Basic) the program can be part of the spreadsheet. The special methods are also useful as part of complicated algorithms that require many solutions to simple problems. For example, solving multiple-facility location problems often requires repeated solution of single-facility location problems. Therefore, a simple approach to solving single-facility location problems is essential for employing such algorithms for the solution of multiple-facility location problems.

Before turning to specific algorithms we elaborate on the issue of distance. Euclidean distance (Equation 1) or straight line distance is the most common distance measure. The rectilinear distance (Equation 3) is used for square grid distances. Another useful distance is the max (or Chebishev) distance. The max distance is: $d_i(x,y) = \max\{ |x - a_i|, |y - b_i| \}$. These distance measures are special cases of the ℓ_p distance: $d_i(x,y) = \sqrt[p]{|x - a_i|^p + |y - b_i|^p}$. Euclidean distances use $p = 2$, rectilinear distances use $p = 1$, and the Chebishev distance uses $p = \infty$. The general ℓ_p distance was found useful in approximating road distances (Brimberg & Love, 1995).

Single-Facility Location Using Euclidean Distances

The single-facility location problem using Euclidean distances is the most basic facility location problem. The commonly used effective procedure for the single-facility problem is the Weiszfeld procedure, first proposed by Weiszfeld (1937). The single-facility location problem consists of minimizing Equation 2:

$$\sum_{i=1}^{n} w_i\sqrt{(x - a_i)^2 + (y - b_i)^2} \qquad (9)$$

The derivatives of this objective function (Equation 9) by x and y are equated to zero, yielding:

$$\sum_{i=1}^{n} w_i\frac{x - a_i}{\sqrt{(x - a_i)^2 + (y - b_i)^2}} = 0; \quad \sum_{i=1}^{n} w_i\frac{y - b_i}{\sqrt{(x - a_i)^2 + (y - b_i)^2}} = 0. \qquad (10)$$

Solving Equation 10 for x and y in the numerators leads to:

$$x = \frac{\displaystyle\sum_{i=1}^{n} \frac{w_i a_i}{\sqrt{(x - a_i)^2 + (y - y_i)^2}}}{\displaystyle\sum_{i=1}^{n} \frac{w_i}{\sqrt{(x - a_i)^2 + (y - y_i)^2}}}; \quad y = \frac{\displaystyle\sum_{i=1}^{n} \frac{w_i b_i}{\sqrt{(x - a_i)^2 + (y - y_i)^2}}}{\displaystyle\sum_{i=1}^{n} \frac{w_i}{\sqrt{(x - a_i)^2 + (y - y_i)^2}}}. \qquad (11)$$

Equation 11 is an implicit solution for x and y, meaning that these variables appear in both sides of the equation. The Weiszfeld algorithm starts from a starting site (x, y) and calculates new x and y using Equation 11 by substituting the previous x and y in the right-hand side of the equation. The Weiszfeld procedure is proven to converge to the solution point, and is very effective. Acceleration methods were proposed for this algorithm (for the latest see Z. Drezner, 1996). This algorithm is very easy to code and can serve as a subroutine for more complicated algorithms.

We mention here that the squared Euclidean distance problem is much simpler. The objective function is:

$$\sum_{i=1}^{n} w_i \left\{ (x - a_i)^2 + (y - b_i)^2 \right\}$$

and it leads to the explicit solution (x and y appear only in the left-hand side of the equation):

$$x = \frac{\sum_{i=1}^{n} w_i a_i}{\sum_{i=1}^{n} w_i}; \quad y = \frac{\sum_{i=1}^{n} w_i b_i}{\sum_{i=1}^{n} w_i}, \tag{12}$$

which is the center of gravity. The center of gravity is a good choice of a starting solution for the Weiszfeld algorithm.

The Generalized Weiszfeld Procedure

In many instances the minimization of transportation cost involves a function of the distance rather than the distance itself. One such example is competitive facility location based on gravity models (Equation 6). We show how to design a Weiszfeld-type procedure for general functions of the Euclidean distance (Equation 1).

The objective is to minimize: $\sum_{i=1}^{n} f_i[d_i(x,y)]$ where $d_i(x,y) =$

$\sqrt{(x - a_i)^2 + (y - b_i)^2}$. By equating the derivatives of the function by x and y to zero and using the chain rule we get:

$$\sum_{i=1}^{n} \frac{\partial f_i}{\partial d_i} \frac{x - a_i}{d_i} = 0; \quad \sum_{i=1}^{n} \frac{\partial f_i}{\partial d_i} \frac{y - b_i}{d_i} = 0, \tag{13}$$

which leads to:

$$x = \frac{\displaystyle\sum_{i=1}^{n} \frac{1}{d_i} \frac{\partial f_i}{\partial d_i} a_i}{\displaystyle\sum_{i=1}^{n} \frac{1}{d_i} \frac{\partial f_i}{\partial d_i}}; \quad y = \frac{\displaystyle\sum_{i=1}^{n} \frac{1}{d_i} \frac{\partial f_i}{\partial d_i} b_i}{\displaystyle\sum_{i=1}^{n} \frac{1}{d_i} \frac{\partial f_i}{\partial d_i}}. \tag{14}$$

Formulas 13 and 14 can be applied in an iterative procedure similar to the Weiszfeld procedure. Note that for the minisum, Euclidean $f_i(d_i) = w_i d_i$ and the formula reduces to the Weiszfeld procedure (Equation 11). For squared Euclidean distances the formula is $f_i(d_i) = w_i d_i^2$ and the formula reduces to the center of gravity formula (Equation 12).

Single-Facility Location Using Rectilinear Distances

The single-facility minisum objective using rectilinear distances (Equations 2 and 3) is the minimization of:

$$\sum_{i=1}^{n} w_i \left(|x - a_i| + |y - b_i| \right). \tag{15}$$

Problem 15 is separable into two independent optimization problems: one for x and one for y. The problem is solved twice, once for each dimension. Consider the solution of the x dimension. The best solution is the median point of the sequence $a_1, \ldots, a_n$, each coordinate with its associated weight. The median point is either at one a_i, or the segment connecting two consecutive coordinates a_i and a_{i+1}. In any case, one of the optimal solutions must be on a point a_i for some i. In order to find the median point all coordinates a_i are sorted, points with the same coordinate are collapsed, and the median found. For the Orange County example problem (Table 4.1), the solution to the x dimension leads to the data in Table 4.5. The median (the point where half of the weight of all points is reached) is at $x = 3$. Similarly, the median for y is $y = 4$. The best location (3, 4) is the one obtained by Excel.

The Single-Facility Minimax Problem
Using Euclidean Distances

The unweighted Euclidean distance (Equation 1) minimax problem is equivalent to finding the smallest circle that surrounds all demand points. Either such a circle is defined by three points, or its diameter is defined by two points. The center of such a circle is the minimax solution. Elzinga and

TABLE 4.5
Calculating the Median Point

x	w
1	42
2	244
3	588
4	430
5	177
6	57
7	48

Hearn (1972) proposed an exchange algorithm for the solution of this problem. The algorithm proceeds as follows:

1. A starting point (center) is selected.

2. The three farthest demand points from the selected center are found.

3. The circle passing through these three points is calculated. (If the triangle is obtuse, the center of the largest side of the triangle is the center of the circle.)

4. If the circle encloses all demand points, then the center of this circle is the optimal solution.

5. If there are points outside this circle (these points are farther from the center than the radius of the circle), select the farthest point from the center as a fourth point.

6. Find the smallest circle enclosing these four demand points. This circle passes through three of these four demand points. There are four possible choices of three points out of four, but the original three demand points cannot be the group enclosing all four points because the newly selected point is outside the circle enclosing the original three points. Therefore, there are only three possible selections of three points out of four to check. Each time one of the original three points is dropped from the group and the circle enclosing the remaining three points is found. The group yielding the largest radius must enclose all four points. This set of three points is the new set of three points and defines a new circle with a new center. Go back to step 4.

This algorithm is empirically fast because few iterations are required for most problems. Even a problem with 10,000 points, which is beyond Excel's capability, is solved in a fraction of a second. The weighted version of the problem is solved in a similar manner (Hearn & Vijay, 1982).

The Single-Facility Rectilinear Distance Minimax

The rectilinear distance (Equation 3) has the following property: If the co-ordinates are rotated in 45°, the rectilinear distance becomes a max distance (also known as Chebishev distance). Therefore, to find the minimax recti-linear distance location, one rotates the coordinates in 45° and finds the smallest enclosing rectangle. The center of this rectangle is one of the optimal solutions. In Z. Drezner (1987b) a simple formula is given for such a solution.

It is interesting that the two-center solution is also very simple to find even though the objective function is not convex. See Z. Drezner (1987b) for the explicit formula for the two-center problem.

Multiple-Facility Location Problems

There are two types of multifacility problems. In one type, each customer is serviced by all facilities. The more useful type is the location of several identical facilities such that each customer is serviced by the facility closest to him or her. We discuss problems of the second type. These problems are the location-allocation problems. Another common name (especially on networks), is the p-median problem for the minisum objective (because the solution to the single-facility problem is the median), and the p-center problem for the minimax multifacility problem (because the solution to the one-facility minimax problem is the center of a circle). These problems are not convex and may have many local optima. It is therefore required to check all possible local minima in order to identify the global minimum. For these problems heuristic algorithms are proposed. A heuristic algorithm is a pro-cedure that terminates with a solution that is usually quite good but is not guaranteed to be optimal. Heuristic procedures are useful when solving a problem to optimality requires prohibitive computer time.

Cooper (1963, 1964) was the first to propose a heuristic approach to solving the location-allocation problem for any distance measure. His idea is as follows:

1. Random locations for p facilities are selected.
2. Each demand point is assigned to its closest facility (this is the allo-cation phase).
3. Each facility defines a set of demand points closest to it.
4. p single-facility problems are solved by finding the best location for each subset of demand points (this is the location phase).
5. If the calculated locations of all p facilities are the same as in the previous iteration, stop with this as a proposed solution. Otherwise go to step 2.

This is a simple and effective heuristic procedure. In order to operationalize this procedure one needs a procedure for solving the single-facility
problem. Note that solution to many single-facility problems (whether
minisum or minimax) is required. Because it is a heuristic algorithm, it is
recommended that the procedure is repeated many times from randomly
generated starting locations, and the best solution among these experiments
selected as the solution to be used.

Voronoi Diagrams

A useful tool in constructing special algorithms for various location problems
is the Voronoi diagram introduced by Voronoi (1907, 1908) and reintroduced
by Shamos and Hoey (1975). For a complete review of Voronoi diagram,
see Okabe, Boots, and Sugihara (1992) and Suzuki and Okabe (1995). To
explain the concept consider a set of n points (demand points or facilities)
in the plane. Each point defines a polygon of *all the points in the plane
that are closest to it*. Some of these polygons are finite and some are open
to infinity. See Fig. 4.12 for an example of such a diagram enclosed in a
square. Constructing such a diagram is done very efficiently by special construction algorithms (Ohya, Iri, & Murota, 1984; Preparata & Shamos, 1985).
The diagram consists of a set of generating points (the original points), and
the sides and vertices of all polygons. In location-allocation models, the
Voronoi diagram generated by the facilities defines the allocation of customers to facilities. An example of the use of a Voronoi diagram is the
solution to the obnoxious facility location problem maximizing the shortest
distance to all demand points. The solution point for this maximin problem

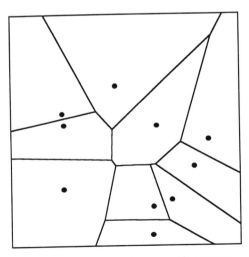

FIG. 4.12. The Voronoi diagram inside a square.

is a vertex of the Voronoi diagram (Preparata & Shamos, 1985; Shamos & Hoey, 1975).

One can construct a Voronoi diagram where each generator point defines a polygon whose points are *farthest* from the generator point. The solution for the single-facility minimax location problem is on a vertex of such a Voronoi diagram (Okabe et al., 1992). The chapter by Suzuki and Okabe (1995) provides a review of the use of Voronoi diagrams in location analysis.

Network Problems

Location problems on a network are usually formulated as integer linear programming models. The Solver option in Excel can solve such problems, but the number of integer variables is large even for small problems and would normally exceed Excel's capacity. Location problems on a network were first introduced by Hakimi (1964, 1965). Hakimi proved the main property of these problems: "The solution for the one facility minisum problem on a network must be on a node of the network." (Note that it is possible to have many equally valued optimal solutions but one of these must be on a node.) This restricts the search for the optimal solution to the finite set of nodes.

Special cases of networks are much easier to analyze. A commonly researched network is a tree network. A tree network does not contain cycles and there is only one way to travel from any node to any other node. Such a network lends itself to simpler algorithms.

Solution algorithms on a network are combinatorial in nature. This means that there are many combinations to be tested and algorithms perform these tests in an efficient way trying to exclude as many trials as possible. For a review of network location problems, see the textbook by Daskin (1995).

Facility Layout

The facility layout problem is different from other location models in that there are only facilities to be located in relation to each other and no demand points. An area is available for the location of facilities, and each facility has a given size (and sometimes given shape). A weight describing the relationship between each pair of facilities is given. This weight quantifies the attraction between pairs of facilities. A large weight means that the two facilities should to be located close to one another, whereas a zero weight (we may have negative weights as well) indicates indifference to the relative location of the two facilities. For example, in the design of an office-building complex, the weight may indicate the amount of traffic between buildings. In planning an instrument panel for an airplane, the weight may indicate the frequency of consecutive or simultaneous watch of a pair of displays.

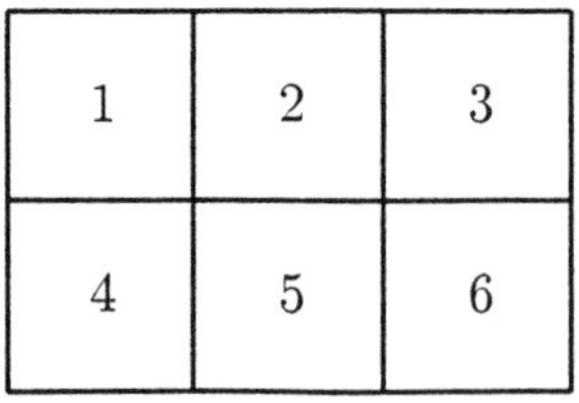

1	2	3
4	5	6

FIG. 4.13. The office layout.

The problem is illustrated by a simple example. Consider the planning of an office-building floor. There are six offices on the floor, three on each side of a corridor. See Fig. 4.13.

The distance between two offices is the rectilinear distance (Equation 3). That means that the distance between offices #1 and #2 is 1, #1 and #5 is 2, and #1 and #6 is 3. There are six people to be placed in these offices each performing a different function (such as accounting, marketing, finance). The weights between various people are given in Table 4.6. The layout problem becomes a permutation question. Which person should be placed in which office? The objective is to minimize the sum of weighted distances between all possible pairs of offices. For a problem with n offices there are $n!$ possible permutations. A problem with six offices can be easily solved by complete enumeration of the 720 possibilities (due to symmetry one needs to check only one fourth of these possibilities). However, for large ns complete enumeration requires a prohibitive amount of time. This problem is considered among the most difficult problems in operations research and exact algorithms have difficulties with problems of more than 15 facilities (see Resende, Ramakrishnan, & Z. Drezner, 1995). The most useful algorithms for this type of problem are heuristic algorithms that find a good solution, but not necessarily the best one, in a reasonable amount of time.

The first heuristic procedure for this problem was CRAFT (Armour & Buffa, 1963). A random arrangement is selected. All pair-wise exchanges of facilities are checked and the exchange that most reduces the objective

TABLE 4.6
Weights Between Different Users

	1	2	3	4	5	6
1	—					
2	3	—				
3	5	0	—			
4	0	10	2	—		
5	0	0	0	7	—	
6	4	2	5	0	0	—

function is performed. The iterations are repeated until no improvement is possible by pair-wise exchanges.

DISCON (Z. Drezner, 1980) is a different approach to formulating and solving the facility layout problem. The locations for the facilities are not prefixed to a certain pattern. A configuration in the plane is obtained by a simulation of the "big bang" that is believed to have created the universe. All facilities are placed at one point and are allowed to explode (the dispersion phase). The configuration is then concentrated back to the center (the concentrated phase) yielding the final configuration. This configuration is finished by the user to fit his or her needs. The configuration is "good" in the sense that facilities that need to be close to each other usually are in the final configuration. DISCON was simplified in Z. Drezner (1987a) where the locations for the facilities are determined by the eigenvectors of a certain matrix. This approach was used in Marcoulides and Z. Drezner (1993) to map n-dimensional data in two dimensions. The weights are calculated as reciprocals of the distances in the n-dimensional space raised to some power and the layout problem is solved. The result is a two-dimensional map where points that are close to one another in the n-dimensional space tend to be close to one another in that two-dimensional solution and vice versa.

Recently, metaheuristic and genetic algorithms were applied to the layout problem (see Pardalos & Wolkowicz, 1994). In particular, simulated annealing (Thonemann & Bolte, 1994) and tabu search (Skorin-Kapov, 1990; Taillard, 1991) are effective in finding good heuristic solutions to the quadratic assignment problem.

The DISCON solution for the office example using the method proposed in Z. Drezner (1987a) is depicted in Fig. 4.14. By inspection it seems that the solution points to one row of users 1,6,3 and the other row of users 2,4,5 in that order. The objective function value for this solution is 47. Applying CRAFT 100 times obtained a solution of 46 in 46 cases out of 100. CRAFT's solution is very similar to DISCON's except that only facilities #3 and #6 are exchanged. Even though the value of the objective function is lower, the pair (2,6) is now at the maximum distance of "3" whereas their weight is "2." In DISCON's solution all pairs with a distance of "3" have zero weight. Therefore, we applied CRAFT using instead the squares of the distances. Using the squares of the distances gives greater emphasis to larger distances. By CRAFT we obtain the best solution with an objective function value of 65 29 times out of 100. There are two solutions with this value of the objective function: the one obtained by DISCON and another that also looks like the DISCON solution (Fig. 4.14). The other one consists of two rows—4,2,1 and 5,3,6—which can be inferred from the DISCON solution (Fig. 4.14). These two solutions have the same value of the objective function when squares of distances are used for CRAFT.

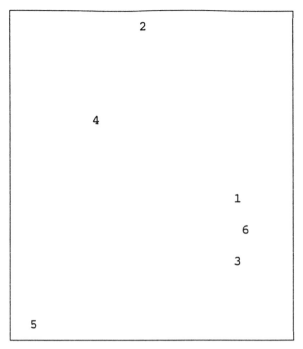

FIG. 4.14. Solution by DISCON.

APPENDIX
NONLINEAR AND INTEGER PROGRAMMING CONCEPTS

Location models are typically formulated as nonlinear programming problems (Zangwill, 1969). Nonlinear programming is a general framework for optimization. A typical nonlinear program consists of an objective function to be maximized or minimized (typically, either maximize profit or minimize cost) subject to a set of constraints that are usually resource limitations. A special case of nonlinear programming is linear programming. In linear programming both the objective function and the constraints are linear. A linear function is a function of the type $a_1x_1 + a_2x_2 + \ldots + a_kx_k$ where a_i are constants (either positive or negative) and x_i are variables. The linear programming model is the most basic optimization model. It is explained in any introductory operations research/management science book (e.g., Anderson, Sweeney, & Williams, 1994). When either the objective function or any of the constraints are not linear, the problem becomes a nonlinear programming problem. A function is not linear if there are products or ratios of variables, or functions of the variables such as squares, square roots, and so forth.

One important issue in nonlinear programming is whether the objective function and the constraints are convex or not. (For a discussion of convexity consult Rockafellar, 1970; Zangwill, 1969.) A function is convex if a line connecting any two points on the function graph is "above" the function graph. Convex functions have only one minimum point and therefore only one solution. (Concave functions have only one maximum point.) Because most location problems deal with minimizing cost, we only mention the convexity property and the reader should be aware that for maximization problems the relevant property is concavity. When constraints are part of the model, the relevant property (for both maximization and minimization) is whether the set of all feasible points is convex or not. When all constraints define a convex region and the objective function is convex, there exists only one optimal solution (there might be several solution points with the same value of the objective function). When the problem is convex, nonlinear programming methods are much more efficient in finding the optimal solution. Note that linear functions are the only functions that are both convex and concave.

Integer linear programming is another case of a model that is not a linear programming model. Integer linear programming is a linear programming formulation with an additional requirement that some of the variables must assume integer values. If all variables must assume integer values, it is an integer linear programming problem. If only some of the variables must assume integer values (and the other ones may have fractional values), the problem is a mixed integer programming problem. A special case of integer linear programming is the case where variables can assume the value 0 or 1. This is sometimes called a 0–1 programming.

Standard nonlinear programming languages (such as AMPL by Fourer, Gay, & Kernighan, 1993), or spreadsheets such as Excel, can be used for the solution of nonlinear programming models. Most of the location literature is concerned with designing special algorithms for solving location optimization problems more efficiently. However, if the problem is not particularly large, standard methods such as Excel can be applied for its solution.

Standard solution methods assume that the objective function is convex and find the optimum under this assumption. When the objective function or any of the constraints are not convex, many local minima may exist. A local minimum is a solution that is locally minimal; that is, the objective function increases in the vicinity of the local minimum and therefore there is no better solution in the neighborhood of the local minimum. However, if the objective function is not convex, there might be another point, in a different region of the area, that is also a local minimum but has a lower value of the objective function. If there are several local minima, the best one is the global minimum. The global minimum is the optimal solution. Convexity guarantees that there is only one local minimum, which is the global one.

If the objective function is not convex, it is recommended to use Excel repeatedly from several (e.g., 100) starting points. Each time Excel converges to a local minimum (depending on the location of the starting solution) and the best solution found in these trials is selected. This approach provides the user with a good result. However, this approach does not guarantee that the optimal solution is found. It is a practical approach if no special algorithm is designed to guarantee that the optimal solution is obtained.

REFERENCES

Anderson, D. R., Sweeney, D. J., & Williams, T. A. (1994). *An introduction to management science: Quantitative approaches to decision making* (7th ed.). Minneapolis/St. Paul: West.

Aneja, Y. P., & Parlar, M. (1994). Algorithm for the Weber facility location problem in the presence of forbidden regions and/or barriers to travel. *Transportation Science, 28,* 70–76.

Armour, G. C., & Buffa, E. S. (1963). A heuristic algorithm and simulation approach to relative location of facilities. *Management Science, 9,* 294–309.

Berman, O., & Simchi-Levi, D. (1990). Conditional location problems on networks. *Transportation Science, 24,* 77–78.

Brimberg, J., & Love, R. F. (1995). Estimating distances. In Z. Drezner (Ed.), *Facility location: A survey of applications and methods* (pp. 9–32). New York: Springer-Verlag.

Burkard, R. E. (1990). Locations with spatial interactions: The quadratic assignment problem. In P. B. Mirchandani & R. L. Francis (Eds.), *Discrete location theory* (pp. 387–437). New York: Wiley.

Chen, R., & Handler, G. Y. (1993). The conditional p-center problem in the plane. *Naval Research Logistics, 40,* 117–127.

Cooper, L. (1963). Location-allocation problems. *Operations Research, 11,* 331–343.

Cooper, L. (1964). Heuristic methods for location-allocation problems. *SIAM Review, 6,* 37–53.

Daskin, M. S. (1995). *Network and discrete location: Models, algorithms, and applications.* New York: Wiley.

Drezner, T. (1995). Competitive facility location in the plane. In Z. Drezner (Ed.), *Facility location: A survey of applications and methods* (pp. 285–300). New York: Springer-Verlag.

Drezner, T., & Drezner, Z. (1997). Replacing discrete demand with continuous demand: The impact on optimal facility location. *Naval Research Logistics, 44,* 81–95.

Drezner, Z. (1980). DISCON—A new method for the layout problem. *Operations Research, 28,* 1375–1384.

Drezner, Z. (1987a). A heuristic procedure for the layout of a large number of facilities. *Management Science, 33,* 909–915.

Drezner, Z. (1987b). On the rectangular p-center problem. *Naval Research Logistics, 34,* 229–234.

Drezner, Z. (1995a). Dynamic facility location: The progressive p-median problem. *Location Science, 3,* 1–7.

Drezner, Z. (Ed.). (1995b). *Facility location: A survey of applications and methods.* New York: Springer-Verlag.

Drezner, Z. (1996). A note on accelerating the Weiszfeld procedure. *Location Science, 3,* 275–279.

Drezner, Z., & Erkut, E. (1995). On the continuous p-dispersion problem. *Journal of the Operational Research Society, 46,* 516–520.

Drezner, Z., & Wesolowsky, G. O. (1978). Facility location on a sphere. *Journal of the Operational Research Society, 29,* 997–1004.

Drezner, Z., & Wesolowsky, G. O. (1981). Optimum location probabilities in the ℓ_p distance Weber problem. *Transportation Science, 15,* 85–97.

Drezner, Z., & Wesolowsky, G. O. (1989). Location of an obnoxious route. *Journal of the Operational Research Society, 40,* 1011–1018.

Drezner, Z., & Wesolowsky, G. O. (1991). Facility location when demand is time dependent. *Naval Research Logistics, 38,* 763–777.

Drezner, Z., & Zemel, E. (1992). Competitive location in the plane. *Annals of Operations Research, 40,* 173–193.

Eiselt, H. A. (1992). Location modeling in practice. *American Journal of Mathematical and Management Sciences, 12,* 3–18.

Eiselt, H. A., & Laporte, G. (1995). Objectives in location problems. In Z. Drezner (Ed.), *Facility location: A survey of applications and methods* (pp. 151–180). New York: Springer-Verlag.

Elzinga, D. J., & Hearn, D. W. (1972). Geometrical solutions for some minimax location problems. *Transportation Science, 6,* 379–394.

Erkut, E., & Neuman, S. (1989). Analytical models for locating undesirable facilities. *European Journal of Operational Research, 40,* 275–291.

Fourer, R., Gay, D. M., & Kernighan, B. W. (1993). *AMPL: A modeling language for mathematical programming.* South San Francisco: The Scientific Press.

Francis, R. L., McGinnis, L. F., Jr., & White, J. A. (1992). *Facility layout and location: An analytical approach* (2nd ed.). Englewood Cliffs, NJ: Prentice-Hall.

Ghosh, A., McLafferty, S., & Craig, C. S. (1995). Multifacility retail networks. In Z. Drezner (Ed.), *Facility location: A survey of applications and methods* (pp. 301–330). New York: Springer-Verlag.

Ghosh, A., & Rushton, G. (1987). *Spatial analysis and location-allocation models.* New York: Van Nostrand Reinhold.

Hakimi, S. L. (1964). Optimal location of switching centers and the absolute centers and medians of a graph. *Operations Research, 12,* 450–459.

Hakimi, S. L. (1965). Optimum distribution of switching centers in a communication network and some related graph theoretic problems. *Operations Research, 13,* 462–475.

Hearn, D. W., & Vijay, J. (1982). Efficient algorithms for the (weighted) minimum circle problem. *Operations Research, 30,* 777–795.

Hotelling, H. (1929). Stability in competition. *Economic Journal, 39,* 41–57.

Huff, D. L. (1964). Defining and estimating a trade area. *Journal of Marketing, 28,* 34–38.

Huff, D. L. (1966). A programmed solution for approximating an optimum retail location. *Land Economics, 42,* 293–303.

Isard, W. (1956). *Location and space economy.* Cambridge, MA: MIT Press.

Katz, I. N., & Cooper, L. (1981). Facility location in the presence of forbidden regions: 1. Formulation and the case of Euclidean distance with one forbidden circle. *European Journal of Operational Research, 6,* 166–173.

Losch, A. (1944). *Die Raumliche Ordnung der Wirtschaft.* Jena, Germany: Verlag.

Losch, A. (1954). *The economics of location.* New Haven, CT: Yale University Press.

Love, R. F., Morris, J. G., & Wesolowsky, G. O. (1988). *Facilities location: Models and methods.* New York: North Holland.

Marcoulides, G., & Drezner, Z. (1993). A procedure for transforming points in multi-dimensional space to two-dimensional. *Educational and Psychological Measurement, 53,* 933–940.

Marsh, M., & Schilling, D. (1994). Equity measurement in facility location analysis: A review and framework. *European Journal of Operational Research, 74,* 1–17.

Mirchandani, P. B., & Francis, R. L. (Eds.). (1990). *Discrete location theory.* New York: Wiley.

Mittal, A. K., & Palsule, V. (1984). Facilities location with ring radial distances. *IIE Transactions, 16,* 59–64.

Ohya, T., Iri, M., & Murota, K. (1984). Improvements of the incremental method for the Voronoi diagram with computational comparisons of various algorithms. *Journal of the Operations Research Society of Japan, 27,* 306–336.

Okabe, A., Boots, B., & Sugihara, K. (1992). *Spatial tessellations. Concepts and applications of Voronoi diagrams*. Chichester, England: Wiley.

Pardalos, P., & Wolkowicz, H. (Eds.). (1994). *Quadratic assignments and related problems*. New York: American Mathematical Society.

Plastria, F. (1995). Continuous location problems. In Z. Drezner (Ed.), *Facility location: A survey of applications and methods* (pp. 225–262). New York: Springer-Verlag.

Preparata, F. P., & Shamos, M. I. (1985). *Computational geometry—An introduction*. New York: Springer-Verlag.

Resende, M. G. C., Ramakrishnan, K. G., & Drezner, Z. (1995). Computational experiments with the lower bound for the quadratic assignment problem based on linear programming. *Operations Research, 43,* 781–791.

Rockafellar, R. T. (1970). *Convex analysis*. Princeton, NJ: Princeton University Press.

Serra, D., & ReVelle, C. (1995). Competitive location in discrete space. In Z. Drezner (Ed.), *Facility location: A survey of applications and methods* (pp. 367–396). New York: Springer-Verlag.

Shamos, M. I., & Hoey, D. (1975). Closest point problems. In *Proceedings of the 16th IEEE Symposium on Foundations of Computer Science* (pp. 151–162).

Skorin-Kapov, J. (1990). Robust tabu search for the quadratic assignment problem. *ORSA Journal on Computing, 2,* 33–45.

Suzuki, A., & Drezner, Z. (1996). On the *p*-center location problem in an area. *Location Science, 4,* 69–82.

Suzuki, A., & Okabe, A. (1995). Using Voronoi diagrams. In Z. Drezner (Ed.), *Facility location: A survey of applications and methods* (pp. 103–118). New York: Springer-Verlag.

Taillard, E. (1991). Robust tabu search for the quadratic assignment problem. *Parallel Computing, 17,* 443–455.

Thonemann, U. V., & Bolte, A. M. (1994). *An improved simulated annealing algorithm for the quadratic assignment problem* (Tech. Rep.). Paderborn, Germany: University of Paderborn, Department of Production and Operations Research.

Voronoi, G. (1907). Nouvelles Applications des Parameters Continus a la Theorie des Formes Quadratiques (Premier Memoire: Sur Quelques Proprietes des Formes Quadratiques Positives Parfaites). *Journal Reine Angew. Math, 133,* 97–178.

Voronoi, G. (1908). Nouvelles Applications des Parameters Continus a la Theorie des Formes Quadratiques (Deuxieme Memoire: Recherches sur les Paralleloedres Primitifs). *Journal Reine Angew. Math, 134,* 198–287.

Ward, J. E., & Wendell, R. E. (1985). Using block norms for location modeling. *Operations Research, 33,* 1074–1090.

Weber, A. (1909). *On the location of industries: 1. Theory of the location of industries* (C. J. Friedeich, Trans.). Chicago: University of Chicago Press.

Weiszfeld, E. (1937). Sur Le Point Pour Lequel La Somme Des Distances De N Points Donnes Est Minimum. *Tohoku Mathematical Journal, 43,* 355–386.

Wesolowsky, G. O. (1983). Location problems on a sphere. *Regional Science and Urban Economics, 12,* 495–508.

Zangwill, W. I. (1969). *Nonlinear programming: A unified approach*. Englewood Cliffs, NJ: Prentice-Hall.

CHAPTER FIVE

Data Envelopment Analysis: An Introduction and an Application to Bank Branch Performance Assessment

Andreas C. Soteriou
Stavros A. Zenios
University of Cyprus

A demanding customer, fierce competition, and market globalization are just a few of the characteristics of the environment organizations face today as they prepare to enter the new millennium. As a result, today's firm constantly seeks new and innovative ways to improve performance and sustain a competitive advantage.

The need to compare performance with some known number or quantity in order to understand how "well" the organization performs brought about the increasing popularity of what is known as performance ratios, that is, the ratio of an output to an input. Ratio analysis, or the use of one or more performance ratios, has widely been used to assess performance for both for-profit and not-for-profit organizations. Such performance ratios can provide a great deal of information regarding performance assessment to management. Two of these, return on assets (ROA) and return on investment (ROI), for example, are extensively used by practitioners to assess financial performance.

Each one of these ratios, however, considers only one input and one output at a time, and is not enough by itself to give a complete picture of performance. Because of the multiinput, multioutput nature of most production processes, a number of these ratios are simultaneously used by management. Summarizing the information produced by ratio analysis and providing the "right" amount of relative importance to each of the ratios still poses a major problem.

In this chapter we introduce a state-of-the-art nonparametric methodology developed in the late 1970s by Charnes, Cooper, and Rhodes (1978), which uses the notion of "relative efficiency" as was originally presented by Farrell (1957). The methodology, known as *Data Envelopment Analysis* (DEA), can be successfully applied to assess performance of units utilizing multiple inputs to produce multiple outputs. DEA can also be applied when the input–output transformation is not known, or when accounting and financial ratios are of little value, and it enjoys a number of advantages over the traditional ratio analysis approach and other parametric approaches to assessing performance (Thanassoulis, Boussofiane, & Dyson, 1996).

Over the last few years, the methodology has gained enormous popularity among both academics and practitioners. A plethora of methodological enhancements to DEA have been made over the last few years by researchers in North America, Europe, and elsewhere. As a result, DEA applications were soon widely spread in different industries, such as education (Thanassoulis, Dyson, & Foster, 1987), health care (Banker, Conrad, & Strauss, 1986), banking (Berger & Humphrey, 1997), and fast-food restaurants (Banker & Morey, 1986a).

It is not the intent of this chapter to provide a detailed description of all the DEA theoretical developments, nor to develop a holistic framework of assessing performance, but rather to provide the reader with a basic understanding of DEA as a modern business research method, along with some guidelines on how it can be used to assess performance. The rest of this chapter proceeds as follows. First, we provide a conceptual understanding of DEA along with its basic mathematical formulation. Some of the generic differences between regression and DEA are also discussed in this section, along with some recent developments of DEA. Next, DEA is applied to a real-life banking environment. We demonstrate how the DEA model's recommendations can be used by the bank's management to improve performance. Concluding remarks follow.

DATA ENVELOPMENT ANALYSIS

The Concept

The DEA methodology was introduced by Charnes et al. in 1978 to evaluate the relative efficiency of a set of decision-making units (DMUs). The term DMU was coined by Charnes et al. to describe homogeneous units, each utilizing a common set of inputs to produce a common set of outputs as shown in Fig. 5.1.

Examples may include the collection of similar firms, departments, or other organizational units. Typical DMUs can consist of, for example, a

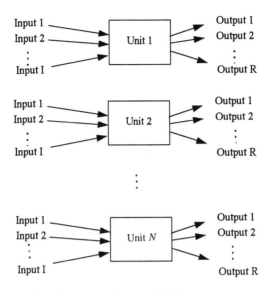

FIG. 5.1. Graphical illustration of a set of DMUs each using a common set of inputs $\{1, 2, \ldots, I\}$ to produce a common set of outputs $\{1, 2, \ldots, R\}$.

group of schools, hospitals, bank branches, and so on. The efficiency of a typical DMU, say unit B, can be defined as follows:

$$E_B = \frac{\sum\limits_{r=1}^{R} u_{rB} y_{rB}}{\sum\limits_{i=1}^{I} v_{iB} x_{iB}}, \tag{1}$$

where, E_B = efficiency of unit B, y_{rB} = amount of output r produced by DMU B, x_{iB} = amount of input i consumed at DMU B, u_{rB} = weight given to output r, v_{iB} = weight given to input i, R = the number of outputs, and I = the number of inputs.

E_B is the ratio of a weighted sum of outputs over a weighted sum of inputs, where the weights u and v can be thought of as the importance that a particular DMU places on a specific input or output in establishing its efficiency measure. Such weights may differ across different DMUs, each exhibiting a unique sub-management system in an attempt to appear as efficient as possible.

This definition of efficiency, as the weighted sum of outputs over the weighted sum of inputs, leads to the following fractional linear program, which can be applied to each DMU B to obtain its relative efficiency vis-à-vis the n DMUs in the set.

(M1):

$$\text{Maximize } E_B = \frac{\displaystyle\sum_{r=1}^{R} u_{rB} y_{rB}}{\displaystyle\sum_{i=1}^{I} v_{iB} x_{rB}} \tag{2}$$

subject to:

$$\frac{\displaystyle\sum_{r=1}^{R} u_{rB} y_{rj}}{\displaystyle\sum_{i=1}^{I} v_{iB} x_{ij}} \leq 1 \text{ for all } j = 1, 2, \ldots n, \tag{3}$$

$$u_{rB}, v_{iB} \geq 0 \text{ for all } i = 1, 2, \ldots I, \text{ and } r = 1, 2, \ldots R. \tag{4}$$

The decision variables for this fractional linear program are the weights of the inputs and outputs v and u, respectively. Thus, for each DMU the model will choose those weights that maximize its efficiency, subject to the constraint that no other DMU using the same set of weights can achieve an efficiency rating of higher than 1. A rating of 1 will deem the DMU efficient, with respect to the rest of the DMUs in the group.

Consider, for example, the DMUs shown in Fig. 5.2. Each DMU consumes a single input to produce a single output. An efficient frontier based on the observed input–output correspondences defines the *Production Possibility Set* (PPS), which contains all feasible input–output correspondences of the production process evident from the DMUs under assessment. Clearly, all DMUs but B and C can improve their efficiencies by either augmenting their output while keeping their input constant, decreasing their input while keeping their output constant, or simultaneously increasing their output while decreasing their input. DMUs B and C find themselves on the efficient frontier constructed under the assumption of constant returns to scale (CRS), which implies that an increase in input (x) is expected to result in a proportionate increase in output (y).[1] These units are relatively efficient. This does not imply that they are efficient in the absolute sense that they cannot improve further. They are efficient when compared with the rest of the group con-

---

[1]Efficient frontier construction under the assumption of variable returns to scale is presented in the following section.

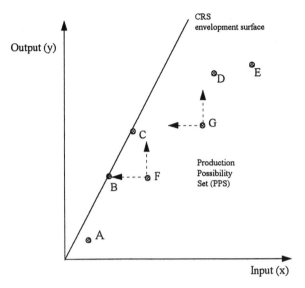

FIG. 5.2. Production possibility set and envelopment surface of example DMUs under the assumption of constant returns to scale (CRS).

sisting of all DMUs. If the group of DMUs is expanded to include other more efficient DMUs, then further possible inefficiencies will in turn appear.

Thus, for each DMU, DEA can provide answers to the following two basic questions:

1. How inefficient is the DMU compared to the rest of the group? That is, how far is the DMU from the constructed efficient frontier?

2. How can an inefficient DMU improve? That is, how much should it augment its outputs and/or decrease its inputs in order to become efficient compared to the rest of the DMUs?

As a result, management can use DEA not only to identify relatively inefficient units and measure the magnitude of their inefficiencies, but also to provide guidelines for improvement. Next we present basic mathematical formulations that can be used to solve (M1) and provide answers to the previous questions.

Linear Programming DEA Formulations

A Constant Returns to Scale (CRS) DEA Formulation. The fractional linear program (M1) is difficult to solve. Notice, however, that in defining the efficiency of DMU B in Equation 2, what is important is the relative magnitudes of the numerator and the denominator and not their actual values. Based on this observation, Charnes et al. (1978) provided the following linear programming (LP) transformation of (M1), by setting the denominator of Equation 2 to an arbitrary constant such as 1, and maximizing the numerator.

(M2):

$$\text{Maximize } E_B = \sum_{r=1}^{R} u_{rB} y_{rB} \tag{5}$$

subject to:

$$\sum_{i=1}^{I} v_{iB} x_{iB} = 1, \tag{6}$$

$$\sum_{r=1}^{R} u_{rB} y_{rj} - \sum_{i=1}^{I} v_{iB} x_{ij} \leq 0 \text{ for all } j = 1, 2, \ldots n, \tag{7}$$

$$u_{rB}, v_{iB} \geq 0 \text{ for all } i = 1, 2, \ldots I, \text{ and } r = 1, 2, \ldots R. \tag{8}$$

where, E_B = efficiency of unit B, y_{rB} = amount of output r observed at DMU B, x_{iB} = amount of input i consumed at DMU B, u_{rB} = weight given to output r, v_{iB} = weight given to input i, R = the number of outputs, and I = the number of inputs.

The resulting LP (M2) is easy to solve and identifies those input–output weights that maximize the efficiency of each DMU, while maintaining that no other DMU can exceed an efficiency rating of 1, using the same weights. (M2) must be solved once for each of the N DMUs under assessment. An alternate linear programming formulation can also result by setting the numerator of Equation 2 to an arbitrary constant such as 1, and minimizing

$$E'_B = \sum_{i=1}^{I} v_{iB} x_{iB}.$$

The concept of LP duality can help provide a different formulation that can not only help with the computational aspects of solving (M2), but can also provide additional insights. Because it is not the purpose of this chapter to cover the theory of LP, the reader is referred to any standard LP book (such as, e.g., Hillier & Lieberman, 1986) for a detailed description of the concept of duality. The dual formulation of (M2) can be expressed as

(M3):

$$\text{Minimize } H_B \tag{9}$$

subject to:

$$\sum_{j=1}^{n} \lambda_{Bj} x_{ij} \leq H_B x_{iB}, \text{ for all } i = 1, 2, \ldots, I, \tag{10}$$

$$\sum_{j=1}^{n} \lambda_{Bj} y_{rj} \geq y_{rB}, \text{ for all } r = 1, 2, \ldots, R, \tag{11}$$

$$\lambda_{Bj} \geq 0, \text{ for all } j = 1, 2, \ldots, n. \tag{12}$$

For each DMU B model (M3) will find the minimum proportion H_B such that for each input, the weighted combination of input of all units does not exceed the proportion H_B of the input of unit B. At the same time, the weighted combination of output of all units is at least as great as that of unit B.

In (M3) a value of $H_B = 1$ deems the unit efficient. However, a value of H_B greater than one implies that the DMU under assessment is underperforming compared to the other DMUs. There exists a weighted combination of actual performance of other units such that no output of unit B exceeds that of the output of the weighted combination. At the same time, we could reduce all inputs of B by the proportion H_B without any input falling below that of the corresponding weighted combination of other units. Clearly, a DMU B with H_B greater than one requires improvement. The value of H_B in (M3) indicates how much we can decrease all the inputs of B, in the same proportion, to achieve the desired weighted combination performance, which in turn is based on the actual performance of the rest of the DMUs.

At optimality, some of the constraints of (M3) will be satisfied as equalities (i.e., those are binding constraints), but some will not. Following LP terminology, the term *slack variable* refers to the amount by which the constraints of (M3) fail to achieve equality at optimality. The following formulation, (M4), also known as the (input-oriented) CCR model, includes the slack variables. The objective function is modified to recognize the fact that at optimality more than one minima may be present, and maximizes these slacks such that the value of H_B is not affected.

(M4):

$$\text{Minimize } H_B - \varepsilon \left(\sum_{r=1}^{R} s_r^+ + \sum_{i=1}^{I} s_i^- \right) \tag{13}$$

subject to:

$$H_B x_{iB} - \sum_{j=1}^{n} \lambda_{Bj} x_{ij} - s_i^- = 0, \text{ for all } i = 1, 2, \ldots, I, \tag{14}$$

$$\sum_{j=1}^{n} \lambda_{Bj} y_{rj} - s_r^+ = y_{rB}, \text{ for all } r = 1, 2, \ldots, R, \tag{15}$$

$$\lambda_{Bj}, s_r^+, s_i^- \geq 0, \text{ for all } j, r, i. \tag{16}$$

where s_r^+ and s_i^- are the slack variables corresponding to the outputs and inputs, respectively.

Input–output target values for inefficient units can easily be set after solving (M4). At optimality, the following input–output values result:

$$x_{iB}^{target} = H_B^* x_{iB} - s_i^{-*}, \text{ for all } i = 1, 2, \ldots, I, \tag{17}$$

$$y_{rB}^{target} = y_{rB} + s_i^{+*}, \text{ for all } r = 1, 2, \ldots, R, \tag{18}$$

where * indicates the optimal value of the corresponding variable. These are input-oriented targets, because the attempt here is to minimize inputs. Output-oriented targets can also be obtained by dividing both x_{iB}^{target} and y_{rB}^{target} by H_B^*. Different approaches have been proposed to set target levels under realistic conditions (Banker & Morey, 1986b; Thanassoulis & Dyson, 1992).

Solving (M4) is typically less time consuming than (M2), because (M4) has only $(R + I)$ constraints compared to $(n + R + I + 1)$ of (M3) and N is typically much larger than $R + I$. However, even though (M4) does provide some computational advantage over (M2), its greater benefit is to provide target values for inefficient units, by comparing them against a composite unit constructed by the actual performance of the rest of the units.

A Variable Returns to Scale (VRS) DEA Formulation. All the formulations presented in the previous section were developed by Charnes et al. (1978) under the assumption of constant returns to scale, which is usually a reasonable assumption. In many cases, however, the scale of operations can influence a DMU's efficiency rating. In such cases, it may not be fair to compare units of different size. Furthermore, providing information as to how much of the DMU's inefficiency is a direct by-product of its scale of operations would also be of great interest to management. Banker, Charnes, and Cooper (1984) extended the CCR model (M4) to account for the inefficiency due to the scale of operations.

Figure 5.3 presents six example DMUs. Clearly, DMU F is inefficient under the assumption of constant returns to scale. A measure of its (input) inefficiency can be obtained by comparing it against unit H because it has the same output level. Following the DEA terminology, the fraction x_H/x_F defines the *pure technical (input)* inefficiency of unit F. In a similar fashion the output technical efficiency can be defined as y_G/y_F. The following input minimization formulation (M5) was presented by Banker et al. (1984) to capture the pure technical efficiency.

(M5):

$$\text{Minimize } H_B - \varepsilon\left(\sum_{r=1}^{R} s_r^+ + \sum_{i=1}^{I} s_i^-\right) \tag{19}$$

subject to:

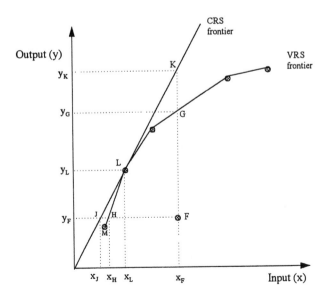

FIG. 5.3. Envelopment surface of example DMUs under the assumption of constant and variable returns to scale.

$$H_B x_{iB} - \sum_{j=1}^{n} \lambda_{Bj} x_{ij} - s_i^- = 0, \text{ for all } i = 1, 2, \ldots, I, \tag{20}$$

$$\sum_{j=1}^{n} \lambda_{Bj} y_{rj} - s_r^+ = y_{rB}, \text{ for all } r = 1, 2, \ldots, R, \tag{21}$$

$$\sum_{j=1}^{n} \lambda_{Bj} = 1, \tag{22}$$

$$\lambda_{Bj}, s_r^+, s_i^- \geq 0, \text{ for all } j, r, i. \tag{23}$$

Note that the only difference between model (M4) and model (M5) is Constraint 22. This additional convexity constraint ensures that the objective function provides a measure of pure technical efficiency by ensuring that DMUs will be compared against a composite unit similar in size. Figure 5.3 also presents the efficient frontier constructed under VRS for the example DMUs. For more detailed description of the VRS formulation, the reader is referred to Banker et al. (1984).

In order to establish the (input) efficiency rating of DMU F in Fig. 5.3, a virtual unit H was constructed on the efficient frontier, based on units M and L. These units form what is known as the peer group of F. This is the set of DMUs that are directly used to construct the composite unit H that defines the inefficiency of unit F.

It is noteworthy to observe that models (M4) and (M5) together can be used to assess the scale efficiency of a DMU. The original CCR model (M4) can provide efficiency ratings that include both scale and technical efficiency. That is, an aggregate measure of *scale* and *technical* efficiency can be defined by the ratio x_j/x_F in Fig. 5.3. Thus to estimate the scale efficiency of each branch B, one needs to only obtain the ratio $E_B^{scale} = E_B^{CRS}/E_B^{VRS}$, where, E_B^{scale}: the scale efficiency rating of branch B, E_B^{CRS}: the CRS efficiency rating of branch B, E_B^{VRS}: the VRS efficiency rating of branch B.

To summarize, the preceding DEA formulations can identify the following:

1. An efficiency rating E for each DMU, which will vary anywhere between 0 and 1. If $E = 1$, then the unit is relatively efficient compared to the rest of the units. It can of course be inefficient when compared with a different group of DMUs. If $E < 1$, then the unit is relatively inefficient.

2. A peer group that is the subset of efficient units that were used to directly compare the inefficient unit against, in order to calculate its efficiency rating. Thus, management can focus its investigation to the peer group of each unit, which consists of a smaller set of real units, in order to understand better the inefficiencies present at the inefficient DMU.

3. Specific guidelines on how inefficient units can move toward the efficient frontier, depending on the model. Different suggestions will, for example, be provided by an output maximization model as compared to an input minimization model. Management can evaluate different models to select an appropriate improvement strategy for inefficient units.

A Simple Example.   To best illustrate the aforementioned formulations, let us consider a simple example where eight units utilize a single input to produce a single output. Actual values are shown in Table 5.1. We use the same example later on to contrast DEA with regression analysis (RA). A graphical illustration is shown in Fig. 5.4.

For each DMU we solve (M4). The input minimization formulation for DMU 3, for example, will be

$$\text{Minimize } H_3 - \varepsilon(s_1^+ + s_1^-) \tag{24}$$

subject to:

$$H_3 x_{13} - (\lambda_{31} x_{11} + \lambda_{32} x_{12} + \ldots + \lambda_{38} x_{18}) - s_1^- = 0, \tag{25}$$

$$(\lambda_{31} y_{11} + \lambda_{32} y_{12} + \ldots + \lambda_{38} y_{18}) - s_1^+ = y_{13}, \tag{26}$$

$$\lambda_{31}, \lambda_{32}, \ldots, \lambda_{38}, s_1^+, s_1^- \geq 0. \tag{27}$$

TABLE 5.1
Observed Performance (Input and Output Values) of Example Units

	Input	Output
DMU1	4.0	14.0
DMU2	2.0	7.0
DMU3	2.5	6.5
DMU4	3.0	10.5
DMU5	4.5	12.0
DMU6	3.5	10.5
DMU7	3.0	9.5
DMU8	6.0	16.0

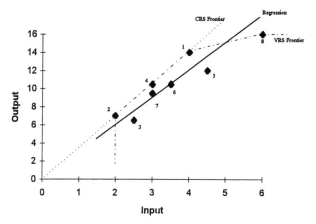

FIG. 5.4. Efficient frontier under constant returns to scale (CRS), variable returns to scale (VRS), and regression, on example DMUs.

Table 5.2 presents the efficiency ratings obtained by solving (M3) and (M5), i.e., under constant and variable returns to scale (VRS), respectively. In the input minimization CRS case, five units have been identified as inefficient, as indicated by their efficiency ratings. Because some part of the CRS and VRS efficient frontiers is common, we observe no differences in the (input or output) efficiency ratings under CRS and VRS for DMUs 1, 2, 4, 6, and 7. DMU 8, however, finds itself on the efficient frontier when assessed under VRS. Also, note how the output maximization efficiency rating for DMU5 and the input minimization efficiency rating for DMU3, respectively, have increased when the assessment changed from CRS to VRS. The VRS efficiency ratings are, on average, higher than the corresponding CRS efficiency ratings.

Table 5.3 also presents the target values for inefficient units. Consider UNIT5, for example, with an input CRS efficiency of 76%. The peer group

TABLE 5.2
CRS and VRS Efficiency Ratings of Example DMUs

	CRS Input Min. Efficiencies	CRS Output Max. Efficiencies	VRS Input Min. Efficiencies	VRS Output Max. Efficiencies
DMU1	100.00	100.00	100.00	100.00
DMU2	100.00	100.00	100.00	100.00
DMU3	74.29	74.29	80.00	74.29
DMU4	100.00	100.00	100.00	100.00
DMU5	76.19	76.19	76.19	82.76
DMU6	85.71	85.71	85.71	85.71
DMU7	90.48	90.48	90.48	90.48
DMU8	76.19	76.19	100.00	100.00

TABLE 5.3
Target Values of Example DMUs for the Input Minimization Case

	Input Actual Values	CRS, Input Min. Input Targets	VRS, Input Min. Input Targets
UNIT1	4.0	4.0	4.0
UNIT2	2.0	2.0	2.0
UNIT3	2.5	1.9	2.0
UNIT4	3.0	3.0	3.0
UNIT5	4.5	3.4	3.4
UNIT6	3.5	3.0	3.0
UNIT7	3.0	2.7	2.7
UNIT8	6.0	4.6	6.0

for UNIT5 consists of UNIT1 and UNIT4. The input target value provided by DEA is 3.4. Thus, UNIT5 could improve its efficiency by reducing its input from 4.5 to 3.4, while keeping the same output.

DEA and Regression Analysis

As DEA has become more popular over the last few years, the need has arisen to compare and contrast the methodology against other established techniques of performance assessment. Such comparisons were the focus of a number of studies comparing, for example, DEA with ratio analysis (Thanassoulis et al., 1996) or DEA with regression analysis[2] (RA) (Levitt & Joyce, 1987; Thanassoulis, 1993). Here we briefly discuss some of the basic differences between DEA and regression analysis, by considering a single-input, single-output case. It is not our intent to exhaustively review the literature on the subject but rather to point out that even though similar in some aspects, the two methods are fundamentally different and can provide different insights to performance assessment.

In general RA is a parametric method where the underlying functional form of the input–output transformation process can and must be specified. The unknown coefficients of this function are typically assumed constant. Violations of this assumption can lead to what is known as *specification errors*. Other assumptions include specific characteristics of the nature of the distribution of the error terms. Given a certain level of the independent variables, RA fits a model estimating the average level of the dependent variable(s). The model includes a random error term of the output or input

---

[2]When RA is used for performance assessment in practice, an output- (input-) dependent variable Y is regressed against a number of input- (output-) independent variables $X_1, X_2, \ldots, X_n$. In the presence of multiple dependent variables, a set of simultaneous equations can be solved.

variables, which in performance assessment is typically assumed to reflect inefficiency. Unfortunately, separating inefficiency from the error term is not an easy procedure, and requires some strong assumptions on the distribution of the inefficiencies.

DEA, on the other hand, is a nonparametric methodology that does not require such strong assumptions. When applying DEA one needs to define a *PPS*, but does not need to prespecify a production functional form. Furthermore, unlike the "average" nature of regression, DEA is a *boundary* method. That is, it defines efficiency based on best-practice units, unlike RA, which estimates an average level for the dependent variable given the levels of the independent or explanatory variables.

Consider for example the DMUs of Fig. 5.4. The resulting regression equation is

$$Output = 2.30^* + 2.37^{**} \; Input + \varepsilon \tag{28}$$

where, $^*p < 0.1$, $^{**}p < 0.001$, and $R^2 = 86\%$. The p values indicate the level of significance of the RA parameters. Here, 86% of the variation of the output can be captured by the level of the input considered. As shown in Fig. 5.4, RA fits the line of efficient units through the data set, whereas DEA constructs the frontier based on the best-practice units. To calculate the RA output efficiencies, we take the ratio of the DMU's fitted output to its actual output. Table 5.4 demonstrates the output efficiencies observed using both methods.

Consider, for example, UNIT1 and UNIT6. UNIT1 is considered 100% efficient by DEA because its observed input–output transformation rate is the best in the group. It is, however, considered inefficient ($E_1 = 84\%$) by RA because it lies away from the "average" line fitted. On the other hand, UNIT6 is deemed efficient by RA being very close to the fitted line, but inefficient by DEA.

Both methods have advantages and disadvantages when used for assessing performance. These stem from the differences in the fundamental as-

TABLE 5.4
Output Efficiencies of Example DMUs Based on Regression and DEA

	Output Efficiency Regression	Output Efficiency DEA
DMU1	0.8414	1.0000
DMU2	1.0057	1.0000
DMU3	1.2654	0.7429
DMU4	0.8962	1.0000
DMU5	1.0804	0.7619
DMU6	1.0090	0.8571
DMU7	0.9905	0.9048
DMU8	1.0325	0.7619

sumptions underlying the two. Some of the advantages of DEA include, among others, that it measures performance against best-practice units and not against average performance, which is the case with RA. DEA does not require a hypothesized functional form for the production function, and can—being a "boundary" method—provide accurate estimates of the relative inefficiencies and targets. Multicollinearity (two or more independent variables being approximately linearly related in the sample data), a common problem when using RA, does not constitute a major threat for DEA.

On the other hand, DEA does not come without limitations. One of its more severe disadvantages is its sensitivity to outliers. Results may not be reliable if an influential outlier modifies the efficient frontier. Thus, the data set must be carefully investigated and outliers treated appropriately. Also, RA provides more stable results and allows for hypothesis testing of the input–output relationships. See Thanassoulis (1993) for further discussion on the relative merits of DEA vis-à-vis RA.

Specifying Input and Output Sets

The major issue when applying DEA to a real-life problem is the choice of inputs and outputs. The group of units to be assessed must use a common set of inputs and outputs as shown in Fig. 5.1. The methodology itself assumes that the choice of inputs and outputs has already been made. Clearly, all relevant inputs and outputs must be included. A number of practical considerations, however, arise when deciding on the input–output sets to be used.

First, a conceptual model describing the input–output transformation process must be constructed in order to be used as the basis for the choice of inputs/outputs. Management can play a critical role to identifying a relevant set of inputs/outputs. Previously developed theoretical models can and should also be consulted if available. Environmental factors that can influence efficiency must also be incorporated in the sets. If, for example, we are interested in school efficiency, a conceptual model from the education literature can be used to help determine relevant inputs and outputs. Table 5.5 presents a some relevant variables that can be used in assessing school efficiency. Environmental variables such as, for example, the socioeconomic environment of the students, can be included in the input set. (A model for bank branch assessment is specified in Section 3.)

Because units typically consume resources to produce certain outputs, these resources must be included in the input set. For example, if we are interested in the operating efficiency of bank branches, relevant inputs can include the number of personnel, number of computers, space, and so on, whereas relevant outputs may include the different products and services offered, that is, different accounts and the like.

TABLE 5.5
Relevant Inputs and Outputs for Assessing School Efficiency

Inputs	*Outputs*
School-Related Variables	% of students passing standardized exams
- Size	Percent of students finding jobs, etc.
- Number of teachers, etc.	Achievement in sports
Student Related Variables	Achievement in music
- Socioeconomic environment such as parents'	Achievement in other relevant activities
education, existence of library at home	
- Quality of students on entry	
Teacher-Related Variables	
- Experience	
- Training	
- Education	

Data availability typically limits our choice of inputs and outputs. In operationalizing some of the variables shown in Table 5.5, for example, we may use the size of the library students have at home as a proxy for the socioeconomic environment. Caution is necessary because the choice of inputs and outputs will limit the interpretability of the model.

Furthermore, the total number of input and output variables will depend on the total number of DMUs to be assessed. If the number of variables chosen is large compared to the number of DMUs in the group, then the model's discriminatory power—discriminating efficient from inefficient units—will suffer. An empirical rule of thumb is that the total number of units available for comparison must exceed the product of the number of inputs and outputs. That is, if three inputs and three outputs are used, more than nine units would be required for the model to adequately discriminate efficient from inefficient units.

Recent DEA Developments

A number of DEA methodological developments were introduced since the appearance of the CCR model in 1978. In this section we briefly discuss some of the recent developments providing references for further reading. This is by no means an extensive literature review of all the recent developments of DEA, but rather a brief overview of the most popular application-oriented enhancements.

In an earlier section we have already discussed model (M5) developed by Banker et al. (1984), which allows for the presence of variable returns to scale. Both (M3) and (M5) are based on the assumption that all inputs and outputs are continuous. If one or more variables are categorical, then problems arise in constructing composite units against which a unit will be compared in order to provide its efficiency rating. If the original DEA models are used, such composite units may be assigned meaningless values for the categorical variables. Banker and Morey (1986) provided a modification of the original DEA model (M3) to address this issue. Additional discussion on the treatment of categorical variables was also given by Kamakura (1988).

We have already seen how target setting can result from DEA using Equations 17 and 18. In 1992, Thanassoulis and Dyson developed DEA formulations to estimate targets when (a) one input or output is given preemptive priority to improve, (b) a unit has a general preference structure over input–output changes, (c) a unit can specify a set of ideal target levels, and (d) certain inputs and outputs are exogenously fixed.

The weights obtained by DEA can also be restricted in order not to allow for inappropriate weighting structures. A number of researchers discuss approaches to weight restrictions (Dyson & Thanassoulis, 1988; Wong & Beasley, 1990). Since then, weight restrictions have been used in a number of applications. Soteriou and S. A. Zenios (1996), for example, have used weight restriction models to provide efficient cost estimates for bank products.

Finally, an approach to capture efficiency changes over time was introduced by Charnes, Clark, Cooper, and Golany (1985). The approach, known as "window analysis," treats each unit as a different one for each time window of m periods. Thus, the effect of time on the efficiency ratings of a group can be observed. Such an approach can be extremely useful to observe time trends and seasonal patterns when data are available over time, which is usually the case. The approach is also extremely useful in increasing the number of units available when the group size to be assessed is small and the data exist over a number of periods.

AN APPLICATION

In this section we present an application of DEA to assess the *operating efficiency* of the branches of a bank. This project is part of a bigger project the authors are currently undertaking that examines issues of operating efficiency, profitability, and quality of bank branches (see Soteriou & S. A. Zenios, 1996, 1997; C. V. Zenios, S. A. Zenios, Agathocleous, & Soteriou, 1995). Two of the most popular approaches in addressing bank branch operating efficiency are the *production* and the *intermediation* approaches. Following the production approach, the branch is considered as a "producer" of banking products and services. Thus, branches are assessed on how well they utilize their resources (personnel, computers, space, etc.) to produce the largest possible number of transactions. Other typical outputs may include the number of different accounts at a branch. The intermediation approach, on the other hand, examines the branches on how well they generate revenue, by considering the various types of costs as inputs. The application we present here is based on C. V. Zenios et al. (1995). A growing body of literature exists on branch efficiency studies focusing on different types of efficiency such as, for example, service processes efficiency (Frei & Harker, 1995). For a review of the state of the art on DEA bank branch studies, the reader is referred to Berger and Humphrey (1997).

The Bank's Environment

The branches we examined belong to a network of a commercial bank. The bank has recently been sensitized to issues of operating efficiency, profitability, and quality, due to the increased local and international competition. The network consists of more than 150 branches located in urban, rural, and tourist areas. All branches offer a full range of services including personal and company accounts, foreign currency accounts, and credit application accounts. Each branch has anywhere between 1 and 40 employees.

Currently, the bank monitors through a computerized online system the operations at each branch, on a monthly basis. More specifically, by using a work measurement program that provides standard times for each task performed, the total work produced at each branch is calculated. This is compared against the number of available personnel hours per month, to generate a measure of personnel efficiency. This measure has been used as an indicator to evaluate operating efficiency. A model that would incorporate additional factors, such as the effect of the computers or the type of personnel on branch efficiency, was clearly necessary, and DEA provided the methodology to do that.

The Model

The bank had already classified the branches based on their geographical location and their size. This classification provided the basis for separating the branches into smaller homogeneous groups. A total of seven groups were formed depending on the branch location (urban, rural, touristic) and size (small, medium, large) as follows:

- Urban branches: (a) small, (b) medium, and (c) large.
- Rural branches: (a) small and (b) medium.
- Touristic branches: (a) small and (b) medium.

We use two broad sets of inputs to the model. One set captures the resources used by the branch. The specific inputs in this set are illustrated in Fig. 5.5. The second set of inputs consists of the number of accounts in different account categories. Although this information is, typically, viewed as an

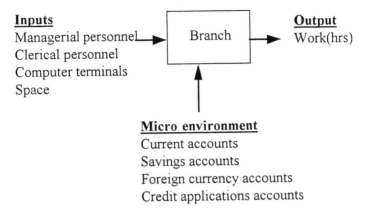

FIG. 5.5. Branch inputs and outputs of the DEA model.

output, we consider it as an input because it reflects the microenvironment of a branch. In particular, it reflects the steady state market conditions for the particular branch reached due to previous efforts. In some sense this information is part of the external environment of the branch. However, the clientele infrastructure is tightly linked to a specific branch, and it changes very slowly with time. Hence, for the purpose of a static analysis (such as the one in this study), this information is part of the internal environment of the branch. This microenvironment of the branch is distinguished from the external macroenvironment (urban, rural, touristic) mentioned earlier. Figure 5.5 also summarizes the types of accounts used as inputs.

The output of the model is the total amount of work produced by the branch. Work is measured in time (hours), through the bank's online computerized system that keeps track of all transactions that take place at each branch during each day. The type and number of tasks required to complete a transaction are known through a work measurement system, and an accurate estimate of the time spent on each transaction is obtained from this system.

Benchmarking the Efficiency of the Bank's Branches

We first run the input minimization formulation (M5) on the branches of each homogeneous group in an attempt to identify both the inefficient branches in each group and the yardstick model branches. Table 5.6, for example, identifies the characteristics of three branches that were identified as group leaders within the small urban group. Note that the organization of the yardstick branch (number of clerical and managerial personnel, number of computer terminals and required working space) varies depending on the mix of accounts (i.e., the microenvironment) of the branch.

TABLE 5.6
Small Urban Group Branch Leaders

Inputs/Outputs	Branch X	Branch Y	Branch Z
Managerial personnel	1	1	1
Clerical personnel	2	1	3
Computer terminals	2	2	4
Working space (m²)	120	40	186
Number of current accounts	107	54	181
Number of savings accounts	331	307	758
Number of foreign company accounts	26	8	71
Number of credit applications accounts	142	39	147
Output time (hrs)	296	220	451

Table 5.7 provides an example of an inefficient branch along with suggested managerial actions that will move it toward the efficient frontier. Whether the suggested actions are feasible or not depends on managerial considerations. For example, it may not be easy to reduce personnel; it may, however, be possible to rotate excess personnel from inefficient branches elsewhere.

Benchmarking the Effects of the Environment

We illustrate now the use of DEA to benchmark the effects of the external environment. Often, performance assessment is associated with the need to contrast alternative policies that characterize various subgroups of the branches used in the assessment. Charnes, Cooper, and Rhodes (1981) proposed an approach to isolate and evaluate school program efficiency. The approach proceeds in three steps:

Step 1: Run the DEA model on two groups operating in two different environments.

TABLE 5.7
Recommendations of DEA Model to Improve Inefficient Unit K

Inputs/Outputs	Branch K (Actual)	Branch K (Target)
Managerial personnel	156 hrs (1 person)	117
Clerical personnel	156 hrs (1 person)	117
Computer terminals	302	226
Working space (m²)	119	34
Number of current accounts	56	42
Number of savings accounts	331	228
Number of foreign accounts	9	7
Number of credit applications accounts	46	33
Output time (hrs)	164	164

Step 2: Combine projected and efficient units from both groups and run the DEA again on the pooled data set.

Step 3: Examine whether the resulting efficiency distributions of the units of each group are different. This can be done using nonparametric tests (such as Mann–Whitney) because the resulting distributions are not likely to follow normality.

The same approach is used here to isolate and assess the impact of the environment on efficiency. The effects of the environment have an impact on strategic planning decisions by the bank in opening new branches or downsizing, and perhaps closing inefficient ones. It is important to identify which groups operate in favorable environments and as a result demonstrate higher efficiencies than other groups operating in less favorable environments. We applied the preceding approach to isolate the effects of the environment on the efficiency ratings of branches operating in urban, rural, and tourist areas. The analysis revealed that urban branches were on average 2% more efficient compared to rural branches ($p < 0.001$). Furthermore, branches operating in tourist areas were, on average, 6% more efficient than urban branches.

These results were obtained during the summer months of 1994. The same analysis was repeated across time, and Mann–Whitney tests were conducted for each month during 1994, to test if the resulting efficiency distributions were different across groups. The results indicated that during the winter months, the aforementioned picture changed. The mean efficiency of urban branches was higher than the corresponding efficiency of the tourist branches. Such results point toward the development of a personnel allocation policy to reduce unfavorable seasonal efficiency gaps at different groups.

Quality and Profitability DEA Models for Bank Branches

In the previous sections we discussed an application of an operating efficiency model to assess branch performance. Clearly, however, operating efficiency is not the sole goal of a branch or any organization. The multiinput, multioutput nature of DEA provides a powerful methodology to capture the multiple objectives of a branch or firm. The authors are currently working toward establishing a general framework that not only develops DEA models to address the existence of multiple goals—that is, operating efficiency, profitability, and quality—but also provides the methodology to capture their linkages (Soteriou & S. A. Zenios, 1997). We next discuss briefly two separate models that can be used to assess branch efficiency when profitability or service quality are the sole performance objectives. We must, however, point out that there is no unique way to build such models. For example, when we refer to profitability, do we measure the efficiency with which costs are transformed to profits, or do we consider revenue growth as well? Similarly, when we talk about service quality (SQ), do we refer to customer-perceived quality, or quality as determined by some objective measures (e.g., queue length and waiting time), or quality as perceived by the branch's personnel (internal customer perceptions)? Answers to these questions, and details on the inputs and outputs of each model, can be determined based on the specific question at hand, and the availability of data.

A Profitability Efficiency Model. Figure 5.6 presents the inputs and outputs of a profitability efficiency model. The input set includes the resources used by the branch—as in the operating efficiency model. Revenue-generating accounts are also included in the input set. The output set includes the profit generated at each branch. More holistic models to include revenue growth, service quality, competition, and so on, can also be developed depending on data availability.

A shortcoming of this model is that it adopts a production—as opposed to financial intermediation—approach to the branch's function, and thus, no measure of *risk* incorporated in the profit measurement is included. Although the model can measure the efficiency with which branches generate profits, it fails to recognize any inefficiencies in the intermediation process as measured by high-risk exposure (for a further discussion of risk-adjusted measures of the efficiency of the financial intermediation process see Holmer & S. A. Zenios, 1995).

This model can be used to provide relative profitability efficiencies on a homogeneous group of branches. The model can also be used to cost the effects of inefficient operations and the cost of offering inappropriate product

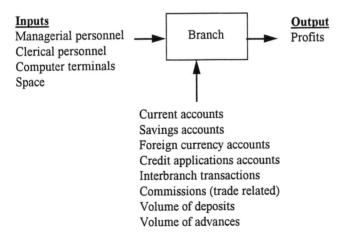

Inputs
Managerial personnel
Clerical personnel
Computer terminals
Space

Branch

Output
Profits

Current accounts
Savings accounts
Foreign currency accounts
Credit applications accounts
Interbranch transactions
Commissions (trade related)
Volume of deposits
Volume of advances

FIG. 5.6. Inputs and outputs of a profitability efficiency model.

mix at each branch, as long as cost information is available for the various resources used. The procedure to do this is outlined as follows:

Step 1: The profitability efficiency model is run and inefficient units are projected onto the efficient frontier.

Step 2: The differences between actual and target profits are calculated. These additional savings in profits derive partially from the reduction in consumable resources and partially from the improvements in the product mix offered at each branch.

Step 3: The differences between the actual and target values of consumable resources (i.e., personnel, computers, space) are computed, and the cost of consumable resources is estimated for each branch, because the unit cost and the level of utilization of resources are known.

Step 4: The total cost of inefficiency due to operations obtained in Step 3 is deducted from the total savings obtained in Step 2, giving the total cost of inefficiency due to product mix.

Using this procedure we are now able to separate the cost of inefficiencies into its two components. When we applied the procedure to the branches of our sample, potential profit increases of the order of 12% were identified. Approximately 40% of this profit increase can be realized by improving operations, whereas the remaining 60% can be achieved by adjustments—if possible—in the product mix.

A Quality Efficiency Model. Achieving high levels of SQ is usually thought of as an important part of banking operations performance. SQ is considered by many as the key to gaining competitive advantage and customer loyalty (Parasuraman, Zeithaml, & Berry, 1994). One of the challenges that banks face today is *how* to deliver services of high quality. Recently, DEA models that take into consideration service quality have been reported in the literature (Athanassopoulos, 1997; Soteriou & Stavrinides, 1997; Soteriou & S. A. Zenios, 1997), demonstrating that DEA can provide an excellent tool toward this direction.

The inputs and outputs of the model are shown in Fig. 5.7. The input set includes SQ drivers such as employee training, technology, and so forth. The output set consists of customer-perceived SQ (Parasuraman et al., 1994). The DEA model we present here can be used (a) to identify those branches that utilize resources in the most efficient way to deliver high-quality services to their customers, and (b) to provide direction for improvement.

For further discussion on the linkages between operations, service quality, and profitability, and for a more detailed discussion of a two-stage DEA model in which both objective and perceived measures of service quality are used, see Soteriou and S. A. Zenios (1997).

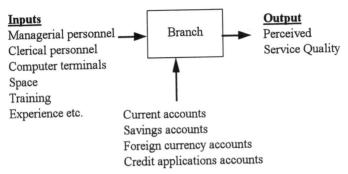

FIG. 5.7.   Inputs and outputs of a service quality model.

CONCLUDING REMARKS

This chapter has provided an introduction on the state-of-the-art methodology of Data Envelopment Analysis. The methodology is extremely useful as a performance assessment tool, because it can not only identify (in)efficiencies in a group of units, but also provide specific direction for improvement. We have described some of the basic DEA formulations and provided the description of an application of the methodology in assessing the operating efficiency of a group of bank branches.

There is already a large body of literature and a continuously growing research activity in DEA methodological developments and empirical applications, in different contexts. DEA is a promising methodology with a number of advantages over traditional performance assessment techniques.

REFERENCES

Athanassopoulos, A. D. (1997). Embodying service quality into operating efficiency for assessing the effort effectiveness in the provision of financial services. *European Journal of Operational Research, 98*(2), 300–313.

Banker, R. D., Charnes, A., & Cooper, W. W. (1984). Some models for estimating technical and scale inefficiencies in data envelopment analysis. *Management Science, 30,* 1078–1092.

Banker, R. D., Conrad, R. F., & Strauss, R. P. (1986). A comparative application of DEA and translog methods: An illustrative study of hospital production. *Management Science, 32,* 30–44.

Banker, R. D., & Morey, R. C. (1986a). Efficiency analysis for exogenously fixed inputs and outputs. *Operations Research, 34,* 513–521.

Banker, R. D., & Morey, R. C. (1986b). The use of categorical variables in data envelopment analysis. *Management Science, 32*(12), 1613–1627.

Berger, A., & Humphrey, D. B. (1997). Efficiency of financial institutions: International survey and directions for future research. *European Journal of Operational Research, 98*(2), 175–212.

Charnes, A., Clark, C., Cooper, W. W., & Golany, B. (1985). A developmental study of data envelopment analysis in measuring the efficiency of maintenance units in the U.S. Air Force. *Annals of Operations Research, 2,* 95–112.

Charnes, A., Cooper, W. W., & Rhodes, E. (1978). Measuring the efficiency of decision making units. *European Journal of Operations Research, 2,* 429–444.

Charnes, A., Cooper, W. W., & Rhodes, E. (1981). Evaluating program and managerial efficiency: An application of data envelopment analysis to program follow through. *Management Science, 27,* 668–697.

Dyson, R., & Thanassoulis, E. (1988). Reducing weight flexibility in data envelopment analysis. *Journal of the Operational Research Society, 39,* 563–576.

Farrell, M. J. (1957). The measurement of productive efficiency. *Journal of the Royal Statistical Society, Series A, 120*(3), 143–155.

Fox, K. J., & Hill, R. J. (1996). *Identifying outlier firms in multiple output–multiple input efficiency models* (Working Paper). Sydney, Australia: University of New South Wales.

Frei, F., & Harker, P. T. (1995). Process design and efficiency: Evidence from retail banking (Working Paper No. 94-18). The Wharton School, University of Pennsylvania.

Hillier, F., & Lieberman, G. (1986). *Introduction to operations research* (4th ed.), San Francisco: Holden Day.

Holmer, M. R., & Zenios, S. A. (1995). The productivity of financial intermediation and the technology of financial product management. *Operations Research, 43*(6), 970–982.

Kamakura, W. (1988). A note on the use of categorical variables in data envelopment analysis. *Management Science, 34*(10), 1273–1276.

Levitt, M. S., & Joyce, M. (1987). *The growth and efficiency of public spending.* Cambridge, England: Cambridge University Press.

Parasuraman, A., Zeithaml, V., & Berry, L. (1994). Reassessment of expectations as a comparison standard in measuring service quality: Implications for further research. *Journal of Marketing, 58,* 111–124.

Soteriou, A. C., & Stavrinides, Y. (1997). An internal customer DEA service quality model for bank branches. *International Journal of Operations and Production Management, 17*(8), 780–789.

Soteriou, A. C., & Zenios, S. A. (1996). *On the costing of bank products* (Working Paper No. 96-04). Nicosia: University of Cyprus, Department of Public and Business Administration.

Soteriou, A. C., & Zenios, S. A. (1997). *Efficiency, profitability and quality in the provision of financial services* (Working Paper No. 97-13). Nicosia: University of Cyprus, Department of Public and Business Administration.

Thanassoulis, E. (1993). A comparison of regression analysis and data envelopment analysis as alternative methods for performance assessment. *Journal of Operational Research Society, 44,* 137–147, 1129–1144.

Thanassoulis, E., Boussofiane, A., & Dyson, R. G. (1996). A comparison of data envelopment analysis and ratio analysis as tools for performance assessment. *Omega, 24,* 229–244.

Thanassoulis, E., & Dyson, R. G. (1992). Estimating preferred target input output levels using data envelopment analysis. *European Journal of Operational Research, 56*(1), 80–98.

Thanassoulis, E., Dyson, R., & Foster, M. J. (1987). Relative efficiency assessments using data envelopment analysis: An application to data on rates departments. *Journal of the Operational Research Society, 38,* 397–411.

Wong, Y. H., & Beasley, J. (1990). Restricting weight flexibility in data envelopment analysis. *Journal of the Operational Research Society, 41,* 829–835.

Zenios, C. V., Zenios, S. A., Agathocleous, K., & Soteriou, A. C. (1995). *Benchmarks of the efficiency of bank branches* (Working Paper No. 95-10). Nicosia: University of Cyprus, Department of Public and Business Administration.

CHAPTER SIX

Heuristic Search Methods

Said Salhi

University of Birmingham, England

Many applications can be modeled reasonably well and usually solved optimally by one of the well-known optimization techniques such as linear programming, integer programming, dynamic programming, and network-based methods, among others. These techniques are widely discussed and explained in most OR/MS texbooks. However, in some situations the combinatorial effect of problems can make the use of these techniques less applicable and the optimal solution intractable. To overcome such potential shortcomings, heuristic methods were devised to provide the user with some reasonable solutions. Although these methods do not guarantee optimality, in some situations they seem to be the only way forward to produce concrete results. To date, heuristic search methods have demonstrated widespread use in business, economic, and industrial problems that were found hard to solve in the past.

The main aim in heuristic search is to construct a model that can be *easily understood* and that provides *good* solutions in a *reasonable* amount of computing time. Unfortunately, this class of methods is both an art and a science because it combines human experience, mathematical logic, computational skills, and common sense. In general, most heuristic search methods fall into one of the following categories: (a) constructive (descent/perturbation/multiphase approach), (b) local search (tabu search, simulated annealing, noisy method), (c) population based (genetic algorithms), (d) mathematically based (lagrangian heuristic/incomplete branch&bound), (e) human/graphical interaction, and (f) hybrid search (combination of any of the preceding).

The purpose of this chapter is to provide an overview of heuristic search methods. In order to accomplish this, some possible methodologies of approach are highlighted along with a discussion on heuristics in practice. Subsequently, the descent method is introduced followed by some of the recently developed constructive heuristics. Finally, the last sections are devoted entirely to so-called modern heuristic methods (e.g., simulated annealing, tabu search, and genetic algorithm). Throughout the chapter, a small example is presented to illustrate each of the heuristic methods.

Possible Methodological Approaches

Most optimization techniques fall into two main categories: exact algorithms and approximate algorithms. Exact algorithms guarantee optimality, but may not be always applicable. Approximate algorithms are capable of producing good solutions to even large problems, but do not guarantee optimality.

In general, there are four rules that can be used to approach real-life problems: (a) an exact method to the exact (true) problem, (b) a heuristic method to the exact problem, (c) an exact method to the (approximate) modified problem, and (d) a heuristic method to the approximate problem. Of course, this list is not exhaustive because combinations of these rules do exist but can be difficult to define explicitly. Thus, the rules (a–d) are put in a priority ordering. However, the main difficulty in practice is the degree of modification of the problem which can be critical to the success of a chosen method. Nevertheless, the preceding hierarchy (a–d) is used to emphasize the need to maintain the problem characteristics as close as possible to the ones of the true problem. This concept does obviously highlight that *it is better to have a good and acceptable solution to a true problem rather than an optimal solution to a simplified problem that may have little resemblance to the original problem.*
There are several reasons for promoting heuristics. These include:

1. Heuristics can be the only way forward to producing concrete solutions to large hard combinatorial problems.
2. They are easily adaptable and accessible for additional modules if need be.
3. Heuristics are usually supported by graphical interface to help the user see what is going on, rather than having a final product from a black box.
4. Management and less specialized users find them reasonably easy to understand and therefore to comment on and to interact with the system.
5. These methods are not difficult to write, validate, and implement.

6. Management can introduce some unquantifiable measures indirectly to see their effect as solutions can be generated reasonably fast.

7. These methods are suitable for producing more than a single solution, and this added information gives more flexibility to the user to choose a few solutions for further investigation.

8. The design of heuristics requires a proper insight of a problem.

Complexity and Performance of Heuristics

Heuristics need not be linked to the terms "quick and dirty" or "guesswork" because heuristics are much wider in conception than these terms. Heuristics need to be carefully devised to represent the full characteristics of a given problem. In addition, heuristics need to be validated and tested, not necessarily on worst scenarios, but extensively on scenarios that have some similarities with the problem under investigation.

The main criteria for evaluating the performance of a new heuristic can best be classified under two headings: the quality of the solutions provided and the computational effort (measured by the central processing unit [CPU] time on a given machine). Of course, other criteria such as simplicity, flexibility, ease of control, interaction and friendliness can also be of interest. For further details, see Eglese (1990), Reeves (1993), Salhi (1994) Barr, Golden, Kelly, Resende, and Stewart (1995), and Johnson (1996).

Solution Quality

As heuristics do not guarantee optimality, several ways of assessing their performance can be used. These include empirical testing, worst case analysis, probabilistic analysis, lower bounds, and benchmarking. The details of each method follow:

1. Empirical testing can be based on the best solutions of some of the existing heuristics when tested on a set of published data. Here one can produce average deviation, worst deviation, the number of best solutions, and so on. This measure, which is one of the most useful approaches in practice, is simple to use and can be effective when published results exist. Although accuracy is guaranteed because the results obtained are known with certainty, this type of analysis can provide only statistical evidence about the performance of the heuristic for other nontested problems.

2. In worst case analysis, a pathological example needs to be generated. This is represented purposely to show the weakness of the algorithm. It is usually very hard to find such an example especially if the problem is complex. One drawback to such an analysis is that in practice the problem under study rarely resembles the worst case example.

3. In probabilistic analysis, the density function of the problem data needs to be determined, and statistical measures derived (e.g., average and worst behavior).

4. One way to use lower bounds analysis is to solve the relaxed problem (where many of the difficult constraints are removed like in linear programming [LP] relaxation), or the transformed problem (which falls into a suitable class of easy problems like lagrangian relaxation). The main difficulty with this analysis is that the lower bound solutions obtained have to be rather tight to tell the quality of the heuristic solution, otherwise misleading conclusions can be drawn.

5. In situations where a benchmark solution already exists, one can see how the heuristic solution compares with the benchmark solution.

Computational Effort

Computational effort is usually measured by the time complexity and the space complexity of a heuristic. The former describes the computing time a heuristic requires for a given instance whereas the latter describes the storage capacity the heuristic needs when solving a given instance. Unfortunately, the latter is seldom discussed in the literature.

Time Complexity. The time complexity of an algorithm is defined by $0(g(N))$ where N denotes the size of the problem. If $g(N)$ is a polynomial function of N (e.g., N^k, $k > 1$), then the problem can be solved optimally within a reasonable amount of computation time. But if $g(N)$ is an exponential function of N, the problem may be difficult to solve optimally within a reasonable amount of time. Such types of problems are usually known to be NP hard; see Garey and Johnson (1979).

Space Complexity. Although this issue is less referenced when compared to time complexity, the way the data are stored and retrieved is an important issue in heuristic design. An efficient data handling not only uses the smallest necessary storage capacity in the computer but it can also save a large amount of computing time by not calculating unnecessary information that is either redundant or already found in earlier iterations.

CONSTRUCTIVE-BASED HEURISTICS

The Descent Method

The first heuristic method considered is the classical descent method (DM). The DM is also known as a hill-climbing heuristic or greedy heuristic. The DM reads as follows:

1. Select an initial solution, say $x \in S$
   (where S is the set of feasible solutions).
2. Choose a solution $x' \in N(x)$ such that $F(x') < F(x)$
   (where $N(x)$ is the neighborhood of x).
   If there is no such x', x is considered as a local optimum and the method stops.
   Else set $x = x'$ and repeat step 2.

Neighborhood Structure. Each solution, say $x \in S$, has an associated set of neighbors, say $N(x) \subset S$, which is called the neighborhood of x. Each solution, x, of $N(x)$, can be obtained directly from x by an operation that is referred to as a move (or transition), say $m(x)$, with $x' = m(x)$. Note that the operation is symmetric as $x' \in N(x) \rightarrow x \in N(x')$.

A move can be defined as: (a) changing the value assigned to a binary variable (e.g., changing $x_j = 1$ to 0 or vice versa), (b) adding or deleting an element from a set (e.g., removing a customer from a route or dropping an existing depot from a configuration), or (c) interchanging the positions of two jobs in a given sequence in scheduling, changing the colors of two vertices in a time-tabling problem, swapping items between knapsacks in a loading problem, and so forth.

In step 2 the choice of the selected solution, x', can be based on either the best improving move:

- Evaluate all or a part of all the neighborhood to select the neighborhood that yields the best solution (discrete case).
- Use the gradient-based formula to generate the next neighbor (continuous case).

Or it can be based on the first improving move:

- Select the first x' that produces $F(x') < F(x)$.

Some Limitations

The preceding DM procedure is efficient when the objective function F is unimodular (one local optimum only). In case F is not unimodular, as often occurs in practice (i.e., several local optima exist), it is not easy to get out of the neighborhood of this local optimum (see Fig. 6.1 for illustration).

One possible approach to solving this problem is to restart the procedure from another initial solution hoping to yield a better local optima. Unfortunately, if not looked at carefully, this process of restarting may lead to already visited local optima. In my view, devising a way to guide the search for generating initial solutions can be worth the effort. One strategy is to develop a dynamic system in which past information (previous initial and found local optimal

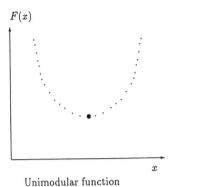
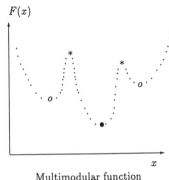

Unimodular function   Multimodular function

- global minima
- *o* local minima
- * local maxima

FIG. 6.1. Local optimality representation for a continuous function.

ones) is integrated to generate the next starting solution. Such a scheme helps in producing useful guidance when searching over unexplored regions.

A Basic Composite Heuristic

This sort of heuristic is similar in principle to the DM except that once the local optimal solution is found, another refinement (called a post optimizer) is used to improve the currently found solution. This process can be repeated between the DM and the refinenemt procedure until no further improvement can be obtained (see Salhi & Rand, 1987, 1993). An example of determining the length of a tour around eight cities including the depot is given to illustrate how a simple composite heuristic works. The aim here is to have a tour with the minimum total distance. The initial tour can be found randomly or using any greedy heuristic. As illustrated in Fig. 6.2, the move from one tour to another is chosen in such a way to improve the current solution (e.g., finding a tour with shorter length). Thus, the move can be defined by exchanging "r" existing arcs in the current tour with "r" new ones while maintaining the structure of the tour; see the following example. In Fig. 6.2, the original tour (i) has been improved using the two-optimal tour procedure (e.g., $r = 2$). The arcs AB and CD are exchanged with the two new arcs AC and BD resulting in a tour with reduced length.

For each possible move all or part of all the neighborhood is explored, the objective function is evaluated, and the best solution is selected. The

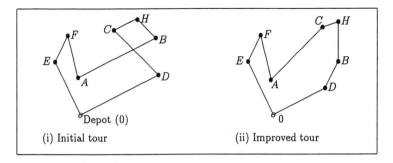

FIG. 6.2. Possible tour improvement.

process is repeated, starting from such a new solution until no further positive improvement is obtained.

It is important to note that the solution in Fig. 6.2(ii) is a local optimal tour with respect to the two-optimal procedure. It is therefore clear that a single neighboring search may not be sufficient to obtain high-quality solutions. In fact, the tour given in Fig. 6.2 (ii) can be improved as follows:

1. Use another neighborhood search (say the three-optimal procedure). This can be done in one step by exchanging three existing arcs (OE, FA, and AC) with three new arcs (OA, AE, and FC) when starting from Fig. 6.2(ii). The optimal tour, for this particular example, is given in Fig. 6.3(ii).

2. Use the same neighboring search. This is carried out in two or more steps by allowing less attractive tours to be formed first, as in Fig. 6.3(i), before reaching the optimal tour given in Fig. 6.3(ii).

A Multilevel Composite Heuristic

In simple composite heuristic, the solution is improved using a given refinement procedure, and the method stops when there is no further improvement. Such a solution is then considered to be the best solution, which

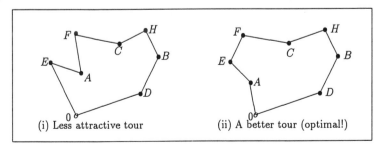

FIG. 6.3. More improvement on the tour construction.

is a local optima with respect to the selected procedure. *One way to direct the search out of a local optima is by using other refinement modules for which current local optimality no longer holds.* The aim here is not to restrict one to using one, two, or at most three modules as usually applied in simple composite heuristics, but to introduce as much distortion to the solution as possible as long as the total computing time remains acceptable. The choice of the refinement procedures and the sequencial order in which they are used can be critical. One possible skeleton of this approach, which is referred to as a multilevel composite heuristic, is given next. For clarity of presentation, p levels are used where the value of p will depend on the problem, and the procedures used within each composite heuristic.

A p-Level Composite Heuristic.

Level 1:   Generate an initial solution.
Level 2:   Apply a composite heuristic of Type I.
Level 3:   Apply a composite heuristic of Type II and go to Level 2.
$\vdots$
Level p: Apply a composite heuritic of Type $p - 1$ and go to Level 2.
Level p + 1:   Record the final solution.

In Level 1, the solution can be generated randomly, by guessing, by experience, or simply by using a suitable greedy heuristic. The solution does not need to be feasible. In case of infeasibility, weights are usually assigned and updated according to the amount by which feasibility is violated. Although the choice of a good initial feasible solution is not a must, it seems logical to start from a good one that can be used at least as a reference solution. It is worth noting that, in heuristic search in general, *there is a lack of firm correlation between the quality of initial solutions and the local optimal ones.* In other words, the superiority of a higher quality solution found at the initial stage will not necessarily be maintained in the final stage (i.e., a better local optimal solution may be generated based on an inferior initial solution). This is an important and a unique property in heuristic design.

In Level 2, the composite heuristic of Type I consists of several refinement modules that are implemented in sequence. These modules need to be fast in their implementation. This can be accomplished either because the procedures themselves are fast, or because they are applied to a small and well-restricted neighborhood.

In Level 3, the composite heuristic of Type II consists of fewer refinements that are usually more powerful but require relatively more computing time. Some of these may be part of the refinements of the previous level but applied to a larger neighborhood. The next levels can be distinguished by using refinement modules that are more and more powerful and that require a larger and larger amount of computing time. This approach was developed by Salhi and Sari (1997) and has proved to be successful when applied to the problem of vehicle routing with multiple depots.

A Perturbation Heuristic

The concept of perturbing an existing solution in an intelligent way provides the search to explore other regions in which better solutions may be generated. The perturbed solution chosen can be the most improved solution, if such a solution exists. If all the perturbed solutions are nonimproved, one can either choose the least nonimproved solution, or one of the worst perturbed solutions picked either randomly or by using past information. For instance, in the simple facility location problem where the objective is to identify the optimal number of depots, the solution is allowed to become infeasible in terms of the number of depots. This is done by accepting solutions with more as well as less the number of depots than the one required by the problem. By solving the relaxed problem (modified problem), we generate infeasible solutions that when transformed into feasible ones may yield a cost improvement. The idea of shifting between feasible and infeasible solutions is also used in strategic oscillation where the amount of infeasibility allowed is dealt with accordingly. This concept is useful particularly when the solution space is disconnected or not convex. The only difference is that we make the solution infeasible in a guided manner. In other words, we continue to do so until either (a) the number of depots remaining open is small or (b) the solution is formed with more than the required number of open depots. In (a) the number of depots is small enough to nearly guarantee that those depots will remain in the final solution, whereas in (b) the solution has a large enough number of depots, most of which are competing depots. When this process is repeated several times, it becomes like *a filtering process* where the most attractive depots will have the tendency to remain in the best depot configuration. Such an approach was developed by Salhi (1997) and it performed rather well when tested on a class of large uncapacitated facility location problems.

SIMULATED ANNEALING

The concept of simulated annealing (SA) is derived from statistical mechanics. In statistical mechanics the study is about the behavior of very large systems of interacting components such as atoms in a fluid in thermal equilibrium, at a finite temperature. The question is what happens to the system at its low-energy ground state. Do the atoms remain fluid, or do they solidify?

Is this solid crystalline or glassy? The way to lower the temperature is crucial in the obtention of a good crystal or glass. The system must be melted and then carefully cooled. This is referred to as an annealing process. In this process, first a high temperature is used to melt the solid and then it is gradually cooled, spending sufficient time for the solid to reach thermal equilibrium, especially when approaching the freezing point. If the process of cooling is too rapid, then defects can be frozen into the solid, and the ground state will not be reached. The resulting solid may be only a metastable (a locally optimal system) a structurally defective crystal or glass. Metropolis et al. (1953) produced an algorithm to provide efficient simulation of a collection of atoms in equilibrium at a given temperature. At each iteration of the algorithm, an atom is given a small random displacement and the resulting change in the energy of the system is evaluated (δ). If δ is negative, the move is systematically accepted and the process continues using the new configuration as the starting configuration. If δ is positive (deterioration of the solution), the new solution will be accepted probabilistically.

Some Ingredients of SA

The Physical Analogy. It was not until 30 years after Metropolis et al.'s (1953) investigation that the analogy between the simulation of the annealing of solids, and the solution of large combinatorial optimization problems was made by Kirkpatrick, Gelat, and Vecchi (1983). In the context of an optimization problem, the process of a body cooling is an analogy for a search process with the solution approaching a global optimum. The energy function becomes the objective function, the configuration of the system's particles becomes the configuration of the problem parameter values, and the search for low-energy configuration becomes the search for optimal solutions. Temperature reduces to the control parameter. Hasty cooling resulting in defective crystal is analogous to the type of neighborhood search that results in a local optimum. Kirkpatrick et al., inspired by these analogies, developed for the context of combinatorial optimization an explicit format for the algorithm that is now widely known as the SA algorithm. The way in which the temperature decreases is called the cooling schedule and the probability function used is that of Boltzmann's law (see Metropolis et al., 1953).

Some Notations.

- δ is the change in the cost function F.
- T_k is the temperature at iteration k.
- $g(T_k)$ is a nonincreasing function of T_k.
- θ is a random number generated from the uniform distribution $U(0,1)$.
- ρ is the acceptance ratio, which has a value in $[0,1]$ but close to 1.

- $\hat{x}$ and $\hat{T}$ denote the best solution and the best temperature for which $\hat{x}$ was found.
- M is the maximum number of iterations.
- T_0 and T_f denote the initial and final temperature values, respectively.

The Basic SA Algorithm.

1. Select an initial solution x, set $k = 0$, and choose an initial temperature T_k.
2. Choose a solution x' in $N(x)$ and compute $\delta = F(x') - F(x)$.
3. If $(\delta \leq 0)$ or $(\delta > 0$ and $e^{-(\delta/T_k)} \geq \theta \in U[0,1])$ then
   accept the new solution x' and set $x = x'$.
   If $F(x') < F(\hat{x})$ then set $\hat{x} = x'$ and $\hat{T} = T_k$.
   Else keep x.
4. If some stopping criteria are satisfied stop.
5. Update the temperature $T_{k+1} = g(T_k) \leq T_k$, set $k = k + 1$, and go to step 2.

An Illustrative Example

Consider for simplicity the minimization of the following one-variable function:

$$IR \rightarrow IR$$
$$x \rightarrow F(x) = \frac{x^6}{6} - \frac{2x^5}{5} - \frac{13x^4}{5} + \frac{14x^3}{3} + 12x^2$$

The sketch of this function is given in Fig. 6.4. The optimal solution can be detected visually at $x* = 4$, which gives $F(x*) = -68.266$. Obviously, for purposes of discussion, one must assume that finding the solution either visually or by differentiation of F is not easily applicable (otherwise there is no point performing this heuristic).

A simple implementation of SA is used here with the following cooling schedules:

- Initial Temperature (T_0):
  $T_0 = 1,000$ (high temperature; uphill moves are likely to be all accepted).
- Updating of the temperature (T_k):
  (a) $T_{k+1} = T_k - t$ $(t = constant = 5)$
  (b) $T_{k+1} = T_k - t_k$ $(t_k$ is randomly chosen in $[0,5]$ at each k).
- Stopping criteria: $T_f \leq 5$ or maximum number of iterations of 3,000, whichever is reached first.

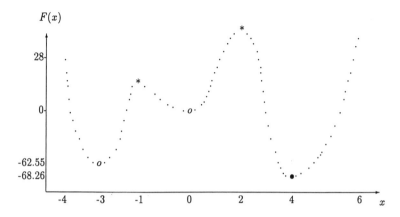

o local minima
• global minima
* local maxima

FIG. 6.4. A sketch of $F(x)$.

A computer program is written to assess the performance of this basic SA heuristic with that of a descent method using several starting solutions. According to the obtained results (see Table 6.1), the use of the DM can be misleading when starting from anywhere with a value less than 2. In fact, three local optima are discovered, from which only one is the optimal solution. In contrast, the SA has the flexibility of going over the hill to reach the global solution from all the initial solutions.

TABLE 6.1
The Effect of Initial Solution When Using Both SA and DM

Initial Solution	SA (Case a)		SA (Case b)		DM	
	x^*	$F(x^*)$	x^*	$F(x^*)$	x^*	$F(x^*)$
−50	4.00	−68.26	3.99	−68.26	−3	−62.55
−45	3.99	−68.26	3.99	−68.26	−3	−62.55
	"	"	"	"	"	"
	"	"	"	"	"	"
↓	"	"	"	"	"	"
−5	4.00	−68.26	3.99	−68.26	−3	−62.55
0	"	"	"	"	0	0
5	"	"	"	"	4	−68.26
↓	"	"	"	"	"	"

The success of the SA heuristic is determined by the choice of the neighborhood and the cooling schedules, which are defined by a number of different parameters including T_0, T_f, T_k, and the stopping criteria. The choice is obviously not unique because this generally depends on the characteristics of the problem. However, in the recent few years several schemes, particularly for the cooling schedules, have been developed with promising results. For further discussion, see Lundy and Mees (1986), van Laarhoven and Aarts (1987), Eglese (1989), Conolly (1990), Downsland (1993), Osman (1993), Osman and Laporte (1996), and Welch and Salhi (1997).

TABU SEARCH METHODS

Tabu search (TS) methods were proposed by Fred Glover (1986) and independently by Pierre Hansen (1986). TS concepts are derived from artificial intelligence where intelligent uses of memory help exploit useful historical information. According to Webster's dictionary, tabu or taboo is defined as "banned on ground of morality or taste or as constituting a risk. . . ." In the context of optimization, TS employs some forms of restrictions for banning some choices from being considered to guide the search process. Such restrictions can vary from problem to problem.

TS shares with SA the flexibility in accepting nonimproving moves. TS and SA are both meta-heuristics that are devised to guide other constructive heuristics to avoid being trapped into a poor local optimum. In TS, attempts to overcome local optimality are made by accepting nonimproving moves and imposing some sort of tabu status for those attributes recently involved in the move. To date, TS methods have proved successful in several areas of optimization, namely scheduling, graph coloring and partitioning, telecommunication path assignment, vehicle routing, quadratic assignment, location problems, and so forth. The obtained solutions are found to be optimal or near optimal (for further discussion see Glover, Laguna, Taillard, & de Werra, 1993).

TS has the following properties:

1. TS selects the next best move in a deterministic manner.
2. TS is more aggressive as it exploits a larger part of the neighborhood.
3. TS tries to avoid cycling by stopping reversal or replicate moves for a certain number of iterations by making such moves tabu.
4. TS is flexible as it accepts tabu moves that have an outcome better than a certain well-defined aspiration level (threshold) by overriding the tabu restrictions.
5. TS takes advantage of historical information of past solutions to form short- and/or long-term memories. These memories are useful guiding

the search to explore other regions via diversification and intensification wherever necessary.

6. TS has the power of searching over nonfeasible regions which, in some situations, can provide an efficient way for crossing the boundaries of feasibility.

Some Terminology

To be familiar with the TS vocabulary, some general terms follow:

A move: a transition from a current solution to its neighboring (or another) solution.

An attribute: the elements that constitute the move; for instance if the move is to add or drop customer i from a vehicle route, the associated attribute is the i^{tb} customer, whereas if the move is formed by exchanging customer i with customer j between their respective routes the attribute can be seen as the pair of customers i and j. The associated vehicle routes may also be used.

Tabu list: a list of moves that are currently tabu.

Tabu list size: the number of iterations for which a recently accepted move is not allowed to be reversed (say $|T_s|$).

Tabu tenure: an integer number telling for how long a given move will remain tabu.

Aspiration level: a threshold (usually the best current objective function value, or an estimate of that, etc.) for which the tabu status of a move can be relaxed (override the tabu restriction).

Admissible move: a move that is nontabu or a move that is tabu active but that can produce a solution well above the aspiration level.

Forbidding strategy: the tabu conditions that forbid a move from being reversed.

Freeing strategy: the conditions that allow a move to become nontabu, because either its tabu status has become not tabu or such a move satisfies an aspiration criterion.

Data structure: the way to record full or partial past information, which helps avoid wasting computing time in recomputing already computed information in future iterations.

A Basic TS Procedure

1. Initialization:
   - Generate an initial solution, say x (which is not necessarily feasible).
   - Set the best current solution $x_{best} = x$.

- Evaluate all the moves in the neighborhood $N(x)$.
- Set values for tabu size, tabu list, and the data structure for candidate list of solutions.
- Set counters: iter = 0 (current iteration) and best iter = 0 (iteration for which the x_{best} is found).

2. Candidate list of solutions:

- Determine strategically, by the use of a special data structure, the candidate list of the best moves in the neighborhood $N'(x) \subseteq N(x)$.
- Update the data structure if necessary.

3. Selection strategy:

- Choose the best admissible solution $x' \in N'(x)$.
- Set $x = x'$ and iter = iter + 1.
- If $F(x') < (x_{best})$, set $x_{best} = x'$ and best iter = iter.
- Update the tabu list.

4. Stopping criterion:
   If a suitable stopping criterion is met go to step 5, else go to step 2.

5. Diversification (optional):
   Apply some forms of diversification on well-defined solutions and go to step 2, or else stop.

Elements of the TS Approach

These TS steps seem to be straightforward to implement. However, the success of the method is dependent on having a good insight into the problem. The following questions may help in being more cautious in the implementation of TS (or any similar local search heuristic):

1. What kind of neighborhood is more representative (fixed or variable) and which size is more appropriate?

2. How is the tabu size defined and what attribute does one want to make tabu?

3. Which aspiration level is most representative (objective function based or using other softer criteria)?

4. What necessary information is needed to make use of the diversification process (frequency, solution quality, chain of attributes, etc.) and possible reduction tests?

Initial Solution. This can be generated randomly, via a suitable heuristic or by an optimal method for a relaxed problem (here the solution may not necessarily be feasible). The idea is to have a solution that can be easily suitable for neighboring search.

Tabu Size ($|T_s|$). This value aims to be small enough to approximately stop a solution from reoccurring. For instance, if the best admissible move is a nonimproving move, it is obvious that, in the next iteration, the reversal move will be an improving move. Such a cycle can be stopped by not allowing this reversal move to be accepted. The value of $|T_s|$ can have a prescribed value, or be determined based on well-designed rules. The choice of the value for $|T_s|$ can be critical to the final solution. For further discussion on these items, see Battiti and Tecchiolli (1994), Osman and Salhi (1996), and Salhi (1997).

Tabu Restriction. A recent accepted move is made tabu using the following representation. $TAB(i)$ denotes the tabu status of the ith attribute. This can be defined by:

(a) $TAB(i) = $ iter $+ |T_s|$ where *iter* is the current number of iterations.

(b) $TAB(i) = \begin{cases} |T_s| \text{ once the move is accepted} \\ TAB(i) - 1 \text{ if } TAB(i) \geq 0 \\ 0 \text{ otherwise.} \end{cases}$

The former setting (a) is much quicker than (b) as no updating is required.

Forbidding Strategy. The move will remain tabu if

$$TAB(i) > \begin{cases} iter & \text{situation (a)} \\ 0 & \text{situation (b)} \end{cases}$$

Freeing Strategy. A move becomes admissible if

(i) $TAB(i) \leq iter$ (case (a)) or $TAB(i) \leq 0$ for case (b).

(ii) The new solution produces a better outcome than the best current solution and therefore the aspiration criterion overrides the tabu restriction.

Stopping Criteria. The heuristic terminates when one of the following stopping criteria occurs:

1. There is no improvement on the current best solution after a prescribed number of successive iterations.
2. There is no improvement on the last improved solution after a prescribed number of successive iterations.
3. The maximum number of iterations or the maximum allowed computing time has been used.

4. The number of diversifications (step 5 calls) allowed has been performed.

Diversification. The idea is to start from a new solution that has as much dissimilarity as possible from the other previously found solutions in order to explore new regions. This can be done using random restarts, solutions found by other greedy heuristics, or solutions obtained using an intelligent search that takes into account past information. Useful ideas on this issue can be found in Kelly, Laguna, and Glover (1994), and Thomas and Salhi (1996).

An Illustrative Example

Consider the example of determining the minimum spanning tree with some restrictions on the interdependency of some specified arcs (this example is taken from Glover, 1990). If there is no restriction, the problem can be solved optimally using the well-known greedy algorithm of Kruskal (1956).

In this example, we have a graph with five vertices ($n = 5$) and seven edges ($m = 7$)—see Fig. 6.5 for an illustration. The additional restrictions include:

$$x_j = \begin{cases} 1 & \text{if arc } x_j \text{ is chosen in the tree.} \\ \text{Else} & 0; \end{cases}$$

$x_1 + x_2 + x_6 \leq 1$ (at most one of the three edges x_1, x_2, x_6 is allowed to be in the tree); $x_1 \leq x_3$ (edge x_1 is allowed in the tree only if edge x_3 is also in the tree).

TS Characteristics for This Example

Initial Solution. This is generated by Kruskal's (1956) greedy algorithm. Although the solution happens to be infeasible (both constraints are violated), this solution is suitable for starting the TS mechanism using a penalty value,

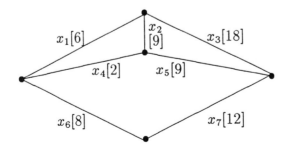

FIG. 6.5. An illustrative example.

say 50, for each unit of infeasibility [e.g., cost = cost + (penalty × number of infeasible units)].

Neighboring Search. Swap x_i with x_j while keeping the structure of the tree (this is an edge swap move).

Tabu Restrictions. For ease of understanding we considered the tabu restriction scenario described in (b). The tabu status of edge x_i is denoted by $TAB(i)$, which is initially set to zero. If edge x_i is selected to be introduced into the tree (and another one, say x_j, is removed from the tree), the value $TAB(i)$ is set to $|T_s|$ (the tabu size). In other words the edge x_i is not allowed to be dropped from the tree during the next $|T_s|$ iterations. The value of $TAB(i)$ will be reduced by one for each iteration until it becomes nontabu and then $TAB(i)$ remains at zero level. Note that other tabu restrictions can also be used. For instance a dropped edge, say x_j, may also be listed in another tabu list, as an edge that is not allowed to be added in the tree only after a certain number of iterations, which is not necessarily the same as $|T_s|$. This can be less restrictive such as $|T_s'| \leq |T_s| \leq n - 1$, or even more restrictive if $T_s \leq T_s' \leq m - n$. Note that $|T_s'|$ cannot be greater than $m - n$ and $|T_s|$ cannot be greater than $n - 1$ as no exchange would be possible except when the aspiration criterion overrides the tabu status.

Tabu Size. $|T_s|$ is set to $[(n - 1)/2]$, which is 2 for our example. This is chosen to show that once an edge is added it will have to remain in the tree for half of the size of that tree. This maintains the solution quality of the solutions while giving flexibility to half of the number of edges in a tree to be candidate for removal once the system is stabilized (e.g., after the first $[(n - 1)/2]$ iterations).

The move from (i) to (ii) in Fig. 6.6 is done by dropping x_1 and adding x_3 resulting in a feasible solution with a total length of 37. The edge x_3 is now made tabu for the following $|T_s|$ iterations. The obtained solution in Fig. 6.7(i) is generated by dropping x_6 and adding x_7.

Updating the Tabu List. $TAB(3) = 1$ (e.g., $|T_s| - 1 = 2 - 1$) and $TAB(7) = 2$. The final solution given in Fig. 6.7(ii) is obtained by dropping x_1 and adding x_2 to the previous solution [the one given in Fig. 6.7(i)]. This move is implemented even though x_3 is still tabu as the aspiration level overrides the tabu status. The tabu list is updated by using $TAB(2) = 2$ and $TAB(7) = 1$. The process continues until a suitable stopping rule is met (e.g., a certain number of iterations without improvement has been performed).

The success of TS methods depends on the choice of the tabu size, the definition of the neighborhood, how diversification schemes are developed and employed, the way previous solutions are identified, the efficiency of

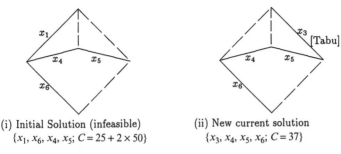

(i) Initial Solution (infeasible)
$\{x_1, x_6, x_4, x_5; C = 25 + 2 \times 50\}$

(ii) New current solution
$\{x_3, x_4, x_5, x_6; C = 37\}$

FIG. 6.6. The first two iterations.

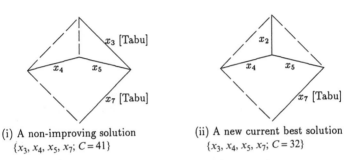

(i) A non-improving solution
$\{x_3, x_4, x_5, x_7; C = 41\}$

(ii) A new current best solution
$\{x_3, x_4, x_5, x_7; C = 32\}$

FIG. 6.7. A better solution via a nonimproving move.

the computer program, and above all a good understanding of the problem. For further details on these issues, see Skorin-Kapov (1990), Dammeyer and Voss (1993), Kelly, Laguna, and Glover (1994), Glover (1989, 1995), Salhi (1994, 1997); Thomas and Salhi (1996), Battiti (1996), and Voss (1996).

GENETIC ALGORITHMS

Genetic algorithms (GAs) were invented to mimic some of the processes observed in natural and biological evolution. GAs are developed from the concepts borrowed from the natural world (Darwinian theory: *survival of the fittest*). Those processes were felt to be good to imitate if organized in a structured manner such as an algorithm. Genetic adaptive search was initially developed by John Holland and his associates at the University of Michigan in the 1970s. It was originally used to solve game theory and pattern recognition problems and formally introduced to the area of optimization in 1975 (see Goldberg, 1989; Holland, 1975).

GA is an adaptive heuristic search method based on population genetics. GA consists of a population of chromosomes that evolve over a number of generations and are subject to genetic operators at each generation. Each chromosome has a fitness value associated with it. A set of best fit chromosomes survive from one generation to the next. The genetic operations that the chromosomes are subjected to are usually crossover and mutation. For a chromosome that is represented by a binary string, the crossover operation takes two strings, randomly cuts at two points of the strings, and exchanges the bit string subset. The mutation operator randomly picks a bit in the chromosome and changes it to its complementary value.

The main idea behind GA is that evolution takes place on chromosomes and there are chromosomal encoding and decoding processes that relate to the problem under study. These features can have different forms from one problem to another. This philosophy is different from the one usually given in the conventional optimization techniques due to the following items:

1. A coding of the parameter set, not the parameters themselves, is directly manipulated (the evolution is based on chromosomes rather than the variable they encode).
2. The search is carried out on a population of points and not on a single point (several solutions are considered simultaneously).
3. There is a payoff (objective function) information, not derivatives or other auxiliary knowledge (the link between chromosomes and the performance of their decoded structures is naturally selected).
4. The transition rules are probabilistic and not deterministic.
5. The process of reproduction from parents to children is the key factor of the evolution.

It is worth noting that randomized search does not necessarily imply directionless search and therefore differs significantly from random search, which can be considered as a blind search.

GA is an iterative procedure that maintains a population of P candidate members (solutions) over many simulated generations (iterations). The population members are string entities of artificial chromosomes. These chromosomes are fixed length strings with binary values (or alleles) at each position (or locus). The allele can take 0 or 1 value in the bit string, and the locus is the position at which the 0 or 1 value is present in each location of the chromosome. Each chromosome has a fitness value associated with it.

Some Terminology

To be familiar with the GA vocabulary, some general terms follow:

Chromosome (genotypes): a string representing a solution to the problem.
Genes (phenotypes): a coding representing the chromosome. This can represent an array of characters (towns), logical bits (0 or 1), or numbers (index of towns).

Alleles: the various values that a gene can take.

Loci: the position of a given allele in the chromosome.

Population (gene-pool): the set of chromosomes used in a given generation (iteration).

Children: the generated chromosomes from the current populations.

Parents: the chromosomes that form the children (current chromosomes).

Fitness: a value of the function to optimize under a given chromosome.

Operators: transformations that generate new solutions based on current ones; the way of reproduction of new solutions. These include *crossover, mutation, reproduction,* and *inversion.*

Schemata: a block or a part of the chromosome (this is done to maintain similarities between parents and children).

The GA Algorithm

A basic genetic algorithm can be summarized in the following steps:

1. Initialize a population of chromosomes (a set of solutions).
2. Evaluate each chromosome in the population.
3. Create new chromosomes by mating current chromosomes using suitable operators.
4. Delete some old chromosomes to maintain the size of the population.
5. Evaluate the new chromosomes and insert them into the population.
6. If certain stopping criteria are met, stop; otherwise go to step 3.

The Main Parts of a GA

The GA process can be organized into three modules:

1. *The evaluation module,* which consists of an evaluation function whose task is to decode a chromosome by converting it into a real or an integer value, say x, and to use this value of x into an objective function, say F, to get $F(x)$.

2. *The population module,* which consists of (a) an encoding technique (how to represent a solution of the problem: these can be binary, integer numbers, or characters, among others), (b) an initialization technique (how are the initial solutions found?), (c) deletion technique (how many and which choromosomes to remove from the population? which decision rule is used for deleting the chromosones?), (d) a reproduction technique (are all solutions replaced?), (e) a parent selection technique (which parent is selected for reproduction?), (f) a fitness technique (evaluation of the objective func-

tion or a related objective function), and (g) the parameters used (population size, desired number of trials, number of chromosomes to be dropped, etc.).

3. *The reproduction module*, which consists of the operators used, such as reproduction, mutation, crossover, and inversion. The probability of choosing any of these operators can be specified a priori or determined dynamically. Usually, a bit mutation rate is relatively smaller than a crossover rate, say 0.005 and 0.70, respectively.

Characterizing a GA Via an Example

In this section we explain the main elements that form a GA using an illustrative example, which is to maximize $F(x) = x^2$ where $x \in [0,31]$.

Coding a Chromosome

There are several possible codings, namely binary, decimal, character, and integer numbers representations. These are put in a string format where bits are represented accordingly. The length of the string that needs to be used has to be fixed. The choice of the length of the string is an issue in GA.

To code a chromosome each bit (gene) must give a piece of information about the chromosome. The simplest and most applicable coding is usually the binary coding. Next, we show how to code an integer number and a continuous function using binary representation.

String Representation of an Integer Number.

Any integer number can be written in decimal system (e.g., in base 10). For instance, the variable $x = 2{,}765$ can also be written as $2{,}765 = 2.10^3 + 7.10^2 + 6.10^1 + 5.10^0$. Similarly, it is also possible to code a number in binary form (e.g., in base 2). For instance, $x = 39 = 1.2^5 + 0.2^4 + 0.2^3 + 1.2^2 + 1.2^1 + 1.2^0$ or simply x can be represented by a string of 6 bits as follows $x = (100111)$. Such a coding is easy to implement as the logical function false and true is used instead. In addition, such a representation requires less computer storage than its counterparts.

String Representation of a Continuous Function.

Minimize $F(x)$ where $x \in [a, b]$.

- Generate a bit string of length k, say 22.
  For instance, this gives $x' = (01011 \ldots 0110)$, hence $x' \in [0, 2^{22} - 1]$.
- Translate x' into $x \in [a, b]$
  $x = a + x' \cdot \frac{b-a}{2^{22}-1}$
- Compute $F(x)$, repeat the process to construct all the parents, say M, and finally use the process of GA to form new and better parents by

well-defined operators such as crossover, mutations, and so on, which we describe in the next subsection.

In our example we use a binary coding and a string of length 4 (maximum $x = 31$, which can be represented by $2^4 + 2^3 + 2^2 + 2^1 + 2^0$).

Selection Mechanism

It is important to know how to select, from one generation to the next, the parents for removal and those ones to mate in order to create the children (e.g., new chromosomes). This choice can be based on the parent relative fitness value (the fitter a parent is, the most likely it will either remain in the population or be used to mate). There are several ways to establish this task but for simplicity we present the following two only:

1. Choose a certain number of parents according to their fitness. This number can be fixed a priori or variable depending on the population average fitness.

2. Use the random nature of the roulette wheel selection. For each parent, say parent k, the probability of being selected can be computed as $F(x)/\bar{F}$ where x is the corresponding value for parent k. The values for all the parents are arranged in a roulette wheel and the parent to choose is recorded according to the outcome. In other words, these values can be put in a list from 0 to 1, a random number in [0,1] is picked, and for whichever range contains such a number, the associated parent will be selected. This process is repeated until the new generation is completed. Consider for instance the probability values found for a generation of four parents (see Fig. 6.8):

$$\text{Probability } (k) = (.20, .15, .47, .18)$$

For illustration, consider the example in Table 6.2 where the four initial chromosomes are generated randomly. A chromosome is considered not fit if

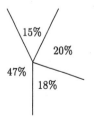

Parents	1	2	3	4
		$\alpha = 0.25$		

0.0   0.15   0.35   0.82   1.0

$\alpha = 0.25 \Rightarrow$ choose parent 2

Roulette Wheel   List Ordering

FIG. 6.8.   Roulette wheel selection.

TABLE 6.2
An Example of Reproduction

String No.	Current Population	x Value	F(x)	P[select]	Expected Count	Actual Count
1	0 1 1 0 1	13	169	0.14	0.58	1
2	1 1 0 0 0	24	579	0.49	**1.97**	2
3	0 1 0 0 0	8	64	0.06	0.22	0
4	1 0 0 1 1	19	361	0.31	1.23	1
Sum			1170	1.00	4.00	4
Average ($\bar{F}$)			293	0.25	1.00	1
Maximum			579	0.49	**1.97**	2

P[select] = $F(x)$ Sum. Expected count = $F(x)/\bar{F}$. Actual count = number found by roulette wheel or simply the nearest integer of the expected count. **Bold** denotes the fittest chromosome.

its expected count is 0. Chromosomes that fail to pass the test (an expected count of at least 1), say N_f, will be removed from the current population. More formally the number of dropped chromosomes can be expressed as N_d = Max $\{K_0, N_f\}$ where K_0 is the minimum number that has to be dropped from one generation to the next. N_f can be found as $|\{k \in Population$ st: P[select k] $\le \gamma$, say $\gamma = 0.10\}|$, where $|E|$ denotes the cardinality of the set E.

The threshold can vary from problem to problem. For instance, parent 3 can be removed and replaced by a new one, which can be formed from the current remaining parents or simply generated completely afresh. The obtention of the new parent is generated via some operators that are described in the next subsection.

Operators

Reproduction. This is a process where certain strings (solutions) are copied fully into the next generation, usually the fittest (the best ones). To determine the fittest, the fitness value for each chromosome and the overall average are computed; a threshold level that distinguishes between the top fittest solutions and the ones that need to be dropped from the population is set. These parents are replaced by the same number of chromosomes. In our example (see Table 6.2), the third chromosome has to die away and this will be replaced by a new one. Note that the reproduction operator aims to keep a certain number of the best current chromosomes from one generation to another.

Bit Mutation. For each bit in each string a random number is generated, say α. If $\alpha \le \beta$ (fixed acceptance probability value, say $\beta = 0.005$), then the value of that bit (allele) may mutate as this will take a value of 0 or 1

TABLE 6.3
An Example of Mutation

String No.	Current Population	Random Numbers	New Bit	New Population	x	F(x)
1	0 1 1 0 1	0.62 0.56 0.23 0.45 0.20	—	0 1 1 0 1	13	169
2	1 1 0 0 0	0.17 **0.01** 0.89 0.72 0.91	0	1 0 0 0 0	16	256
3	0 1 0 0 0	0.25 0.16 0.49 **0.04** 0.36	0	0 1 0 0 0	8	64
4	0 1 0 0 0	0.31 0.59 0.12 0.39 0.66	—	0 1 0 0 0	8	64
5	1 0 0 1 1	0.27 0.75 **0.03** 0.86 0.51	1	1 0 1 1 1	27	729

Note. **Bold** represents the bits that pass the probability mutation test.

randomly. Note that the value of that bit may not necessarily change although it has passed the first probability test. If $\alpha > \beta$ this particular bit is kept unchanged and the next bit of the string is tested and the process is repeated.

According to the example given in Table 6.3, it is only three bits that have passed the first probability mutation test. Among those, the bit in the third chromosome failed to change its allele as the bit generated is the same as the existing one. The new population has a different spread of solutions. According to these results both the third and the fourth chromosomes will die away and be replaced by two other ones. The old second chromosome has lost some of its fitness, whereas the old fifth chromosome has increased its fitness by inverting the gene at loci 3 of this string from 0 to 1.

One-Point Crossover. In nature, crossover occurs when two parents exchange parts of their corresponding chromosomes. GA imitates this process very closely. The operator one-point crossover, which was initially used by John Holland, is used to swap all the alleles of two parent chromosomes located after a given selected point to obtain two children; see Fig. 6.9 for illustration.

From the example of binary coded chromosomes, it is easy to see how the children are generated. For instance, consider the following two chromosomes represented by strings of five bits and assume that the crossover

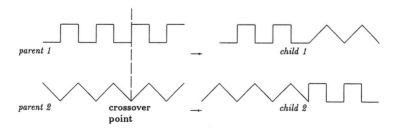

FIG. 6.9. A representation of the 1-point crossover.

$$\begin{cases} \text{parent } 1 : (0\,1\,0\,|\,0\,1) & \rightarrow \\ \text{parent } 2 : (1\,0\,1\,|\,0\,1) & \rightarrow \end{cases} \begin{cases} \text{child } 1 : (0\,1\,0\,0\,1) \\ \text{child } 2 : (1\,0\,1\,0\,1) \end{cases}$$

FIG. 6.10. A binary representation of the 1-point crossover.

point is at after the second position in the string; see Fig. 6.10. Child 1 and child 2 are different from their parents and these provide more diversification leading to new solutions.

An example where the one-point crossover operator may have no effect on the solution is shown in Fig. 6.11. Each child was found to be exactly the same as his or her parent because the genes associated with both parents after the crossover point happens to be the same. It is therefore important to have an idea on how to position the crossover point.

This process can be repeated until a suitable stopping criterion is met. The selection of parents for mating is critical to the success of GA. An entire new population can also be formed using this process as many pairs of parents can be used. Note that one parent could be selected more than once to mate with other parents.

Consider in this illustrative example, the population generated by the reproduction operator given previously as our current population. The parents to mate and their crossover points are selected randomly. The new population is shown in Table 6.4. Both parents 2 and 3 produced their associated children with better fitness values than theirs. The other parents unfortunately lost their best genes to produce less fit children. Those two less fit chromosomes will die away and will be replaced by two other ones, which are either selected randomly or copied directly from the best current chromosomes. By keeping the best fit chromosomes in the population, we are hoping to make even fitter chromosomes. This is obviously not theoretically proved; but it seems logical that if the less promising part of the choromosone (building block) is detected, replacing it by a healthier part (building block) from another chromosome may improve the current solution. The question is how to detect such a crossover point and which parent to mate with in order to yield such a successful outcome.

Inversion. This operator works on a single chromosome. It generates two positions in the string (locus) randomly or via a process, and then all the elements between those two points will have their alleles inverted (from 0 to 1 and vice versa); see the following example for illustration.

$$\begin{cases} \text{parent } 1 : (0\,1\,|\,0\,0\,1) & \rightarrow \\ \text{parent } 2 : (1\,0\,|\,1\,0\,0) & \rightarrow \end{cases} \begin{cases} \text{child } 1 : (0\,1\,1\,0\,0) \\ \text{child } 2 : (1\,0\,0\,0\,1) \end{cases}$$

FIG. 6.11. A bad positioning of the crossover point.

TABLE 6.4
An Example of the One-Point Crossover

Population After Reproduction	Mate Selected	Crossover Point	New Population	x Value	F(x)	P[select]	Expected Count
0 1 1 0 I 1	2	4	0 1 1 0 0	12	144	0.08	0.33
1 1 0 0 I 0	1	4	1 1 0 0 1	25	625	0.35	1.44
1 1 I 0 0 0	4	2	1 1 0 1 1	27	**729**	0.41	1.66
1 0 I 0 1 1	3	2	1 0 0 0 0	16	256	0.14	0.58
Sum					1754	1.00	
Average ($\bar{F}$)					439	0.25	
Maximum					729	0.41	

parent 1 : (1 0 0 1 0 0 1 1)   →   child 1 : (1 0 0 **0 1 1 0** 1)
                *   *

where "*" is the inversion points. An example of inversion is also given in Table 6.5.

Research in GA concentrates on several sensitive parts of the method, such as how to better represent a solution of a given problem, the development of new operators, and how to integrate operators with the choice of the parents for mating. For instance, Agar and Salhi (1997) have developed a scheme in which good and bad schemas are identified within a given chromosome. Such information, when used efficiently to avoid premature convergence, produced a powerful GA. For further details on these aspects, see Grefenstette (1986), Goldberg (1989), Dasgupta and McGregor (1994), Thangiah (1996), Salhi, Thangiah, and Rahman (1997), and Agar and Salhi (1997).

TABLE 6.5
An Example of Inversion

Population After Reproduction	Inversion Points (Chosen Randomly)	New Population	x Value	F(x)	P[select]	Expected Count
0 **1 1 0** 1	2 3	0 0 0 0 1	1	1	0.001	0.004
1 1 **0 0** 0	3 4	1 1 1 1 0	30	**900**	0.85	3.396
0 1 **0** 0 0	2 3	0 0 1 0 0	4	16	0.02	0.060
1 0 0 1 1	1 2	0 **1 1** 0 0	12	144	0.14	0.543
Sum				1061	1.00	
Average ($\bar{F}$)				265	0.25	
Maximum				900	0.85	

REFERENCES

Agar, M., & Salhi, S. (1997, July). *Combining genetic algorithms and lagrangian heuristics to solve location problems.* Paper presented at Euro XV/Informs XXXIV meeting, Barcelona.

Barr, W. S., Golden, B. L., Kelly, J. P., Resende, M. G. C., & Stewart, W. R. (1995). Designing and reporting on computational experiments with heuristic methods. *Journal of Heuristics, 1*, 9–32.

Battiti, R. (1996). Reactive tabu search: Toward self-tuning heuristics. In V. J. Rayward-Smith, I. H. Osman, C. R. Reeves, & G. D. Smith (Eds), *Modern heuristic search techniques* (pp. 61–83). New York: Wiley.

Battiti, R., & Tecchiolli, G. (1994). The reactive tabu search. *ORSA Journal on Computing, 6*, 126–140.

Conolly, D. T. (1990). An improved simulated annealing technique for the QAP. *European Journal of Operational Research, 46*, 93–100.

Dammeyer, F., & Voss, S. (1993). Dynamic tabu list management using the reverse elimination technique. *Annals of Operations Research, 41*, 31–46.

Dasgupta, D., & McGregor, D. R. (1994). A more biological motivated genetic algorithm: The models and some results. *Cybernetics & Systems, 25*, 447–469.

Downsland, K. A. (1993). Some experiments with simulated annealing techniques for packing problems. *European Journal of Operational Research, 68*, 389–399.

Eglese, R. (1990). Simulated annealing: A tool for operational research. *European Journal of Operational Research, 46*, 271–281.

Garey, M. R., & Johnson, D. S. (1979). *Computers and intractability: A guide to the theory of NP-completeness,* San Francisco: Freeman.

Glover, F. (1986). Future paths for integer programming and links to artificial intelligence. *Computers and Operations Research, 13*, 533–549.

Glover, F. (1989). Tabu search—Part I. *ORSA Journal on Computing, 1*, 190–206.

Glover, F. (1990). Tabu search: A tutorial. *Interfaces 20*, 74–94.

Glover, F. (1995). Tabu thresholding: Improved search for nonmonotonic trajectories. *ORSA Journal on Computing 7*, 426–442.

Glover, F., Laguna, M., Taillard, E., & de Werra, D. (Eds.) (1993). Tabu search. *Annals of Operations Research, 41.*

Goldberg, D. E. (1989). *Genetic algorithms in search, optimisation, and machine learning.* New York: Addison-Wesley.

Grefenstette, J. J. (1986). Optimization of control parameters for genetic algorithms. *IEEE Transactions on Systems, Man and Cybernetics, 16*, 122–128.

Hansen, P. (1986). *The steepest ascent, mildest descent heuristic for combinatorial programming.* Paper presented at the congress on Numerical Methods in Combinatorial Optimization, Capri, Italy.

Holland, J. H. (1975). *Adaptation in natural and artificial systems.* Ann Arbor: University of Michigan Press.

Johnson, D. S. (1996). *A theoretical guide to the experimental analysis of algorithms* (AT & T Research Report).

Kelly, J., Laguna, M., & Glover, F. (1994). A study of diversification strategies for the quadratic assignment problem. *Computers and Operations Research 21*, 665–893.

Kirkpatrick, S., Gelat, C. D., & Vecchi, M. P. (1983). Optimization by simulated annealing. *Science, 220*, 671–680.

Kruskal, J. B. (1956). On the shortest spanning subtree of a graph and the travelling salesman problem. *Proceedings of the American Mathematical Society, 7*, 48–50.

Laarhoven, P. J. M. van, & Aarts, E. H. L. (1987). *Simulated annealing: Theory and applications.* Rotterdam: Reidel.

Lundy, M., & Mees, A. (1986). Convergence of an annealing algorithm. *Mathematical Programming, 34,* 111–124.

Metropolis, N., Rosenbluth, A., Rosenbluth, M., Teller, A., & Teller, E. (1953). Equations of state calculations by fast computing machines. *Journal of Chemical Physics, 21,* 1087–1092.

Osman, I. H. (1993). Metastrategy simulated annealing and tabu search algorithms for the vehicle routing problem. *Annals of Operations Research, 41,* 421–451.

Osman, I. H., & Laporte, G. (1996). Metaheuristics: A bibliography. *Annals of Operations Research, 63,* 513–623.

Osman, I. H., & Salhi, S. (1996). Local search strategies for the vehicle fleet mix problem. In V. J. Rayward-Smith, I. H. Osman, C. R. Reeves, & G. D. Smith (Eds.), *Modern heuristic search techniques* (pp. 131–154). New York: Wiley.

Reeves, C. R. (1993). *Modern heuristic techniques for combinatorial problems.* Oxford, England: Blackwell Scientific Publications.

Salhi, S. (1994). Heuristic search methods. In *Topics in management mathematics* (pp. 135–191). Birmingham, England: University of Birmingham Press.

Salhi, S. (1997, May). *An attempt in defining tabu size and aspiration level: Application to location problems.* Paper presented at INFORMS meeting, San Diego.

Salhi, S. (1997). A perturbation heuristic for a class of location problems. *Journal of the Operational Research Society, 48,* 1233–1240.

Salhi, S., & Rand, G. K. (1987). Improvements to vehicle routing heuristics. *Journal of the Operational Research Society, 38,* 293–295.

Salhi, S., & Rand, G. K. (1993). Incorporating vehicle routing into the vehicle fleet composition problem. *European Journal of Operational Research, 66,* 313–330.

Salhi, S., & Sari, M. (1997). A multi-level composite heuristic for the multi-depot vehicle fleet mix problem. *European Journal of Operational Research, 103,* 78–95.

Salhi, S., Thangiah, S. R., & Rahman F. (1997). A genetic clustering method for the multi-depot vehicle routing problem. In G. Smith et al. (Eds.), *The Third International Conference on Artificial Neural Networks and Genetic Algorithms (ICANNGA'97).*

Skorin-Kapov, J. (1990). Tabu search applied to the quadratic assignment problem. *ORSA Journal on Computing, 2,* 33–45.

Thangiah, S. R. (1996). Genetic algorithms for vehicle routing problems with time windows. In L. Chambers (Ed.), *Applications handbook of genetic algorithms: New frontiers* (Vol 2). Florida: CRC Press.

Thomas, P., & Salhi, S. (1996). *A tabu search heuristic for the resource constrained project scheduling problem.* Working Paper. Birmingham, England: University of Birmingham.

Voss, S. (1996). Observing logical interdependencies in tabu search—Methods and results. In V. J. Rayward-Smith, I. H. Osman, C. R. Reeves, & G. D. Smith (Eds.), *Modern heuristic search techniques* (pp. 41–59). New York: Wiley.

Welch, S., & Salhi, S. (1997). The obnoxious p facility network location problem with facility interaction. *European Journal of Operational Research, 102,* 302–319.

Factor Analysis: Exploratory and Confirmatory Approaches

Ronald H. Heck

University of Hawaii at Manoa

Researchers are often concerned with identifying constructs and investigating relationships among them. Constructs are theoretical concepts or abstractions that help us explain and organize our environment (National Council on Measurement, 1984; Pedhazur & Schmelkin, 1991). They are frequently mentioned in the literature in discussions about intelligence or anxiety, people's attitudes toward political and religious issues, consumers' buying habits, and the assessment of learning. Because constructs are theoretical abstractions, they cannot be directly observed. Instead, they must be indirectly defined through their observed manifestations. For example, a researcher might be interested in studying test anxiety. Although test anxiety itself cannot be observed, it might be hypothesized that indicators of it are nail biting, trembling hands, inability to concentrate on the test, or other such physical or psychological symptoms.

Because many social and behavioral phenomena are conceived as structural processes operating among unobserved (latent) constructs, factor analy - sis (FA) is often a useful method for investigating these relationships because it provides a model that links the observations or manifestations of the processes to the theories and constructs through which we interpret and understand them (Ecob & Cuttance, 1987). More specifically, FA is an analytic technique used to express latent variables through defining and measuring their observed indicators. After these relationships are established, it is possible to investigate relationships among the underlying variables (called factors) further, or to examine the relationships between the set of factors and other processes the researcher may be interested in studying.

In general, there are two basic approaches to the investigation of under-lying factors: the exploratory approach and the confirmatory approach. The exploratory approach is useful when the researcher's intent is to identify a set of latent factors that may be responsible for relationships (i.e., correlations or covariances) among a set of observed variables. In this manner, the structure of the data is simplified by exploring which subsets of observed variables may be grouped together by a common, underlying factor. In contrast, when a researcher already has a specific theoretical model in mind and can specify the relationships among the underlying factors and their observed indicators beforehand, he or she can then attempt to "confirm" its existence with the data by using confirmatory FA.

The intent of this chapter is to provide an overview that contrasts these two factor-analytic approaches as means of identifying or confirming (i.e., validating) a set of constructs that represent a theoretical model. More spe-cifically, the purposes are to describe the exploratory and confirmatory ap-proaches for doing factor analysis in some detail, and to contrast the two approaches by presenting an exploratory factor-analytic study to develop a theoretical model and then testing its validity and generalizability with con-firmatory FA within single and multigroup samples.

AN OVERVIEW OF FACTOR ANALYSIS

FA begins when a researcher believes that a larger set of observed variables may be related to one or more underlying variables. These underlying factors are hypothesized to be responsible for the specific pattern of correlations (or covariances) present among the observed variables. Both exploratory and confirmatory FA attempt to reproduce the set of either correlations or covariances present in the original data by clustering subsets of the observed variables with a relatively small set of underlying factors. Through this new system of relations, the dimensionality of the original data is simplified, and the set of theoretical relations may be discovered (or confirmed) that ac-counts for the patterns in the data.

Perhaps the most basic difference in the two approaches is that in ex-ploratory FA one generally begins with the pattern of correlations present in the data and seeks to discover the number of underlying factors that need to be retained in order to reproduce this observed correlation matrix, using a variety of criteria to help in this judgment. In this process, the researcher can also determine which subsets of observed variables are related to which underlying factors by observing how strongly each observed variable "loads" on, or is related to, each underlying factor. In the exploratory approach, therefore, the structure of the factor model is discovered from the structure of the data.

An example may help illustrate this point. A researcher may have six items from a questionnaire that he or she wants to group together in some fashion in order to create more valid and reliable constructs. The researcher believes there is some underlying set of theoretical relations present, but is unsure how many factors would be needed to adequately reproduce the intercorrelations among these six variables. The observed variables may result from two factors, possibly three factors, or maybe only one general factor. Moreover, the researcher does not know whether the factors are well measured by these indicators and, additionally, whether the factors may be correlated with each other. When the relationships among observed indicators and underlying factors are not well known (e.g., when the theory is not well explicated), the analysis is said to exploratory because the researcher must make certain assumptions in attempting to define the relationships between observed variables and the factors, the intercorrelations among factors, and the relationships among observed variables, factors, and measurement errors.

The assumptions considerably restrict the flexibility the researcher has in defining a theoretical model. They do, however, aid in helping to discover a preliminary underlying factor structure. More specifically, the assumptions of the exploratory approach are that all observed variables must be directly affected by all common factors (i.e., load on all factors), that all common factors are either correlated or not correlated at all, and that all factors are uncorrelated with all error terms. Because the exploratory factor model is able to incorporate only a few theoretical constraints into the development of a final substantive model (e.g., the number of factors to be retained and whether or not they are to be intercorrelated), it is most appropriately used in new research where little is known about the structure of underlying constructs, and the goal is to decide how many factors exist in a set of theoretical relations.

The limitations of exploratory FA, however, have now been largely overcome by the development of the confirmatory factor model (e.g., Jöreskog, 1970, 1971). Whereas in exploratory FA mathematical criteria based on the previously outlined assumptions are used to create factor models from the data, confirmatory FA allows the researcher to develop factor models that are more closely related to existing theories because they must be specified before being actually tested with the data. Returning to our discussion about test anxiety and questionnaire items, a researcher may have a particular model in mind that represents a set of theoretical relations developed from previous research. The researcher might believe that three items from the questionnaire represent manifestations of test anxiety. The other three items may represent measures of performance.

After specifying the set of relationships in the model (i.e., two underlying factors, each with three observed indicators, a correlation between the two factors), it can be tested against the actual data. If the model fits the data well (i.e., it reproduces the observed variation present among the variables), the researcher has preliminary evidence of its adequacy in representing a set of theoretical relations. This process is referred to as confirming a model's structure and is one means of establishing the construct validity of a proposed model. Construct validity concerns inferences that can be made about underlying variables through measuring observed indicators of them. It occurs "when one evaluates a test or other set of operations in light of the specified construct" (National Council on Measurement, 1984, p. 23). Construct validation takes place when an investigator believes that his or her instrument reflects a particular construct, to which are attached certain meanings. The proposed interpretation generates specific testable hypotheses (e.g., about relations among constructs), which are a means of confirming or disconfirming the claim (Cronbach & Meehl, 1955).

In the confirmatory factor-analytic approach to construct validation, the researcher imposes theoretically motivated constraints on the specification of the underlying dimensions in a proposed model. These constraints determine before the model is tested which factors will be correlated (and which ones may be uncorrelated), which observed variables are affected by which factors, and whether the unique factors (error terms) should be correlated. The researcher therefore has tremendous control over the specification of the exact theoretical model to be tested. Statistical tests can then be performed to determine if the sample data confirm the hypothesized factor model.

Because these theoretical constraints are delineated prior to testing the model, the procedure is thought of as confirmatory. In practice, the researcher may not have only one model in mind, but rather, a series of competing models. The confirmatory approach allows the researcher to test each model to find the one that most closely corresponds to the patterns in the data. In addition, by relaxing constraints one at a time, one may find the best-fitting model to describe the data through a specification search (e.g., allowing a variable that was specified to load on only one factor to load on another also). By relaxing all of the constraints on the parameters in the model (e.g., allowing all items to load on all factors), the researcher would be performing an exploratory FA.

After determining that a model represents the data reasonably well, an examination of the factor loadings, factor intercorrelations, and unique factors enables the researcher to identify and then label the underlying variables that explain the observed covariances (or correlations) in the data. Because of the emphasis on theory inherent in this approach, it is important to work with clear definitions about constructs, using previous research and theoretical models as guides in defining the constructs. In operationalizing constructs, however, it is important to keep in mind that the observed indicators are not the construct itself, but only a set of possible manifestations of it.

Once a model's preliminary construct validity has been established in one sample, the researcher could also investigate whether the same model fits across different subgroups (e.g., age, ethnicity, gender), samples, or settings. This process is referred to in the literature as testing a model's generalizability and is a second way of investigating its construct validity. Testing the gneralizability of a model helps extend the usefulness of a theory by confirming and, if necessary, modifying a set of proposed relationships in a variety of different settings and groups.

EXPLORATORY FACTOR ANALYSIS

In this section, a general introduction to conducting exploratory factor analysis (EFA) is presented. The literature on EFA is vast, contrasting, often complex, with a lack of uniformity in terminology and notation (Pedhauzer & Schmelkin, 1991). The introduction is not formal; rather, it focuses on presenting some of the basic concepts in the process through means of an actual example. As suggested previously, where little is known about the underlying structure of the data, conducting an EFA may be an important first step in identifying a set of underlying relationships. The major goal of an EFA is to extract the minimum number of factors needed to reproduce the variation present in a set of observed variables. The factors are viewed as a set of independent, underlying variables that are responsible for the correlations among a set of observed indicators (the dependent variables). The procedure implies that there is some set of theoretical relations present in the data that may be uncovered. In the process of identifying the patterns present in the data, its structure is simplified. This does not mean, however, that the technique should be applied without any regard to theory, hoping that something meaningful will result (Pedhazur & Schmelkin, 1991).

Generally, one should have at least a basic plan in mind before applying FA. For example, items from a section in a questionnaire involving anxiety and performance could be subjected to an EFA because there is some expected belief that the items will reflect the structure. It is important to emphasize, however, that one would not simply factor analyze the whole questionnaire at once to see what "fell out."

EFA simplifies the structure of the data by grouping together observed variables that are intercorrelated under one "common" factor. Of course, the clearest solution would be if all the observed variables reduced to one factor. In most applications, however, this is unlikely. By eyeballing a correlation matrix, often one can partially determine a common factor structure by seeing what observed variables clump together as one possible factor (due to their stronger intercorrelations) and which ones may form another factor.

Some basic discussion of matrices is necessary in developing an understanding of the FA procedures. A matrix is a two-dimensional (rows × columns) representation of correlations (or covariances) among a set of observed variables. Several types of matrices are referred to in conducting an FA. EFA generally proceeds from a correlation matrix summarizing relationships between pairs of observed variables. The observed correlation matrix (R) is called a square matrix (i.e., having same number of rows and columns) that is also symmetric, because each row in the matrix has a corresponding column.

The correlation matrix in Table 7.1 consists of 10 questionnaire items regarding administrators' perceptions about work issues. This data set is used in the discussion of EFA. Note that the diagonals of the correlation matrix contain ones (1.0). Because correlations are standardized with mean of 0 and standard deviation of 1, the ones in the diagonals represent the variance of each variable (or correlation with itself). Off-diagonal elements are the correlations between pairs of observed variables. Because R matrices are square and symmetric, the correlations above the diagonals are redundant; therefore, usually only the lower (or upper) triangle is presented in a table.

In contrast to the observed R matrix, the "reduced" correlation matrix is produced from the factors. This matrix is generated from how well the observed variables are related to the set of factors. The more the factors influence the observed variables, the better this matrix will be reproduced. The aim of the FA is to generate the correlations in this reproduced matrix adequately with as few factors as possible. The "residual" correlation matrix is the difference in fit between the observed and reproduced correlation matrices. In a good FA, the residual, or error, matrix should be small. Thus, the reproduced matrix results from decomposing the original correlation matrix into two other matrices: a matrix of factor loadings (called a factor pattern matrix) and a matrix of errors.

If the reader studies the matrix in Table 7.1 a bit more closely, he or she will notice that the correlations among gender discrimination (SEXDIS), ethnic discrimination ETHDIS), and age discrimination (AGEDIS) are fairly strong, ranging from .64 to .82. Similarly, their relationships with the other variables in the matrix are relatively weak. This pattern of interrelationships may suggest that these three observed variables result from an underlying "discrimination" factor.

Let us suppose that this underlying factor were responsible for the observed correlations among SEXDIS (called x_1), ETHDIS (x_2), and AGEDIS (x_3). If these variables were measured without error, the factor would perfectly account for the observed interrelationships among x_1, x_2, and x_3 seen in the R matrix (Table 7.1). In most settings, however, these observed variables usually will not be measured without error, so there is some amount of error present in each one. We refer to the error component as a unique factor, whereas the construct is the common factor. Visually, these relationships can be summarized in Fig. 7.1.

TABLE 7.1
Correlation Matrix

	AGEDISC	ETHDISC	EXCAND	HIRE	PERCRIT	PROACT	PROMO	RESOURCE	SEXDISC	STAFF
AGEDISC	1.00									
ETHDISC	.64	1.00								
EXCAND	.07	.09	1.00							
HIRE	-.03	.02	.59	1.00						
PERCRIT	-.25	-.17	.36	.56	1.00					
PROACT	-.19	-.16	.26	.41	.56	1.00				
PROMO	-.32	-.27	.25	.48	.70	.62	1.00			
RESOURCE	-.11	-.13	.23	.31	.39	.41	.44	1.00		
SEXDISC	.68	.82	.08	-.04	-.22	-.18	-.34	-.18	1.00	
STAFF	.32	.29	.23	.17	.02	.00	-.07	.05	.31	1.00

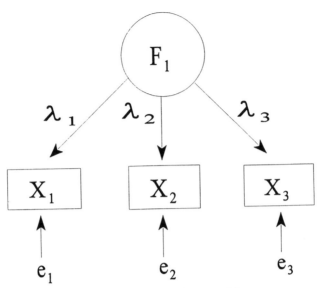

FIG. 7.1. Exploratory factor model.

A visual diagram provides a nice representation of what can be a fairly complex set of algebraic equations by the time all factors and observed indicators in a model are considered. For example, mathematically, these relationships implied in the figure are represented in the following three equations:

$$x_1 = \lambda_1 F_1 + e_1$$
$$x_2 = \lambda_2 F_1 + e_2$$
$$x_3 = \lambda_3 F_1 + e_3.$$

Each lambda (λ) represents the loading for each observed variable on the factor. In matrix form, this would be written as $x = \lambda f + e$, called the factor equation, which can be written out in matrix form like this:

$$\begin{bmatrix} x_1 \\ x_2 \\ x_3 \end{bmatrix} = \begin{bmatrix} \lambda_1 \\ \lambda_2 \\ \lambda_3 \end{bmatrix} F_1 + \begin{bmatrix} E_1 \\ E_2 \\ E_3 \end{bmatrix}.$$

Note that this notation implies no correlation between the factor and errors of measurement and no correlation among the various errors associated with each observed variable (Marcoulides & Hershberger, 1997). Given these assumptions, the variance-covariance matrix of observed variables is represented by

$$\Sigma = XX' = \begin{bmatrix} \sigma^2_{x1} & & \\ \sigma_{x2x1} & \sigma^2_{x2} & \\ \sigma_{x3x1} & \sigma_{x3x2} & \sigma^2_{x3} \end{bmatrix}.$$

which can be expressed as

$$\Sigma = XX' = (\lambda f + e)(\lambda f + e)' = \Lambda \Phi \Lambda' + \Theta$$

where Λ refers to a matrix of factor loadings, Φ represents the variance and covariances (e.g., correlation) among common factors, and Θ refers to a matrix of the variances and covariances among the unique factors (or errors). Λ' represents the transpose of the Λ matrix.

If the factors are assumed to be uncorrelated (i.e., orthogonal), the off-diagonal elements of the matrix Φ would be restricted to zeros (i.e., $\Phi =$ an identity matrix). For orthogonal factors, the expression reduces to

$$\Sigma = \Lambda \Lambda' + \Theta.$$

Because a correlation matrix is usually used, the observed variables are standardized before the FA is conducted. When the observed variables are standardized, the decomposition of the variance-covariance matrix Σ can be written as a decomposition of a correlation matrix R:

$$R = ZZ' = \Lambda \; \Phi \; \Lambda' + \Theta.$$

With uncorrelated factors, this would be written as

$$R = \Lambda \Lambda' + \Theta.$$

It is important to understand these mathematical representations with respect to the goal of FA. The left side of the equation contains a matrix of observed variances and covariances among observed variables (e.g., in this case a set of correlations). The observed R matrix is then decomposed into the matrices on the right side of the equation. These matrices contain a set of possible factor loadings (Λ), a matrix of variances and covariances among factors (Φ) if they are assumed to be correlated, and a matrix of unique factors (Θ).

If the observed variables could be measured without error, the correlation matrix R could be perfectly reproduced ($R = \Lambda \Lambda'$). To do so, however, would generally require the factor-loading matrix to be the same size as R (i.e., containing as many common factors as observed variables). Because we expect errors in the measurement of the observed variables, however, we must also take the error matrix (Θ) into consideration. Because of the assumption of no correlations among unique factors required in EFA, the Θ

matrix is a diagonal matrix containing values that when added to the diagonal values in the ($\Lambda\Lambda'$) product matrix will always sum to 1 (i.e., the diagonals in the R matrix).

Eigenvalues and Eigenvectors

Because FA involves the decomposition and transformation of a correlation or covariance matrix, some discussion of the mathematical means through which this is accomplished is helpful in interpreting the computer output generated. The eigenequation is the primary mathematical tool through which matrix decomposition is accomplished (Kim & Mueller, 1978). In solving this equation, a correlation matrix R (or a variance-covariance matrix) is decomposed into a matrix product consisting of diagonal matrix of its characteristic roots (called eigenvalues) and a square matrix consisting of corresponding eigenvectors. An eigenvalue may be defined as the sum of the squared loadings of the indicators on the factor with which the eigenvalue is associated. The factor loadings (λs) of observed variables in the factor pattern matrix are then obtained via the eigenvalues and eigenvectors of the reduced correlation matrix through matrix multiplication (Loehlin, 1992).

In FA, therefore, the variance in the correlation matrix is condensed into eigenvalues and their corresponding eigenvectors. Although the calculation of eigenvalues and eigenvectors is best left to computers, they are useful in determining how much common variance is accounted for by the factor solution.[1] Because the sum of the eigenvalues is always equal to the number of observed variables in the correlation matrix, summing the eigenvalues of the factors retained gives the proportion of common variance accounted for by the factor solution. The factors with the largest eigenvalues contain the most common variance among the observed indicators; those with small or negative eigenvalues are then dropped from the factor solution.

Extracting Factors

There are several methods available for extracting the number of factors needed to reproduce the correlation matrix. These include principal axis factoring, maximum likelihood, alpha, image, and unweighted least squares, to name a few (see Kim & Mueller, 1978; Loehlin, 1992, for more detailed explanations of each method). One should not necessarily count on the default methods of extraction available in different computer programs. For example, the default method in SPSS is principal components analysis, which is generally not viewed as an appropriate technique for investigating under-

---

[1]A formal discussion of how eigenvalues and eigenvectors are calculated is outside the scope of this chapter, as it relies on considerable matrix algebra. See Loehlin (1992) or Marcoulides and Hershberger (1997) for further discussion.

lying theoretical structures. Although principal axis factoring has been the most widely used method in the past, maximum likelihood (ML) estimation has a number of desirable features that make it the currently preferred method for conducting both exploratory and confirmatory FAs.

The ML method attempts to find the most likely population parameter estimates that produced the observed correlation matrix, assuming that the observed correlation matrix is from a sample drawn from a multivariate normal population (see Lawley & Maxwell, 1963). The problem of estimation involves finding parameter values (i.e., factor loadings, factor intercorrelations, and unique factors) such that the predicted correlation matrix is as close as possible to the observed correlations contained in the R matrix (see Long, 1983, for further discussion of this issue).

As has been suggested exploratory factor analytic approaches attempt to account for the common variance, or variance that is shared among a set of observed variables. In actuality, we do not know ahead of performing the analysis how much of a variable's variance is shared (referred to as its communality) with other variables in the correlation matrix and how much of the variance is unique. Factor extraction begins with making some initial estimates of each variable's communality and uniqueness. In the ML approach, an adjusted R matrix is used. This matrix is readjusted at every iteration by assigning greater weight to variables with greater communality (or less error variance). In most circumstances, eventually a solution is reached that represents the required number of factors necessary to reproduce the correlation matrix and corresponding optimal parameter estimates (i.e., factor loadings, errors, factor intercorrelations). It should be noted that sometimes a considerable number of iterations is required to reach a satisfactory solution, and under some circumstances, the program will fail to converge on a solution.

How Well Does the Model Fit?

We can determine whether the optimal number of factors has been retained in the exploratory factor solution in several ways. Any one criterion is unlikely to be sufficient in deciding upon a solution, so it is recommended that the analyst look at several criteria. First, one can examine the proportion of variance contributed by each factor and the set of factors as a group. Although we know that all variables together would account for 100% of the common variance, the goal is to account for as much of the common variance as possible with the fewest number of factors. For practical purposes, if the factors account for 80% of the variance, the rest is meaningless. Most solutions do not account for this much variance, however (50% to 80% is probably more reasonable).

Second, we use the Kaiser–Eigenvalue Criterion, which involves retaining factors whose eigenvalues of the correlation matrix are greater than one

(1.0). Eigenvalues represent variance, and because the variance of each standardized variable in the correlation matrix is one, a quick estimate is to retain that number of factors, because they would be more important than a single observed variable (Tabachnick & Fidell, 1996). Used alone, this criterion may over- or underestimate the number of factors, however, especially because the ones in the diagonals of the correlation matrix are initially replaced by estimates of each indicator's communality (which is expected to be less than one because the uniqueness has been removed). This could result in eliminating a factor that is potentially important, because its eigenvalue falls below 1.0 (which is the default in the SPSS program).

Third, we can use Cattell's (1966) scree test, which is a visual representation of descending eigenvalues (or variance accounted for) associated with each factor. When the descending eigenvalues reach a horizontal line, those factors would not account for further meaningful variance. Metaphorically, they are considered as rubble or "scree" at the bottom of the mountain. Sometimes, the eigenvalues will level off at 1.0, which is consistent with the Kaiser–Eigenvalue criterion, but there could be occasions where they level off somewhat below that point. The scree test, therefore, might show a factor that would have be eliminated using the Kaiser–Eigenvalue criterion.

For most methods of factor extraction, the analyst is limited to these three previously mentioned criteria. However, one of the desirable properties of the ML approach is that there is a chi-square test of the number of factors retained in the model. The larger the value of chi-square, the more the number of factors retained in the solution disagrees with an ideal model (e.g., models with probability values < .05 are generally rejected as ill-fitting). Because chi-square values are related to sample size, however, with larger data sets, good models could be rejected as ill-fitting if this criterion is used alone. Another factor would then be extracted based on this statistical criterion, which might be unnecessary by several of the other criteria.

Ultimately, after considering all of these practical and statistical criteria, one should remember that a good solution "makes sense" in that it appears to fit what is known about the phenomenon being studied. This is related to the construct validity of the model. For example, the "right" items appear to load highly on the right factor, and not very well on the other factors. That is why it is important to remember that theory should be a guide, even when performing EFA. In this manner, we can avoid the criticism that this method is sometimes referred to as "garbage in, and garbage out."

Example Output

To demonstrate how to conduct an EFA, we use data from an investigation of a number of work-related issues believed to affect college administrators' morale. There were 850 midlevel administrators in the data set. Because of the size of the data set, the sample was randomly split into smaller subsamples in order to run additional "confirming" tests after the preliminary model has been developed through EFA. For the initial EFA, 335 subjects were chosen. Other subsets of the remaining 500 or so subjects are used in the second part of the chapter to demonstrate the use of confirmatory FA.

As suggested earlier, 10 items from the larger study were selected for purposes of the presentation (see Table 7.1). Although it is ideal to have interval data in developing factor models, the reality is that in the social sciences researchers are often dealing with ordinal scales (e.g., people's attitudes, beliefs, preferences). There is an extensive literature on the analysis of ordinal data. Researchers differ as to the exact number of points on a scale that are optimal in these analyses, but 5-point scales are often seen as sufficient to conduct analyses using ML (Boomsma, 1987). Suffice it to say that where there are a greater number of points on a scale, ordinal data begin to behave very similarly to interval data.

ML estimation methods have been shown to be robust to mild to moderate departures from normality in generating appropriate factor solutions (e.g., Boomsma, 1987). As Jöreskog and Sörbom (1993) suggested, there are also a variety of transformations that can be used to condition the set of ordinal variables differently (e.g., replacing the correlation matrix with correlations based on optimal scores for each pair, or using a matrix of polychoric correlations). There are also other methods of estimation that may be appropriately applied to ordinal measures (i.e., weighted least squares).

The following EFAs were conducted using SPSS for Windows, Version 6.1 (see Appendix for the SPSS syntax needed to conduct the analysis). Because EFA generally proceeds from a correlation matrix, the interested reader can reproduce this analysis by entering the correlation matrix in Table 7.1 as input for the FA in any of several possible computer programs. Slight discrepancies might result, however, in developing solutions across computer routines or between analyses run with raw data versus those conducted using correlation matrices (e.g., coefficients in the correlation matrix often have been rounded off).

Table 7.2 presents the descriptive information on the items that are used in the FA. As can be seen, the items are all within normal limits, with skewness ranging from −.44 to .30 and kurtosis ranging from −1.48 to −.13. Under conditions of mild skewness (+1 to −1) or kurtosis (+2 to −2), researchers have held that factor models may be developed appropriately with ordinal measures (e.g., Boomsma, 1987). Given the information presented in Table 7.1, all of the observed variables were judged to be within normal limits so that the FA could proceed.

Besides a statistical test of fit, another point to keep in mind is that ML estimation can be used in both EFAs and confirmatory factor analyses (CFAs). Previously, one of the problems with developing factor models through EFA

TABLE 7.2
Skewness and Kurtosis of Observed Variables

Variable	Skewness	Kurtosis
ETHDIS	.30	−.46
SEXDIS	.26	−.49
AGEDIS	.06	−.34
PROMO	.03	−1.48
PERCRIT	−.23	−.81
PROACT	−.44	−.75
RESOURCE	−.07	−1.02
HIRE	−.10	−.63
EXCAND	−.16	−.13
STAFF	.08	−.39

and then attempting to confirm them with CFA has been that different methods of extraction were used in each type of analysis (e.g., principal axis factoring with EFA and ML with CFA). Because it is one method of estimation commonly used in both approaches, ML was used in the present analysis to show how similar results (i.e., confirmation) can be achieved through using both the exploratory and confirmatory approaches as a means of developing and testing theory.

Communalities and Factor Pattern Matrix

In Table 7.3 the initial and final estimates of the communalities are presented. We can compute the proportion of the variance for each observed variable explained by the three-factor model. This is referred to as its communality. Notice, that there is a set of initial communality estimates used in extracting the number of factors and there is a set of final estimates. As suggested previously, the initial communality estimates are placed in the diagonals of the adjusted R matrix and reestimated each time the computer program iterates to find a solution that results in the best reproduced correlation matrix. These two sets of communalities are different, because all of the common variance is not explained when only a smaller set of factors (e.g., 3) is retained.

Table 7.4 summarizes the relationships among the factors and their observed indicators. The coefficients may be considered as standardized regression coefficients. We can immediately see that some variables are well defined with a factor (SEXDIS, AGEDIS, ETHDIS with Factor 1). For some variables, however, the relationships are not as clear. For example, EXCAND appears to load on Factor 2 (.58) and Factor 3 (.49). HIRE has the same problem. It is important to note that this initial factor matrix is unrotated. Later, we rotate the matrix to improve our ability to interpret the loadings, that is, to maximize the high loading of each observed variable on one factor and minimize the loadings on the other factors.

TABLE 7.3
Communalities and Eigenvalues

Variable	Initial Statistics		Final Statistics		Pct.of Var.	Cum. Pct.
	Communality	Eigenvalue	Communality	Eigenvalue		
ETHDIS	.68899	3.58549	.77412			
SEXDISC	.72634	2.48018	.87006			
AGEDIS	.51278	.88743	.54618			
HIRE	.51562	.77785	.67328			
PERCRIT	.57959	.64793	.65957			
PROACT	.43913	.45401	.49721			
PROMO	.61682	.38332	.79305			
EXCAND	.37925	.33846	.57686			
RESOURCE	.24885	.27477	.25606			
STAFF	.17107	.17056	.18801			
Factor 1				3.81328	38.1	38.1
Factor 2				2.30571	23.1	53.2
Factor 3				.51541	5.2	58.3

Note. Determinant of correlation matrix = .0109792.

The overall goodness of fit of the model should also be considered. Several criteria can be used in determining the model's fit. From Table 7.3, one can see that the three factors account for about 58% of the common variance among the observed variables. Similarly, the final estimates of the communalities and their respective factor loadings may also be considered as evidence about how well the observed variables measure the factors. Higher communalities estimates and high loadings concentrated on one factor (as opposed to spread across all factors) suggest stronger measures of the factors. Looking

TABLE 7.4
Unrotated Factor Matrix

	Factor 1	Factor 2	Factor 3
SEXDISC	.86	.34	−.08
ETHDISC	.79	.37	−.08
AGEDISC	.70	.23	.03
HIRE	−.28	.69	.33
PROMO	−.51	.56	−.27
PERCRIT	−.44	.62	−.08
EXCAND	−.09	.58	.49
PROACT	−.44	.52	−.18
RESOURCE	−.34	.37	−.06
STAFF	.27	.28	.19

Note. ML required five iterations. Test of fit of the three-factor model: Chi-square = 18.3078, $df = 18$, $p = .4356$.

at SEXDIS, for example, its final communality estimate (.87006) is calculated by summing the squares of its loading on the three factors.

$$(.86)^2 + (.34)^2 + (-.08)^2 = .87 \text{ (with rounding)}.$$

The adequacy of the model can also be determined by examining the scree plot in Fig. 7.2. After three factors are retained, the eigenvalues of the rest of the factors attain almost a horizontal line (scree). Therefore, these additional factors would add little to the model.

The chi-square statistic is another important measure of the model's fit. For this solution, the chi-square value 18.31 (with 18 degrees of freedom), and the significance level is above .05. The insignificant chi-square statistic suggests that retaining three factors will adequately reproduce the observed correlation matrix.

We can also assess the adequacy of the factor model by looking at the reproduced correlation matrix in Table 7.5 and comparing it to the observed correlation matrix (see Table 7.1). For example, the observed correlation between ETHDIS and AGEDIS in Table 7.1 is .64 (rounded) and the reproduced correlation in Table 7.5 it is .63976.

After considering all of the available criteria, the three-factor model can be viewed as an adequate representation of the data on administrative work life. Moreover, substantively, the factor solution appears to make sense. For example, the observed indicators SEXDIS, ETHDIS, and AGEDIS appear to

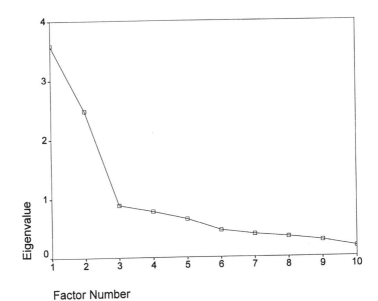

FIG. 7.2. Factor scree plot.

TABLE 7.5
Reproduced Correlation Matrix

	AGEDISC	ETHDISC	EXCAND	HIRE	PERCRIT
ETHDISC	.63976	.77412*	−.00904	.01175	−.00049
EXCAND	.07746	.09904	.57686*	.00103	−.00694
HIRE	−.03024	.00825	.58897	.67328*	.01026
PERCRIT	−.22173	−.16951	.36694	.54974	.65957*
PROACT	−.19606	−.14109	.25058	.42267	.56506
PROMO	−.32630	−.27363	.25180	.47855	.69941
RESOURCE	−.15854	−.13029	.21608	.33260	.41021
SEXDISC	.68273	.81903	.07370	−.03413	−.22610
STAFF	.25972	.30424	.22743	.18150	.01924

	PROACT	PROMO	RESOURCE	SEXDISC	STAFF
AGEDISC	.00606	.00630	.04854	−.00273	.06028
ETHDISC	−.01891	.00363	.00029	.00097	−.01424
EXCAND	.00942	−.00180	.01392	.00630	.00257
HIRE	−.01267	.00145	−.02260	−.00587	−.01150
PERCRIT	−.00506	.00059	−.02021	.00610	.00076
PROACT	.49721*	−.00135	.05759	.00901	.00898
PROMO	.62135	.79305*	−.00012	−.00313	−.00350
RESOURCE	.35241	.44012	.25606*	−.01352	.05088
SEXDISC	−.18901	−.33687	−.16648	.87006*	−.00465
STAFF	−.00898	−.06650	−.00088	.31465	.18801*

Note. The lower left triangle contains the reproduced correlation matrix. The diagonal contains reproduced communalities. The upper right triangle contains residuals between the observed correlations and the reproduced correlations. There are three (6.0%) residuals (above diagonal) with absolute values > 0.05.

result from a more general "Discrimination" factor (Factor 1). PROMO (opportunities for promotion), PROACT (support for professional activities), PERCRIT (clear performance expectations and criteria), and RESOURCE (resource support for unit) appear to result from a "Professional Support" factor (Factor 2). HIRE (beliefs about hiring), EXCAND (preference for hiring external candidates), and STAFF (staffing needs) could comprise a "Hiring Practices" factor (Factor 3).

Methods of Rotation

Although we can see an initial pattern in the data from the various factor loadings in Table 7.4, some variables are not yet clearly defined as belonging with one underlying factor. We may be able to clean up the solution some, making the interpretation of the factor structure a bit easier. Some of these problems can be shown visually by plotting the factor loadings along a set of axes representing the factors. Because our solution would require three

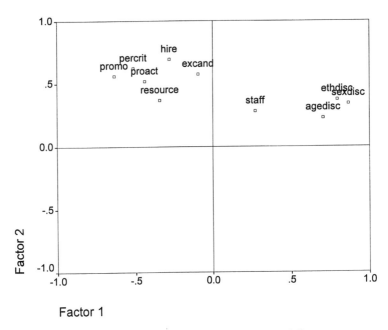

FIG. 7.3. Unrotated factor plot (Factors 1 and 2).

dimensions to represent all three factors simultaneously, to make this easier to visualize, in Fig. 7.3 we only plot the loadings on only the first two factors (Factor 1 and Factor 2).

We can easily identify the cluster of variables representing discrimination (e.g., SEXDIS, ETHDIS, AGEDIS). These all loaded highly on Factor 1. Notice, however, that they are not right on the axis for Factor 1. Instead, they are all a bit off the center of the axis, suggesting that they also load somewhat on Factor 2. Similarly, it appears that some of the other items are even more split between the two axes. They appear to load positively on Factor 2 and negatively on the other factor. In looking back at Table 7.4, for example, one can see that PROMO loads positively on Factor 2 (.56) and negatively on Factor 1 (−.51).

Through rotation, we would like to get items to be identified more strongly with one or the other factor, that is, to cluster them with higher loadings on either axis. Once that is accomplished, the solution should be easier to interpret, and the data's simplified structure will be determined. It is important to note that rotation will not change this set of relationships mathematically—only visually, by rotating the axes through the clusters of variables. The unrotated factor loading matrix is simply multiplied by a transformation matrix to reproduce the rotated loading matrix (Tabachnick & Fidell, 1996).

There are three basic approaches to rotation including (a) graphic, which is difficult to apply when clustering of variables is unclear or there are more that two factors (Kim & Mueller, 1978), (b) analytic, which consists of orthogonal and oblique schemes, and (c) rotation to a target matrix, where the researcher has a pattern of relationships already in mind. All three attempt to yield a simple structure that increases ease of interpretation. Due to space restrictions, we concentrate on analytic rotation, as it is the most widely used method. For the interested reader, however, discussions of the other methods may be found in Kim and Mueller (1978) or Marcoulides and Hershberger (1997).

Orthogonal Rotation

The axes for Factor 1 and Factor 2 presented in Fig. 7.3 can be thought of as representing uncorrelated factors (i.e., they are separated by 90°). The goal of orthogonal rotation is to maintain the 90° of separation between the clusters of variables but to get each set of variables clustered on an axis. This tends to maximize their loadings on one factor and minimize their loading on the other factor or factors. For orthogonal rotations, therefore, the factor correlation matrix is defined as an identity matrix (i.e., with ones in the diagonals and zeros off the diagonals, indicating no correlations among factors).

Because of the assumption of uncorrelated factors, orthogonal rotation has often been criticized, as it is unlikely that factors in the real world would be completely uncorrelated. Orthogonal rotation can be applied inappropriately in many EFA applications—especially where correlations among factors are likely to exist. In spite of this potential limitation, this approach has the appeal of simplicity, provided that the correlations among factors are indeed low or nonexistent in the data set.

The most commonly used rotation scheme for orthogonal factors is Varimax, which attempts to minimize the number of variables that have high loadings on one factor. This is accomplished by developing high loadings for some indicators on a particular factor (e.g., .8 or .9) and minimizing their loadings on all the other factors (e.g., .0 or .1). With Varimax rotation, the goal is to extract a few factors that maximize common variance, as opposed to one general factor. In accomplishing this, the variance tends to be reapportioned among the factors, so that they become more equal in importance (Tabachnick & Fidell, 1996).

Other schemes include Quartimax, which emphasizes the simple interpretation of variables by limiting the number of factors needed to explain a variable. In contrast to Varimax, therefore, Quartimax rotation often results in a general factor with moderate to high loadings, which would be problematic in situations where the researcher hopes for a two- or three-factor solution. The researcher should not use Varimax, therefore, when a general factor (e.g., like a scale) is being developed. Another is rotation scheme is

Equamax, which is a combination of Varimax (simplifying factors) and Quartimax (simplifying variables).

Rotation does not affect the final communality estimates of the observed variables. Because the factors themselves are by definition not correlated, the communality of a variable is simply the sum of its squared loadings on all the factors. This can be seen examining the rotated factor matrix in Table 7.6 to calculate the final communalities presented previously in Table 7.3. For example, examining the first item (SEXDIS), we can see that it now loads .92 on Factor 2, −.16 on Factor 1, and .02 on Factor 3. The reader can compare these slightly different loadings with the ones in the unrotated factor matrix in Table 7.4. The final communality for SEXDIS is still calculated by summing the squares of its loadings, which produces the final communality estimate of .87 (with rounding) printed in Table 7.3. The reader may also notice that through rotation, the items comprising the discrimination factor are now on the y-axis (Factor 2), as opposed to the x-axis (Factor 1) in the unrotated solution. This reconfiguration makes no difference in the interpretation of the solution.

One can see the suitability of this rotated solution by looking at a graph of the results in Fig. 7.4 and comparing it with the unrotated solution in Fig. 7.3. After rotation, the three indicators of discrimination still load very strongly on Factor 2. Notice that through rotation PROMO, PROACT, PERCRIT, and RESOURCE now have higher loadings on Factor 1 and have moved much closer to the axis. Their negative loadings on the other factor have been considerably reduced as well. In Fig. 7.4, one can see that the rotation has managed to maintain 90° of separation between the two axes, which is required by the assumption of orthogonality (even those the factors have exchanged axes).

Figure 7.4 also indicates that STAFF and EXCAND have relatively low loadings on both Factors 1 and 2. This is because these variables now have higher loadings on Factor 3. This is not shown in the figure, but can be

TABLE 7.6
Varimax Rotated Factor Matrix

	Factor 1	Factor 2	Factor 3
SEXDISC	−.15869	.91905	.01512
ETHDISC	−.09861	.87355	.03629
AGEDISC	−.20575	.70616	.07202
PROMO	.85973	−.21935	.07619
PROACT	.68989	−.08845	.11589
PERCRIT	.76011	−.11905	.26007
RESOURCE	.47271	−.10197	.14904
HIRE	.51008	.04038	.64145
EXCAND	.25935	.11337	.70480
STAFF	−.01622	.33504	.27476

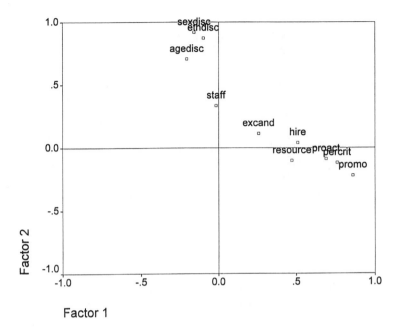

FIG. 7.4. Orthogonal (Varimax) rotation.

seen by examining Table 7.6 more closely. HIRE is a bit more problematic, however, with moderate loadings on Factor 1 and Factor 3.

It is easy to reproduce the correlation between two variables, whether using an orthogonal or oblique rotation scheme. For example, for the orthogonal rotation, if ETHDIS and AGEDIS are correlated .64 (see Table 7.1), their reproduced correlation is simply the factor loadings of ETHDIS and AGEDIS on each factor multiplied and summed across factors. This product is equal to approximately .64 (allowing for rounding):

$$(-.10)(-.21) + (.87)(.71) + (.04)(.07) = .64.$$

Oblique Rotation

Where factors are intercorrelated, which is likely in the real world, using oblique rotation generally simplifies interpretation of the factor pattern matrix. Its advantage over orthogonal rotation is that after making the rotation, if the resulting factors are uncorrelated, the researcher can feel confident that the orthogonality is not a result of the rotational method (Kim & Mueller, (1978). When oblique rotation is used, however, there are two matrices that are created in the rotational process. This is because the factor-loading matrix (i.e., factor pattern matrix) and the factor variable correlations (i.e., the factor structure matrix) are no longer identical. The factor loadings are still partial

regression coefficients, but because the factors are now allowed to be correlated, the partial regression coefficients are no longer the same as the factor
variable correlations. Because these matrices differ somewhat in oblique rotations, it is common practice to interpret (i.e., report) the pattern matrix. If
the researcher reports the pattern matrix and the factor correlations, however,
the interested reader can calculate the coefficients in the structure matrix if desired.

Like orthogonal rotation, oblique rotation also preserves the communalities of the variables. Calculating the communalities becomes a bit more
difficult because one has to take into consideration the factor loadings and
the correlations. One multiplies the loading and the correlation on each
factor and sums them across the number of factors. However, the higher
the correlation among factors, the more ambiguous are attempts to partition
the communality (Pedhauzer & Schmelkin, 1991).

Table 7.7 provides the factor loadings (pattern matrix), the correlations
of observed items with the factors (structure matrix), and factor intercorrelations using oblique rotation (called direct oblimin in SPSS). The orthogonal
pattern matrix in Table 7.6 and the oblique pattern matrix in Table 7.7 are
of course a little different. One can notice that the factors are not truly
orthogonal. In fact, some of the factor correlations are moderate, ranging
from −.33 to .41. This fact accounts for the slightly higher variable loadings
on the factors resulting from the oblique rotation.

Figure 7.5 presents the graphic results of the oblique rotation. As one
can see, the items loading on Factors 1 and 2 are placed even closer to the

TABLE 7.7
Oblimin Rotation

	Pattern Matrix			Structure Matrix		
	Factor 1	Factor 2	Factor 3	Factor 1	Factor 2	Factor 3
SEXDISC	.95	.02	−.07	.93	−.32	.17
ETHDISC	.91	.07	−.05	.73	−.32	.16
AGEDISC	.69	−.10	.04	.73	−.32	.16
PROMO	−.03	.91	−.10	−.36	.88	.28
PROACT	.05	.73	−.02	−.20	.70	.29
PERCRIT	−.01	.74	.13	−.23	.80	.44
RESOURCE	−.03	.46	.07	−.17	.50	.26
HIRE	−.04	.33	.63	.00	.60	.76
EXCAND	−.05	.03	.76	.12	.36	.76
STAFF	.27	−.06	.29	.35	−.03	.33

Factor Correlation Matrix			
	Factor 1	Factor 2	Factor 3
Factor 1	1.00		
Factor 2	−.33	1.00	
Factor 3	.24	.41	1.00

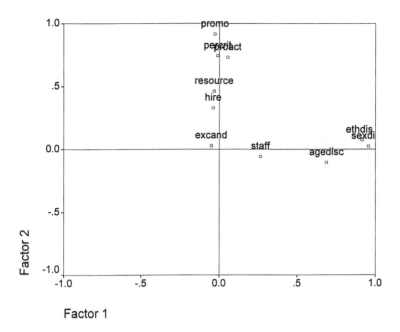

FIG. 7.5. Oblique (oblimin) rotation.

reference axes through this rotational scheme (once again, the factors have changed axes). Moreover, the items loading on Factor 3 (i.e., HIRE, EXCAND) are clustered even closer to the origin (0.0), suggesting that their loadings have been maximized on Factor 3. STAFF, however, appears to load on both Factor 1 and Factor 3 (see Table 7.7 also).

Orthogonal solutions have often been preferred in past FAs, but some of the problems of this approach have been identified. Thus, it is often best to look at both types of rotated solutions, starting with the oblique rotation. If the factors are uncorrelated, then it would be appropriate to retain the orthogonal solution. Very little difference will be noted between the pattern and structure matrices of the oblique solution and the pattern matrix of the orthogonal solution in this case. Where factors are correlated, then the oblique solution can be retained.

CONFIRMATORY FACTOR ANALYSIS

Our attention now shifts to the CFA approach. Once again, the presentation is more informal, because of the need to use matrix algebra and complex statistical theory (e.g., maximum likelihood) in estimating model parameters. This approach involves confirming the existence of a specific factor structure. In contrast to exploratory factor analysis (EFA), which is concerned with the minimum number of factors required to reproduce the observed correlations in the data, CFA requires a proposed theoretical model that the researcher must specify prior to actually testing it with the data. In the last section, several constraints were identified in the EFA approach. Some of these included the need to have items load on all factors simultaneously, the need to have all factors correlated (oblique) or uncorrelated (orthogonal), and the need for unique (error) factors to be uncorrelated.

CFA begins with the researcher specifying the sets of relationships in the model such as the number of common factors, the factors with which the observed variables are to be associated, the particular pattern of correlations between factors, the relationships among unique factors and observed variables, and even possible relationships among the set of unique factors (Long, 1983). These relationships are often postulated on the basis of knowledge of theory, previous research, or some combination of both. CFA is therefore very useful in investigating the construct validity of theoretical models in both single-group and multiple-group analyses.

Because of its focus on linking observed variables to their underlying (unobserved) factors, CFA is often the first part of a structural equation modeling (SEM) analysis. CFA is used to develop the measurement model, where the latent variables are defined by their observed indicators. Then the second model, the structural model, may be used to estimate structural relations among the latent variables. Further descriptions of SEM can be found in Bollen (1989), Pedhazur and Schmelkin (1991), Marcoulides and Hershberger (1997), and Marcoulides and Schumacker (1996).

There are several statistical packages that can perform CFA, sometimes referred to as covariance structure analysis (see chap. 9 in this volume on SEM). Each package may develop a sightly different presentation for specifying and testing CFA models. For example, the LISREL program (Jöreskog & Sörbom, 1989) requires the use of matrices and Greek notation to specify the model to be tested. This is the program that was used in analyzing the data that follows in this chapter. Other packages (e.g., Amos, CALIS, EQS) may or may not use the matrix and Greek notation approach.

Proposing a Model

To demonstrate how a CFA proceeds, we use the exploratory factor model on administrative worklife as a starting point. In the previous section, we determined that a three-factor model adequately reproduced the observed correlations among 10 indicators of the factors. Using ML estimation and an oblique rotation we observed the pattern matrix and factor correlations contained in Table 7.8.

This solution suggests that almost all of the 10 indicators are primarily concerned with one factor in particular. For example, SEXDIS loads highly

TABLE 7.8
Factor Pattern Matrix From Oblimin Rotation

	F1	F2	F3
SEXDISC	.95	.02	−.07
ETHDISC	.91	.07	−.05
AGEDISC	.69	−.10	.04
PROMO	−.02	.91	−.10
PROACT	.05	.73	−.02
PERCRIT	−.01	.74	.13
RESOURCE	−.03	.46	.07
HIRE	−.04	.33	.63
EXCAND	−.05	.03	.76
STAFF	.27	−.06	.29

on Factor 1 (.95), but almost not at all on Factor 2 (.02) and Factor 3 (−.07). Although the EFA is useful in determining the adequate number of factors in a theoretical model, it does not provide a statistical test of how well the individual items fit with each particular factor. In the LISREL (Jöreskog & Sörbom, 1989) approach to CFA and SEM, we can specify a restricted set of relationships between items and factors, for example, by "fixing" SEXDIS's loadings on Factor 2 and Factor 3 to zero (0) and allowing the program to estimate only those parameters that we desire (i.e., its loading on Factor 1). Then we can statistically test how well this restricted model fits the data.

Mathematically, these sets of relationships may be defined very similarly to the exploratory factor model. The factor equation for CFA is

$$x = \Lambda \, \xi + \delta$$

where x is a set of observed variables, Λ is a matrix of factor loadings of x, ξ is a set of latent factors, and δ a matrix of unique factors. Thus, the mathematical relationship for x_1, for example, is given as

$$x_1 = \lambda_{11} \, \xi_1 + \delta_1.$$

Parameters (i.e., factor loadings) to be estimated are labeled as λ (lambda).

As the name covariance structure analysis implies, the relationships among the observed variables are characterized by the covariances among these variables contained in a sample covariance matrix. This matrix is decomposed by a model that assumes that unobserved variables are generating the pattern or structure among the observed variables (Long, 1983). In contrast to EFA, one generally analyzes a covariance matrix in CFA, rather than a correlation matrix. This is because statistical theory underlying SEM is based on covariances, and it is questionable the extent to which it can be generalized to correlations (e.g., Marcoulides & Hershberger, 1997). Moreover, correlations remove information concerning variability (i.e., through standardization). In many practical applications, however, a correlation matrix is analyzed because researchers are unable to attach substantive meaning to the units of measurement that they are using (Jöreskog & Sörbom, 1989; Pedhazur & Schmelkin, 1991).

The form of the covariance structure equation used in specifying relationships between the observed and latent variables is generally represented as

$$\Sigma = \Lambda \; \Phi \; \Lambda' + \psi$$

where Σ is a variance-covariance matrix, Φ is a matrix of factor variances and covariances, and ψ is a variance-covariance matrix of measurement errors (e.g., Jöreskog & Sörbom, 1989). It should be clear that these relationships are very similar to the EFA approach, except as suggested that variance-covariance matrices are generally analyzed in CFA. A second distinction is that in CFA the researcher specifies a particular pattern of observed variable loadings on the factors, which results in many cells in the matrix being fixed (i.e., not estimated). Fixing paths is what provides the test of a particular model and in most cases is needed to identify a unique solution to the set of equations.

A final difference is that the error matrix in CFA is not restricted to being diagonal (i.e., error terms represented in the diagonals and zeros off the diagonals). This permits the specification of correlated error terms for different pairs of variables in the model within the ψ matrix. This final difference, however, also makes model identification (i.e., determining whether a unique solution exists) more difficult than in the exploratory approach because there are many more possible parameters that can be estimated.

In the LISREL approach to CFA, a series of matrices is used to specify the sets of relationships implied in the theoretical model. The complete specification of our factor model may be written in matrix form as:

$$
\begin{bmatrix} x_1 \\ x_2 \\ x_3 \\ x_4 \\ x_5 \\ x_6 \\ x_7 \\ x_8 \\ x_9 \\ x_{10} \end{bmatrix}
=
\begin{bmatrix}
\lambda_{1,1} & 0 & 0 \\
\lambda_{2,1} & 0 & 0 \\
\lambda_{3,1} & 0 & 0 \\
0 & \lambda_{4,2} & 0 \\
0 & \lambda_{5,2} & 0 \\
0 & \lambda_{6,2} & 0 \\
0 & \lambda_{7,2} & 0 \\
0 & 0 & \lambda_{8,3} \\
0 & 0 & \lambda_{9,3} \\
0 & 0 & \lambda_{10,3}
\end{bmatrix}
\begin{bmatrix} \xi_1 \\ \xi_2 \\ \xi_3 \end{bmatrix}
+
\begin{bmatrix} \delta_1 \\ \delta_2 \\ \delta_3 \\ \delta_4 \\ \delta_5 \\ \delta_6 \\ \delta_7 \\ \delta_8 \\ \delta_9 \\ \delta_{10} \end{bmatrix}.
$$

In examining this specification, one can see that each observed variable has been restricted to load on only one common factor, with loadings on other common factors being specified as equal to zero. Notice that we have fixed SEXDIS (x_1), ETHDIS (x_2), and AGEDIS (x_3) to belong only with Factor 1. PROMO (x_4), PROACT (x_5) PROCRIT (x_6), and RESOURCE (x_7) are defined as belonging with Factor 2, and HIRE (x_8), EXCAND (x_9), and STAFF (x_{10}) are defined as belonging with Factor 3. Because these restrictions are imposed on the model, the model becomes confirmatory, in that the various fit indices will describe how this particular model fits the data, as opposed to some other model that we might propose.

Of course, we could decide that some observed indicators were to be associated with more than one factor. For example, we could have allowed STAFF (x_{10}) to also load of Factor 1 because the exploratory solution suggested that it is divided between the two factors. For the moment, however, we restrict it to load only on Factor 3. If we replaced all zeros in the ξ matrix with λs, we would approach an exploratory type of analysis; this is called testing an "unrestricted" model. As is shown later, after testing this original model, it turned out that a substantial improvement in overall model fit was achieved by allowing STAFF to also load on Factor 1 by freeing and then estimating an additional path ($\lambda_{10,1}$).

Each observed indicator also has a unique factor (or error term). Through using matrix specification, one may choose whether or not particular error terms are to be correlated (e.g., δ_1 and δ_2). Similarly, one may also decide which factors are to be correlated (e.g., ξ_1 and ξ_3). We could actually even specify the strength of the relationships for certain parameters (e.g., loadings, factor variances and covariances) ahead of time and test whether these estimates fit the actual data. Thus, there is tremendous flexibility afforded by this approach.

A visual representation of this model is given in Fig. 7.6. A drawing of the proposed model often facilitates understanding the full set of relationships that

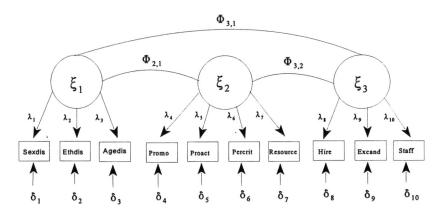

FIG. 7.6. Proposed model of administrative worklife.

are specified. Observed variables are enclosed in rectangles and latent variables in ovals. Covariances between factors are indicated by curved lines.

Testing the Model

Once the model has been specified, we may test the model with data. Estimation proceeds like in EFA. Initial values are obtained for parameters in the model. Through iteration, these estimates are refined until they are optimal, and there is little difference between the structure implied by the proposed model and the reproduced sample covariance matrix. This should be very close to the original sample matrix. If one considers the sample matrix (S) to represent the population matrix Σ, then the difference between the reproduced sample matrix and the sample matrix should be very small if the model is consistent with the data.

The evaluation of difference between the observed and reproduced covariance matrices depends on which method of estimating the model's parameters is used. A function that measures how close a given reproduced covariance matrix is to the sample covariance matrix is called a fitting function (see Long, 1983, for further discussion of estimation). Several fitting functions are available for estimating the parameters of the model. ML is the most frequently used. Other possibilities include unweighted least squares (ULS), generalized least squares (GLS), and weighted least squares (WLS). Each one has conditions under which it is best employed to estimate a theoretical model. This is important to keep in mind, because the methods can result in varying parameter estimates and fit indices, especially in models that are only marginally acceptable. A thorough discussion of these various methods of estimation can be found in sources such as Long (1983), Bollen (1989), Byrne (1989), and Jöreskog and Sörbom (1989).

Identification

In testing the proposed model against the data, it is necessary to make sure that the model is identified properly. This is a complicated issue that has been widely discussed in the SEM literature (e.g., Bollen, 1989; Bollen & Long, 1993; Jöreskog & Sörbom, 1989; Long, 1983; Marcoulides & Hershberger, 1997; Shumacker & Lomax, 1996). Identification has to do with the adequacy of the information for parameter estimation. If a model were not identified (called underidentified), it would be possible to find an infinite number of values for the parameters, each set of which would be consistent with the covariance equation (Long, 1983).

Estimation assumes that the model has been identified. Either there is just enough information to solve each parameter (just-identified) or there is more than enough information (overidentified). In a general sense, the problem is often dealt with by restricting the number of parameters actually estimated from the total number of parameters that could be estimated. The restriction is that the number of parameters estimated must be less than or equal to $q(q + 1)/2$, where q is the number of observed variables in the model. Thus, there is one covariance equation for each of the independent elements of the $q \times q \Sigma$ matrix (Long, 1983). If there are more parameters to be estimated than covariance equations, there will be many solutions to the covariance equation and the model will not be identified. It should be pointed out, however, that satisfying this constraint is a necessary, but not sufficient, condition to guarantee model identification.

In actually testing models, determining whether a model is identified or not can be somewhat challenging, especially when models are more complicated. Sometimes an underidentified model can be identified by imposing additional constraints on some of its elements (e.g., fixing off-diagonal elements in the error matrix to 0). Fortunately, most computer programs provide clues regarding the identifiability of a model being tested, often checking whether certain assumptions of identification have been met (e.g., Pedhauzer & Schmelkin, 1991).

The easiest way to approach the issue of model identification is to think of it in terms of algebraic equations. For example, if we have the following equations with two unknowns (x, y):

$$x + y = 8$$
$$x - y = 4$$

there is one specific answer $(x = 6, y = 2)$, and the model would be just-identified in that there are as many equations as unknowns. A just-identified model always fits the data perfectly, so the model cannot be tested for fit. If, however, we have two unknowns and only one equation $(x + y = 8)$, we could substitute any numbers for values of x and y, as long as they summed to 8. The model would then be underidentified because there are more unknown parameters than equations provided. If we have the same equations as the just-identified model and now add other pieces of information (i.e., more than necessary to find the solution), the model becomes overidentified.

Overidentified models have more than enough available variances-covariances than are needed to obtain a unique solution; that is, for at least one of the parameters in the model there is more than one equation the solution to the parameter must satisfy. Because of this, there will be positive degrees of freedom in the model. This is another way of considering the necessary, but not sufficient, condition of having more than enough parameters for model identification. As suggested, only overidentified models may be tested for their fit (see Bollen, 1989, or Long, 1983, for more technical discussions of model identification).

The problem of model identification did not surface during EFA because of the lack of control that the researcher has in specifying the model to be tested. Instead of being able to specify intercorrelations between error terms for individual variables, for example, in EFA a constraint is imposed on the nature of the unique factor (Θ) matrix, by making it diagonal. This has the effect of always eliminating all but one set of possible parameters, thereby guaranteeing that a solution can be determined. This is, however, a relatively arbitrary constraint, and is one of the weaknesses of the exploratory factor model that has been discussed. In contrast, in the confirmatory approach constraints that are imposed on the model are due to substantive issues, as opposed to mathematical ones. One achieves identification by substantially reducing the number of parameters to be estimated.

Determining the Adequacy of the Model

Our primary concern in CFA is with the overall fit of the proposed model to the data. If the model does not fit at least adequately, the researcher would have to reconceptualize the model. As suggested, the researcher attempts to impose a hypothesized structure on the actual data and then determines how closely the data fit this proposed model. In actuality, it is quite unlikely that the fit will be perfect (i.e., unless the model is just-identified). The difference between the model implied by the series of specified mathematical relationships (the theoretical model) and the model tested with the data is termed the residual (Byrne, 1989).

There are various statistical and practical criteria that can be used in determining the fit of the data to the proposed theoretical model (i.e., currently there are over 30). Each index defines fit in a slightly different manner, or has been constructed to provide a particular correction, for example, because of the effects of sample size. As Marcoulides and Hershberger (1997) summarized these indices, most are concerned with the discrepancy between the observed and implied covariance (or correlation) matrices. Others combine this concern with a parsimony criterion (i.e., models are favored that are more parsimonious). Still others define goodness of fit in terms of model complexity.

Perhaps the best known of the fit indices is the chi-square statistic because of its widespread use in hypothesis testing. There are, however, several assumptions involved in this test that make its use as a sole criterion of model fit problematic (e.g., multivariate normality, larger samples required for testing). In testing proposed factor models, one wishes to accept the null hypothesis that there is no difference between the proposed set of relationships and the actual data (i.e., an insignificant chi-square value for the degrees of freedom in the model). As suggested during the earlier discussion on EFA, however, because the chi-square statistic is affected by sample size, with large samples the accompanying level of significance is often low (i.e., $p < .05$), even though the other model criteria indicate a strong fit.

One alternative that has been widely used is the chi-square/degrees of freedom ratio. Researchers, however, do not agree on the appropriateness of this index. On one hand, although this index is also affected by sample size because of its reliance on chi-square, it is not associated with an exact test of significance. The chi-square/degrees of freedom ratio therefore provides a rough estimate of the statistical fit of the model (i.e., the error present) versus the number of parameters estimated (i.e., degrees of freedom). Better models will have a lower ratio. Researchers have proposed accepting larger ratios with larger sample sizes (e.g., ratios of 2:1 for samples of 400 and 3:1 for samples of 800).

On the other hand, a more recently developed alternative is the root mean square error of approximation (RMSEA). This index makes an adjustment for the "exact" fit of the chi-square statistic and its relationship to sample size. The RMSEA index allows for a discrepancy of fit per degree of freedom, which provides a bit more room for acceptance of the model than does the chi-square statistic alone (e.g., Marcoulides & Hershberger, 1997). After making this adjustment, it has the desirable property of still using a statistical test that provides a region for rejecting ill-fitting models on statistical grounds.

A few other commonly used indices should also be mentioned. These do not depend on a region of rejection like chi-square types of tests. Instead, the researcher must look at a variety of these indices and use judgment in determining whether the range on indices provide evidence of an adequate-fitting model. Statistical criteria include the goodness-of-fit index (GFI), adjusted goodness-of-fit index (AGFI), the chi-square/degrees of freedom ratio, and the root mean square residual (RMR). Practical criteria include the comparative fit index (CFI). The GFI, AGFI, and CFI can be considered as measurements of the relative amount of variance and covariance in the data accounted for by the proposed model. For example, a model that fit the data perfectly would provide a coefficient of 1.00. Values above .90 are often considered as evidence of good model fit. In contrast, the RMR and RMSEA are measures of the average unexplained variances and covariances in the model. These indices should be close to zero for a good-fitting model.

It is important to mention that the value of these various indices are likely to differ (e.g., providing larger or smaller values of chi-square), depending on the method of estimation used. This is especially true in the case of marginal or ill-fitting models. Strong models will be more likely to result in index similarity across methods of estimation used to fit the model to the data.

Example Output

The remaining data set ($N = 521$) was subjected to a confirmatory FA. Our proposed three-factor model was tested with LISREL 8 (Jöreskog & Sörbom, 1993) with ML estimation and a correlation matrix as input because all data were ordinal scales. The correlation matrix is provided in Table 7.9, for those who wish to compare it to the correlation matrix for the EFA (see Table 7.2).

Evidence of the model's fit is provided in Table 7.10. The initial model resulted in a marginal fit of the model to the data (e.g., GFI = .94, AGFI = .89, RMR = .069). The RMSEA coefficient of .085 (with p value of .003) also indicated that the model should be rejected. Most programs provide a modification index (MI), which can help the researcher locate poor parameters in the model that cause it to be ill-fitting. Caution is recommended, however, in using the MI to "find" a better fitting model on statistical grounds alone. One should not simply use the MI blindly because the modification may make little sense substantively. If the MI is used, it is recommended that one modification be made at a time. In this case, the change in chi-square ($\Delta\chi^2$) with 1 degree of freedom (the parameter freed) can be evaluated for statistical significance (i.e., a drop in χ^2 of 3.84 would indicate a significant improvement at $p = .05$).

In this case, the MI (not tabled) suggested that a large source of error could be eliminated if a path between STAFF and Factor 1 were freed. If the reader looks back at the exploratory factor analysis presented in Table 7.7, for example, he or she can see that STAFF loaded highest on Factor 3, but also loaded almost the same on Factor 1. These are the types of problems one frequently encounters in working with actual data. The conceptual solution is not quite as clear as we would first hope. It appears, therefore that "forcing" STAFF to load on only one factor in the confirmatory FA was not the "correct" model. Therefore, this one parameter was freed, and the model was reestimated.

Table 7.9 shows that this resulted in a significant improvement in model fit (e.g., $\Delta\chi^2$ = 17.36, GFI = .95, AGFI = .91, RMR = .041). The RMSEA of .074 and corresponding significance level of .04, however, suggested that the model also could be rejected as ill-fitting on purely statistical grounds. Once again, the MI indicated a few parameters that could be freed to improve the model. Often, with models that are obviously close to adequate, these modifications concern the presence of correlated error terms between observed variables. In most cases, the researcher would probably stop at this point, because there generally is no substantive reason for estimating paths between error terms associated with individual observed variables.

To demonstrate the procedure, however, the largest error term (between PROMO and PERCRIT) was freed, and the model was once again reestimated. This additional change resulted in another significant improvement in model fit ($\Delta\chi^2$ = 16.61, GFI = .96, AGFI = .92, RMR = .037). The RMSEA of .06 and corresponding significance level of .24 suggested that this model could now be accepted on statistical grounds as well.

Given the variety of criteria used to evaluate the model, we could now accept this model (with these two modifications) as one plausible representation of the data. It is important to note that although better-fitting

TABLE 7.9
Correlation Matrix for Confirmatory FA

	AGEDISC	ETHDISC	EXCAND	HIRE	PERCRIT	PROACT	PROMO	RESOURCE	SEXDISC	STAFF
AGEDIS	1.00									
ETHDIS	.73	1.00								
EXCAND	.13	.14	1.00							
HIRE	-.05	-.01	.59	1.00						
PERCRIT	-.18	-.15	.33	.54	1.00					
PROACT	-.15	-.12	.21	.39	.55	1.00				
PROMO	-.29	-.23	.20	.43	.63	.59	1.00			
RESOURCE	-.15	-.10	.15	.25	.33	.42	.44	1.00		
SEXDIS	.74	.86	.12	-.07	-.18	-.11	-.27	-.12	1.00	
STAFF	.31	.33	.25	.16	.03	.07	-.06	.04	.34	1.00

TABLE 7.10
Goodness-of-Fit Indices

Index	Model 1	Model 2[a]	Model 3[b]
χ^2	90.11	72.75	56.54
$\Delta\chi^2$ (p)	NA	17.36 (< .01)	16.21 (< .01)
GFI	.94	.95	.96
AGFI	.89	.91	.92
CFI	.94	.96	.97
RMR	.069	.041	.037
RMSEA (p)	.085 ($p = .003$)	.074 ($p = .04$)	.06 ($p = .24$)

[a]Path between STAFF and Factor 1 freed. [b]Path between STAFF and Factor 1 freed; path between error terms for PROMO and PERCRIT freed.

statistical models could be developed, they might make little substantive sense in light of the original model proposed and then tested. The researcher therefore needs to exercise caution in making model changes, or the final model accepted will not represent any type of valid test of the proposed theory.

Now that the fit of the model has been determined, the parameter estimates (i.e., factor loadings, error terms, and squared multiple correlations) may be more closely investigated. These are provided in Table 7.11. The estimates show that the model fits very well with the estimates from the ML oblimin rotation in Table 7.7. For comparative purposes those estimates are provided in parentheses. The estimates suggest that the observed variables are substantially associated with the factors, with loadings ranging generally

TABLE 7.11
Parameter Estimates for Confirmatory FA
(Exploratory Factor Loadings With Oblimin Rotation in Parentheses)

Variable	Factor Loadings			SMC	Error
	Factor 1	Factor 2	Factor 3		
SEXDIS	.89 (.95)			.80	.20
ETHDIS	.91 (.91)			.84	.16
AGEDIS	.81 (.69)			.66	.34
PERCRIT		.82 (.74)		.68	.32
PROACT		.82 (.73)		.67	.33
PROMO		.72 (.91)		.51	.49
RESOURCE		.41 (.46)		.17	.83
HIRE			.82 (.63)	.67	.33
EXCAND			.62 (.76)	.38	.62
STAFF	.26 (.27)		.34 (.29)	.17	.83

from .4 to .9. The one exception is STAFF, which loads below .4 on both Factor 1 and Factor 3 (notice the similarities of both solutions for this variable). The reader might have noticed that the chi-square values are not the same in the two model tests (χ^2 = 28.54 in the exploratory analysis and χ^2 = 56.54 in the confirmatory test). This is because in the exploratory case, it represents a test only of the number of factors, as opposed to a test of the complete measurement model.

The CFA also provides information about the error terms and squared multiple correlations (like communality estimates). In general, the squared multiple correlations are relatively high (except for RESOURCE and STAFF). Similarly, the error terms are generally low, except for RESOURCE and STAFF. This suggests that these two variables are not as reliable as measures of the factors. The squared multiple correlation (SMC), which is very similar to the communality estimate in EFA, is simply the square of the loading on the factor, so that high loadings may be seen as sharing more variance with the factor (i.e., SMC = 1 − uniqueness).

Given all of the various criteria and parameter estimates, we would argue that the CFA tends to support the original factor model developed through EFA quite closely. Because of the goal in CFA of verifying factor structures, a basic question arises about whether the model is similar across other samples or groups (Marcoulides & Hershberger, 1997).

Simultaneous Model Tests Across Samples or Groups

The ultimate test of EFA in choosing the number of factors to extract is that it selects factors that will be found again in new samples of subjects and new sets of tests (Loehlin, 1992). Comparing how a model fits from one sample or setting to another is often referred to as testing its invariance and is one means of investigating its construct validity. Current SEM software packages (e.g., LISREL) provide several means for comparing models across samples or groups.

When differences in samples (e.g., measurements taken at different points in times) or groups (e.g., managers in different countries) are considered, assumptions are generally made that the constructs being measured are similar for all groups examined. If the constructs measured are not similar across the groups examined, this failure to measure the same construct may be an indication of the lack of construct validity of the measurement, a difference in the sample, or an indication that the groups are different. Thus, comparative studies involving different groups yield not only information about potential group or sample differences, but also additional insight into the construct validity of measures. The value of a proposed model, therefore, is greatly enhanced if it can be replicated in samples from the same and different populations. If the model is not similar, we can determine to what degree it differs. In the methodological literature this is referred to as testing the invariance of a theoretical model.

Although we have initially developed and confirmed the three-factor model, it could, for example, be further investigated to see if the same model exists for males and females, or other subgroups. Moreover, we could also establish if the patterns of factor loadings and intercorrelations between factors are the same across both groups, and if the items are equally well measured across groups. More fully efficient estimates of the parameters are provided as well as possible differences discovered if the model is tested across samples or groups simultaneously (Jöreskog & Sörbom, 1989). Structural relations across models can also be tested (e.g., equal mean structures or equal paths between latent factors).

As a prerequisite to doing model tests across groups or samples, it is often useful to develop baseline models for each group. Of course, this has already been done in the context of presenting the material in the chapter. Because instruments are often group specific and sample sizes may be different, we would not expect baseline models to be exactly the same (Byrne, 1989). Although the two approaches to FA appeared to produce very similar results, we can test whether they can be considered statistically equivalent by examining the patterns of factors, loadings, factor intercorrelations, and error terms across the samples. For example, although the loadings appear similar in each analysis, we don't have comparative information about the error terms, or the reliability of measurement, in each model.

In tests of model invariance, the researcher imposes constraints on particular parameters of interest across the groups and estimates these parameters simultaneously. The same pattern of fixed and free parameters used from the original baseline model is fit to the covariance matrices of successive groups. The fit of the model is subsequently examined in order to determine whether its structure is the same across the different groups.

More specifically, the researcher can proceed to test a series of hypotheses about substantive aspects of the model, using several indices of model fit to test these hypotheses. In this case, the proposed hypotheses were an invariant number of factors and loadings on the factors (H_1), invariant intercorrelations among factors (H_2), and invariant errors of measurement (H_3). These hypotheses could also be extended to a test of factor means across groups if desired. It should be noted that tests of model invariance conducted using LISREL 8 (Jöreskog & Sörbom, 1993) require covariance matrices as input (remember that either covariance or correlation matrices can be used in single-group tests).

The results of the simultaneous test of model fit across two different samples is presented in Table 7.12. The first hypothesis tested concerned an invariant number of factors and invariant item loadings on the factors. This hypothesis was considered tenable (e.g., GFI = .99, RMR = .033). Moreover, the chi-square

TABLE 7.12
Goodness-of-Fit Indices for Multisample Tests

Hypothesis	χ^2	df	χ^2/df ratio	GFI	CFI	RMR
			Indices			
1. Invariant Factors and Factor Loadings	83	72	1.2	.99	.99	.033
2. Invariant Factors, Factor Loadings, and Factor Correlations	87	75	1.2	.99	1.00	.026
3. Invariant Factors, Factor Loadings, Factor Correlations, and Errors	4,072	86	47.0	.80	0.00	.340

statistic suggested the model did not differ from an ideal model ($\chi^2 = 83$, $p = .18$). The second hypothesis concerned equal factors, item loadings, and factor correlations. Once again, this hypothesis could not be rejected (GFI = .99, RMR = .026, $\chi^2 = 87$, $p = .19$). This suggests the pattern of correlations between the factors was similar across both samples.

Finally, the hypothesis of invariant error terms across samples was also added (H_3). Unfortunately, this hypothesis could not be supported (GFI = .80, RMR = .34, $\chi^2 = 4,072$, $p = .000$). Notice in particular the large jump in chi-square. This suggests that despite considerable similarity in the model's structure across the two samples, the constructs are not equally well measured. It is also possible that this significant result is related to differences in sample sizes. Because of these issues, the criterion of invariant error matrices across groups is generally considered too stringent in most tests of model invariance.

CLOSING REMARKS

FA is an important analytic tool in the investigation of underlying constructs and their observed indicators. In this chapter, two basic approaches were presented. EFA is often the appropriate choice when the underlying structure among a set of observed variables is not well known. In contrast, the ability to test specific underlying structures using CFA gives it an important advantage over the exploratory method. Some of the similarities and differences in these approaches were highlighted in the chapter as a means of introducing the method in relatively simple terms.

It is important to keep in mind the role of theory in defining and testing factor models. CFA is a powerful statistical tool, but it can be easily misused (e.g., by relying solely upon modification indices to improve model fit.)

Although the factor model investigated in this chapter was necessarily simple, of course, complexity can be added by increasing the number of observed variables, the number of factors, and the various relationships among the factors. As shown in the chapter, the basic confirmatory factor model can also be easily adapted to comparing factor structures across groups or temporal conditions. Moreover, techniques are now becoming available to allow the extension of the model to multilevel or individual growth analyses (e.g., see McArdle & Hamagami, 1996, or Willett & Sayer, 1996).

ACKNOWLEDGMENTS

The author is grateful to George A. Marcoulides and Victoria Rosser for comments made on earlier versions of the manuscript.

REFERENCES

Bollen, K. (1989). *Structural equations with latent variables.* New York: Wiley.

Bollen, K., & Long, J. (1993). *Testing structural equation models.* Newbury Park, CA: Sage.

Boomsma, A. (1987). The robustness of maximum likelihood estimation in structural equation models. In P. Cuttance & R. Ecob (Eds.), *Structural equation modeling by example: Applications in educational, sociological, and behavioral research* (pp. 160–188). Cambridge, England: Cambridge University Press.

Byrne, B. (1989). *A primer of LISREL: Basic applications and programming for confirmatory factor analytic models.* New York: Springer-Verlag.

Cattell, R. (1966). The Scree Test for the number of factors. *Multivariate Behavioral Research, 1,* 245–276.

Cronbach, L., & Meehl, P. (1955). Construct validity in psychological tests. *Psychological Bulletin, 52,* 281–302.

Ecob, R., & Cuttance, P. (1987). An overview of structural equation modeling. In P. Cuttance & R. Ecob (Eds.), *Structural modeling by example.* Cambridge, England: Cambridge University Press.

Jöreskog, K. (1970). A general method for analysis of covariance structures. *Biometrika, 57,* 239–251.

Jöreskog, K. (1971). Simultaneous factor analysis in several populations. *Psychometrika, 36,* 409–426.

Jöreskog, K., & Sörbom, D. (1989). *LISREL 7: User's reference guide.* Chicago: Scientific Software.

Jöreskog, K., & Sörbom, D. (1993). *LISREL 8: User's reference guide.* Chicago: Scientific Software.

Kim, J., & Mueller, C. (1978). *An introduction to factor analysis* (Sage Series on Quantitative Applications in the Social Sciences No. 13). Newbury Park, CA: Sage.

Lawley, D., & Maxwell, A. (1963). *Factor Analysis as a statistical method.* London: Butterworth.

Loehlin, J. (1992). *Latent variable models: An introduction to factor, path, and structural models.* Hillsdale, NJ: Lawrence Erlbaum Associates.

Long, S. (1983). *Confirmatory factor analysis* (Sage Series on Quantitative Applications in the Social Sciences No. 33). Newbury Park, CA: Sage.

Marcoulides, G., & Hershberger, S. (1997). *Multivariate statistical methods: A first course.* Hillsdale, NJ: Lawrence Erlbaum Associates.

Marcoulides, G., & Schumacker, R. (1996). *Advanced structural equation modeling.* Mahwah, NJ: Lawrence Erlbaum Associates.

McArdle, J., & Hamagami, F. (1996). Multilevel models from a multiple group structural equation perspective. In G. Marcoulides & R. Schumacker (Eds.), *Advanced structural equation modeling: Issues and techniques* (pp. 89–124). Hillsdale, NJ: Lawrence Erlbaum Associates.

National Council on Measurement in Education. (1984). *Standards for educational and psychological testing.* Washington, DC: American Psychological Association.

Pedhazur, E., & Schmelkin, L. (1991). *Measurement, design, and analysis: An integrated approach.* Hillsdale, NJ: Lawrence Erlbaum Associates.

Schumacker, R., & Lomax, R. (1996). *A beginner's guide to structural equation modeling.* Mahwah, NJ: Lawrence Erlbaum Associates.

Tabachnick, B., & Fidell, L. (1996). *Using multivariate statistics* (3rd ed.). New York: Harper-Collins College Publishers.

Willett, J., & Sayer, A. (1996). Cross-domain analyses of change over time: Combining growth modeling and covariance structure analysis. In G. Marcoulides & R. Schumacker (Eds.), *Advanced structural equation modeling: Issues and techniques* (pp. 125–158). Hillsdale, NJ: Lawrence Erlbaum Associates.

APPENDIX

SPSS Windows 6.1 Syntax

```
Matrix data
 VARIABLES agedisc ethdisc excand hire percrit proact promo resource
  sexdisc staff
 /format free lower diagonal
 /contents corr N_Scaler.
Begin data.
1.00
 .64 1.00
 .07 .09 1.00
-.03 .02 .59 1.00
-.25 -.17 .36 .56 1.00
-.19 -.16 .26 .41 .56 1.00
-.32 -.27 .25 .48 .70 .62 1.00
-.11 -.13 .23 .31 .39 .41 .44 1.00
 .68 .82 .08 -.04 -.22 -.18 -.34 -.18 1.00
 .32 .29 .23 .17 .02 .00 -.07 .05 .31 1.00
335
End data.
list.
Factor matrix in (cor=*)
/ANALYSIS agedisc ethdisc excand hire
  percrit proact promo resource sexdisc staff
/PRINT INITIAL DET EXTRACTION ROTATION
/CRITERIA FACTORS(3)
/EXTRACTION ML
/CRITERIA ITERATE (25)
/ROTATION VARIMAX
/PLOT ROTATION(1,2).
```

CHAPTER EIGHT

Dynamic Factor Analysis

Scott L. Hershberger

University of Kansas

Dynamic factor analysis (DFA) is a latent variable modeling technique that joins together the power of multivariate time series analysis and factor analysis. In short, DFA refers to the factor analysis of multivariate time series, the purpose of which is to understand the common, latent sources of change in a set of observed variables across time. Factor analytic approaches to serially dependent data are not new. Earlier approaches were discussed by, among others, Ahamad (1967), Priestly, Subba Rao, and Tong (1973), Brillinger (1975), Geweke (1977), Geweke and Singleton (1981), Sims (1981), Box and Tiao (1977), and Velu, Reinsel, and Wichern (1986). What distinguishes the current formulation of DFA from other formulations is its acknowledged dependence on the factor analytic tradition embodied by the work of Cattell (1952). This tradition views factor analysis not so much as a data reduction technique but as a method for understanding the covariance structure underlying the data: The factors or components extracted from data do not simply summarize the data, they explain it in some meaningful way.

The DFA approaches discussed in this chapter derive most directly from the *P*-technique analysis proposed by Cattell (1952). As originally proposed, *P*-technique factor analysis involves the factor analysis of correlations among variables, produced from an occasion by variable data matrix for a single person. Subsequently, variations on *P*-technique were introduced, such as chain P-technique (Cattell & Scheier, 1961), in which the series of several subjects are concatenated. Although P-technique has been applied in numerous contexts (cf. Jones & Nesselroade, 1990), it has been criticized for its failure to incorporate the lagged covariance structure of the time series (Anderson, 1963; Holtzman, 1963). In P-technique, in which the correlations are of 0-lag (the correlations are among measurements taken within the same occasion), the obtained factor structure represents the simultaneous relation among variables. Incorporating lagged covariances (1 or greater) would open up the possibility of uncovering relations among variables across a specified interval of time, an interval defined by the order of the lag.

The purpose of this chapter is to describe the stationary DFA model proposed by Molenaar (1985) to incorporate the lagged covariance structure missing from P-technique. We describe classical P-technique, then the stationary DFA and its extension, the nonstationary DFA model (Molenaar, De Gooijer, & Schmitz, 1992). All three models are then applied to a data example. Before discussing the factor models, however, a brief overview of a number of concepts important to time series modeling and DFA are reviewed, as well as the autoregressive integrated moving average (ARIMA) approach to time series modeling.

DEFINITIONS

This section defines some basic terminology and concepts important to time series modeling and DFA.

Lagged Covariances/Correlations

The covariances (or correlations) among a set of variables provide the essential information in a multivariate analysis concerning the strength of relationship among the variables at any occasion. On the other hand, lagged covariances (correlations) provide information concerning how strongly variables measured at earlier occasions are related to measures at later occasions, and thus form the cornerstone of all time series analyses. The order of the lag signifies the distance between the occasions: A first-order lagged covariance is the covariance between variable Y at occasion t and the same variable Y at occasion $t + 1$; a second-order lagged covariance is the covariance between variable Y at occasion t and variable Y at occasion $t + 2$; a third-order lagged covariance is the covariance between variable Y at occasion t and variable Y at occasion $t + 3$, or the kth-order lagged covariance is the covariance between variable Y at occasion t and variable Y at occasion

$t + k$. Specifically, the lag k covariance (cov_k) is computed for times series Y_t as:

$$cov_k = \frac{\sum\limits_{t=1}^{N-k} (Y_t - \bar{Y})(Y_{t+k} - \bar{Y})}{N}.$$

Comparably, the lag k correlation (r_k) is:

$$r_k = \frac{\sum\limits_{t=1}^{N-k} (Y_t - \bar{Y})(Y_{t+k} - \bar{Y})}{\sum\limits_{t=1}^{N} (Y_t - \bar{Y})^2}.$$

These formulae are, respectively, the traditional formulas for the covariance and Pearson product-moment correlation between two variables. In the context of the lagged covariance of a variable with itself, the covariance is referred to as an *autocovariance*.

As an illustration of a lagged-covariance (autocovariance), consider the short times series:

$$[1\ 3\ 5\ 7\ 9].$$

The first-order lagged covariance is computed between the product sum between the two vectors (first deviated from their mean):

$$\begin{bmatrix} 1 \\ 3 \\ 5 \\ 7 \\ 9 \end{bmatrix} \cdot \begin{bmatrix} 1 \\ 3 \\ 5 \\ 7 \\ 9 \end{bmatrix}^T \quad \downarrow \quad = \quad \begin{bmatrix} 3 \\ 5 \\ 7 \\ 9 \end{bmatrix} \cdot \begin{bmatrix} 1 \\ 3 \\ 5 \\ 7 \end{bmatrix}^T.$$

Note what has occurred. The original column vector has been shifted down one number relative to itself, resulting in the loss of number "1" in the left vector and the loss of number "9" in the right vector. For the second-order lagged covariance,

$$
\begin{bmatrix} 1 \\ 3 \\ 5 \\ 7 \\ 9 \end{bmatrix} \cdot \begin{bmatrix} 1 \\ 3 \\ 5 \\ 7 \\ 9 \end{bmatrix}^{T} \quad \downarrow \; = \; \begin{bmatrix} 5 \\ 7 \\ 9 \end{bmatrix} \cdot \begin{bmatrix} 1 \\ 3 \\ 5 \end{bmatrix}^{T}
$$

resulting in the loss of two numbers, "1" and "3" in the left vector and "7" and "9" in the right vector. Similarly for the third-lagged covariance,

$$
\begin{bmatrix} 1 \\ 3 \\ 5 \\ 7 \\ 9 \end{bmatrix} \cdot \begin{bmatrix} 1 \\ 3 \\ 5 \\ 7 \\ 9 \end{bmatrix}^{T} \quad \downarrow \; = \; \begin{bmatrix} 7 \\ 9 \end{bmatrix} \cdot \begin{bmatrix} 1 \\ 3 \end{bmatrix}^{T}
$$

three numbers are lost from each vector in the computation of the covariance. The fourth-lagged covariance is [9] [1], resulting in the loss of four numbers from each vector. No higher order lagged covariances are possible: The maximum number of lags calculable from a time series is always equal to one less than the total number of occasions. The zero-lagged covariance is simply the covariance between the variable's vector and the same vector nonshifted, which is of course the variable's variance:

$$\begin{bmatrix} 1 \\ 3 \\ 5 \\ 7 \\ 9 \end{bmatrix} \cdot \begin{bmatrix} 1 \\ 3 \\ 5 \\ 7 \\ 9 \end{bmatrix}^{T}.$$

In the preceding illustration, the univariate time series Y_t was lagged on itself. However, DFA is concerned principally with the analysis of multivariate time series; thus interest more frequently lies with the lagged relation between two different time series. If we consider a time series X_t ([4, 10, 15, 18, 25]) and its first-lagged covariance with Y_t, we have:

$$\begin{bmatrix} 4 \\ 10 \\ 15 \\ 18 \\ 25 \end{bmatrix} \cdot \begin{bmatrix} 1 \\ 3 \\ 5 \\ 7 \\ 9 \end{bmatrix}^{T} \quad \downarrow = \begin{bmatrix} 10 \\ 15 \\ 18 \\ 25 \end{bmatrix} \cdot \begin{bmatrix} 1 \\ 3 \\ 5 \\ 7 \end{bmatrix}^{T}.$$

Two difficulties with the interpretation of lagged covariances are apparent. First, the calculation of a lagged covariance results in the loss of two data points (occasions) for every unit increase in the order of the lag. This loss of data places a limit on the desirable interval size of the lag. Further, it would seem reasonable to calculate each lagged covariance using a sample size that represents the actual number of data points contributing to the covariance because it yields an unbiased estimator. However, use of the full sample (occasions) N is preferable because it yields an estimate that often has a smaller mean square error (Jenkins & Watts, 1968). In practice, the order of the lag is so minor as not occasion concern about the size of the N used. Second, lagged covariances between two different variables are not generally symmetric; for example,

$$
\begin{bmatrix} 4 \\ 10 \\ 15 \\ 18 \\ 25 \end{bmatrix} \cdot \begin{bmatrix} 1 \\ 3 \\ 5 \\ 7 \\ 9 \end{bmatrix}^{T} \;\Downarrow=\; \begin{bmatrix} 10 \\ 15 \\ 18 \\ 25 \end{bmatrix} \cdot \begin{bmatrix} 1 \\ 3 \\ 5 \\ 7 \end{bmatrix}^{T} \;\neq\; \Downarrow \begin{bmatrix} 4 \\ 10 \\ 15 \\ 18 \\ 25 \end{bmatrix} \cdot \begin{bmatrix} 1 \\ 3 \\ 5 \\ 7 \\ 9 \end{bmatrix}^{T} = \begin{bmatrix} 4 \\ 10 \\ 18 \\ 25 \end{bmatrix} \cdot \begin{bmatrix} 3 \\ 5 \\ 7 \\ 9 \end{bmatrix}^{T}
$$

As discussed in the section Block-Toeplitz Matrices, this lack of symmetry places special restrictions on the type of covariance matrix used.

Although not directly used in DFA, the concept of a partial autocovariance or partial autocorrelation is important for the proper transformation of the data prior to a DFA. A lag-k partial autocorrelation is a correlation between an observation at time t (Y_t) and one at time $t - k$ (Y_{t-k}) after the effects of the intermediate observations ($Y_{t-1}, Y_{t-2}, \ldots, Y_{t-k+1}$) have been removed. Thus a lag-k partial autocorrelation is merely the partial correlation of a variable with itself lagged k times. The formulas for a lag-one, lag-two, and lag-three partial autocorrelation are, respectively:

$$
r_{1}, \quad \frac{r_2 - r_1^2}{1 - r_1^2}, \quad \frac{r_3 + r_1 r_2^2 + r_1^3 - 2 r_1 r_2 - r_1^2 r_3}{1 + 2 r_1^2 r_2 - r_2^2 - 2 r_1^2}.
$$

Beyond the third lag, the formula for the partial autocorrelation becomes extremely complicated and is generally estimated as a solution to the Yule–Walker equation system (Box & Jenkins, 1976).

Autocorrelation functions play an important role in time series model identification. An autocorrelation function is constructed by plotting the values of successive k-lagged autocorrelations. Closely related to the autocorrelation function is the *partial autocorrelation function,* in which successive k-lagged partial autocorrelations are plotted. Another plot, useful for detecting when a series has been overcorrected for a deterministic trend, is the *inverse autocorrelation function.* This function may be best understood as the autocorrelation function of a series whose parameters are the complements of the series (Schmitz, 1990). Confidence intervals typically of one standard error in magnitude are constructed around each correlation in the functions. Inspection of all three plots is helpful in determining the presence and order of significant serial dependency in the data.

Block-Toeplitz Matrices

As discussed later, the solution of the dynamic factor model relies on structural equation modeling (SEM) methodology. In order to exploit SEM for this purpose, we are required to specify a symmetric covariance matrix that contains the lagged covariances, seemingly a difficult task to accomplish given the inherently asymmetric character of the lagged covariances. One solution lies in the organization of the lagged covariance matrices as a block-Toeplitz matrix. A block-Toeplitz matrix replicates the symmetric blocks of 0-lagged covariances and higher order asymmetric blocks of lagged covariances so as to construct a variance-covariance matrix that is square and symmetric, overcoming the difficulties presented by the asymmetry of lagged covariances. Let $A(0)$ represent a symmetric variance-covariance matrix of 0-lagged covariances, $A(1)$ an asymmetric variance-covariance matrix of first-order lagged covariances, and $A(s)$ an asymmetric matrix of higher order ($s > 1$) lagged covariances. The incorporation of $A(0)$, $A(1)$, and $A(s)$ into a block-Toeplitz matrix produces:

$$A = \begin{bmatrix} A(0) & & & \\ A(1) & A(0) & & \\ A(s) & A(1) & A(0) & \\ A(s+1) & A(s) & A(1) & A(0) \end{bmatrix}.$$

By duplicating the blocks of variance-covariance matrices in a diagonal fashion, the square symmetry of a typical variance-covariance matrix is created. As a concrete example, consider the block-Toeplitz matrix when the number of variables (p) is equal to eight and the number of lags (s) is equal to three. The corresponding block-Toeplitz matrix is 32×32 ($p * (s + 1) \times p * (s + 1)$) and appears as

$$\begin{bmatrix} A(0) & & & \\ A(1) & A(0) & & \\ A(2) & A(1) & A(0) & \\ A(3) & A(2) & A(1) & A(0) \end{bmatrix}.$$

To our knowledge, no standard statistical software program exists that will directly compute the lagged covariance matrices and organize them in block-Toeplitz form. In this chapter, a FORTRAN program was used to conduct these tasks. One alternative has been provided by Wood and Brown (1994) who provided a program written in the SAS (Statistical Analysis System) Macro (SAS, 1990a) and SAS IML (SAS, 1990b) languages to construct the lagged covariances and block-Toeplitz matrices, among other important tasks required in modeling time series.

Stationarity

A p-dimensional observed time series of length t may be defined by the transposed vector:

$$y(t) = \{y_1(t_1), \ldots, y_p(t_k)\}'$$

where p refers to the number of variables measured on an individual at each of the k occasions. It is assumed that $y(t)$ is generated by the finite-dimensional probability distributions

$$P(y;t) = Prob[y(t) < y],$$
$$P(y_1,y_2;t_1,t_2) = Prob[y(t_1) < y_1;y(t_2) < y_2], \; etc.$$

As a random, time-dependent function, $y(t)$ has first-order mean and second-order covariance functions. If the mean function is a constant,

$$E[y(t)] = c_y,$$

then $y(t)$ is referred to as first-order stationary. When the covariance function depends only on the order of the lag between t_1 and t_2, $y(t)$ is referred to as second-order stationary:

$$E[y(t_1),y(t_2)'] = C_y(t_2 - t_1) = C_y(s), s = t_2 - t_1.$$

If $y(t)$ is both first- and second-order stationary, it is called weakly stationary. When all of $y(t)$'s other, higher order moments are stationary as well, $y(t)$ is called strictly stationary. Identifying a time series as at least weakly stationary is critical for appropriately estimating its mean and covariance from any single realization (observation) of the series. This implies that the series has no deterministic trend (a rising or falling mean), and that its covariance function is invariant under a translation along the time axis.

The necessity for stationarity is particularly compelling when considered in light of the purpose for computing cross-lagged correlations between two series. Nonstationarity in either series implies that future observations are predictable from past observations within the same series. Thus a series with significant nonstationary can "predict itself." On the other hand, the magnitude of the cross-lagged correlation between two series represents the degree to which one series can predict the other. Our interpretation of the importance of the cross-series relation should consider whether one series can add to the predictability of the other, beyond that obtained from using the series to predict itself. Thus, before evaluating the cross-series predictability, the within-series predictability should be removed.

The DFA model assumes weak stationarity; that is, no deterministic trend is present and there is sequential covariance homogeneity across time (i.e., adjacent observations are similarly correlated throughout the series). One extension of the model, nonstationary DFA, allows the series to have a deterministic trend but still requires sequential covariance homogeneity. Both models are discussed in this chapter. A model in which the assumption of weak stationarity is removed has been described (Molenaar, 1994) but is not applied here. There are two primary reasons for staying within the realm of weakly stationary models. First, the statistical theory of weakly stationary models is the most highly developed within time series analysis. Second, parameter estimation of weakly stationary models can be conducted by a number of commercially available SEM programs. Dispensing altogether with the assumption of weak stationary does not preclude the solution of these models with some SEM programs, but difficulty in specifying these models does increase greatly.

Disturbances (Random Shock, White Noise, Innovations)

Nearly all time series models incorporate a stochastic component, referred to as a *disturbance* (or sometimes a *random shock, white noise,* an *innovation*), to denote the novelty of this effect at a particular occasion. Disturbances (ε) are assumed to have the following properties:

$$E(\varepsilon_t) = 0,$$

$$var(\varepsilon_t) = \sigma_\varepsilon^2,$$

$$\gamma_k = E(\varepsilon_t \varepsilon_{t+k}) = \begin{cases} \sigma_\varepsilon^2, k = 0, \\ 0, k \neq 0, \end{cases}$$

$$\rho_k = \frac{\gamma_k}{\sigma_\varepsilon^2} = \begin{cases} 1, k = 0, \\ 0, k \neq 0, \end{cases}$$

where γ and ρ are general covariance and correlation functions, respectively.

TIME SERIES MODELING

In this section, a very general introduction is given to time series modeling using the ARIMA approach developed principally by Box and Jenkins (1976). Some familiarity with ARIMA modeling is important for conducting and interpreting the results of a DFA. This is because, as noted earlier, the DFA model assumes weak stationarity. Thus, before conducting a dynamic analysis, the time series should be examined for the presence of a deterministic trend and heterogeneity in the sequential covariance pattern. If either are found, they should be removed prior to the DFA. ARIMA modeling provides an efficient system for detecting violations to the assumption of weak stationarity and for correcting the data for their presence. Essentially, the correction is done by explicitly modeling the problematic characteristics of the data, and creating a time series residualized for these characteristics. The residualized series is then weakly stationary and appropriate for DFA. The residualization depends on the correct identification of the order of three different parameters: p, d, and q, where p refers to the order of the autoregressive (AR) process, d refers to the number of times the data must be differenced (integrated) to remove deterministic trends, and q refers to the order of the moving average (MA) process. These three parameters are used in combination to explain the mean trend (d) and covariation (p, q) of the series.

The univariate equation for an $AR(p)$ is:

$$y_t = \phi y_{t-1} + \phi y_{t-2} + \ldots + \phi y_{t-p} + \varepsilon_t,$$

where ϕ and ε are scalars. This equation expresses the relation between one occasion and p preceding occasions, the number of preceding occasions corresponding to the order of the autoregressive process. An $AR(p)$ process is required to be stationary. In order for an $AR(p)$ process to be stationary, the ϕ_p scalars must meet the so-called *bounds of invertibility* condition, where $|\phi_p| < 1$. Figure 8.1 shows the autocorrelation, partial autocorrelation, and inverse autocorrelation functions expected when $AR(p) = 2$. For stationary models, the AR autocorrelation function should decrease exponentially or sinusoidally, the partial correlations corresponding to lag $> p$ should equal zero, and the inverse autocorrelation function should decrease sinusoidally.

A multivariate autoregressive process of order P $(AR(P))$ may be expressed as:

$$y_t = \Phi_1 y_{t-1} + \phi_p y_{t-p} + \varepsilon_t$$

where Φ_i, $i = 1, \ldots, p$ are $p \times p$ matrices of parameters and ε_t is a $p \times 1$ disturbance vector. Both Φ_p and ε_t provide information concerning the univariate process of each variable, and the multivariate processes occurring among the variables. Significant diagonal elements in Φ indicate the order of the autoregressive process for each variable, and the off-diagonal elements indicate the order of the lagged relation between the variables. The diagonal elements in ε indicate the existence of a disturbance for a variable; the off-diagonal elements indicate whether a simultaneous relation exists between variables.

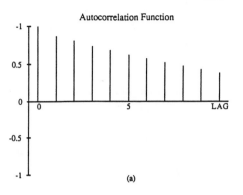

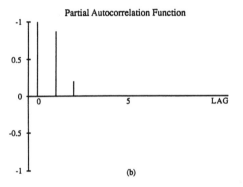

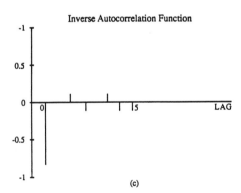

FIG. 8.1. Autocorrelation functions for *AR(2)* model.

In practice, autocorrelation, partial autocorrelation, and inverse autocorrelation functions for the *cross-correlations* among the variables would be inspected to determine *AR(P)*. This approach is preferable to the inspection of univariate autocorrelation functions when a set of variables is involved. The requirement for a stationary *AR(P)* process is the stationarity of the variables' cross-correlation functions and not their individual correlation functions (Harvey, 1981).

The univariate equation for a *MA(q)* process is:

$$y(t) = \varepsilon_t - \theta_1\varepsilon_{t-1} - \theta_2\varepsilon_{t-2} - \ldots - \theta_q y_{t-q}.$$

This equation expresses the relation between one occasion and a weighted average of θ_q preceding disturbances, the number of preceding disturbances corresponding to the order of the MA process. θ_q and ε_t are again scalars. In order for an *MA(q)* process to be stationary, θ must meet the invertibility condition $|\theta| < 1$. Figure 8.2 shows the autocorrelation, partial autocorrelation, and inverse autocorrelation functions expected when *MA(q)* = 2. For stationary models, the MA autocorrelation function should equal zero for lags greater than *q*, the partial correlation should decrease exponentially or sinusoidally, and the inverse autocorrelation function should decrease sinusoidally.

A multivariate MA *(MA(Q))* may be expressed as:

$$y_t = \varepsilon_t - \Theta_1\varepsilon_{t-1} - \Theta_2\varepsilon_{t-2} - \ldots - \Theta_Q\varepsilon_{t-Q},$$

where Θ is a $p \times p$ matrix of parameters and ε is defined as a $p \times 1$ vector of disturbances.

As noted earlier, stationarity is required for time series analyses. Frequently, a nonstationary time series may be made so by differencing the time series, $y_t - y_{t-d}$, where *d* refers to the order of the difference. A nonstationary time series is most easily detected when the slope of the autocorrelation plot is fairly flat. Conversely, an overdifferenced time series is most easily detected by an exponentially decreasing inverse autocorrelation plot (Cleveland, 1972). When both *AR* and *MA* processes co-occur in a differenced time series, the univariate *ARIMA (p,d,q)* equation is:

$$y_t = \phi_1 Y_{t-1} + \phi_2 y_{t-2} + \ldots \phi_p y_{t-p} + \varepsilon_t - \theta_1\varepsilon_{t-1} - \theta_2\varepsilon_{t-2} - \ldots - \theta_q\varepsilon_{t-q},$$

where *d* may be of any order $< k - 2$. The comparable multivariate *ARIMA (P,D,Q)* equation is:

$$y_t = \Phi_1 y_{t-1} + \Phi_2 y_{t-2} + \ldots + \Phi_p y_{t-p} + \varepsilon_t - \Theta_1\varepsilon_{t-1} - \Theta_2\varepsilon_{t-2} - \ldots - \Theta_Q\varepsilon_{t-Q}.$$

Note that when the series is stationary, and therefore does not require differencing, it is referred to as either an *ARMA (p,q)* or *ARMA (P,Q)* process.

It is important to identify *seasonal or cyclical* processes in the data if they exist. These processes occur at consistent points in the time series. For example, each year, retail sales increase in the 4-week period prior to Christmas. This is a deterministic trend and should be removed. Instead of differencing observations one or two occasions removed, observations 12 months apart would need to be differenced in order to remove this yearly cycle.

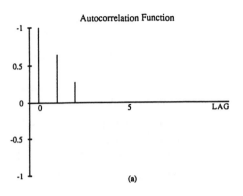

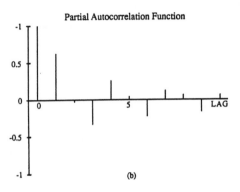

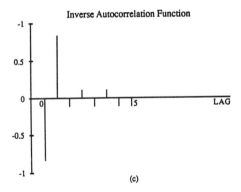

FIG. 8.2. Autocorrelation functions
for *MA(2)* model.

Model-Fitting Criteria

One of the most important questions to address in time series modeling and
dynamic factor analysis is: How well does the model fit the data? Harvey
(1989) has enumerated six criteria that can be used to judge whether the
model selected should be the "final" model retained to describe the data:

1. Parsimony: A parsimonious model is a model that uses relatively few parameters to describe the data.
2. Data coherence: Coherent data are data predicted by a model that closely match the observed data.
3. Consistency with prior knowledge: Models should be consistent with accepted theory and prior knowledge.
4. Data admissibility: Models should not imply impossible values for the data.
5. Structural stability: A structurally stable model for a time series fits other sampled occasions for the same variables.
6. Encompassing: A good model encompasses competing models. It explains aspects of the data accounted for by competing models *and* provides additional explanation.

Numerous statistical indices for comparing the relative fit of models fit have been proposed. A common approach, when dealing with hierarchically nested models, is to compute a chi-square difference test. Hierarchically nested models are two or more models that be derived from each other by imposing constraints on the more highly parameterized model. A chi-square value based on the likelihood of each model is typically computed. The difference between the chi-squares of nested models is itself distributed as a chi-square with degrees of freedom equal to the difference in degrees of freedom of the two models. In the simplest case, where the significance of a single parameter is in question, the chi-square difference is evaluated with 1 degree of freedom. A nonsignificant difference in chi-square implies that the parameter may be removed from the model without a significant decrement in model fit.

Various information indices are useful in comparing non-nested models. Common to all information indices is a comparison between the fit of the model and the number of parameters that were used to obtain that fit. Models with smaller information indices are to be preferred; that is, the fit of these models is similar to the fit of competing models but this fit was obtained with fewer parameters. Three information indices are commonly reported:

- *Akaike's* (1987) *Information Criterion (AIC):*

$$\chi^2_{target} - 2df_{target},$$

- *Schwarz's* (1978) *Bayesian Information Criterion (SBIC):*

$$\chi^2_{target} - \ln(N)df_{target},$$

• *Hannan–Quinn* (1979) *Criterion (HQ):*

$$\chi^2_{target} - c\,(\ln(\ln(N)))\,2df_{target}\; c = 1.$$

FACTOR ANALYSIS MODELS

P-Technique Factor Analysis

P-technique was an early approach to the factor analysis of time series introduced by Cattell (1952). As a factor analytic technique, it was hoped that *P*-technique might reveal the latent structure underlying the observed correlations among a set of variables measured over time. *P*-technique factor analysis involves the factor analysis of covariances among variables, produced from occasion by variable data matrices for a single entity (e.g., a person, business, etc.). This is to be contrasted with traditional *R*-technique factor analysis in which the latent variable structure among a set of variables is also examined, but the correlation matrix is constructed from an entity by variable data matrix obtained from one occasion of measurement. Interestingly, factoring the same set of variables using *P*- and *R*-technique will not necessarily result in the same latent structure responsible for the variable intercorrelations. *P*-technique reveals the latent sources of within-entity variability across time, whereas *R*-technique reveals the latent sources of between-entity variability at one time.

The *P*-technique factor analysis model may be expressed as:

$$y(t) = \Lambda\eta(t) + \varepsilon(t),\ t = 0, \pm 1, \ldots,$$

with Λ, $(p \times q)$, η, $(q \times 1)$, and ε, $(p \times 1)$. Λ is a matrix of factor loadings relating p variables to q factors, η is a vector of scores on the factors, and ε is a vector of disturbance terms.

The covariance function of the model is:

$$C(0) = \Lambda\Xi(0)\Lambda^T + \Theta(0),$$

with *COV(0)* a $p \times p$ matrix of nonlagged covariances, Ξ a $q \times q$ matrix of factor variances and covariances, and Θ a $p \times p$ matrix of disturbance variances and covariances. Figure 8.3 shows a path diagram representation of the *P*-technique model. In this diagram, Y_1, Y_2, and Y_3 are three observed measures, whose covariance at any point in time is due to their common association with the factor, labeled *Day K*. λ_{1y}, λ_{2y}, and λ_{3y} represent the regression of the observed variables on their common factor (i.e., factor loadings) and ζ, the variance of the factor. When solved under an exploratory approach, two restrictions are generally imposed on the *P*-technique model:

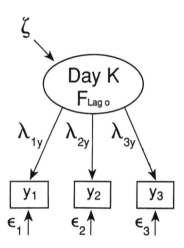

FIG. 8.3. Path diagram of P-technique model.

One, the factors are scaled to have unit variance (although they may be correlated), and two, Θ is restricted to be a diagonal matrix (the disturbance terms are uncorrelated). This latter restriction is not likely to be valid, however, given the sequential nature of the data. Under a confirmatory factor analytic approach, Θ may be specified as nondiagonal, if restrictions are placed on the pattern on factor loadings. In either case, the P-technique model assumes weak stationarity in the data.

As an example, consider a four-factor ($q = 4$) model in which $p = 20$. Variables 1 through 5 load on the first factor, variables 6 through 10 load on the second factor, variables 11 through 15 load on the third factor, and variables 16 through 20 load on the fourth factor. The factors are permitted to be correlated with each other, and disturbances are permitted to be correlated within factors. The matrix representation of this model is:

$$COV = [COV(0)];\ (28 \times 28)$$

$$\lambda = [\lambda(0)];\ (20 \times 4) =$$

$$
\begin{bmatrix}
\lambda_{1,1} & 0 & 0 & 0 \\
\vdots & \vdots & \vdots & \vdots \\
0 & \lambda_{6,2} & 0 & 0 \\
\vdots & \vdots & \vdots & \vdots \\
0 & 0 & \lambda_{11,3} & 0 \\
\vdots & \vdots & \vdots & \vdots \\
0 & 0 & 0 & \lambda_{20,4}
\end{bmatrix}
$$

$$\Theta = [\Theta(0)]; \ (28 \times 28) =$$

$$
\begin{bmatrix}
\theta_{1,1} \\
\theta_{2,1} & \theta_{2,2} \\
\theta_{3,1} & \theta_{3,2} & \theta_{3,3} \\
\theta_{4,1} & \theta_{4,2} & \theta_{4,3} & \theta_{4,4} \\
\theta_{5,1} & \theta_{5,2} & \theta_{5,3} & \theta_{5,4} & \theta_{5,5} \\
0 & 0 & 0 & 0 & 0 & \theta_{6,6} \\
0 & 0 & 0 & 0 & 0 & \theta_{7,6} & \theta_{7,7} \\
0 & 0 & 0 & 0 & 0 & \theta_{8,6} & \theta_{8,7} & \theta_{8,8} \\
0 & 0 & 0 & 0 & 0 & \theta_{9,6} & \theta_{9,7} & \theta_{9,8} & \theta_{9,9} \\
0 & 0 & 0 & 0 & 0 & \theta_{10,6} & \theta_{10,7} & \theta_{10,8} & \theta_{10,9} & \theta_{10,10} \\
0 & 0 & 0 & 0 & 0 & 0 & 0 & 0 & 0 & 0 & \theta_{11,11} \\
0 & 0 & 0 & 0 & 0 & 0 & 0 & 0 & 0 & 0 & \theta_{12,11} & \theta_{12,12} \\
0 & 0 & 0 & 0 & 0 & 0 & 0 & 0 & 0 & 0 & \theta_{13,11} & \theta_{13,12} & \theta_{13,13} \\
0 & 0 & 0 & 0 & 0 & 0 & 0 & 0 & 0 & 0 & \theta_{14,11} & \theta_{14,12} & \theta_{14,13} & \theta_{14,14} \\
0 & 0 & 0 & 0 & 0 & 0 & 0 & 0 & 0 & 0 & \theta_{15,11} & \theta_{15,12} & \theta_{15,13} & \theta_{15,14} & \theta_{15,15} \\
0 & 0 & 0 & 0 & 0 & 0 & 0 & 0 & 0 & 0 & 0 & 0 & 0 & 0 & 0 & \theta_{16,16} \\
0 & 0 & 0 & 0 & 0 & 0 & 0 & 0 & 0 & 0 & 0 & 0 & 0 & 0 & 0 & \theta_{17,16} & \theta_{17,17} \\
0 & 0 & 0 & 0 & 0 & 0 & 0 & 0 & 0 & 0 & 0 & 0 & 0 & 0 & 0 & \theta_{18,16} & \theta_{18,17} & \theta_{18,18} \\
0 & 0 & 0 & 0 & 0 & 0 & 0 & 0 & 0 & 0 & 0 & 0 & 0 & 0 & 0 & \theta_{19,16} & \theta_{19,17} & \theta_{19,18} & \theta_{19,19} \\
0 & 0 & 0 & 0 & 0 & 0 & 0 & 0 & 0 & 0 & 0 & 0 & 0 & 0 & 0 & \theta_{20,16} & \theta_{20,17} & \theta_{20,18} & \theta_{20,19} & \theta_{20,20}
\end{bmatrix}
$$

$$\Xi = [\phi]; \ (4 \times 4) =$$

$$
\begin{bmatrix}
1 \\
\phi_{2,1} & 1 \\
\phi_{3,1} & \phi_{3,2} & 1 \\
\phi_{4,1} & \phi_{4,2} & \phi_{4,3} & 1
\end{bmatrix}.
$$

Note that the typical issue of rotating the initial factor pattern to achieve interpretabilty of the solution is rendered moot by the confirmatory approach taken in this example. That is, a specific pattern of variable-factor associations were imposed prior to the analysis. After obtaining the factor pattern matrix, it is often desirable to compute factor scores directly in the interest of graphing the latent time series directly.

Stationary Dynamic Factor Analysis

The *stationary dynamic factor analysis* (SDFA) model may be considered a generalization of the *P*-technique factor analysis model that includes the lagged-covariance structure among the variables (Molenaar, 1985). Under ordinary *P*-technique, in which the covariances are of 0-lag (the covariances are among measurements taken within the same occasion), the obtained factor structure represents the simultaneous relation among variables. The incorporation of lagged covariances in SDFA opens up the possibility of uncovering relations among variables across a specified interval of time, an interval defined by the order of the lag.

The SDFA model with q factors and s lags of p observed variables can be expressed as:

$$y(t) = \Lambda(0)\,\eta(t) + \Lambda(1)\,\eta(t-1) + \ldots + \Lambda(s-1)\,\eta(t-s+1) + \varepsilon(t) =$$

$$y(t) = \sum_{u=0}^{s} \Lambda(u)\eta(t-u) + \varepsilon(t),$$

where $y(t)$ is the observed p-variate time series, $\eta(t)$ is the latent q-variate factor time series, $\varepsilon(t)$ is a p-variate vector of disturbances, and $\Lambda(u)$, $u = 0, 1, \ldots, s-1$, are $p \times q$ matrices of lagged factor loadings. Each of the Λ differ from each other, suggesting the factor structure differs for each of the lags. To put it simply, the latent "causes" of the time series differ depending on the length of time observed between two time points.

The covariance function of the *SDFA* model is:

$$COV(u) = \sum_{v=0}^{s} \Lambda(v)\Xi\Lambda(u-v)' + \Theta(u),$$

where $\Lambda(u)$ is a series of $(p \times q)$ matrices of lagged loadings on the latent factors, $\Xi(u)$ is a series of $(q \times q)$ matrices of lagged covariances among the latent factors, and $\Theta(u)$ is a series of diagonal $(p \times p)$ disturbance matrices.

Figure 8.4 shows a path diagram of the SDFA model. Note that within any single occasion, the covariances among the observed variables are a function (Λ) of the 0-lagged factors, and across occasions, the covariances

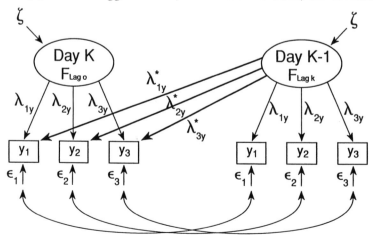

FIG. 8.4. Path diagram of dynamic factor analysis model.

are a function (Λ^*) of the higher order lagged factors. Note also that a 0-lag disturbance is correlated with its higher order lag counterpart.

Transforming the SDFA model into a form appropriate for SEM involves two essential steps. First, a symmetric covariance matrix that incorporates the lagged covariances of the observed multivariate time series must be constructed. This is the block-Toeplitz matrix described earlier. Second, an SEM must be specified that places constraints on the model parameters consistent with the redundancies in the block-Toeplitz matrix.

The SEM for the SDFA model can be specified as follows: Λ, the matrix of factor loadings, is of order $p(s + 1) \times q(2s + 1)$, where s = the number of lags. Λ consists of $s + 1$ $p \times q$ blocks of lag-0 loadings, $s + 1$ $p \times q$ blocks of lag-1 loadings, $s + 1$ $p \times q$ blocks of lag-2 loadings, and so on. The factor covariance Ξ is symmetric and of order $q(2s + 1)$. In order to achieve identification of the model, the latent factors are scaled to have variances of unity (1s are fixed on the diagonal of Ξ) and the factors are left uncorrelated. The disturbance variance-covariance Θ is symmetric and of order $p(s + 1)$. Θ has the same block-Toeplitz pattern and dimensions as the covariance matrix among the observed variables but all the blocks are diagonal $p \times p$ dimensional matrices.

As an example, consider a four-factor, two-lag model for 20 observed variables; that is, $q = 4$, $s = 2$, $p = 20$:

$$COV = \begin{bmatrix} COV(0) & & \\ COV(1) & COV(0) & \\ COV(2) & COV(1) & COV(0) \end{bmatrix}; (60 \times 60)$$

$$\Lambda = \begin{bmatrix} \Lambda(0) & \Lambda(1) & \Lambda(2) & 0 & 0 \\ 0 & \Lambda(0) & \Lambda(1) & \Lambda(2) & 0 \\ 0 & 0 & \Lambda(0) & \Lambda(1) & \Lambda(2) \end{bmatrix}; (60 \times 20)$$

$$\Theta = \begin{bmatrix} \Theta(0) & & \\ \Theta(1) & \Theta(0) & \\ \Theta(2) & \Theta(1) & \Theta(0) \end{bmatrix}; (60 \times 60)$$

$$\Xi = I_q; (20 \times 20).$$

In this model, the covariance matrix and Θ are of order 60×60 because there are 60 observed variables (each of the 20 observed variables for the 0, first, and second lags), and therefore, the Λ matrix is of order 60×20 because each lag is represented by four factors, $q(2s + 1) = 4 * (2 * 2 + 1) = 20$.

Although DFA allows in principle confirmatory analyses (like the P-technique example give earlier), in practice most analyses will be exploratory (as in the preceding example) due to the likely differences among the factor structures across the various lags and the consequent difficulty many researchers would have in specifying such differences. Thus typically, all identified factor loadings will be evaluated. Analogous to the situation that exists for exploratory factor analyses, the initial DFA solution will often be difficult to interpret, requiring a rotation to achieve interpretability. For any orthogonal transformation matrix, the rotated DFA solution will be statistically equivalent to the unrotated solution. As a practical matter, under most analytic rotations, the 0-lag factor pattern will capture a majority of the variance from the higher order lagged factor patterns if the factor patterns are rotated simultaneously. Thus, factor patterns of different lags should be rotated separately. A theoretical rational exists for the independent rotation of factor solutions of different lags as well: The factor structures of each of the lags represents a distinct process.

Scores on the factors in DFA are generally not as easily computed when compared with the computation of factor scores from analyses using only the 0-lag covariances. Once higher order lagged covariances are introduced, Kalman filtering procedures are necessary to obtain factor scores (Dolan & Molenaar, 1991).

Nonstationary Dynamic Factor Analysis Model

Molenaar et al. (1992) proposed a nonstationary extension of the SDFA model. In the *nonstationary dynamic factor analysis* (NDFA) model, the temporal effects of trends are not removed prior to the analysis, but instead incorporated as an influence on the latent factor series. It is still assumed, however, that the assumption of homogenous sequential covariances is still met. Repeating the equation for the SDFA model given earlier:

$$y(t) = \sum_{u=0}^{s} \Lambda(u)\eta(t-u) + \varepsilon(t),$$

we add the linear trend model:

$$\eta(t) = \gamma\tau(t) + w(t),$$

where γ is $(q \times 1)$, $\tau(t)$ denotes the linear trend, and $w(t)$ is a stochastic term. The covariance function of the NDFA model is then:

$$COV(u) = \sum_{v=0}^{s} \Lambda(v)\{\varpi\varpi' + I_{(2s+1)q}\}\Lambda' + \Theta$$

where ϖ is the $(2s + 1)$ q-dimensional vector. Note that $w(t)$ is a diagonal matrix with fixed ones.

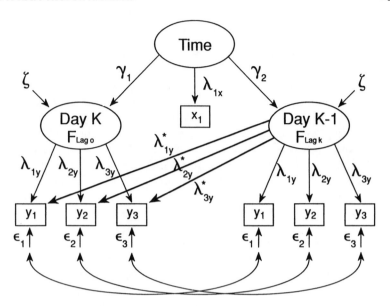

FIG. 8.5. Path diagram of nonstationary dynamic factor analysis model.

Implementation of the NDFA model requires a simple addition to the SDFA model: the construction of a time-ordered vector equal in length to that of the observed series, and the addition of this new variable to the existing set of variables. For example, if the time series consisted of 60 observations, we created a new variable with values from 1 to 60. The scaling of this time variable is completely arbitrary. During the construction of the block-Toeplitz matrix, both the original form and the lagged form of this time variable are added to the matrix, although it is only necessary to select the nonlagged form of the time variable for the analysis. With this new observed variable, one then creates a second-order factor model in which the observed variable is equated to a latent exogenous variable; the exogenous latent variable is allowed to influence all the lower order lagged and nonlagged factors. The values of the γ coefficients connecting the higher and lower order factors provide the values of the trend coefficients unique to each factor. Figure 8.5 presents a path diagram of the NDFA model (an extension of Fig. 8.4). In order to parameterize the NDFA model as an SEM, Λ and Θ are dimensionalized as in the SDFA model. Γ is symmetric and of order $(2s + 1)q$:

$$\Gamma \begin{bmatrix} \gamma & 0 & \cdots & 0 \\ 0 & \gamma & \cdots & 0 \\ \vdots & \vdots & \vdots & \vdots \\ 0 & 0 & \cdots & \gamma \end{bmatrix}.$$

EMPIRICAL EXAMPLE

For the analysis of this example, the SEM program LISREL (Jöreskog & Sörbom, 1993) is used. The example we use to illustrate the application of the dynamic factor models concerns a chain of appliance stores in a particular state. The data are not real but were manufactured to provide a relatively clear example of the methods. The corporation owning these stores was interested in determining what were the factors affecting the volume of weekly sales of a certain brand of refrigerator. Eighty weeks of data were collected. Each time point in the multivariate series was the weekly average for that variable. Twenty-eight variables were measured: (a) number of units sold, (b) sales price, (c) price relative to the most popular brand of refrigerator, (d) price increase relative to the week before, (e) price decrease relative to the week before, (f) amount of "regular" (ordinary), and (g) "special" (for holidays, unusual price reductions) advertising on television, (h) amount of regular and (i) special advertising on radio, (j) amount of regular and (k) special advertising in newspapers, (l) amount of regular and (m) special advertising on the Internet, (n) increase in total amount of advertising relative to the week before, (o) decrease in total advertising relative to the week before, (p) area unemployment rate (q) change in area unemployment rate from week before, (r) median area income, (s) degree of inclement weather, (t) whether the week contained a national holiday, (u) average household size, (v) area ratio of the number of apartments to households, (w) number of competing appliance stores in the area, (x) a prestige score for the target brand, (y) total number of the same units available, (z) total number of other brand units available, (aa) a favorableness rating of the target brand, and (bb) a recognition rating of the target brand, both from a survey conducted by a national marketing company.

Before the DFA can proceed, the assumption of weak stationary in the multivariate time series must be confirmed. We do not review the analytic details concerned with confirming the assumption of weak stationarity. It should be emphasized that in these data, the presence of a seasonal trend is highly likely, and the data should be examined with this expectation. Such a seasonal trend was removed from the data before conducting the factor analyses.

Once the data have been appropriately corrected for departures from weak stationarity, the 0-lagged covariances among the 28 variables can be subjected to a P-technique factor analysis. Appendix A provides the LISREL program for a P-technique analysis, specifying four factors and one lag. Throughout the analyses, we assume that four factors is the correct dimensionality of the latent variable structure and that single-lagged covariances capture adequately the cross-time associations among the observed variables.

In the first P-technique model, an orthogonal four-factor structure was rejected: $\chi^2(350, N = 104) = 668.50$, $p < .001$. Significant improvement in fit occurred with the addition of either an oblique factor structure (χ^2_{344} = 591.67, $p < .001$; $\chi^2_{diff,6}$ = 76.62, $p < .001$), or correlated disturbances within each of the factors (χ^2_{345} = 653.95, $p < .001$; $\chi^2_{diff,5}$ = 14.54, $p < .05$). In the correlated disturbances model, the disturbances of some of the observed indicators of a factor were allowed to correlate with each other within the factor; disturbances were not allowed to correlate across factors. Allowing disturbances to correlate in this way would, if all possible disturbance correlations were evaluated, completely explain the within-time correlations among the observed variables. The detection of significant correlated disturbances within factors suggests an unmodeled source of commonality among the observed variables. This commonality could in theory be attributable to the influence of higher order (lagged) processes in the data.

Appendix B provides the LISREL program for an SDFA model. The SDFA model was evaluated by first constructing a block-Toeplitz matrix with 0, 1-lagged covariances. This model was rejected: $\chi^2(1,484) = 2,538.07$, $p < .001$. Still, it is of some value to compare the SDFA model with the P-technique to see if any improvement in fit was obtained. Because P-technique factor analysis (with uncorrelated factors and measurement errors) and SDFA use different covariance matrices, it is strictly inappropriate to conduct a chi-square difference test between the two models (the models are not nested). We can compare their information indices: $AIC_p = -36.05$, $AIC_{SDFA} = -429.93$; $SBIC_p = -857.85$, $SBIC_{SDFA} = -3,964.86$; $HQ_p = -365.53$, $HQ_{SDFA} = -1,847.18$. All three information indices indicate that the increase in chi-square for the SDFA model was more than compensated by the increase in degrees of freedom, relative to the P-technique factor analysis.

Although the SDFA model did not fit the data, it is of some value to examine the factor pattern matrix from this analysis as an example of how to interpret the results of a SDFA. This matrix is given in Table 8.1. In Table 8.1, all factor loadings that had standardized values of .30 or greater on a factor are indicated by an "X." Under the 0-lag solution, Factor I may be interpreted as a price factor: The number of units sold is associated with the current sale price, and the price of the target brand relative to the most popular brand. Under the 1-lag solution, Factor I' may also be interpreted as a price factor, but in this case reflecting week-to-week changes. Thus, the number of units sold is still related to the current sale price and the price relative to the most popular brand, but in addition, sales are also associated with increases and decrease in the sale price from the previous week. Under the 0-lag solution, Factor II is clearly an advertising factor: The volume of advertising from all four media, whether of the regular or special variety, has an effect on sales. Factor II' is also an advertising factor, additionally indexing how week-by-week changes in advertising influences sales. The third 0-lag factor is a local conditions factor: Local unemployment, median income, amount of inclement weather, the appearance of a national

TABLE 8.1
Dynamic Factor Analysis Factor Pattern

Variable	0-lag				1-lag			
	I	II	III	IV	I'	II'	III'	IV'
Units sold	X	X	X	X	X	X	X	X
Sales price	X				X			
Relative price	X				X			
Price increase					X			
Price decrease					X			
Reg. TV adv.		X				X		
Reg. radio adv.		X				X		
Reg. paper adv.		X				X		
Reg. internet adv.		X				X		
Spec. TV adv.		X				X		
Spec. radio adv.		X				X		
Spec. paper adv.		X				X		
Spec internet adv.		X				X		
Increase total adv.						X		
Decrease total adv.						X		
Unemployment								
Unemployment change			X				X	
Income			X				X	
Weather			X				X	
National holiday			X				X	
Household size			X					
Dwelling ratio			X					
Store competition			X					
Prestige				X				X
No. of same units				X				X
No. of other units				X				X
Favorableness rating				X				X
Recognition rating				X				X

Note. Xs indicate standardized factor loadings that were .30 or higher.

holiday, the average household size, the ratio of apartments to houses in the area, and the number of other appliance stores in the area are all related to the number of units sold on this factor. Factor III' under the 1-lag solution is an abbreviated form of this factor: Unemployment change, income, weather, and national holiday load on this factor whereas the other local condition variables do not. Possibly, this is due to the lack of week-to-week variability in these measures. For instance, we would expect the local ratio of number of apartments to number of houses to not fluctuate significantly except over long periods of time. Labeling the fourth factor in both the 0-lag and 1-lag solutions is a somewhat more difficult task than labeling the other factors due to the eclectic nature of the relevant variables: Brand reliability may be a good descriptor. Prestige certainly indicates this. The number of units of the same brand available at time of purchase may also indicate reliability depending on how a consumer interprets this number. For example, if a consumer sees many units of the same brand available, the consumer may believe other consumers are not buying the brand because it is not very good. Conversely, if few units remain, the brand appears popular and perhaps reliable in the consumer's eyes. This same reasoning will of course apply to other brands in the same store: More units of another brand available may enhance the desirability of the target brand; fewer units of another brand may detract from the desirability of the target brand. Not surprisingly, the target brand's favorableness and recognition ratings are related to the number of units.

The one-lagged, four-factor NDFA model (provided in Appendix C) was also rejected: $\chi^2(1,528) = 2,709.21$, $p < .001$. The information indices were: $\text{AIC}_{\text{NDFA}} = -346.79$; $\text{SBIC}_{\text{NDFA}} = -3,986.53$; $\text{HQ}_{\text{NDFA}} = -1,806.09$. When these information indices are compared with their counterparts for the SDFA model, it is not surprising that they differ minimally: The ARIMA modeling previously removed the deterministic trend from the data. Consistent with this lack of improvement in fit was the nonsignificance of the linear trend parameter in the model.

A final note concerns the comparability of the 0- and 1-lag factor solutions. Each 0-lag factor was matched with a conceptually similar or identical factor in the 1-lag solution. This will rarely be the case in real data. But that is precisely the reason why DFA is conducted: to discover how the latent variable structure of the higher order lagged factor series differs from the more typically evaluated zero order factor series.

REFERENCES

Ahamad, B. (1967). An analysis of crimes by the method of principal components. *Applied Statistics, 16,* 17–39.

Akaike, H. (1987). Factor analysis and AIC. *Psychometrika, 52,* 333–342.

Anderson, T. W. (1963). The use of factor analysis in the statistical analysis of multiple time series. *Psychometrika, 28,* 1–25.

Box, G. E. P., & Jenkins, G. M. (1976). *Time series analysis: Forecasting and control.* San Francisco: Holden-Day.

Box, G. E. P., & Tiao, G. C. (1977). A canonical analysis of multiple time series. *Biometrika, 64,* 355–365.

Brillinger, D. R. (1975). *Time series: Data analysis and theory.* New York: Holt.

Cattell, R. B. (1952). *Factor analysis.* New York: Harper.

Cattell, R. B., & Scheier, I. H. (1961). *The meaning and measurement of neuroticism and anxiety.* New York: Ronald.

Cleveland, W. W. (1972). The inverse autocorrelation of a time series and their applications. *Technometrics, 14*, 277–293.

Dolan, C. V., & Molenaar, P. C. M. (1991). A note on the calculation of latent trajectories in the quasi-Markov simplex model by means of the regression method and the discrete Kalman filter. *Kwantitative Methoden, 38*, 29–44.

Geweke, J. (1977). The dynamic factor analysis of economic time series models. In D. J. Aigner & A. S. Goldberger (Eds.), *Latent variables in socio-economic models*. New York: North Holland.

Geweke, J., & Singleton, K. (1981). Maximum likelihood confirmatory factor analysis of economic time series. *International Economic Review, 2*, 37–54.

Hannan, E. J., & Quinn, B. G. (1979). The determination of the order of an autoregression. *Journal of the Royal Statistical Society, 41*, 190–195.

Harvey, A. C. (1981). *Time-series models*. Oxford, England: Philip Alan.

Harvey, A. C. (1989). *Forecasting, structural time series models and the Kalman filter*. Cambridge, England: Cambridge University Press.

Holtzman, W. H. (1963). Statistical models for the study of change in the single case. In C. W. Harris (Ed.), *Problems in measuring change* (pp. 191–211). Madison: University of Wisconsin Press.

Jenkins, G. M., & Watts, D. G. (1968). *Spectrum analysis and its applications*. San Francisco: Holden-Day.

Jones, C. J., & Nesselroade, J. R. (1990). Multivariate, replicated, single-subject designs and P-technique factor analysis: A selected review of intraindividual change studies. *Experimental Aging Research, 16*, 171–183.

Jöreskog, K. G., & Sörbom, D. (1993). *LISREL VIII user's reference guide*. Chicago: Scientific Software International.

Molenaar, P. C. M. (1985). A dynamic factor model for the analysis of multivariate time series. *Psychometrika, 50*, 181–202.

Molenaar, P. C. M. (1994). Dynamic latent variable models in developmental psychology. In A. Von Eye & C. C. Clogg (Eds.), *Latent variables analysis: Applications for developmental research* (pp. 155–180). Thousand Oaks, CA: Sage.

Molenaar, P. C. M., de Gooijer, J. G., & Schmitz, B. (1992). Dynamic factor analysis of nonstationary multivariate time series. *Psychometrika, 57*, 333–349.

Priestly, M. B., Subba Rao, T., & Tong, H. (1973). Identification of the structure of multivariable stochastic systems. In P. R. Krishnaiah (Ed.), *Multivariate analysis III* (pp. 351–368). New York: Academic Press.

Schmitz, B. (1990). Univariate and multivariate time-series models: The analysis of intraindividual variability and interindividual relationships. In A. Von Eye (Ed.), *Statistical methods in longitudinal research: Vol. 2. Time series and categorical longitudinal data* (pp. 351–386). San Diego: Academic Press.

Schwarz, G. (1978). Estimating the dimension of a model. *Annals of Statistics, 6*, 461–464.

Sims, C. A. (1981). An autoregressive index model for the US, 1948–1975. In J. Kmenta & J. B. Ramey (Eds.), *Large scale macro-economic models* (pp. 283–327). Amsterdam: North Holland.

Statistical Analysis System. (1990a). *SAS guide to macro processing* (2nd ed.). Cary, NC: SAS Institute.

Statistical Analysis System. (1990b). *SAS/IML software*. Cary, NC: SAS Institute.

Velu, R. P., Reinsel, G. C., & Wichern, D. W. (1986). Reduced rank models for multiple time series. *Biometrika, 73*, 105–118.

Wood, P., & Brown, D. (1994). The study of intraindividual differences by means of dynamic factor models: Rationale, implementation, and interpretation. *Psychological Bulletin, 116*, 166–186.

APPENDIX A

LISREL Program for Four-Factor *P*-Technique Factor Analysis

```
P-TECHNIQUE FACTOR ANALYSIS - FOUR FACTORS
UNCORRELATED FACTORS AND DISTURBANCES
DA NI = 28 MA = CM NO = 80
MO NY = 28 NE = 4 LY = FU,FR PS=DI,FI TE = DI
FIX LY(1,2) LY(1,3) LY(1,4) LY(2,3) LY(2,4) LY(3,4)
ST 1 ALL
ST 1 PS(1,1) PS(2,2) PS(3,3) PS(4,4)
OU NS
```

APPENDIX B

LISREL Program for Four-Factor, 0, 1 Lagged Dynamic Factor Analysis

```
DYNAMIC FACTOR ANALYSIS - FOUR FACTORS, 0, 1-LAGS
DA NI = 56 MA = CM NO = 80
MO NY = 56 NE = 12 LY = FU,FI PS=DI,FI TE = FU,FI
FR TE(1,1) TE(2,2) TE(3,3) TE(4,4) TE(5,5) TE(6,6) TE(7,7)
FR TE(8,8) TE(9,9) TE(10,10) TE(11,11) TE(12,12) TE(13,13)
FR TE(14,14) TE(15,15) TE(16,16) TE(17,17) TE(18,18) TE(19,19)
FR TE(20,20) TE(21,21) TE(22,22) TE(23,23) TE(24,24) TE(25,25)
FR TE(26,26) TE(27,27) TE(28,28)
FR TE(29,1) TE(30,2) TE(31,3) TE(32,4) TE(33,5) TE(34,6) TE(35,7)
FR TE(36,8) TE(37,9) TE(38,10) TE(39,11) TE(40,12) TE(41,13)
FR TE(42,14) TE(43,15) TE(44,16) TE(45,17) TE(46,18) TE(47,19)
FR TE(48,20) TE(49,21) TE(50,22) TE(51,23) TE(52,24) TE(53,25)
FR TE(54,26) TE(55,27) TE(56,28)
FR LY(1,2) LY(29,6)
FR LY(2,1) LY(30,5)
FR LY(3,4) LY(31,8)
FR LY(4,1) LY(32,5)
FR LY(5,1) LY(33,5)
FR LY(6,2) LY(34,6)
FR LY(7,1) LY(35,5)
FR LY(8,3) LY(36,7)
FR LY(9,1) LY(37,5)
FR LY(10,2) LY(38,6)
FR LY(11,1) LY(39,5)
FR LY(12,1) LY(40,5)
FR LY(13,4) LY(41,8)
FR LY(14,3) LY(42,7)
FR LY(15,2) LY(43,6)
FR LY(16,1) LY(44,5)
FR LY(17,4) LY(45,8)
```

```
FR LY(18,3) LY(46,7)
FR LY(19,1) LY(47,5)
FR LY(20,2) LY(48,6)
FR LY(21,2) LY(49,6)
FR LY(22,4) LY(50,8)
FR LY(23,4) LY(51,8)
FR LY(24,4) LY(52,8)
FR LY(25,3) LY(53,7)
FR LY(26,3) LY(54,6)
FR LY(27,3) LY(55,7)
FR LY(28,4) LY(56,8)
FR LY(1,6) LY(29,10)
FR LY(2,5) LY(30,9)
FR LY(3,8) LY(31,12)
FR LY(4,5) LY(32,9)
FR LY(5,5) LY(33,9)
FR LY(6,6) LY(34,10)
FR LY(7,5) LY(35,9)
FR LY(8,7) LY(36,11)
FR LY(9,5) LY(37,10)
FR LY(10,6) LY(38,10)
FR LY(11,5) LY(39,9)
FR LY(12,5) LY(40,9)
FR LY(13,8) LY(41,12)
FR LY(14,7) LY(42,11)
FR LY(15,6) LY(43,10)
FR LY(16,5) LY(44,9)
FR LY(17,8) LY(45,12)
FR LY(18,7) LY(46,11)
FR LY(19,5) LY(47,9)
FR LY(20,6) LY(48,10)
FR LY(21,6) LY(49,10)
FR LY(22,8) LY(50,12)
FR LY(23,8) LY(51,12)
FR LY(24,8) LY(52,12)
FR LY(25,7) LY(53,11)
FR LY(26,6) LY(54,10)
FR LY(27,7) LY(55,11)
FR LY(28,8) LY(56,12)
EQ LY(1,2) LY(29,6)
EQ LY(2,1) LY(30,5)
EQ LY(3,4) LY(31,8)
EQ LY(4,1) LY(32,5)
EQ LY(5,1) LY(33,5)
EQ LY(6,2) LY(34,6)
EQ LY(7,1) LY(35,5)
EQ LY(8,3) LY(36,7)
EQ LY(9,1) LY(37,5)
EQ LY(10,2) LY(38,6)
EQ LY(11,1) LY(39,5)
EQ LY(12,1) LY(40,5)
EQ LY(13,4) LY(41,8)
```

```
EQ LY(14,3) LY(42,7)
EQ LY(15,2) LY(43,6)
EQ LY(16,1) LY(44,5)
EQ LY(17,4) LY(45,8)
EQ LY(18,3) LY(46,7)
EQ LY(19,1) LY(47,5)
EQ LY(20,2) LY(48,6)
EQ LY(21,2) LY(49,6)
EQ LY(22,4) LY(50,8)
EQ LY(23,4) LY(51,8)
EQ LY(24,4) LY(52,8)
EQ LY(25,3) LY(53,7)
EQ LY(26,3) LY(54,6)
EQ LY(27,3) LY(55,7)
EQ LY(28,4) LY(56,8)
EQ LY(1,6) LY(29,10)
EQ LY(2,5) LY(30,9)
EQ LY(3,8) LY(31,12)
EQ LY(4,5) LY(32,9)
EQ LY(5,5) LY(33,9)
EQ LY(6,6) LY(34,10)
EQ LY(7,5) LY(35,9)
EQ LY(8,7) LY(36,11)
EQ LY(9,5) LY(37,10)
EQ LY(10,6) LY(38,10)
EQ LY(11,5) LY(39,9)
EQ LY(12,5) LY(40,9)
EQ LY(13,8) LY(41,12)
EQ LY(14,7) LY(42,11)
EQ LY(15,6) LY(43,10)
EQ LY(16,5) LY(44,9)
EQ LY(17,8) LY(45,12)
EQ LY(18,7) LY(46,11)
EQ LY(19,5) LY(47,9)
EQ LY(20,6) LY(48,10)
EQ LY(21,6) LY(49,10)
EQ LY(22,8) LY(50,12)
EQ LY(23,8) LY(51,12)
EQ LY(24,8) LY(52,12)
EQ LY(25,7) LY(53,11)
EQ LY(26,6) LY(54,10)
EQ LY(27,7) LY(55,11)
EQ LY(28,8) LY(56,12)
EQ TE(1,1) TE(29,29)
EQ TE(2,2) TE(30,30)
EQ TE(3,3) TE(31,31)
EQ TE(4,4) TE(32,32)
EQ TE(5,5) TE(33,33)
EQ TE(6,6) TE(34,34)
EQ TE(7,7) TE(35,35)
EQ TE(8,8) TE(36,36)
EQ TE(9,9) TE(37,37)
```

```
EQ TE(10,10)  TE(38,38)
EQ TE(11,11)  TE(39,39)
EQ TE(12,12)  TE(40,40)
EQ TE(13,13)  TE(41,41)
EQ TE(14,14)  TE(42,42)
EQ TE(15,15)  TE(43,43)
EQ TE(16,16)  TE(44,44)
EQ TE(17,17)  TE(45,45)
EQ TE(18,18)  TE(46,46)
EQ TE(19,19)  TE(47,47)
EQ TE(20,20)  TE(48,48)
EQ TE(21,21)  TE(49,49)
EQ TE(22,22)  TE(50,50)
EQ TE(23,23)  TE(51,51)
EQ TE(24,24)  TE(52,52)
EQ TE(25,25)  TE(53,53)
EQ TE(26,26)  TE(54,54)
EQ TE(27,27)  TE(55,55)
EQ TE(28,28)  TE(56,56)
ST 1 ALL
ST 1 PS(1,1) PS(2,2) PS(3,3) PS(4,4) PS(5,5) PS(6,6)
ST 1 PS(7,7) PS(8,8) PS(9,9) PS(10,10)
ST 1 PS(11,11) PS(12,12)
OU NS
```

APPENDIX C

LISREL Program for Four-Factor, 0, 1 Lagged Nonstationary Dynamic Factor Analysis

```
NONSTATIONARY DYNAMIC FACTOR ANALYSIS - FOUR FACTORS, 0, 1-LAGS
DA NI = 57 MA = CM NO = 80
MO NY = 56 NE = 12 NX = 1 NK = 1 LY = FU,FI PS=DI,FI TE = FU,FI C
  GA = FU,FI PH=SY,FI LX = FU,FR TD = ZE
VA 1.00 PH(1,1)
FR GA(1,1) GA(2,1) GA(3,1) GA(4,1) GA(5,1) GA(6,1) GA(7,1)
FR GA(8,1) GA(9,1) GA(10,1) GA(11,1) GA(12,1)
FR TE(1,1) TE(2,2) TE(3,3) TE(4,4) TE(5,5) TE(6,6) TE(7,7)
FR TE(8,8) TE(9,9) TE(10,10) TE(11,11) TE(12,12) TE(13,13)
FR TE(14,14) TE(15,15) TE(16,16) TE(17,17) TE(18,18) TE(19,19)
FR TE(20,20) TE(21,21) TE(22,22) TE(23,23) TE(24,24) TE(25,25)
FR TE(26,26) TE(27,27) TE(28,28)
FR TE(29,1) TE(30,2) TE(31,3) TE(32,4) TE(33,5) TE(34,6) TE(35,7)
FR TE(36,8) TE(37,9) TE(38,10) TE(39,11) TE(40,12) TE(41,13)
FR TE(42,14) TE(43,15) TE(44,16) TE(45,17) TE(46,18) TE(47,19)
FR TE(48,20) TE(49,21) TE(50,22) TE(51,23) TE(52,24) TE(53,25)
FR TE(54,26) TE(55,27) TE(56,28)
VA 1.00 LY(1,2) LY(29,6)
VA 1.00 LY(2,1) LY(30,5)
VA 1.00 LY(3,4) LY(31,8)
```

```
FR LY(4,1) LY(32,5)
FR LY(5,1) LY(33,5)
FR LY(6,2) LY(34,6)
FR LY(7,1) LY(35,5)
VA 1.00 LY(8,3) LY(36,7)
FR LY(9,1) LY(37,5)
FR LY(10,2) LY(38,6)
FR LY(11,1) LY(39,5)
FR LY(12,1) LY(40,5)
FR LY(13,4) LY(41,8)
FR LY(14,3) LY(42,7)
FR LY(15,2) LY(43,6)
FR LY(16,1) LY(44,5)
FR LY(17,4) LY(45,8)
FR LY(18,3) LY(46,7)
FR LY(19,1) LY(47,5)
FR LY(20,2) LY(48,6)
FR LY(21,2) LY(49,6)
FR LY(22,4) LY(50,8)
FR LY(23,4) LY(51,8)
FR LY(24,4) LY(52,8)
FR LY(25,3) LY(53,7)
FR LY(26,3) LY(54,6)
FR LY(27,3) LY(55,7)
FR LY(28,4) LY(56,8)
FR LY(1,6) LY(29,10)
FR LY(2,5) LY(30,9)
FR LY(3,8) LY(31,12)
FR LY(4,5) LY(32,9)
FR LY(5,5) LY(33,9)
FR LY(6,6) LY(34,10)
FR LY(7,5) LY(35,9)
FR LY(8,7) LY(36,11)
FR LY(9,5) LY(37,10)
FR LY(10,6) LY(38,10)
FR LY(11,5) LY(39,9)
FR LY(12,5) LY(40,9)
FR LY(13,8) LY(41,12)
FR LY(14,7) LY(42,11)
FR LY(15,6) LY(43,10)
FR LY(16,5) LY(44,9)
FR LY(17,8) LY(45,12)
FR LY(18,7) LY(46,11)
FR LY(19,5) LY(47,9)
FR LY(20,6) LY(48,10)
FR LY(21,6) LY(49,10)
FR LY(22,8) LY(50,12)
FR LY(23,8) LY(51,12)
FR LY(24,8) LY(52,12)
FR LY(25,7) LY(53,11)
FR LY(26,6) LY(54,10)
FR LY(27,7) LY(55,11)
```

```
FR LY(28,8) LY(56,12)
EQ LY(4,1) LY(32,5)
EQ LY(5,1) LY(33,5)
EQ LY(6,2) LY(34,6)
EQ LY(7,1) LY(35,5)
EQ LY(9,1) LY(37,5)
EQ LY(10,2) LY(38,6)
EQ LY(11,1) LY(39,5)
EQ LY(12,1) LY(40,5)
EQ LY(13,4) LY(41,8)
EQ LY(14,3) LY(42,7)
EQ LY(15,2) LY(43,6)
EQ LY(16,1) LY(44,5)
EQ LY(17,4) LY(45,8)
EQ LY(18,3) LY(46,7)
EQ LY(19,1) LY(47,5)
EQ LY(20,2) LY(48,6)
EQ LY(21,2) LY(49,6)
EQ LY(22,4) LY(50,8)
EQ LY(23,4) LY(51,8)
EQ LY(24,4) LY(52,8)
EQ LY(25,3) LY(53,7)
EQ LY(26,3) LY(54,6)
EQ LY(27,3) LY(55,7)
EQ LY(28,4) LY(56,8)
EQ LY(1,6) LY(29,10)
EQ LY(2,5) LY(30,9)
EQ LY(3,8) LY(31,12)
EQ LY(4,5) LY(32,9)
EQ LY(5,5) LY(33,9)
EQ LY(6,6) LY(34,10)
EQ LY(7,5) LY(35,9)
EQ LY(8,7) LY(36,11)
EQ LY(9,5) LY(37,10)
EQ LY(10,6) LY(38,10)
EQ LY(11,5) LY(39,9)
EQ LY(12,5) LY(40,9)
EQ LY(13,8) LY(41,12)
EQ LY(14,7) LY(42,11)
EQ LY(15,6) LY(43,10)
EQ LY(16,5) LY(44,9)
EQ LY(17,8) LY(45,12)
EQ LY(18,7) LY(46,11)
EQ LY(19,5) LY(47,9)
EQ LY(20,6) LY(48,10)
EQ LY(21,6) LY(49,10)
EQ LY(22,8) LY(50,12)
EQ LY(23,8) LY(51,12)
EQ LY(24,8) LY(52,12)
EQ LY(25,7) LY(53,11)
EQ LY(26,6) LY(54,10)
EQ LY(27,7) LY(55,11)
```

```
EQ LY(28,8) LY(56,12)
EQ TE(1,1) TE(29,29)
EQ TE(2,2) TE(30,30)
EQ TE(3,3) TE(31,31)
EQ TE(4,4) TE(32,32)
EQ TE(5,5) TE(33,33)
EQ TE(6,6) TE(34,34)
EQ TE(7,7) TE(35,35)
EQ TE(8,8) TE(36,36)
EQ TE(9,9) TE(37,37)
EQ TE(10,10) TE(38,38)
EQ TE(11,11) TE(39,39)
EQ TE(12,12) TE(40,40)
EQ TE(13,13) TE(41,41)
EQ TE(14,14) TE(42,42)
EQ TE(15,15) TE(43,43)
EQ TE(16,16) TE(44,44)
EQ TE(17,17) TE(45,45)
EQ TE(18,18) TE(46,46)
EQ TE(19,19) TE(47,47)
EQ TE(20,20) TE(48,48)
EQ TE(21,21) TE(49,49)
EQ TE(22,22) TE(50,50)
EQ TE(23,23) TE(51,51)
EQ TE(24,24) TE(52,52)
EQ TE(25,25) TE(53,53)
EQ TE(26,26) TE(54,54)
EQ TE(27,27) TE(55,55)
EQ TE(28,28) TE(56,56)
ST 1 ALL
OU NS
```

CHAPTER NINE

Structural Equation Modeling

Edward E. Rigdon

Georgia State University

Like many multivariate statistical techniques, *structural equation modeling* (SEM) is a relatively recent innovation. Despite this, SEM has taken up a prominent role in the academic literatures of many fields, including marketing and management, and it is beginning to have an impact in finance and accounting. Whenever researchers deal with relations between constructs such as satisfaction, role ambiguity, or attitude, SEM is likely to be the methodology of choice.

The purpose of this chapter is to provide a basic introduction to structural equation modeling. The chapter demonstrates the methodology in a realistic commercial research context. The chapter also looks at weaknesses of the methodology. Finally, the chapter identifies sources of further information for those who are considering applying SEM techniques in their own research.

WHAT IS STRUCTURAL EQUATION MODELING?

SEM, also called *causal modeling, latent variable structural equation* (LVSE) modeling, and *analysis of covariance structures,* is a method for representing, estimating, and testing a theoretical network of (mostly) linear relations between variables, where those variables may be either observable or directly unobservable, and may only be measured imperfectly. SEM is a generalization of both regression and factor analysis, and subsumes most linear modeling methods as "special cases." This means that many researchers are already using simplified versions of SEM on a daily basis. However, because of the simplifications in those other methods, these researchers cannot take full advantage of the potential benefits of the methodology.

SEM proceeds by assessing whether a sample covariance or correlation matrix is consistent with a hypothetical matrix implied by the model specified by the user. So the inputs to SEM are either raw data or sample moments computed from the data, and a model to be evaluated. The sample moments will include either variances and covariances or correlations, and may also include means and higher order moments, as well. The model consists of a network of proposed equations, with some parameters fixed to particular values and others "free to be estimated." The outputs from SEM fall into five general groups: (a) estimates of the designated model parameters, (b) estimates of the standard errors for the estimated parameters, (c) for the dependent variables, estimates of the proportion of variance explained, often called *squared multiple correlations* (or SMCs), which are akin to the R^2 statistic in regression, (d) overall goodness-of-fit statistics, which assess the overall consistency between the specified model and the data, and (e) diagnostic statistics, which aid in pinpointing the sources of any fit problems. In SEM, parameter estimates are optimized to maximize fit, not variance explained. Sometimes a model will fit well while having little explanatory power. Nevertheless, good fit is essential to interpretation. If a structural equation model fits poorly, the parameter estimates may be uninterpretable.

What SEM Is Not

Before going further, it is important to state what SEM is not. SEM is not *LISREL*. LISREL is a computer program for conducting SEM analysis, created by Karl Jöreskog—one of the founders of SEM—and Dag Sörbom. Although SEM is sometimes identified with LISREL, there are many computer packages for SEM, and there is no consensus regarding which one is "best" under all circumstances.

In addition, SEM is not *latent class analysis*. In SEM, the dependent variables or constructs must be (at least conceptually) continuous—matters of degree. If the dependent variables are essentially categorical—buyer versus nonbuyer, for example—then latent class analysis is the appropriate technique. For more information on latent class analysis, see McCollam (chap. 2 of this volume).

Finally, SEM is not *partial least squares* (PLS; see Chin, chap. 10 of this volume). PLS is an alternative approach, originally developed by Herman Wold, Karl Jöreskog's mentor and a pioneer in econometrics. SEM and PLS have been applied to similar problems, but the two methods have different strengths and weaknesses.

WHY USE SEM?

Convenient, Flexible Modeling

SEM, as a general framework for linear modeling, offers a number of advantages over some more familiar methods. First, the method is highly flexible. It is designed for working with multiple, related equations simultaneously. Within the limits of *identification* (discussed later in this chapter), SEM allows great flexibility in how the equations are specified. This includes allowing reciprocal relationships (where, e.g., "customer satisfaction" directly affects "perceived value" whereas "perceived value" directly affects "customer satisfaction") and allowing the disturbances for different equations to be either correlated or uncorrelated. The methodology also allows researchers to compare the performance of a model across multiple populations. Thus, researchers can explicitly test whether a given model is equally appropriate for members of different market segments, for new hires versus veteran employees, or for both control and treatment groups in an experiment. Within the multigroup context, structural equation models can also test hypotheses about the means of both the *observed* and *latent* variables (see later discussion). This gives the researcher additional flexibility in modeling different types of interaction relationships or experimental effects.

Explicit Modeling of Measurement Error

Second, SEM allows researchers to explicitly recognize the imperfect nature of their measures. Particularly when measuring abstract psychological variables such as "customer satisfaction" or "role conflict," most researchers accept that the behavior of a given measure is driven by a number of other components, aside from the trait that the researcher intended to measure. These other components include both unreliability, or random measurement error, and threats to validity, which include contamination by other traits and the influence of factors arising from the measurement process itself. Ignoring these additional influences on even one measure may bias parameter estimates all across the model (Bollen, 1989; Gillespie & Fox, 1980; Rigdon, 1994b).

SEM gives researchers the ability to account for these additional influences (and thus avoid the potential bias) by interposing a flexible factor analytic measurement model between the measures and the traits being measured. This model may be expressed as:

$$X = \Lambda_x \xi + \delta$$

where X is the original measures, ξ is a set of common factors/*constructs*/latent variables that affect the measures/manifest variables, and δ is a set of measurement error terms. The common factors represent purified versions of the measures, with error terms and contamination removed. Modeling relations between the common factors, rather than between the measures directly, protects those *structural* parameter estimates from imperfections in the measures (as long as those imperfections are correctly modeled). At the same time, estimates of the parameters of this *measurement model* provide important information about the quality of the measures, which can help researchers to improve their research instruments over time.

To fully exploit this factor analytic measurement model, researchers must administer multiple measures of each factor of interest. That is, instead of employing only one item or question to represent a factor, SEM users will employ responses to two, three, four, or more items. In fact, each of these multiple measures may itself be the sum of responses to several items. For some researchers, this requirement will represent an additional burden.

Resolution of Multicollinearity

For others, however, the SEM measurement model will give rise to a third important advantage—the means to resolve thorny problems of multicollinearity. Many researchers often include multiple items in a questionnaire in an attempt to guarantee that key variables are tapped appropriately. These multiple measures tend to be highly correlated. Including these multiple measures as predictors in the same regression equation leads to the familiar consequences of multicollinearity, including biased parameter estimates and inflated standard errors. In the context of stepwise regression, researchers may observe a great deal of instability in terms of which of the several measures are included in the regression equation. This, in turn, may lead researchers to unwieldy solutions such as estimating several regression equations, where each measure is included in a different equation—and where no equation truly represents the relationship of interest. In SEM, the multiple items are modeled as measures of the same common factor, and only the factor is used as a (single) structural variable. Thus, all of the multiple measures are included in the model, but only one variable enters the prediction equation. High correlations among the multiple items actually improve the stability of the factor analytic measurement model.

Use of SEM as a modeling framework may also help researchers to deal with multicollinearity at the structural level, as well. The SEM approach may give researchers the information they need to diagnose the problem and the flexibility they need to respecify a set of equations, in order to resolve the problem.

Evocative Graphical Language

Fourth, the development of SEM as a statistical method has been accompanied by the development of an evocative graphical language. This language provides a convenient and powerful way to present complex relationships to others not familiar with SEM. Some researchers who are familiar with SEM use this graphical language on an everyday basis, and it is easy to see the influence of this graphical language in Bagozzi's (1984) attempt to develop a general system for representing research problems. Figure 9.1 shows an example of a structural equation model. (This diagram adheres to the most well-known convention in SEM—for one alternative, see McArdle & McDonald, 1984.) This model includes five common factors—Loyalty, Satisfaction, Value, Price, and Quality. The arrows in the diagram show the direct dependencies in the model, and the arrowheads indicate the direction of influence. As the diagram shows, Loyalty is directly dependent on Value and Satisfaction. Value, in turn, is dependent on Price and Satisfaction, whereas Satisfaction is dependent on Value and Quality. Thus, the model proposes a reciprocal relationship between Value and Satisfaction. The structural component of the model could also be represented as three equations:

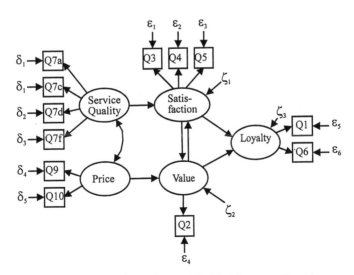

FIG. 9.1. A structural equation model of Satisfaction and Loyalty.

$$\text{Satisfaction} = \beta_{12} * \text{Value} + \gamma_{11} * \text{Quality} + \zeta_1$$
$$\text{Value} = \beta_{21} * \text{Satisfaction} + \gamma_{22} * \text{Price} + \zeta_2$$
$$\text{Loyalty} = \beta_{31} * \text{Satisfaction} + \beta_{32} * \text{Value} + \zeta_3$$

Here, the Greek βs (betas) and γs (gammas) represent regression parameters. (The SEM literature includes conflicting conventions for linking symbols to model components. This presentation adopts one common convention.) The Greek ζs (zetas), here and in the diagram, are error terms, reflecting the modeler's knowledge that the dependent variable in each equation is not perfectly predicted by the independent variables.

The two-headed arrow between Price and Quality indicates that those two common factors covary, but that this covariance is not explained or predicted by other variables within the model. In SEM, researchers expect that independent common factors will covary among themselves to some degree, due to common causes or antecedents that lie outside the model's frame of reference. This is not required, however. Particularly in the context of an experiment, where the administration of treatments is randomized to ensure independence, common factors may be modeled as not covarying with other independent factors. Further, within the limits of identification, even dependent constructs, such as Value and Satisfaction in Fig. 9.1, may be allowed to have covariance with other common factors that is not explained within the model. Graphically, this would be represented by a two-headed arrow between the error terms for the respective constructs.

The diagram also depicts the measurement model for these variables. The diagram shows two measures associated with Loyalty, one with Value, three with Satisfaction, two with Price, and four with Quality. As the arrowheads indicate, and consistent with the factor model, each measure is itself a *dependent* variable, dependent on its associated common factor and an error term, represented by the Greek δ (delta) or ε (epsilon). (In some cases, it will be more appropriate to represent the common factor as dependent on the measure. Bollen and Lennox, 1991, discussed this issue in the context of SEM; however, this alternative *principal components model* of measurement is easier to estimate using PLS methods.) Thus, Fig. 9.1 represents not only the 3 structural model equations but also 12 measurement model equations, each of the form:

$$Q\# = \lambda_i * \text{common factor} + \delta_i \text{ or } \varepsilon_i.$$

Thus, the graphical language of SEM allows one diagram to represent 15 equations. Many researchers will find that they prefer this graphical approach for communicating research objectives and results.

HOW DO I USE STRUCTURAL EQUATION MODELING?

Conducting SEM in an efficient, reliable, and successful manner demands a systematic approach. Researchers who fail to think through the entire process beforehand, or who fail to carefully document each step, will sooner or later find themselves mired in a swamp of conflicting models, meanings, and printouts, and questioning the value of the methodology itself.

Conceptualization

The first stage of the process is conceptualization. First, the researcher must make certain that his or her research objectives are consistent with SEM, and that the risks and limitations of SEM (discussed in a later section) are acceptable. Next, the researcher must conceptualize the structure of the model. Will the model involve one group of subjects or more than one? Multiple-group analysis gives added richness to the analysis, whereas single-group studies share all the weaknesses of one-shot, cross-sectional research. Even researchers conducting after-the-fact research with secondhand data may find that there are distinct subpopulations represented in the data set, and that comparisons between those groups are revealing.

Choice of Dependent and Independent Variable(s).   Next, the researcher should identify dependent variables for the analysis. The choice of dependent variables may be based partially on questions of managerial relevance, but it may also be determined by the contents of the data set being analyzed. In a sense, the choice of independent or predictor variables is far more important and offers the researcher less freedom. Failing to include an important predictor (or an important relationship) in the model will lead to bias in the model's parameter estimates, if the excluded predictor is correlated with other predictors that *are* included in the model. This is the "excluded predictor" or "missing variable" problem, which is familiar to researchers in regression and econometrics. This problem means that there may be a price to pay for arbitrarily excluding variables from a model. Bollen (1989) provided a discussion of this problem in the context of SEM.

Identification.   Researchers must also ensure that their structural model is identified. A model is identified if it is consistent with one unique set of parameter estimates. For a familiar example, solve the algebraic equation $X + Y = 10$ for X and Y. Any number of pairs of values for X and Y are consistent with this equation—the equation is not identified. But with a system of two independent equations, such as:

$$X + Y = 10$$
$$X - Y = 4,$$

there is a unique solution: $X = 7$, $Y = 3$. The system of two equations is identified or just identified. If a third independent equation is added, such as:

$$X + 2Y = 13,$$

then the system has *more* equations than it has unknown values to estimate, so the system of equations is said to be overidentified.

Evaluating the identification status of a structural equation model is a mathematically difficult task (Bekker, Merckens, & Wansbeek, 1994). However, a number of heuristics and rules of thumb are available to help researchers check identification in specific situations (Rigdon, 1995). Most SEM software packages will issue warning messages if analysis indicates that the model being estimated is not identified. But researchers who are forewarned about possible identification problems may be able to modify the design of their model in order to minimize the possibility of a negative result.

Functional Form of Relations. Researchers also should consider the functional form of relations between the variables in the model. SEM is chiefly used for modeling linear relations, although there is an emerging literature on specifying quadratic and interaction terms. Currently, however, those alternative specifications usually entail an increase in complexity and a confrontation with some unresolved methodological problems (Kenny & Judd, 1984; Ping, 1996; Rigdon, Schumacker, & Wothke, in press). Although linear equations sometimes provide good approximations to nonlinear equations, at least within certain ranges, those approximations can also conceal relationships that would be significant if modeled at a nonlinear level. If the researcher has data on an important moderating variable, this may also give rise to a multiple-group analysis, where each group is characterized by a different value (or range of values) for the moderating variable.

Importance of Alternative Models. Although it may seem difficult enough to conceptualize one structural model, there are advantages to conceptualizing plausible alternative models for the selected variables, as well. Estimating alternative, competing models with the same data gives the researcher additional perspective on the results of each separate analysis. With just one model, researchers may take a positive result to indicate that their one model is the only correct model for a set of data, or they may take a negative result to indicate that their model is hopelessly inappropriate. With competing models, researchers can see whether the alternative models fit just as well, or better, or worse, than the primary model. There are always alternative models that are identical in fit to a given model. These are called *equivalent models* (Stelzl, 1986), and they represent one limitation of SEM methodology, in that they cannot be empirically distinguished, based on fit, even though they may have profoundly different managerial implications.

If the competing models are *nested*, then researchers may have access to an inferential technique for distinguishing between the models in terms of their consistency with the data. Two models are nested if the free parameters in one model are a strict subset of the free parameters in the other. Put another way, if a researcher can start with one model and produce the other model *just* by imposing restrictions on the first model, then the two models are nested. Figure 9.2 presents three alternative models for a set of six manifest variables. Model A in the diagram is nested within Model C—the two models are identical except that Model A excludes two paths between the common factors and the manifest variables. On the other hand, Model

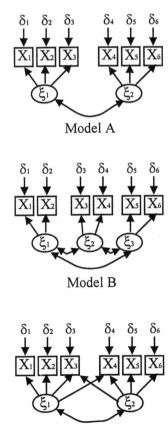

Model A

Model B

FIG. 9.2. Three models for six measured variables.

Model C

B does not have a nesting relationship with either Model A or Model C. Researchers should be cautious about ruling out the possibility of a nesting relationship between two models, however, because such relationships are not always obvious.

Authorities in SEM (Anderson & Gerbing, 1988a; James, Mulaik, & Brett, 1982) strongly recommend proposing and testing a series of nested models, as a way to better understand the implications of their research results for the primary model of interest, and obtain more diagnostic information from the analysis. Researchers can construct a series of nested models by assigning a likelihood or level of confidence to each possible path between the common factors. The primary model should then include the most likely paths, but other, competing models can be chosen, which either include some less likely paths or exclude some more likely paths. Color coding the model's paths, with, perhaps, green paths representing high confidence, yellow paths indicating moderate confidence, and red paths indicating low confidence, may facilitate this process in a group setting.

It is worth emphasizing that SEM is best seen as a confirmatory, rather than an exploratory, technique. The freedom that SEM grants to researchers in specifying models for analysis also assures that *some* model will fit any given data set. The diagnostic information provided by SEM software makes it easy for researchers to modify a rejected model in order to achieve good fit to the data at hand. Typically, though, such models tend to be *overfitted* to the sample, with the result that they will not replicate well in other, independent samples. Further, Steiger (1990) pointed out that model modifications designed to improve fit may not actually yield the true model. Instead, the resulting model may be merely equivalent to the correct one, but again, with substantively different managerial implications. Either way, *good fit* may be meaningless.

On the other hand, a substantial research stream has been devoted precisely to developing an exploratory approach to SEM. The *TETRAD* program (Spirtes, Glymour, & Scheines, 1993) includes software with algorithms for finding all models that are consistent with a given data set, under certain constraints. This approach may be an option for researchers who have substantial databases but who do not have specific models in mind (see Wood, chap. 13 of this volume).

Choose Measures for the Variables.   After establishing a set of structural models, researchers must then choose measures for each of the common factors in their model. In the ideal case, these measures will be designed specifically to be consistent with the researchers' understanding of the common factors in their model. Contributions in the field of psychometrics, including those of Nunnally (1967; Nunnally & Bernstein, 1994) and Churchill (1979) provide detailed procedures for developing sound measures of abstract constructs. Unfortunately, researchers often must work with data that have already been collected. The process of measure development is then a matter of identifying those manifest variables within a predefined set that will best serve as measures of the common factors.

How can researchers identify good measures? First, the variables must be conceptually associated with the common factor. Determining this will be easier if researchers have a deep understanding of the latent variables in their model. Researchers using secondary data may have to rely on the wording of the items in a questionnaire.

Second, good measures will be reliable, meaning that they are relatively free of random error. Some researchers will have prior information on measure reliability, especially if they form their measures out of sets of items. In such cases, researchers can compute Cronbach's coefficient alpha or another reliability index.

Finally, when employed in a structural equation model, measures must behave in a manner that is consistent with the model. Typically, this means that the measure must be *unidimensional* (Anderson & Gerbing, 1988a, 1988b), loading on only one construct, so that all association or covariance between the various measures is entirely mediated by the common factors. It also means that a measure will have relatively high correlations with other measures of the same common factor (this demonstrates *convergent validity*) and rather lower correlations with measures of different factors (which demonstrates *discriminant validity*) (Campbell & Fiske, 1959). (Note that this rule does not apply for the alternate measurement model, where the structural variable is dependent on its measures.) Further, the common factors that arise from valid measures will correlate with other common factors in a manner consistent with what the researcher knows about the factors. For example, in a study of Satisfaction and Loyalty, one would expect a positive correlation between these factors. A negative correlation, then, could be taken as evidence that the measures of one factor or the other are invalid.

This presents a well-known quandary for SEM researchers. To validate measures against prior knowledge (or theory), researchers must assume that their model is correct. But when researchers are using SEM to test their model, they must assume that their measures are valid. Thus, researchers cannot validate their measures *and* test their model in the same analysis. Researchers are advised to develop their measures and their models in stages over the course of several studies. Lacking this luxury, researchers should consider a cross-validation approach (Cudeck & Browne, 1983) dividing the available data into calibration and validation samples. A caution here is that each sample should be large enough to meet the minimum sample size guidelines for SEM analysis.

Another likely question for researchers is: How many measures does one need for each common factor? Here, the literature is somewhat mixed. Bentler and Chou (1987) and Hair, Anderson, Tatham, and Black (1995) indicated that researchers are not likely to obtain good results from SEM with models that have more than 20 or so measures altogether. This implies a constraint on the number of measures per common factor and/or the number of common factors.

On the other hand, based on simulation research, Marsh, Hau, and Balla (1996) argued that having more measures is always better, all other things equal. Further, there are clear practical reasons to prefer two measures over one, three measures over two, and four measures over three. For one thing, there is the issue of identification. Just as the structural model must be identified, researchers must also beware of identification problems in the measurement model. With only one measure for a factor, researchers typically lose the ability to estimate the degree of random error in the measure from within SEM itself. With only two measures, identification hinges on the common factor being correlated with at least one other factor (Bollen, 1989), or on arbitrary restrictions imposed on the factor model. With three sound measures per factor, identification is assured; as a consequence and a side benefit, researchers will see substantially smaller standard errors for estimates of the parameters of the measurement model. With four measures per factor, the measurement model for each common factor is overidentified, which gives researchers additional ability to evaluate the soundness of the measurement model (Stanley Mulaik, January 17, 1996, message to SEMNET). On a practical level, with four or more measures per construct, researchers gain flexibility in being able to discard measures whose performance is disappointing.

Execution

With latent variables, model structure, and manifest variables selected, the researcher is ready to initiate SEM analysis.

Data Distributions. As with other statistical methods, analysis should always begin with a look at the data itself. Before engaging in more elaborate analysis, one should study the distribution of the data, looking for outliers and for extreme levels of skew or kurtosis. Bollen (1989) made the point that, even with fairly large sample sizes, a few unlikely cases can be highly influential.

At the univariate and bivariate levels, researchers can employ the usual tools to seek out unlikely values. At the multivariate level, however, outliers may be less apparent. Bollen (1989) suggested computing the matrix A:

$$A = Z * (Z' * Z)^{-1} * Z'$$

where Z is a data matrix with one case per row and all variables expressed as deviations from their means, and A is a square matrix with one row and one column per case. The diagonal elements of A can then be interpreted as measures of the *extremeness* of each case. The *sum* of the diagonal values of A will be equal to the number of variables in the data set, and the *average* of these values will be equal to the number of variables divided by the sample size. Values that are "large" relative to this benchmark may be influential and certainly invite closer scrutiny.

Researchers should also examine the degree of skewness and kurtosis in their data. Extreme levels of skewness and, especially, kurtosis may bias results from SEM analysis, and may call for special measures in that analysis. Again, authorities differ. Satorra and Bentler (1988) have argued for taking specific steps when a data set is found not to be multivariate normal. Others observe that the *maximum likelihood* (ML) estimation method (see later discussion)—the most widely used method in practice—is reasonably robust to moderate departures from normality. Some research topics, such as studies of Customer Satisfaction among a firm's current customers, are well known for leading to highly skewed distributions, with most Satisfaction scores clustering at the upper end of the response scale. At least, it is better to have distributional information before the analysis proceeds, rather than being surprised later.

Ordinal Data. More significant questions arise when some or all measures are only ordinally scaled. For example, suppose a questionnaire includes the item, "How satisfied are you with your experience?" with response categories labeled, "Not Satisfied," "Somewhat Satisfied" and "Very Satisfied." These response categories may not represent equally spaced points along the Satisfaction continuum. The researcher may only be sure of the *order* of the response categories, not their interval. A large body of literature shows that ignoring the special attributes of such data can lead to bias in virtually all of the statistical outputs from SEM analysis. Researchers differ on what sorts of scales should be considered ordinal, and there are certainly cases where the presence of *ordinal variables* is not a critical issue. Johnson and Creech (1983) and others indicated that problems are minimized when there are five or more response categories and when the distribution of the data mimics a bell curve. With few response categories, however, problems can be severe, and that has led to an extensive search for solutions.

Most of this literature has focused on the *polychoric correlation coefficient.* This coefficient is specifically designed for assessing the degree of association between ordinal variables. (For correlations between an ordinal variable and a continuous variable, there is an analogous *polyserial correlation coefficient.*) Whereas ordinary Pearson correlations tend to be attenuated when computed for ordinal variables, the polychoric correlation coefficient is unbiased for such data, when assumptions hold (Olsson, 1979). These assumptions include a relatively large sample size and normal distributions for the hypothetical continuous variables that are supposed to underlie the observed ordinal variables. Use of the polychoric correlation coefficient is known to lead to unbiased parameter estimates (Babakus, Ferguson, & Jöreskog, 1987), but it does not necessarily eliminate problems with standard error estimates and goodness-of-fit statistics. In fact, the remaining problems in this regard (discussed later) are so severe that some researchers will choose to simply ignore the problem and accept a certain approximateness in the outputs of SEM analysis with ordinal variables.

Missing Data. One other issue relating to data is the problem of missing data. With a large number of measures in a model, there are many opportunities for cases to be incomplete. Listwise deletion (where an entire case is discarded if any value in the case is missing) can take a tremendous toll on sample size, and may induce additional bias. Pairwise deletion (where each correlation or covariance is computed from all cases that have valid values for the two variables involved) can lead to input matrices that behave poorly in statistical terms, and is inconsistent with some SEM estimation methods. Currently, SEM is experiencing rapid advances in terms of sophisticated procedures for replacing individual missing values with *likely* values—a procedure known as *imputation* (Rubin, 1987). These methods outperform simple mean-replacement approaches in simulation studies, in terms of minimizing biases resulting from missing data and replacement. Aside from the missing data routines incorporated within SEM software packages, an imputation procedure based on the iterative *EM algorithm* (Dempster, Laird, & Rubin, 1977) is available free on the Internet.

Discrepancy Functions/Estimation Methods. With data questions resolved, the researcher next must choose one of several available methods for estimating model parameters. All methods attempt to minimize the difference between the empirical covariance or correlation matrix and the matrix implied by the model. Browne (1982) demonstrated that the different methods are all variations on a common, general discrepancy function:

$$F = (s - \hat{\sigma})' * W^{-1} * (s - \hat{\sigma})$$

where s is a vector or list of the unique (nonredundant) elements of the sample covariance or correlation matrix, $\hat{\sigma}$ is a parallel vector of elements from the model-implied matrix, and W is a matrix of weights. Thus, the estimation methods in SEM are analogous to the generalized least squares method used in advanced regression contexts (Bollen, 1989). There is an important difference, however. When SEM researchers speak of *residuals,* they are usually referring to covariance residuals—differences between s and $\hat{\sigma}$—whereas in regression, residuals usually means data point residuals—differences between Y and $\hat{Y}$. In other words, the elements of the sample covariance matrix serve the same role in SEM that data points serve in regression.

Different SEM software packages offer different choices of estimation method. If the estimated model is correct in the population, sample size is large enough, and data assumptions are met, then all of these methods will produce comparable results. If not, then substantive differences can be observed, but in such cases there is no broad consensus regarding which method produces "better" results. Furthermore, new approaches continue to appear in the literature.

The two most widely used estimation methods are the ML method and the *generalized least squares* (GLS) method. In principle, use of these methods requires that the elements of the sample moment matrix must have a joint Wishart distribution. This condition is met when the sample matrix is a covariance matrix computed from a sufficiently large sample of data that follow a multivariate normal distribution. Scattered evidence and personal experience suggest that ML and GLS are rather robust even when data are moderately nonnormal. Further, in many cases, researchers can use a Pearson correlation matrix just as well as a covariance matrix, although use of a correlation matrix will lead some programs to produce inaccurate estimated standard errors (James Steiger, message to SEMNET, April 5, 1996; Lawley & Maxwell, 1971).

The *asymptotically distribution free* (ADF) or *weighted least squares* (WLS) method (the terms are almost synonymous), on the other hand, requires little more than that all variables are continuously distributed. To use this method, the researcher must derive an estimate of the asymptotic covariance matrix of the elements of the sample covariance matrix. In other words, to complement the second-order moments (the covariances) of the distribution, the researcher must also supply the fourth-order moments (the covariances of the covariances).

This explicit weight matrix tends to be quite large. The model in Fig. 9.1, for example, involves $p = 12$ measures. That means there will be $k = 1/2 * p * (p + 1) = 78$ nonredundant elements of the sample covariance matrix, so the explicit weight matrix will have dimension 78 × 78, with $1/2 * k * (k + 1) = 3{,}081$ nonredundant elements. Unfortunately, obtaining an adequate estimate of this matrix is demanding, in terms of both computational burden and sample size. Muthén and Kaplan (1985, 1992) indicate that, even with models involving only a handful of variables, sample sizes in the thousands are required for stable estimation. Yung and Bentler (1994) have suggested that these requirements can be reduced through *bootstrapping*. This procedure involves drawing repeated samples from the data set, computing a number of sample covariance matrices, then estimating the asymptotic weight matrix based on the degree of variability actually observed across those computed matrices.

Finally, *unweighted least squares* (ULS) involves weighting all elements of the covariance or correlation matrix equally—a "know nothing" approach to estimation. This method should be used only when analyzing correlation matrices; without compensating weights, measures scaled in large units will have much more influence on the estimation process than measures scaled in small units. Further, there is no statistical theory behind ULS to support the computation of standard errors or an overall goodness-of-fit test. Still, some research (Rigdon & Ferguson, 1991, 1992) suggests that ULS is a relatively stable estimation method, which may produce some results when other estimation methods fail entirely. In particular, ULS may be a choice for researchers analyzing polychoric correlations who cannot use ADF/WLS methods and who obtain unacceptable or suspicious results from GLS or ML estimation.

SEM Software. Researchers also face a choice in terms of the SEM software they will use. The available products in this field—Amos, Proc CALIS, Cosan, EQS, Lincs, Liscomp, LISREL, Mecosa, Mx, Ramona, SEPath, and others—are far from interchangeable. Currently, there is a trend toward graphical interfaces and greater ease of use. Leaders in this direction include products such as Amos (SmallWaters Corporation) and EQS (Multivariate Software), which allow researchers to specify and modify the model to be tested by drawing it, using simple graphical tools. Even Jöreskog's venerable LISREL (Scientific Software) package currently offers graphical model modification and a Microsoft Windows version. Where a command line interface is used, most programs have adopted a *natural language* approach, in place of arcane syntaxes dominated by cryptic keywords and matrix algebra. Table 9.1, for example, demonstrates the specification of the model in Fig. 9.1 using the old-style command language of LISREL8 and the newer *natural language/line equation* Simplis command language. The LISREL package interprets either command language, although the two cannot be mixed in the same program. As tends to be true with SEM software, there are many ways to specify exactly the same model, even within a given language or package, so Table 9.1 shows just two of many approaches to specifying this model.

Some programs have special features that make them stand out. For example, the EQS package incorporates innovations developed by the package's author, Peter Bentler, that have not been adopted by other packages. Amos features exceptional missing-data handling procedures, and comes with a highly readable manual that incorporates a series of lessons on SEM. EQS, LISREL, and Liscomp include procedures for dealing with ordinal data, including facilities for computing polychoric correlations and the appropriate

TABLE 9.1
Command Lines for the Model in Fig. 9.1

LISREL8 Command Lines:

---

(1) Marcoulides chapter example in LISREL8 command language
(2) DA NI=12 NO=275 MA=KM
(3) KM=MARCSEM1.KMM
(4) LA
(5) Q3 Q4 Q5 Q2 Q1 Q6 Q7a Q7c Q7d Q7f Q9 Q10
(6) MO NY=6 NE=3 NX=6 NK=2 PS=SY TE=SY BE=FU TD=SY GA=FI
(7) LE
(8) SATISFAC VALUE LOYALTY
(9) LK
(10) QUALITY PRICE
(11) FR LY(2,1) LY(3,1) LY(6,3)
(12) FR LX(2,1) LX(3,1) LX(4,1) LX(6,2)
(13) VA 1.0 LY(1,1) LY(4,2) LY(5,3) LX(1,1) LX(5,2)
(14) FI TE(4,4)
(15) VA 0.20 TE(4,4)
(16) FR BE(1,2) BE(2,1) BE(3,2) BE(3,1) GA(1,1) GA(2,2)
(17) OU SC RS EF

Simplis Command Lines:

---

(1) !Marcoulides chapter example in SIMPLIS command language
(2) Observed Variables: Q3 Q4 Q5 Q2 Q1 Q6 Q7a Q7c Q7d Q7f Q9 Q10
(3) Correlation matrix from file MARCSEM1.KMM
(4) Sample size: 275
(5) Latent Variables: SATISFAC VALUE LOYALTY QUALITY PRICE
(6) Relationships:
(7) SATISFAC = VALUE QUALITY
(8) VALUE = SATISFAC PRICE
(9) LOYALTY = SATISFAC VALUE
(10) Q3 = 1***SATISFAC**
(11) Q4 - Q5 = SATISFAC
(12) Q2 = 1***VALUE**
(13) Q1 = 1***LOYALTY**
(14) Q6 = LOYALTY
(15) Q7a = 1***QUALITY**
(16) Q7c - Q7f = QUALITY
(17) Q9 = 1***PRICE**
(18) Q10 = PRICE
(19) Set the Error Variance of Q2 to 0.20
(20) Print Residuals
(21) End of Problem

---

asymptotic weight matrices. Some SEM software is integrated with more general statistical packages—Amos with SPSS, Proc CALIS with SAS, SEPath with Statistica. Mx, a program written by Michael Neale, has the unique virtue of being distributed at no cost, over the Internet. Whereas Mx has previously utilized an old-fashioned interface, testing for a new graphical interface is currently underway.

Interpretation

A systematic approach is also important when interpreting SEM results. SEM analysis typically leads to a variety of outputs, which must be interpreted holistically. Interpreting each element in isolation can lead to frustration, wasted time, and embarrassing errors.

Interpreting Error Messages. First, the researcher should scan the output looking for error or warning messages. Unfortunately, the same "warning" issued by SEM software can indicate either that things have gone well, or that things have gone badly, depending on the situation. For example, in the model in Fig. 9.1, the common factor Value has only one indicator. With only one indicator, the measurement error variance may not be identified, so its value must be specified a priori. Suppose the researcher assumes *no* error variance (usually a poor assumption), and sets this value at zero. Then the covariance matrix of the measurement error terms in this model would be "not positive definite," meaning, essentially, that the determinant of this matrix would be zero. Because proper covariance matrices should have positive determinants, many SEM programs will flag this with an error message. However, because this is just what the modeler intended, the error message is, in fact, a "no error" message. Other examples may exist, as well.

Evaluating Fit. The next step is to evaluate the model's overall fit, because parameter estimates may only be meaningful if the model's fit is acceptable. The literature of SEM offers a stunning number of alternative fit indices, many of which have fallen out of favor over time. Three that deserve special attention are the chi-square statistic (Jöreskog, 1969), the root mean square error of approximation (RMSEA; Browne & Cudeck, 1993; Steiger & Lind, 1980), and the comparative fit index (CFI; Bentler, 1990). The chi-square statistic can be computed as $(N-1) * \hat{F}$, where N is sample size and $\hat{F}$ is the minimum value of an appropriately used ML, GLS, or ADF discrepancy function. The overall chi-square statistic provides a test of whether the sample covariance matrix is equivalent to the model-implied covariance matrix, within sampling error. One unusual feature of this test is that the proposed model represents the null hypothesis in the test, not the alternative (Fornell, 1983). Thus, the aim of the researcher is to not reject the null hypothesis. A "good" value for the chi-square, then, is one that is not much larger than the statistic's degrees of freedom, and one that is associated with a "large" p-value. Typical rules of thumb look for p-values larger than .05 or .10. (The model's degrees of freedom are a function of the structure of the model and the number of measures—see Rigdon, 1994a—but *not* of sample size.) A positive result here implies that the model is consistent with the data—but it does *not* imply that the tested model is a correct representation of the phenomena in question. The chi-square test cannot confirm a model—it merely fails to reject it.

Furthermore, it is important to remember that what the chi-square statistic tests is not the free parameters in the model but the restrictions. The chi-square test does not "test" whether parameter estimates are correct. It tests whether the restrictions in the model—the paths that are excluded, and the constraints placed on estimated parameters—are consistent with the data. With highly *saturated* models, where almost every variable has a direct relation to almost every other variable, there are few restrictions, so little in the model is actually being tested. For the model in Fig. 9.1, adding only two structural paths (from Quality to Loyalty, and from Price to Loyalty) would make the structural model completely saturated. If both of those paths were added to the model, then the chi-square would not be testing the structural model at all, but only the restrictions implied by the measurement model. Following a form of Occam's razor, researchers prefer *parsimonious* models, which have many restrictions and relatively few free parameters. Parsimony gives researchers more confidence in interpreting model results (Anderson & Gerbing, 1988a). Specifying parsimonious models also reduces the number of *equivalent* models.

Well-known problems with the chi-square statistic have led researchers to interpret it with caution. If the proposed model is not *perfectly* correct in the statistical population, the behavior of the chi-square is very much a function of sample size. Large sample sizes then produce large chi-square values, which favor rejecting the proposed model, and small sample sizes produce small chi-square values, which favor not rejecting the model. Because proposed models typically represent simplified approximations to reality rather than exact representations (MacCallum & Tucker, 1991), a strong sample size influence on the chi-square is the rule rather than the exception. Other violated assumptions, such as using non-normal data with the ML or GLS estimation methods, can also induce this behavior.

Alternative fit indices have been proposed in an effort to minimize this and related problems. The RMSEA attempts to minimize the impact of sample size, and to shift the research focus from exact fit to approximate fit. RMSEA is computed as:

$$RMSEA = \sqrt{\frac{\chi^2 - d}{(N-1) \times d}}$$

where d is degrees of freedom (df). Dividing by sample size is designed to remove the sample size influence. Dividing by degrees of freedom is intended to produce a measure of nonfit per degree of freedom, to allow for comparisons across different model structures. RMSEA is a statistic whose distribution is linked to the *noncentral* chi-square distribution (Steiger, Shapiro, & Browne, 1985), a distribution that arises when a model is only approximately correct. Browne and Cudeck (1993) suggested that RMSEA values between 0 and .05 imply good approximate overall fit, whereas values above .10 indicate significant fit problems. Because RMSEA has a known distribution, it is possible to construct confidence intervals for this statistic, which provide a more complete picture of a model's performance.

Bentler (1990) created CFI as a means for researchers to compare the fit of their model to a "worst case" alternative, but under the same conditions of sample size and data distribution. CFI is computed as:

$$CFI = 1 - \frac{\chi^2_k - d_k}{\chi^2_i - d_i}$$

where χ^2_k and d_k are the chi-square and degrees of freedom for the model of interest, and χ^2_i and d_i are those values derived from a *baseline* model. The typical baseline model is one where every measure is modeled as being uncorrelated with every other measure. This is also known as the *independence* or *null* baseline model. In Bentler's formulation, there is a further restriction that the denominator in the formula must always be as large or larger than the numerator, so that CFI always ranges between 0 and 1. Values near 1 imply that the model is doing a reasonable job of explaining covariance among the measures. Although there is a well-established rule of thumb saying that CFI values of .90 or above indicate adequate fit, Hu and Bentler (1995) failed to find evidence to support the use of this rule. Informal proposals (Mulaik, message to SEMNET, February 24, 1995) have called for raising the minimal acceptable value to .95.

Besides consulting overall fit indices, researchers should also examine the detailed diagnostics provided by their software. Good overall fit may conceal a specific fit problem that has implications for the interpretability of the solution. Examining the individual residuals (as previously noted, these residuals are the differences between the sample values and model-implied values for each element of the covariance matrix) may help to pinpoint the locations of fit problems. *Standardized residuals* (sometimes called *normalized residuals*) are the residuals divided by their estimated standard errors. These standardized residuals should follow (approximately) a standard normal or Z distribution. Standardized residuals that are greater than ±3, or that stand as outliers from the generally symmetric distribution of these values in a stem-leaf plot, demand closer scrutiny. *Modification indices* are values associated with constrained or fixed parameters, and that indicate the minimum amount that the overall chi-square statistic would decline (improve) if the constraint were removed or the parameter were freely estimated in the model. Because removing one restriction from the model would cause the loss of 1 degree of freedom, modification indices can be interpreted as following a $\chi^2_{(1)}$ distribution. Rules of thumb suggest that values above 5 or 10 require closer examination.

The larger the sample size, and the larger the model, the more opportunities there are for large standardized residuals and modification indices to occur based on pure random sampling error. Thus, researchers must exercise judgment. Recent SEM software has also incorporated an *expected parameter change* (EPC) statistic, to indicate how much the value of a fixed parameter would likely change if it were freely estimated. Kaplan (1990—see also the accompanying commentaries) has suggested that if both a modification index and the associated EPC statistic are large, then a serious fit problem may be present.

Interpreting Parameter Estimates. If all of these tests are passed, the researcher can move on to interpreting the parameter estimates. However, the researcher's first look at the parameter estimates is actually an extension of the evaluation of fit (Jöreskog & Sörbom, 1989). Before going further, researchers should make certain that the estimates appear reasonable. Some model parameters represent variances, and all free parameters of this type should be positive in sign. All parameters should be examined to ensure that their signs and magnitudes are reasonable, given the researcher's prior knowledge about the variables involved. Unlikely or unexpected values may signal a problem relating to command syntax, fit, identification, or multicollinearity. If all estimates are reasonable, then it is appropriate to interpret them, and also to interpret ancillary results such as the SMC values and measures of indirect and total effects.

Factor Scores. Finally, researchers may wish to generate and interpret *factor scores* for individual cases or respondents. Factor scores give each case a value on the common factors, derived from the model's structure and the case's scores on the measures. Unfortunately, the computation of factor scores includes a degree of uncertainty or indeterminacy, which is inherent in the common factor model (Bollen, 1989). There are competing formulas for computing factor scores, and whereas the different formulas tend to yield similar scores, different formulas may yield different rank orders for the cases. Thus, researchers should be cautious in using factor scores for sensitive tasks such as assessing employee performance.

Model Modification. Before looking at an example application, it is important to revisit the issue of modifying a structural equation model to improve its fit. Researchers may observe that their model seems to fit poorly, but that making certain changes in the model would substantially improve fit. Researchers must be cautious in interpreting results from such modified models, due in part to the danger that the modifications are only sample-specific. Model modifications designed to improve the fit of the model in a given sample may compromise the model's generalizability, and thus, its overall value. Again, a cross-validation approach with holdout samples will minimize this risk. Researchers should also examine the solution for the modified model in detail. Modifications that improve overall fit may produce unlikely or unacceptable values for individual parameter estimates. Finally, researchers should make certain that the modified model's form is still consistent with the researchers' prior knowledge regarding the research situation. Otherwise, researchers may face a major challenge in defending the validity and meaningfulness of their results.

EXAMPLE

In this example, a data set of 275 observations is used to compute a correlation matrix (Table 9.2), which is then used to test the model in Fig. 9.1. A correlation matrix is used here for the sake of clarity, although it would be best to analyze a covariance matrix. The researcher expects that (a) Value and Quality will both have positive effects on Satisfaction, (b) Satisfaction should have a positive effect on Value whereas Price will have a negative effect, and (c) both Satisfaction and Value will have positive effects on Loyalty. In addition, some alternative models are proposed. Because Price may be a key variable in determining Loyalty, one alternative model adds a direct effect from Price to Loyalty. Finally, based on experience in similar research settings, the researcher suspects that Satisfaction and Loyalty derive primarily from *hedonic* or experiential factors, rather than from utilitarian

TABLE 9.2
Correlation Matrix for Example Analysis

	Q3	Q4	Q5	Q2	Q1	Q6	Q7a	Q7c	Q7d	Q7f	Q9	Q10
Q3	1.00											
Q4	0.57	1.00										
Q5	0.44	0.41	1.00									
Q2	0.29	0.27	0.15	1.00								
Q1	0.53	0.51	0.44	0.23	1.00							
Q6	0.42	0.39	0.36	0.17	0.72	1.00						
Q7a	0.47	0.30	0.26	0.05	0.32	0.29	1.00					
Q7c	0.29	0.23	0.13	−0.03	0.24	0.17	0.51	1.00				
Q7d	0.40	0.11	0.17	−0.03	0.04	0.04	0.30	0.24	1.00			
Q7f	0.40	0.28	0.18	−0.03	0.26	0.25	0.73	0.60	0.36	1.00		
Q9	−0.08	−0.07	−0.04	−0.41	−0.11	−0.06	0.13	0.17	0.12	0.16	1.00	
Q10	0.06	0.05	0.00	−0.32	−0.03	0.02	0.18	0.21	0.16	0.23	0.74	1.00

factors like Price and Value, so another alternative model deletes the paths from Value to Satisfaction and from Value to Loyalty (see Fig. 9.3).

The measures for this study were selected from a questionnaire chiefly on the basis of their wording, augmented by exploratory factor analysis. The correlation matrix (Table 9.2) shows that, as urged by Campbell and Fiske (1959), correlations between measures of the same common factor tend to be higher than correlations between measures of different common factors—although there are exceptions in this correlation matrix. The correlation matrix also confirms an expectation that, based on the wording of the items, the measures of Price will have negative correlations with the measure of Value.

The command files for the original model (shown in Table 9.1) include two special features that are worth noting. First, because there is only a single measure of Value, the researcher must specify the degree of measurement error for that measure. Based on prior experience with this measure, the researcher assigns a reliability of .80 to the measure. This means that 80% of the variance of the measure is systematic, and 20% is attributed to

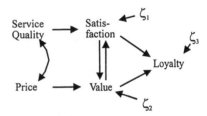

Original or Target Model

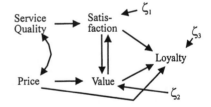

Model with Direct Effect of Price on Loyalty

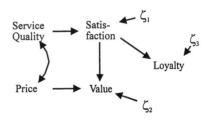

FIG. 9.3. Alternative structural models of Satisfaction and Loyalty.

Model with No Effects from Value

measurement error. Thus, the researcher must set the error variance for this measure to .20 times the total variance of the measure. Because we are analyzing a correlation matrix, the measure's variance is 1, so the error variance is set to .20 * **1** = .20. Lines 14 and 15 in the LISREL code and line 19 in the Simplis code set this value.

Second, both command files (line 13 in the LISREL commands, and lines 10, 12, 13, 15, and 17 in the Simplis commands) fix the value of some measurement *loadings* (parameters linking measures to common factors) to 1. The purpose of this is to give a variance or *scale* to the common factors. Inherently, the variances of these unobserved variables are not identified. The researcher can solve this problem either by directly assigning variances to the common factors, or by fixing one loading to a nonzero constant. Either way, the value typically used is 1. Some SEM packages automatically standardize the common factors, but with others researchers may be required to fix loadings. These specifications do not bias the results—they merely rescale them. No essential information is lost.

The researchers first estimated their original or target model. A scan of the output (see Appendix A) shows no error or warning messages, and a careful look at the parameter estimates indicates that the model had been set up correctly. LISREL8 reports values for about 30 overall fit indices. In particular, the chi-square statistic, with 48 degrees of freedom, is equal to 97.11, which has a p-value of .000035. In other words, it is very *unlikely* that we would obtain such a large chi-square value, given the degrees of freedom, if the model were exactly correct in the population and if other assumptions held. This suggests that the model may be invalid. This is consistent with the RMSEA of .061, which is beyond the rule-of-thumb .05 value for this index. On the other hand, the "p-value for test of close fit" for this model is .14. This means that an 86% $(1 - .14)$ confidence interval for RMSEA would include the .05 value, so perhaps the fit is acceptable, after all. Like many SEM packages today, LISREL8 automatically computes a chi-square value for the null or independence baseline model, which then allows the software to compute CFI and related indices. The null model's chi-square value is 1,349.52, with 66 degrees of freedom, so CFI is equal to .96, which is better than even the strict .95 rule-of thumb value for this index. Although the chi-square value for the model is discouraging, the other indices suggest adequate overall fit.

A look at the detailed diagnostics suggests that the model may have some specific fit problems. The stem-leaf plot of the standardized residuals generally follows the *bell curve* of a normal distribution, suggesting good fit:

- 2 | 510
- 1 | 9886443333200
- 0 | 98876554433320000000000000
  0 | 111222333355666777888

1 | 0003446679
2 | 00123
3 | 8
4 | 7

but some extreme values on the positive end argue for taking a closer look. The summary of extreme values provided by LISREL8 shows that both of the largest standardized residual values (3.80 and 4.70) are for elements of the correlation matrix involving Q3, a measure of Satisfaction, and Q7a and Q7d, two measures of Quality. Large models with many measures may produce standardized residuals of this magnitude purely by chance, but this model involves only 12 measures, so these values, standing as outliers in the stem-leaf plot, invite closer scrutiny.

Most of the modification indices are quite small, but clearly one stands out. The value for the covariance between the measurement error terms for Q3 and Q7d is 35.93, well above any rule of thumb. This value means that, for this data set, modifying the model by allowing those error terms to correlate would reduce the chi-square value by at least 35.93, at the cost of only 1 degree of freedom. Further, the expected parameter change statistic or expected value for the parameter would be .24. This represents a substantial share of the variance of both Q3 and Q7d. These results all suggest that these measures have either substantially more or substantially less in common with each other than the tested model allows.

A look at the parameter estimates for the LISREL and Simplis approaches (see Appendix B) highlights a key difference between the two. The LISREL parameter estimates are presented in a matrix algebra format, whereas the Simplis estimates are presented in equation format. (The Simplis package also offers options for displaying parameter estimates either in the LISREL matrix format or on a path diagram similar to that shown in Fig. 9.1.) To an extent, the choice between formats is a choice between the comprehensiveness of the matrix algebra format and the convenience of the equation/graphical format. Researchers should keep such distinctions in mind when evaluating SEM software.

The parameter estimates for the structural model (labeled *Beta* and *Gamma* in the LISREL output) lead to these structural equations:

$$\text{Value} = .15 * \text{Satisfaction} - .47 * \text{Price} + \zeta_1$$
$$\text{Satisfaction} = .29 * \text{Value} + .54 * \text{Quality} + \zeta_2$$
$$\text{Loyalty} = .00 * \text{Value} + .83 * \text{Satisfaction} + \zeta_3$$

(Readers who are familiar with matrix algebra will note that the positions of the parameter estimates in these matrices are consistent with the subscripts used in the earlier presentation of the structural equations.) In both the LISREL and Simplis displays, the top number is the parameter estimate, the number in parentheses is the standard error, and the bottom number—the t-value—can be interpreted against the standard normal distribution, as with the standardized residuals. Thus, whereas all of the parameter point estimates have the expected signs, not all of them appear to be statistically significant. However the R^2s for the three equations are .43, .31, and .51 for Satisfaction, Value, and Loyalty, which are certainly respectable, especially given the small number of predictor factors in the model. Note that these parameter estimates are unstandardized, based on common factors with differing variances. Standardized estimates are also available from nearly all SEM packages.

At this point, the researcher is confronted with various options, complicated by the desire to compare alternative models under identical conditions. Allowing the measurement error terms for Q3 and Q7d to covary in the model would improve fit, but also would hurt parsimony, and, perhaps, replicability. The researcher might also consider deleting one of the two measures from the model. The SMC for Q7d is only .16, meaning that only 16% of the variance of Q7d is directly associated with its common factor, Quality. Thus, it seems that little would be lost by eliminating this variable. In general, however, deleting offending measures presents the same risks as modifying the paths in the model.

The best approach is to test the competing models under both conditions—with the correlated measurement error term, and without it. Table 9.3 presents overall fit indices for the three competing models, under both conditions. Notice that the three models are nested, so researchers could perform chi-square difference tests to compare the three models under each condition. In a comparison between a less restricted model (with lower degrees of freedom) and a more restricted model (with higher degrees of freedom), a significant chi-square difference indicates that the additional restrictions contained in the latter model are not empirically supported. Thus, a significant chi-square difference favors the less restricted model, whereas a nonsignificant result indicates that the additional restrictions are consistent with the empirical evidence.

For example, compare the model with a *direct price effect* on Loyalty (the *DPE* model) with the original model, under the original specification. The DPE model includes one additional freely estimated parameter, so it is the less restricted model. The DPE model has 47 degrees of freedom, whereas the original model has 48, so the chi-square difference will have 48 − 47 = 1 degree of freedom. The difference in the chi-square values for the two models (see Table 9.3) is 1.90. With 1 degree of freedom, the p-value is .168, which is not likely to be considered significant. Thus, this comparison favors the more restricted, original model. Comparing the original model with the alternative model with the *Value paths deleted* (the *VPD* model)

TABLE 9.3
Fit Indices and Chi-Square Differences for Competing Models

		Original Specification	With Correlated Measurement Error
Direct Price Effect	χ^2 (DF)	95.21 (47)	56.24 (47)
(DPE) Model	p-value	<.001	.14
	RMSEA	.061	.029
	CFI	.96	.96
Original Model	χ^2 (DF)	97.11 (48)	57.98 (47)
	p-value	<.001	.13
	RMSEA	.061	.029
	CFI	.96	.99
Value Paths	χ^2 (DF)	107.58 (50)	69.48 (49)
Deleted (VPD)	p-value	<.001	.029
Model	RMSEA	.065	.039
	CFI	.96	.98

Chi-Square Differences

χ^2 (p-value)	DF	Original Specification	With Correlated Measurement Error
DPE Model vs. Original Model	1	1.90 (0.168)	1.74 (0.187)
Original Model vs. VPD Model	2	10.47 (0.005)	11.50 (0.003)
DPE Model vs. VPD Model	3	12.37 (0.006)	13.24 (0.004)

leads to a $\chi^2_{(2)}$ of 10.47 and a p-value of .005. This significant result favors the less restricted model—again, the original model. Table 9.3 also shows that incorporating the correlated measurement error term into the three models does not alter the substantive results of these comparisons, although the chi-square values do change somewhat.

With many models under consideration, of course, researchers will need to take account of the number of comparisons when choosing an overall significance level. In such cases, researchers may also wish to adopt Anderson and Gerbing's (1988a) model comparison decision tree, in order to avoid confusion.

LIMITATIONS OF SEM

Although SEM offers a number of attractive features, it also has features that may give researchers pause. First, as may be clear from the preceding discussion, the methodology of SEM is still "under construction." Significant gaps remain. For example, SEM researchers are only now developing procedures for incorporating nonlinear relations into their models, or for modeling dynamic, time-dependent phenomena. The process of developing and testing a structural equation model calls for judgment throughout, and SEM authorities often disagree, even on points that are fundamental to the application of the method. Researchers who like their methodology neat and well established will be tempted to look elsewhere.

Second, researchers using SEM face the real possibility that a given model will fail to produce an interpretable result. Even when a model is well identified, and other assumptions are met, it is possible that SEM's iterative estimation methods will fail to converge on a solution, or may converge on a solution involving unacceptable parameter estimates. Alternatively, a model may fit so poorly that it is inappropriate to interpret the parameter estimates. Researchers can forestall such problems through methodical model development and careful data preparation, but the risk remains, especially in studies where researchers have only one model of interest and where data are drawn from previous research, where the use of such a demanding analytical technique was not contemplated.

Third, SEM requires much larger sample sizes than are needed for more specialized methods, such as regression. Rules of thumb call for 5 or 10 cases per estimated parameter. Using ADF methods dramatically increases the necessary sample size. Bootstrapping may overcome this problem to a degree, but a literature on the practical value of this approach is only beginning to emerge.

Fourth, short of adopting ADF methods, SEM tends to involve the unrealistic assumption of a multivariate normal distribution in the data. This assumption is commonly violated, but the impact of violations is not entirely clear. Researchers also regularly violate the assumption that the model is correct in the population—in fact, SEM researchers expect most models to be simplifications of a complex reality—but again, the exact penalty for violating this assumption is unknown.

Fifth, some researchers will find the indeterminacy of factor scores frustrating. Once the researcher has translated a problem into latent variable terms, it seems there is no single way to return to the level of the observables—the level likely to be of greatest interest to the research sponsor. Researchers who need their feet planted firmly in the world of observables may prefer an alternate technique, like PLS, although a combination of cautious interpretation and the use of holdout samples may mitigate the researcher's concerns.

Sixth, full mastery of SEM methodology requires more than the ability to use a computer program. To be fully confident in using this technique, researchers must have a background in matrix algebra. This is often the only way to understand negative outcomes—or to tell when a seemingly negative outcome is actually a positive one. The ability to successfully troubleshoot SEM models comes only with experience. Researchers who want to add SEM to their modeling toolkit should look forward to a significant period of study and practice. On the brighter side, though, researchers will find that the study of SEM illuminates their understanding of other techniques, as well.

FOR MORE INFORMATION

There are many ways to learn more about the methodology of SEM. One way is to become familiar with at least one of three textbooks—Loehlin (1992), Bollen (1989), or Hayduk (1987). Bollen's and Hayduk's texts are somewhat dated, but second editions of Bollen's and Loehlin's texts are in development. Hoyle (1995) and Marcoulides and Schumacker (1996) have recent volumes comprised of contributed chapters, and Schumacker and Lomax (1996) have written a text aimed at beginners in SEM. Additional texts are also available that present SEM in the context of a specific software package (e.g., Byrne, 1994). For more compact treatments, consider overview articles by Anderson and Gerbing (1988a) or Bentler and Chou (1987).

For more active learning, consider the workshops on SEM sponsored by the Inter-University Consortium for Political and Social Research (ICPSR), hosted every summer by the University of Michigan, at Ann Arbor. In recent years, these 2-week workshops have been led by Kenneth Bollen, who developed his popular text from notes for these sessions. Bollen leads both introductory and advanced workshops, and both are highly recommended. Local universities may also offer courses on SEM.

Articles presenting either methodological developments in SEM or outstanding applications of the approach can be found in a number of journals. As the references for this chapter indicate, leading SEM journals include *Psychometrika* (for highly technical treatments), *Psychological Bulletin* (since 1996, methodological papers appear in a separate publication, *Psychological Methods*), *Educational and Psychological Measurement*, *Multivariate Behavioral Research*, *Sociological Methods & Research*, *British Journal of Mathematical and Statistical Psychology*, and *Journal of Marketing Research*. A rather new journal, *Structural Equation Modeling*, may be especially useful for SEM novices. This journal often includes articles aimed at teaching aspects of this method, and its editorial review board is almost a "Who's Who" of active SEM researchers.

A variety of SEM resources is available over the Internet. Many software and text publishers maintain World Wide Web sites to provide information and upgrades. Michael Neale's Mx Web site, located at http://griffin. vcu.edu/mx/, offers free downloads of a full-scale and fully functional SEM program, with accompanying documentation. A number of other privately maintained Web sites also provide useful information and hyperlinks. An electronic mailing list known as SEMNET is devoted to topics in SEM. This list has more than 1,300 subscribers worldwide, including many of the leading figures in SEM today. SEMNET welcomes both basic and advanced questions, ranging from inquiries about the philosophy of SEM to requests for help in debugging particular SEM programs. More information about SEM-NET is available from the World Wide Web, at http://www.gsu.edu/~mkteer/semnet.html, or from the author (erigdon@gsu.edu). A SEM "frequently asked questions" Web site is also available, at http://www.gsu.edu/~mkteer/semfaq.html. This site includes short discussions of basic issues in SEM, many of them drawn from SEMNET exchanges. Readers can expect to see more sites established as this dynamic field continues to mature.

REFERENCES

Anderson, J. C., & Gerbing, D. W. (1988a). Structural equation modeling in practice: A review and recommended two-step approach. *Psychological Bulletin, 103,* 411–423.

Anderson, J. C., & Gerbing, D. W. (1988b). An updated paradigm for scale development incorporating unidimensionality and its assessment. *Journal of Marketing Research, 25*(2), 186–192.

Babakus, E., Ferguson, C. E., Jr., & Jöreskog, K. G. (1987). The sensitivity of confirmatory maximum likelihood factor analysis to violations of measurement scale and distributional assumptions. *Journal of Marketing Research, 28,* 222–229.

Bagozzi, R. P. (1984). A prospectus for theory construction in marketing. *Journal of Marketing, 48,* 11–29.

Bekker, P. A., Merckens, A., & Wansbeek, T. J. (1994). *Identification, equivalent models, and computer algebra.* New York: Academic Press.

Bentler, P. M. (1990). Comparative fit indices in structural models. *Psychological Bulletin, 107*(3), 238–246.

Bentler, P. M., & Chou, C.-P. (1987). Practical issues in structural modeling. *Sociological Methods & Research, 16,* 78–117.

Bollen, K. A. (1989). *Structural equations with latent variables.* New York: Wiley.

Bollen, K. A., & Lennox, R. (1991). Conventional wisdom on measurement: A structural equation perspective. *Psychological Bulletin, 110,* 305–314.

Browne, M. W. (1982). Covariance structures. In D. M. Hawkins (Ed.), *Topics in applied multivariate analysis* (pp. 72–141). Cambridge, England: Cambridge University Press.

Browne, M. W., & Cudeck, R. (1993). Alternative ways of assessing model fit. In K. A. Bollen & J. S. Long (Eds.), *Testing structural equation models* (pp. 136–162). Newbury Park, CA: Sage.

Byrne, B. M. (1994). *Structural equation modeling with EQS and EQS/Windows: Basic concepts, applications, and programming.* Newbury Park, CA: Sage.

Campbell, D. R., & Fiske, D. W. (1959). Convergent and discriminant validation by the multitrait-multimethod matrix. *Psychological Bulletin, 56,* 81–105.

Churchill, G. A., Jr. (1979). A paradigm for developing better measures of marketing constructs. *Journal of Marketing Research, 16*(1), 64–73.

Cudeck, R., & Browne, M. W. (1983). Cross-validation of covariance structures. *Multivariate Behavioral Research, 18,* 147–167.

Dempster, A. P., Laird, N. M., & Rubin, D. B. (1977). Maximum likelihood from incomplete data via the EM algorithm. *Journal of the Royal Statistical Society, Series B, 39,* 1–22.

Fornell, C. (1983). Issues in the application of covariance structure analysis: A comment. *Journal of Consumer Research, 9,* 443–448.

Gillespie, M. W., & Fox, J. (1980). Specification errors and negatively correlated disturbances in "parallel" simultaneous-equation models. *Sociological Methods & Research, 8,* 273–308.

Hair, J. F., Jr., Anderson, R. E., Tatham, R. L., & Black, W. C. (1995). *Multivariate data analysis with readings* (4th ed.). Englewood Cliffs, NJ: Prentice-Hall.

Hayduk, L. A. (1987). *Structural equation modeling with LISREL: Essentials and advances.* Baltimore: Johns Hopkins University Press.

Hoyle, R. M. (Ed.). (1995). *Structural equation models: Concepts, issues and applications.* Thousand Oaks, CA: Sage.

Hu, L., & Bentler, P. M. (1995). Evaluating model fit. In R. M. Hoyle (Ed.), *Structural equation models: Concepts, issues and applications* (pp. 76–99). Thousand Oaks, CA: Sage.

James, L. R., Mulaik, S. A., & Brett, J. M. (1982). *Causal analysis: Assumptions, models and data.* Beverly Hills, CA: Sage.

Johnson, D. R., & Creech, J. C. (1983). Ordinal measures in multiple indicators models: A simulation study of categorization error. *American Sociological Review, 48,* 398–407.

Jöreskog, K. G. (1969). A general approach to confirmatory maximum likelihood factor analysis. *Psychometrika, 34,* 183–202.

Jöreskog, K. G., & Sörbom, D. (1989). *LISREL 7: A guide to the program and applications* (2nd ed.). Chicago: SPSS.

Kaplan, D. (1990). Evaluating and modifying covariance structure models: A review and recommendation. *Multivariate Behavioral Research, 25,* 137–155.

Kenny, D. A., & Judd, C. M. (1984). Estimating the nonlinear and interactive effects of latent variables. *Psychological Bulletin, 96,* 201–210.

Lawley, D. N., & Maxwell, A. E. (1971). *Factor analysis as a statistical method.* London: Butterworths.

Loehlin, J. C. (1992). *Latent variable models: An introduction to factor, path, and structural analysis.* Hillsdale, NJ: Lawrence Erlbaum Associates.

MacCallum, R. C., & Tucker, L. R. (1991). Representing sources of error in the common-factor model: Implications for theory and practice. *Psychological Bulletin, 109,* 502–511.

Marcoulides, G. A., & Schumacker, R. E. (1996). *Advanced structural equation modeling: Issues and techniques.* Mahwah, NJ: Lawrence Erlbaum Associates.

Marsh, H. W., Hau, K.-T., & Balla, J. R. (1996). *Is more ever too much: The number of indicators per factor in confirmatory factor analysis.* Unpublished manuscript.

McArdle, J. J., & McDonald, R. P. (1984). Some algebraic properties of the reticular action model. *British Journal of Mathematical and Statistical Psychology, 37,* 234–251.

Muthén, B., & Kaplan, D. (1985). A comparison of methodologies for the factor analysis of non-normal Likert variables. *British Journal of Mathematical and Statistical Psychology, 38,* 171–189.

Muthén, B., & Kaplan, D. (1992). A comparison of some methodologies for the factor analysis of non-normal Likert variables: A note on the size of the model. *British Journal of Mathematical and Statistical Psychology, 45,* 19–30.

Nunnally, J. C. (1967). *Psychometric theory.* New York: McGraw-Hill.

Nunnally, J. C., & Bernstein, I. H. (1994). *Psychometric theory* (3rd ed.). New York: McGraw-Hill.

Olsson, U. (1979). Maximum likelihood estimation of the polychoric correlation coefficient. *Psychometrika, 44,* 443–460.

Ping, R. A. (1996). Latent variable interactions and quadratic effect estimation: A two-step technique using structural equation analysis. *Psychological Bulletin, 119,* 166–175.

Rigdon, E. E. (1994a). Calculating degrees of freedom for a structural equation model. *Structural Equation Modeling, 1,* 274–278.

Rigdon, E. E. (1994b). Demonstrating the effects of unmodeled random measurement error. *Structural Equation Modeling, 1,* 375–380.

Rigdon, E. E. (1995). A necessary and sufficient identification rule for structural models estimated in practice. *Multivariate Behavioral Research, 30*, 359–384.

Rigdon, E. E., & Ferguson, C. E., Jr. (1991). The performance of the polychoric correlation coefficient and selected fitting functions in confirmatory factor analysis with ordinal data. *Journal of Marketing Research, 28*, 491–497.

Rigdon, E. E., & Ferguson, C. E., Jr. (1992). *Analysis of ordinal data with PRELIS and LISREL7.* Unpublished manuscript.

Rigdon, E. E., Schumacker, R. E., & Wothke, W. (in press). Modeling latent variable interaction: A comparative review. In R. E. Schumacker & G. Marcoulides (Eds.), *Advanced structural equation modeling: Interaction models.* Mahwah, NJ: Lawrence Erlbaum Associates.

Rubin, D. B. (1987). *Multiple imputation for nonresponse in surveys.* New York: Wiley.

Satorra, A., & Bentler, P. M. (1988). Scaling corrections for chi-square statistics in covariance structure analysis. *Proceedings of the American Statistical Association, 308–313.*

Schumacker, R. E., & Lomax, R. G. (1996). *A beginner's guide to structural equation modeling.* Mahwah, NJ: Lawrence Erlbaum Associates.

Spirtes, P., Glymour, C., & Scheines, R. (1993). *Causation, prediction, and search.* New York: Springer-Verlag.

Steiger, J. H. (1990). Structural model evaluation and modification: An interval estimation approach. *Multivariate Behavioral Research, 25*, 173–180.

Steiger, J. H., & Lind, J. C. (1980, May). *Statistically-based tests for the number of common factors.* Handout presented at the spring meeting of the Psychometric Society, Iowa City.

Steiger, J. H., Shapiro, A., & Browne, M. W. (1985). On the multivariate asymptotic distribution of sequential chi-square statistics. *Psychometrika, 50*, 253–264.

Stelzl, I. (1986). Changing a causal hypothesis without changing the fit: Some rules for generating equivalent path models. *Multivariate Behavioral Research, 21*, 309–331.

Yung, Y.-F., & Bentler, P. M. (1994). Bootstrap-corrected ADF test statistics in covariance structure analysis. *British Journal of Mathematical and Statistical Psychology, 47*, 63–84.

APPENDIX A

Edited LISREL8 Output for the Original Model

```
Marcoulides chapter example in LISREL8 command language
Number of Iterations = 9

LISREL ESTIMATES (MAXIMUM LIKELIHOOD)

        LAMBDA-Y

                SATISFAC      VALUE      LOYALTY
                --------     -----      -------
        Q3        1.00        - -         - -

        Q4        0.87        - -         - -
                 (0.08)
                 11.01

        Q5        0.68        - -         - -
                 (0.08)
                  8.58

        Q2         - -        1.00        - -
```

Q1	- -	- -	1.00
Q6	- -	- -	0.80
			(0.07)
			11.43

LAMBDA-X

	QUALITY	PRICE
	------	-----
Q7a	1.00	- -
Q7c	0.81	- -
	(0.07)	
	11.14	
Q7d	0.49	- -
	(0.08)	
	6.37	
Q7f	1.10	- -
	(0.08)	
	14.40	
Q9	- -	1.00
Q10	- -	0.90
		(0.10)
		9.27

BETA

	SATISFAC	VALUE	LOYALTY
	-------	-----	-------
SATISFAC	- -	0.29	- -
		(0.08)	
		3.49	
VALUE	0.15	- -	- -
	(0.11)		
	1.38		
LOYALTY	0.83	0.00	- -
	(0.09)	(0.07)	
	9.53	0.03	

GAMMA

	QUALITY	PRICE
	------	-----
SATISFAC	0.54	- -
	(0.07)	
	7.88	

```
VALUE              - -          -0.47
                               (0.07)
                               -6.63


LOYALTY            - -          - -
```

COVARIANCE MATRIX OF ETA AND KSI

	SATISFAC	VALUE	LOYALTY	QUALITY	PRICE
SATISFAC	0.66				
VALUE	0.27	0.80			
LOYALTY	0.55	0.23	0.89		
QUALITY	0.35	-0.03	0.29	0.66	
PRICE	-0.02	-0.39	-0.02	0.17	0.82

SQUARED MULTIPLE CORRELATIONS FOR STRUCTURAL EQUATIONS

SATISFAC	VALUE	LOYALTY
0.43	0.31	0.51

THETA-EPS

Q3	Q4	Q5	Q2	Q1	Q6
0.34	0.49	0.69	0.20	0.11	0.42
(0.05)	(0.05)	(0.07)		(0.06)	(0.05)
6.73	9.11	10.61		1.68	7.81

SQUARED MULTIPLE CORRELATIONS FOR Y - VARIABLES

Q3	Q4	Q5	Q2	Q1	Q6
0.66	0.50	0.31	0.80	0.89	0.58

THETA-DELTA

Q7a	Q7c	Q7d	Q7f	Q9	Q10
0.34	0.57	0.84	0.20	0.18	0.34
(0.04)	(0.05)	(0.07)	(0.04)	(0.08)	(0.07)
7.68	10.36	11.39	4.79	2.17	4.80

SQUARED MULTIPLE CORRELATIONS FOR X - VARIABLES

Q7a	Q7c	Q7d	Q7f	Q9	Q10
0.66	0.43	0.16	0.80	0.82	0.66

GOODNESS OF FIT STATISTICS

CHI-SQUARE WITH 48 DEGREES OF FREEDOM = 97.11 (P = 0.000035)
ESTIMATED NON-CENTRALITY PARAMETER (NCP) = 49.11

```
MINIMUM FIT FUNCTION VALUE = 0.35
POPULATION DISCREPANCY FUNCTION VALUE (F0) = 0.18
ROOT MEAN SQUARE ERROR OF APPROXIMATION (RMSEA) = 0.061
P-VALUE FOR TEST OF CLOSE FIT (RMSEA < 0.05) = 0.14


EXPECTED CROSS-VALIDATION INDEX (ECVI) = 0.57
ECVI FOR SATURATED MODEL = 0.57
ECVI FOR INDEPENDENCE MODEL = 5.01


CHI-SQUARE FOR INDEPENDENCE MODEL WITH 66 DEGREES OF FREEDOM = 1349.52
INDEPENDENCE AIC = 1373.52
MODEL AIC = 157.11
SATURATED AIC = 156.00
INDEPENDENCE CAIC = 1428.92
MODEL CAIC = 295.61
SATURATED CAIC = 516.11


ROOT MEAN SQUARE RESIDUAL (RMR) = 0.049
STANDARDIZED RMR = 0.049
GOODNESS OF FIT INDEX (GFI) = 0.95
ADJUSTED GOODNESS OF FIT INDEX (AGFI) = 0.91
PARSIMONY GOODNESS OF FIT INDEX (PGFI) = 0.58


NORMED FIT INDEX (NFI) = 0.93
NON-NORMED FIT INDEX (NNFI) = 0.95
PARSIMONY NORMED FIT INDEX (PNFI) = 0.67
COMPARATIVE FIT INDEX (CFI) = 0.96
INCREMENTAL FIT INDEX (IFI) = 0.96
RELATIVE FIT INDEX (RFI) = 0.90


CRITICAL N (CN) = 208.91
```

CONFIDENCE LIMITS COULD NOT BE COMPUTED DUE TO TOO SMALL P-VALUE FOR CHI-SQUARE

Marcoulides chapter example in LISREL8 command language

FITTED RESIDUALS

	Q3	Q4	Q5	Q2	Q1	Q6
Q3	0.01					
Q4	0.00	0.00				
Q5	−0.01	0.01	0.00			
Q2	0.01	0.03	−0.04	0.00		
Q1	−0.02	0.03	0.07	0.00	0.00	
Q6	−0.01	0.00	0.06	−0.02	0.00	0.00
Q7a	0.12	−0.01	0.02	0.08	0.03	0.06
Q7c	0.01	−0.02	−0.06	0.00	0.00	−0.01
Q7d	0.23	−0.04	0.06	−0.02	−0.10	−0.07
Q7f	0.02	−0.06	−0.08	0.01	−0.05	0.00
Q9	−0.06	−0.06	−0.02	−0.01	−0.09	−0.05
Q10	0.07	0.06	0.02	0.03	−0.01	0.04

```
    FITTED RESIDUALS

                Q7a      Q7c      Q7d      Q7f       Q9      Q10
                ------   ------   ------   ------   ------   ------
    Q7a        0.00
    Q7c       -0.03     0.00
    Q7d       -0.02    -0.02     0.00
    Q7f        0.00     0.02     0.00     0.00
     Q9       -0.04     0.03     0.03    -0.03     0.00
    Q10        0.03     0.09     0.09     0.06     0.00     0.00
```

SUMMARY STATISTICS FOR FITTED RESIDUALS
SMALLEST FITTED RESIDUAL = -0.10
  MEDIAN FITTED RESIDUAL = 0.00
 LARGEST FITTED RESIDUAL = 0.23

```
STEMLEAF PLOT
 - 1 | 0
 - 0 | 987666655
 - 0 | 444332222222211111110000000000000000000000
   0 | 11111222233333334
   0 | 6666677899
   1 | 2
   1 |
   2 | 3
```

```
    STANDARDIZED RESIDUALS

                Q3       Q4       Q5       Q2       Q1       Q6
                ------   ------   ------   ------   ------   ------
    Q3         0.33
    Q4        -0.02     0.12
    Q5        -0.55     0.48     0.05
    Q2         0.61     0.80    -0.83     1.01
    Q1        -1.44     1.43     2.17     0.23     0.04
    Q6        -0.79     0.17     1.66    -0.45     1.01     0.09
    Q7a        3.80    -0.22     0.52     2.11     0.84     1.40
    Q7c        0.28    -0.37    -1.31    -0.05     0.07    -0.28
    Q7d        4.70    -0.73     1.02    -0.33    -1.97    -1.33
    Q7f        0.62    -1.75    -1.89     0.16    -1.61    -0.02
     Q9       -1.44    -1.25    -0.43    -2.49    -2.06    -0.99
    Q10        1.63     1.29     0.29     2.30    -0.29     0.68
```

```
    STANDARDIZED RESIDUALS

                Q7a      Q7c      Q7d      Q7f       Q9      Q10
                ------   ------   ------   ------   ------   ------
    Q7a        0.00
    Q7c       -1.82     0.00
    Q7d       -0.90    -0.62     0.00
    Q7f        0.74     1.96     0.02     0.00
     Q9       -1.33     0.78     0.64    -1.30     0.00
    Q10        0.73     1.86     1.61     1.96    -1.01     0.00
```

```
SUMMARY STATISTICS FOR STANDARDIZED RESIDUALS
SMALLEST STANDARDIZED RESIDUAL = -2.49
  MEDIAN STANDARDIZED RESIDUAL =  0.03
 LARGEST STANDARDIZED RESIDUAL =  4.70

STEMLEAF PLOT
 - 2|510
 - 1|9886443333200
 - 0|98876554433320000000000000
   0|11122233355666777888
   1|0003446679
   2|00123
   3|8
   4|7
LARGEST POSITIVE STANDARDIZED RESIDUALS
RESIDUAL FOR    Q7a AND    Q3   3.80
RESIDUAL FOR    Q7d AND    Q3   4.70
```

Marcoulides chapter example in LISREL8 command language
MODIFICATION INDICES AND EXPECTED CHANGE

            MODIFICATION INDICES FOR LAMBDA-Y

	SATISFAC	VALUE	LOYALTY
Q3	- -	0.00	3.46
Q4	- -	0.38	1.30
Q5	- -	0.70	4.72
Q2	- -	- -	2.42
Q1	0.32	0.32	- -
Q6	0.32	0.32	- -

              EXPECTED CHANGE FOR LAMBDA-Y

	SATISFAC	VALUE	LOYALTY
Q3	- -	0.00	-0.21
Q4	- -	0.04	0.12
Q5	- -	-0.06	0.22
Q2	- -	- -	-0.26
Q1	-18.89	0.04	- -
Q6	15.20	-0.03	- -

            MODIFICATION INDICES FOR LAMBDA-X

	QUALITY	PRICE
Q7a	- -	0.81
Q7c	- -	1.52
Q7d	- -	1.04
Q7f	- -	0.00
Q9	5.10	- -
Q10	6.32	- -

```
          EXPECTED CHANGE FOR LAMBDA-X

               QUALITY      PRICE
               -------      -----
     Q7a         - -       -0.05
     Q7c         - -        0.07
     Q7d         - -        0.07
     Q7f         - -        0.00
      Q9       -0.15        - -
     Q10        0.15        - -


          MODIFICATION INDICES FOR BETA

               SATISFAC     VALUE    LOYALTY
               -------      -----    -------
SATISFAC         - -         - -       0.93
   VALUE         - -         - -       1.87
 LOYALTY         - -         - -       - -


          EXPECTED CHANGE FOR BETA

               SATISFAC     VALUE    LOYALTY
               -------      -----    -------
SATISFAC         - -         - -       0.14
   VALUE         - -         - -      -0.26
 LOYALTY         - -         - -       - -


          MODIFICATION INDICES FOR GAMMA

               QUALITY      PRICE
               -------      -----
SATISFAC         - -        1.02
   VALUE        1.02        - -
 LOYALTY        0.93        1.87


          EXPECTED CHANGE FOR GAMMA

               QUALITY      PRICE
               -------      -----
SATISFAC         - -       -0.08
   VALUE        0.14        - -
 LOYALTY       -0.09       -0.10


          MODIFICATION INDICES FOR THETA-EPS

                    Q3       Q4       Q5       Q2       Q1       Q6
                  -----    -----    -----    -----    -----    -----
          Q3       - -
          Q4      0.17      - -
          Q5      0.55     0.14      - -
          Q2      0.64     0.13     1.64     1.05
          Q1      1.39     1.79     1.57     0.51      - -
          Q6      0.02     0.42     0.33     0.02      - -       - -
```

EXPECTED CHANGE FOR THETA-EPS

	Q3	Q4	Q5	Q2	Q1	Q6
Q3	- -					
Q4	-0.02	- -				
Q5	-0.03	0.02	- -			
Q2	0.04	0.02	-0.06	0.33		
Q1	-0.04	0.04	0.04	-0.03	- -	
Q6	0.00	-0.02	0.02	-0.01	- -	- -

MODIFICATION INDICES FOR THETA-DELTA-EPS

	Q3	Q4	Q5	Q2	Q1	Q6
Q7a	2.66	1.00	0.81	1.21	0.02	0.31
Q7c	0.56	0.39	0.85	0.01	2.00	1.21
Q7d	35.93	3.96	0.61	0.71	6.27	0.41
Q7f	0.71	0.00	2.54	0.07	0.98	0.79
Q9	2.06	0.66	0.42	0.09	0.00	0.32
Q10	2.22	1.67	0.69	0.37	1.20	0.80

EXPECTED CHANGE FOR THETA-DELTA-EPS

	Q3	Q4	Q5	Q2	Q1	Q6
Q7a	0.05	-0.03	0.03	0.04	0.00	0.02
Q7c	-0.03	0.02	-0.04	0.01	0.04	-0.04
Q7d	0.24	-0.09	0.04	-0.04	-0.09	-0.02
Q7f	-0.02	0.00	-0.05	-0.01	-0.02	0.02
Q9	-0.04	-0.03	0.02	-0.02	0.00	-0.02
Q10	0.04	0.04	-0.03	0.04	-0.03	0.03

MODIFICATION INDICES FOR THETA-DELTA

	Q7a	Q7c	Q7d	Q7f	Q9	Q10
Q7a	- -					
Q7c	3.30	- -				
Q7d	0.80	0.39	- -			
Q7f	0.54	3.83	0.00	- -		
Q9	0.07	0.39	0.00	0.72	- -	
Q10	0.06	0.08	0.67	0.30	1.02	- -

EXPECTED CHANGE FOR THETA-DELTA

	Q7a	Q7c	Q7d	Q7f	Q9	Q10
Q7a	- -					
Q7c	-0.08	- -				
Q7d	-0.04	-0.03	- -			
Q7f	0.05	0.10	0.00	- -		

```
Q9     0.01    0.02    0.00    -0.02    - -
Q10   -0.01    0.01    0.03     0.01   -0.80    - -
```

MAXIMUM MODIFICATION INDEX IS 35.93 FOR ELEMENT (3, 1) OF THETA DELTA-EPSILON

APPENDIX B

Edited Simplis Output for the Original Model

!Marcoulides chapter example in SIMPLIS command language
Number of Iterations = 9

LISREL ESTIMATES (MAXIMUM LIKELIHOOD)

Q3   =   1.00*SATISFAC, Errorvar. =   0.34   , $R\acute{y}$ = 0.66
                                                    (0.050)
                                                     6.73

Q4   =   0.87*SATISFAC, Errorvar. =   0.49   , $R\acute{y}$ = 0.50
            (0.079)   (0.054)
             11.01   9.11

Q5   =   0.68*SATISFAC, Errorvar. =   0.69   , $R\acute{y}$ = 0.31
            (0.079)   (0.065)
             8.58   10.61

Q2   =   1.00*VALUE, Errorvar. =   0.20   , $R\acute{y}$ = 0.80

Q1   =   1.00*LOYALTY, Errorvar. =   0.11   , $R\acute{y}$ = 0.89
                                                    (0.063)
                                                     1.68

Q6   =   0.80*LOYALTY, Errorvar. =   0.42   , $R\acute{y}$ = 0.58
            (0.070)   (0.054)
             11.43   7.81

Q7a   =   1.00*QUALITY, Errorvar. =   0.34   , $R\acute{y}$ = 0.66
                                                    (0.044)
                                                     7.68

Q7c   =   0.81*QUALITY, Errorvar. =   0.57   , $R\acute{y}$ = 0.43
            (0.073)   (0.055)
             11.14   10.36

Q7d   =   0.49*QUALITY, Errorvar. =   0.84   , $R\acute{y}$ = 0.16
            (0.077)   (0.074)
             6.37   11.39

Q7f   =   1.10*QUALITY, Errorvar. =   0.20   , $R\acute{y}$ = 0.80
            (0.076)   (0.043)
             14.40   4.79

Q9   =   1.00*PRICE, Errorvar. =   0.18 , Rý = 0.82
                                                         (0.081)
                                                         2.17

Q10   =   0.90*PRICE, Errorvar. =   0.34 , Rý = 0.66
              (0.097)   (0.070)
              9.27   4.80

SATISFAC =   0.29*VALUE + 0.54*QUALITY, Errorvar. =   0.37 , Rý = 0.43
              (0.083)   (0.069)   (0.062)
              3.49   7.88   6.03

VALUE   =   0.15*SATISFAC - 0.47*PRICE, Errorvar. =   0.55 , Rý = 0.31
              (0.11)   (0.071)   (0.078)
              1.38   -6.63   7.00

LOYALTY   =   0.83*SATISFAC + 0.0018*VALUE, Errorvar. = 0.44 , Rý = 0.51
              (0.087)   (0.068)   (0.078)
              9.53   0.026   5.67

COVARIANCE MATRIX OF INDEPENDENT VARIABLES

	QUALITY	PRICE
QUALITY	0.66	
	(0.09)	
	7.60	
PRICE	0.17	0.82
	(0.05)	(0.12)
	3.23	7.11

COVARIANCE MATRIX OF LATENT VARIABLES

	SATISFAC	VALUE	LOYALTY	QUALITY	PRICE
SATISFAC	0.66				
VALUE	0.27	0.80			
LOYALTY	0.55	0.23	0.89		
QUALITY	0.35	-0.03	0.29	0.66	
PRICE	-0.02	-0.39	-0.02	0.17	0.82

GOODNESS OF FIT STATISTICS

CHI-SQUARE WITH 48 DEGREES OF FREEDOM = 97.11 (P = 0.000035)
ESTIMATED NON-CENTRALITY PARAMETER (NCP) = 49.11

MINIMUM FIT FUNCTION VALUE = 0.35
POPULATION DISCREPANCY FUNCTION VALUE (F0) = 0.18
ROOT MEAN SQUARE ERROR OF APPROXIMATION (RMSEA) = 0.061
P-VALUE FOR TEST OF CLOSE FIT (RMSEA < 0.05) = 0.14

EXPECTED CROSS-VALIDATION INDEX (ECVI) = 0.57

```
                 ECVI FOR SATURATED MODEL = 0.57
                 ECVI FOR INDEPENDENCE MODEL = 5.01

CHI-SQUARE FOR INDEPENDENCE MODEL WITH 66 DEGREES OF FREEDOM = 1349.52
                    INDEPENDENCE AIC = 1373.52
                       MODEL AIC = 157.11
                     SATURATED AIC = 156.00
                   INDEPENDENCE CAIC = 1428.92
                      MODEL CAIC = 295.61
                    SATURATED CAIC = 516.11

              ROOT MEAN SQUARE RESIDUAL (RMR) = 0.049
                   STANDARDIZED RMR = 0.049
                GOODNESS OF FIT INDEX (GFI) = 0.95
           ADJUSTED GOODNESS OF FIT INDEX (AGFI) = 0.91
          PARSIMONY GOODNESS OF FIT INDEX (PGFI) = 0.58

                  NORMED FIT INDEX (NFI) = 0.93
                NON-NORMED FIT INDEX (NNFI) = 0.95
             PARSIMONY NORMED FIT INDEX (PNFI) = 0.67
                COMPARATIVE FIT INDEX (CFI) = 0.96
                INCREMENTAL FIT INDEX (IFI) = 0.96
                 RELATIVE FIT INDEX (RFI) = 0.90

                     CRITICAL N (CN) = 208.91

CONFIDENCE LIMITS COULD NOT BE COMPUTED DUE TO TOO SMALL P-VALUE FOR CHI-SQUARE

!Marcoulides chapter example in SIMPLIS command language

        FITTED RESIDUALS

             Q3        Q4        Q5        Q2        Q1        Q6
           ------    ------    ------    ------    ------    ------
     Q3     0.01
     Q4     0.00      0.00
     Q5    -0.01      0.01      0.00
     Q2     0.01      0.03     -0.04      0.00
     Q1    -0.02      0.03      0.07      0.00      0.00
     Q6    -0.01      0.00      0.06     -0.02      0.00      0.00
     Q7a    0.12     -0.01      0.02      0.08      0.03      0.06
     Q7c    0.01     -0.02     -0.06      0.00      0.00     -0.01
     Q7d    0.23     -0.04      0.06     -0.02     -0.10     -0.07
     Q7f    0.02     -0.06     -0.08      0.01     -0.05      0.00
     Q9    -0.06     -0.06     -0.02     -0.01     -0.09     -0.05
     Q10    0.07      0.06      0.02      0.03     -0.01      0.04

        FFITTED RESIDUALS

             Q7a       Q7c       Q7d       Q7f       Q9        Q10
           ------    ------    ------    ------    ------    ------
     Q7a    0.00
     Q7c   -0.03      0.00
```

Q7d	-0.02	-0.02	0.00			
Q7f	0.00	0.02	0.00	0.00		
Q9	-0.04	0.03	0.03	-0.03	0.00	
Q10	0.03	0.09	0.09	0.06	0.00	0.00

SUMMARY STATISTICS FOR FITTED RESIDUALS
SMALLEST FITTED RESIDUAL = -0.10
  MEDIAN FITTED RESIDUAL = 0.00
 LARGEST FITTED RESIDUAL = 0.23

STEMLEAF PLOT
- 1|0
- 0|987666655
- 0|4443322222221111111000000000000000000000
  0|11111222233333334
  0|6666677899
  1|2
  1|
  2|3

STANDARDIZED RESIDUALS

	Q3	Q4	Q5	Q2	Q1	Q6
	------	------	------	------	------	------
Q3	0.33					
Q4	-0.02	0.12				
Q5	-0.55	0.48	0.05			
Q2	0.61	0.80	-0.83	1.01		
Q1	-1.44	1.43	2.17	0.23	0.04	
Q6	-0.79	0.17	1.66	-0.45	1.01	0.09
Q7a	3.80	-0.22	0.52	2.11	0.84	1.40
Q7c	0.28	-0.37	-1.31	-0.05	0.07	-0.28
Q7d	4.70	-0.73	1.02	-0.33	-1.97	-1.33
Q7f	0.62	-1.75	-1.89	0.16	-1.61	-0.02
Q9	-1.44	-1.25	-0.43	-2.49	-2.06	-0.99
Q10	1.63	1.29	0.29	2.30	-0.29	0.68

STANDARDIZED RESIDUALS

	Q7a	Q7c	Q7d	Q7f	Q9	Q10
	------	------	------	------	------	------
Q7a	0.00					
Q7c	-1.82	0.00				
Q7d	-0.90	-0.62	0.00			
Q7f	0.74	1.96	0.02	0.00		
Q9	-1.33	0.78	0.64	-1.30	0.00	
Q10	0.73	1.86	1.61	1.96	-1.01	0.00

SUMMARY STATISTICS FOR STANDARDIZED RESIDUALS
SMALLEST STANDARDIZED RESIDUAL = -2.49
  MEDIAN STANDARDIZED RESIDUAL = 0.03
 LARGEST STANDARDIZED RESIDUAL = 4.70

```
STEMLEAF PLOT
 - 2|510
 - 1|9886443333200
 - 0|98876554433320000000000000
   0|11122233355666777888
   1|0003446679
   2|00123
   3|8
   4|7
```

LARGEST POSITIVE STANDARDIZED RESIDUALS
RESIDUAL FOR   Q7a AND   Q3   3.80
RESIDUAL FOR   Q7d AND   Q3   4.70

THE MODIFICATION INDICES SUGGEST TO ADD AN ERROR COVARIANCE

BETWEEN	AND	DECREASE IN CHI-SQUARE	NEW ESTIMATE
Q7d	Q3	35.9	0.24

THE PROBLEM USED   19384 BYTES (= 0.1% OF AVAILABLE WORKSPACE)

TIME USED: 0.7 SECONDS

CHAPTER TEN

The Partial Least Squares Approach to Structural Equation Modeling

Wynne W. Chin
University of Houston

Among *structural equation modeling* (SEM) techniques, by far the most well known are covariance-based methods as exemplified by software such as LISREL, EQS, AMOS, SEPATH, and RAMONA. In fact, to many social science researchers, the covariance-based procedure is tautologically synonymous with the term SEM. Yet, an alternative and less widespread technique known as *partial least squares* (PLS) is also available for researchers interested in doing SEM-based analysis. Depending on the researcher's objectives and epistemic view of data to theory, properties of the data at hand, or level of theoretical knowledge and measurement development, the PLS approach can be argued to be more suitable.

PLS can be a powerful method of analysis because of the minimal demands on measurement scales (i.e., do measures need to be at an interval or ratio level?), sample size, and residual distributions (Wold, 1985). Although PLS can be used for theory confirmation, it can also be used to suggest where relationships might or might not exist and to suggest propositions for testing later. Compared to the better known factor-based covariance-fitting approach for latent structural modeling, the component-based PLS avoids two serious problems: inadmissible solutions and factor indeterminacy (Fornell & Bookstein, 1982). Because the iterative algorithm performed in a PLS analysis generally consists of a series of ordinary least squares (OLS) analyses, identification is not a problem for recursive models nor does it presume any distributional form for measured variables. The utility of the PLS method has been documented elsewhere (Falk & Miller, 1992) as possibly more appropriate for a large percentage of the studies and data sets typically used among researchers.

The objective of this chapter, therefore, is to provide a nontechnical introduction to the PLS approach. As a logical base for comparison, the PLS approach for structural path estimation is contrasted to the covariance-based approach. In so doing, a set of considerations are then provided with the goal of helping the reader understand the conditions under which it might be reasonable or even more appropriate to employ this technique. This chapter builds up from various simple two latent variable models to a more complex one. The formal PLS model is provided along with a discussion of the properties of its estimates. Finally, for further clarification, an empirical example is provided as a basis for highlighting the various analytic considerations when using PLS and the set of tests that one can employ in assessing the validity of a PLS-based model. This chapter concludes with a summary discussion of the PLS approach and associated issues for the future.

HISTORICAL BACKGROUND

In general, the SEM-based method has been viewed as a coupling of two traditions: an econometric perspective focusing on prediction and a psychometric emphasis that models concepts as latent (unobserved) variables that are indirectly inferred from multiple observed measures (alternately termed as indicators or manifest variables). This coupling, thus, allowed social scientists to perform path analytic modeling with latent variables which, in turn, has led some to describe this approach as an example of "a second generation of multivariate analysis" (Fornell, 1987, p. 408).

The advantage that SEM-based procedures have over first-generation techniques such as principal components analysis, factor analysis, discriminant analysis, or multiple regression is the greater flexibility that a researcher has for the interplay of theory and data. When theoretical knowledge is strong, the researcher can allow greater reliance on a theory in analyzing data. Alternatively, when one has less confidence in a theory, the researcher might wish to let the data have a stronger say.

Essentially, second-generation multivariate techniques such as SEM involve generalizations and extensions of first-generation procedures. By applying certain constraints or assumptions on one or more particular second-generation techniques, one would result in a first-generation procedure with correspondingly less flexibility in modeling theory with data. For example, Knapp (1978) has shown how various constraints applied on a canonical correlation analysis would be equivalent to performing a multiple regression, multiple discriminant analysis, analysis of variance or covariance, or principle components analysis. In turn, canonical correlation has been shown to be a special case of PLS (Wold, 1975) and covariance-based SEM (Bagozzi, Fornell, & Larcker, 1981).

In general, SEM-based approaches provide the researcher with the flexibility to perform the following: (a) model relationships among multiple predictor and criterion variables, (b) construct unobservable latent variables, (c) model errors in measurements for observed variables, and (d) statistically test a priori substantive/theoretical and measurement assumptions against empirical data (i.e., confirmatory analysis).

The covariance-based approach for SEM modeling can be traced back to the original development by Jöreskog (1973), Keesling (1972), and Wiley (1973). Its widespread popularity is due in large part to the availability of the LISREL III program developed by Jöreskog and Sörbom in the mid-1970s and subsequent updates (see Jöreskog & Sörbom, 1989). Recent alternate programs such as EQS, CALIS, AMOS, and SEPATH have further increased the accessibility of this approach. Typically using a *maximum likelihood* (ML) function, covariance-based SEM attempts to minimize the difference between the sample covariances and those predicted by the theoretical model (i.e., $\hat{\Sigma} - \Sigma(\Theta)$). Therefore, the parameters that are estimated by this procedure attempt to reproduce the covariance matrix of the observed measures. But such an attempt makes the underlying assumptions that the observed variables follow a specific multivariate distribution (normality in the case of the ML function) and that observations are independent of one another.

The PLS approach has its origins back in 1966 when Herman Wold presented two iterative procedures using *least squares* (LS) estimation for single- and multicomponent models and for canonical correlation. Then in 1971, upon seeing the LISREL approach to latent variable path modeling, Wold stated:

> It struck me that it might be possible to estimate models with the same arrow scheme by an appropriate generalization of my LS algorithms for principal components and canonical correlations. The extension involved two crucial steps, namely from two to three LVs and corresponding blocks of indicators, and from one to two inner relations. Once these steps were taken, the road to an iterative LS algorithm of general scope for estimation of path models with latent variables observed by multiple indicators was straightforward. (Wold, 1982a, p. 200)

The impetus for Wold's development of PLS was a desire to "take an intermediate position between data analysis and traditional modeling based on the 'hard' assumption that the observables are jointly ruled by a specified probability distribution. The PLS approach is distribution-free . . ." (Wold, 1982a, p. 200). Originally termed NIPALS (*nonlinear iterative partial least squares*), Wold felt that "in comparison with other approaches, and in particular the maximum likelihood method, NIPALS is often more general, and typically so since it works with a smaller number of zero intercorrelation assumptions between residuals and variables. Hence the NIPALS approach makes for models that give a closer fit to the given observations, as is reflected in successful application to real-world data" (Wold, 1973, p. 384). The basic PLS design was completed in 1977 (Wold, 1982b) and has subsequently been extended in various ways. Lohmöller (1984, 1989) covered various inner weighting schemes. Wold discussed nonlinearities among latent variables whereas Hui (1978, 1982) used a fixed-point PLS method to model nonrecursive (i.e., interdependent) relations. In accord with this chapter's objective of providing a simple introduction to the PLS method, subsequent discussions are restricted to the basic design involving recursive models.

**EXAMPLE 1: CHOICE OF ESTIMATION
FOR A TWO-BLOCK MODEL**

As a starting point for understanding the PLS approach for SEM modeling, let's examine a simple hypothetical two-block model. By two blocks, we are referring to the situation where the researcher is able to partition indicators (i.e., observed variables) into two groups where each block of indicators is felt to capture some underlying issue or construct. Thus, we have two latent variables each being represented by a block of indicators.

Figure 10.1 depicts a path diagram of a two-block model with two indicators per block. When modeling path diagrams, it is important to consider the path relations among constructs as well as between constructs and their respective indicators. In this example, a one-way causal relationship is hy-

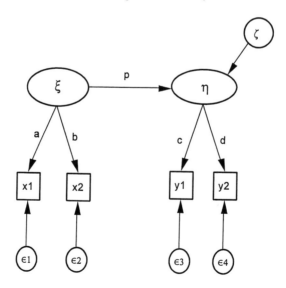

FIG. 10.1. Two-block model with reflective indicators.

pothesized between two latent variables (ξ and η). As a concrete example, this structural model might represent a simple attitude model where ξ is a cognitive belief regarding the ease of use of a specific information technology (IT) and η the intention to use that IT in the future. Inasmuch as ξ can only explain a portion of the variance in η, the residual variance at this structural level is assumed to reside in ζ.

The measurement model consists of the relationship between the constructs and their respective indicators. Both the attitudinal constructs of belief and intention, considered as latent variables, are modeled as phenomena that cannot be directly measured. Instead, each latent variable is indirectly measured by two indicators. In Fig. 10.1, the indicators, being observed variables, are modeled as influenced by two unrelated (i.e., orthogonal) factors: the underlying construct they are intended to measure and a composite of all other factors (including error term) that they may also tap into. The extent to which these indicators do a good job at "reflecting" or "tapping" their respective construct is determined to a large extent by the size of the loadings (i.e., *a*, *b*, *c*, and *d*). As discussed later, the PLS approach also allows one to model the indicator-construct relationship in the opposite direction (in a "formative" or "causal" sense).

Given a sample data set of observed indicators, the task, therefore, is to devise a procedure for estimating parameters for the measurement model (e.g., loadings *a*, *b*, *c*, and *d*) and structural model (e.g., path coefficient *p* and variance ζ). Three essential distinctions to be brought forth between the PLS and covariance-based approaches are (a) whether the underlying constructs are modeled as indeterminate or determinate, (b) the extent to which one is confident in one's theoretical model and auxiliary theory linking measures to constructs, and (c) whether one is parameter oriented or prediction oriented. If, in each instance, one's answer is the latter, then the PLS approach is likely more suitable.

Covariance-Based Solution

For the covariance-based approach, a covariance matrix is calculated from the sample data set. Parameter estimates for a given model are then selected such that the implied covariance based on the model parameter estimates is as similar as that of the sample data set. For example, let's assume that the product moment correlations from our sample data set resulted in those given in Table 10.1. Based on Fig. 10.1, we would start to select parameter estimates that come as close as possible to reproducing the sample correlations. Prior to starting, for scale identification purposes (Bollen, 1989), we need to set the variance of ξ and loading *c* at 1.

Starting with indicators *x*1 and *x*2, we note the model only allows these indicators to covary through ξ. Given that the variance of ξ is set at 1 and assuming the model to be correct, the correlation between *x*1 and *x*2 must be

TABLE 10.1
Hypothetical Sample Correlation Matrix

	x1	x2	y1	y2
x1	1.00			
x2	.81	1.00		
y1	.576	.586	1.00	
y2	.576	.576	.64	1.00

equivalent to $a*b$. As a first guess, we might try setting a and b each at .90 because that would yield an implied correlation of .81 consistent with the sample data set. In a similar manner, we equate each sample correlation to the implied correlation based on the parameters of our model (see Table 10.2).

In the case of the correlation between x1 and y1, the model only allows them to be linked via the route consisting of the loading a (thus far estimated at .90), path p, and loading c (set at 1.0). We might try estimating p at .64 because it would yield an implied correlation identical to the sample set correlation of .576. With p at .64 and a at .90, we might set d at 1.0 in order to obtain an implied correlation for x1 and y2 identical to the sample correlation. So far so good. Unfortunately, our estimates thus far also imply a correlation of .576 between x2 and y2 whereas the sample correlation is .586. Thus, the parameter estimates based on the proposed model does not perfectly fit the observed correlations. This lack of fit can be attributed to an incorrect model or sampling variation because we used the sample correlation for estimation purposes instead of the "true" population correlations (which could be .576 if our model is correct).

The covariance-based procedure, therefore, consists of continually guessing at parameter estimates in order to minimize a fitting function between the sample correlations (S) and those implied by the parameter estimates (Σ) until no further improvement is made. By using the fitting function $\ln |\Sigma|$

TABLE 10.2
Model Implied Covariance Matrix

	x1	x2	y1	y2
x1	$var\xi*a^2 + var\varepsilon1$ $= a^2 + var\varepsilon1$			
x2	$a*var\xi*b$ $= a*b$	$var\xi*b^2 + var\varepsilon2$ $= b^2 + var\varepsilon2$		
y1	$a*var\xi*p*c$ $= a*p*c$	$b*var\xi*p*c$ $= b*p*c$	$var\eta*c^2 + var\varepsilon3$	
y2	$a*var\xi*p*d$ $= a*p*d$	$b*var\xi*p*d$ $= b*p*d$	$a*var\eta*b$	$var\eta*d^2 + var\varepsilon4$

$+ \ trace\left(\dfrac{S}{\Sigma}\right) - \ln|S| - p$ where p is the number of indicators, we obtain ML-based estimates that are asymptotically unbiased, consistent, and efficient under the empirical conditions that the indicators follow a multivariate normal distribution and independence of observations (Bollen, 1989).

In summary, if the hypothesized structural and measurement model is correct in the sense of explaining the covariation of all the indicators, the covariance-based procedure provides optimal estimations of the model parameters. Yet, there is an inherent indeterminacy in the procedure. In other words, case values for the latent variables are never obtained in the process. Thus, the ability to estimate scores for the underlying latent variables and, in turn, be able to predict the observed indicators is not provided. In fact, an infinite set of possible scores can be created that is consistent with the parameter estimates, which may or may not be viewed as problematic (see Maraun, 1996, and the two rounds of commentary). Furthermore, under conditions of small sample size and violations in distributional assumptions, improper solutions such as negative variance estimates can often result (Dillon, Kumar, & Mulani, 1987; Van Driel, 1978). Finally, all indicators must be treated in a reflective manner where they are causally influenced by an underlying construct. To model otherwise would create a situation where we are unable to explain the covariances of all indicators, which is the rationale for this approach.

Partial Least Squares-Based Solution

The PLS approach, in part, starts off with a different goal: to help the researcher obtain determinate values of the latent variables for predictive purposes. Under this perspective, our model in Fig. 10.1 is viewed and used differently. Instead of using the model for explaining the covariation of all the indicators, we switch to minimizing the variance of all dependent variables (i.e., variables with arrows pointing toward them). Thus, parameter estimates are obtained based on the ability to minimize the residual variances of dependent variables (both latent and observed).

We start by saying each latent variable is approximated by its respective block of indicators. Therefore, we should create latent variable component scores based on a weighted sum of their indicators. What constitutes the best weighting scheme for each block of indicators depends on the model being estimated. In the case of our model in Fig. 10.1, indicators $x1$ and $x2$ should be combined to create the best component score of ξ such that this score can, in turn, optimally predict η as well as $x1$ and $x2$. In other words, we wish to find the appropriate weights for $x1$ and $x2$ that creates a score that jointly accounts for as much variance as possible in $x1$, $x2$, and η. For indicators $y1$ and $y2$, we wish to find the best weights such that the sum forms the best estimate of η in the sense that it can both account for as much variance in $y1$ and $y2$ as possible and also be predicted (correlated) by ξ.

To obtain the weights and subsequent loading and path estimates, the PLS approach uses a three-stage estimation algorithm. In the first stage, an iterative scheme of simple and/or multiple regressions contingent on the particular model is performed until a solution converges on a set of weights used for estimating the latent variables (LV) scores. Once the LV estimates are obtained, stages 2 and 3 are simple noniterative applications of OLS regression for obtaining loadings, path coefficients, and mean scores and location parameters for the LV and observed variables. Until stage 3, the LV and indicators are treated as deviations from their means.

Referring back to Fig. 10.1, we would start with equal weights for each block of indicators. The weights, in each iteration, are scaled to obtain unit variance for the latent variable scores over the N cases in our sample. This step is known as the *outside approximation*. Once that is done, we create proxies for each LV variable based on its association with other LVs. In other words, we combine the components scores for all LVs associated (i.e., having path relations) with each specific LV to obtain a proxy estimate. This is called the *inside approximation* and various weighting schemes for combining LV components are discussed later. In our model, there is only one LV connected to η, which is ξ and vice versa. Thus we would use η as a proxy or instrumental variable for ξ and ξ as a proxy for η. With our proxy estimates replacing each LV in our model, we perform the appropriate regression as dictated by the model in order to obtain new weights. In our example, $y1$ and $y2$ are individually regressed on ξ whereas $x1$ and $x2$ are individually regressed on η. If, for example, the arrow directions for $x1$ and $x2$ had been reversed and modeled as pointing toward its LV, we would have performed a multiple regression with η (the proxy of ξ) on $x1$ and $x2$ instead. We then take these new regression estimates as the basis for new weights for another round of outside approximation for each LV. The iteration stops when the weights converge using a conventional stopping rule such as the percentage change from the previous round for each weight is less than 10^{-3}. If the covariance matrix is used instead of the raw data as input, the covariances between the indicators and LV would then be estimated using the same procedure yielding the same estimates with only loss in the ability to estimate the LV scores (for more details see Lohmöller, 1989).

Thus, the PLS procedure iterates back and forth between two ways of estimating a LV. The outside approximation attempts to provide an estimate of the LV via an aggregation of its indicators whereas the inside approximation yields an estimate by combining "neighboring" LVs. The first approach (i.e., outside approximation) occurs under situations where the researchers is handed a set of measures supposedly capturing a particular construct. Without additional information, the best initial estimate of the construct would be a summation of the measures. The second approach represents the situation where a researcher is not provided with the outer set of measures, but instead scores of LVs that are considered to be most closely related with the construct in question. If asked to give the best initial estimate of that construct, we would also aggregate the scores given. The PLS procedure, thus, utilizes information at both levels in estimating a component score for each LV.

In summary, the PLS approach provides a means for directly estimating LV component scores. The procedure is partial in a least squares sense because each step of the procedure minimizes a residual variance with respect to a subset of the parameters being estimated given proxies or fixed estimates for the other parameters. It is coherent in a predictive sense where its objective is to minimize the variances of the dependent variables (observed or latent). Because LV scores are determinate, we can also model what have been termed *cause* or *formative* indicators where the observed indicators are assume to cause or form the LV (Bollen, 1989). In this situation, with arrows directed toward the construct from their indicators, the PLS algorithm provides LV weight estimates such that the LV score is maximally predicted by its block of indicators. Furthermore, the determinate nature of the PLS approach avoids parameter identification problems that can occur under covariance-based analysis (Bollen, 1989).

EXAMPLE 2: ESTIMATION RESULTS
FOR A TWO-BLOCK MODEL

PLS, as noted earlier, is argued as more deeply rooted in the observed data set. As opposed to the covariance-based approach, it does not rigidly adhere to an underlying theoretical model (i.e., to the extent of explaining all observed correlations). Rather, the objective of PLS is to aggregate indicators within blocks in a predictive sense. The extent to which the theoretical model is true is determined partly by the strength of the path relations among LV components scores and loadings for "reflective" indicators as estimated by the procedure.

As a further example of the difference between PLS and the covariance-based approach, consider the sample correlation matrix in Table 10.3, which was obtained from a data set of size 1,000. All correlations, given the sample size, are significant but quite low ranging from .087 to .272. If we use the theoretical model as depicted in Fig. 10.1, what would be the path estimate p linking ξ and η? The covariance-based estimate resulted in a standardized estimate of p at .83 whereas the PLS estimate was .22. The standardized loadings of a, b, c, d using the covariance procedure were .33, .26, .46, and .59 as opposed to .81, .66, .73, and .85 under PLS with corresponding weights

TABLE 10.3
Sample Data Set

	x1	x2	y1	y2
x1	1.00			
x2	.087	1.00		
y1	.140	.080	1.00	
y2	.152	.143	.272	1.00

Note. N = 1,000.

of .75, .60, .54, and .71. In the case of the covariance estimates, the path estimate of .83 is much larger than the observed correlations between the x and y variables where the highest is .152. In the case of PLS, the estimate of .22 is much closer to the observed correlations. Which estimate should we place confidence in?

The decision of which solution to use depends largely on the how much confidence one has in the underlying model. If the researcher, based on strong substantive knowledge, believes that both the underlying structural model is correct and the indicators for each block covary only through their respective LV (i.e., no other shared factors), then we should accept the path estimate of .83. Essentially, that's how the covariance procedure views the sample correlation matrix. By assuming the model to be correct, the only way to reproduce the small x-y correlations is to assign low loadings thereby resulting in the measures only sharing between 7% and 35% of the variance with their respective LV. If, on the other hand, we are not as confident in the underlying structural model or in agreeing that the measures are that poor, and also would like to obtain the best summed estimates of the LV for predictive purposes, we would use the PLS estimates. The answer thus depends on the judgment and level of understanding that the researcher brings to the phenomena under consideration.

ADDITIONAL TWO-BLOCK MODELS
AND CORRESPONDING ARROW SCHEME

The previous examples demonstrate the importance in the theoretical-conceptual design of the model (as depicted in Fig. 10.1). We now examine the implications and interpretations for the various two-block designs. Termed the *arrow scheme* by Wold (1985), such graphical models provide all the information concerning the "inner relations" among latent variables and the "outer relations" relating each latent variable and their respective indicators. Within the PLS approach, it then becomes a rather simple matter to take a particular arrow scheme and write down the corresponding formal model and estimation algorithm. Given the objectives of the PLS approach, it is clear that the arrow scheme is used quite differently from that of a covariance analysis. For the covariance approach, we saw that the arrow scheme became a rigid constraint on how parameters are estimated, because it dictates the paths by which indicators are associated in a correlational sense. In the PLS approach, the parameters appear as a result of the attempt to minimize the variances as outline by the scheme. The arrow scheme, therefore, is used to determine which set of residuals are to be minimized (i.e., which LV components and indicators) in order to come up with the set of weights necessary to create the LV components.

Mode A (Reflective Indicators)

Because the arrows relating indicators to their LVs can go in either direction, various combinations or modes can be formed. In our earlier example, all LVs consisted of indicators in a reflective mode. Among PLS users, models where only reflective indicators are used have been termed mode A.

Reflective indicators are typical for the classical true score test theory and factor analysis models. These indicators are created under the perspective that they all measure the same underlying phenomenon (i.e., LV). Should the actual level of the phenomenon change (say decrease in magnitude), then all the indicators should also change in the same direction. The magnitude in which each indicator shifts relative to the shift in the underlying phenomenon is based on how well the indicator reflects or taps into the LV. This, in turn, can be determined by the loading, which is proportional to the amount of variance in that indicator that the LV is able to account.

Whether the indicators should be modeled as reflective depends on several considerations. One consideration is the substantive theory behind the measurement model. The question concerns how the researcher conceptualizes the LV relative to the indicators. If the LV is viewed as giving rise to those observed measures, the arrow scheme for the model should be specified in this "outward" manner. Attitude, for example, is typically treated in this fashion where responses to the indicators are viewed as being influenced by it. In addition to the theoretical understanding, another consideration is the objective of the study. If the objective is explanation/prediction of observed measures, a reflective design would be specified that minimizes the trace of the residual variances for measurement model equations. A final consideration relates to the empirical conditions. The stability of estimates can be affected contingent on the sample size and multicollinearity among indicators in each block. If this is of concern, modeling reflective indicators would minimize this complication because parameter estimates would be based on simple regressions.

For the two-block scenario, as depicted in Fig. 10.2, the weights for each block are calculated to obtain LV component scores such that these scores

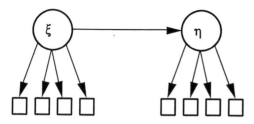

FIG. 10.2. Interbattery factor analysis (mode A).

are able to predict as much variance as possible in their respective observed measures. This is equivalent to Tucker's (1958) interbattery factor model, which assumes an LV is measured by two batteries of tests (say xs and ys). Tucker derived his model from two different interpretations, the first being a covariance structure approach and the second a data structure approach. The PLS estimate of this model represents the data-analytical derivation.

For LVs with reflective indicators, the loadings should be inspected for determining the appropriateness of the indicators. Essentially, each loading represents the correlation between the indicator and the component score. Indicators with low loadings essentially imply that they have little relationship in terms of shared variance with the LV component score.

Mode B (Formative Indicators)

Mode B refers to models consisting only of formative indicators. In contrast to reflective indicators, formative indicators are not assumed to be correlated nor do they measure the same underlying phenomenon. Instead, formative indicators are viewed as the cause variables that provide the condition under which the LV they are connected to is formed. A good example was provided by P. Cohen, J. Cohen, Teresi, Marchi, and Velez (1990) where the observed measures—number of children in a family, illness of the mother, and hours of maternal employment—are examples of valid and reliable indicators of a mother's availability to interact with and monitor any given child. In this situation, the mother's availability represents an LV that emerges from these indicators. It is also clear that the number of children in a family is not necessarily related to the health (i.e., illness indicator) of the mother. Because the LV is viewed as an effect rather than a cause of the indicator responses, examinations of correlations or internal consistency have been argued as inappropriate and illogical (Bollen, 1984). Cohen et al. showed that a substantial number of SEM-based published research had indeed used formative indicators and mistakenly or unknowingly treated them as reflective through the application of covariance-based analysis.

The decision as to whether indicators should be modeled in a formative mode may again rely on the three considerations of theory/substantive knowledge, research objective, and empirical conditions. The indicators are

directed in an "inward" fashion toward the LV if the indicators are conceptualized as the mix of variables that in combination led to the formation of
the LV. To help in this determination, one can ask the question as to whether
a change in the underlying LV will necessarily result in similar changes in
all the indicators. If not, the indicators may be modeled as formative. But
one would still need to consider whether this set of indicators are indeed
the critical antecedent variables for the formation of the LV. Substantive
knowledge, of course, helps in this deliberation. Another consideration is
whether one's research objective is to focus at the abstract level. In the PLS
sense, formative indicators might be applied if the researcher wishes to
account for the "unobserved" or component-level variance rather than the
observed indicators. Finally, whether the indicators are relatively independent of one another (i.e., no multicollinearity problems) and the sample
size is large enough must be taken into account. Lack of multicollinearity
is important if the researcher is concerned with understanding the formation
process of the LV. Otherwise, it can be ignored if the focus is on the structural
path relations. The formative modeling option may be moot if estimates for
the measurement model are not stable.

Figure 10.3 provides the arrow scheme for a two-block, mode B analysis.
In this model, no attempt is made to explain the variances of the observed
indicators. Instead, the goal is to maximize the variance explained at the LV
component level. Thus, indicators for each block are weighted optimally in
order to maximize the correlation between the two LV component scores
for ξ and η. Therefore, the results from applying the PLS algorithm to this
model are equivalent to performing a canonical correlation analysis.

The interpretation of LVs with formative indicators in any PLS analysis
should be based on the weights. As in the case of a canonical correlation
(Harris, 1989), the weights provide information as to what the makeup and
relative importance are for each indicator in the creation/formation of the
component. To that extent, the researcher applies an operation-based interpretation of the meaning of the component score. The loadings are misleading
because the intraset correlations for each block were never taken into account
in the estimation process. Thus, it makes no sense to compare loadings among
indicators within a block. At best, loadings can be used for identifying which
indicator makes the best surrogate for the component score.

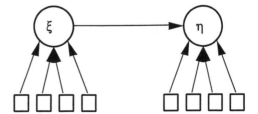

FIG. 10.3. Canonical correlation
analysis (mode B).

Mode C (Formative and Reflective)

Finally, we can have an arrow scheme that uses both formative and reflective indicators. Labeled as mode C, such models can be viewed as reflecting a compromise between maximizing the predictiveness of the observed variables (mode A) and the LV component scores (mode B). This, of course, may be due to the substantive/theoretical understanding of the indicators as they relate to the constructs. But under conditions of low theoretical knowledge where the researcher desires to follow a mode C approach, Wold (1980) suggested modeling indicators for all exogenous (i.e., independent) LVs in mode B and for all endogenous (i.e., dependent) LVs in mode A.

Figure 10.4 represents a two-block mode C model. Performing a PLS analysis on this model is equivalent to performing a redundancy analysis (Fornell, Barclay, & Rhee, 1988; Van den Wollenberg, 1977). Here, redundancy refers to the mean variance in the η block of indicators being predicted by the linear composite of the ξ set of indicators.

Essentially, the information is redundant in the sense that the information is double given the two blocks of indicators. The formative set, as discussed earlier, is viewed at that set of indicators that give rise to the underlying LV. That LV is then also measured by reflective indicators. The extent to which both sets approximate the underlying construct well is determined by the structural path linking the two component scores.

MULTIBLOCK EXAMPLE

We now move on to the situation of more than two blocks. As discussed earlier, the PLS procedure results in estimating weights to yield components for the LVs in the model. As part of this process, the relationships among the blocks of indicators as depicted at the structural level must be taken into account. This is accomplished by the inside approximation process discussed earlier, which creates proxies for each LV in the model which, in turn, are used for performing the next round of weight estimates (i.e., outside approximation). In the case of the two-block model, we simply use the component score for the other LV as the proxy. But in the multiblock case, a particular LV may have more than one LV connected to it at the structural level. Under these conditions, we need

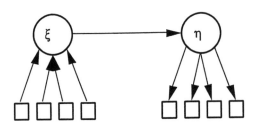

FIG. 10.4. Redundancy analysis (mode C).

to consider procedures for combining more than one component score to obtain the best proxy for the LV under consideration.

There have been three primary inside approximation weighting schemes developed thus far for combining neighboring LVs to obtain the proxy for a specific LV: *centroid weighting, factor weighting,* and *path weighting.* Although each weighting scheme follows a particular logic, it has been noted that its choice tends to have little influence on the results: .005 or less for structural paths and .05 or less for measurement paths (Noonan & Wold, 1982).

The centroid-weighting scheme was the original procedure used by Wold. It considers only the sign direction of the correlations between the LV and the neighboring LVs. The strength of the correlations and the direction of the structural model are not taken account. It is computationally simple because the proxy estimates are obtained by adding up all connected LVs with weights of either +1 or −1 depending on the sign of their correlation, which leads each LV to become similar to the centroid factor (Lohmöller, 1989). Thus, if a structurally linked LV is correlated −.24, the weight assigned to it would be −1.

This approach is considered advantageous (relative to the path weighting scheme discussed later) when the LV correlation matrix is singular, because the weights are based only on the bivariate correlations among component scores. A disadvantage arises when a LV correlation is close to zero and thus may oscillate during iterations from a small positive to a small negative and back. Under this situation, these values are magnified by the corresponding +1 and −1 weights.

The factor-weighting scheme, therefore, uses the correlation coefficients between the focal LV and its neighboring LVs as the weights. The LV becomes the "principal component" of its neighboring LVs. According to Lohmöller (1989), the factor-weighting scheme maximizes the variance of the principal component of the LVs when the number of the LVs goes to infinity.

Finally, the path-weighting scheme differentially weights neighboring LVs depending on whether they are antecedents or consequents of the focal LV. This scheme, thus, attempts to produce a component that can both ideally be predicted (as a predictand) and at the same time be a good predictor for subsequent dependent variables. To do this, all independent variables impacting the target LV are weighted by the multiple regression coefficients, whereas all dependent LVs are weighted by the correlation coefficients. In a sense, the focal LV becomes the best mediating LV between the source and target LVs.

Therefore, as the only procedure among the three that takes into account the directionality of the structural model, the path-weighting scheme is often used for models with hypothesized causal relations. If, on the other hand, no propositions are made regarding the associations among the LVs, the factor-weighting scheme would be the logical choice.

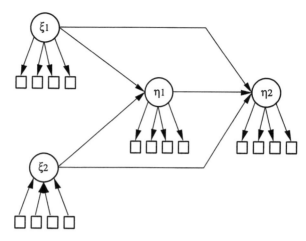

FIG. 10.5. Multiblock model (mode C).

As a further example of how PLS deals with the multiblock case, let's look at the model given in Fig. 10.5. As depicted, the measures are partitioned into four blocks (two exogenous ξs and two endogenous ηs). As a starting point, we do an initial outside approximation estimation of the LVs by summing the indicators in each block with equal weights. The weights, in each iteration, are scaled to obtain unit variance for the latent variable scores over the N cases in the sample. Using the estimated scores for each LV as given, we now perform an inside approximation estimate of the LVs.

Under a factor-weighting scheme, for example, the inner proxy for ξ1 would be the sum of the outside approximation scores for η1 and η2 weighted by their respective correlation coefficients with ξ1. ξ2 is not included in the estimate because there is no link between it and ξ1. η1, on the other hand, is a weighted estimated of the other three LVs because it has structural paths with all three.

Under a path-weighting scheme, we see three different inside approximation situations. For both ξ1 and ξ2, being exogenous constructs, they are weighted by correlations coefficients. So, for example, the proxy estimate for ξ1 would follow the same procedure as under the factor-weighting scheme. In the case of η2, being a pure endogenous (dependent) variable, we perform a multiple regression with the outside approximation scores for ξ1, ξ2, and η1 on η2. The multiple regression coefficients are then used as the weights for combining the outside approximation scores of ξ1, ξ2, and η1 to obtain the proxy estimate for η2. Finally, the proxy for η1 uses both multiple regression coefficients and correlational coefficients as weights. We would regress η1 on ξ1 and ξ2 to obtain weights for ξ1, ξ2 and take the simple correlation between η1 on η2 for the weight of η2.

We now use the LV proxies from the inside approximation to obtain a new set of weights for a new round of outside approximation. Taking the proxy scores as fixed, we perform either simple or multiple regression depending on whether the block of indicators is in mode A or B. Because $\xi 1$, $\eta 2$, and $\eta 1$ are modeled as mode A with arrows directed toward the indicators, each indicator in each block would be individually regressed on its respective proxy (i.e., inside approximation score). In the case of $\xi 2$, being in mode B with arrows directed inward, we would perform a multiple regression of the proxy estimate of $\xi 2$ on its indicators. The simple or multiple regressions coefficients are then used as new weights for an outside approximation of each LV.

SAMPLE SIZE REQUIREMENTS BASED ON THE INSIDE AND OUTSIDE APPROXIMATIONS

At this point, having gone through the inside/outside estimation process, we should make a comment on the issue of sample size under PLS. As the previous example demonstrates, we perform either simple or multiple regressions depending on the mode for each block of indicators and the inner weighting scheme. Due to the partial nature of the estimation procedure where only a portion of the model is involved, we need find only that part that required the largest multiple regression. In Fig. 10.5, the use of a factor-weighting scheme will lead only to performing simple regression between the LVs in calculating the weights to be used in performing the inside approximation. Under the path-weighting scheme, we had to perform two multiple regressions: two independent variables on $\eta 1$ and three on $\eta 2$. For the outside approximation, weights for all reflective indicators in mode A are obtained through simple regressions. For $\xi 2$, we perform a multiple regression with four indicators. Therefore, in this example, the largest number of parameters being estimated was the multiple regression on $\xi 2$. In general, one simply has to look at the arrow scheme and find the largest of two possibilities: (a) the block with the largest number of formative indicators (i.e., largest measurement equation) or (b) the dependent LV with the largest number of independent LVs impacting it (i.e., largest structural equation). If one were to use a regression heuristic of 10 cases per predictor, the sample size requirement would be 10 times either (a) or (b), whichever is the greater. If one is *not* using a path-weighting scheme for inside approximation, then only the measurement model with formative indicators are considered for the first stage of estimation. At the extreme, we see that a factor- or centroid-weighting scheme with all reflective (mode A) measures will involve only a series of simple regressions. Under this condition, it may be possible to obtain stable estimates for the weights and loadings of each component independent of the final estimates for the structural model.

FORMAL SPECIFICATION OF THE PLS MODEL

Now that we have covered the estimation procedure that PLS uses, we can give the formal model specification that guides the process. All latent variable path models in PLS consist of three sets of relations: (a) the inner model, which specifies the relationships between latent variables (LVs), (b) the outer model, which specifies the relationships between LVs and their associated observed or manifest variables (MVs), and (c) the weight relations upon which case values for the LVs can be estimated. Without loss of generality, it can be assumed that LVs and MVs are scaled to zero means and unit variances so that location parameter (i.e., constant parameter terms) can be eliminated in the following equations.

Inner Model

The *inner model* (also termed the inner relations, structural model, substantive theory) depicts the relationship among latent variables based on substantive theory,

$$\eta = \beta_0 + \beta\eta + \Gamma\xi + \zeta \tag{1}$$

where η represents the vector of endogenous (i.e., dependent) latent variables, ξ is a vector of the exogenous latent variables, and ζ is the vector of residual variables (i.e., unexplained variance).

Because the basic PLS design assumes recursive (i.e., one-way arrowed) relations among LVs, each dependent latent variable η_j in this often termed *causal chain system* of LVs can be specified as follows:

$$\eta_j = \Sigma_i \, \beta_{ji}\eta_i + \Sigma_i \, \gamma_{jh}\xi_h + \zeta_j \tag{2}$$

where β_{ji} and γ_{jh} are the path coefficients linking the predictor endogenous and exogenous latent variables ξ and η over the range specified by the indices i and h, and ζ_j is the inner residual variable.

For example, the inner model specification for Fig. 10.5 would be as follows:

$$\begin{pmatrix}\eta 1 \\ \eta 2\end{pmatrix} = \begin{pmatrix}0 & 0 \\ \beta_{21} & 0\end{pmatrix}\begin{pmatrix}\eta 1 \\ \eta 2\end{pmatrix} + \begin{pmatrix}\gamma_{11} & \gamma_{12} \\ \gamma_{21} & \gamma_{22}\end{pmatrix}\begin{pmatrix}\xi 1 \\ \xi 2\end{pmatrix} + \begin{pmatrix}\zeta 1 \\ \zeta 2\end{pmatrix}. \tag{3}$$

This represents a simple example of the causal chain system, because the one-way arrow relationship among endogenous latent variables can be seen in the matrix β where it can be arranged as a lower triangular matrix with zero diagonal elements.

The inner model of Equation 1 is subject to predictor specification (Wold, 1988):

$$E(\eta_j \mid \forall \eta_i, \xi_h) = \Sigma_i \beta_{ji} \eta_i + \Sigma_i \gamma_{ji} \xi_h. \tag{4}$$

Thus, it is assumed that each LV is a linear function of its predictors and that there is no linear relationship between the predictors and the residual,

$$E(\zeta_j \mid \forall \eta_i, \xi_h) = 0 \text{ and } Cov(\zeta_j, \eta_i) = Cov(\zeta_j, \xi_h) = 0 \tag{5}$$

for the indices i and h ranging over all predictors.

The structural form of the inner model can be also be written in reduced form by subtracting $\beta\eta$ from both sides of Equation 1 and premultiplying by $(I - \beta)^{-1}$ yielding:

$$\eta = (I - \beta)^{-1}\Gamma\xi + (I - \beta)^{-1} = \beta^*\xi + \zeta^* \tag{6}$$

where β^* represents the total effect of the exogenous latent variable ξ.

To make predictor specification possible for both the structural and reduced forms, the assumption is made that $E(\zeta_j^* \mid \forall \xi_h) = 0$ for all j endogenous LVs as they relate to the exogenous LVs impacting in the first j relations given in the structural form given in Equation 2.

Outer Model

The *outer model* (also referred to as outer relations or measurement model) defines how each block of indicators relates to its latent variable. The MVs are partitioned into nonoverlapping blocks. For those blocks with reflective indicators, the relationships can be defined as:

$$\begin{aligned} x &= \Lambda_x\xi + \varepsilon_x \\ y &= \Lambda_y\eta + \varepsilon_y \end{aligned} \tag{7}$$

where x and y are the MVs for the exogenous and endogenous LVs ξ and η respectively. Λ_x and Λ_y are the loadings matrices representing simple regression coefficients connecting the LV and their measures. The residuals for the measures ε_x and ε_y, in turn, can be interpreted as measurement errors or noise.

Predictor specification, as in the case for the inner model, is assumed to hold for the outer model in reflective mode as follows:

$$\begin{aligned} E[x \mid \xi] &= \Lambda_x\xi \\ E[y \mid \eta] &= \Lambda_y\eta. \end{aligned} \tag{8}$$

For those blocks in a formative mode, the relationship is defined as:

$$\xi = \Pi_\xi x + \delta_\xi$$
$$\eta = \Pi_\eta y + \delta_\eta \quad (9)$$

where ξ, η, x, and y are the same as those used in Equation 7. Π_x and Π_y are the multiple regression coefficients for the LV on its block of indicators and δ_x and δ_y are the corresponding residuals from the regressions. Predictor specification is also in effect as:

$$E[\xi \mid x] = \Pi_\xi x$$
$$E[\eta \mid y] = \Pi_\eta y \quad (10)$$

As opposed to the weight relations discussed next, the formative specification for outer relations refer to the MV and the true LV. This, in turn, provide the basis for the manner in which the weights are determined within the PLS estimation algorithm estimating the LV.

Weight Relations

Whereas the inner and outer models provide the specifications that are followed in the PLS estimation algorithm, we need, for completeness, to define the weight relations. The case value for each LV is estimated in PLS as follows:

$$\hat{\xi}_b = \Sigma_{kb} \, w_{kb} x_{kb}$$
$$\hat{\eta}_i = \Sigma_{ki} \, w_{ki} y_{ki} \quad (11)$$

where w_{kb}, w_{ki} are the k weights used to form the LV estimates of ξ_b and η_i.

Thus, the LV estimates are linear aggregates of their observed indicators whose weights are obtained via the PLS estimation procedure as specified by the inner and outer models where η is a vector of the endogenous (i.e., dependent) latent variables, ξ is a vector of the exogenous (i.e., independent) latent variables, ζ is a vector of residuals, and B and Γ are the path coefficient matrices.

PREDICTOR SPECIFICATION

Predictor specification (Presp), therefore, forms the basis for PLS modeling. Whereas the covariance-based ML estimation rests on the assumptions of a specific joint multivariate distribution and independence of observations, the

PLS approach does not make these hard assumptions. Instead, the PLS technique of model building uses very general, soft distributional assumptions, which often led to this approach being termed *soft modeling*. Thus, as Lohmöller (1989) noted, "it is not the concepts nor the models nor the estimation techniques which are 'soft', only the distributional assumptions" (p. 64).

Presp "is imposed on relations that the investigator wants to use for prediction, be it in theoretical or estimated form, and Presp provides the ensuing predictions" (Wold, 1988, p. 589). Lohmöller (1989) further stated that:

> [Presp] starts with the purpose of prediction (not primarily a structural expla-nation) [and] sets up a system of relations preferably linear, where the structure of the relations must be founded in the substance of the matter, and the predictive purpose should not jeopardize a structural-causal interpretation of the relation (causal-predictive relation). (p. 72)

Presp adopts the statistical assumptions for a linear conditional expectation relationship between dependent and independent variables, which can be summarized as:

$$y = \alpha + Bx + v, \; \hat{y} \equiv E[y \mid x] = \alpha + Bx$$
$$\Rightarrow E[v] = 0$$
$$\Rightarrow Cov[x,v] = Cov[\hat{y},v] = 0$$
$$\Rightarrow Cov[x,y] = Cov[x,\hat{y}] = B var[x]$$

(12)

where y and x are $(m \times 1)$ and $(n \times 1)$ matrix of dependent and independent variables, v is a $(m \times 1)$ matrix of residuals, and B the $(m \times n)$ matrix of coefficient relations between y and x. The implications are that for a given x and y: (a) x is a predictor (cause or stimulus) of y, and not the other way around (nonreversability), (b) $\hat{y}$ is the systematic part of y, with respect to x, and (c) the systematic part, $\hat{y}$, is a linear function of x.

The observational or empirical representation of Equation 12 would follow simply by including the index n for observations $1, \ldots, N$:

$$y = \alpha + \beta x_n + v_n, \; \hat{y}_n \equiv E[y_n \mid x_n] = \alpha + \beta x_n$$
$$\Rightarrow E[v_n] = 0$$
$$\Rightarrow Cov[x_n,v_n] = Cov[\hat{y}_n,v_n] = 0$$
$$\Rightarrow Cov[x_n,y_n] = Cov[x_n,\hat{y}_n] = \beta var[x_n].$$

(13)

Therefore, it should be noted that identical distributions are not assumed. For any two cases, say n and $n + 1$, no assumption is made that the residuals v_n and v_{n+1} have the same distribution. Nor is independence of cases re-quired because no specification was made regarding the correlation between two different cases (i.e., $Cov[v_n, v_{n+1}]$). In general, a sufficient condition for consistency in LS estimates is that as the number of observations go toward infinity, the sum of the correlations between cases must stay below infinity (i.e., $\Sigma_i \mid cor(v_n, v_{n+i}) \mid < \infty$; Wold, 1988, p. 589).

Thus, predictor specification can be viewed as an LS counterpart to the distributional assumptions of ML modeling. It avoids the assumptions that observations follow a specific distributional pattern and that they are independently distributed. Therefore, no restrictions are made on the structure of the residual covariances and under LS modeling the residual variance terms are minimized. In summary, Wold (1988) stated that Presp "provides a general rationale for (I*) LS specification and (ii*) LS estimation, and thereby also for the application of (iii*) the cross-validation test for predictive relevance . . . and (iv) the assessment of SEs by Tukey's jackknife" (p. 587), which are used for model evaluation.

MODEL EVALUATION

Because PLS makes no distributional assumption, other than predictor specification, in its procedure for estimating parameters, traditional parametric-based techniques for significance testing/evaluation would not be appropriate. Instead, Wold (1980, 1982b) argued for tests consistent with the distribution-free/predictive approach of PLS. In other words, rather than based on covariance fit, evaluation of PLS models should apply prediction-oriented measures that are also nonparametric. To that extent, the R-square for dependent LVs, the Stone–Geisser (Geisser, 1975; Stone, 1974) test for predictive relevance, and Fornell and Larcker's (1981) average variance extracted measure are used to assess predictiveness, whereas resampling procedures such as jackknifing and bootstrapping are used to examine the stability of estimates.

R-Square

In assessing a PLS model, we can start by looking at the R-squares for each dependent LV provided by PLS for the structural model. This is obtained because the case values of the LVs are determined by the weight relations. The interpretation is identical to that of traditional regression. The corresponding standardized path estimates can also be examined and interpreted in the same manner. Finally, the change in R-squares can be explored to see whether the impact of a particular independent LV on a dependent LV has substantive impact. Specifically, the effect size f^2 can be calculated as:

$$f^2 = \frac{R^2_{included} - R^2_{excluded}}{1 - R^2_{included}} \tag{14}$$

where $R^2_{included}$ and $R^2_{excluded}$ are the R-squares provided on the dependent LV when the predictor LV is used or omitted in the structural equation respectively. f^2 of .02, .15, and .35, similar to J. Cohen's (1988) operational definitions for multiple regression, can be viewed as a gauge for whether a predictor LV has a small, medium, or large effect at the structural level.

Q^2 Predictive Relevance

Besides looking at the magnitude of the LS regression R-square as a criterion for predictive relevance, we can also apply the predictive sample reuse technique as developed by Stone (1974) and Geisser (1975). This technique represents a synthesis of cross-validation and function fitting with the perspective that "the prediction of observables or potential observables is of much greater relevance than the estimation of what are often artificial construct-parameters" (Geisser, 1975, p. 320). The sample reuse technique has been argued as fitting the soft modeling approach of PLS "like hand in glove" (Wold, 1982b, p. 30).

The PLS adaptation of this approach follows a blindfolding procedure that omits a part of the data for a particular block of indicators during parameter estimations and then attempts to estimate the omitted part using the estimated parameters. This procedure is repeated until every data point has been omitted and estimated. As a result of this procedure, a generalized cross-validation measure and jackknife standard deviations of parameter estimates can be obtained.

The blindfolding procedure takes a block of say N cases and K indicators and takes out a portion of the N by K data points. Using an omission distance D, we would omit the first point (case 1 indicator 1) and then omit every other D data point as we move across each column and row. This continues until we reach the end of the data matrix. With the remaining data points, estimates are obtained by treating the missing values via pairwise deletion, mean substitution, or an imputation procedure. The sum of squares of prediction error (E) is calculated when the omitted data points are then predicted. The sum of squares errors using the mean for prediction (O) is also calculated. The omitted data points are returned and we shift over to the next data point in the data matrix (case 1 indicator 2) as the starting point for a new round of omission. A new E and O are calculated. This continues until D sets of Es and Os are obtained. The predictive measure for the block becomes:

$$Q^2 = 1 - \frac{\Sigma_D E_D}{\Sigma_D O_D} \qquad (15)$$

Thus, without any loss of freedom, Q^2 represents a measure of how well-observed values are reconstructed by the model and its parameter estimates. $Q^2 > 0$ implies the model has predictive relevance, whereas $Q^2 < 0$ represents a lack of predictive relevance. As in the case of f^2, changes in Q^2 can be used to assess the relative impact of the structural model on the observed measures for each dependent LV:

$$q^2 = \frac{Q^2_{included} - Q^2_{excluded}}{1 - Q^2_{included}} \qquad (16)$$

Different forms of Q^2 can be obtained depending on the form of prediction. A cross-validated communality Q^2 is obtained if prediction of the data points is made by the underlying latent variable score, whereas a cross-validated redundancy Q^2 is obtained if prediction is made by those LVs that predict the block in question. One would use the cross-validated redundancy measure to examine the predictive relevance of one's theoretical/structural model.

According to Wold (1982b), the omission distance D should be a prime integer between the number of indicators K and cases N. Furthermore, the choice of the omission distance D need not be large. Experience shows that D from 5 to 10 as long as N is large is feasible.

As a by-product of estimating each blindfolded sample, jackknifing standard deviations can also be obtained. Because a set of weights, loadings, structural paths, and latent component scores and correlations is obtained during each round, jackknife estimates of standard errors can be calculated. The smaller the error the more stable and more precise the parameter estimates.

Jackknifing

In general, the jackknife is an inferential technique that assesses the variability of a statistic by examining the variability of the sample data rather than using parametric assumptions. Developed in the late 1940s and 1950s, the jackknife can be used to provide both estimates and compensate for bias in statistical estimates by developing robust confidence intervals. The general approach, in contrast to the blindfolding procedure, is "delete n cases" where n is typically 1. Parameter estimates are calculated for each instance and the variation in the estimates are analyzed.

The basic steps for performing jackknife on a parameter estimate θ of the population value θ_p (e.g., factor weight or loading, structural path) is as follows:

1. Calculate the parameter using the entire sample data. Let's call this θ.

2. Partition the sample into subsamples according to the deletion number d. The first subsample represents the full sample with the first d cases removed. The second subsample has the next d cases deleted. Thus, a full sample set of 100 cases with a deletion number of 2 results in 50 subsamples where each subsample has 98 cases.

3. For each of the n subsamples (say the ith subsample), calculate the pseudo-jackknife value J_i as follows:

$$J_i = n*\theta - (n-1)\theta_i. \qquad (17)$$

4. Calculate the mean of the pseudovalues to yield the jackknife estimate JM of the population parameter θ_p as follows:

$$JM = \frac{\Sigma J_i}{n} = n*\theta - (n-1)*\frac{\Sigma \theta_i}{n}. \qquad (18)$$

5. Treat the pseudovalues as approximately independent and identically randomly distributed (Tukey, 1958) and calculate the standard deviation (SD) and standard error (SE) as follows:

$$SD = \frac{\sqrt{\Sigma_i(J_i - JM)^2}}{n-1}$$
$$SE = \frac{SD}{\sqrt{n}}. \qquad (19)$$

6. The jackknifed t-statistic with $n - 1$ degrees of freedom (where n is the number of subsamples) is used to test the null hypothesis that θ_p is not different from θ_0.

$$t\text{-}statistic = \frac{(JM - \theta_0)}{SE} \qquad (20)$$

where θ_0 is normally zero.

Although the pseudovalues are asymptotically independent, Gray and Schucany (1972) advised adjusting the t-statistic to account for possible interdependence. If the intraclass correlation between pseudovalues is r, the t-statistic should be adjusted by multiplying it with the following correction factor:

$$\sqrt{\frac{1-r}{1-(n-1)*r}}. \qquad (21)$$

Gray and Schucany suggested the use $1/n$ for r, which results in the correction factor as follows:

$$\sqrt{\frac{n-1}{2n-1}} \, .$$

(22)

Bootstrapping

The bootstrap represents yet another nonparametric approach for estimating the precision of the PLS estimates. N samples sets are created in order to obtain N estimates for each parameter in the PLS model. Each sample is obtained by sampling with replacement from the original data set (typically until the number of cases are identical to the original sample set). Various approaches for estimating confidence intervals have been developed (see Efron & Tibshirani, 1993, for more details).

In comparing the bootstrap to the jackknife, you need to consider the trade-off between computational time and efficiency. Jackknife estimation tends to take less time for standard error estimation under the joint assumption that the bootstrap procedure utilizes a confidence estimation procedure other than the normal approximation and the number of resamples are larger than those of the jackknife. Conversely, the jackknife is viewed as less efficient than the bootstrap because it can be considered as an approximation to the bootstrap (Efron & Tibshirani, 1993). In general, both the jackknife and bootstrap standard errors should converge.

Composite Reliability

In assessing the internal consistency for a given block of indicators, we can calculate the composite reliability developed by Werts, Linn, and Jöreskog (1974). Using the normal PLS output, which standardizes the indicators and LV, the composite reliability is:

$$\rho_c = \frac{(\Sigma \, \lambda_i)^2}{(\Sigma \, \lambda_i)^2 + \Sigma_i var(\varepsilon_i)}$$

(21)

where λ_i is the component loading to an indicator and $var(\varepsilon_i) = 1 - \lambda_i^2$. In comparison to Cronbach's alpha, this measure does not assume tau equivalency among the measures with its assumption that all indicators are equally weighted. Therefore, alpha tends to be a lower bound estimate of reliability, whereas ρ_c is a closer approximation under the assumption that the parameter estimates are accurate. Finally, being a measure of internal consistency and as discussed earlier, ρ_c is only applicable for LVs with reflective indicators (i.e., mode A blocks).

Average Variance Extracted

Another measure that has been proposed is the *average variance extracted* (AVE) created by Fornell and Larcker (1981). It attempts to measure the amount of variance that an LV component captures from its indicators relative to the amount due to measurement error. Therefore, as in the case of the composite reliability measure, AVE is only applicable for mode A (outward-directed) blocks. Assuming standardized indicators and LV estimates, the AVE is calculated as follows:

$$AVE = \frac{\Sigma \lambda_i^2}{\Sigma \lambda_i^2 + \Sigma_i var(\varepsilon_i)} \tag{22}$$

where λ_i is the component loading to an indicator and $var(\varepsilon_i) = 1 - \lambda_i^2$.

When all the indicators are standardized, this measure would be the same as the average of the communalities in the block. Fornell and Larcker (1981) suggested that this measure can also be interpreted as a measure of reliability for the LV component score and tends to be more conservative than ρ_c. It is recommended that AVE should be greater than .50 meaning that 50% or more variance of the indicators should be accounted for. Furthermore, they suggested that as a means of evaluating discriminant validity, the AVEs of the LVs should be greater than the square of the correlations among the LVs, which indicates that more variance is shared between the LV component and its block of indicators than with another component representing a different block of indicators.

Cross-Loadings

Another test of discriminant validity for mode A blocks can be obtained by calculating the correlations between LV component scores and other indicators besides its own block. If an indicator loads higher with other LVs than the one it is intended to measure, the researcher may wish to reconsider its appropriateness because it is unclear which construct or constructs it is actually reflecting. Furthermore, we should expect each block of indicators to load higher for its respective LV than indicators for other LVs.

AN EMPIRICAL APPLICATION OF PLS:
THE CASE OF PERCEIVED RESOURCES

As a final example of the use of PLS in an empirical study, a portion of the results produced recently by Mathieson, Peacock, and Chin (1996) is examined. The purpose of the study was to extend an existing model for predicting individual usage of information technology (IT) by including a construct called perceived resources. For illustrative purposes, we examine a subset of the model that predicts attitude and intention to use the IT.

The baseline model (see Fig. 10.6) developed by Davis, Bagozzi, and Warshaw (1989) suggests that an individual's intention to use an IT is predicted by both one's attitude (in an evaluative sense) toward usage (labeled Attitude) and one's cognitive belief that the use of the IT will lead to performance gains (labeled Usefulness). Attitude is seen as partially mediating the impact of Usefulness. In addition, one's belief in the Ease of Use of the IT is modeled indirectly impacting Intention through attitude and usefulness. A number of past empirical studies have demonstrated the generalizability of the model and validity of the measures (e.g., Adams, Nelson, & Todd, 1992; Chin & Gopal, 1995; Mathieson, 1991).

Mathieson et al. (1996), borrowing from Ajzen's (1991) work on the theory of planned behavior decided to extend the model in order to enhance predictiveness under conditions where the ability to use an IT is not entirely under the volition of the individual. To that extent, they developed a new construct called *perceived resources*. Perceived resources (*R*) is defined as "the extent to which an individual believes that he or she has the personal and organizational tools needed to use an IT" (Mathieson et al., p. 6). Thus, separate from the notion of assessing one's own ability, *R* attempts to capture how the perception of the presence or absence of resources or opportunities can impact one's attitude and intention toward using an IT.

The study examined the attitudes and intentions toward an electronic bulletin board system (BBS) developed by the Institute for Management Accountants (IMA). The IMA is the principal professional organization for management accountants, with approximately 83,000 members worldwide in over 300 chapters. Surveys were mailed to 1,172 IMA members along

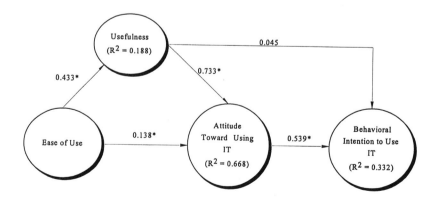

FIG. 10.6. Baseline model.

TABLE 10.4
The Resource Instrument

Reflective Items

R1. I have the resources, opportunities, and knowledge I would need to use a database package in my job.
R2. There are no barriers to my using a database package in my job.
R3. I would be able to use a database package in my job if I wanted to.
R4. I have access to the resources I would need to use a database package in my job.

Formative Items

R5. I have access to the hardware and software I would need to use a database package in my job.
R6. I have the knowledge I would need to use a database package in my job.
R7. I would be able to find the time I would need to use a database package in my job.
R8. Financial resources (e.g., to pay for computer time) are not a barrier for me in using a database package in my job.
R9. If I needed someone's help in using a database package in my job, I could get it easily.
R10. I have the documentation (manuals, books etc.) I would need to use a database package in my job.
R11. I have access to the data (on customers, products, etc.) I would need to use a database package in my job.

Note. Fully-anchored Likert scales were used. Responses to all items ranged from Extremely Likely (7) to Extremely Unlikely (1).

with other IMA documents. A total of 401 usable replies were received for a response rate of 34.2%.

Two sets of items were developed to measure R (see Table 10.4). One set of four indicators ($R1$ through $R4$) consisted of reflective measures that tap into the general feeling of having enough resources, whereas the other set ($R5$ through $R11$) attempted to capture a comprehensive set of formative indicators that help create that perception.

The results of the baseline model using an inner model path weighting scheme shows a substantial R-square of .67 for Attitude, a more moderate level of .33 for Intention, and a weak level of .19 for Usefulness. We opted to use bootstrap resampling (500 resamples) throughout this study for significance testing of path estimates. All structural paths were found to be significant except for one. Contrary to past research, no direct influence was found for Usefulness to Intention. For completeness, the loadings, weights, composite reliability, AVE, and Q^2 should be presented. But due to space limitations, we go on to the results using the R measures.

The first analysis is to compare the two sets of measures via a two-block redundancy model. The redundancy model is specified based on the original design of the questions. In other words, one set was designed with reflective indicators in mind whereas the other was meant to be formative. The extent to which both modes of assessing R are successful can be partly determined by the structural path linking them. In general, we would expect a path of .80 or above to be suggestive of securing an adequate set of formative measures assuming convergent validity (i.e., adequate loadings) for the reflective set. A path of .90 or above would indicate an extremely strong sign.

Figure 10.7 provides the results of the redundancy analysis. The path of .87 between the two modes of assessing R indicates a strong convergence and implies an adequate coverage of the perceptions in the formative set. The first of the two estimates for each measurement path represents the regression estimates in the direction of the arrows. Thus, for the formative case, the estimates represent the regression weights as opposed to the component loadings for the reflective case. In turn, the numbers in the parentheses for the formative block represent the component loadings (simple regression between the indicator and the LV component scores). Conversely, for the reflective block, the parentheses contain the weights. Bootstrap resampling was performed to examine the significance of the weights for the formative block and loadings for the reflective block. Overall, the loadings for the reflective set were uniformly high around .9 with a composite reliability ρ_c of .95 and an AVE of .81. Among the formative measures, $R5$, $R6$, $R7$, and $R8$ were all significant ($\alpha = .01$) with weights of .59, .27, .13, and .10 respectively. This empirically suggests that the overall impression of available resources for IT usage is primarily formed by access to necessary hardware, software, and knowledge.

The next step is to examine the validity of the R measures as applied to the basic model. We start by placing R (mode A) into the model. Although R was theoretically developed to predict the Attitude and Intention constructs, we can also include structural paths to Usefulness and Ease of Use in an exploratory sense. What we found were significant paths of .22 and

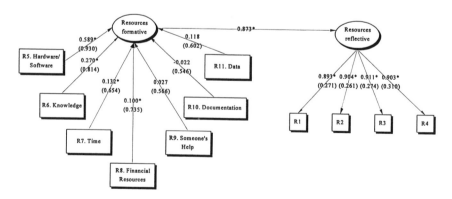

FIG. 10.7. Redundancy analysis of perceived resources (*indicates significant estimates).

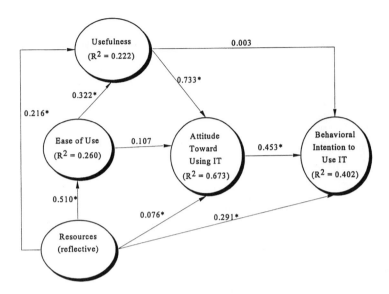

FIG. 10.8. Impact of including perceived resources (reflective measures).

.51, respectively. The full structural level results are presented in Fig. 10.8. All paths going from R were found to be significant. But in terms of substantive effects, R had more impact on Intention than Attitude. This is determined in terms of changes in both the R-squares and Q^2 as measured by f^2 and q^2. The f^2 for Intention and Attitude were .12 and .04. Thus, R has an approximately medium effect on Intention above and beyond the contributions provided by Usefulness and Attitude. The impact on Attitude, on the other hand, was small.

In calculating q^2, we performed blindfold analyses with varying omission distances. Specifically, D of 7, 37, and 97 were used. The results were very similar (i.e., to the third decimal point). The cross-validated redundancy Q^2 went from .15 to .26 when we included R implying a q^2 of .15 reflecting, again, a medium impact. Similarly, the q^2 for Attitude was small with an effect of .026 for Q^2 increasing from .60 to .61.

The validity of the measurement model is then assessed by examining the loading and cross-loadings of indicators in Table 10.5. Because all measures are reflective (i.e., mode A analysis), we can examine the individual loadings for each block of indicators. Individual item reliability should be considered. In general, one would like to have each indicator share more variance with the component score than with error variance. This implies that standardized loadings should be greater that .707. This condition was met in this study. But it should also be noted that this rule of thumb should not be as rigid at early stages of scale development. Loadings of .5 or .6 may still be acceptable if there exist additional indicators in the block for comparison basis. Once the

TABLE 10.5
Loadings and Cross-Loadings for the Measurement (Outer) Model

	USEFUL $(\rho_c = .98)$	EASE OF USE $(\rho_c = .97)$	RESOURCES $(\rho_c = .95)$	ATTITUDE $(\rho_c = .99)$	INTENTION $(\rho_c = .99)$
U1	**.95**	.40	.37	.78	.48
U2	**.96**	.41	.37	.77	.45
U3	**.95**	.38	.35	.75	.48
U4	**.96**	.39	.34	.75	.41
U5	**.95**	.43	.35	.78	.45
U6	**.96**	.46	.39	.79	.48
EOU1	.35	**.86**	.53	.42	.35
EOU2	.40	**.91**	.44	.41	.35
EOU3	.40	**.94**	.46	.40	.36
EOU4	.44	**.90**	.43	.44	.37
EOU5	.44	**.92**	.50	.46	.36
EOU6	.37	**.93**	.44	.42	.33
R1	.42	.51	**.90**	.41	.42
R2	.37	.50	**.91**	.38	.46
R3	.31	.46	**.91**	.35	.41
R4	.28	.38	**.90**	.33	.44
A1	.80	.47	.39	**.98**	.54
A2	.80	.44	.41	**.99**	.57
A3	.78	.45	.41	**.98**	.58
I1	.48	.38	.46	.58	**.97**
I2	.47	.37	.48	.56	**.99**
I3	.47	.37	.48	.56	**.99**

individual reliabilities are considered, the composite reliability ρ_c is next. In this study, ρ_c for each construct was above .95.

If items with low loadings in a mode A block are encountered, possible reasons are that (a) the item is simply unreliable, (b) it may be influenced by additional factors such as a method effect or some other concept, or (c) the construct itself is multidimensional in character (thus items were created capturing different issues). For the last situation, one might partition the items into more coherent blocks or simply remove the item. For the first situation, keeping the item will likely still increase predictiveness because it will still weight it to the extent it helps minimize residual variance as long as other more reliable indicators exist. This, of course, assumes the poor loading is due only to noise. This would not be the case if the indicator cross-loads higher with other LVs. Only in situation (b) would you have to remove it for lack of discriminant validity.

Going down the columns of Table 10.5, we find that the loadings for the indicators in each block are higher than any other indicators from other blocks, implying that the LV component score does indeed predict each indicator in its block better than indicators in other blocks. Going across,

TABLE 10.6
Correlation Among Construct Scores (AVE Extracted in Diagonals)

	Usefulness	*Ease of Use*	*Resources*	*Attitude*	*Intention*
Usefulness	**.91**				
Ease of Use	.43	**.83**			
Resources	.38	.51	**.82**		
Attitude	.81	.46	.41	**.97**	
Intention	.48	.38	.48	.58	**.97**

we see each indicator also loads higher with its respective LV. The next step in examining discriminant validity is to calculate the AVE and compare it to the square of the correlations among constructs. Table 10.6 provides this information with the AVE given in the diagonals.

As discussed earlier, an indicator of discriminant validity is to have all AVE measures be larger than the square of the correlations. Alternatively, you can take the square root of the AVE when comparing with the correlations. Given that the AVE was already larger than the correlations, we didn't need to make the transformation. But earlier in our redundancy analysis, we did have an AVE of .81, which was smaller than the path estimate (i.e., correlation) of .87. This square of the correlation does result in a number (.76) that is smaller than the AVE.

Finally, we can replace the mode A measures with the mode B measures of R. If the mode A measures do approximate R well, the pattern of structural relationships we saw with the reflective measures should also appear. The only difference would be an increase in the magnitude of the paths connected to R because mode B minimizes the residuals at the structural level. The results, as provided in Fig. 10.9, did occur as expected. In particular, we see the R-square increase from .40 to .44 for Intention, .67 to .69 for Attitude, .26 to .35 for Ease of Use, and .22 to .324 for Usefulness.

As we look at the weights and loadings associated with our model using the formative measures of R (see Table 10.7), we notice that only indicators $R6$, $R7$, and $R10$ have a significant impact with .23, .56, and .41, respectively. Substantively, this would suggest that time is the most important resource, followed by documentation, and then knowledge in forming an overall perception of resources that facilitate or hinder using an IT. We also see a difference in the impact of these measures relative to the earlier Redundancy model. Whereas, in both analyses, Knowledge ($R6$) and Time ($R7$) were factors influential in forming one's overall perception of resources, the significance of the other factors varied. It is beyond the scope of this chapter to discuss the substantive issues, but it does highlight the importance of the nomological context in which measures are used. Whether formative or reflective, loadings and weights can change for a given construct as it is applied in different contexts and associated constructs distinct from those originally developed.

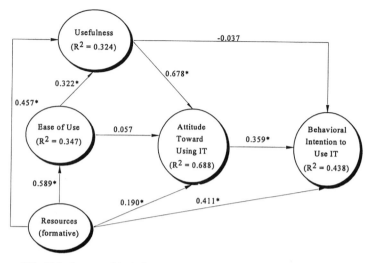

FIG. 10.9. Impact of including perceived resources (formative measures).

TABLE 10.7
Outer Model Weights and Loadings for Model Using Formative R Measures

Indicator	Weights	Loadings
U1	.18	.95
U2	.17	.96
U3	.17	.95
U4	.17	.96
U5	.18	.95
U6	.18	.96
EOU1	.18	.86
EOU2	.18	.90
EOU3	.18	.93
EOU4	.19	.89
EOU5	.20	.91
EOU6	.18	.92
A1	.34	.98
A2	.34	.99
A3	.34	.98
I1	.34	.96
I2	.35	.98
I3	.34	.98
R5. Hardware/Software n.s.	.00	.58
R6. Knowledge	.23	.73
R7. Time	.56	.85
R8. Financial Resources n.s.	−.10	.56
R9. Someone's Help n.s.	.07	.59
R10. Documentation	.41	.76
R11. Data n.s.	.09	.68

Note. n.s. = nonsignificant.

In summary, this empirical study provides an example of how PLS can be used in a confirmatory sense. An existing theoretical model with an established set of measures was used as the basis for further theoretical and measurement development. Both formative and reflective sets of measures were created to estimate the same underlying construct, which demonstrates the importance of having both sets of measures. Without the reflective measures, there would be less evidence as to whether the researcher was successful in estimating the particular construct. With only formative measures, a researcher can demonstrate only the predictive capabilities of that block of measures. But by providing a set of reflective measures, we were able to demonstrate that both sets converged toward the same LV by means of the redundancy analysis and substitutability in a nomological network. It is less problematic if we only had reflective measures. Under that condition, we can also examine the validity of the indicators via the individual loadings, composite reliability, and AVE. Finally, the use of the cross-validated redundancy measures provides a strong contrast to that of the AVE and R-square measures. Whereas the latter two have the inherent bias of being assessed on the same data that were used to estimate its parameters (thus the potential of overinflation), the sample reuse approach of the q^2 measure is more informative of the generalizability toward predicting future observations.

PROPERTIES OF THE PLS ESTIMATES:
THE ISSUE OF CONSISTENCY AT LARGE

Although one of the benefits of the PLS procedure can be argued to be its ability to estimate LV case values, it also represents a bias in obtaining parameter estimates. Essentially, the case values for the LVs are "inconsistent" due to the fact that they are aggregates of the observed variables, which in part include measurement error. This bias tends to manifest itself in higher estimates for component loadings (outer model relations) and lower estimates at the structural level (inner model relations). The estimates will approach the "true" latent variable scores as the number of indicators per both block and sample size increase. This limiting case is termed "consistency at large" (Wold, 1982b, p. 25). Intuitively, the larger the number of indicators in a block, the more the "essence" of the LV is confirmed by the data. But the sample size also needs to increase, as in the usual asymptoptic notion of consistency, in order for the sample covariance matrix to become a better estimate of the population covariance matrix. Thus, in PLS, better estimates cannot be obtained simply by increasing the sample size. Both are needed. Furthermore, increasing the block size not only approaches the "true" parameter scores, but also lowers the standard errors, which have been shown to vary inversely with the square root of the block size (Lyttkens, 1966, 1973).

Although closed-form solutions for estimating the amount of bias are not available for multiblock heterogenous loadings conditions, bias formulas for the PLS estimates relative to the parameter-oriented ML estimates in the single- and two-block models have been provided (for derivations see Lohmöller, 1989). In the single-block case, the overestimating loading bias is:

$$bias(\lambda)_{single\ block} = \frac{PLS_{estimate}}{ML_{estimate}} = \sqrt{\frac{s + (1 - s)/K}{s}} \qquad (23)$$

where s is the correlation coefficient assumed identical across all indicators in the block and K the number of indicators. In the two-block case, the underestimating bias for the correlation between LVs is:

$$bias(\rho)_{two\ block} = \frac{PLS_{estimate}}{ML_{estimate}} = \frac{s}{s + (1 - s)/K} \qquad (24)$$

where s is the correlation coefficient assumed identical across all indicators (within and between blocks) and K the number of indicators. The loading bias for the two-block case is simply the inverse square root of the loadings:

$$bias(\lambda)_{twoblock} = \frac{1}{\sqrt{bias(\rho)_{two\ block}}} \qquad (25)$$

which is the same as Equation 23.

Two points become clear from these formulas: The bias decreases as the loadings become more reliable, and the bias decreases as the number of indicators increase. We also see that the predicted correlation between indicators from different blocks is unbiased because the loading and correlation biases cancel each other out. The general proof that this canceling effect occurs even under conditions of unequal block sizes, weights, and loadings has been given by Areskoug (1982).

Therefore, we again see the distinction between prediction orientation versus parameter orientation. The parameter estimation accuracy of the PLS procedure relative to the covariance-based ML procedure increases under consistency at large. Yet one side point should be made. The bias measures just presented are relative to the ML estimators, which presupposes that the underlying model that generates the data is covariance based. Schneeweiss (1990) has argued that the consistency at large notion is really a "justification for using PLS as an estimation method to estimate LISREL parameters in cases where the number of manifest variables is large" (p. 38). Instead, Schneeweiss argued, PLS can be seen as a consistent estimator of parameters and latent variables as long as we ask the question of which population parameters we are attempting to estimate. If we are estimating the parameters for the population model as defined by PLS, then we have the advantage of "treating PLS as a method for defining descriptive parameters in situations where blocks of manifest variables are related to each other" (p. 38), even if the data cannot be regarded as stemming from a LISREL model. Under this situation, the PLS estimation method will estimate the PLS parameters consistently. If, on the other hand, the data are generated from a covariance-based model, the PLS estimates will result in inconsistent estimates.

Therefore, though PLS can be used in a confirmatory sense following a covariance-based orientation, it can also be used for testing the appropriateness of a block of indicators in a predictive sense and for suggesting potential relations among blocks without necessarily making any assumptions regarding which LV model generated the data. As Wold (1980) noted:

> The arrow scheme is usually tentative since the model construction is an evolutionary process. The empirical content of the model is extracted from the data, and the model is improved by interactions through the estimation procedure between the model and the data and the reactions of the researcher. Consequently, the researcher should begin with a generous number of observables-indicators in the various blocks. To use many observables makes for rich empirical content of the model and is favorable to the accuracy of the PLS estimation procedure. In the interaction between the data and the original model it will become apparent which indicators are relevant and which should be omitted. (p. 70)

SUMMARY DISCUSSION

As mentioned at the beginning of this chapter, by far the most dominant approach to SEM has been the covariance-based procedures such as LISREL. Yet, the PLS procedure may be more suitable under certain circumstances. As we covered the PLS model and estimation procedure in this chapter, we were able to contrast many differences.

Programs such as LISREL are covariance-based procedures with the objective of obtaining optimal parameter accuracy. The level of theoretical/substantive knowledge that the researcher brings to the study is a major factor inasmuch as any given model becomes the basis for explaining the covariances among all the indicators. In order to obtain consistent parameter estimates, the empirical conditions of the data require multivariate normal distribution (under an ML function) and independence of observations. Finally, indicators are typically required to be modeled, as reflective and unique case values for LVs cannot be obtained (i.e., factor indeterminacy).

PLS was developed as a counterpart to the covariance-based approach. In general, it can be viewed as complementary to LISREL because its main objective is prediction. PLS's focus under predictor specification is on the variance of dependent variables and no assumptions are made regarding the joint distribution of the indicators or the independence of sample cases. Because of its prediction orientation, factors are determinate and unique case values for the LVs are estimated. Indicators can be modeled in either direction (i.e., formative or reflective).

We also saw that sample size requirements under PLS can be quite minimal relative to a LISREL. Computationally, PLS is an order of magnitude faster given that its procedure involves only a series of LS estimations. And, by virtue of the fact that at any moment only a subset of the parameters are being estimated, PLS can handle much larger/complex models with many LVs and indicators in each block. Models consisting of over 200 indicators can be easily executed.

In addition, as the number of indicators per block increase along with the sample size, we saw that the PLS estimates tend to become more stable as they converge to the "true" parameter values. LISREL, conversely, will tend to reject the model (based on covariance fit). This rejection occurs, in part, because the model needs to account for more covariances. As the number of indicators increases and as sample size increases, the power to detect even minor model misspecification increases.

In summary, PLS should not be viewed as simply a distribution-free alternative to LISREL. Rather, it represents a different approach to empirical modeling—a descriptive, prediction-oriented one. But it is not just pure prediction. For, if one values predictiveness above all else, a simple multiple regression will always lead to the highest R^2. However, the ability to predict and understand the role and formation of individual constructs and their relationships among each other would be lost. The decision, thus, becomes one of assessing which is of greater value, model complexity or parsimonious prediction, and whether the use of each LV makes theoretical and substantive sense.

McDonald (1996) recently stated that:

> The PLS methods are difficult to describe and extremely difficult to evaluate, partly because PLS constitutes a set of ad hoc algorithms that have generally not been formally analyzed, or shown to possess any clear global optimizing properties (except in the well understood case of just two composites), and partly because these devices are represented as a form of path analysis with latent variables, and it can be difficult to determine what properties of latent variable models they posses, if any. (p. 240)

But as Wold (1980) said, "In the limit, the PLS estimation procedure is coherent in the sense that all the residual variances are minimized jointly. However, the PLS procedure remains partial in the sense that no total residual variance or other overall criterion is set up for optimization" (p. 67).

Therefore, echoing McDonald's (1996) statement, one major goal for the future is to examine how PLS performs under varying conditions of sample sizes, number of blocks, and modes. Monte Carlo-based simulations will need to be conducted to examine these varying conditions because closed-form solutions are likely not available. Perhaps the current lack of understanding of the statistical properties of the PLS method beyond the two-block models may be a contributing factor to its relative obscurity. Another factor may be the access to software. Whereas there are a number of software packages for performing covariance-based analysis, the accessibility of PLS-based software is somewhat limited. One hopes this problem will change in the future with the release of PLS-Graph—a Windows-based version currently under development by the author (contact the author for information or via the World Wide Web at: http://www.ucalgary.ca/~chin).

In conclusion, the PLS methodology will likely grow in usage in the future. As a least square alternative, it is substantially less complex to understand than the covariance-based procedures when it comes to specifying a model (e.g., checking model identification, scaling, and other constraints vs. partitioning blocks and specifying the arrow directions) and interpretation of results (variance-explained vs. model fit indices). The approach is likely congruent with a large percentage of social science research where the phenomena in question are: (a) relatively new or changing and where the theoretical model or measures are not well formed, or (b) the model is relatively complex with large numbers of indicators and/or LVs, or (c) there is an epistemic need to model the relationship between LV and indicators in different modes (i.e., formative and reflective measures), or (d) the data conditions relating to normal distribution, independence, or sample size are not met, or (e) there is a need for more flexibility in modeling beyond those afforded by first-generation techniques. What remains is to make researchers aware of this approach, which is the goal of this chapter.

REFERENCES

Adams, D. A., Nelson, R. R., & Todd, P. A. (1992). Perceived usefulness, ease of use, and usage of information technology: A replication. *MIS Quarterly, 16*(2), 227–247.

Ajzen, I. (1991). The theory of planned behavior. *Organizational Behavior and Human Decision Processes, 50,* 179–211.

Areskoug, B. (1982). The first canonical correlation: Theoretical PLS analysis and simulation experiments. In K. G. Jöreskog & H. Wold (Eds.), *Systems under indirect observations: Causality, structure, prediction* (Part 2, pp. 95–118). Amsterdam: North-Holland.

Bagozzi, R. P., Fornell, C., & Larcker, D. F. (1981). Canonical correlation analysis as a special case of structural relations model. *Multivariate Behavioral Research, 16,* 437–454.

Bollen, K. A. (1984). Multiple indicators: Internal consistency or no necessary relationship? *Quality & Quantity, 18,* 377–385.

Bollen, K. A. (1989). *Structural equations with latent variables.* New York: Wiley.

Chin, W. W., & Gopal, A. (1995). Adoption intention in GSS: Relative importance of beliefs. *DATA BASE, 26*(2 & 3), 42–63.

Cohen, J. (1988). *Statistical power analysis for the behavioral sciences* (2nd ed.). Hillsdale, NJ: Lawrence Erlbaum Associates.

Cohen, P., Cohen, J., Teresi, J., Marchi, M., & Velez, C. N. (1990). Problems in the measurement of latent variables in structural equations causal models. *Applied Psychological Measurement, 14,* 183–196.

Davis, F. D., Bagozzi, R. P., & Warshaw, P. R. (1989). User acceptance of computer technology: A comparison of two theoretical models. *Management Science, 35,* 982–1003.

Dillon, W. R., Kumar, A., & Mulani, N. (1987). Offending estimates in covariance structure analysis: Comments on the causes of and solutions to Heywood cases. *Psychological Bulletin, 101*(1), 126–135.

Efron, B., & Tibshirani, R. J. (1993). *An introduction to the bootstrap (monographs on statistics and applied probability, #57).* New York: Chapman & Hall.

Falk, R. F., & Miller, N. B. (1992). *A primer for soft modeling.* Akron, OH: University of Akron Press.

Fornell, C. (1987). A second generation of multivariate analysis: Classification of methods and implications for marketing research. In M. J. Houston (Ed.), *Review of marketing* (pp. 407–450). Chicago: American Marketing Association.

Fornell, C., Barclay, D. W., & Rhee, B.-D. (1988). A model and simple iterative algorithm for redundancy analysis. *Multivariate Behavioral Research, 23,* 349–360.

Fornell, C., & Bookstein, F. (1982). Two structural equation models: LISREL and PLS applied to consumer exit-voice theory. *Journal of Marketing Research, 19,* 440–452.

Fornell, C., & Larcker, D. (1981). Evaluating structural equation models with unobservable variables and measurement error. *Journal of Marketing Research, 18,* 39–50.

Geisser, S. (1975). The predictive sample reuse method with applications. *Journal of the American Statistical Association, 70,* 320–328.

Gray, H. L., & Schucany, W. R. (1972). *The generalized jackknife statistic.* New York: Marcel Dekker.

Harris, R. J. (1989). A canonical cautionary. *Multivariate Behavioral Research, 24*(1), 17–39.

Hui, B. S. (1978). *The partial least squares approach to path models of indirectly observed variables with multiple indicators.* Unpublished doctoral thesis, University of Pennsylvania, Philadelphia.

Hui, B. S. (1982). On building partial least squares models with interdependent inner relations. In K. G. Jöreskog & H. Wold (Eds.), *Systems under indirect observations: Causality, structure, prediction* (Part 2, pp. 249–272). Amsterdam: North-Holland.

Jöreskog, K. G. (1973). A general method for estimating a linear structural equation system. In A. S. Goldberger & O. D. Duncan (Eds.), *Structural equation models in the social sciences* (pp. 85–112). New York: Academic Press.

Jöreskog, K. G., & Sörbom, D. (1989). *LISREL 7: A guide to the program and applications.* Chicago: SPSS, Inc.

Keesling, J. W. (1972). *Maximum likelihood approaches to causal analysis.* Unpublished doctoral dissertation, University of Chicago, Chicago.

Knapp, T. R. (1978). Canonical correlation analysis: A general parametric significance-testing system. *Psychological Bulletin, 85*(2), 410–416.

Lohmöller, J.-B. (1984). *LVPLS, program manual. Latent variables path analysis with partial least-squares estimation.* Köln, Germany: Zentralarchiv für empirische Sozialforschung.

Lohmöller, J.-B. (1989). *Latent variable path modeling with partial least squares.* Heidelberg, Germany: Physica-Verlag.

Lyttkens, E. (1966). On the fixed-point property of Wold's iterative estimation method for principal components. In P. R. Krishnaiah (Ed.), *Multivariate analysis: Proceedings of an international symposium held in Dayton, Ohio, June 14–19, 1965* (pp. 335–350). New York: Academic Press.

Lyttkens, E. (1973). The fixed-point method for estimating interdependent systems with the underlying model specification. *Journal of the Royal Statistical Society, Series A, 136*, 353–394.

Maraun, M. D. (1996). Metaphor taken as math: Indeterminacy in the factor analysis model. *Multivariate Behavioral Research, 31*(4), 517–538, 539–689.

Mathieson, K. (1991). Predicting user intentions: Comparing the technology acceptance model with the theory of planned behavior. *Information Systems Research, 2*, 173–191.

Mathieson, K., Peacock, E., & Chin, W. (1996). *Extending the technology acceptance model: The influence of perceived user resources* (Working Paper No. WP 96-18). Calgary, Canada: University of Calgary.

McDonald, R. P. (1996). Path analysis with composite variables. *Multivariate Behavioral Research, 31*(2), 239–270.

Noonan, R., & Wold, H. (1982). PLS path modeling with indirectly observed variables: A comparison of alternative estimates for latent variables. In K. G. Jöreskog & H. Wold (Eds.), *Systems under indirect observations: Causality, structure, prediction* (Part 2, pp. 75–94). Amsterdam: North-Holland.

Schneeweiss, H. (1990). Models with latent variables: LISREL versus PLS. *Contemporary Mathematics, 112*, 33–40.

Stone, M. (1974). Cross-validatory choice and assessment of statistical predictions. *Journal of the Royal Statistical Society, Series B, 36*(2), 111–133.

Tucker, L. R. (1958). An inter-battery method of factor analysis. *Psychometrika, 23*, 111–136.

Tukey, J. W. (1958). Bias and confidence in not-quite large samples. *Annals of Mathematical Statistics, 29*, 614.

Van den Wollenberg, A. L. (1977). Redundancy analysis: An alternative for canonical correlation analysis. *Psychometrika, 42*, 207–219.

Van Driel, O. P. (1978). On various causes of improper solutions in maximum likelihood factor analysis. *Psychometrika, 43*, 225–243.

Werts, C. E., Linn, R. L., & Jöreskog, K. G. (1974). Intraclass reliability estimates: Testing structural assumptions. *Educational and Psychological Measurement, 34*, 25–33.

Wiley, D. E. (1973). The identification problem for structural equation models with unmeasured variables. In A. S. Goldberger & O. D. Duncan (Eds.), *Structural equation models in the social sciences* (pp. 69–83). New York: Academic Press.

Wold, H. (1966). Estimation of principal components and related models by iterative least squares. In P. R. Krishnaiah (Ed.), *Multivariate analysis: Proceedings of an international symposium held in Dayton, Ohio, June 14–19, 1965* (pp. 391–420). New York: Academic Press.

Wold, H. (1973). Nonlinear iterative partial least squares (NIPALS) modeling: Some current developments. In P. R. Krishnaiah (Ed.), *Multivariate analysis: II. Proceedings of an international symposium on multivariate analysis held at Wright State University, Dayton, Ohio, June 19–24, 1972* (pp. 383–407). New York: Academic Press.

Wold, H. (1975). Path models with latent variables: The NIPALS approach. In H. M. Blalock, A. Aganbegian, F. M. Borodkin, R. Boudon, & V. Cappecchi (Eds.), *Quantitative sociology: International perspectives on mathematical and statistical modeling* (pp. 307–357). New York: Academic Press.

Wold, H. (1980). Model construction and evaluation when theoretical knowledge is scarce: Theory and application of partial least squares. In J. Kmenta & J. B. Ramsey (Eds.), *Evaluation of econometric models* (pp. 47–74). New York: Academic Press.

Wold, H. (1982a). Models for knowledge. In J. Gani (Ed.), *The making of statisticians* (pp. 190–212). London: Applied Probability Trust.

Wold, H. (1982b). Soft modeling: the basic design and some extensions. In K. G. Jöreskog & H. Wold (Eds.), *Systems under indirect observations: Causality, structure, prediction* (Part 2, pp. 1–54). Amsterdam: North-Holland.

Wold, H. (1985). Partial least squares. In S. Kotz & N. L. Johnson (Eds.), *Encyclopedia of statistical sciences* (Vol. 6, pp. 581–591). New York: Wiley.

Wold, H. (1988). Specification, predictor. In S. Kotz & N. L. Johnson (Eds.), *Encyclopedia of statistical sciences* (Vol. 8, pp. 587–599). New York: Wiley.

CHAPTER ELEVEN

Methods for Multilevel Data Analysis

David Kaplan
University of Delaware

Researchers interested in the study of organizations are becoming increasingly aware of the fact that many types of social institutions are hierarchically structured. For example, in the context of business organizations, employees are nested in work units and work units are nested in organizations. In still another example, students are nested in classrooms, which in turn are nested in schools, and so forth. Moreover, data generated from these types of systems are typically obtained through some form of clustered random sampling. Until relatively recently, common approaches to the analysis of hierarchically organized social science data would be to either disaggregate data to the individual (e.g., employee) level or aggregate data to the organizational (e.g., work unit or firm) level. Neither approach is adequate for a proper analysis of the actual structure of the data. In the former case, units within an organization will have the same values on observed and unobserved organizational-level variables. As such, the usual regression assumption of independence of errors is violated—leading to biased regression coefficients. In the latter case, where within-unit data are aggregated and analyzed at the between-unit level, a great deal of information on within-unit variation is lost. The result of aggregation is that relationships among between-unit variables may appear stronger than they really are.

To overcome the limitations associated with aggregated and disaggregated data, methodologists and statisticians have made significant advances in the analysis of hierarchical data that allow for proper modeling of organization systems such as businesses. These methods have appeared under many different names such as *multilevel linear models, mixed-effects* and *random-effects models, random coefficient models,* and *covariance components models.* These terms also reflect the fact that they have been utilized in many different research settings, such as sociology, biometrics, econometrics, and statistics, respectively (see Bryk & Raudenbush, 1992, for an overview of the history of these methods). In addition to statistical developments, advances have also been made in providing software for the estimation of multilevel models. With the advent of software programs such as HLM (Bryk, Raudenbush, & Congdon, 1996) it is now possible to analyze hierarchically structured data in a straightforward and statistically appropriate fashion.

In addition to the multilevel structure of data arising from settings such as businesses or schools, it is often the case that data generated from these systems exhibit the usual problems associated with the reliability and validity of the measures. These problems can sometimes be ameliorated through the incorporation of factor analytic methodologies. Recent advances now allow one to capture multilevel effects within the factor analysis setting (Muthén, 1991b). Moreover, it is also true that such systems possess complex structural relationships that cannot adequately be captured by simple linear regression-based methods. Here too, recent advances by Muthén and his colleagues (see, e.g., Muthén, 1989; Muthén & Satorra, 1989) now allow researchers to combine full structural equation models (e.g., Jöreskog, 1977) with multilevel models in order to simultaneously handle sampling, structure, and measurement issues.

The purpose of this chapter is to provide an overview of the basic ideas and research issues surrounding multilevel modeling. The organization of this chapter is as follows. The first section gives an overview of multilevel regression modeling. A number of models can be covered, however in this section we concentrate on the simple two-level *slopes- and intercepts-as-outcomes* model discussed in Bryk and Raudenbush (1992). This model is arguably the most applicable to business settings. The next section gives a brief overview of the basic concepts of structural equation modeling. The third section provides a discussion of multilevel factor analysis, multilevel structural equation modeling. Multilevel structural equation modeling is described in the simple case of multilevel path analysis model wherein within-organization-level parameters are modeled as a function of between-organization variables following their own path model. In the fourth section, the topic changes to an analysis of longitudinal data. Here, the analysis of longitudinal data is discussed in the context of both standard multilevel modeling and structural equation modeling. Along the way, examples taken primarily from research on educational organizations are provided. The final section concludes with a discussion of the potential of multilevel methodology for business research.

BASIC CONCEPTS IN MULTILEVEL
REGRESSION ANALYSIS

To set the groundwork for the remainder of this chapter, consider the analysis of institutional settings such as educational systems. In the United States, large national surveys are often conducted to obtain policy-relevant information regarding education policies and outcomes—especially those concerned with student learning. One such survey is the National Educational Longitudinal Study of 1988 (NELS:88; National Center for Educational Statistics [NCES], 1988). For NELS:88, a form of clustered random sampling is utilized where schools are randomly sampled, followed by the sampling of teachers within schools. Finally, students are sampled in classrooms. Treating data arising from such surveys as though simple random sampling was used leads to predictable biases as mentioned earlier. Recognizing the importance of properly modeling data generated from clustered sampling schemes, extraordinary advances in social organization research have resulted from the application of *multilevel linear regression* methods (see, e.g., Aitken & Longford, 1986; Bock, 1989; Bryk & Raudenbush, 1992). The advantage of applying multilevel methods to such data is that they mitigate many of the problems associated with aggregation and disaggregation bias by explicitly modeling the clustered sampling mechanism that generates student-, classroom-, and school-level data. Of course, the same advantages would hold for business data generated from clustered sampling.

To fix ideas consider a simple two-level model where, for example, we are interested in modeling achievement for the ith student in the gth school.[1] Such a model can be specified as follows: Following Bryk and Raudenbush (1992), let

$$y_{ig} = \beta_{0g} + \beta_{ig} x_{ig} + r_{ig} \qquad (1)$$

where y_{ig} is the ith student's science achievement score in the gth school, x_{ig} is a vector of student-level predictors such as socioeconomic status (SES), ethnicity, gender, the number of semesters of science classes, the degree to which students are involved in experiments versus lectures, and so on, β_{0g} is the expected science achievement score for a student with scores of zero on the predictors, and β_{1g} is the SES-achievement slope for school g. Assume

---

[1]Again, it's important to note that the discussion can also be extended to other organizational systems. We can consider employees nested in work units or other large aggregates such as firms.

also that x_{ig} is centered around the group mean so that the intercept, β_{0g}, can be interpreted as the unadjusted mean for group g (see Bryk & Raudenbush, 1992).[2]

Note the subscript g on the intercept β_{0g} and slope β_{1g} in Equation 1. This implies that the g schools vary both in their levels of achievement and their rates of achievement given the predictor variables. Thus, there may be school-level variables that explain variation in the intercept and slope. These variables might include school characteristics such as the sector of the school, average teacher salary, or other policies and practices of the school. For simplicity, let W_g represent whether the school g is public or private, where public schools are coded zero and private schools coded one, and let Z_g be a measure of the average teacher salary for school g. Then, the g intercepts and slopes in Equation 1 can be modeled as

$$\beta_{0g} = \gamma_{00} + \gamma_{01}W_g + \gamma_{02}Z_g + u_{0g}, \tag{2}$$

and

$$\beta_{1g} = \gamma_{10} + \gamma_{11}W_g + \gamma_{12}Z_g + u_{1g}, \tag{3}$$

where γ_{00} is the mean science achievement score for public schools with a hypothetical teacher salary of zero, γ_{01} is the gap between public and private schools on levels of achievement (termed the private school *effectiveness* advantage), γ_{02} is the effect of average teacher salary on average level of achievement, γ_{10} is the average SES-achievement slope for public schools with teacher salaries of zero, γ_{11} is the average difference in SES-achievement slopes between public and private schools (termed the private school *equity* advantage), and γ_{12} is the effect of teacher salary on the SES-achievement slopes (see Bryk & Raudenbush, 1992).

To see more clearly the usefulness of this multilevel model for understanding the hierarchically organized social structures such as schools or businesses, we can substitute Equations 2 and 3 into Equation 1 yielding the general model

$$y_{ig} = \gamma_{00} + \gamma_{01}W_g + \gamma_{02}Z_g + \gamma_{10}x_{ig} + \gamma_{11}W_g x_{ig} + \gamma_{12}Z_g x_{ig} + u_{0g} + u_{1g}x_{ig} + r_{ig}. \tag{4}$$

This model, then, relates the achievement score of the ith student in the gth school as a function of the main effect of the student SES, the main effect

---

[2]This interpretation follows from the centering of the predictor variables. If variables are not centered such that there is a meaningful zero point, then the intercepts will have arbitrary meanings. On the other hand, the research can choose from a variety of different ways of centering that will result in different interpretations for the intercept. These centering choices are discussed in Bryk and Raudenbush (1992). See also, Kreft (1995).

of the type of the school, the main effect of the average teacher salary of the school, as well as cross-level interactions of student characteristics, school characteristics, and school policies. With estimates of the unknown parameters available, analysts can, for example, study the effects of a change in average teacher salary on student achievement or examine such a change in combination with changes in other school-level or student-level variables.

An Example of Multilevel Modeling

Lee and Bryk (1989) provided an example of the intercept- and slopes-as-outcomes model examining the social distribution of achievement in public and Catholic high schools. Specifically, Lee and Bryk examined, among other things, the claim by Coleman et al. (1982) that academic achievement was more equitably distributed in Catholic schools than in public schools. Using data from the High School and Beyond Survey, Lee and Bryk estimated a Level 1 model (Equation 1) that modeled mathematics achievement (MATHACH) as a function of a dummy variable representing the student minority status (MINORITY; 1 = African-American or Hispanic), the socioeconomic status of the student (SES), and a composite measure of student academic background up to entry into high school (BACKGROUND).

The Level 2 models (Equations 2 and 3) included separate equations for the intercept and the three slopes (one each for MINORITY, SES, BACKGROUND). The model for the intercept (the school mean achievement model) included a measure of the average social class of the students within the school (AVGSES), a measure of whether the school had high minority enrollment (HIMIN), a measure of the average academic background of the students within the school (AVGBCK), and a measure of the sector of the school (SECTOR; 1 = Catholic, −1 = public). In addition, interaction terms were also included.

The slope relating MATHACH to MINORITY (the minority achievement gap model) was modeled as a function of the HIMIN, SECTOR, and the interaction of the two. The slope relating mathematics achievement to SES (the social class differentiation model) was modeled as a function of the AVGSES, SECTOR, and the interaction of the two. Finally, the slope relating mathematics achievement to academic background was modeled as a function of the AVGBCK, SECTOR, and the interaction of the two (the academic differentiation model).

To summarize the results, Lee and Bryk (1989) found that for the school mean achievement model, mean achievement was significantly related to average academic background with higher average background associated with greater mean achievement. Schools with high minority enrollment were associated with lower overall mean achievement. Catholic schools were found to have overall higher levels of achievement but an interaction was also observed between the sector of the school and the average SES of the school.

For the minority achievement gap model, Lee and Bryk (1989) found that the African-American versus White achievement gap was smaller in Catholic schools than in public schools after controlling for students' SES and academic background. For the social class differentiation model, the results showed that the relationship between math achievement and the SES of the student was significantly related to the joint effects of the average SES of the school and the sector of the school. Specifically, the achievement-SES relationship was lower in high social class Catholic schools than in low social class Catholic schools. The converse was true for public schools—namely there was a steeper relationship between achievement and SES for high social class public schools compared to lower social class public schools. Finally, Lee and Bryk found no significant predictors in the academic differentiation model.

BASIC IDEAS IN STRUCTURAL EQUATION MODELING

Structural equation modeling represents a major methodological breakthrough in the study of complex interrelationships among variables (Jöreskog, 1977). Structural equation modeling represents the unification of two methodological traditions: Thurstonian factor analysis originating from psychology and psychometrics, and simultaneous equations (path analytic) modeling originating from econometrics and tracing its way to social and behavioral science research primarily through sociology (see, e.g., Goldberger & Duncan, 1973). The standard specification of a structural equation model is composed of two parts—the *structural model* and the *measurement model*. The structural model can be written as

$$\eta = \alpha + B\eta + \Gamma\xi + \zeta, \qquad (5)$$

where η is a vector endogenous factors, α is a vector of intercepts, B is a matrix of regression coefficients relating the endogenous factors to other endogenous factors, ξ is a vector of exogenous factors, Γ is a matrix of regression coefficients relating the endogenous factors to the exogenous variables, and ζ is a vector of disturbances.

Specific student-level outcome and input factors are linked to observed measures via a measurement model, which can be written as

$$y = \Lambda_y \eta + \varepsilon, \qquad (6)$$

and

$$x = \Lambda_x \xi + \delta, \qquad (7)$$

where y may be a vector of individual items on an achievement test and x may be items on survey of student attitudes toward school. Each item is assumed to be measured with error that is captured by the vectors ε and δ, respectively. The observed measures y and x are linked to the underlying factors η and ξ through their respective factor loading matrices, Λ_y and Λ_x. It should be noted that when observed measures (or scales) are utilized for structural equation modeling it is not necessary to make use of the specification of the measurement part of the model as given in Equations 6 and 7. Instead, the general model in Equation 5 reduces to the standard simultaneous equations (path analytic) model developed in the field of econometrics and written as

$$y = \alpha + \mathbf{B}y + \Gamma x + \zeta. \tag{8}$$

The specification of the full structural equation model given previously in Equations 5–7 was presented in Jöreskog (1977). Details regarding identification, estimation, and testing can be found in, for example, Bollen (1989). Good discussion of current topics in structural equation modeling can be found in Bollen and Long (1993), Hoyle (1995), and Marcoulides and Schumacker (1996).

An Example of Structural Equation Modeling

A recent article of relevance to business provides a nice example of standard structural equation modeling. Specifically, Settoon, Bennett, and Liden (1996) utilized structural equation modeling to ascertain the relative contribution of measures of employee–organization exchange and subordinate–supervisor exchange. The dependent constructs consisted of a measure of organizational commitment (Mowday, Steers, & Porter, 1979), a measure of inrole behavior (Williams & Anderson, 1991), and a measure of citizenship behavior (Williams & Anderson, 1991). Each of these constructs was measured by one manifest variable. Exogenous constructs included a measure of perceived organizational support (Eisenberger, Huntington, Hutchison, & Sowa, 1986) and a set of measures that tap leader-member exchange (Liden & Maslyn, 1993).

The final sample for the Settoon et al. (1996) study consisted of 102 employees from 28 work groups in a regional U.S. hospital. There were 26 supervisors who completed a number of questionnaires for their employees. In this study, the employees completed the perceived organizational support, leader-member exchange, and organizational commitment scales, whereas the supervisors provided responses to the citizenship and inrole behavior scales.

After a small series of nested model comparisons, Settoon et al. (1996) found positive and significant effects of perceived organizational support to organizational commitment, leader-member exchange to inrole behavior, and leader-member exchange to citizenship behavior. A small and nonsignificant effect of perceived organizational support to inrole behavior was observed. From the standpoint of hierarchical linear modeling, the Settoon et al. (1996) article is suggestive of the level-of-analysis problem. That is, in this article there is a mixture of levels—namely supervisors and employees with supervisors rating more than one employee. Because subordinates within supervisors share observed and unobserved supervisor characteristics, the errors within the equations are not independent of one another. Biases in estimates and tests of model fit could be expected. What is needed, therefore, is a method that combines multilevel modeling with structural equation modeling. This method is discussed in the next section.

BASIC IDEAS IN MULTILEVEL STRUCTURAL EQUATION MODELING

From the previous discussion, it is evident that a full understanding of the complexities of organizations cannot be obtained from an application of structural equation modeling or multilevel modeling methods separately. Use of either methodology alone would result in different but perhaps equally serious misspecifications. In particular, the use of multilevel modeling alone would preclude the analyst from studying complex indirect and simultaneous effects within and across levels of the system. Utilizing structural equation modeling alone would ignore the clustered sampling schemes that are often used to generate educational data and would result in biased structural regression coefficients (Muthén, 1989). Clearly what is required is a method that combines the best of both methodologies.

In recent years attempts have been made to integrate multilevel modeling with structural equation modeling so as to provide a general methodology that would account for issues of measurement error and simultaneity as well as clustered sampling and population heterogeneity. One of the earliest attempts was Schmidt (1969), who provided maximum likelihood estimation of a general multilevel covariance structure model but did not attempt to introduce group-level variables into the model. More recently, Longford and Muthén (1992) provided computational results for multilevel factor analysis models. Muthén and Satorra (1989) were the first to show the variety of possible special cases of multilevel covariance structure modeling and Muthén (1989) suggested, among other things, how such models could be estimated with existing software.

Multilevel Factor Analysis

As noted earlier, multilevel linear regression models are not capable of explicitly dealing with issues of measurement error. Yet it is not uncommon to find empirical measures of attitudes or behavior to be unreliable. It is well known that measurement error in an outcome variable will affect precision whereas measurement error in input variables will affect the accuracy of the estimates. In any preliminary investigation utilizing structural equation modeling, it may be of interest to examine the reliability and validity of the measurements. One way that this can be accomplished is via factor analysis. The results of a factor analytic investigation can provide valuable information about the contribution of each item to the reliability of the scale, as well as provide evidence for construct validity.

As with the standard application of linear regression to data arising from clustered sampling, the application of factor analysis must also account for clustered effects. For example, a battery of attitude items administered to employees within a sample of businesses can exhibit between business variability. Ignoring the between-business variability in the scores of employees within businesses will result in predictable biases in the parameters of the factor analysis model. To see this, we can consider a general form for a multilevel factor analytic model, described in Muthén and Satorra (1989; see also Muthén, 1991b). Consider the factor analytic model of Equation 6 written as

$$y_{ig} = v + \Lambda \eta_{ig} + \varepsilon_{ig}, \tag{9}$$

where here y_{ig} is a vector of, say, items on a employee attitude survey for the ith employee in the gth business, v is a vector of measurement intercepts, Λ is a matrix of factor loadings, η_{ig} is a vector of latent variables for the ith employee in the gth business, and ε_{ig} is a vector of unique variables for the ith employee in the gth business. We assume that businesses are randomly sampled, and as such, the factor means can be viewed as random effects (varying over businesses). Thus,

$$\eta_{ig} = \kappa_g + \zeta_{ig}, \tag{10}$$

where κ_g is a random component capturing business effects, and ζ_{ig} is a random factor. The factor mean κ_g is allowed to vary across businesses. The between-business variation in the business factor means can be further modeled as a function of business-level variables z_g as

$$\kappa_g = \kappa + \Gamma z_g + \delta_{\kappa g}, \tag{11}$$

where κ is a vector of grand latent variable means, Γ is a matrix of regression coefficients, and $\delta_{\kappa g}$ is a vector of disturbance terms.

Note how this model differs from the one described in Equation 6. Specifically, the model in Equation 11 allows for the factor means to vary across businesses and for there to exist variables at the business level to predict this variation. Thus, the model in Equation 11 represents a very flexible approach for modeling business-level variation in latent variables.

Multilevel Structural Equation Modeling

As noted earlier, multilevel regression models are not capable of capturing the structural complexity within and between levels of organizations. For example, it may be reasonable to assume that variation in the parameters of a structural model at the employee level can be accounted for by variation in business-level variables. Moreover, it may also be reasonable to assume that an entirely different model holds for the relationships among the business variables.

For the purposes of this chapter, we concentrate our discussion on multilevel path analysis. By focusing on this model we are assuming that reliable and valid measures of the variables are available. We recognize that this assumption may be unreasonable for most organizational studies, but as shown in the previous section, multilevel measurement models exist that allow one to examine heterogeneity in measurement structure. Indeed, it may be very informative to examine heterogeneity in measurement structure before forming scales to be used in multilevel path analysis. Moreover, it is possible to combine multilevel factor analysis with multilevel path analysis so as to allow for the specification of a full multilevel structural equation model.

We consider the simple case of the multilevel path analysis model described in Kaplan and Elliott (1997a) and applied to a specific educational problem in Kaplan and Elliott (1997b) in which it is assumed that the levels of the within-group endogenous and exogenous variables vary over between-group units and that there exists a model that holds at the between-group level that is hypothesized to explain variation in the means of the within-group variables. This specific model has been alluded to by Muthén (1994) but has not been explicitly demonstrated. We believe that this particular specification illustrates the broad potential that multilevel structural equation modeling has for study of organizations.

Following Muthén (1994) consider the within-groups model written as

$$y_{ig} = \alpha_g + B_y y_{ig} + \varepsilon_{ig}, \tag{12}$$

where, utilizing the educational achievement example given in Kaplan and Elliott (1997b), y_{ig} is a vector of within-group variables (e.g., science achievement, time spent on homework, etc.) for, say, the ith student in the gth school, α_g is a vector of intercepts or means of the student-level variables that are assumed to vary over schools, B is a matrix of regression coefficients relating the student-level variables to each other, and ε_{ig} is a disturbance term for the student-level equation.

In the language of structural equation modeling via LISREL (Jöreskog & Sörbom, 1993), Equation 12 is referred to as an "all-y" model. In the all-y specification, all variables are treated as endogenous variables. Thus, y_{ig} is a p-dimensional vector of variables, where the first, say, $p - q$ variables are endogenous variables, whereas the last q variables are exogenous variables. The remaining matrices are given appropriate dimensions. So, for example, the first $p - q$ elements of α_g are intercepts in the usual sense of the word, whereas the last q elements of α_g are the means of the exogenous variables. For the purposes of this study, the all-y specification is used to simplify the notation and does not result in any loss of generality (see Kaplan & Elliott, 1997a).

The model as expressed in Equation 12 was referred to by Kaplan and Elliott (1997b) as the *structural form* of the within-school part of the model, representing the statistical relationships among the variables as they are implied by the generic model. The direct effects embodied by the B matrix are those that are typically displayed in path diagrams. For the purposes of this study we wish to model variation in the means of the student-level variables. To accomplish this, it is useful to reexpress Equation 12 in the form

$$y_{ig} = (I - B)^{-1}\alpha_g + (I - B)^{-1}\varepsilon_{ig}, \tag{13}$$

where it is assumed that the inverse of $(I - B)$ exists (see Muthén, 1994). Within the field of econometrics, the specification of Equation 13 is referred to as the *reduced form* of the model.

As stated earlier, we assume that the levels of the student-level variables (contained in α_g) vary across the g schools and that this variation can be explained by school-level variables. Thus, we write a between-school model for the intercepts and means as

$$\alpha_g = \alpha + B_\alpha z_g + \delta_g, \tag{14}$$

where, assuming z_g is centered around the grand mean, α is the grand mean vector across the g schools, z_g are school-level variables (such as school resources and professional teaching conditions), B_α is a matrix of regression coefficients relating z_g to the intercepts of the student variables, and δ_g is a vector of disturbances for the intercept equation.

The model described in Equations 12, 13, and 14 allows intercepts to be expressed as a function of school-level variables. A unique feature of the model presented here, and alluded to by Muthén (1994), is that the between-school variables z_g are allowed to follow a separate between-school simultaneous equation model that can be written as

$$z_g = \tau + B_z z_g + u_g, \tag{15}$$

where, assuming that the inverse of $(I - B_z)$ is nonsingular, can be reexpressed in reduced form as

$$z_g = (I - B_z)^{-1}\tau + (I - B_z)^{-1}u_g, \tag{16}$$

where τ is a vector of intercepts and means for the school-level equations, B_z a matrix of coefficients relating school-level variables to each other, and u_g is a vector of disturbances for the school-level equation.

After a series of substitutions, Kaplan and Elliott (1997a) arrived at the expression for the ith student's score in the gth school taking into account the structural relationships within as well as between schools. This final model can be written as

$$y_{ig} = (I - B_y)^{-1}\alpha + \Pi\tau + \Pi u_g + (I - B_y)^{-1}\delta_g + (I - B_y)^{-1}\varepsilon_g, \tag{17}$$

where $\Pi = (I - B_y)^{-1}B_\alpha(I - B_z)^{-1}$. Kaplan and Elliott referred to Π as a *multilevel total effects matrix,* where the total effects of changes in between-group exogenous variables on within-group endogenous variables are manifested through other between- and within-group variables. Technical details regarding parameter estimation can be found in Muthén (1994) (see also Kaplan & Elliott, 1997a).

An Example of Multilevel Structural Equation Modeling

The model described in Equations 12–17 was recently applied to a problem in education policy analysis. Specifically, Kaplan and Elliott (1997b) used this model to examine the validity of education indicators of science achievement. The problem was motivated by an increasing desire to monitor the quality of science education in the United States through the collection of policy-relevant measures of students, teachers, and schools (see, e.g., Shavelson, McDonnell, & Oakes, 1989).

Kaplan and Elliott (1997b), building on suggestions by de Neuville (1978), argued that it was essential for the assessment of the validity of these indicators to embed them in an explicit model of the education system. Clearly, given the complexities of the education system in the United States, such a model would be multilevel as well as structural. Utilizing data from NELS:88 (NCES, 1988), Kaplan and Elliott (1997b) specified separate within-school and between-school models via Equations 12 and 15 that were found to have adequate fit. These models were then linked together in a full multilevel structural model via Equation 14. This full multilevel model was found to fit the data quite well, but the parameter estimates of the cross-level effects were quite small.

A unique feature of the Kaplan and Elliott (1997b) example was the use of Equation 17 for what they termed *policy-relevant simulations*. Specifically, following de Neuville's (1978) suggestion, Kaplan and Elliott (1997b) specified policy-relevant changes in between-school exogenous variables and examined changes in between-school and within-school endogenous variables. As noted before, these changes are manifested through the multilevel total effects matrix Π. The results of the simulations were modest but encouraging. Specifically, changes in the between-school exogenous variables resulted in very small changes in the outcome variables of interest. It was argued that these modest effects were due to a complexity of factors including specification errors within and between the levels of the system as well as measurement issues in the outcome variables themselves. Nevertheless, Kaplan and Elliott argued that multilevel structural equation modeling in conjunction with policy-relevant simulations showed great promise in increasing our understanding of the structure of organizations.

GROWTH MODELING AS A MULTILEVEL STRUCTURAL MODEL

Growth curve modeling has been advocated for many years by researchers such as Bryk and Raudenbush (1987), Rogosa, Brandt, and Zimowski (1982), and Willett (1988) for the study of interindividual differences in change (see also Willett & Sayer, 1994, for a review). The specification of growth models also can be viewed as falling within the class of multilevel linear models (Bryk & Raudenbush, 1992). Under this specification, time is viewed as a *Level 1* unit of analysis. That is, the individual becomes the context within which changes in that individual over time are observed. The Level 1 model can be written as

$$y_{ip} = \pi_{0p} + \pi_{1p} t_i + \varepsilon_{ip}, \tag{18}$$

where y_{ip} is the outcome of interest for person p at time i, π_{0p} represents the initial status at time $t = 0$, π_{1p} represents the growth trajectory, and ε_{ip} is the disturbance term. Quadratic growth can be incorporated into the model by extending the specification as

$$y_{ip} = \pi_{0p} + \pi_{1p} t_i + \pi_{2p} t_i^2 + \varepsilon_{ip}, \tag{19}$$

where π_{2p} captures the curvilinearity of the growth trajectory. Higher order terms can also be incorporated.

The specification of Equation 18 can be further extended to handle predictors of individual differences in the initial status and growth trajectory parameters. In the terminology of multilevel modeling, individuals would be considered *Level 2* units of analysis. In this case, two models are specified, one for the initial status parameter and one for the growth trajectory parameter. Consider, for example, a single time-invariant predictor of initial status and growth for person p, denoted as x_p. An example of such a predictor might be gender. Then, the Level 2 model can be written as

$$\pi_{0p} = \mu_{\pi0} + \gamma_{\pi0}x_p + \zeta_{0p}, \tag{20}$$

and

$$\pi_{1p} = \mu_{\pi1} + \gamma_{\pi1}x_p + \zeta_{1p}, \tag{21}$$

where $\mu_{\pi0}$ and $\mu_{\pi1}$ are intercept parameters representing population true status and population growth when x_p is zero; $\gamma_{\pi0}$ and $\gamma_{\pi1}$ are slopes relating x_p to initial status and growth, respectively.

The model just specified can be further extended to allow individuals to be nested in groups. In this case, groups become a *Level 3* unit of analysis. Finally, the model can incorporate time-varying predictors of change. In the achievement example, such a time-varying predictor might be absenteeism rates across the four grades. Thus, this model can be used to study such issues as the influence of school-level characteristics and student-level invariant and varying characteristics on initial status and growth in achievement over time.

The models described in Equations 18–21 can be incorporated in such standard multilevel modeling programs as HLM (Bryk et al., 1996). Recently, work by Muthén (1991a) and Willett and Sayer (1994) has shown how the general growth model described earlier can be incorporated into a structural equation modeling framework. The advantages of utilizing a structural equation modeling perspective are (a) it is easy to implement with existing software such as LISREL (Jöreskog & Sörbom, 1993) or LISCOMP (Muthén, 1987), (b) it provides maximum likelihood estimates of the parameters of the growth model, and (c) the goodness-of-fit statistics and other auxiliary measures generally available in structural equation modeling software allow for a wide variety of substantively interesting hypotheses to be tested, including the general test of whether the growth model fits the observed mean vector and covariance matrix of the data.

In what follows, the specification proposed by Willett and Sayer (1994) is described. The broad details of the specification are provided, however the reader is referred to Willett and Sayer's article for more detail. It should be noted that the specification proposed by Willett and Sayer utilizes LISREL notation. As they correctly pointed out, the growth model proposed in their article and discussed here can be reparameterized to fit into other full latent variable structural equation modeling software programs such as LISCOMP and EQS (Bentler, 1989).

The Level 1 individual growth model given in Equation 1 can be written in the form of a LISREL measurement model as

$$y = \tau_y + \Lambda_y \eta + \varepsilon, \tag{22}$$

where y is a vector of variables representing the empirical growth record for person p. For example, y could be science achievement scores for person p at the 7th, 8th, 9th, and 10th grades. In this specification, τ_y is a null vector, Λ_y is a fixed matrix containing a column of ones and a column of constant time values. Assuming that time is centered at the 7th grade, the time constants would be 0, 1, 2, and 3. The matrix η contains the parameters π_{0p} and π_{1p} and the vector ε contains measurement errors, where it is assumed that $Cov (\varepsilon)$ is a diagonal matrix of constant measurement error variances. Because this specification results in the growth parameters being absorbed into the latent variable vector η, this model is sometimes referred to as a latent variable growth model (see, e.g., Muthén, 1991a).

Next, it is possible to utilize the standard LISREL structural model specification to handle the Level 2 components of the growth model, corresponding to Equations 20 and 21. Considering the Level 2 model without the vector of predictor variables x, the model can be written as

$$\eta = \alpha + B\eta + \zeta, \tag{23}$$

where η is specified as before, α contains the population initial status and growth parameters $\mu_{\pi 0}$ and $\mu_{\pi 1}$, B is a null matrix, and ζ is a vector of deviations of the parameters from their respective population means. Again, this specification has the effect of parameterizing the true population initial status parameter and growth parameter into LISREL's α vector. Finally, the covariance matrix of ζ contains the variances and covariances of true initial status and growth.

The Level 2 model given in Equation 23 does not contain predictor variables. The latent variable growth model can, however, be extended to include exogenous predictors of initial status and growth. To incorporate exogenous predictors requires using the x-measurement model in LISREL. Specifically, the model is written as

$$x = \tau_x + \Lambda_x \xi + \delta, \tag{24}$$

where here x is a vector of exogenous predictors, τ_x contains the mean vector, Λ_x is an identity matrix, ξ contains the exogenous predictors deviated from their means, and δ is a null vector. This specification has the effect of placing the centered exogenous variables in the ξ (Willett & Sayer, 1994).

Finally, the full specification of the structural equation model given in Equation 15 can be utilized to model the predictors of true initial status and true growth, where, due to the centering of the exogenous predictors, it retains its interpretation as the population mean vector of the individual initial status and growth parameters (see Willett & Sayer, 1994).

An Example of Growth Modeling

Recently, Kaplan and George (in press) provided an example of growth modeling to an educational problem. Specifically, Kaplan and George were interested in modeling the increase in science achievement scores from 7th grade to 11th grade suggested by data from the Longitudinal Study of American Youth (Miller, Hoffer, Sucher, Brown, & Nelson, 1992). In addition, Kaplan and George (in press) provided *ex post simulation* statistics from the economic forecasting literature (see Pindyck & Rubinfeld, 1991) to evaluate the quality of the model. These ex post simulation statistics provide a variety of measures for gauging the fit of the model-predicted trajectory to the observed trajectory by capturing overall mean, variation, and covariation differences between the two trajectories.

Kaplan and George (in press) proposed six models to describe the increase observed in science achievement scores over the five grades. The first model (Model 1) was a baseline no-predictor model that simply fits Equation 18 to the observed trend. The Model 1 predicted line was found to fit the observed trend fairly well as revealed by the ex post simulation statistics. However, the observed trend shows a slight curvilinearity with science achievement flattening out around the 9th grade. A curvilinear model (Model 2) was fit based on Equation 19. The Model 2 predicted trajectory was found to fit better than Model 1.

In addition to the no-predictor models, Kaplan and George (in press) fit four models that included time-invariant and time-varying predictors. Model 3 was a time-invariant model including background variables of gender, mother's education, and a measure of science resources in the home. This model was proposed to explain the variation in the initial status and growth trajectory and corresponds to Equations 20 and 21. Kaplan and George (in press) found this model to actually degrade the fit compared to Models 1 and 2.

Next, the time-varying predictors models were then explored. Model 4 included measures of the students' attitudes toward science and measures of the degree to which the students' peers "push" the student in science. These measures were obtained at each time point. The time-invariant measures were not included. The model-generated trajectory was found to fit the observed trajectory fairly well on the basis of the ex post simulation statistics. Model 5 included measures of the degree to which parents push their children academically and measures of the degree to which their science teacher pushes them in science. Model 5 was found to fit better overall compared to Model 4. Finally, Model 6 included all of the time-invariant and time-varying predictors. This model was only a marginal improvement compared to Model 5. Kaplan and George (in press) concluded on the basis of the ex post simulation statistics and other measures of model fit that Model 5 (parent and teacher push) best captured the growth trajectory science achievement scores.

CONCLUSION: THE POTENTIAL OF MULTILEVEL METHODS FOR BUSINESS RESEARCH

The purpose of this chapter was to provide a general overview of multilevel methods—including multilevel regression modeling and extensions to multilevel structural modeling and growth modeling. The examples given in this chapter have come primarily from the field of education, reflecting the author's expertise as well as the fact that the major developments and applications have come from the education field. Nevertheless, it is worth considering how multilevel methods might illuminate business research.

Clearly, businesses constitute hierarchically organized social systems with employees nested in work units that are in turn nested in businesses. Consider the simple issue of whether employee satisfaction with work conditions influences productivity. We might first be interested in the measurement properties of an employee satisfaction survey. As we noted earlier in the section on multilevel factor analysis, concern might center on whether the measurement parameters vary over businesses. Assuming enough employees within work units (or businesses), a multilevel factor analysis could lead one to first study the role that work-unit-level variables play in explaining variation in the measurement parameters. If significant work-unit-level effects are present, one might need to interpret the employee satisfaction survey separately for each work unit under investigation.

Assuming that the employee satisfaction survey can be reasonably applied to the whole sample of employees, the next question to be answered is the relationship between employee satisfaction and productivity. Here one might wish to employ the intercept- and slopes-as-outcomes model. The Level 1 model would specify the relationship between productivity and employee satisfaction (and perhaps other predictors of productivity) for each employee. The intercept would represent average productivity when employee satisfaction is zero (or some other reasonable choice of centering). The slope is then the relationship between employee satisfaction and productivity. It may be of interest to specify a Level 2 between-work-unit model that accounts for variation in the intercept and slope across work units in terms of work-unit-level variables. Such work-unit-level variables might include attitudes and dispositions of the supervisors such as the degree of autonomy that supervisors give subordinates.

As the number of predictors in either level of the equation increase, it might be desirable to entertain the possibility that certain structural (i.e., causal) relationships exist within levels. That is, it may be reasonable to assume that predictor variables in the productivity equation are, in fact, outcomes for other equations. This type of reasoning would then yield a system of structural equations and then naturally to multilevel structural equation modeling. It may be relatively straightforward to consider this possibility for the employee-level model. In this case one can simply let the parameters of the employee-level structural model vary over work units without necessarily specifying a separate work-unit-level model (see, e.g., Muthén, 1994). If one can isolate a work-unit-level outcome as an important predictor of variation within work units, and if this outcome itself can be expressed as a structural model, then the specification described earlier and applied in Kaplan and Elliott (1997b) might be useful.

Finally, it may be reasonable to assume that a large business organization would wish to track the productivity of its workforce over a specified period of time. Such data would constitute a longitudinal study of the factors that determine initial rate of productivity as well as the growth rate in productivity over the time span. As we noted in the section Growth Modeling as a Multilevel Structural Model, we can model initial productivity and the rate of change in productivity as a function of time-invariant predictors. Such time-invariant predictors might include the educational background of the employee. In addition, one may wish to model the impact of time-varying variables on productivity at each time point. Such time-varying variables in this context might very well include employee satisfaction, which we could argue changes over time.

These examples do not exhaust the range of studies that are possible using multilevel methods. Indeed, numerous interesting submodels were not explored in this chapter. Moreover, there exist a number of important methodological issues that might limit the utility of this method to business data. A major problem that could conceivably plague business researchers interested in this methodology is the issue of sample size. Specifically, sufficient numbers of within-group and between-group units must be available to ensure stable estimates of parameters. In addition, the problem of unequal within-group units must be considered. Research into these issues is underway and guidelines are not yet readily available. It is only a matter of time, however, when methodologists and statisticians will provide advice that will serve to circumscribe the use of these methods.

These methodological issues notwithstanding, what will determine the success of multilevel methodology will depend on whether it illuminates our understanding of the substantive problem of interest. We have witnessed how multilevel regression models provided great insights into the process of schooling. It remains to be seen if multilevel structural modeling, in the forms presented in this chapter, can also yield insights into the complex structure of organizational systems.

ACKNOWLEDGMENT

This material is based on work supported by the National Science Foundation under Grant REC-9550472. Any opinions, findings, and conclusions or recommendations are those of the author and do not necessarily reflect the views of the National Science Foundation.

REFERENCES

Aitkin, M., & Longford, N. (1986). Statistical modelling issues in school effectiveness studies (with discussion). *Journal of the Royal Statistical Society, Series A, 149,* 1–43.

Bentler, P. M. (1989). *EQS structural equations program manual.* Los Angeles: BMDP Statistical Software.

Bock, R. D. (1989). *Multilevel analysis of educational data.* San Diego: Academic Press.

Bollen, K. A. (1989). *Structural equations with latent variables.* New York: Wiley.

Bollen, K. A., & Long, J. S. (1993). *Testing structural equation models.* Newbury Park, CA: Sage.

Bryk, A. S., & Raudenbush, S. W. (1987). Application of hierarchical linear models to assessing change. *Psychological Bulletin, 101,* 147–158.

Bryk, A. S., & Raudenbush, S. W. (1992). *Hierarchical linear models: Applications and data analysis models.* Newbury Park, CA: Sage.

Bryk, A. S., Raudenbush, S. W., & Congdon, R. T. (1996). *HLM: Hierarchical linear modeling with the HLM/2L and HLM/3L programs.* Chicago: Scientific Software, Inc.

Coleman, J. S., Hoffer, T., & Kilgore, S. B. (1982). *High school achievement: Public, Catholic, and other private schools compared.* New York: Basic Books.

de Neuville, J. I. (1978). Validating policy indicators. *Policy Sciences, 10,* 171–188.

Eisenberger, R., Huntington, R., Hutchison, S., & Sowa, D. (1986). Perceived organizational support. *Journal of Applied Psychology, 71,* 500–507.

Goldberger, A. S., & Duncan, O. D. (1973). *Structural equation models in the social sciences.* New York: Seminar Press.

Hoyle, R. H. (1995). *Structural equation modeling: Concepts, issues, and applications.* Newbury Park, CA: Sage.

Jöreskog, K. G. (1977). Structural equation modeling in the social sciences: Specification, estimation, and testing. In P. R. Krishnaiah (Ed.), *Applications of statistics* (pp. 265–287). Amsterdam: North-Holland.

Jöreskog, K. G., & Sörbom, D. (1993). *LISREL 8: User's reference guide.* Chicago: Scientific Software, Inc.

Kaplan, D., & Elliott, P. E. (1997a). A didactic example of multilevel structural equation modeling applicable to the study of organizations. *Structural Equation Modeling: A Multidisciplinary Journal, 4,* 1–24.

Kaplan, D., & Elliott, P. E. (1997b). A model-based approach to validating educational indicators using multilevel structural equation modeling. *Journal of Educational and Behavioral Statistics, 22,* 323–348.

Kaplan, D., & George, R. (in press). Evaluating latent variable growth models through ex-post simulation. *Journal of Educational and Behavioral Statistics.*

Kreft, I. G. G. (1995). *The effects of centering in multilevel analysis: Is the public school the loser or the winner.* Paper presented at the annual meeting of the American Educational Research Association, San Francisco.

Lee, V. E., & Bryk, A. S. (1989). A multilevel model of the social distribution of high school achievement. *Sociology of Education, 62,* 175–192.

Liden, R. C., & Maslyn, J. M. (1993, August). *Scale development for a multidimensional measure of leader-member exchange.* Paper presented at the annual meeting of the Academy of Management, Atlanta.

Longford, N. T., & Muthén, B. (1992). Factor analysis for clustered observations. *Psychometrika, 57,* 581–597.

Marcoulides, G. A., & Schumacker, R. E. (1996). *Advanced structural equation modeling: Issues and techniques.* Mahwah, NJ: Lawrence Erlbaum Associates.

Miller, J. D., Hoffer, T., Sucher, R. W., Brown, K. G., & Nelson, C. (1992). *LSAY codebook: Student, parent, and teacher data for 1992 cohort two for longitudinal years one through four (1987–1991).* IL: Northern Illinois University.

Mowday, R. T., Steers, R. M., & Porter, L. W. (1979). The measurement of organizational commitment. *Journal of Vocational Behavior, 14,* 224–247.

Muthén, B. (1987). *LISCOMP. Analysis of linear structural equations using a comprehensive measurement model.* Chicago: Scientific Software, Inc.

Muthén, B. (1989). Latent variable modeling in heterogenous populations. *Psychometrika, 54,* 557–585.

Muthén, B. (1991a). Analysis of longitudinal data using latent variable models with varying parameters. In L. Collins & J. Horn (Eds.), *Best methods for the analysis of change: Recent advances, unanswered questions, future directions* (pp. 1–17). Washington, DC: American Psychological Association.

Muthén, B. (1991b). Multilevel factor analysis of class and student achievement components. *Journal of Educational Measurement, 28,* 338–354.

Muthén, B. (1994). Multilevel covariance structure analysis. *Sociological Methods & Research, 22,* 376–398.

Muthén, B., & Satorra, A. (1989). Multilevel aspects of varying parameters in structural models. In R. D. Bock (Ed.), *Multilevel analysis of educational data* (pp. 87–99). San Diego: Academic Press.

National Center for Education Statistics. (1988). *National education longitudinal study of 1988.* Washington, DC: Author.

Pindyck, R. S., & Rubinfeld, D. L. (1991). *Econometric models and economic forecasts.* New York: McGraw-Hill.

Rogosa, D. R., Brandt, D., & Zimowski, M. (1982). A growth curve approach to the measurement of change. *Psychological Bulletin, 90,* 726–748.

Schmidt, W. H. (1969). *Covariance structure analysis of the multivariate random effects model.* Unpublished doctoral dissertation, University of Chicago, Chicago.

Settoon, R. P., Bennett, N., & Liden, R. C. (1996). Social exchange in organizations: Perceived organizational support, leader-member exchange, and employee reciprocity. *Journal of Applied Psychology, 81,* 219–227.

Shavelson, R. J., McDonnell, L. M., & Oakes, J. (1989). *Indicators for monitoring mathematics and science education*. Santa Monica, CA: Rand Corporation.

Willett, J. B. (1988). Questions and answers in the measurement of change. In E. Rothkopf (Ed.), *Review of research in education* (Vol. 15, pp. 345–422). Washington, DC: American Educational Research Association.

Willett, J. B., & Sayer, A. G. (1994). Using covariance structure analysis to detect correlates and predictors of individual change over time. *Psychological Bulletin, 116*(2), 363–381.

Williams, L. J., & Anderson, S. E. (1991). Job satisfaction and organizational commitment as predictors of organizational citizenship and in-role behaviors. *Journal of Management, 17,* 601–617.

CHAPTER TWELVE

Modeling Longitudinal Data by Latent Growth Curve Methods

John J. McArdle
University of Virginia

SUMMARY

The purpose of this chapter is to introduce some recent trends in Latent Growth Curve Models (LGM). Basic features of Structural Equation Modeling (SEM) are used to describe these models. To illustrate this type of longitudinal data analysis, a small sample of data from the National Institutes of Health (NIH) are used. These data include the budgets of 20 NIH Institutes and up to 6 occasions of measurement (1992 to 1998). These data are analyzed using maximum-likelihood estimation (MLE) available with the LISREL-8 (Jöreskog & Sörbom, 1993) and Mx (Neale, 1993) computer programs. In a first analysis, standard autoregressive changes models are described and fitted. In a second analysis, standard LGMs are fitted to the same data using average cross-products (i.e., moments). In a third analysis, these same data are then explored using raw data and fitted with unbalanced pedigree techniques (Neale, 1993). More complex dynamic model extensions are also described.

INTRODUCTION

Overview

There are many ways to collect data on changes over time. This includes long-term longitudinal studies of exactly the same individuals measured on exactly the same variables, as well as a variety of approximations to this ideal design (see McArdle & Woodcock, 1997; Nesselroade & Baltes, 1979). Longitudinal data are now often collected by a thorough reexamination of historical or archival records (see Elder, Pavalko, & Cliff, 1991; Hill, 1992). There are also many ways to look for and understand patterns and broad trends in such data. One common approach used throughout all sciences— the physical, biological, and social sciences—is the use of mathematical and statistical models. There are a wide variety of alternative models for the analysis of longitudinal data (see Collins & Horn, 1991; Diggle, Liang, & Zeger, 1994; Dwyer, Feinleib, Lippert, & Hoffmeister, 1992; Jones et al., 1991; Lindsey, 1993; Varian, 1993). This chapter provides an introduction to longitudinal analyses using *latent growth models* (LGM; see McArdle & Epstein, 1987; Meredith & Tisak, 1990).

The LGMs examined here are based on organizing trends around group and individual differences in growth and change functions. These models have a long history in psychometrics (see Tucker, 1966), statistics (Rao, 1958), and economics (see McArdle, 1988), but they have only recently been used in a wide variety of applications (see Browne & Arminger, 1995; McArdle, 1988, 1989; McArdle & Aber, 1990; McArdle & Anderson, 1990; McArdle & Hamagami, 1991, 1992; McArdle & Woodcock, 1997; Meredith & Tisak, 1990). Part of the reason for this recent upsurge of interest in LGMs is the possibility of fitting these models using standard computer software for *structural equation models* (SEM; see Jöreskog & Sörbom, 1993; Neale, 1993). These relatively new techniques are illustrated here and only minimal technical details are presented.

A small sample of longitudinal data on financial budgets is presented for the purposes of illustration. Following a brief description of a standard autoregressive model, the same data are analyzed with three alternative latent growth models for longitudinal data. These models are compared and contrasted using the numerical examples, and a variety of alternative models are also discussed.

These longitudinal analyses are initially carried out using the *LISREL-8* computer program by Jöreskog and Sörbom (1979, 1993). The LISREL computer program series is well known and may be the most widely used computer program for SEM. LISREL input scripts are now available in many published sources (e.g., McArdle & Hamagami, 1992; Neale & Cardon, 1992).

These analyses are also carried out using the *Mx* computer program by Neale (1993). Mx is a much newer program but it accomplishes many of the same tasks in the same way, and it is still in the public domain (i.e., free; see Hamagami, 1997). But Mx is also used here because it includes advanced provisions for *raw scores* and *unbalanced data* (i.e., a pedigree approach modeled after Lange et al., 1976). This feature allows a direct examination of SEM *outliers* as well as structural analysis with *incomplete data*.

The term *structure* in an SEM refers to the precise way a model proscribes a pattern for the statistical expectations about the data (see McArdle & Aber,

1990; Wright, 1982). The algebraic approach to generating model expectations here is based on a simplified SEM approach termed *RAM notation* (McArdle & Boker, 1990; McArdle & McDonald, 1984). Perhaps most critically, this RAM approach to algebra and graphics makes models with covariances and means, including latent growth models, easier to understand and analyze.

Computer program scripts for a variety of longitudinal analyses are listed and discussed here. These are not standard programs but use only the most basic principles presented here. This simple approach also allows us to deal with some further complexities of multilevel longitudinal data (for examples, see McArdle & Hamagami, 1996; McArdle & Prescott, 1996; McArdle & Woodcock, 1997). These illustrations are not intended to be advanced or technical, but are designed to convey a few of the main themes of longitudinal analysis with latent growth models.

A Sample of Longitudinal Data

In any longitudinal analysis we typically assume some subjects ($n = 1$ to N) have been independently sampled with observed scores $Y_{n,t}$ at time t. The scores Y are usually assumed to have been repeatedly measured under the same conditions and in the same units at all times t. From such measurements we should be able to create a variety of statistical indicators describing the time series, including means (M_t), standard deviations (S_t), and pairwise correlations ($R_{t,t+j}$).

All longitudinal data for all analyses presented here are listed in Table 12.1. This table is a copy of one of the budget pages of a recent publication of the National Institutes of Health (NIH) (from Dr. Virginia Cain, OBSSR-NIH; personal communication, May 1997). The first column lists the acronyms of 20 specific institutes at NIH (e.g., NCI stands for the "National Cancer Institute"). The next seven columns give the actual or best estimate of the total budget allocation for each of the past 7 years. Due to the size of the budget at some of these institutes (e.g., NIDA, NCI, etc.), these allocations are listed in thousands of dollars each. The last column lists the percentage change in the last year (1997–1998), and the last row lists the total dollar amounts.

There are many questions that can be examined using these data, and one of these deals with the possibility of a "long-run trend" in the funding cycles of these institutes. In order to be clearer about this focus, these longitudinal trends are plotted in Fig. 12.1. In Fig. 12.1(a), the data for the current estimates (year 1997) are presented in a stem-and-leaf form (Tukey, 1977). This plot shows something that is hard to see in the table—the extreme skewness of the raw dollar figures. In Fig. 12.1(b), the raw score data of Table 12.1 are redisplayed using a connected line for each institute. This plot also shows a few patterns that are hard to understand from the table of numbers. For

TABLE 12.1
DHHS—National Institutes of Health: Health and Behavior Research

Participating ICDs	1992 Actual	1993 Actual	1994 Actual	1995 Estimate	1996 Actual	1997 Estimate	1998 Estimate	Change 97/98
NCI	$80,173	118,914	129,428	129,887	140,729	144,700	149,000	3.0%
NHLBI	67,929	79,225	84,854	87,300	87,200	92,450	94,700	2.4%
NIDR	6,261	6,142	6,367	6,522	9,567	10,262	10,714	4.4%
NIDDK	16,600	16,900	17,600	18,100	25,600	27,000	27,500	1.9%
NINDS	40,357	34,421	31,134	32,030	22,114	22,929	23,406	2.1%
NIAID	6,314	8,340	11,057	11,378	8,299	8,631	8,804	2.0%
NIGMS	4,313	4,313	4,041	4,150	4,389	4,637	4,745	2.3%
NICHD	56,000	58,194	56,954	58,700	72,761	77,400	79,400	2.6%
NEI	6,484	9,142	9,219	9,555	5,952	6,325	6,474	2.4%
NIEHS	7,022	9,800	7,390	7,390	9,392	9,815	10,060	2.5%
NIA	61,029	65,051	66,936	68,940	69,324	71,400	72,110	1.0%
NIAMS	6,604	5,805	4,591	4,730	7,495	7,870	8,060	2.4%
NIDCD	7,725	10,560	6,720	6,976	5,425	5,760	5,944	3.2%
NIMH*	163,433	156,638	52,277	54,204	72,658	78,010	81,501	4.5%
NIAAA	33,027	34,000	56,945	59,000	66,343	67,000	67,000	0.0%
NIDA	168,472	163,210	179,363	185,600	189,442	202,000	215,500	6.7%
NCRR	22,982	24,069	21,216	21,913	27,817	29,811	30,606	2.7%
NINR	20,376	21,377	21,463	22,200	8,321	8,900	9,120	2.5%
FIC	697	568	905	932	1,454	1,547	1,562	1.0%
NLM	2,650	6,544	7,600	8,166	6,502	6,502	6,502	0.0%
TOTAL	778,448	833,213	776,060	797,673	840,784	882,949	912,708	3.4%

Note. Dollars in thousands. From NIH Budget Office. Reprinted by permission. *NIMH revised its 1994–1995 figures due to a definition clarification/change.

Fig.[1a]: NIH Institute Budgets in 1997

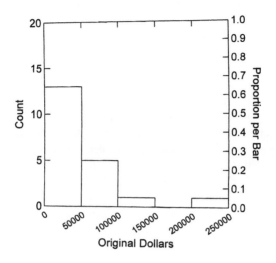

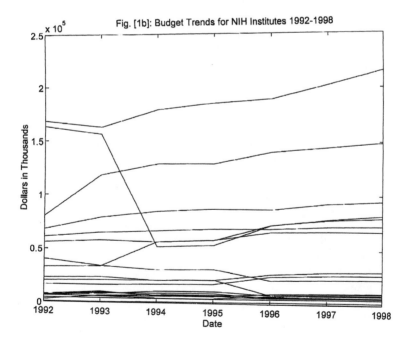

FIG. 12.1. (a) NIH institute budgets in 1997. (b) Budget trends for NIH institutes 1992–1998.

example, the top line is the budget trend for NIDA, and it certainly looks as if this is increasing over the time period 1992–1998. The next highest initial line is for NIMH, and this line shows a rapid change in 1993.

The visual approach is very effective in describing important aspects of the longitudinal data (see Cleveland, 1993). Given data at this level of aggregation, we might be best off to simply describe the pattern of each separate curve. Although this kind of descriptive analysis is useful, and it might tell us a great deal about each institute, this approach might not be the most effective method for dealing with the broader trends apparent in all NIH budgets. In order to move in this direction we deal with these data on a more formal statistical basis.

Excluding the last row and column, Table 12.1 includes 140 independent pieces of information that can be placed in a 20×7 raw data matrix (Y). These data are "counts" of dollars with no possible negatives, and these may be effectively transformed before further analysis. That is, "Since we are dealing with COUNTS, we always START by at least taking (square) ROOTS" (Tukey, 1977, p. 543). Figure 12.2(a) is a histogram of the original data transformed using (a) a rescaling into millions of dollars followed by (b) taking the square root of these numbers (i.e., $Y_t = \sqrt{\$_t / 1,000}$). As expected, this new plot displays less skewness and is more nearly symmetric about the center. Figure 12.2(b) next redisplays the transformed data in a longitudinal connected line for each of the 20 institutes. In contrast to the raw data in Fig. 12.1(b), this transformation allows the trends for all 20 institutes to be more clearly displayed in the same plot [Fig. 12.2(b)]. Other transformations (e.g., logs) have a similar behavior and may be appropriate as well.

Some statistical features of these transformed data are listed in Table 12.2. These include the mean (M_t) and standard deviations (D_t) at all 7 years, as well as a matrix of correlations ($R_{t,t+k}$) among all pairs of time points. This is an unusual correlation matrix because all of these correlations are high ($r > .9$), and some are almost unity ($r > .999$). This result obtains in part because we have a small aggregate sample where the budget lines do not cross very much; that is, there is a high degree of *tracking* in these trends. Unfortunately, the lack of individual differences in these data lead to a nearly singular correlation matrix (i.e., one or more of the eigenvalues are close to zero) and we can run into numerical problems in later analyses. Incidentally, the untransformed data were also ill-conditioned (the determinant $|R| = 1.67 * 10^{-16}$), and these square root data are slightly better conditioned ($|R| = 1.74 * 10^{-16}$). Other transformations have similar problems (i.e., using log transformations, $|R| = 4.43 * 10^{-17}$) but still might be appropriate on a substantive basis.

Table 12.2 also includes a covariance matrix (C) formed from the deviations and correlations (C = DRD'). This matrix is used in analyses where we want to retain the information in the changes in the variance over time. Finally, the final matrix in Table 12.2 is an average *sums of squares and*

Fig.[2a]: Transformed Budgets in 1997

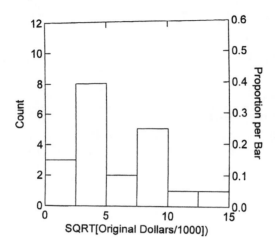

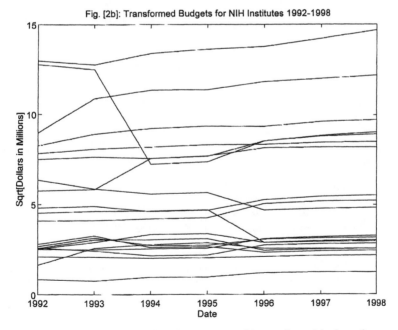

FIG. 12.2. (a) Transformed budgets in 1997. (b) Transformed budgets for NIH institutes 1992–1998.

TABLE 12.2
Selected Statistics Calculated From Budget Reports
From the National Institutes of Health

(a) Means and Standard Deviations (N = 20; Y = √$/1000)

Year	1992	1993	1994	1995	1996	1997	1998
Means	5.192	5.435	5.278	5.355	5.440	5.575	5.654
SDs	3.549	3.572	3.395	3.436	3.619	3.709	3.793

(b) Correlations Over Time (N = 20; Y = √$/1000)

Year	1992	1993	1994	1995	1996	1997	1998
1992	1.0000						sym.
1993	0.989	1.0000					
1994	0.905	0.931	1.0000				
1995	0.906	0.932	0.999	1.0000			
1996	0.913	0.936	0.982	0.982	1.0000		
1997	0.917	0.939	0.981	0.981	0.999	1.0000	
1998	0.919	0.940	0.981	0.981	0.999	0.999	1.0000

(c) Resulting Covariance Matrix

Year	1992	1993	1994	1995	1996	1997	1998
1992	12.60						sym.
1993	12.54	12.76					
1994	10.90	11.29	11.52				
1995	11.05	11.44	11.66	11.80			
1996	11.72	12.10	12.06	12.20	13.10		
1997	12.07	12.44	12.36	12.50	13.42	13.76	
1998	12.37	12.74	12.63	12.78	13.72	14.07	14.39

(d) Resulting Augmented Moment (Average Cross-Products) Matrix

Year	K = 1	1992	1993	1994	1995	1996	1997	1998
K = 1	1.000							sym.
1992	5.192	39.552						
1993	5.435	40.757	42.298					
1994	5.278	38.300	39.979	39.379				
1995	5.355	38.847	40.537	39.922	40.474			
1996	5.440	39.967	41.666	40.774	41.335	42.693		
1997	5.575	41.008	42.733	41.777	42.353	43.749	44.836	
1998	5.654	41.722	43.464	42.473	43.059	44.479	45.588	46.355

cross-products (SSCP) or central moments matrix (W). This moments matrix is conveniently formed from the means and covariances (W = C + MM′) or directly from the raw data (W = YY′N^{-1}). A unit contrast (K = 1) has been added as a variable to these data so we can easily separate out the mean vector in the first column from the rest of the covariances and mean squares in the other parts of the matrix.

Structural Equation Modeling Programs

There are many statistical approaches for dealing with the previous longitudinal data. In this presentation we discuss only approaches based on contemporary structural equation modeling (see Jöreskog & Sörbom, 1979; Loehlin, 1992). There are now many different SEM computer programs, including some with friendly and colorful names (see Hamagami, 1997). But all such computer programs have common technical features and many of these programs can be used for further analysis here.

One relatively easy way to input these kinds of models to the SEM computer programs used here is to write the model equations in a matrix form using RAM notation (McArdle & Boker, 1990). This notation allows the user to describe any linear system of equations using only three parameter matrices (A, S, and F). Although these three model matrices are not intended to have any substantive meaning, they are each directly related to the graphic elements in a *path diagram*: (a) all one-headed arrows are included in A, (b) all two-headed arrows are included in S, and (c) the separation of the squares from the circles is included in F. This approach is practically useful because it is an easy way to *automatically* generate structural expectations for the covariances and means of a model (see Appendix).

These SEM programs allow us to obtain optimal statistical estimates for model parameters defined in the previous fashion. Estimation of parameters, especially optimal estimation, turns out to be a relatively complex issue. (Instead of detailing these issues here, we provide references to other work and a few critical details in the Appendix.)

In broad terms, the SEM computer programs used here (e.g., LISREL-8 and Mx) provide *maximum-likelihood estimates* (MLE) of all model parameters by iteratively minimizing a *fitting function* ($\mathcal{F}_{ml}$) based on weighted differences between the observations and the expectations. At some final solution point, the obtained numerical results are then used to form an approximate *likelihood ratio test* (LRT) statistic

$$LRT \approx 2(N - 1) \times \mathcal{F}_{ml} \tag{1}$$

with the *degrees of freedom* (df) for v observed variables and p unknown parameters calculated by

$$df = \frac{v * (v + 1)}{2} - p. \tag{2}$$

Under assumptions often based on the multivariate normality of the random error terms (U_t here), this statistical model provides an index of the *goodness of fit* between the overall model and the data (see Appendix).

These *LRT* indices and their differences (*dLRT*) are usually compared to a chi-square (χ^2) distribution for a probability interpretation of the adequacy of specific models. The associated chi-square test of fit examines a very rigid hypothesis of "perfect fit," so we can also employ an index of "close fit" proposed by Browne and Cudeck (1993). As the reader will note, a rigorous use of probability values is not presented here, but enough information is presented for several alternative ways to view the question of fit.

ANALYSIS 1: AN AUTOREGRESSIVE MODEL APPROACH

An Autoregressive Change Model

It is useful to relate these models for longitudinal data to others that have emerged from the extensive literature on regression modeling approaches to time-series analysis (e.g., Dielman, 1989; Jones, 1993; Pankratz, 1991). For simplicity here, we also initially examine one popular SEM—the *auto-regressive change model* (see Jöreskog & Sörbom, 1979; McArdle & Aber, 1990).

In a typical application of this model, we first "de-trend" a time series by removing the mean score at each time point. In this notation we first define deviation scores $Y^*_{n,t} = Y^*_{n,t} - M_t$, and we write

$$Y^*_{n,t} = A_t \times Y_{n,t-1} + U_{n,t},\tag{3}$$

so any score at time t is simply a proportional function (A_t) of the individual's previous score at time $t - 1$ plus some new unique error ($U_{n,t}$) at each time. The random scores $U_{n,t}$ are assumed to have constant variance V_u and zero correlations with all other variables in the model.

The simplicity of this model can also be seen in the path diagrams of Fig. 12.3. In these diagrams (a) *squares* are used to represent observed or measured variables, (b) *circles* are used to represent unobserved or theoretical variables, (c) *one-headed arrows* are used to represent asymmetric regression coefficients, and (d) *two-headed arrows* are used to represent symmetric variance, covariance, or correlation coefficients. The first diagram (3a) shows this pattern of predictive relationships over time for four measured variables. The second diagram (3b) is more explicit by adding the unique unobserved variables (inside circles) and labels for all the model parameters (e.g., variance V_1, deviation D_u). The third diagram (3c) is an equivalent but more compact version of the same model, and here no explicit unique term is included, but the variance of the uniqueness is implied by the addition of the two-headed arrow (labeled V_u) attached to each variable.

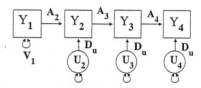

Current Path Diagram

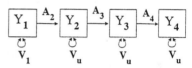

Complete RAM Diagram

FIG. 12.3. Some path diagrams of
the autoregressive change model.

Compact but Equivalent Diagram

Using this model with the NIH budget data, we may write a series of equations based on the date of observation where

$$Y^*_{n,93} = A_{93} \times Y_{n,92} + U_{n,93},$$
$$Y^*_{n,94} = A_{94} \times Y_{n,93} + U_{n,94},$$
$$Y^*_{n,95} = A_{95} \times Y_{n,94} + U_{n,95},$$
$$Y^*_{n,96} = A_{96} \times Y_{n,95} + U_{n,96},$$
$$Y^*_{n,97} = A_{97} \times Y_{n,96} + U_{n,97}, \text{ and}$$
$$Y^*_{n,98} = A_{98} \times Y_{n,97} + U_{n,98},$$

$$(4)$$

so the budget for each year is predicted only from the budget for the previous year plus some residual error.

Alternative Autoregressive Models

Before we fit this first model, let us consider two simplifications of this model. If we can assume the same autoregressive coefficient is invariant (i.e., $A_t = A$) over all time points, we can write

$$Y^*_{n,t} = A \times Y_{n,t-1} + U_{n,t},$$

$$(5)$$

and it can be shown that the structure of any covariance over time is now simplified. In the specific example of the NIH budget data, we may now write

$$Y^*_{n,93} = A \times Y_{n,92} + U_{n,93},$$

$$Y^*_{n,94} = A \times Y_{n,93} + U_{n,94},$$

$$Y^*_{n,95} = A \times Y_{n,94} + U_{n,95},$$

$$Y^*_{n,96} = A \times Y_{n,95} + U_{n,96}, \tag{6}$$

$$Y^*_{n,97} = A \times Y_{n,96} + U_{n,97}, \text{ and}$$

$$Y^*_{n,98} = A \times Y_{n,97} + U_{n,98},$$

which is obviously simpler because it requires fewer parameters for the same data. Due to its roots in the time-series literature, this simple predictive model has been termed a *first-order autoregressive* model or a *Markov simplex* model (see Jöreskog, 1970; McArdle & Aber, 1990).

As an even simpler model, let us assume the autoregressive coefficient is zero over all time points

$$Y^*_{n,t} = 0 \times Y_{n,t-1} + U_{n,t}, \tag{7}$$

(i.e., $A_t = 0$), and this is a commonly used *null baseline* against which to judge the fit of other substantive models.

Of course, it is possible to consider more complicated models at this point, including a *second-order autoregressive* model written as

$$Y^*_{n,t} = A_1 \times Y_{n,t-1} + A_2 \times Y_{n,t-2} + U_{n,t}, \tag{8}$$

where a second lagged score is used in the prediction. But these and other time series models can be represented in the same fashion described here, so no further details on these extensions are presented here.

Structural Covariance Expectations

This kind of autoregressive change model also makes a different kind of explicit prediction—there is a specific *pattern of covariances* that should be found in the data if this autoregressive model is appropriate. That is, in this model the expected covariance ($\mathcal{E}\{C\}$) for any two time periods can be written as the product

$$\mathcal{E}\{C_{t,t+j}\} = V_t \times \left[\prod_{i=t}^{t+j} A_i \right]. \tag{9}$$

Although at first this appears complicated, the pattern of the expected co-variances for any pair of specific time points (e.g., t and $t + j$) is determined only by the distance between points (j) and the coefficients (A_i) between these points.

This model leads to a pattern of expected covariances where

$$\mathcal{E}\{C_{92,93}\} = V_{92} \times A_{93},$$
$$\mathcal{E}\{C_{92,94}\} = V_{92} \times A_{93} \times A_{94},$$
$$\mathcal{E}\{C_{92,95}\} = V_{92} \times A_{93} \times A_{94} \times A_{95},$$
$$\mathcal{E}\{C_{92,96}\} = V_{92} \times A_{93} \times A_{94} \times A_{95} \times A_{96}, \quad (10)$$
$$\mathcal{E}\{C_{92,97}\} = V_{92} \times A_{93} \times A_{94} \times A_{95} \times A_{96} \times A_{97},$$
$$\mathcal{E}\{C_{92,98}\} = V_{92} \times A_{93} \times A_{94} \times A_{95} \times A_{96} \times A_{97} \times A_{98},$$

and so on for all pairs. The complete patterning of all covariances is not listed here but can be examined using the computer programs described here.

Under the alternative Markov simplex model (i.e., $A_t = A$) it can be shown that the expected structure of any covariance over time is now the less complex product

$$\mathcal{E}\{C_{t,t+j}\} = V_t \times A^j, \quad (11)$$

so the expected covariance is a power function based on the interval of time (j) between occasions. In this example, this model leads to a pattern of expected covariances where

$$\mathcal{E}\{C_{92,93}\} = V_{92} \times A,$$
$$\mathcal{E}\{C_{92,94}\} = V_{92} \times A^2,$$
$$\mathcal{E}\{C_{92,95}\} = V_{92} \times A^3,$$
$$\mathcal{E}\{C_{92,96}\} = V_{92} \times A^4, \quad (12)$$
$$\mathcal{E}\{C_{92,97}\} = V_{92} \times A^5,$$
$$\mathcal{E}\{C_{92,98}\} = V_{92} \times A^6,$$

so the expected covariance is entirely based on the distance between time points.

Finally, in the null model, the structure of any covariance over time is expected to be

$$\mathcal{E}\{C_{t,t+j}\} = 0 \times V_t = 0, \quad (13)$$

and this highly restrictive structure of zero covariances can also be compared to the observed covariances. If this simple model fits the data, there would probably be no reason to pursue the analysis any further, but it is often used as a structural baseline (see Browne & Cudeck, 1993).

Results From the Autoregressive Models

Table 12.3 is a list of numerical results for three alternative autoregressive change models fitted to the (7 × 7) covariance matrix (of Table 12.2's resulting covariance matrix) using the LISREL-8 or Mx computer programs.

The first model evaluated is a null baseline or *unique only* model. This model assumes that individual differences over time are independent of one another and only one unique variance term (V_u) is needed. This model results in an estimate $V_u = 12.9$, and an $LRT = 681$ on $df = 27$. This highly restrictive model does not fit these data very well.

The second model evaluated is an *equal autoregressive* model which, in addition to the initial level and random error, includes a single first-order regression term (A) for pairs of adjacent time points. This model results in estimates for $A = 1.0$, $V_{92} = 12.6$, and $V_u = .4$, and an $LRT = 289$ on $df = 25$. Although this highly restrictive model also does not fit these data very well, the change in fit due to the addition of these two parameters seems relatively large ($dLRT = 391$ on $ddf = 2$).

The third model evaluated is a *free autoregressive* model, which includes six first-order regression terms (A_t) for pairs of adjacent time points. This

TABLE 12.3
Numerical Results From Autoregressive
Markov Models for Rescaled NIH Budget Data

Model Parameters	Unique Only		Equal Auto		Free Auto	
Regression[1992]	0.0		0.0		0.0	
Regression[1993]	0.0		1.0	(.02)	1.0	(.04)
Regression[1994]	0.0		1.0	(==)	0.9	(.04)
Regression[1995]	0.0		1.0	(==)	1.0	(.04)
Regression[1996]	0.0		1.0	(==)	1.0	(.04)
Regression[1997]	0.0		1.0	(==)	1.0	(.04)
Regression[1998]	0.0		1.0	(==)	1.0	(.04)
Initial Variance	12.9	(2.)	12.6	(4.)	12.6	(4.)
Unique Variance	12.9	(==)	.40	(.1)	.38	(.1)
Params	1		3		8	
LRT Fit	681.		289.		279.	
DF Fit	27		25		20	
dLRT Fit	—		391.		10.	
dDF Fit	—		2		5	

Note. These results have been fitted using LISREL-8 and Mx with the covariance matrix (see Table 12.A1).

model results in estimates for A_t, V_{92}, and V_u, which are all very similar to the previous model, and an $LRT = 279$ on $df = 8$. Although this model seems better than the first ($dLRT = 401$ on $ddf = 7$), the change in fit between the second and third models is not large ($dLRT = 10$ on $ddf = 5$).

From this simple illustration we might conclude that an appropriate model for these NIH data is a highly simple one—the current budget is entirely predicted by the budget from the previous year with coefficient $A = 1.0$. This interpretation can lead to a number of other calculations such as, say, the explained variance (squared correlation) over time

$$R_{98}^2 = \frac{V_{92} - (t \times V_u)}{V_{92}} = \frac{12.6 - (6 \times .4)}{12.6} = \frac{10.2}{12.6} = .81. \tag{14}$$

In sum, this model suggests only a small and random change in the deviations in the budgets from one time to the next. Of course, this simple interpretation must be tempered by the fact that this simple model does not completely fit the data. But rather than pursue the more complex ARIMA models here, let us turn to consider a different approach for the organization of these changes.

ANALYSIS 2: A LATENT GROWTH MODEL APPROACH

A Latent Growth Model

Let us now start from another direction. Here we write a basic *latent growth model,* which can initially be written as a difference equation

$$\frac{\Delta Y_n}{\Delta B_t} = \frac{Y_{n,t} - Y_{n,t-j}}{B_t - B_{t-j}} = S_n, \tag{15}$$

where the ΔY_n is the change in the score on Y for subject n, the ΔB_t is the specific basis or unit of time during which the change takes place, and S_n is the *linear slope for individual n* over this time period. This simple model can be fitted to a time sequence of data [such as in Fig. 12.2(b)] by writing the corresponding trajectory (or integral) equation as

$$Y_{n,t} = L_n + B_t \times S_n + U_{n,t}. \tag{16}$$

In this representation L_n is the individual's unique starting point or level, and $U_{n,t}$ is a unique random component at each time. This trajectory implies that any change in the score is based on the individual slope but is also directly proportional to the basis coefficients or saturation coefficients (B_t).

A path diagram of the general latent growth curve model is presented in Fig. 12.4, and this diagram illustrates a few additional assumptions about

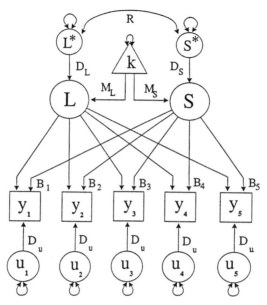

FIG. 12.4. A latent growth model.

the unobserved scores. Assume (a) the level scores (L_n) have a mean (M_l) and variance (V_l), (b) the slope scores (S_n) have a mean (M_s) and variance (V_s), (c) the level and slope scores have a possibly nonzero covariance (C_{ls}) or correlation (R_{ls}), and (d) the random scores $E_{n,t}$ have zero mean, constant variance (V_e), and zero correlations with all other components. In order to deal with this model we have added a new graphic device—a triangle is used to represent the constant ($K = 1$), and this new variable allows the means and intercepts to be incorporated into the model as regression coefficients (one-headed arrows from the constant to the variable). The two-headed arrow associated with this constant (and labeled 1) is not a variance term but is an average cross-product.

In the specific example of the NIH budget data, we may now write the model as

$$Y_{n,92} = L_n + B_{92} \times S_n + U_{n,92},$$

$$Y_{n,93} = L_n + B_{93} \times S_n + U_{n,93},$$

$$Y_{n,94} = L_n + B_{94} \times S_n + U_{n,94},$$

$$Y_{n,95} = L_n + B_{95} \times S_n + U_{n,95},$$ (17)

$$Y_{n,96} = L_n + B_{96} \times S_n + U_{n,96},$$

$$Y_{n,97} = L_n + B_{97} \times S_n + U_{n,97}, \text{ and}$$

$$Y_{n,98} = L_n + B_{98} \times S_n + U_{n,98},$$

where the unobserved level (L) and slope (S) scores are constant features of each institute, but the basis coefficients (B) may change depending on the year of interest.

Alternative Latent Growth Models

A variety of options are now available using this basic organization. The set of basis coefficients (B_t) are used to define an interval for changes over time, and these can either be defined on an a priori basis or *estimated* from the data (as in McArdle, 1988; Meredith & Tisak, 1990). A variety of alternative models are also possible from this basic starting point.

As a first alternative let us assume that there is no second component (i.e., $M_s = 0$, $V_s = 0$, $C_{ls} = 0$) and we can fit a *no-growth* or *level-only* model. This simplified model can be written as

$$\frac{\Delta Y_n}{\Delta B_t} = 0 \quad so \quad Y_{n,t} = L_n + U_{n,t}. \tag{18}$$

It follows that this no-growth model is appropriate for time-sequence data where there is a constant mean (M_l), constant variance ($V_l + V_u$), and constant variance (V_l) or correlation over time. This simple model is often used as a baseline against which to judge the size of the growth components.

A second model we may be interested in is a traditional *linear growth model* where we assume a constant slope S_n for each individual score but we fix the basis B_t at some observed time-based coefficients (i.e., $B_t = t$). More formally we write

$$\frac{\Delta Y_n}{\Delta B_t} = S_n \quad so \quad Y_{n,t} = L_n + B_t \times S_n + U_{n,t}. \tag{19}$$

Using this model, we can obtain estimates of the mean of the linear slopes (M_s) and variance of the linear slopes (V_s). These coefficients B_t are fixed (not free to vary) at a specific set of values defined by the investigator and this simplifies the structural expectations for the means, variances, and co-variances. In this example we fix the basis coefficients at "year(t) − 1992" by defining $B_t = [0, 1, 2, 3, 4, 5, 6]$. Using this basis we can evaluate the fit of a "straight line" trend over calendar time.

It is important to understand that by estimating the B_t coefficients from the data we can obtain curvatures that are *not necessarily linear*. That is, the B_t loadings obtained might suggest a different organization of the individual and group differences. However, in order to achieve the gain we need to recognize at least one limitation in the model: The B_t values cannot all be estimated uniquely. As in any model of this kind, at least some of the model parameters need to be fixed to obtain a unique solution. In all cases here, we fix (a) $B_1 = 0$, to allow a separation of the level and slope components, and (b) $B_7 = 6$, to provide a scale of measurement for the slopes (i.e., in "years"). This representation of the basis is similar to the linear model, except here B = $[0, B_2, B_3, B_4, B_5, B_6, 6]$, and five of the coefficients are free to take on the form of a complex trend. These basis coefficients are described in more detail as results are obtained.

A variety of more complex latent growth models are possible using this general form, including options for more complex curvature (e.g., quadratic, exponential, etc.). For example, we could fit a model with

$$Y_{n,t} = Y_{n,0} + [1 - e^{[-(t-1)(1-A)]}] \times Y_{n,a} + U_{n,t}, \tag{20}$$

where an arbitrary constant starting level ($L_n = Y_{n,0}$) is assumed, and an exponential change over time ($B_t = 1 - e^{[-(t-1)(1-A)]}$) is expected until some asymptotic value ($S_n = Y_{n,a}$) is reached. The complexity of this model is seen in the calculation of the exponential form of the time relationship, and comments are made about this model later (but see McArdle & Hamagami, 1992, 1996; Meredith & Tisak, 1990).

Structural LGM Expectations

In the case of the latent growth model, it is worthwhile describing the structural pattern of the model expectation in more detail. When the appropriate linear algebra is carried out (e.g., using RAM notation, etc.) we obtain a definition of the *expected means over time* as

$$\begin{aligned} \mathcal{E}\{M_t\} &= \mathcal{E}\{Y_{n,t}\} \\ &= \mathcal{E}\{L_n + B_t \times S_n + U_{n,t}\} \\ &= \mathcal{E}\{L_n\} + B_t \times \mathcal{E}\{S_n\} + \mathcal{E}\{U_{n,t}\} \\ &= M_l + B_t \times M_s. \end{aligned} \tag{21}$$

This model assumes a mean level (M_l) plus a change in the mean (M_s) whose impact on the observations is directly proportional to the basis coefficients (B_t). If we place numerical values into the locations for the parameters (M_l, B_t, M_s) then we can obtain numerical values for the expected means at each time (M_0, M_1, M_2, M_3, etc.).

In the same way we can define the *expected variance over time* as

$$\begin{aligned} \mathcal{E}\{V_t\} &= \mathcal{E}\{(Y_{n,t} - M_t) \times (Y_{n,t} - M_t)'\} \\ &= \mathcal{E}\{(L_n + B_t \times S_n + U_{n,t} - M_t) \times (L_n + B_t \times S_n + U_{n,t} - M_t)'\} \\ &= V_l + (B_t^2 \times V_s) + (2 \times B_t \times C_{ls}) + V_u. \end{aligned} \tag{22}$$

This variance structure is a bit more complicated than that of the mean, but it basically has four components: (a) a starting variance level (V_l), (b) an impact of the slope variance (V_s) proportional to the basis coefficients (B_t^2), (c) a covariance component for the level and slope correlation, and (d) the error variance (V_e). Again, if we place numerical values into the locations for the parameters $(V_l, B_t, V_s, C_{ls}, V_u)$ then we can obtain numerical values for the expected variances at each time $(V_0, V_1, V_2, V_3,$ etc.).

We also can define the *expected covariance over time* between pairs of time points t and $t + j$, which can be written as

$$\mathcal{E}\{C_{t,t+j}\} = \mathcal{E}\{(Y_{n,t} - M_t) \times (Y_{n,t+j} - M_{t+j})'\},$$
$$= \mathcal{E}\{(L_n + B_t \times S_n + U_{n,t} - M_t) \times (L_n + B_{t+j} \times S_n + U_{n,t+j} - M_{t+j})'\}$$
$$= V_l + (B_t \times V_s \times B_{t+j}) + (2 \times B_t \times C_{ls} \times B_{t+j}). \tag{23}$$

This covariance structure basically has three components: (a) a starting variance level (V_l), (b) an impact of the slope variance (V_s) proportional to two basis coefficients (B_t, B_{t+j}), and (c) a covariance component for the level and slope correlation. Once again, if we place numerical values into the locations for the parameters $(V_l, B_t, B_{t+j}, V_s, C_{ls})$ then we can obtain numerical values for the expected covariances at each time $(C_{01}, C_{02}, C_{12}, C_{13},$ etc.).

Other aspects of the model can be calculated from the previous expectations. For example, expected standard deviation can be obtained as the square root of this variance expectation (i.e., $\mathcal{E}\{D_t\} = \sqrt{\mathcal{E}\{V_t\}}$). Similarly, we can define the *expected correlation over time* between pairs of time points t and $t + j$ as

$$\mathcal{E}\{R_{t,t+j}\}$$
$$= \mathcal{E}\left\{ \frac{(Y_{n,t} - M_t)}{\sqrt{V_t}} \times \frac{(Y_{n,t+j} - M_{t+j})'}{\sqrt{V_{t+j}}} \right\}$$
$$= \frac{V_l + (B_t \times V_s \times B_{t+j}) + (2 \times B_t \times C_{ls} \times B_{t+j})}{\sqrt{V_l + (B_t^2 \times V_s) + (2 \times B_t \times C_{ls}) + V_e} \sqrt{V_l + (B_{t+j}^2 \times V_s) + (2 \times B_{t+j} \times C_{ls}) + V_e}}, \tag{24}$$

but this turns out to be far more complex than desired. In contrast, and perhaps more important, the *reliability of the growth curve* at time t can be obtained as a simple ratio

$$\mathcal{E}\{r_{tt}\} = \mathcal{E}\left\{ \frac{V_t - V_u}{V_t} \right\}, \tag{25}$$

and this index can be useful in a variety of ways (see McArdle, 1996; Meredith & Tisak, 1990). In all cases, if we place numerical values into the locations for the five parameters (V_l, B_t, B_{t+j}, V_s, C_{ls}) then we can obtain numerical values for the expected correlations at each time (R_{01}, R_{02}, R_{12}, R_{13}, etc.).

Each alternative structural model leads to a different set of expectations for the means, deviations, and correlations over time. The linear growth model expectations basically substitute the fixed set of coefficients A_t for the free (or partially free) set of coefficients B_t. In contrast, the no-growth model expectations C_0 lead to the simplified set of structural expectations written as

$$\mathcal{E}\{M_t\} = M_l,$$
$$\mathcal{E}\{V_t\} = V_l + V_u, \text{ and}$$
$$\mathcal{E}\{C_{l,t+j}\} = V_l, \text{ so} \tag{26}$$
$$\mathcal{E}\{R_{l,t+j}\} = \frac{V_l}{V_l + V_u}.$$

These expectations are certainly simpler because they assume a constant mean, variance, and covariance (or correlation) over all times. However, the question remains: How well can this simple model approximate the available data? To answer this and other similar question, we next turn to some numerical results.

Results From Latent Growth Analyses

The three alternative growth models were first fitted to the moment matrix using the LISREL-8 and Mx programs, and the initial results are given in Table 12.4. In general, these programs include the algebra needed for the automatic generation of covariance expectations. However, there are a variety of ways to use these programs so that they can carry out the automatic generation of mean and covariance expectations. This is a nontrivial addition to the numerical technique because it allows us to simultaneously evaluate hypotheses about both the covariances and the mean structures (for further details, see McArdle, 1988; Meredith & Tisak, 1990; Sörbom, 1978).

The first model evaluated is a no-growth model. This model assumes that individual differences over time are a function of the individual's unique starting point, plus a random error at each time of evaluation. This model results in estimates for $M_l = 5.4$, $D_l = 3.5$, and $V_u = .6$, and these lead to an *LRT* = 365 on *df* = 32. This highly restrictive model does not fit these data very well.

The second model evaluated is a linear growth model which, in addition to the initial level and random error, includes a linear age-based slope for each person. This model results in revised estimates for $M_l = 5.2$, $D_l = 3.4$, and $V_u = .3$, as well as new estimates for $M_s = .07$, $D_s = .2$, and $R_{ls} = .1$. These new estimates show a small but positive linear change per year in

TABLE 12.4
Numerical Results From Latent Growth Models Fitted to NIH Budget Data

Model Parameters	Level Only		Linear Growth		Latent Growth		
Loadings[1992]	1.0	0.0	1.0	0.0	1.0	0.0	(−)
Loadings[1993]	1.0	0.0	1.0	1.0	1.0	1.1	(.5)
Loadings[1994]	1.0	0.0	1.0	2.0	1.0	5.7	(.6)
Loadings[1995]	1.0	0.0	1.0	3.0	1.0	5.7	(.6)
Loadings[1996]	1.0	0.0	1.0	4.0	1.0	5.9	(.6)
Loadings[1997]	1.0	0.0	1.0	5.0	1.0	6.0	(.6)
Loadings[1998]	1.0	0.0	1.0	6.0	1.0	6.0	(−)
Mean Level	5.4	(.8)	5.2	(??)	5.3		(.8)
Mean Slope	—	—	.07	(.8)	.03		(.1)
Deviation Level	3.5	(.6)	3.4	(.2)	3.5		(.6)
Deviation Slope	—	—	.2	(5.)	.2		(.1)
Correlation(L,S)	—	—	.1	(4.)	−.2		(.2)
Unique Variance	.6	(.1)	.3	(.1)	.2		(.0)
Num. Free Params.	3		6		11		
LRT Fit	366.		326.		284.		
DF Fit	32		29		24		
dLRT Fit	—		40.		42.		
dDF Fit	—		3		5		

Note. These results have been fitted using LISREL-8 and Mx with moments matrix (see Tables 12.A2 and 12.A3).

the overall NIH budget (M_s = .07), but also suggest a small but potentially systematic set of individual differences in these changes (D_s = .2), but the parameters related to the slope are very small compared to their standard errors. In any case, these new estimates lead to an LRT = 324 on df = 29, and this is an improvement in fit over the previous model with $dLRT$ = 40 on ddf = 3. So, although this linear model still does not fit these data very well, we do find some improvement over the previous growth model.

The third model evaluated in Table 12.4 is a latent growth model where the change in the individual is based on a linear slope with an unknown but flexible basis. This model results in revised estimates for M_l = 5.3, D_l = 3.5, and V_u = .2, as well as new estimates for M_s = .03, D_s = .2, and R_{ls} = .2. These new estimates still show a smaller but positive linear change per year in the overall NIH budget (M_s = .03), and also suggest a small but potentially systematic set of individual differences in these changes (D_s = .2). But the most informative parameters here are the five estimated basis coefficients: B = [0, 1.1, 5.7, 5.7, 5.9, 6.0, 6]. These results can be interpreted to mean that the single *optimal curve* in these data can be written where the budget changes are largest between 1992 and 1994, and then are relatively flat from 1994 to 1998.

In any case, these new estimates lead to an $LRT = 284$ on $df = 24$, and this is an improvement in fit over the previous model with $dLRT = 42$ on $ddf = 5$. So, although this latent model still does not fit these data very well, we again find some improvement over the previous growth model. Also, this last model is not totally devoid of substance—in comparison to an increasing linear trend, this model can be interpreted to mean that any increases in NIH budgets came in the first two years of the new Democratic administration, and these increases have not continued or declined since that time.

ANALYSIS 3: FITTING GROWTH MODELS TO RAW DATA

Individual-Level Structural Equation Models

A great deal of literature has emerged about the importance of fitting structural models using all available data. One often overlooked aspect of SEM is the practical use of all individual-level information. However, such an individual SEM approach is desirable in many cases, and especially in dealing with individual growth curves (see McArdle & Hamagami, 1992). In such an approach the model is fitted in the usual way and the same estimates are obtained. However, the overall likelihood function can also be decomposed into individual components and the contribution to the overall likelihood can be evaluated. One theoretical benefit of this approach is that it broadens our understanding and interpretation of the statistical indices (e.g., LRT). One practical benefit of this approach is that it permits a thorough analysis of outliers or subgroups.

This approach also naturally leads to the possibility of fitting the model in situations where some of the data are incomplete. Let us assume we wish to make an inference about a model with t total variables but we may have only measured a subset of these variables in any single subject. At this point we make no special assumption about the reason for the patterns of incomplete data. The same basic ideas have been stated in many different ways, including Rubin's *theorems for incomplete groups* and Pearson–Aiken–Lawley's *selection theorems* (for overviews, see Little & Rubin, 1987; McArdle, 1994). Basically, the available information for any subject on any data point (i.e., any variable measured at any occasion) is used to build up the likelihood function and optimize the model parameters with respect to the available data.

In this special case of a latent growth model with incomplete data we can write

$$Y_{g,n} = F_n \times Y_{t,n}$$
$$= F_n \times (L_n + B_t \times S_n + U_{n,t}), \tag{27}$$

where $F_n = [I_g, O_{t-g}]$ is the nth binary filter vector selecting g_n observed variables for person n. This basically allows all subjects to have any *subset of the observed data*. Using this general approach, we can write the filtering of the individually observed summary statistics into the total summary statistics as

$$\mathcal{E}\{Y_g\} = \mathcal{E}\{M_g\} = F_n \times \mathcal{E}\{Y_t\} = F_n \times \mathcal{E}\{M_t\}, \text{ and}$$
$$\mathcal{E}\{Y_g, Y_g\} = \mathcal{E}\{C_{g,g}\} = F_n \times \mathcal{E}\{Y_t, Y_t\} \times F'_n = F_n \times \mathcal{E}\{C_{t,t}\} \times F'_n. \tag{28}$$

This means the relation between the individually measured variables and the total variables is based on the individual filtering. The individual filtering procedure also allows all means and covariances to be written for any group g of persons $N^{(g)}$ with identical filter matrices $F^{(g)}$.

Following Lange et al. (1976; see also Neale, 1993) we can write a log–likelihood function for raw scores for separate *pedigrees*. The general statistical features of this approach required the use of *accumulated information from the individual likelihood*. The overall difference between two nested models can be indexed by the difference in the obtained likelihoods and, under standard normal theory assumptions about the distribution of the error, we can compare this difference to a chi-square variate (degrees of freedom are usually based on the difference in the numbers of parameters and subjects).

Results From Raw Data Growth Models

In this analysis we have refit the previous LGMs using the (20×7) raw data matrix as input to the Mx program (using the RAW data option). In Table 12.5 we present results from the three models. As the careful reader will note, these results for all three models are almost exactly the same as results presented in Table 12.4. The main exception here is that the indices of fit are somewhat different, and these require a brief explanation.

In the first column of Table 12.5, we can see that the level-only model with three parameters now yields an $\mathcal{L} = 415$ on $df = 137$. This is larger than the result for the comparable model of the previous table ($LRT = 366$ on $df = 32$). The difference comes because this raw data index is a *likelihood of the model* ($\mathcal{L}_m$) whereas the previous index was a likelihood ratio (LRT) comparison of the likelihood of the model ($\mathcal{L}_m$) to the likelihood of the data ($\mathcal{L}_d$). The raw data include 140 pieces of information, and only 3 are used in this model, so the difference accounts for the $df = 137$. The same interpretation follows for the linear model, where the six parameters now yield an $\mathcal{L} = 373$ on $df = 134$. This is an improvement in fit that is indexed by the difference $dLRT = (\mathcal{L}_1 - \mathcal{L}_2) = (415 - 373) = 42$, on $ddf = (df_1 - df_2) = (137 - 134) = 3$. This change in the fit is almost exactly what was found

TABLE 12.5
Numerical Results From Latent Growth Models Fitted to NIH Budget Data

Model Parameters	Level Only		Linear Growth		Latent Growth		
Loadings[1992]	1.0	0.0	1.0	0.0	1.0	0.0	(–)
Loadings[1993]	1.0	0.0	1.0	1.0	1.0	1.1	(.5)
Loadings[1994]	1.0	0.0	1.0	2.0	1.0	5.6	(.6)
Loadings[1995]	1.0	0.0	1.0	3.0	1.0	5.6	(.6)
Loadings[1996]	1.0	0.0	1.0	4.0	1.0	5.9	(.6)
Loadings[1997]	1.0	0.0	1.0	5.0	1.0	6.0	(.6)
Loadings[1998]	1.0	0.0	1.0	6.0	1.0	6.0	(–)
Mean Level	5.4	(.8)	5.2	(.8)	5.3		(.8)
Mean Slope	—	—	.07	(.1)	.03		(.1)
Deviation Level	3.4	(.6)	3.3	(.6)	3.5		(.6)
Deviation Slope	—	—	.2	(.0)	.2		(.0)
Correlation(L,S)	—	—	.1	(.3)	–.2		(.2)
Unique Variance	.6	(.1)	.3	(.0)	.2		(.0)
Num. Free Params.	3		6		11		
$\mathcal{L}'$ Fit	415.		373.		329.		
DF Fit	137		134		129		
dLRT Fit	—		42.		44.		
dDF Fit	—		3		5		

Note. These results have been fitted by using Mx-96 with raw data (see Table 12.A4).

by the previous moment-matrix models in Table 12.4. The same principles apply to the fitting of the latent growth model, and the resulting improvements in fit over the linear model.

An important benefit here is the individual analysis of the misfit. The individual likelihood indices were calculated for all 20 institutes on all models (by Mx and saved using a standard OUTPUT option). The numerical results from the latent growth model are plotted sequentially for each of the 20 institutes in Fig. 12.5.

This plot shows an informative result: The misfit for each of the 20 institutes is not the same. Whereas many of the institutes have low to moderate misfit ($\mathcal{L}_n < 20$), a few institutes seem to have exceedingly large misfits. The worst misfit is seen for institute 14 ($\mathcal{L}_n < 47$), which by itself contains 5% of the data (1/20) but contributes 14% (47/329) of the overall misfit. Institutes 18 and 1 are also potentially problematic in this regard.

In looking back to Table 12.1 we find an interesting substantive issue: The 14th institute is the NIMH, and this label includes an asterisk that says, "NIMH revised its 1994–1995 figures due to a definition clarification/change." If we then look at the budget values included for NIMH in Table 12.1, or even in the longitudinal plots of Figs. 12.1 and 12.2, we can see a dramatic shift in the size of the NIMH budget due to this clarification (e.g., a drop from $156,638 to $52,277 between 1993 and 1994). Basically this means that

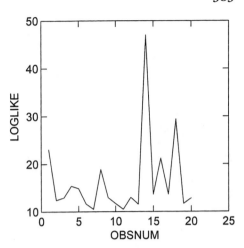

FIG. 12.5. Individual likelihoods from NIH-LAT model.

the NIMH budget data for the first two dates are *not consistent in coding* with the data for the last five dates. This is a reasonable problem that can be taken care of in a number of ways. This analysis of individual misfits certainly provides some useful information about these outliers.

Results From Incomplete Data Growth Models

There are many ways to deal with the previous *change of coding* problems, and not all such approaches can be presented here. However, at least one reasonable approach would be to remove the entire institute 14 (NIMH) vector from the data set. We could then recalculate the necessary statistical matrices (in Table 12.2) and rerun the SEM analyses. This approach is a common solution but has a weakness—eliminating data that we believe is actually correct (the last 5 data points). So, as a contemporary alternative approach, we now fit the same model to the same raw data, except here we eliminate the two data points for NIMH that logically seemed to create the misfit problems. The results for this incomplete matrix approach are presented in Table 12.6.

These results were obtained using the same Mx programs as before but with the elimination of the two NIMH values (these two were replaced by a dot in the raw data matrix input to Mx). This means there are now 138 independent pieces of information in the raw data set. These results show some distinct changes in the parameter estimates, as well as some changes in the fit indices. Most important here, the linear model now exhibits a much improved fit over the level-only model ($dLRT = 105$ on $ddf = 3$) and includes a much larger positive linear slope ($M_s = .12$) and almost nonexistent unique variance at each time ($V_u = .1$). Also, the latent growth model now shows a more nearly linear pattern: B = [0, 1.3, 2.7, 3.0, 5.2, 5.7, 6], and it does not fit the data substantially better than the linear model ($dLRT = 15$ on *ddf*

TABLE 12.6

Numerical Results From Latent Growth Models Fitted to NIH Budget Data

Model Parameters	Level Only		Linear Growth		Latent Growth		
Loadings[1992]	1.0	0.0	1.0	0.0	1.0	0.0	(–)
Loadings[1993]	1.0	0.0	1.0	1.0	1.0	1.3	(.4)
Loadings[1994]	1.0	0.0	1.0	2.0	1.0	2.7	(.4)
Loadings[1995]	1.0	0.0	1.0	3.0	1.0	3.0	(.4)
Loadings[1996]	1.0	0.0	1.0	4.0	1.0	5.2	(.4)
Loadings[1997]	1.0	0.0	1.0	5.0	1.0	5.7	(.4)
Loadings[1998]	1.0	0.0	1.0	6.0	1.0	6.0	(–)
Mean Level	5.4	(.8)	5.0	(.7)	4.9		(.7)
Mean Slope	—	—	.12	(.1)	.11		(.1)
Deviation Level	3.4	(.6)	3.0	(.5)	3.0		(.5)
Deviation Slope	—	—	.2	(.0)	.2		(.0)
Correlation(L,S)	—	—	.5	(.2)	.4		(.2)
Unique Variance	.3	(.0)	.1	(.0)	.1		(.0)
Num. Free Params.	3		6		11		
$\mathcal{L}$ Fit	346.		242.		227.		
DF Fit	135		132		127		
dLRT Fit	—		105.		15.		
dDF Fit	—		3		5		

Note. These results have been fitted using Mx-96 with missing raw data (see Table 12.A5).

TABLE 12.7
Numerical Results From Latent Growth Models Fitted to NIH Budget Data

Model Parameters	Level Only		Linear Growth		Latent Growth		
Loadings[1992]	1.0	0.0	1.0	0.0	1.0	0.0	(–)
Loadings[1993]	1.0	0.0	1.0	1.0	1.0	1.1	(??)
Loadings[1994]	1.0	0.0	1.0	2.0	1.0	5.7	(??)
Loadings[1995]	1.0	0.0	1.0	3.0	1.0	5.7	(??)
Loadings[1996]	1.0	0.0	1.0	4.0	1.0	5.9	(??)
Loadings[1997]	1.0	0.0	1.0	5.0	1.0	6.0	(??)
Loadings[1998]	1.0	0.0	1.0	6.0	1.0	6.0	(–)
Mean Level	5.4	(.8)	5.4	(??)	5.0		(??)
Mean Slope	—	—	-.03	(??)	-.02		(??)
Deviation Level	3.4	(.6)	3.4	(??)	3.3		(??)
Deviation Slope	—	—	.0	(??)	.0		(??)
Correlation(L,S)	—	—	.3	(??)	.6		(??)
Unique Variance	.5	(.1)	.5	(??)	.4		(??)
Num. Free Params.	3		6		11		
$\mathcal{L}$ Fit	211.		211.		205.		
DF Fit	57		54		49		
dLRT Fit	—		0.		6.		
dDF Fit	—		3		5		

Note. These results have been fitted using Mx-96 with sparse raw data (see Tables 12.A6 and 12.A7).

= 5). It now appears that the two coding errors had a substantial impact on the model interpretation.

In order to examine modeling incomplete data in a more extreme fashion, additional pieces of the full data set were removed (following the techniques of McArdle, 1994, and McArdle & Hamagami, 1992). This included the elimination of an essentially random set of 4 scores for each institute—leaving only 3 consecutive measures for each institute, and a set of only 60 scores. The pattern of the time of measurement was kept intact, however, so the same models could, at least in theory, be fitted to the now sparse data set. The numerical results from this sparse data analysis are listed in Table 12.7, and they are not very appealing. After losing so much of the longitudinal data, we cannot easily estimate the model parameters or standard errors, and it is no longer possible to distinguish between the fit of the alternative models.

DISCUSSION

Conclusions

The chapter was designed as an introduction to the topic of latent growth curve analyses, so it is not all-inclusive. The initial autoregressive approach showed one way to evaluate a simple predictive system of equations using standard SEM software. The initial latent growth model approach extended these ideas in a slightly different direction, and found some interesting nonlinear results. The raw data approach used a more general way to deal with these problems, and found at least one outlier, and an important change in the results. Also, in theory, the raw data approach to fitting latent growth models does not require all data for all persons but, in practice, some aspects of the data are needed for an adequate longitudinal analysis.

The illustrations here were intended to be based on a real example, but further efforts are needed to make a clear substantive interpretation from these analyses. Nevertheless, these examples illustrate how the SEM computer programs can work in a variety of different approaches. We also showed how the latent growth models used here permit the expression of many key features of longitudinal data analysis (see Nesselroade & Baltes, 1979).

Practical Issues

There are a number of ways latent growth model results can be useful for the researcher and practitioner alike. In broad terms, we have emphasized how the SEM approach is used as a way to distinguish between different models for the same data. These calculations of discrepancies among different models for the same data is a fundamental empirical result. Hopefully, these SEM analyses can be turned into some practical uses designed to better describe and understand the phenomena of interest (e.g., budget trends).

The final parameters of any of these growth models can also be used for practical *forecasting* purposes as well. For example, we can look at the initial linear growth model for the NIH budgets from Table 12.4. These results can be written in numerical terms as

$$\mathcal{E}\{M_t\} = M_I + B_t \times M_s,\ so$$
$$= 5.22 + .07 \times (t - 1992),\tag{29}$$

where the mean score at time t depends on the model parameters and the number of years ($t - 1992$) since the start of the series studied here. This calculation can also lead to predictions about the means of the untransformed budgets, which can be written as

$$\mathcal{E}\{\$1992\} = (5.22 + .07 \times 0)^2 = 5.22^2 = \$27.25\ millions,$$
$$\mathcal{E}\{\$1993\} = (5.22 + .07 \times 1)^2 = 5.29^2 = \$27.98\ millions,$$
$$\mathcal{E}\{\$1994\} = (5.22 + .07 \times 2)^2 = 5.36^2 = \$28.73\ millions,$$
$$\mathcal{E}\{\$1995\} = (5.22 + .07 \times 3)^2 = 5.43^2 = \$29.48\ millions,$$
$$\mathcal{E}\{\$1996\} = (5.22 + .07 \times 4)^2 = 5.50^2 = \$30.25\ millions,\tag{30}$$
$$\mathcal{E}\{\$1997\} = (5.22 + .07 \times 5)^2 = 5.57^2 = \$31.02\ millions,$$
$$\mathcal{E}\{\$1998\} = (5.22 + .07 \times 6)^2 = 5.63^2 = \$31.70\ millions,\ and\ even$$
$$\mathcal{E}\{\$1999\} = (5.22 + .07 \times 7)^2 = 5.70^2 = \$32.49\ millions,$$

and these may be plotted as a small but geometrically increasing trend in terms of real dollars. Although this change may be viewed as small by some standards, these changes would probably be noticeable for some NIH institutes (e.g., "A million here, a million there, and pretty soon we're talking about real money"; The Honorable Mr. E. Dirkson, 1973). The careful reader will notice that we have also included a budget projection for the next year by simply applying the model to 1999 (i.e., $B_t = 1999 - 1992 = 7$).

These predictions can also be considered in the context of individual differences between institutes, and this requires a calculation of the variance of the budgets over time. Using the previous formulas we can write the general expression

$$\mathcal{E}\{V_t\} = V_I + (B_t^2 \times V_s) + (2 \times B_t \times C_{ls}) + V_u,\ so$$
$$= (3.4)^2 + (t - 1992)^2 \times (.2)^2 + 2 \times (t - 1992) \times 0 + .3,\tag{31}$$
$$= 10.2 + (t - 1992)^2 \times .04 + .3,$$

where the estimated D_l and D_s deviations have been squared to form variances. Because the model was fitted to the square roots, this expression leads to a set of systematic expressions for the standard deviations of the untransformed budgets written as

$$\mathcal{E}\{D_{92}\} = 10.2 + (0^2 \times .04) + .3 = 10.50,$$
$$\mathcal{E}\{D_{93}\} = 10.2 + (1^2 \times .04) + .3 = 10.54,$$
$$\mathcal{E}\{D_{94}\} = 10.2 + (2^2 \times .04) + .3 = 10.66,$$
$$\mathcal{E}\{D_{95}\} = 10.2 + (3^2 \times .04) + .3 = 10.86,$$
$$\mathcal{E}\{D_{96}\} = 10.2 + (4^2 \times .04) + .3 = 11.14,$$
$$\mathcal{E}\{D_{97}\} = 10.2 + (5^2 \times .04) + .3 = 11.50,$$
$$\mathcal{E}\{D_{98}\} = 10.2 + (6^2 \times .04) + .3 = 11.94,$$
$$\mathcal{E}\{D_{99}\} = 10.2 + (7^2 \times .04) + .3 = 12.46,$$

(32)

and this shows small increases like a *fan-spread* in the individual growth around the predictions. These estimated deviations can also be used to form confidence boundaries around the estimated means. The same kinds of extensions can be made for a more practical use of any model parameters.

Future Directions

There are many possibilities for future work in this area. The LGMs are directly related to repeated measures analysis of variance models. Here we also ask some questions about group differences and sampling heterogeneity. These questions are phrased as, "To what degree do the variables measure the same dynamic patterns in several important subgroups?" Standard models from item-response theory and common factor analysis (see McArdle, 1996) can be used to deal with these kinds of questions. In the first case we use standard techniques in structural factor analysis, including estimation via MLE and comparison of alternative models through the likelihood ratio test.

Many interesting aspects on the relationships between the autoregressive change model can be explored in more detail. For parallels with growth models, it may also be useful to express any model as a *difference* (or differential) equation where ΔY_n is the change in the score and B_t is some explicit value defining the time interval between occasions. Under this form of the model, the expected changes over all times can be expressed as a *trajectory* (or integral) equation. In the case of autoregression, an exponential change over time (in mean deviations) is expected. A more general exponential growth model has often been used because it may have particular biological interpretation (e.g., in growth of cancer cells), physical interpretation (e.g., the decay of radioactive materials), or economic interpretation (e.g., the compound interest function). Recent attempts to use latent growth models with a priori nonlinear basis are described by Browne and DuToit (1991) and McArdle and Hamagami (1996).

After an initial dynamic growth structure is determined, we will be interested in the equality of the factor loadings (i.e., growth patterns) over different groups. This is an important set of analyses in this context. If the same set of factor loadings B_t can be used to account for the data in each separate group, then we have some evidence that the factor is *invariant over groups*—that is, we can say that we are measuring the same growth curve and dynamic processes in all subgroups (i.e., dropouts and persisters, males and females, healthy and nonhealthy, etc.).

These models can also be generalized to fit dynamic growth models among different longitudinal growth models (see McArdle & Hamagami, 1992; McArdle & Neale, 1996). The interrelationships of the levels (asymptotes) and slopes (or distances) across different variables at different ages form the basis of a dynamic interpretation of the developmental influences of variables X_t on Y_t, and vice versa. The statistical models used are based on a structural equation model based on Coleman's (1968) differential equations model of bivariate change (also see Arminger, 1987).

These and other kinds of dynamic coupling models typically require much larger amounts of raw data than we have available here (e.g., see Dwyer et al., 1992; cf. McArdle & Hamagami, 1996). However, a structural modeling approach using the longitudinal and cross-sectional data can yield reasonable results from a variety of points of view. These results must be considered in the context of potential problems such as the potential instability of the statistical parameters (i.e., to be evaluated by bootstrapping techniques), or some potential artifacts of measurement and scaling (i.e., the exponential form is not invariant to changes in scale). When such issues are carefully considered, all recent trends in latent growth models are positive and rapidly growing.

ACKNOWLEDGMENTS

The work described here has been supported since 1980 by the National Institute on Aging (Grants AG-04704 and AG-07137).

REFERENCES

Arminger, G. (1987). Linear stochastic differential equation models for panel data with unobserved variables. In N. B. Tuma (Ed.), *Sociology methodology, 1987* (pp. 187–212). San Francisco: Jossey-Bass.

Browne, M., & Arminger, G. (1995). Specification and estimation of mean-and-covariance structure models. In G. Arminger, C. C. Clogg, & M. E. Sobel (Eds.), *Handbook of statistical modeling for the social and behavioral sciences* (pp. 185–250). New York: Plenum.

Browne, M., & Cudeck, R. (1993). Alternative ways of assessing model fit. In K. Bolen & S. Long (Eds.), *Testing structural equation models* (pp. 136–162). Newbury Park, CA: Sage.

Browne, M., & DuToit, S. (1991). Analysis of learning curves. In L. Collins & J. L. Horn (Eds.), *Best methods for the analysis of change*. Washington, DC: APA Press.

Cleveland, W. S. (1993). *Visualizing data*. Summit, NJ: Hobart.

Coleman, J. S. (1968). The mathematical study of change. In H. M. Blalock & A. Blalock (Eds.), *Methodology in social research* (pp. 428–478). New York: McGraw-Hill.

Collins, L., & Horn, J. L. (Eds.). (1991). *Best methods for the analysis of change*. Washington, DC: APA Press.

Dielman, T. E. (1989). *Pooled cross-sectional and times series data analysis*. New York: Marcel-Dekker.

Diggle, P. J., Liang, K.-Y., & Zeger, S. L. (1994). *Analysis of longitudinal data*. New York: Oxford University Press.

Dwyer, J. H., Feinleib, M., Lippert, P., & Hoffmeister, H. (1992). *Statistical models for longitudinal studies of health*. New York: Oxford University Press.

Elder, G. H., Pavalko, E. K., & Clipp, E. C. (1991). *Working with archival data: Studying lives*. Newbury Park, CA: Sage.

Hamagami, F. (1997). A review of the Mx computer program for structural equation modeling. *Structural Equation Modeling, 4*(2), 157–175.

Hill, M. S. (1992). *The panel study of income dynamics: A user's guide*. Newbury Park, CA: Sage.

Jones, K., Albert, M., Aldwin, C., Duffy, F., Naeser, M., & Hyde, M. (1991). Modeling age using cognitive, physiological and psychosocial variables. *Expert Aging Research, 17,* 227–242.

Jones, R. H. (1993). *Longitudinal data with serial correlation: A state-space approach*. London: Chapman & Hall.

Jöreskog, K. G. (1970). Estimation and testing of simplex models. *British Journal of Mathematical and Statistical Psychology, 23,* 121–146.

Jöreskog, K. G., & Sörbom, D. (1979). *Advances in factor analysis and structural equation models*. Cambridge, MA: Abt Books.

Jöreskog, K. G., & Sörbom, D. (1993). *LISREL-VIII Users' Guide*. Mooresville, IN: Scientific Software, Inc.

Lange, K., Westlake, J., & Spence, M. A. (1976). Extensions to pedigree analysis: III. Variance components by the scoring method. *Annals of Human Genetics, 39,* 485–491.

Lindsey, J. K. (1993). *Models for repeated measurements*. New York: Oxford University Press.

Little, R. T. A., & Rubin, D. B. (1987). *Statistical analysis with missing data*. New York: Wiley.

Loehlin, J. C. (1992). *Latent variable modeling*. Hillsdale, NJ: Lawrence Erlbaum Associates.

McArdle, J. J. (1988). Dynamic but structural equation modeling of repeated measures data. In J. R. Nesselroade & R. B. Cattell (Eds.), *The handbook of multivariate experimental psychology* (Vol. 2, pp. 561–614). New York: Plenum.

McArdle, J. J. (1989). Structural modeling experiments using multiple growth functions. In P. Ackerman, R. Kanfer, & R. Cudeck (Eds.), *Learning and individual differences: Abilities, motivation, and methodology* (pp. 71–117).

McArdle, J. J. (1994). Structural factor analysis experiments with incomplete data. *Multivariate Behavioral Research, 29*(4), 409–454.

McArdle, J. J. (1996). Current directions in structural factor analysis. *Current Directions in Psychological Science, 5*(1), 10–17.

McArdle, J. J., & Aber, M. S. (1990). Patterns of change within latent variable structural equation modeling. In A. von Eye (Ed.), *New statistical methods in developmental research* (pp. 151–224). New York: Academic Press.

McArdle, J. J., & Anderson, E. (1990). Latent variable growth models for research on aging. In J. E. Birren & K. W. Schaie (Eds.), *The handbook of the psychology of aging* (pp. 21–43). New York: Plenum.

McArdle, J. J., & Boker, S. M. (1990). *RAMpath: A computer program for automatic path diagrams.* Hillsdale, NJ: Lawrence Erlbaum Associates.

McArdle, J. J., & Epstein, D. B. (1987). Latent growth curves within developmental structural equation models. *Child Development, 58*(1), 110–133.

McArdle, J. J., & Hamagami, E. (1991). Modeling incomplete longitudinal data using latent growth structural equation models. In L. Collins & J. L. Horn (Eds.), *Best methods for the analysis of change* (pp. 276–304). Washington, DC: APA Press.

McArdle, J. J., & Hamagami, E. (1992). Modeling incomplete longitudinal and cross-sectional data using latent growth structural models. *Experimental Aging Research, 18*(3), 145–166.

McArdle, J. J., & Hamagami, F. (1996). Multilevel models from a multiple group structural equation perspective. In G. Marcoulides & R. Schumacker (Eds.), *Advanced structural equation modeling techniques* (pp. 89–124). Mahwah, NJ: Lawrence Erlbaum Associates.

McArdle, J. J., & McDonald, R. P. (1984). Some algebraic properties of the Reticular Action Model for moment structures. *The British Journal of Mathematical and Statistical Psychology, 37*, 234–251.

McArdle, J. J., & Neale, M. C. (1996). *Estimating longitudinal growth curves from individual level structural equation models* (Working Paper).

McArdle, J. J., & Prescott, C. A. (1992). Age-based construct validation using structural equation models. *Experimental Aging Research, 18*(3), 145–166.

McArdle, J. J., & Prescott, C. A. (1996). Contemporary research on biometric genetic analyses of human cognitive ability. In D. P. Flanagan, J. L. Genshaft, & P. L. Harrison (Eds.), *Beyond traditional intellectual assessment: Contemporary and emerging theories, tests and issues.* New York: Guilford.

McArdle, J. J., & Woodcock, J. R. (1997). Expanding test-rest designs to include developmental time-lag components. *Psychological Methods.*

Meredith, W., & Tisak, J. (1990). Latent curve analysis. *Psychometrika, 55*(1), 107–122.

Neale, M. C. (1993). *Mx statistical modeling.* Unpublished program manual, Department of Human Genetics, Medical College of Virginia, Virginia Commonwealth University, Richmond, VA.

Neale, M. C., & Cardon, L. R. (1992). *Methodology for genetic studies of twins and families.* London: Kluwer Academic Press.

Nesselroade, J. R., & Baltes, P. B. (Eds.). (1979). *Longitudinal research in the study of behavior and development.* New York: Academic Press.

Pankratz, A. (1991). *Forecasting with dynamic regression models.* New York: Wiley.

Rao, C. R. (1958). Some statistical methods for the comparison of growth curves. *Biometrics, 14*, 1–17.

Sörbom, D. (1978). An alternative to the methodology for analysis of covariance. *Psychometrika, 43*(3), 381–396.

Tucker, L. R. (1966). Learning theory and multivariate experiment: Illustration by determination of parameters of generalized learning curves. In R. B. Cattell (Ed.), *The handbook of multivariate experimental psychology* (pp. 476–501). Chicago: Rand-McNally.

Tukey, J. W. (1977). *Exploratory data analysis.* Reading, MA: Addison-Wesley.

Varian, H. R. (Ed.). (1993). *Economic and financial modeling with Mathematica.* New York: Springer-Verlag.

Wright, S. (1982). On "Path analysis in genetic epidemiology: A critique." *American Journal of Human Genetics, 35*, 757–762.

APPENDIX

Computer Input Scripts

A variety of input scripts for the LISREL-8 and Mx programs are included at the author's FTP site (FTP: virginia.edu/mcardle/marco97). Each of these input scripts is associated with a table of results using the same number—for example, some variations using Table 12.A1 were used to produce the numerical results of Table 12.3. (See Tables 12.A2 through 12.A7 for other examples of scripts.)

Specifying the Required Model Matrices

In this initial autoregressive model, we can automatically generate the expected structural equations by using the following steps:

1. Define all model variables in a (1×7) vector

$$v = [Y_{92}^* \ Y_{93}^* \ Y_{94}^* \ Y_{95}^\# \ Y_{96}^* \ Y_{97}^* \ Y_{98}^*]. \qquad (A1)$$

These variables can be placed in any order as long as that order is retained throughout the rest of the matrix specification.

2. Place all one-headed arrows in a matrix A where *the column variable is input to the row variable*. This is defined for the LGMs as the (7×7) asymmetric matrix

$$A = \begin{bmatrix} 0 & 0 & 0 & 0 & 0 & 0 & 0 \\ A_{93} & 0 & 0 & 0 & 0 & 0 & 0 \\ 0 & A_{94} & 0 & 0 & 0 & 0 & 0 \\ 0 & 0 & A_{95} & 0 & 0 & 0 & 0 \\ 0 & 0 & 0 & A_{96} & 0 & 0 & 0 \\ 0 & 0 & 0 & 0 & A_{97} & 0 & 0 \\ 0 & 0 & 0 & 0 & 0 & A_{98} & 0 \end{bmatrix}. \qquad (A2)$$

3. Place all two-headed arrows in a matrix S where the column and row variables are connected. In this example we write the (8×8) symmetric matrix

$$S = \begin{bmatrix} V_{92} & & & & & & sym. \\ 0 & V_u & & & & & \\ 0 & 0 & V_u & & & & \\ 0 & 0 & 0 & V_u & & & \\ 0 & 0 & 0 & 0 & V_u & & \\ 0 & 0 & 0 & 0 & 0 & V_u & \\ 0 & 0 & 0 & 0 & 0 & 0 & V_u \end{bmatrix}. \qquad (A3)$$

4. Distinguish the squares and circles by defining a unit value where the *row variable (from the data) is the same as the column variable (from the model)*. In this simple case where all variables in the model are observed, we write the (7×7) identity matrix $F = I$.

Specifying the Latent Growth Model

To provide an automatic calculation of the expectations, as well as an estimation of optimal parameters, we can write the LGM equations in a matrix form using the following steps:

1. Define all model variables in a (1×10) vector

$$v = [\, K \; Y_{92} \; Y_{93} \; Y_{94} \; Y_{95} \; Y_{96} \; Y_{97} \; Y_{98} \; L \; S \,], \tag{A4}$$

where the K is a label for the unit constant, and the last two variables are the unobserved level and slope variables. These variables can be placed in any order as long as that order is retained throughout the rest of the matrix specification.

2. Place all one-headed arrows in a matrix A where *the column variable is input to the row variable*. This is defined for the LGMs as the (10×10) asymmetric matrix

$$A = \begin{bmatrix} 0 & 0 & 0 & 0 & 0 & 0 & 0 & 0 & 0 & 0 \\ 0 & 0 & 0 & 0 & 0 & 0 & 0 & 0 & 1 & B_1 \\ 0 & 0 & 0 & 0 & 0 & 0 & 0 & 0 & 1 & B_2 \\ 0 & 0 & 0 & 0 & 0 & 0 & 0 & 0 & 1 & B_3 \\ 0 & 0 & 0 & 0 & 0 & 0 & 0 & 0 & 1 & B_4 \\ 0 & 0 & 0 & 0 & 0 & 0 & 0 & 0 & 1 & B_5 \\ 0 & 0 & 0 & 0 & 0 & 0 & 0 & 0 & 1 & B_6 \\ 0 & 0 & 0 & 0 & 0 & 0 & 0 & 0 & 1 & B_7 \\ M_l & 0 & 0 & 0 & 0 & 0 & 0 & 0 & 0 & 0 \\ M_s & 0 & 0 & 0 & 0 & 0 & 0 & 0 & 0 & 0 \end{bmatrix}, \tag{A5}$$

which includes all the basis loadings (last two columns) as well as the latent means (from the constant in the column to the variable in the row).

3. Place all two-headed arrows in a matrix S where the column and row variable are connected. In this example, we write the (10×10) symmetric matrix

$$
S = \begin{bmatrix}
1 & & & & & & & & & sym. \\
0 & V_u & & & & & & & & \\
0 & 0 & V_u & & & & & & & \\
0 & 0 & 0 & V_u & & & & & & \\
0 & 0 & 0 & 0 & V_u & & & & & \\
0 & 0 & 0 & 0 & 0 & V_u & & & & \\
0 & 0 & 0 & 0 & 0 & 0 & V_u & & & \\
0 & 0 & 0 & 0 & 0 & 0 & 0 & V_u & & \\
0 & 0 & 0 & 0 & 0 & 0 & 0 & 0 & V_l & \\
0 & 0 & 0 & 0 & 0 & 0 & 0 & 0 & C_{ls} & V_s
\end{bmatrix}, \tag{A6}
$$

where the matrix includes all variance and covariance terms as well as one cross-product (the unit value).

4. Distinguish the squares and the circles by defining a unit value where the *row variable (from the data) is the same as the column variable (from the model)*. In this case we write the (8 × 10) binary matrix

$$
F = \begin{bmatrix}
1 & 0 & 0 & 0 & 0 & 0 & 0 & 0 & 0 & 0 \\
0 & 1 & 0 & 0 & 0 & 0 & 0 & 0 & 0 & 0 \\
0 & 0 & 1 & 0 & 0 & 0 & 0 & 0 & 0 & 0 \\
0 & 0 & 0 & 1 & 0 & 0 & 0 & 0 & 0 & 0 \\
0 & 0 & 0 & 0 & 1 & 0 & 0 & 0 & 0 & 0 \\
0 & 0 & 0 & 0 & 0 & 1 & 0 & 0 & 0 & 0 \\
0 & 0 & 0 & 0 & 0 & 0 & 1 & 0 & 0 & 0 \\
0 & 0 & 0 & 0 & 0 & 0 & 0 & 1 & 0 & 0
\end{bmatrix}, \tag{A7}
$$

so the last two columns are completely zero and act to filter out the expectations dealing with the latent level and slope variables.

Generating Model Expectations

This matrix specification of A, S, and F can be used in most any SEM program (e.g., LISREL, Mx, etc.) to *automatically* generate structural expectations and other features of the model by using the following steps:

1. Define the *total effects* matrix from the one-headed arrows as

$$
E = (I - A)^{-1}. \tag{A8}
$$

2. Define a *total variables connections* matrix from all model parameters as

$$
\mathcal{E}\{C_{vv}\} = E \times S \times E'. \tag{A9}
$$

3. Define the *observed variables connections* matrix by filtering (if needed)

$$\mathcal{E}\{C\} = F \times \mathcal{E}\{C_{vv}\} \times F'. \tag{A10}$$

More details on the interpretation of these algebraic and graphic relations can be found in McArdle and McDonald (1984) and McArdle and Boker (1990).

Obtaining Statistical Estimates

In a next phase of the analysis, we would like to obtain optimal statistical estimates for the parameters that minimize the differences between the observations and the expectations. Due to the complexity of this problem, we usually use a computer program with a numerical algorithm that can find parameters that minimize these kinds of discrepancies. The computer programs used here (LISREL-8 and Mx) provide MLEs by minimizing a *fitting function* written as

$$\mathcal{F}_{ml} = [ln \mid \mathcal{E}\{C\} \mid - ln \mid C \mid] + [tr(\mathcal{E}\{C\}^{-1} \times C) - q], \tag{A11}$$

where, for q measured variables, the expected covariance matrix is based on p independent parameters (note that the matrix operators $ln(x)$ is the natural logarithm, $\mid x \mid$ is the matrix determinant, and $tr(x)$ is the trace for matrix x). This numerical result is then used to form an approximate LRT statistic

$$LRT \approx 2(N-1) \times \mathcal{F}_{ml} \tag{A12}$$

with the degrees of freedom calculated by

$$df = \frac{q*(q+1)}{2} - p. \tag{A13}$$

Under assumptions of multivariate normality of the random error terms (U_i here), this statistical model provides an index of the goodness of fit between the overall model and the data. These LRT indices and their differences (dLRT) are usually compared to a chi-square distribution for a probability interpretation of the adequacy of specific models.

In models including means as well as covariances, we use the same basic approach. Initially we add a constant ($K = 1$) to the data set. Following this matrix model specification, we can use the same matrix algebra for the calculations of the total effects matrix ($E = (I - A)^{-1}$), the total connections matrix ($\mathcal{E}\{C_w\}$ = ESE$'$), and the expected covariance matrix (C = F$\mathcal{E}\{C_w\}$F$'$). However, because the previous model matrices explicitly include a constant (K) these same algebraic calculations automatically result in a model for the expected moments matrix ($\mathcal{E}\{W\}$). The computer programs used here (LIS-REL-8 and Mx) minimize a fitting function written as

$$\mathcal{F}_{ml} = [ln \mid \mathcal{E}\{W\} \mid - ln \mid W \mid] + [tr(\mathcal{E}\{W\}^{-1} \times W) - (q+1)]$$
$$= [ln \mid \mathcal{E}\{C\} \mid - ln \mid C \mid] + [tr(\mathcal{E}\{C\}^{-1} \times C) - q]$$
$$+ [(\mathcal{E}\{M\} - M) \times \mathcal{E}\{C\}^{-1} \times (\mathcal{E}\{M\} - M)'], \tag{A14}$$

where the same fitting function is apparent, but a third term is added based on mean square distances (as in Hotelling's T^2 or Mahalanobis distance D^2). That is, although the same model matrices are used to form the expected means and covariances, this resulting estimation based on discrepancies actually uses a more complex fitting function.

A Likelihood Difference Approach

When dealing with models fitted to the raw data, we need to recognize that these same likelihood expressions can be written in a different way. If we assume we have measured a vector Y composed of q scores for N individual subjects we can write a *multivariate normal pdf* for all observations as

$$\mathcal{L}(\mu, \Sigma) = \prod_{n=1}^{N} \frac{1}{2\pi^{\frac{q}{2}} \mid \Sigma \mid^{\frac{1}{2}}} \exp\left(-\frac{1}{2}(Y_n - \mu)'\Sigma^{-1}(Y_n - \mu)\right), \tag{A15}$$

where μ is a $(1 \times q)$ expected mean vector, Σ is a $(q \times q)$ expected covariance matrix, and $\mathcal{L}(\mu, \Sigma)$ is the normal *likelihood function*.

To simplify this expression for further calculations, we take the natural logarithm (ln) of $\mathcal{L}(\mu, \Sigma)$ and write the scalar summation

$$-2ln\mathcal{L}(\mu, \Sigma) = -\sum_{n=1}^{N} k * ln(2\pi) - ln \mid \Sigma \mid + (Y_n - \mu)'\Sigma^{-1}(Y_n - \mu), \tag{A16}$$

often termed the *log likelihood function for the model.* If we now substitute the sample statistics for the expected mean $\mu = \bar{Y}$ and for the expected covariance $\Sigma = C$, we obtain

$$-2ln\mathcal{L}(\bar{Y}, C) = -\sum_{n=1}^{N} k * ln(2\pi) - ln \mid C \mid + (Y_n - \bar{Y})'C^{-1}(Y_n - \bar{Y}), \tag{A17}$$

and this can be termed the *log likelihood function for the data*. Because the previous likelihoods are written as simple scalar functions, the change in fit between the observed summary statistics and the expected statistics can be written as

$$\mathcal{F}(\mu, \Sigma) = [-2ln\mathcal{L}(\mu, \Sigma)] - [-2ln\mathcal{L}(\bar{Y}, C)] \tag{A18}$$

which, due to the use of the natural logarithm, this *likelihood difference* is monotonically equivalent to the ratio of the original likelihoods

$$\mathcal{F}(\mu, \Sigma) \approx \frac{\mathcal{L}(\mu, \Sigma)}{\mathcal{L}(\bar{Y}, C)} \tag{A19}$$

so it is often termed the *likelihood ratio*. These equations can be simplified by assuming $\bar{Y} = \mu = 0$, and rearranging the terms to yield the LISREL $\mathcal{F}(ml)$ expression presented initially.

One of the benefits of this raw data expression is that we can rewrite the log likelihood expression in terms of the N individual subjects.

$$-2ln\mathcal{L}(\mu, \Sigma) = -\sum_{n=1}^{N} k * ln(2\pi) - ln \mid \Sigma \mid + (Y_n - \mu)'\Sigma^{-1}(Y_n - \mu),$$

$$= -N[k\, ln(2\pi) - ln \mid \Sigma \mid] - \sum_{n=1}^{N} (Y_n - \mu)'\Sigma^{-1}(Y_n - \mu)$$

$$= -N[k\, ln(2\pi) - ln \mid \Sigma \mid] - \sum_{n=1}^{N} d_n^2(\mu, \Sigma) \tag{A20}$$

where the scalar quantity

$$d_n^2(\mu, \Sigma) = (Y_n - \mu)'\Sigma^{-1}(Y_n - \mu) \tag{A21}$$

is an individual index of the covariance weighted distance between the individual scores and the group averages.

TABLE 12.A1
LISREL Input Script for Autoregressive Markov Model

```
REGs.LS8: Full Auto Only Change Models for NIH SQRT (Budgets) by McArdle (1997)

DAta NIndicators=7 NOservations=20 MAatrix=CMatrix
SDeviations
3.5492     3.5723     3.3947     3.4355     3.6189     3.7094     3.7931
KMatrix SYmmetric
1.0000
0.9891     1.0000
0.9046     0.9314     1.0000
0.9060     0.9318     0.9999     1.0000
0.9126     0.9359     0.9818     0.9816     1.0000
0.9165     0.9385     0.9812     0.9811     0.9998     1.0000
0.9187     0.9399     0.9810     0.9810     0.9995     0.9999     1.0000

MOdel NY[manifest]=7 NE[total]=7 be=fi,fu ps=fi,sy ly=fi,fu te=ze
LE[labels_for_all_variables]
't92','t93','t94','t95','t96','t97','t98'

start[filter] 1 ly 1 1 ly 2 2 ly 3 3 ly 4 4 ly 5 5 ly 6 6 ly 7 7

free[unique_variances] ps 1 1 ps 2 2 ps 3 3 ps 4 4 ps 5 5 ps 6 6 ps 7 7
equal[unique_variances] ps 2 2 ps 3 3 ps 4 4 ps 5 5 ps 6 6 ps 7 7
start[unique_variances] 2 ps 1 1 ps 2 2 ps 3 3 ps 4 4 ps 5 5 ps 6 6 ps 7 7

free[auto_regs] be 2 1 be 3 2 be 4 3 be 5 4 be 6 5 be 7 6
equal[auto_regs] be 2 1 be 3 2 be 4 3 be 5 4 be 6 5 be 7 6
start[auto_regs] .1 be 2 1 be 3 2 be 4 3 be 5 4 be 6 5 be 7 6

output ns ml se tv pt pc rs xm  ad=off
```

TABLE 12.A2
LISREL-8 Input Script for Latent Growth Models

```
LGMS.LS8: A Latent Growth Models for SQRT NIH Budgets by McArdle (1997)
          Using RAM notation and augmented moment matrix with LISREL

DAta  NIndicators=8 NObservations=20 MAtrix = MMoments
MEans
   1       5.1918    5.4348    5.2778    5.3546    5.4403    5.5746    5.6540
SDeviations
   0       3.5492    3.5723    3.3947    3.4355    3.6189    3.7094    3.7931
KMatrix SYmmetric
      1.0
      0.0  1.0000
      0.0  0.9891    1.0000
      0.0  0.9046    0.9314    1.0000
      0.0  0.9060    0.9318    0.9999    1.0000
      0.0  0.9126    0.9359    0.9818    0.9816    1.0000
      0.0  0.9165    0.9385    0.9812    0.9811    0.9998    1.0000
      0.0  0.9187    0.9399    0.9810    0.9810    0.9995    0.9999    1.0000

MOdel NY[manifest]=8 NE[total]=12 be=fi,fu ps=fi,sy ly=fi,fu te=ze
LE[labels_for_all_variables]
'con','t92','t93','t94','t95','t96','t97','t98','lev','slope','level*',
  'slope*'

start[filter] 1 ly 1 1 ly 2 2 ly 3 3 ly 4 4 ly 5 5 ly 6 6 ly 7 7 ly 8 8

start[level] 1 be 2 9 be 3 9 be 4 9 be 5 9 be 6 9 be 7 9 be 8 9

start[linear] 0 be 2 10
start[linear] 1 be 3 10
start[linear] 2 be 4 10
start[linear] 3 be 5 10
start[linear] 4 be 6 10
start[linear] 5 be 7 10
start[linear] 6 be 8 10

free[latent_deviations] be 9 11 be 10 12
start[latent_dev_level] 3.38 be 9 11
start[latent_dev_slope] 1.26 be 10 12

start[constant_moment] 1 ps 1 1
start[scaling] 1 ps 11 11 ps 12 12
free[latent_corr] ps 11 12
start[latent_corr] .04 ps 11 12

free[latent_means] be 9 1 be 10 1
start[latent_mean_level] 5.22 be 9 1
start[latent_mean_slope] .07 be 10 1

free[unique_variances] ps 2 2 ps 3 3 ps 4 4 ps 5 5 ps 6 6 ps 7 7 ps 8 8
equal[unique_variances] ps 2 2 ps 3 3 ps 4 4 ps 5 5 ps 6 6 ps 7 7 ps 8 8
start[unique_variances] 1 ps 2 2 ps 3 3 ps 4 4 ps 5 5 ps 6 6 ps 7 7 ps 8 8
```

(Continued)

398

TABLE 12.A2

(Continued)

```
free[slope] be 3 10 be 4 10 be 5 10 be 6 10 be 7 10

IRestriction be 10 12 > 0
IRestriction ps 11 12 < 1 > -1

free[constant_moment] ps 1 1

output ns ml se tv pt pc fd it=100 ad=off rs xm ep=.00001
```

TABLE 12.A3

Mx-96 Input Script for Moment Matrix Form of Latent Growth Models

```
LGMS_MOM.MX = Latent Growth models using Pre-calculated Moments.

DAta NG=1 NO=20 NI=8
CMatrix SYmmetric
 1.0000
 5.1918   39.5516
 5.4348   40.7570   42.2984
 5.2778   38.3003   39.9788   39.3792
 5.3546   38.8471   40.5368   39.9218   40.4744
 5.4403   39.9666   41.6661   40.7743   41.3346   42.6933
 5.5746   41.0083   42.7330   41.7772   42.3525   43.7488   44.8358
 5.6540   41.7224   43.4641   42.4725   43.0585   44.4794   45.5875   46.3553

Select  1 2 3 4 5 6 7 8 /

Begin Matrices;
F  FUll  8   12
A  Full  12  12
S  Symm  12  12
I  Iden  12  12
End Matrices;

Labels Row F
K $92 $93 $94 $95 $96 $97 $98
Labels Col F
K $92 $93 $94 $95 $96 $97 $98 $L $S $L* $S*
Matrix F
1 0 0 0 0 0 0 0 0 0 0 0
0 1 0 0 0 0 0 0 0 0 0 0
0 0 1 0 0 0 0 0 0 0 0 0
0 0 0 1 0 0 0 0 0 0 0 0
0 0 0 0 1 0 0 0 0 0 0 0
0 0 0 0 0 1 0 0 0 0 0 0
0 0 0 0 0 0 1 0 0 0 0 0
0 0 0 0 0 0 0 1 0 0 0 0

Labels Row A
K $92 $93 $94 $95 $96 $97 $98 $L $S $L* $S*
```

(Continued)

TABLE 12.A3
(Continued)

```
Labels Col A
K $92 $93 $94 $95 $96 $97 $98 $L $S $L* $S*
Specify A
 0 0 0 0 0 0 0 0 0 0 0 0
 0 0 0 0 0 0 0 0 0 0 0 0
 0 0 0 0 0 0 0 0 0 7 0 0
 0 0 0 0 0 0 0 0 0 8 0 0
 0 0 0 0 0 0 0 0 0 9 0 0
 0 0 0 0 0 0 0 0 0 10 0 0
 0 0 0 0 0 0 0 0 0 11 0 0
 0 0 0 0 0 0 0 0 0 0 0 0
 5 0 0 0 0 0 0 0 0 0 1 0
 6 0 0 0 0 0 0 0 0 0 0 2
 0 0 0 0 0 0 0 0 0 0 0 0
 0 0 0 0 0 0 0 0 0 0 0 0
Matrix A
0    0 0 0 0 0 0 0  0   0  0
0    0 0 0 0 0 0 1. 0   0  0
0    0 0 0 0 0 0 1. 1.  0  0
0    0 0 0 0 0 0 1. 2.  0  0
0    0 0 0 0 0 0 1. 3.  0  0
0    0 0 0 0 0 0 1. 4.  0  0
0    0 0 0 0 0 0 1. 5.  0  0
0    0 0 0 0 0 0 1. 6.  0  0
5.   0 0 0 0 0 0 0  0   2. 0
.1   0 0 0 0 0 0 0  0   0  1.
0    0 0 0 0 0 0 0  0   0  0
0    0 0 0 0 0 0 0  0   0  0


Labels Row S
K $92 $93 $94 $95 $96 $97 $98 $L $S $L* $S*
Labels Col S
K $92 $93 $94 $95 $96 $97 $98 $L $S $L* $S*
Specify S
12
0 3
0 0 3
0 0 0 3
0 0 0 0 3
0 0 0 0 0 3
0 0 0 0 0 0 3
0 0 0 0 0 0 0 3
0 0 0 0 0 0 0 0 0
0 0 0 0 0 0 0 0 0 0
0 0 0 0 0 0 0 0 0 0 0
0 0 0 0 0 0 0 0 0 0 4 0
```

(Continued)

TABLE 12.A3
(Continued)

```
Matrix S
1.
0 2.
0 0 2.
0 0 0 2.
0 0 0 0 2.
0 0 0 0 0 2.
0 0 0 0 0 0 2.
0 0 0 0 0 0 0 2.
0 0 0 0 0 0 0 0 0
0 0 0 0 0 0 0 0 0 0
0 0 0 0 0 0 0 0 0 0 1.
0 0 0 0 0 0 0 0 0 0 .01 1.

Boundary -1 1 S 11 12
Boundary  0 2 A 10 12

COvariance F * (I − A)~ * S * (I − A)~' * F' ;

Options RSiduals SErrors DRaw=c:\lgms\lgms_mom.ram
End Group;
```

TABLE 12.A4
Mx-96 Input Script for Raw Data Latent Growth Models

```
LGMS_RAW.MX = Latent Growth Models from Raw data

DAta NG=1 NO=20 NI=7
REctangular
    8.9539    10.9048    11.3766    11.3968    11.8629    12.0291    12.2066
    8.2419     8.9008     9.2116     9.3434     9.3381     9.6151     9.7314
    2.5022     2.4783     2.5233     2.5538     3.0931     3.2034     3.2732
    4.0743     4.1110     4.1952     4.2544     5.0596     5.1962     5.2440
    6.3527     5.8669     5.5798     5.6595     4.7026     4.7884     4.8380
    2.5128     2.8879     3.3252     3.3731     2.8808     2.9379     2.9672
    2.0768     2.0768     2.0102     2.0372     2.0950     2.1534     2.1783
    7.4833     7.6285     7.5468     7.6616     8.5300     8.7977     8.9107
    2.5464     3.0236     3.0363     3.0911     2.4397     2.5150     2.5444
    2.6499     3.1305     2.7185     2.7185     3.0646     3.1329     3.1718
    7.8121     8.0654     8.1814     8.3030     8.3261     8.4499     8.4918
    2.5698     2.4094     2.1427     2.1749     2.7377     2.8054     2.8390
    2.7794     3.2496     2.5923     2.6412     2.3292     2.4000     2.4380
   12.7841    12.5155     7.2303     7.3623     8.5240     8.8323     9.0278
    5.7469     5.8310     7.5462     7.6811     8.1451     8.1854     8.1854
   12.9797    12.7754    13.3926    13.6235    13.7638    14.2127    14.6799
    4.7940     4.9060     4.6061     4.6811     5.2742     5.4599     5.5323
    4.5140     4.6235     4.6328     4.7117     2.8846     2.9833     3.0199
    0.8349     0.7537     0.9513     0.9654     1.2058     1.2438     1.2498
    1.6279     2.5581     2.7568     2.8576     2.5499     2.5499     2.5499
Select  1 2 3 4 5 6 7 /
```

(Continued)

TABLE 12.A4
(Continued)

```
Begin Matrices;
F  FUll 7  11
A  Full 11  11
S  Symm 11  11
M  Full 11  1
I  Iden 11  11
End Matrices;


Labels Row F
$92 $93 $94 $95 $96 $97 $98
Labels Col F
$92 $93 $94 $95 $96 $97 $98 $L $S $L* $S*
Matrix F
1 0 0 0 0 0 0 0 0 0 0
0 1 0 0 0 0 0 0 0 0 0
0 0 1 0 0 0 0 0 0 0 0
0 0 0 1 0 0 0 0 0 0 0
0 0 0 0 1 0 0 0 0 0 0
0 0 0 0 0 1 0 0 0 0 0
0 0 0 0 0 0 1 0 0 0 0


Labels Row A
$92 $93 $94 $95 $96 $97 $98 $L $S $L* $S*
Labels Col A
$92 $93 $94 $95 $96 $97 $98 $L $S $L* $S*
Specify A
 0 0 0 0 0 0 0 0  0 0
 0 0 0 0 0 0 0 7  0 0
 0 0 0 0 0 0 0 8  0 0
 0 0 0 0 0 0 0 9  0 0
 0 0 0 0 0 0 0 10 0 0
 0 0 0 0 0 0 0 11 0 0
 0 0 0 0 0 0 0 0  0 0
 0 0 0 0 0 0 0 0  1 0
 0 0 0 0 0 0 0 0  0 2
 0 0 0 0 0 0 0 0  0 0
 0 0 0 0 0 0 0 0  0 0
Matrix A
 0 0 0 0 0 0 0 1. 0  0  0
 0 0 0 0 0 0 0 1. 1. 0  0
 0 0 0 0 0 0 0 1. 2. 0  0
 0 0 0 0 0 0 0 1. 3. 0  0
 0 0 0 0 0 0 0 1. 4. 0  0
 0 0 0 0 0 0 0 1. 5. 0  0
 0 0 0 0 0 0 0 1. 6. 0  0
 0 0 0 0 0 0 0 0  2. 0
 0 0 0 0 0 0 0 0  0  1.
 0 0 0 0 0 0 0 0  0  0
 0 0 0 0 0 0 0 0  0  0
```

(Continued)

TABLE 12.A4
(*Continued*)

```
Labels Row S
$92 $93 $94 $95 $96 $97 $98 $L $S $L* $S*
Labels Col S
$92 $93 $94 $95 $96 $97 $98 $L $S $L* $S*
Specify S
3
0 3
0 0 3
0 0 0 3
0 0 0 0 3
0 0 0 0 0 3
0 0 0 0 0 0 3
0 0 0 0 0 0 0 0
0 0 0 0 0 0 0 0 0
0 0 0 0 0 0 0 0 0 0
0 0 0 0 0 0 0 0 0 4 0
Matrix S
2.
0 2.
0 0 2.
0 0 0 2.
0 0 0 0 2.
0 0 0 0 0 2.
0 0 0 0 0 0 2.
0 0 0 0 0 0 0 0
0 0 0 0 0 0 0 0 0
0 0 0 0 0 0 0 0 1.
0 0 0 0 0 0 0 0 .01 1.

Labels Row M
$92 $93 $94 $95 $96 $97 $98 $L $S $L* $S*
Labels Col M
K
Specify M
0
0
0
0
0
0
0
5
6
0
0
Matrix M
0
0
0
```

(*Continued*)

TABLE 12.A4
(Continued)

```
0
0
0
0
5.
.1
0
0


Boundary -1 1 S 10 11
Boundary  0 2 A 9  11

MEan F * (I - A)~ * M ;
COvariance F * (I - A)~ * S * (I - A)~' * F' ;

Options RSiduals SErrors MX%P=c:\lgms\lgms_raw.fit
End Group;
```

TABLE 12.A5
Mx-96 Input Script for Missing Data Latent Growth Models

```
LGMS_MIS = Latent Growth including some Missing raw data.

DAta NG=1 NO=20 NI=7
REctangular
      8.9539    10.9048    11.3766    11.3968    11.8629    12.0291    12.2066
      8.2419     8.9008     9.2116     9.3434     9.3381     9.6151     9.7314
      2.5022     2.4783     2.5233     2.5538     3.0931     3.2034     3.2732
      4.0743     4.1110     4.1952     4.2544     5.0596     5.1962     5.2440
      6.3527     5.8669     5.5798     5.6595     4.7026     4.7884     4.8380
      2.5128     2.8879     3.3252     3.3731     2.8808     2.9379     2.9672
      2.0768     2.0768     2.0102     2.0372     2.0950     2.1534     2.1783
      7.4833     7.6285     7.5468     7.6616     8.5300     8.7977     8.9107
      2.5464     3.0236     3.0363     3.0911     2.4397     2.5150     2.5444
      2.6499     3.1305     2.7185     2.7185     3.0646     3.1329     3.1718
      7.8121     8.0654     8.1814     8.3030     8.3261     8.4499     8.4918
      2.5698     2.4094     2.1427     2.1749     2.7377     2.8054     2.8390
      2.7794     3.2496     2.5923     2.6412     2.3292     2.4000     2.4380
         .          .       7.2303     7.3623     8.5240     8.8323     9.0278
      5.7469     5.8310     7.5462     7.6811     8.1451     8.1854     8.1854
     12.9797    12.7754    13.3926    13.6235    13.7638    14.2127    14.6799
      4.7940     4.9060     4.6061     4.6811     5.2742     5.4599     5.5323
      4.5140     4.6235     4.6328     4.7117     2.8846     2.9833     3.0199
      0.8349     0.7537     0.9513     0.9654     1.2058     1.2438     1.2498
      1.6279     2.5581     2.7568     2.8576     2.5499     2.5499     2.5499
Select  1 2 3 4 5 6 7 /

<NOTE:  The same as previous Raw Data Mx-script from here on>
```

TABLE 12.A6
Mx-96 Input Script for Sparse Data Latent Growth Models

```
LGMS_SPA = Latent Growth including a Sparse Pattern of Missing raw data.
DAta NG=1 NO=20 NI=7
REctangular
        8.9539     10.9048     11.3766        .           .           .           .
           .         8.9008      9.2116      9.3434        .           .           .
           .            .        2.5233      2.5538      3.0931        .           .
           .            .           .        4.2544      5.0596      5.1962        .
           .            .           .           .        4.7026      4.7884      4.8380
        2.5128          .           .           .           .        2.9379      2.9672
        2.0768       2.0768         .           .           .           .        2.1783
        7.4833       7.6285      7.5468         .           .           .           .
           .         3.0236      3.0363      3.0911        .           .           .
           .            .        2.7185      2.7185      3.0646        .           .
           .            .           .        8.3030      8.3261      8.4499        .
           .            .           .           .        2.7377      2.8054      2.8390
        2.7794          .           .           .           .        2.4000      2.4380
       12.7841      12.5155         .           .           .           .        9.0278
        5.7469       5.8310      7.5462         .           .           .           .
           .        12.7754     13.3926     13.6235        .           .           .
           .            .        4.6061      4.6811      5.2742        .           .
           .            .           .        4.7117      2.8846      2.9833        .
           .            .           .           .        1.2058      1.2438      1.2498
        1.6279          .           .           .           .        2.5499      2.5499
Select  1 2 3 4 5 6 7 /
<NOTE:  The same as previous Raw Data Mx-script from here on>
```

```
LGMS_SVL = Latent Growth including a Sparse Variable Length of Missing raw data
DAta NG=1 NO=20 NI=7
VLength
3
1 2 3
 8.9539     10.9048     11.3766
3
2 3 4
 8.9008      9.2116      9.3434
3
3 4 5
 2.5233      2.5538      3.0931
3
4 5 6
 4.2544      5.0596      5.1962
3
5 6 7
 4.7026      4.7884      4.8380
```

(Continued)

405

TABLE 12.A7
(Continued)

```
3
1 6 7
  2.5128    2.9379    2.9672
3
1 2 7
  2.0768    2.0768    2.1783
3
1 2 3
  7.4833    7.6285    7.5468
3
2 3 4
  3.0236    3.0363    3.0911
3
3 4 5
  2.7185    2.7185    3.0646
3
4 5 6
  8.3030    8.3261    8.4499
3
5 6 7
  2.7377    2.8054    2.8390
3
1 6 7
  2.7794    2.4000    2.4380
3
1 2 7
 12.7841   12.5155    9.0278
3
1 2 3
  5.7469    5.8310    7.5462
3
2 3 4
 12.7754   13.3926   13.6235
3
3 4 5
  4.6061    4.6811    5.2742
3
4 5 6
  4.7117    2.8846    2.9833
3
5 6 7
  1.2058    1.2438    1.2498
3
1 6 7
  1.6279    2.5499    2.5499

Select  1 2 3 4 5 6 7 /

<NOTE:  The same as previous Raw Data Mx-script from here on>
```

406

CHAPTER THIRTEEN

Structural and Configural Models for Longitudinal Categorical Data

Phillip K. Wood
University of Missouri–Columbia

Although the importance of longitudinal research designs in the construction and testing of management and psychological theory appears to be gaining increasing recognition, there seems to be little consensus as to how to specify and evaluate models from such data. Part of the difficulty in choosing and evaluating various approaches to longitudinal categorical models stems from different views of how time affects the constructs under study. In the simplest form, for example, longitudinal models of categorical data could view repeated measurements of the same constructs as merely repeated measurements of a dependent variable that are related to selected independent variables of interest (as is implicit in standard loglinear repeated measures models). More elementary models in this category assume that the error associated with any given measurement occasion is independent of any other occasion, whereas more sophisticated models allow for autoregressive error, or prespecified patterning of error.

Although such standard approaches are useful if the research questions and data conform to such a model, two new approaches that consider how response patterns may be structured over time have been proposed. One technique, *configural frequency analysis* (CFA), assumes that patterns of response across categorical variables over time may be used to uncover "types" or "syndromes" of response in the data (von Eye, 1990a, 1990b; von Eye & Spiel, 1996; von Eye, Spiel, & Wood, 1996). CFA approaches are a method of residual analysis in that they define such types based on a discrepancy between the observed frequency of response in the data and the

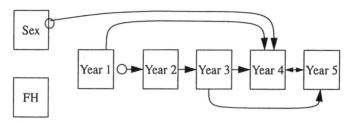

FIG. 13.1. POIPG of a 5-year study of alcohol abuse/dependence, gender, and family history (FH).

predicted frequency of response based on a null model (usually a null model of marginal independence). As such, configural frequency models usually result in the identification of one or more patterns of response over the entire trajectory of a longitudinal study.

Bayesian belief systems, by contrast, are exploratory techniques designed to identify patterns of conditional dependence in categorical data by means of structural diagrams that represent causal relationships between the variables under study (Spirtes, Glymour, & Scheines, 1993; Spirtes, Scheines, Meek, & Glymour, 1994). These conditional dependencies are represented by means of a POIPG, or *partially oriented inducing path graph*. One example of such a graph is given in Fig. 13.1.

This chapter examines how these two approaches can be used to explore relationships between categorical variables in an extended longitudinal study. On one hand, the basic assumptions of these two approaches result in conceptual different patterns of results. However, the two approaches can be used in tandem to produce a clearer picture of the data: The power of the Tetrad approach to detect relatively proscribed patterns of conditional dependence provides interesting alternatives to configural frequency approaches. Configural frequency models, on the other hand, can be used to identify and operationalize categorical variables that are defined across measurement occasions and, as such, can be used to define "clusters" or "types" of individuals as an alternative to complicated patterns of conditional dependence.

This chapter begins with a brief introduction to CFA, by presenting a CFA of a simple two-wave longitudinal study. This example is then extended to a five-wave longitudinal study of the same data. Following that, a Bayesian belief network representation for the same data is presented. The conditional independence model of CFA has a ready structural representation as a Bayesian belief network. After that, the belief network generated by the *Tetrad* program for these data is presented. Additional Tetrad analyses are then described in which types of response identified by a CFA are used to generate a simpler and more interpretable graph of conditional relationships. Fortunately in these data, the Tetrad approach also identifies local patterns of conditional independence not identified by a global CFA. These relationships are also used as the basis for a CFA conducted on a subset of the available time measurements.

Configural Frequency Analysis of a 2 × 2 Table. In order to better understand the logic of CFA for multiwave longitudinal designs, it is helpful to first consider the analysis of a simple longitudinal design with two measurement occasions. Table 13.1 presents the data from a longitudinal study (described in more detail later) of the incidence of 12-month alcohol use disorder in a sample of young adults measured on two occasions. In the 2 × 2 contingency table of such a study, CFA involves the evaluation of four tests, one for each cell, as opposed to more familiar global tests of association such as Pearson's X^2. Although many of the conventionally used global tests of association reject the hypothesis that these two variables are independent (X^2_1 = 186.99, $p <$ .001; Λ_1 = 168.304, $p <$ .001; Fisher's exact test (2-tailed) = $1.0*10^{38}$), such a relationship does not inform the researcher whether such a pattern of association is due to the fact that individuals who do not diagnose for alcoholism tend not to on later occasions, whether those who diagnose at the first occasion tend to continue to diagnose, whether both of these relationships obtain, or whether some other pattern of contingency is present.

Identification of Types and Antitypes. CFA tests are designed to test for the presence of significant departures from a null or base model that reflect such systematic patterns. Most often, such a null model involves the assump-

TABLE 13.1
12-Month Alcohol Diagnosis at Two Times of Testing

Time 2	Time 1		
	No Diagnosis	Diagnosis	Marginals
No Diagnosis	315[a]	24	
	263.75[b]	75.25	339
	70.63%[c]	5.38%	76.01%
	59.14%[d]	16.87%	
Diagnosis	32	75	
	83.25	23.75	107
	7.17%	16.82%	23.99%
	18.66%	5.33%	
Marginals	347	99	446
	77.80%	22.20%	

[a]denotes observed frequency. [b]denotes expected frequency under independence. [c]denotes the observed proportion. [d]denotes the expected proportion under independence model.

tion that the proportion of individuals in each cell of the contingency table is the product of the marginal frequencies. Such a model is termed *first-order CFA* to distinguish it from *zero-order CFA,* which assumes that all marginal frequencies are equally likely. One CFA statistic for residuals is the familiar z-score statistic, which involves testing whether the cell X^2 contributions for given cells are statistically significant. This is usually done by recognizing that X^2 is calculated by summing the component one-degree-of-freedom chi-square statistics associated with each cell of the contingency table. The z-score statistic for such component X^2 tests is calculated by noting that the X^2 distribution is the result of squaring the elements of a standard normal (mean = 0, $SD = 1$) distribution. Accordingly, if $X_1{}^2 = (o - np)2/Npq$, then $z = (o - np)/\mathrm{sqrt}(Npq)$. Application of the z test to the four cells of Table 13.1 yields two types and two antitypes. For cells 00 and 11, for example, $z = 4.94$ and 10.81, respectively. The two other cells of the contingency table have z scores lower than their expected values (for cell 01, $z = -6.48$, and for cell 10, $z = -6.23$). In all cases, $p(z) < \alpha*$, where $\alpha*$ represents a Bonferroni-corrected significance level.

Binomial Probabilities. Initially, CFA theorists (Haberman, 1973; Krauth & Lienert, 1973) introduced the binomial test as a "best" or "most accurate" test for the identication of types and antitypes. This is based on the probability distribution under the assumption that a fixed population proportion exists that determines the observed frequency in the sample. It is possible to calculate the critical region associated with the binomial distribution using the Probbeta function in SAS™. In such applications, the probability of the cell is calculated under the null model (i.e., $p = e/N$ where N is the sample size and e is the expected frequency under the chance model). For a 2×2 table, $e = N*pi.*p.j$ where $pi.*p.j$ indicates the product of the marginal proportions associated with the cell. For the first cell of the contingency table, computation of the probability of 75 individuals diagnosing on both occasions under the marginal independence null model is:

$p11 = .7601*.7780$; *calculates joint probability under marginal independence model;

$\mathrm{prob}11 = \mathrm{probbeta}(p11,75,446-75+1)$.

Again, $p11$ is the proportion of individuals in cell 11 under the model of marginal independence. If the probability associated with such a model is low, this is again taken as evidence for the existence of a type associated with that cell. For the data of Table 13.1, if the obtained significance levels are again corrected for family-wise error rates, two types again emerge: 00, individuals who did not diagnose for alcoholism at either time; and 11, individuals who diagnosed for alcoholism at both times. Two antitypes also emerge, consisting of those individuals who diagnosed at one, but not the other occasion. If the researcher desires some statement of the population incidence of patterns identified with CFA, Wood, Sher, and von Eye (1993) developed and demonstrated Bayesian highest density regions, which represent maximum likelihood values for the obtained type (or antitype) proportions.

Problems of Inference With CFA Models. The example just presented is shown only to demonstrate the general logic and computations behind the CFA approach. Limitations of the general approach and execution of CFA, however, have been the object of much discussion. For the analysis of longitudinal data with CFA, these concerns may be grouped around the central themes of: (a) how many types may be logically identified in a cross-tabulation table, (b) concerns regarding the underlying distribution used for CFA, (c) concerns regarding choice of an appropriate null model, (d) questions about which variables to include in a CFA, and (e) questions as to whether global types exist over all occasions of measurement, or whether types exist over only a restricted time period. These are discussed in turn in the sections that follow.

How Many Types May Be Present in a Contingency Table? It has often been mentioned that one of the main difficulties with CFA is that residual analysis of contingency table data does not allow for simultaneous testing of whether each cell of the contingency table constitutes a type or antitype (Kieser & Victor, 1991; Victor, 1989). For example, in the 2×2 example given earlier, if a researcher correctly identifies a "type" of respondent who is considered a non-alcohol-abuser on both occasions, the hypothesis of independence based on marginal proportions no longer obtains. Because this contingency table has, under the main effect model, only one degree of freedom, no further independence hypotheses based on collapsed information may be made. (Although, as Netter, 1996, pointed out, the one-degree-of-freedom limitation does not extend to the analysis of three or more times of measurement with dichotomous data.) Several extensions of the model have been proposed to deal with this. Victor proposed an extension of traditional CFA models that involves the sequential identification of types and antitypes for large sample data sets. In the first step of the procedure, types and antitypes are identified as before. In subsequent steps, however, frequencies for this cell are excluded from the contingency table. This cell is then treated as a structural zero for subsequent tests of quasi-independence. Analysis then proceeds to testing for types and antitypes under this modified base model. Netter and Lienert (1984) proposed the use of local or prediction CFA, in which only certain cells of the contingency table are analyzed. Finally, Wood, Sher, and von Eye (1994) considered another sequential modification of the base model for CFA by testing whether the subsequent cells of a contingency table are equally likely.

Is the Binomial Distribution Appropriate? A second problem with CFA concerns the fact that a particular contingency table may violate the marginal independence model or that the binomial distribution may not be an appropriate model for the observed frequencies of response. Specifically, if the contingency table presented in Table 13.1 is actually condensed from a larger contingency table (as might happen, e.g., if alcohol use patterns for men and women were significantly different over time), the resulting cell frequencies in the reduced contingency table are not necessarily binomially distributed. Variants of CFA have been developed to address these issues (Kieser & Victor, 1991; Victor, 1989). Unfortunately, these approaches are based on asymptotic theory, which requires the use of large samples.

Is the Base Model Appropriate? Third, the confidence that a researcher may have in the identified types and antitypes depends on whether the chosen base model is appropriate. This point was discussed most clearly by Mellenbergh (1996) in which he demonstrated that the identified types and antitypes of a cross-tabulation table were different, depending on the nature of the assumed base model. For longitudinal data, for example, it seems particularly relevant to consider if the obtained pattern of results represents a Markovian process, wherein the probability of subsequent observations is conditional on immediately preceding observation for the individual. For example, in the contingency table of Table 13.1, such a Markovian model would assume that the joint expected proportion for not diagnosing at Time 1 (O_1) or Time 2 (O_2) may be expressed as: $P(O_1 O_2) = P(O_1)P(O_2 \mid O_1)$. Unfortunately, such a Markovian model for 2×2 contingency tables represents a fully saturated model for such an experiment (i.e., the predicted cell frequencies under the Markovian model are identical to the observed frequencies by definition). In the case of more than two measurement occasions, however, the Markovian model of adjacent time periods can be used as a base model in a CFA analysis (as is shown later).

Which Variables Should Be Included in the Analysis? In addition, little guidance has been given to researchers as to how to select variables for inclusion in the CFA. On one hand, selection of too few variables may result in a coarse division of the data, which may obscure useful patterns in the data. By contrast, inclusion of too many variables risks splintering the observations into many different cells of the contingency table, where they may not occur in sufficient numbers to result in identification as a systematic pattern.

Must Types Span All Times of Measurement, or Only a Few Measurement Occasions? A final point related to all of the second through fourth points just discussed is that it is quite possible that types or antitypes may exist for only a subset of measurement occasions, or that base models for the data may be appropriate for only some measurement occasions, but not the entire timeline of the study. It is possible, for example, that only some of the adjacent measurement occasions require conditional probabilities, or that a selected subset of the variables may be conditionally independent of other variables in the study. It is also possible to consider models in which multiple time-delimited Types may be present in the data, or models in which the base model for some measurement occasions may be different than the most appropriate one for other occasions (as might occur, e.g., in studies that span periods of transition over time as well as measurement occasions with relatively stable patterns).

Summary. From the preceding discussion of questions and limitations, it should be evident that any given application of CFA to research data must be carefully thought through. On one hand, the question of when to interpret residual frequencies is a logical limitations of the method, although workarounds for such problems have been advanced. More critical to the existence of claimed types, however, are the questions concerning whether the level of aggregation of the table is appropriate, whether the base model chosen is defensible, whether the appropriate variables have been chosen for analysis, and whether the types and antitypes that have been identified represent consistent patterns of performance over the duration of the study, or may be more parsimoniously expressed as a subset of measurement occasions.

Tetrad analysis of contingency table data appears a promising tool to explore these concerns within a particular data set. Specifically, the Tetrad program can be used to identify contingent relationships between variables in a study, and thereby provide some information about the level of appropriate aggregation for the data. Tetrad can also be used to identify those subsets of the data that have significant interrelationships. Tetrad can also be used to specify the probabilities that would result from a model of adjacent conditional probabilities, such as the Markovian model described earlier. Tetrad models can also be used as a way to generate a conceptual model that is an alternative to the types identified under a CFA. Finally, Tetrad can be used to allow the researcher to easily specify mixed models in which some variables are conditionally related to adjacent variables, and where types are included in the model in either a time-limited, or global fashion. Conversely, the logic of CFA can also be used to guide reparameterizations of a Bayesian belief network in order to make it more conceptually interpretable.

To show how this can be accomplished, data from a five-wave longitudinal study are presented and analyzed using the traditional CFA model. An alternative base model using adjacent conditional probabilities is estimated, and the resulting types from this CFA compared with the original. Finally, the structural model proposed by Tetrad's Build option are reported. Although this model represents an even better fit to the data than the model of adjacent conditional relationships, its conceptual interpretation is not readily apparent. To remedy this, additional categorical variables are added to the analysis that represent the types identified under both the Markovian and Tetrad-generated base models.

The Data. Table 13.2 presents the data from a five-wave longitudinal study of participants who were first-time freshmen enrolled at a midwestern research university. (This study is discussed in further detail in Sher, Walitzer, Wood, & Brent, 1991.) Participants were selected based on sex and family history of alcoholism (scored as 1 = present and 0 = absent). In addition, participants were classed based on their 12-month alcoholism diagnosis at each measurement occasion. At each time of testing, subjects were diagnosed as either having a 12-month alcohol use disorder diagnosis or not having such a disorder. Alcohol use disorder was operationally defined for this study as either a 12-month alcohol abuse or dependence diagnosis. For these data, then, the resulting 2 × 2 × 2 × 2 × 2 × 2 × 2 contingency table represents information on sex and family history of alcoholism as well as all patterns of alcohol diagnosis over the five occasions of measurement. Longitudinal diagnoses are described by a five-digit code indicating diagnosis of alcohol use disorder (1) or no diagnosis (0). An individual who diagnosed at only the first occasion, then, would receive a longitudinal diagnosis of 10000, for example.

Traditional CFA Results. In the interests of simplicity, a traditional first-order CFA of the data was conducted using probabilities estimated under the binomial distribution (as described previously). The expected frequencies for the configurations of alcohol use disorder for family history positive and negative individuals are given in the fourth and eighth columns of Table 13.2. Holms correction was used in order to control for experimentwise error, assuming an experimentwise alpha of .05. For purposes of comparison, other probability estimates described in von Eye (1990a) were calculated as well, but because the pattern of recovered types was identical to the binomial estimates, only these are reported. Under traditional CFA, 10 types (which are shaded in Table 13.2) are classified: Three types were composed of individuals who did not diagnose at any wave (00000) and were either females (both Family History negative and positive), or Family History negative males; three types were composed of individuals who diagnose at all waves (11111), and were either family history positive females, or males (both Family History negative and positive); three types were composed of individuals who diagnosed at the first four waves, but not the last wave (11110), and were found among family history positive females, and in both family history positive and negative males. Finally, weak evidence was also found among family history positive males for a type corresponding to

TABLE 13.2

CFA Observed and Expected Frequencies for Traditional Type I CFA, Markov, and Tetrad Models

| | | Family History Negative Participants | | | | Family History Positive Participants | | | |
| | | Obs. Freq. | Expected Frequencies[b] | | | Obs. Freq. | Expected Frequencies | | |
Gender	Longitudinal Diagnosis[a]		Trad. CFA	Markov	Tetrad		Trad. CFA	Markov	Tetrad
Male	00000	61	**33.5785**	59.9595	61.4563	46	35.1188	51.2717	52.5516
	00001	2	6.5717	5.2210	3.3573	4	6.8751	4.4645	2.8709
	00010	5	7.7917	2.5533	3.8240	2	8.1491	2.1833	3.2699
	00011	1	1.5249	2.8085	1.9117	2	1.5949	2.4015	1.6347
	00100	0	8.6074	2.1284	1.0927	2	9.0023	1.8200	0.9344
	00101	1	1.6846	0.1853	0.5962	0	1.7618	0.1585	0.5098
	00110	4	1.9973	1.8474	1.7386	3	2.0889	1.5797	1.4867
	00111	1	0.3909	2.0320	2.7656	0	0.4088	1.7376	2.3649
	01000	1	9.5800	1.8070	1.6128	2	10.0195	1.5451	1.3791
	01001	1	1.8749	0.1573	0.0881	0	1.9609	0.1345	0.0753
	01010	0	2.2230	0.0769	0.2835	0	2.3250	0.0658	0.2424
	01011	0	0.4351	0.0846	0.1417	0	0.4550	0.0724	0.1212
	01100	1	2.4557	1.2789	1.2038	1	2.5684	1.0936	1.0294
	01101	0	0.4806	0.1114	0.6568	0	0.5027	0.0952	0.5616
	01110	1	0.5698	1.1100	0.7182	0	0.5960	0.9492	0.6141
	01111	0	0.1115	1.2210	1.1424	0	0.1166	1.0441	0.9769
	10000	5	10.5985	7.0843	7.1852	1	11.0847	11.0899	11.2480
	10001	0	2.0742	0.6169	0.3925	5	2.1694	0.9657	0.6145
	10010	0	2.4593	0.3017	0.5052	0	2.5721	0.4722	0.7908
	10011	0	0.4813	0.3318	0.2525	0	0.5034	0.5194	0.3953
	10100	1	2.7168	0.2515	0.0947	1	2.8414	0.3937	0.1482
	10101	0	0.5317	0.0219	0.0517	0	0.5561	0.0343	0.0809
	10110	1	0.6304	0.2183	0.2260	1	0.6593	0.3417	0.3537

(Continued)

TABLE 13.2
(Continued)

Gender	Longitudinal Diagnosis[a]	Family History Negative Participants				Family History Positive Participants			
		Obs. Freq.	Expected Frequencies[b]			Obs. Freq.	Expected Frequencies		
			Trad. CFA	Markov	Tetrad		Trad. CFA	Markov	Tetrad
	10111	1	0.1234	0.2401	0.3594	1	0.1290	0.3758	0.5626
	11000	2	3.0238	6.5660	3.6627	2	3.1625	10.2786	5.7338
	11001	2	0.5918	0.5717	0.2001	1	0.6189	0.8950	0.3132
	11010	1	0.7017	0.2796	2.5754	3	0.7338	0.4377	4.0315
	11011	1	0.1373	0.3075	1.2875	2	0.1436	0.4814	2.0155
	11100	3	0.7751	4.6472	2.0831	2	0.8107	7.2748	3.2609
	11101	1	0.1517	0.4047	1.1365	4	**0.1587**	0.6335	1.7791
	11110	3	**0.1799**	4.0335	3.9767	3	**0.1881**	6.3142	6.2253
	11111	8	**0.0352**	**4.4367**	6.3257	18	**0.0368**	**6.9453**	**9.9024**
Female	00000	90	**36.0773**	**72.8301**	79.3609	73	**37.7322**	**60.0165**	65.3982
	00001	1	7.0607	6.3417	4.3355	4	7.3846	5.2259	3.5727
	00010	2	8.3715	3.1013	1.2740	2	8.7555	2.5557	1.0499
	00011	0	1.6384	3.4113	0.6369	0	1.7136	2.8111	0.5249
	00100	3	9.2480	2.5853	3.7856	1	9.6722	2.1304	3.1196
	00101	1	1.8099	0.2251	2.0654	2	1.8930	0.1855	1.7020
	00110	0	2.1459	2.2439	0.6452	1	2.2444	1.8491	0.5317
	00111	0	0.4200	2.4682	1.0263	1	0.4392	2.0339	0.8457
	01000	4	10.2930	2.1948	2.4487	3	10.7651	1.8087	2.0179

Pattern								
01001	0	2.0144	0.1911	0.1338	1	2.1068	0.1575	0.1102
01010	0	2.3884	0.0935	0.0000	0	2.4980	0.0770	0.0000
01011	0	0.4674	0.1028	0.0000	0	0.4889	0.0847	0.0000
01100	1	2.6385	1.5534	2.5066	2	2.7595	1.2801	2.0656
01101	3	0.5164	0.1353	1.3676	0	0.5401	0.1115	1.1270
01110	0	0.6122	1.3483	0.2493	1	0.6403	1.1111	0.2055
01111	0	0.1198	1.4831	0.3966	0	0.1253	1.2221	0.3268
10000	1	11.3872	1.1175	0.9590	8	11.9096	6.36764	5.46452
10001	0	2.2286	0.0973	0.0524	1	2.3308	0.55446	0.29853
10010	1	2.6423	0.0476	0.2023	1	2.7636	0.27115	1.15287
10011	0	0.5171	0.0523	0.1011	1	0.5409	0.29826	0.57635
10100	1	2.9190	0.0397	0.0498	1	3.0529	0.22604	0.28370
10101	0	0.5713	0.0035	0.0272	0	0.5975	0.01968	0.15479
10110	0	0.6773	0.0344	0.0149	0	0.7084	0.19619	0.08462
10111	0	0.1326	0.0379	0.0236	1	0.1386	0.21580	0.13460
11000	1	3.2488	1.0358	1.0272	7	3.3978	5.90181	5.85291
11001	0	0.6358	0.0902	0.0561	0	0.6650	0.51390	0.31974
11010	0	0.7539	0.0441	0.0903	1	0.7884	0.25132	0.51436
11011	0	0.1475	0.0485	0.0451	0	0.1543	0.27644	0.25714
11100	1	0.8328	0.7331	0.4140	2	0.8710	4.17708	2.35913
11101	0	0.1630	0.0638	0.2259	0	0.1705	0.36372	1.28713
11110	0	0.1932	0.6363	0.5763	4	**0.2021**	3.62549	3.28406
11111	0	0.0378	0.6999	0.9168	3	**0.0396**	3.98789	5.22387

aEach five-digit number represents the pattern of 12-month alcoholism diagnosis at time 1–5 with 0 indicating no alcoholism diagnosis and 1 indicating a diagnosis. bBold cells indicate a Type under the model, meaning that the expected frequency under the base model is significantly less than the actual frequency.

diagnosing at the first three waves, not diagnosing at the fourth wave, and diagnosing at the fifth wave (11101), although it should be noted that this type was barely significant, and the number of individuals for the 11110 and 11101 patterns were fairly small ($N <= 4$). Overall, these types correspond roughly to everyday notions that some individuals do not diagnose for alcohol use disorder, that other consistently diagnose for such a disorder, and that still others may evidence an alcohol use disorder during the college years, but that such disorder is "developmentally limited" and is not found in assessments after college (Zucker, 1987).

Graphical Representation of Marginal Independence. As mentioned earlier, there is some question, however, whether such categorical longitudinal data must be represented by only marginal independence or the presence of such global types. Structural relationships between longitudinal categorical variables may be present at only some measurement occasions, and not others, for example. To see this, it helps to visualize the study presented in Table 13.2 as a POIPG, as is done in the Tetrad program. Specifically, if no conditional relationships are present in the study, the POIPG no relationships are indicated in the POIPG, and the diagram for the study is represented as in Fig. 13.2.

Under this model, neither Sex, Family History (FH), nor any previous alcohol abuse/dependence diagnosis is related to any subsequent diagnosis. Conditional probabilities of any given variable are equal to their overall baserate, or marginal, probabilities. The probability for the instantiation of any particular configuration of Sex, Family History, and diagnosis pattern over time is equal to the product of the proportions associated with each variable. Further, the expected frequencies associated with any possible configuration of these variables is equal to the overall sample size multiplied by the probability for the configuration.

Alternative Analyses: Markov Models. Although use of the marginal independence structural model of Fig. 13.2 resulted in the identification of types that appear to have a ready conceptual interpretation, it is by no

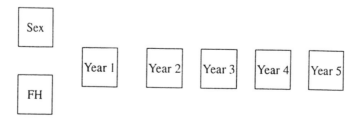

FIG. 13.2. POIPG of a 5-year study of alcohol abuse/dependence under marginal independence.

means clear that such a structural model is the only appropriate diagram for such data. It could be, for example, that diagnosis for an alcohol use disorder at any given occasion affects the probability of diagnosis on a subsequent occasion and that Sex and Family History have an affect on the baserates of diagnosis only via their effect on the initial diagnosis. Such a Markovian model of the relationships between variables is expressed in the POIPG of Fig. 13.3. From a CFA approach, this means that the appropriate analysis for the data is not an analysis of all measurement occasions and variables, but rather a series of smaller analyses that examine only adjacent diagnoses, as well as the relationship of Sex and Family History to Year 1 diagnosis. Of course, as discussed earlier, a skeptic of the CFA approach could argue that such two-wave CFA analyses merely represent the presence of conditional probabilities in the 2 × 2 tables of such an analysis, but if a CFA analysis of such a model of adjacent conditional probabilities still reveals the presence of types, a stronger (but not absolute) claim regarding the presence of such types may be made. A skeptic must either accept that types exist in the data, that some measurement occasions (such as Year 1 diagnosis) have additional prospective influences (such as to Year 4 diagnosis), or that some other unmeasured construct affects the constructs over multiple measurement occasions. In order to generate the expected frequencies for this model, the raw data of the study as well as the POIPG of Fig. 13.3 were input to Tetrad and the joint probabilities for all configurations of Sex, Family History, and alcohol use disorder were generated using the Estimate module of Tetrad. These probabilities were then multiplied by the overall sample size to calculate the expected frequencies for each cell. Inspection of the frequencies for the Markov model in columns 5 and 9 of Table 13.2 reveal a much closer correspondence to the observed frequencies than was found for the traditional CFA. Nevertheless, four types were still found under this model. Two types reflecting diagnosis on every measurement occasion (11111) were found for men, regardless of their family history of alcoholism, and two types reflecting no alcohol use disorder for women were found, again regardless of family history of alcohol use disorder. Even though the expected frequencies for these cells are closer to their obtained

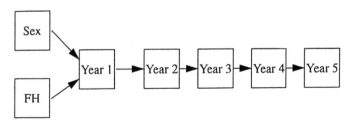

FIG. 13.3. POIPG of a 5-year study of alcohol abuse/dependence, sex, and family history (FH).

values for many cells, the discrepancies between the actual frequencies and the predicted frequencies are fairly substantial for these types. For example, for the family history positive males who diagnose consistently over the study, the Markov model predicts 6.9453 individuals whereas 18 individuals occurred. Similarly, the Markov model predicts only 72.8 family history negative individuals would not diagnose at all during the study, but 90 individuals actually showed this pattern.

Tetrad Search Results.   It is possible that the Markovian model shown in Fig. 13.3 fails to include some relationships in the data that would result in a failure to correctly model the probabilities associated with the longitudinal configurations of the data. One of the major uses of Tetrad is to use exploratory search techniques to recover the underlying structure of the data. For this reason, the Build module of Tetrad was used to construct a model of conditional dependencies for the data. The POIPG that Tetrad generated for these data is given in Fig. 13.1. In some ways, the general form of the resulting diagram is heartening, in that the graph correctly orients the times of measurement of the study. In other ways, however, this POIPG does not represent a readily interpretable explanation of the data. First, several of the diagnosis effects predict subsequent years that are not adjacent. Second, the findings of no relationship of family history to alcohol abuse are surprising, given the overall pattern of alcohol diagnosis in the data. When the five-wave longitudinal data of the study are analyzed with Proc Catmod, for example, pronounced family history and sex effects are found for the data. Finally, the sex effect that predicts only Year 4 seems puzzling, given that there is no a priori reason to suspect this relationship. In order for the conditional probabilities of the model to be estimated under Tetrad, a unidirectional graph was produced, in which ambiguous unidirectional arrows in the POIPG (denoted by a circle-based arrow in Fig. 13.1) were converted to directed arrows and the double-headed arrow between Years 4 and 5 was converted to a single-headed arrow. Conditional probabilities under this model were then estimated using the Estimate module of Tetrad, and the expected frequencies associated with each cell of the contingency table shown in the 6th and 10th columns of Table 13.2. As can be seen from the table, the expected frequencies under this model are even closer to the actual frequencies estimated under the Markov model, however one type still emerged, corresponding to male, family history positive, consistent diagnosers on all five measurement occasions. The presence of this type would appear to have some research support, given alcohol research hypotheses concerning the intergenerational transmission of alcohol use disorders (Sher et al., 1991).

In order to modify the Tetrad model so that the presence of this residual type is explicitly included, a new categorical variable, Type, was defined for the study, in which male family history positive participants who diagnosed over all measurement occasions were awarded a score of 1 and

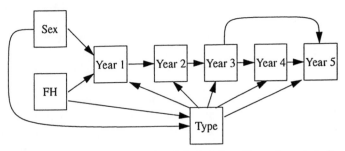

FIG. 13.4. POIPG of a 5-year study of alcohol abuse/dependence including Type information.

everyone else was awarded a score of 0. Inclusion of this variable in the analysis corresponds generally to Victor's (1989) notion of a type as an increased probability mass associated with a particular cell of the contingency table. When this variable is included in the analysis, the POIPG that results from the analysis appears much more interpretable, as seen in Fig. 13.4. In this diagram, the Year 4 diagnosis is no longer dependent on both Year 1 and Year 3 diagnoses and both Year 1 and Type variables appear to be conditional on Gender and Family History. The only exception to the pattern of autoregressivity was the Year 3 to Year 5 relationship, which was consistent with the initial POIPG for the data, and indicates that alcohol abuse disorder diagnosis may be stable for Years 4 and 5. When Year 4 and 5 diagnoses were substituted for a variable scored as 1 if a diagnosis occurred during either Years 4 or 5, the resulting POIPG yielded the same conditional relationship between Sex, Family History, and Year 1, relationships from the Type variable to each measurement occasion, and adjacent conditional relationships. When a CFA was conducted based on the conditional probabilities expressed in Fig. 13.4 as well as the modified model collapsing Years 4 and 5, no statistically significant types emerged. Clearly, the model represented in Fig. 13.4 could be further modified by the inclusion of additional time-delimited types, such as types representing consistent alcohol diagnosis from Years 1 to 2, for example. Although such analyses may well be appropriate for some research situations, the CFA of the resulting path diagram failed to find any differential relationships of these time-limited types to later measurement occasions, meaning that the impact of such times did not appear to be influential over the long term.

DISCUSSION

Given the differences in assumptions and analysis of the CFA and Tetrad approaches, it is helpful to revisit the general logic underlying each approach. The CFA model attempts, via analysis of the discrepancy of the residuals associated with particular cells of a contingency table, to establish that a particular configuration of response occurs significantly more (or less) than that expected under a base model. Although the most often-used base model is that of marginal independence, there are plausible reasons to believe, particularly for longitudinal data, that the model of marginal independence may not be appropriate. One plausible alternative to the model of marginal independence that has not been addressed as a plausible CFA model is a model of adjacent conditional probabilities, termed a Markovian base model. In two-wave longitudinal research it is not possible to differentiate the CFA model from the Markovian model because both models perfectly recapture the observed frequencies in the data. For multiple wave data, however, it is possible to enunciate such a model and to use it as the base model for a CFA. The Tetrad program's Graph and Estimate modules can be used to generate the conditional probabilities for such a base model.

The Tetrad program can also be used as an exploratory analysis technique for the analysis of contingency data. The fact that a POIPG containing no arrows is equivalent to a model of marginal independence makes it easy to understand connections between CFA approaches, loglinear approaches, and use of Tetrad models as a base for CFA. On one hand, it is tempting to use the Build module of Tetrad to generate plausible conditional models for the data. As seen, though, although the search algorithm of Build attempts to produce a best possible explanation for the conditional probabilities of the model, it is not true that Tetrad will necessarily identify patterns of longitudinal data that span multiple measurement occasions. This is because the alternative explanations developed by the CFA approach involve the specification of new categorical variables that span the categorical variables of the study. Although the Tetrad program allows for the specification of latent variables in the analysis of categorical data, the Estimate module does not generate joint probability estimates for such models.

Rather than view an analysis of these two techniques as competing with each other, it is more helpful to consider one approach as providing a basis for skeptical consideration of models developed by the other approach. For example, Mellenbergh's (1996) reanalysis of a proposed CFA resulted in a model of no identified types when a slightly different base model was considered. When the categorical data from a larger study are considered that may constitute a mix of longitudinal assessments and various constructs, it may not be clear which associations in the model may be used to respecify a new, more skeptical base model for the analysis. Conversely, the POIPG produced by the Tetrad approach may also be open to reevaluation in light of the presence of significant and conceptually plausible types as identified under a CFA. The effect of the presence of such Types in a data set appears to have a substantial effect on the influence paths identified by Tetrad.

In spite of the utility of conducting and evaluating such approaches to categorical data, much work in this area remains to be done. As mentioned earlier, the widespread use of the binomial distribution (or less computationally intensive approximations) has not been extensively evaluated under situations when this assumption is violated (as in the case of analysis of a contingency table collapsed from a higher order table). Although Tetrad analyses of such data can inform the researcher whether such collapsing has been done across relatively independent variables, bootstrapping approaches to the generation of standard errors is probably called for. Second, more work is needed in order to integrate the Tetrad and CFA approaches in the analysis of longitudinal data. Specifically, it seems likely that many "true" models of growth and development may be a mix of the longitudinal categorization of types as identified by CFA and conditional transition patterns as recovered under Tetrad models. Although the models proposed here represent a reasonable step in this direction, it would be relatively easy to generate alternative categorizations of types and conditional probabilities that would recover the observed frequencies of response for this study and others like it.

REFERENCES

Haberman, S. J. (1973). The analysis of residuals in cross-classified tables. *Biometrics, 29,* 205–220.

Kieser, M., & Victor, N. (1991). A test procedure for an alternative approach to configural frequency analysis. *Methodika, 5,* 87–97.

Krauth, J., & Lienert, G. A. (1973). *KFA. Die Konfigurationsfrequenzanalyse und ihre Anwendung in Psychologie und Medizin* [Configural frequency analysis and its application in psychology and medicine]. Freiburg, Germany: Alber.

Mellenbergh, G. J. (1996). Other null model, other (anti)type. *Applied Psychology: An International Review, 45,* 329–330.

Netter, P. (1996). Prediction CFA as a search for types: History and specifications. *Applied Psychology: An International Review, 45,* 338–344.

Netter, P., & Lienert, G. A. (1984). Die Konfigurationsfrequenzanalyse XXIa. Streßinduzierte Katecholaminreactionen bei Hyper- und Normotonikern [Configural frequency analysis XXIa: Stress-inducted catecholamine reactions in hypertonic and normal individuals]. *Zeitschrift für Klinische Psychologie, Psychopathologie und Psychotherapie, 33,* 47–58.

Sher, K. J., Walitzer, K. S., Wood, P. K., & Brent, E. E. (1991). Characteristics of children of alcoholics: Putative risk factors, substance use and abuse, and psychopathology. *Journal of Abnormal Psychology, 100,* 427–448.

Spirtes, P., Glymour, C., & Scheines, R. (1993). *Causation, prediction and search.* New York: Springer.

Spirtes, P., Scheines, R., Meek, C., & Glymour, C. (1994). *TETRAD II: Tools for causal modeling.* Hillsdale, NJ: Lawrence Erlbaum Associates.

Victor, N. (1989). An alternative approach to configural frequency analysis. *Methodika, 3,* 61–73.

von Eye, A. (1990a). *Configural frequency analysis.* New York: Cambridge University Press.

von Eye, A. (1990b). Configural frequency analysis of longitudinal multivariate responses. In A. von Eye (Ed.), *New statistical methods for longitudinal research* (Vol. 1, pp. 545–570). New York: Academic Press.

von Eye, A., & Spiel, C. (1996). Standard and nonstandard log-linear symmetry models for measuring change in categorical variables. *The American Statistician, 50,* 300–305.

von Eye, A., Spiel, C., & Wood, P. K. (1996). Configural frequency analysis in applied psychological research. *Applied Psychology: An International Review, 45,* 301–352.

Wood, P. K., Sher, K., & von Eye, A. (1994). Conjugate and other distributional methods in configural frequency analysis. *Biometrical Journal, 26,* 387–410.

Zucker, R. A. (1987). The four alcoholisms: A developmental account of the etiologic process. In P. C. Rivers (Ed.), *Nebraska symposium on motivation 1986: Alcohol and addictive behavior* (pp. 27–83). Lincoln: University of Nebraska Press.

Author Index

Subject Index

A

Analysis of covariance structure, *see* Structural equation modeling
ANOVA approach, 6, 9-11

B

Bentler-Bonett index, *see* Evaluation of fit
Block-Toeplitz matrices, *see* Dynamic factor analysis
Bootstrapping, *see* Structural equation modeling

C

Capacitated plant location, *see* Location theory
Causal analysis, *see* Structural equation modeling
Chi-square, *see* Evaluation of fit
Classical test theory, 2-4, 24-25
    reliability coefficients, 2-3, 57
    true scores, 2
Classification, *see* Location theory
Competitive facility location, *see* Location theory
Composite heuristic, *see* Heuristic search methods
Computer programs, 10-409
    CRAFT, 115
    DISCON, 115-116
    EQS, 266
    EXCEL, 88-93
    LISREL, 10, 202-204, 207-213, 239, 243-249, 267, 282-294

Mx, 271-280
    PLS-Graph, 333
    SAS, 6, 10, 223
    TETRAD, 260, 408-409
Communalities, *see* Factor analysis
Conditional location problem, *see* Location theory
Configural frequency analysis, 407-423
    binomial probabilities, 410-411
    Markov models, 418-420
    problems of inference, 411
    results, 414-418
Confirmatory factor analysis, 199-213
Constructive-based heuristics, *see* Heuristic search methods
Construct validity, 17, 179-181, 261-262
Convergent validity, 17-18

D

Data envelopment analysis, 121-144
    an application, 137-144
    decision-making units, 122-125
    recent developments, 136-137
    regression analysis, 133-135
    slack variable, 127
    specification errors, 133
Descent method, *see* Heuristic search methods
DISCON, *see* Computer programs
Divergent validity, 17
Dynamic factor analysis, 217-249
    Block-Toeplitz matrices, 223-225
    lagged covariances, 218-222
    model fitting criteria, 229-231
    p-technique factor analysis, 231-233
    stationarity, 224-225, 233-237

431

About the Authors

Wynne W. Chin is a professor in the Department of Decision and Information Sciences at the University of Houston. His research interests include information systems and latent variable modeling using the partial least squares approach.

Tammy Drezner is a lecturer in the Department of Marketing at California State University, Fullerton. She received her B.A. from McMaster University, Canada, and her M.A. and Ph.D. degrees from the University of Michigan. Her research interests are in the location of retail facilities and consumer behavior. Her recent publications have appeared in the *Journal of Retailing* and *The Journal of Regional Science*.

Zvi Drezner is Professor of Management Science/Information Systems at California State University, Fullerton. He received his B.Sc. in Mathematics and Ph.D. in Computer Science from the Technion, Israel Institute of Technology. His research interests are in location theory and computational statistics. He has published over 100 articles in such journals as *Operations Research, Management Science, IIE Transactions*, and *Naval Research Logistics*.

Ronald H. Heck is Professor of Educational Administration at the University of Hawaii at Manoa. His professional interests include the application of modeling techniques to studying organizations, educational policy, and educational politics. Recent publications include "Leadership and culture: Conceptual and methodological issues in comparing models across cultural settings" in the *Journal of Educational Administration*.

Scott L. Hershberger is Assistant Professor of Quantitative Psychology in the Department of Psychology at the University of Kansas. His research interests include structural equation modeling, psychometric theory, and developmental behavior genetics.

David Kaplan is Associate Professor in the Department of Educational Studies at the University of Delaware. He specializes in statistics and psychometrics. He has published extensively on the problem of nonnormality, specification error, and power in covariance structure models. His papers have appeared in the *British Journal of Mathematical and Statistical Psychology, Educational and Psychological Measurement, Journal of Behavioral and Educational Statistics, Multivariate Behavioral Research,* and *Sociological Methods and Research.* His current program of research focuses on the development of multilevel simultaneous equation systems with applications to policy simulation modeling.

John M. Linacre is Associate Director of the MESA (Measurement, Analysis and Statistical Analysis) Psychometric Laboratory at the University of Chicago, and editor of *Rasch Measurement Transactions.* After a career in business, he became interested in the problem of drawing sound inferences from social science data. His initial work centered on achievement data for children in the Headstart program. Recently he has focused on measuring the quality of life of medical patients. He now works closely with Benjamin D. Wright, the best-known proponent of the Rasch model as a means for transforming ordinal observations into linear measures.

Mary E. Lunz is currently Psychometrician and Director of Examination Activities at the Board of Registry of the American Society of Clinical Pathologists. She also works with medical specialty boards and other organizations who use the principles of objective measurement in their evaluation or research protocols. The emphasis of her current research is multifacet analysis of performance examinations and surveys. Previously, she completed a systematic national study of computerized testing that was the basis for a series of articles on aspects of computerized adaptive testing.

George A. Marcoulides is Professor of Statistics at California State University, Fullerton, and Adjunct Professor at the University of California, Irvine. He is the recipient of the 1991 UCEA William J. Davis Memorial Award for outstanding scholarship. He is currently the Editor of the *Methodology for Business and Management* Book Series, Editor of *Structural Equation Modeling,* Associate Editor for three other scholarly journals, and on the editorial board of numerous measurement and statistics journals. His research interests include generalizability theory and structural equation modeling.

John J. McArdle is a professor in the Department of Psychology at the University of Virginia. His research interests include structural equation modeling and individual differences.

Karen M. Schmidt McCollam is an assistant professor in the Experimental Psychology: Quantitative Methods program at the University of Virginia. Her research deals with interfacing cognitive test design with IRT models, methods for studying spatial ability, and examining cognitive ability structure change over time.

Edward E. Rigdon is Associate Professor of Marketing at Georgia State University in Atlanta. He teaches a doctoral seminar in structural equation modeling (SEM), serves as methodological specialist on dissertation committees, and consults with commerical researchers on SEM problems. His SEM research has been published in *Journal of Marketing Research, Multivariate Behavioral Research,* and *Structural Equation Modeling.* He is also a cofounder of and frequent contributor to SEMNET, an Internet-based discussion list devoted to SEM.

Said Salhi is a lecturer in Management Mathematics/Operational Research at the University of Birmingham, UK. He held the post of Senior Lecturer in Industrial Engineering at Algiers Polytechnic from 1987 to 1990. He obtained his M.Sc. and Ph.D. in Operational Research from Southampton and Lancaster Universities, respectively. His interests include heuristic design applied to logistic systems and project management. He has published articles in the *European Journal of Operational Research, Journal of the Operational Research Society, Omega, Location Science,* the *Studies in Locational Analysis,* and in edited books and proceedings.

Andreas C. Soteriou is Assistant Professor of Management Science in the Department of Public and Business Administration at the University of Cyprus. He received his B.Sc. in Electrical and Biomedical Engineering and his Ph.D. in Business Administration from the University of Southern California. His research interests are in service management, quality and service quality improvement, and capacity acquisition and planning.

Phillip K. Wood received his doctoral degree from the University of Minnesota specializing in measurement and statistics in 1985. He was a National Institute of Aging postdoctoral trainee at Pennsylvania State University where he specialized in statistical methods for longitudinal data. His methodology interests include the analysis and design of longitudinal data.

Stavros A. Zenios is Professor of Management Science in the Department of Public and Business Administration at the University of Cyprus. He completed his undergraduate studies at the Higher Technical Institute of Cyprus (H.N.D.), at the University of London (B.Sc.), and at the Council of Engineering Institutions, UK (B.Eng.). He received his M.A. and Ph.D. from Princeton University. He has served on the faculty at the Wharton School, University of Pennsylvania, and has worked as a Visiting Scientist at the Operations Research Center at M.I.T. His research interests are in the application of management science in planning financial operations, parallel and vector supercomputing, large scale optimization of planning under uncertainty and parallel algorithms, network optimization, matrix balancing, and image reconstruction.